ALCOHOL AND PLEASURE

International Center For Alcohol Policies
Series on Alcohol in Society

Grant and Litvak—*Drinking Patterns and Their Consequences*
Grant—*Alcohol and Emerging Markets: Patterns, Problems, and Responses*
Peele and Grant—*Alcohol and Pleasure: A Health Perspective*

ALCOHOL AND PLEASURE: A HEALTH PERSPECTIVE

Edited by

Stanton Peele
Psychologist and Consultant
Morristown, New Jersey, USA

and

Marcus Grant
International Center for Alcohol Policies
Washington, DC, USA

BRUNNER/MAZEL
Taylor & Francis Group

USA	Publishing Office:	BRUNNER/MAZEL
		A member of the Taylor & Francis Group
		325 Chestnut Street
		Philadelphia, PA 19106
		Tel: (215) 625-8900
		Fax: (215) 625-2940
	Distribution Center:	BRUNNER/MAZEL
		A member of the Taylor & Francis Group
		47 Runway Road, Suite G
		Levittown, PA 19057
		Tel: (215) 269-0400
		Fax: (215) 269-0363
UK		BRUNNER/MAZEL
		A member of the Taylor & Francis Group
		1 Gunpowder Square
		London EC4A 3DE
		Tel: +44 171 583 0490
		Fax: +44 171 583 0581

ALCOHOL AND PLEASURE: A Health Perspective

1 2 3 4 5 6 7 8 9 0

Printed by Edwards Brothers, Ann Arbor, MI, 1999.

Cover design by Nancy Abbott.

A CIP catalog record for this book is available from the British Library.
⊗ The paper in this publication meets the requirements of the ANSI Standard Z39.48-1984 (Permanence of Paper).

Library of Congress Cataloging-in-Publication Data

Alcohol and pleasure : a health perspective / edited by Stanton Peele, Marcus Grant.
    p.   cm. -- (Series on alcohol in society)
    Includes bibliographical references and index.
    ISBN 1-58391-015-8 (case)
    1. Alcoholism--Psychological aspects Congresses.   2. Alcohol--Physiological aspects Congresses.   3. Drinking of alcoholic beverages--Psychological aspects Congresses.   I. Peele, Stanton.
II. Grant, Marcus.   III. Series.
RC565.A3926   1999
362.292--dc21   99-12975
                                                         CIP

ISBN 1-58391-015-8

Contents

PART 2—PLEASURE AND ALCOHOL CROSS-CULTURALLY

PART 3—ALCOHOL AND MEDICAL, PSYCHOLOGICAL, AND SOCIAL HEALTH

PART 6—CONCLUSIONS

Contributors

IRINA ANOKHINA
Research Institute on Addictions
Moscow, Russia

JOSEPH ASARE
Ministry of Health
Accra, Ghana

ARCHIE BRODSKY
Harvard Medical School
Massachusetts Mental Health Center
Boston, Massachusetts, USA

CARLOS A. CAMARGO, JR.
Harvard Medical School
Boston, Massachusetts, USA

CYNTHIA CHASOKELA
Ministry of Health
Harare, Zimbabwe

MICHAEL DAUBE
Ministry of the Premier and Cabinet
Perth, Western Australia

JEAN-PAUL DAVID
Vin-Santé-Plaisir de Vivre
Macon, France

MARCUS GRANT
International Center for Alcohol
   Policies
Washington, D.C., USA

ALAN HAWORTH
National Mental Health Resource Center
University of Zambia
Lusaka, Zambia

DWIGHT B. HEATH
Brown University
Providence, Rhode Island, USA

MOHAN ISAAC
National Institute of Mental Health and
   Neurosciences
Bangalore, India

ROSS KALUCY
Flinders Medical Center
Bedford Park, Southern Australia

ARTHUR L. KLATSKY
Kaiser Permanente Medical Center
Oakland, California, USA

BARBARA C. LEIGH
Alcohol and Drug Abuse Institute
University of Washington
Seattle, Washington, USA

GEOFF LOWE
University of Hull
Hull, UK

JOHN LUIK
Independent Consultant
Fairfax Station, Virginia, USA

DAVE MACDONALD
University of Botswana
Gaborone, Botswana

G. ALAN MARLATT
Addictive Behaviors Research Center
University of Washington
Seattle, Washington, USA

DAVINDER MOHAN
All India Institute of Medical Sciences
New Delhi, India

LOUIS MOLAMU
University of South Africa
Pretoria, South Africa

JENNIFER MOYO
Mental Health Services
Harare, Zimbabwe

LOUISE NADEAU
University of Montreal
Montreal, Québec, Canada

BIOLA ODEJIDE
University of Ibadan
Ibadan, Nigeria

OLABISI A. ODEJIDE
University College Hospital
Ibadan, Nigeria

JOHN ORLEY
Division of Mental Health and Prevention
   of Substance Abuse
World Health Organization
Geneva, Switzerland

STANTON PEELE
Psychologist and Consultant
Morristown, New Jersey, USA

NII-K PLANGE
School of Social and Economic
   Development
University of the South Pacific
Suva, Fiji

HENRY POMEROY
Allied Domecq PLC
Bristol, England

HAYDÉE ROSOVSKY
National Council on Addictions
Mexico City, Mexico

NORMAN SARTORIUS
World Psychiatric Association
Geneva, Switzerland

HARI KESH SHARMA
All India Institute of Medical
   Sciences
New Delhi, India

NAOTAKA SHINFUKU
Kobe University School of Medicine
Kobe, Japan

ERIC SINGLE
University of Toronto
Toronto, Ontario, Canada

OLE-JØRGEN SKOG
University of Oslo
Oslo, Norway

JAN SNEL
University of Amsterdam
The Netherlands

TIM STOCKWELL
National Center for Research into the
   Prevention of Drug Abuse
Perth, Australia

EVA TONGUE
International Council on Alcohol and
   Addictions
Lausanne, Switzerland

DAVID M. WARBURTON
University of Reading
Reading, UK

Preface

This book is based on a conference organized by the International Center for Alcohol Policies (ICAP) that took place in New York from June 28 to July 1, 1998. It was exactly 2 years previously—at a board meeting in Amsterdam—that ICAP actually decided to organize the conference. Many factors entered into the decision, but the principal factor was the sense that the time had come to turn a new page in the long story of alcohol and society.

Most people who reach for a drink do so in the expectation that it will satisfy them and provide a source of personal pleasure. This simple, undeniable truth somehow has been obscured by the vast literature on health and social problems associated with alcohol abuse. Exploring the vast territory between the pleasure of most people's drinking experiences and the tragic consequences of alcohol abuse has been fraught with confusion and uncertainty. How much is too much? Are there "safe" limits to drinking? Is less necessarily better? In what ways is alcohol good for you?

These were some of the questions that the conference was intended to address. In the two years of planning and preparation, ICAP was assisted by a number of eminent experts. The key architect of the scholarly program of the conference was my coeditor, Dr. Stanton Peele, whose erudition is matched only by his intellectual daring. From a few scribbled notes that I had made in Amsterdam on a sheet of hotel notepaper, he was able to create the impressive edifice that is reported in this volume.

Dr. Peele was assisted in this task by an international advisory group consisting of Dr. Joe Asare (Ghana), Dr. Michael Daube (Australia), Dr. Arthur Klatsky (United States), Dr. Barbara Leigh (United States), Dr. Eric Single (Canada), Dr. Eva Tongue (Switzerland), Mr. Ragnar Waahlberg (Norway), and Dr. David Warburton (United Kingdom). Not only did the group help with the planning of the conference, but—as is apparent from reading this volume—they all became sufficiently committed to the success of the event to play an active part in the conference itself.

In order to create the right climate for discussion, we decided to involve a wide range of individuals and at the same time limit the total number of participants. In the end, more than 30 countries were represented among the 150 participants, including scientists, scholars, public health advocates, government officials, medical specialists, and executives of beverage alcohol companies. Many members of this assembled group joined the debate to share their different perspectives on the relationship between alcohol and pleasure within a health perspective. We also were fortunate to have a dedicated group of session chairs and rapporteurs—mainly from developing countries—who provided the structure within which these discussions took place.

In compiling this volume, we have attempted to do more than provide final versions of the papers presented at New York. We also have tried to capture some of the creativity and energy of the many discussions that took place there in reports prepared by the rapporteurs for each session, which are placed at the end of each of the parts of the volume.

There are those who believe that the function of a conference proceedings volume is simply to chronicle an event, so that those who were there can point to their contributions and those who were not can regret whatever circumstances kept them away. Our hope is that this volume is something more than that. Never before has this theme been addressed so comprehensively at an international level. Never before has such an imposing array of speakers from such a wide range of disciplines been encouraged to share their perspectives and to search for a new way of describing the relationship between alcohol and pleasure.

Our hope is that we have succeeded in our aim of turning a new page in the story of alcohol and society, at least to the extent that we have demonstrated how much more needs to be done to fill in the page that we have turned. Neither the conference nor this volume provides final answers to any of the questions the conference addressed. But both the conference and the volume are vivid evidence of how relevant and significant these questions are.

I suppose that all those who met in New York shared a common view that alcohol has a legitimate place in society and a common concern that accurate and balanced information should be available to individuals to guide their drinking choices. There is no simple threshold between the experience of drinking and the pleasure it can bring on the one hand and the pain and suffering caused by alcohol abuse on the other. But if we are to understand the role of alcohol in society, then at the very least we need to acknowledge the pleasure as well as the pain. If nothing else, this volume is testimony to the respectability of pleasure as a motive for drinking and as its main consequence for most people.

This volume is divided into five substantive sections, together with a summary and conclusions section and an appendix devoted to a session on the media and alcohol. In brief, the book's sections and chapters are as follows. Part 1, Pleasure and Health, sets the stage by developing notions of pleasure in relation to health and culture. David Warburton surveys data showing an intimate relationship between people's experience of pleasure and their resistance to disease and general well-being. In his contribution, John Luik takes modern health promotion to task as being moralistically motivated. Michael Daube contests this viewpoint and provides a rationale for a noncoercive model of health promotion. Finally, Norman Sartorius closes this section by reflecting on the variety of cultural meanings of pleasure.

In Part 2, Pleasure and Alcohol Cross-Culturally, Dwight Heath reviews cross-cultural perspective on alcohol and pleasure and the virtually infinite ways different societies have organized the consumption of alcohol. This perspective then is filled in with case examples from Botswana (Dave Macdonald and Louis Molamu), the Latin American region (Haydée Rosovsky), India (Hari Kesh Sharma and Davinder Mohan), Japan (Naotaka Shinfuku), Ghana (Joe Asare), and France (Jean-Paul David). As a rule, these case examples explore the variety of indigenous means that various societies have to regulate alcohol consumption in the service of pleasurable social interactions.

Part 3, Alcohol and Medical, Psychological, and Social Health, reviews the by now extensive literature showing that alcohol benefits health. In their contributions, Arthur Klatsky and Carlos Camargo, Jr., carefully sift through the medical evidence (important parts of which they have generated) to show under what conditions, and for which drinkers, alcohol's benefits exceed its risks. Ole-Jørgen Skog, on the other hand, questions whether the cumulative impact of even healthy drinking by many is a boon for public health. Archie Brodsky and Stanton Peele, for their part, expand the arena of potential benefits from drinking by exploring the empirical basis for positive social and psychological effects associated with alcohol.

Drinking Expectations and Contexts (Part 4) elucidates the role of individual and cultural set and setting for drinking. *Set* refers to the cognitive map with which people approach drinking, which—as Barbara Leigh shows—is often as important as (or more important than) alcohol's pharmacology in producing the effects of drinking. G. Alan Marlatt completes this picture by contrasting the expectations and experiences of problematic and pleasurable drinking, each of which is self-fulfilling in its own way. Geoff Lowe describes pleasurable experiences with alcohol, and the very different experiences people seek at different times in their lives. Eric Single and Henry Pomeroy review the complex ways in which the setting of the drinking event impinges on the way alcohol is consumed; Jan Snel looks at the human being in flux, and how individuals with different characteristics use substances in seeking to create desired states. Ross Kalucy is concerned about the self-imposition of restraints on pleasure, and about maladies that restraint on its own may cause. Finally, in this section dealing with the varieties of alcohol and pleasure experiences, Louise Nadeau explores alcohol use among women, in patterns tied to the sometimes distinct realities that separate the genders.

In the last substantive section (Part 5), Pleasure and Alcohol Policy, John Orley reviews the process by which the World Health Organization conceived and carried out the measurement of quality of life. Olabisi and Biola Odejide tackle the challenging case of pleasure as a component of alcohol policy in a developing nation (Nigeria). Tim Stockwell and Eric Single review an array of alcohol policies to minimize the harms that result from drinking. Their tack is dictated by a recognition that people use alcohol for specific, often positive, purposes, and that a policy directed at having people cease or reduce their use of alcohol will be limited in its effectiveness. In a parallel chapter, Stanton Peele examines governing images of alcohol, and how negative images of alcohol may cause the problems said to be the reasons for fearing this substance. He also presents an integrated view of alcohol within a generally life-enhancing framework as one that seems to offer the most secure guarantee that drinking will be a pleasurable experience.

The entire roster of speakers who have contributed chapters to this book has turned not one but several new pages in the story of alcohol and society. The discussion of drinking problems and pleasures contained in this volume, I am sure, represents an exciting point of departure for research, policy, and advocacy in the years to come.

Marcus Grant
President, ICAP
Washington, DC
November 11, 1998

Acknowledgments

The editors wish to acknowledge the substantial editorial input of Linda Schmidt and David Thompson, both of whom worked tirelessly to help in the process of converting conference presentations into scholarly chapters. Their attention to detail was combined with a sensitivity to the place of each author's contribution in the overall theme of the book. Archie Brodsky provided additional editorial assistance.

The efforts of many others combined to create the conference on which the book is based. The members of the international advisory group (whose names are listed in the preface) and the staff and consultants of the International Center for Alcohol Policies all brought particular skills to many different parts of the process. Without their dedication to the development of the theme and theater of the conference, there would have been no book.

Introduction

Stanton Peele

Like the conference on which it is based, this book is designed to address the concept of pleasure in relation to beverage alcohol. Colloquially, pleasure seems to be an important ingredient in alcohol consumption. Yet it rarely has been incorporated in research or public health models. The book's aim is to bring together existing knowledge on the role of pleasure in drinking and to determine whether the concept is useful for scientific understanding and policy consideration by professionals in government, public health, research, and other fields, in both the developing and developed world, who are concerned with the consumption of alcohol.

WHY IS THIS TOPIC WORTHWHILE?

Pleasure Is an Important Motivation for Drinking Alcohol

In their surveys of drinking behavior in the United States, the Alcohol Research Group in Berkeley, California, has asked ordinary drinkers about their "experiences after drinking." Among current drinkers, by far the most common response was "felt happy and cheerful" (Cahalan, 1970, p. 131; see Chapter 15). The Mass Observation studies begun in the 1940s questioned ordinary drinkers closely about their drinking experiences and expectations (Mass Observation, 1943, 1948; see Chapter 18). Some focused on the contents of the beverage ("It tastes good"), some on the mood it engenders ("It relaxes me, makes me feel good"), some on the ritual or social elements ("I like relaxing at home over a drink" or "I like getting together with my friends and downing a few at the

1

pub"). This straightforward approach of asking drinkers about their current motivations for and experiences of drinking is represented in expectancy research
(Goldman, Brown, & Christiansen, 1987; see Chapter 16), including especially
younger drinkers (Foxcroft & Lowe, 1991). *Most* people who consume alcohol indicate that they anticipate a positive change in experience from drinking,
although this means different things for different groups.

Pleasure Plays a Role in Both Ordinary and Problematic Drinking

Cahalan (1970) divided drinkers into those who have never experienced problems
from drinking, those who have experienced such problems in the past but not at
present, and those who experience substantial drinking problems currently. *For
all groups among both genders, pleasure (feeling happy and cheerful) remained
the single most common drinking experience.* More problem drinkers gave pleasure as a response to questions on motivation, but they gave higher rates of
response to every type of drinking experience and consequence. This may be
because they drink more and have more of all such experiences. At the same
time, pleasure may motivate both normal, social drinking and problematic drinking, but heavy or problem drinkers may define pleasure differently (Critchlow,
1986; see Chapter 17). Younger drinkers more often drink for effect than for
ritual pleasure (Foxcroft & Lowe, 1991), although all drinkers emphasize the
socially pleasurable functions of drinking (see Chapter 18).

Issues to be Engaged

- Is pleasure a useful concept for explaining alcohol consumption?
- What distinguishes pleasure as a healthful or harmful motivation in
drinking behavior?
- Can the concept of pleasure be used to encourage healthy drinking?

WHY ARE NEW APPROACHES TO ALCOHOL CONSUMPTION REQUIRED?

Alcohol Consumption Will Always Be a Critical Public Health Issue Worldwide

Although the World Health Organization Regional Office for Europe (Edwards
et al., 1994; WHO, 1993) and other health agencies worldwide officially have
adopted reduced national alcohol consumption as a target, the elimination of all
beverage alcohol is not a possibility, and even the goal of reduced consumption
may be hard to achieve. In developed nations, alcohol consumption increased
dramatically from about 1950 to the middle to late 1970s, although in the longer
historical perspective, the 1970s was not an all-time high period of consumption

(Musto, 1996). Following the 1970s, many, but far from all, developed countries showed decreases in consumption. However, "the more recent declines in consumption typical of many developed countries have not appeared in many developing nations," where consumption is still increasing (Smart, 1998, p. 27). Nonetheless, developing nations still consume less alcohol per capita than developed nations. Thus styles, patterns, and levels of consumption and motivations for drinking in relation to these questions will remain critical public health issues. This may be particularly so in developing nations, which have perhaps fewer moderating traditions and yet in which consumption is increasing rapidly (see Part 2 and Chapter 24).

Public Health Policy Ignores the Almost Universal Motivation to Drink

Although people in most cultures seem strongly motivated to drink alcohol with expectations of positive effects (see Chapter 16), this attraction to alcohol is largely ignored by the public health sector. What makes this apparent oversight more puzzling is that a large percentage of those involved in alcohol policy and research themselves drink—if drinking behavior evinced at the conference upon which this volume is based may be used as a yardstick. This suggests that personal or cultural ambivalence may be a worthwhile point for investigation, and may need to be confronted by policy professionals, as policies that ignore the almost universal motivation to consume alcohol face long odds against succeeding (see Chapter 25).

Issues to be Engaged

- What is the impact of pleasure on the nature of and trends in drinking in the developing world, and does pleasure mean something different—have a different impact—there than in the developed world?
- What has prevented professionals from using pleasure as a policy tool and scientific concept, and is this continuing lacuna detrimental?

WHY DISCUSS DRINKING AND PLEASURE NOW?

Change and Stasis in the Alcohol Debate

The benefits of alcohol for coronary artery disease (CAD) are now quite broadly accepted (Doll, 1997; WHO, 1994; see Chapter 12). The CAD benefits of moderate drinking may well prolong life (Poikolainen, 1995). Nonetheless, the debate persists over whether to present such benefits to the public (see Chapter 14), and notably the concern that children should not be exposed to information about possible benefits of drinking. Thus, at the same time that the 1995 U.S. dietary guidelines (U.S. Department of Agriculture/Department of Health and Human Services, 1995) discussed coronary-disease benefits of alcohol consumption, as did the British sensible drinking guidelines (Department of Health and Social Security, 1995) and standards established by other Western nations (International Center for Alcohol Policies, 1996a, 1996b), this discussion is still controversial. Already, interest groups have mounted campaigns to reverse the language in the U.S. guidelines when these are reconsidered after 5 years, just as the current guidelines reversed those from 5 years earlier.

Current Approaches Towards Alcohol Are Almost Totally Problem-Oriented

There has been an ongoing process in the United States and throughout the world of identifying and addressing the problematic nature of alcohol consumption. Although there still may be room to extend this problem focus to new groups, and to deepen the depiction of the severity of worldwide drinking problems, we have proceeded quite a long way in this direction. At the same time, in the West and much of the rest of the world, alcohol production and consumption are legal, commercially marketed, and informally encouraged. Thus, considerable contention is built into the consideration of beverage alcohol. Yet broad agreement also seems attainable through the recognition of benefits from drinking among public health advocates and the recognition in turn by alcohol producers that problem drinking leads to serious and widespread social and health consequences.

One recent development that suggests the value of pleasure as a public health concept is the health-economics view of quality of life as a measurable and important ingredient in health (Nussbaum & Sen, 1993; see Chapter 23). For health economists, years survived alone do not describe the outcome of a disease event or intervention (Orley, 1994). Pleasure may be one reflection of quality-of-life considerations in drinking decision making and outcomes. To suggest this is to be conscious of the great differences in the apparent enjoyment of drinking events—from a shouting, angry public inebriate, to a person guiltily sneaking a drink alone, to a person drinking pleasantly in a shared experience within the family or with friends, for instance. These differences are reflected in cross-cultural, national, and group differences in the experience of alcohol, suggesting that they can be detailed and utilized (Douglas, 1987; Hartford & Gaines, 1982; Heath, 1995; see Chapter 5).

Issues to be Engaged

- Does an understanding of pleasure in drinking offer a route to moderate the current polarization in views of the role of alcohol in society?
- Can important individual, group, cultural, and situational differences in the pleasure of drinking experiences be understood and related to positive outcomes so that these can be encouraged as a part of health policies?

WHY A CONFERENCE?

This volume is based on a conference, one that seemed exciting and novel. The rationale for the conference was to explore a broad topic not thoroughly examined previously, to expose and interpret existing research related to the topic, and to outline the state of knowledge and areas in which future investigation is necessary. Because it is unlikely that the evidence on the conference topics covered in this volume will prove definitive, it is important to air different perspectives and interpretations in order to determine whether a new approach appears to have promise and deserves further attention. Among the topics the conference opened for discussion are the following:

- *The meaning of pleasure in cultural context:* How do people define pleasure? How central a motivator is pleasure for them? Are there differences in the definitions and importance of pleasure in different cultures (East versus West, for example; see Chapters 8 and 9)? Is pleasure useful as a health concept (see Chapter 11)?
- *Pleasure and drinking:* How do people define pleasure in relation to drinking? Are there differences in pleasurable drinking levels and styles according to situation (e.g., a wedding versus a fraternity party; see Chapter 19), group (e.g., male versus female; see Chapters 13 and 22), or culture (e.g., Nordic versus Mediterranean; see Chapter 5)? How do people vary in their expectations of pleasure when drinking (see Chapter 16)? Do differences in views of pleasure and its association with drinking explain different patterns of drinking (see Chapter 17)?
- *Pleasure and public health:* Is pleasure a worthwhile goal to encourage in drinkers? How does pleasurable drinking affect the likelihood of drinking problems (see Chapter 26)? Does pleasure offer a point of departure for respecting cultural differences (see Chapters 6, 7, and 10), for offering drinkers with different values a way to orient and control their drinking (see Chapter 21), and for communicating effectively with drinkers (see Chapter 25)? How does the consideration of pleasure in drinking policy affect individuals, educators, families, clinicians, communities, nations, and the planet as a whole (see Chapter 26)?

CONCLUSION

After a longstanding period of public health attention to alcohol, one primarily concerned with the problematic aspects of drinking, alcohol consumption remains both a major public health concern and a popular, widespread, and irreducible activity. Even the sternest public health advocates cannot reasonably expect to eliminate or indefinitely reduce drinking worldwide, nor do the data clearly show that such a goal would produce a public health gain. It is clearly established, for example, that drinking is associated with reduced heart disease epidemiologically in all parts of the Western world (Criqui & Ringel, 1994).

Pleasure in drinking is an understudied phenomenon. In addition to its appeal as a lay explanation for drinking, surveys of motivation also indicate that it is the primary goal in alcohol consumption. This volume and the conference on which it is based propose that enhancing our understanding of conceptions and differences in conceptions of pleasure, the actual role of pleasure as a motivator, and pleasure as a communication and a public health tool could advance our understanding of and ability to deal with beverage alcohol.

REFERENCES

Cahalan, D. (1970). *Problem drinkers*. San Francisco: Jossey-Bass.

Criqui, M. H., & Ringel, B. L. (1994). Does diet or alcohol explain the French paradox? *Lancet, 344*, 1719–1723.

Critchlow, B. (1986). The powers of John Barleycorn: Beliefs about the effects of alcohol on social behavior. *American Psychologist, 41*, 751–764.

Department of Health and Social Security (1995). *Sensible drinking: The report of an interdepartmental working group*. London: Her Majesty's Stationery Office.

Doll, R. (1997). One for the heart. *British Medical Journal, 315*, 1664–1668.

Douglas, M. (Ed.). (1987). *Constructive drinking: Perspectives on drink from anthropology*. Cambridge, UK: Cambridge University Press.

Edwards, G., Anderson, P., Babor, T. F., Casswell, S., Ferrence, R., Giesbrecht, N., Godfrey, C., Holder, H. D., Lemmens, P., Mäkelä, K., Midanik, L. T., Nöstrom, T., Österberg, E., Romelsjö, A., Room, R., Simpura, J., & Skog, O.-J. (1994). *Alcohol policy and the public good*. Oxford, UK: Oxford University Press.

Foxcroft, D. R., & Lowe, G. (1991). Adolescent drinking behaviour and family socialization factors: A meta-analysis. *Journal of Adolescence, 14*, 255–273.

Goldman, M. S., Brown, S. A., & Christiansen, B. A. (1987). Expectancy theory: Thinking about drinking. In H. T. Blane & K. E. Leonard (Eds.), *Psychological theories of drinking and alcoholism* (pp. 181–126). New York: Guilford.

Hartford, T. C., & Gaines, L. S. (Eds.). (1982). *Social drinking contexts* (Research Monograph 7). Rockville, MD: National Institute on Alcohol Abuse and Alcoholism.

Heath, D. (1995). *International handbook on alcohol and culture*. Westport, CT: Greenwood Press.

International Center for Alcohol Policies. (1996a). *Safe alcohol consumption: A comparison of* Nutrition and your health: Dietary guidelines for Americans *and* Sensible drinking (ICAP Reports 1). Washington, DC: Author.

International Center for Alcohol Policies. (1996b). *Safe alcohol consumption: A comparison of* Nutrition and your health: Dietary guidelines for Americans *and* Sensible drinking (ICAP Reports 1, Suppl.). Washington, DC: Author.

Mass Observation. (1943). *The pub and the people*. Falmer, UK: University of Sussex Mass Observation Archive.

Mass Observation. (1948). *Drinking habits*. Falmer, UK: University of Sussex Mass Observation Archive.

Musto, D. F. (1996, April). Alcohol and American history. *Scientific American*, 78–82.

Nussbaum, M., & Sen, A. (Eds.). (1993). *Quality of life*. New York: Oxford University Press.

Orley, J. (1994). *Quality-of-life assessment: International perspectives*. Secaucus, NJ: Springer-Verlag.

Poikolainen, K. (1995). Alcohol and mortality. *Journal of Clinical Epidemiology, 48*, 455–465.

Smart, R. (1998). Trends in drinking and patterns of drinking. In M. Grant & J. Litvak (Eds.), *Drinking patterns and their consequences* (pp. 25–41). Washington, DC: Taylor & Francis.

U.S. Department of Agriculture/Department of Health and Human Services. (1995). *Nutrition and your health: Dietary guidelines for Americans* (4th ed.). Washington, DC: U.S. Government Printing Office.

WHO. (1993). *European alcohol action plan.* Copenhagen, Denmark: WHO Regional Office for Europe.

WHO. (1994). *Cardiovascular disease risk factors: New areas for research. Report of a WHO Scientific Group* (WHO Technical Report Series, No. 841). Geneva, Switzerland: Author.

Part One

Pleasure and Health

The idea that pleasure has public health significance is a novel one, but not without precedent. Healthful aspects of drinking have been noted historically and cross-culturally since antiquity, as reported in Part 2. Current evidence and policy implications concerning the healthfulness of drinking are treated in Parts 3, 4, and 5.

In this first part, David Warburton compiles evidence from epidemiology, immunology, and other medical sciences that pleasure contributes to health. In making this case, Warburton describes pleasure as a fundamental biological mechanism. Michael Daube explores the concrete uses of pleasure in public health. Daube, like Warburton, sees the resistance to pleasure by health specialists as a cultural blind spot, one that makes health policy and education less effective than it otherwise could be. John Luik presents the opposing point of view that government should be excluded from decisions about individual health behaviors, just as modern society has moved towards excluding government from decisions about personal pleasure. Luik's and Daube's opposing positions stimulated considerable discussion and disputation at the conference, as reflected in the rapporteur's report at the end of this section.

Finally, Norman Sartorius broadens the conception of pleasure by relating it to its cultural, familial, social, and personal meanings. Although Sartorius stresses the relativity of the concept of pleasure, his long involvement in the field nonetheless points for him to the importance of pleasure as a consideration in public health.

Chapter 1

Pleasure for Health

David M. Warburton

This chapter summarizes evidence of the positive contribution of pleasure to individuals' health and so to the quality of everyday life (see also Warburton & Sherwood, 1996). The evidence comes from anthropology, neurochemistry, oncology, psychology, psychoimmunology, psychoendocrinology, and psychopharmacology.

For the anthropologist, pleasure must be seen as a subjective experience, because ethnic and cultural groups enjoy different things. It is also, however, a common experience and is part of the emotional vocabulary of all cultures (Tiger, 1992). This commonality among cultures indicates that pleasure is a universal human phenomenon.

From the viewpoint of psychology, pleasure has three components: (a) anticipation or the expectation of the pleasurable experience, (b) the pleasurable experience itself (often fleeting), and (c) retrospection. Recall of the pleasurable experience is often the most potent of pleasurable experiences and can be thought of as scanning the scrapbook of the mind.

Viewed from a psychopharmacological perspective, pleasurable experiences are clearly emotional states that map onto a neurochemical state in the brain. Studies on the neurochemistry of pleasure suggest that all pleasurable experiences can be related to the same neurochemical systems of the brain. There are two main strands of evidence for this proposition.

First, all pleasures can be lost under certain pathological conditions and then regained with treatment by certain types of drugs. One pathological condition marked by the loss of pleasurable experience is depression. Depression occurs in all cultures and is defined by a standard set of symptoms (American Psychiatric Association, 1994). Not all of these symptoms occur in every depressed individual, but a person is considered to have a major depressive episode if he or she exhibits a loss of pleasure in all, or almost all, usual activities. The universality of the pleasure loss by persons suffering from depression in all activities (from sexual activities and social interaction to musical and intellectual pursuits) suggests mediation by a common brain system.

Second, drug treatment can reinstate all the personal pleasures of an individual, whatever they may be. The restoration of pleasure in all typically pleasurable activities supports the notion of a common neurochemical system or systems for all pleasures. Thus, the only difference between brain states for pleasurable acts is quantitative.

Although there is a vast literature showing that negative psychological states are deleterious for physical health, the words "pleasure" and "happiness" are almost totally absent from the medical vocabulary. It is becoming clear, however, that pleasure is essential for physical and mental health. Pleasure can proactively promote good physical and mental health and protect against ill health, that is, serve as inoculation. Pleasure also can aid the process of unwinding, thereby lowering levels of stress hormones and protecting against potential adverse effects on the body. In this manner, pleasure acts as antidote against past stressors.

NEGATIVE PSYCHOLOGICAL STATES AND HEALTH

A good deal of evidence exists on the association of negative psychological states with ill health.

Stressors

Studies have shown a 259% increase in illness episodes following the onset of stress episodes in comparison with what would be expected by chance (Roghmann & Haggerty, 1973). This reactivity to stress increases, for example, the likelihood of childhood respiratory illnesses (Boyce et al., 1995). Similarly, other research has shown that children's life-event stress is associated with a longer duration of illness (Boyce et al., 1977). An important study has shown that stressor levels prior to inoculation with the common cold virus are positively associated with the onset of the symptoms of an upper respiratory infection (Cohen, Tyrrell, & Smith, 1991). This finding has been replicated in a smaller study (Stone et al., 1992).

Interestingly, the measure of life-event stressors in this research predicted infection symptoms, whereas negative affect and perceived stress levels predicted infection incidence (Cohen, Tyrrell, & Smith, 1993; Totman, Kiff, Reed, & Craig, 1980). The symptoms of upper respiratory infection cause people to seek medical help and to buy medication, but it is the incidence of infection that determines the size of the pool of contagious individuals and thereby the spread of infection throughout the population.

Although the acute stressor of parachuting decreases the number of natural killer cells (Schedlowski et al., 1993), more chronic stressful life changes actually reduce natural killer-cell activity (Locke et al., 1984).[1] Relatedly, familial caregivers for patients with Alzheimer's disease have weaker immune systems, as shown, for example, by an enhanced antibody response to the Epstein-Barr virus antigen (Kiecolt-Glaser et al., 1987); this reduction in immunity predicts adverse health consequences in the long term (Kiecolt-Glaser, Dura, Speicher, Trask, & Glaser, 1991).

Anxiety

The anticipatory anxiety of examinations reduces the activity of natural killer cells and the number of helper T lymphocytes, which directly or indirectly defend the body against viruses. Such changes are a predictor of acute infections (Glaser et al., 1987).

Bereavement

There is depressed lymphocyte proliferation response after bereavement (Bartrop, Lockhurst, Lazarus, Kiloh, & Penny, 1977) and suppression of lymphocyte production in response to an antigen challenge (Schleifer, Keller, Camerino, Thornton, & Stein, 1983). Irwin, Daniels, Smith, Bloom, and Weiner (1987) examined immune function in three groups: (a) women whose husbands had died of lung cancer within the previous 6 months, (b) women whose husbands currently were being treated for lung cancer, and (c) a control group of women whose husbands were in good health. In line with previous studies, the first group—those recently widowed—had impaired natural killer-cell activity.

Depression and Immunity

Depression, whose defining characteristic is a loss of interest and pleasure in all activities, decreases natural killer-cell activity (Irwin, Daniels, Bloom, Smith, & Weiner, 1987). In comparison with control subjects, patients with major depression have more circulating leukocytes and granulocytes, fewer natural killer cells, and less natural killer-cell activity. As a result, these individuals are more susceptible to viral infections normally controlled by such activity (Bartlett, Schleifer, Demetrikopoulos, & Keller, 1995; Schleifer, Keller, Bartlett, Eckholdt, & Delaney, 1996).

Negative Mood State and Immunity

All of the psychological states described previously are extremes on the spectrum of negative emotions, but recent studies indicate that everyday negative moods also weaken the immune system. For example, Stone et al. (1994) demonstrated reduced salivary immunoglobulin-A antibody response to oral antigen challenge on days marked by negative mood states. In turn, low secretory immunoglobulin-A levels in saliva were found to be associated with frequent viral infections of the upper repiratory tract. In another study (Knapp et al., 1992), the induction of a negative mood state in healthy volunteers resulted in short-term suppression of the immune system. Mood induction was created by asking subjects to recall or imagine "the most stressful, disturbing, painful, turmoil-filled time or times you can." The ensuing negative emotion produced significant decline in lymphocyte reactivity.

PLEASURE INOCULATION

There is an expanding literature on the effects of positive mood states on body systems, resulting in lower cortisol levels and increased immunocompetence.

Short Term

In the short term, techniques that promote relaxation have been demonstrated, for example, to produce a significant increase in natural killer-cell activity (Kiecolt-Glaser et al., 1986). Mirthful laughter has been found to lower serum cortisol levels (Berk, Tan, Fry, et al., 1989), raise T-lymphocyte levels, increase the number and activity of natural killer cells, and expand the count of T cells that have helper or suppressor receptors (Berk, Tan, Napier, & Eby, 1989). Watching a funny film increases the salivary levels of immunoglobulin A (Dillon, Minchoff, & Baker, 1985), especially in those with a strong sense of humor (Lefcourt, Davidson-Katz, & Kueneman, 1990). In our laboratory, we asked subjects to recall either a happy autobiographical memory or one associated with feelings of guilt ($n = 20$ in each group). In the happy condition, subjects experienced an elevation of salivary immunogobulin-A secretion for 3 hours following the recall, guilty memories suppressed immunoreactions for a similar period (Figure 1.1).

Longer Term

As studies previously have demonstrated (Stone, Cox, Valdimarsdottir, Jandorf, & Neale, 1987; Stone et al., 1994), the salivary immunoglobulin-A antibody response to an oral antigen challenge is enhanced on days on which subjects experience a positive mood and lowered on days dominated by a highly negative mood. Moreover, the positive effect of pleasurable events on salivary immunoglobulin A has a 1- to 2-day carryover. Thus, it is not surprising that earlier studies had shown either an increase in unhappy events or a decrease in pleasurable events during the 3- to 5-day period prior to the onset of upper respiratory infection symptoms (Stone, Reed, & Neale, 1987).

Evans, Pitts, and Smith (1988) found a drop in the incidence of pleasurable events but not an increase in undesirable events prior to the onset of an upper

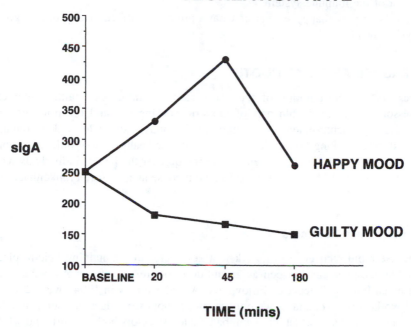

SALIVARY IMMUNOGLOBULIN-A SECREATION RATE

Figure 1.1 Immune response to "happy" and "guilty" autobiographical memories. *Secretion rate* refers to secretion over a 2-minute period as measured in micrograms per minute. The baseline (40 μg/min) is the prerecall baseline, that is, the "normal" baseline for individuals prior to laboratory testing.

respiratory infection. Evans and Edgerton (1991) found, by contrast, a decrease in happy events and a trend towards an increase in unhappy events in the days before an upper respiratory infection.

A provocative study about the influence of lifestyle in a random population survey in Northern Ireland ($N = 1787$) collected samples of serum immunoglobulin-A, along with reported beverage-alcohol and cigarette consumption (McMillan, Douglas, Archbold, McCrum, & Evans, 1997). The population then was classified into the following groups: no beverage alcohol, 8 to 160 g beverage alcohol per week, 168 to 320 g beverage alcohol per week, and more than 320 g beverage alcohol per week (less than 8% of the sample). The median serum immunoglobulin-A concentrations showed a significant increase with beverage-alcohol consumption ($p = .0001$); subjects who consumed more than 320 g per week showed an increase of 12% over the no-alcohol group. There was no significant relation with cigarette consumption.

We must be cautious in assuming that the participants differed only in their beverage-alcohol consumption, as numerous other variables are associated with imbibing. Nevertheless, these data are consistent with the hypothesis that beverage-alcohol consumption and its associated lifestyle strengthen this component of the immune system.

In summary, happy events can have protective effects and promote good physical health.

PLEASURE AS AN ANTIDOTE

Stressors and the duration of the stress response influence health outcomes. Stressors are an inevitable part of modern working life and the price people pay for high achievement. Yet, although the body's stress level does remain high during working hours, the critical factor for health is how quickly people unwind after work. The key seems to be the quicker the better; individuals who are slow to unwind have more adverse health consequences (see Frankenhaeuser, 1986).

Some Stress Reducers

Because rapid recovery from work is a key factor in maintaining health, pleasurable activities can be seen as an antidote to stressors. In an Associates for Research Into the Science of Enjoyment (ARISE) survey in 1994, over 5296 office workers in 16 countries were interviewed about workplace pressures and the pleasurable ways in which they combated such stressors both at work and while unwinding at the end of the day. Activities mentioned by those surveyed fell into four categories: (a) social pleasures, such as chatting; (b) passive pleasures, such as listening to music, reading, watching television, or having a shower; (c) active pleasures, such as exercising, dining out, play with children, or shopping; and (d) enjoyment of "pleasure products" such as coffee, tea, cigarettes, beverage alcohol, or chocolate (Table 1.1).

Little research has been done to assess the mood-enhancing effects of these activities, let alone their impact on the immune system. Nevertheless, laboratory tests for assessing potential antianxiety drugs and antidepressants have shown that a cup of coffee, a glass of wine, a cigarette, some sugar, and a few pieces of chocolate all make people calmer, more relaxed, and generally happier. This is not surprising, because these products exert a mild pharmacological action on the brain's pleasure pathways (Warburton, 1996). It is known that these same pathways are common for all pleasures, ranging from food to music, because pleasure is not experienced by people with depression regardless of the activity (American Psychiatric Association, 1994).

Enjoying Them Together

The lists in Table 1.1 imply that these activities occur separately, but this is clearly not the case. For example, many studies have demonstrated that alco-

Table 1.1   Pleasurable activities chosen by office workers in 16 countries to combat stress.

Social	Passive	Active	Products
Chatting, 76%	Music, 76%	Exercise, 59%	Coffee, 37%
	Reading, 74%	Eating out, 58%	Tea, 30%
	Television, 70%	Playing with children, 51%[a]	Tobacco, 28%
	Bath/shower, 63%[b]	Shopping, 39%[c]	Alcohol, 25%[e]
		Buying self present, 37%[d]	Chocolate, 24%[f]
		Playing cards, etc., 26%	
		Meditation, 12%	

[a]This was the only unwinding activity for which the United States was *not* significantly below the global mean.
[b]Women 69%; men 57%.
[c]Women 47%; men 30%.
[d]Women 44%; men 29%.
[e]Women 18%; men 32%.
[f]Women 28%; men 19%.
Source: Associates for Research Into the Science of Enjoyment (1994).

hol consumption, coffee drinking, and smoking are associated activities (see Chapter 20).

The ARISE survey revealed the importance of meals for unwinding and relaxation at the end of the day. Moreover, pleasure products accompany many meals. Thus, significant aspects of a good meal mentioned in the survey for relaxing and unwinding were an alcoholic drink, a cup of coffee, a cigarette, and chocolate. Such pleasurable items often combine and interact with the more spiritual components of a meal—for example, with the conviviality and sociability of conversation, joking, and maybe the enjoyment of music.

Mood States and Cognition

Research has demonstrated that mood states can influence the way we think and what we remember (Teasdale & Barnard, 1993). Research at our laboratory employed small doses of beverage alcohol to modify the mood state of individuals independent of measurable changes in both attentional and mnemonic processing of words. The positive mood changes with alcohol—for example, increased calmness and happiness—were greater if expectancies were enhanced by set (participants were told they receiving alcohol) and setting (the alcohol was taken in a pleasant, sociable environment).

In the first study of mood state and cognition, we found that alcohol abolished the Emotional Stroop Effect, that is the slowing of processing by emotive words such as *cancer* in comparison with neutral words such as *cover*. The calm mood state engendered by alcohol lowered the impact of the threat words and so there was no slowing of word processing. In a second study, alcohol specifically enhanced memory for "happy" (i.e., mood-congruent) words. Thus, subjects who had consumed a social amount of alcohol (8 g) showed normal

2a. Amnesic Effect

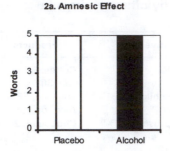

2b. Word Type

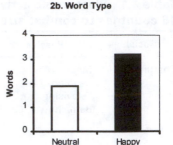

Figure 1.2 Impact of social drinking on memory of "happy" words. *Words* refers to the number of words recalled from a mixed list of 20 happy and neutral words.

memory overall yet were able to recall a higher percentage of happy than neutral words (Figure 1.2). Mood-congruent memory was greatest for the participants if the expectancy of receiving alcohol matched actual alcohol consumption and the alcohol was drunk in a pleasant sociable setting.

In summary, pleasurable activities must be seen as additive and interactive. One activity may have a small impact, but the effects of pleasurable activities combine. The importance of inducing positive mood states to aid unwinding and the impact of pleasant events in general cannot be overestimated (Miller & Berman, 1983; Rehm, 1978). The 1994 ARISE survey revealed that the United States had the most stressed population, not because it was lowest on enjoying any one activity, but because it rated significantly lower on 15 out of the 16 pleasurable activities listed in Table 1.1.

NEGATIVE MOOD STATES AND CHRONIC ILLNESS

Research has established the impact of anxiety and depression on health. As suggested previously, the essential feature of a major depressive episode is the loss of pleasure in all, or nearly all, activities. One note of caution is that anxiety and depression are not independent, and comorbidity may be as high as 30% (U.S. Department of Health and Human Services, 1993).

Meta-analysis of the relationship between anxiety and a number of illnesses has found highly significant associations of anxiety with arthritis, asthma, coronary heart disease, headaches, and ulcers (Friedman & Booth-Kewley, 1987; Steptoe, 1981).

Patients with major depressive disorders also have more physical illnesses than other primary-care patients. As with anxiety, a meta-analysis of the relationship between depression and a number of illnesses found highly significant associations of depression with arthritis, asthma, coronary heart disease, headache, and ulcers (Friedman & Booth-Kewley, 1987). This finding has been confirmed by several studies. Depression is associated with increased incidence of morbidity from almost all physical illnesses, including respiratory problems and cardiovascular disease (Lee & Murray, 1988; Sims, 1988; Sims & Prior, 1978; Wells et al., 1989).

Indeed, reports of individuals' health status bear out this association. In 1993, 48% of depressed people surveyed by the U.S. Department of Health and Human Services (1993) reported their health as only fair or poor—a considerably higher percentage than that in the general population (19%). In addition, 23% of depressed primary-care patients and only 5% of the general population reported that their health had kept them in bed for all or part of one day. Thus, the level of healthcare utilization is higher for depressed people in comparison with other primary-care patients.

A number of studies show that unhappiness caused by job and life dissatisfaction is a predictor of coronary heart disease and general mortality rate (Botwinnick, West, & Storandt, 1978; Kaplan & Camandro, 1983; Zuckerman, Kasl, & Ostfeld, 1984). If accidents and suicides are excluded, clinically depressed patients have a higher than expected mortality risk, particularly in respects to cardiovascular disease (Avery & Winokur, 1976; Roose & Dalack, 1992).

A 30- to 40-year follow-up study of 182 persons suffering from depression and 109 matched controls in Iowa revealed dramatic differences in death rates (Winokur & Tsuang, 1975). At the end of the study, 66% of the controls were still alive; 34% had died. In contrast, 27% of the depressive persons were still alive and 73% had died (8% through suicide and 65% from other causes). Another study found that patients with major depressive disorders had a 59% greater likelihood of death in the first year following admission to hospital with depression and that patients 55 years or older had a mortality rate over four times greater than nondepressed, age-matched controls in the 15 months after diagnosis (U.S. Department of Health and Human Services, 1993).

In summary, individuals experiencing persistent negative mood states face a higher risk of injury and mortality compared to the general population.

PLEASURE, HAPPINESS, AND LONGEVITY

Prospective studies have shown that happiness is a predictor of longevity, even if current state of health is controlled for (Botwinnick et al., 1978; Deeg, 1987; Kaplan & Camandro, 1983; Lehr & Schmitz-Scherer, 1974; Lehr, Schmitz-Scherer, & Zimmerman, 1983; Palmore, 1974, 1982, 1985; Veenhoven, 1988; Zuckerman et al., 1984). Because the evidence reviewed here suggests that happier people are also healthier, this work indicates that contentment contributes to longevity even apart from its impact on health.

CONCLUSION

Several types of evidence indicate that pleasure is beneficial for health. This chapter reviews many of these, including the following:

- Stressors (e.g., bereavement) and negative psychological states depreciate health.
- Pleasurable events and experienced enjoyment enhance immunological resistance to disease.
- Pleasurable activities and their resulting enjoyment relieve stress, thereby contributing to health.
- Chronically anxious and depressed individuals suffer more disease and die earlier.
- Happier people live longer, even when current health status is factored out.

Notwithstanding this evidence, we must realize that pleasure should be enjoyed in its own right as part of a well-balanced life. The medical evidence that pleasure is good for people is a useful riposte to the moralistic self-righteousness of those who believe that there is only one way to live life—denial.

ACKNOWLEDGMENT AND DISCLAIMER

Much of the research for the preparation of this chapter was funded by the Associates for Research Into the Science of Enjoyment (ARISE). Nonetheless, the views expressed here are solely those of the author and not necessarily those of the International Center for Alcohol Policy, its sponsoring companies, or ARISE.

NOTE

1. Natural killer cells are white blood cells that engulf and destroy cells that have been infected by a virus or have been transformed into cancer cells. Thus, natural killer cells are the body's first defense against the development of malignant tumors.

REFERENCES

American Psychiatric Association. (1994). *Diagnostic and statistical manual of mental disorders* (4th ed.). Washington, DC: Author.

Associates for Research Into the Science of Enjoyment. (1994). Stress, relaxation, and pleasure. [Online]. Available: http://www.arise.org.

Avery, D., & Winokur, G. (1976). Mortality in depressed patients treated with electroconvulsive therapy and antidepressants. *Archives of General Psychiatry, 33,* 1029–1037.

Bartlett, J. A., Schleifer, S. J., Demetrikopoulos, M. K., & Keller, S. E. (1995). Immune differences in children with and without depression. *Biological Psychiatry, 38,* 771–774.

Bartrop, R. W., Lockhurst, E., Lazarus, L., Kiloh, L. G., & Penny, R. (1977). Depressed lymphocyte function after bereavement. *Lancet, i,* 834–836.

Berk, L., Tan, S. A., Fry, W. F., Napier, B. J., Lee, J. W., Hubbard, R. W., Lewis, J. E., & Eby, W. C. (1989). Neuroendocrine and stress hormone changes during mirthful laughter. *American Journal of Medical Sciences, 298,* 390–396.

Berk, L., Tan, S. A., Napier, B. J., & Eby, W. C. (1989). Eustress of mirthful laughter modifies natural killer cell activity. *Clinical Research, 37,* 115.

Botwinnick, J., West, R., & Storandt, M. (1978). Predicting death from behavioral test performance. *Journal of Gerontology, 33,* 755–762.

Boyce, W. T., Chesney, M., Alkon, A., Tschann, J. M., Adams, S., Chesterman, B., Cohen, F., Kaiser, P., Folkman, S., & Wara, D. (1995). Psychobiologic reactivity to stress and childhood respiratory illnesses: Results of two prospective studies. *Psychosomatic Medicine, 57,* 411–422.

Boyce, W. T., Jensen, E., Cassel, J., Collier, A., Smith, A., & Ramey, C. (1977). Influence of life events and family routines on childhood respiratory tract illness. *Pediatrics, 60,* 609.

Cohen, S., Tyrrell, D. A. J., & Smith, A. P. (1991). Psychological stress and susceptibility to the common cold. *New England Journal of Medicine, 325,* 606–612.

Cohen, S., Tyrrell, D. A. J., & Smith, A. P. (1993). Negative life events, perceived stress, negative affect and susceptibility to the common cold. *Journal of Personality and Social Psychology, 64,* 131–140.

Deeg, D. (1987). En ze leefden nog lang en gelukkig: Satisfactie als predictor voor overlevingsduur bij bejaarden [And they lived long and happily ever after: Satisfaction as a predictor of survival rates among the elderly]. *Gezondheid en Samenleving, 7,* 98–107.

Dillon, K., Minchoff, B., & Baker, K. (1985). Positive emotional states and enhancement of the immune system. *International Journal of Psychiatry in Medicine, 15,* 13–18.

Evans, P., & Edgerton, N., (1991). Life events and mood as predictors of the common cold. *British Journal of Medical Psychology, 64,* 35–44.

Evans, P. D., Pitts, M. K., & Smith, K. (1988). Minor infection, minor life events, and the four day desirability dip. *Journal of Psychosomatic Research, 32,* 533–539.

Frankenhaeuser, M. (1986). A psychobiological framework for research on human stress and coping. In M. H. Appley & R. Trumbell (Eds.), *Dynamics of stress* (pp. 101–116). New York: Plenum.

Friedman, M., & Booth-Kewley, S. (1987). *The disease-prone personality.* New York: Knopf.

Glaser, R., Rice, J., Sheridan, J., Post, A. Fertel, R., Stout, J., Speicher, C. E., Kotur, M., & Kiecolt-Glaser, I. K. (1987). Stress-related immune suppression: Health implications. *Brain, Behavior, and Immunity, 1,* 7–20.

Irwin, M., Daniels, M., Bloom, E., Smith, T., & Weiner, H. (1987). Life events, depressive symptoms, and immune function. *American Journal of Psychiatry, 4,* 144.

Irwin, M., Daniels, M., Smith, T., Bloom, E., & Weiner, H. (1987). Impaired natural killer cell activity during bereavement. *Brain, Behavior, and Immunity, 1,* 98–104.

Kaplan, G. A., & Camandro, T. (1983). Perceived health and mortality: A nine-year follow-up of the Human Population Laboratory Control. *American Journal of Epidemiology, 117,* 292–304.

Kiecolt-Glaser, J. K., Dura, J. R., Speicher, C. E., Trask, O. J., & Glaser, R. (1991). Spousal caregivers of dementia victims: Longitudinal changes in immunity and health. *Psychosomatic Medicine, 53,* 345–362.

Kiecolt-Glaser, J. K., Glaser, R., Shuttleworth, E. C., Dyer, C. S., Ogrocki, P., & Speicher, C. E. (1987). Chronic stress and immunity in family caregivers of Alzheimer's disease victims. *Psychosomatic Medicine, 49,* 523–535.

Kiecolt-Glaser, J. K., Glaser, R., Strain, E., Stout, J., Tarr, K., Holliday, J., & Speicher, C. E. (1986). Modulation of cellular immunity in medical students. *Journal of Behavioral Medicine, 9,* 5–21.

Knapp, P. H., Levy, E. M., Giorgi, R. G., Black, P. H., Fox, B. H., & Heeren, T. C. (1992). Short-term immunological effects of induced emotion. *Psychosomatic Medicine, 54,* 133–148.

Lee, A. S., & Murray, R. M. (1988). The long-term outcome of Maudsley depressives. *British Journal of Psychiatry, 153,* 741–751.

Lefcourt, H., Davidson-Katz, K., & Kueneman, K. (1990). Humor and immune system functioning. *International Journal of Humor Research, 3,* 305–321.

Lehr, U., & Schmitz-Scherer, R. (1974). Psycho-soziale Korrelate der Langlebigkeit [Psychosocial correlates of longevity]. *Aktuelle Gerontologie, 4,* 261–268.

Lehr, U., Schmitz-Scherer, R., & Zimmerman, E. (1983). *Sozial-psychologische Korrelate der Langlebigkeit* [Social-psychological correlates of longevity]. Bonn, Germany: Psychological Institute, University of Bonn.

Locke, S. E., Kraus, L., Leserman, J., Hurst, M. W., Heisel, J. S., & Williams, R. M. (1984). Life change stress, psychiatric symptoms, and natural killer cell activity. *Psychosomatic Medicine, 46*, 441–453.

McMillan, S. A., Douglas, J. P., Archbold, G. P. R., McCrum, E. E., & Evans, A. E. (1997). Effect of low to moderate levels of smoking and alcohol consumption on serum immunoglobulin concentrations. *Journal of Clinical Pathology, 50*, 819–822.

Miller, R. C., & Berman, J. S. (1983). The efficacy of cognitive behavior therapies: A quantitative review of the research evidence. *Psychological Bulletin, 94*, 39–53.

Palmore, E. (1974). Predicting longevity: A new method. In E. Palmore (Ed.), *Normal aging II: Report from Duke longitudinal studies 1970–1975*. Durham, NC: Duke University Press.

Palmore, E. B. (1982). Predictors of the longevity difference: A 25-year follow-up. *Gerontologist, 6*, 513–518.

Palmore, E. B. (1985). How to live longer and like it. *Journal of Applied Gerontology, 4*, 1–8.

Rehm, L. P. (1978). Mood, pleasant events, and unpleasant events: Two pilot studies. *Journal of Consulting and Clinical Psychology, 46*, 854–859.

Roghmann, K., & Haggerty, R. (1973). Daily stress, illness, and use of health services in young families. *Pediatric Research, 23*, 520–526.

Roose, S. P., & Dalack, G. W. (1992). Treating the depressed patient with cardiovascular problems. *Journal of Clinical Psychiatry, 53*(Suppl. 9), 25–31.

Schedlowski, M., Jacobs, R., Stratmann, G., Richter, S., Hadicke, A., Tewes, U., Wagner, T. O. F., & Schmidt, R. E. (1993). Changes of natural killer cells during acute psychological stress. *Journal of Clinical Immunology, 13*, 119–126.

Schleifer, S. J., Keller, S. E., Bartlett, J. A., Eckholdt, H. M., & Delaney, B. R. (1996). Immunity in young adults with major depressive disorder. *American Journal of Psychiatry, 153*, 477–482.

Schleifer, S. J., Keller, S. E., Camerino, M., Thornton, J. C., & Stein, M. (1983). Suppression of lymphocyte stimulation following bereavement. *Journal of the American Medical Association, 15*, 374–377.

Sims, A. C. (1988). The mortality associated with depression. *International Clinical Psychopharmacology, 3*(Suppl. 2), 1–13.

Sims, A., & Prior, P. (1978). The pattern of mortality in severe neuroses. *British Journal of Psychiatry, 133*, 299–305.

Steptoe, A. (1981). *Psychological factors in cardiovascular disorders*. London: Academic Press.

Stone, A., Bovbjerg, D., Neale, J., Napoli, A., Valdimarsdottir, H., Cox, D., Hayden, F., & Gwaltney, J., Jr. (1992). Development of common cold symptoms following experimental rhinovirus infection is related to prior stressful life events. *Behavioral Medicine, 18*, 115–120.

Stone, A., Cox, D., Valdimarsdottir, H., Jandorf, L., & Neale, J. (1987). Evidence that secretory IgA antibody is associated with daily mood. *Journal of Personality and Social Psychology, 52*, 988–993.

Stone, A., Neale, J., Cox, D., Napoli, A., Valdimarsdottir, H., & Kennedy-Moore, E. (1994). Daily events are associated with a secretory response to an oral antigen in men. *Health Psychology, 13*, 440–446.

Stone, A., Reed, B. R., & Neale, J. M. (1987). Changes in daily event frequency precede episodes of physical symptoms. *Journal of Human Stress, 13*, 70–74.

Teasdale, J. D., & Barnard, P. J. B. (1993). *Affect, cognition, and change*. Hove, UK: Lawrence Erlbaum Associates.

Tiger, L. (1992). *The pursuit of pleasure*. London: Little, Brown and Company.

Totman, R., Kiff, J., Reed, S., & Craig, J. (1980). Predicting experimental colds in volunteers from different measures of recent life stress. *Journal of Psychosomatic Research, 24*, 155.

U.S. Department of Health and Human Services. (1993). *Depression in primary care: Vol. 1* (AHCPR Publication No. 93-0550). Washington, DC: U.S. Government Printing Office

Veenhoven, R. (1988). The utility of happiness. *Social Indicators Research, 20*, 333–354.

Warburton, D. M. (1996). The functions of pleasure. In D. M. Warburton & N. Sherwood (Eds.), *Pleasure and quality of life* (pp. 1–10). Chichester, UK: John Wiley.

Warburton, D. M., & Sherwood, N. (Eds.). (1996). *Pleasure and quality of life*. Chichester, UK: John Wiley.

Wells, K. B., Stewart, A., Hays, R. D., Burnam, M. A., Rogers, W., Daniels, M., Berry, S., Greenfield, S., & Ware, J. (1989). The functioning and well-being of depressed patients: Results from the Medical Outcomes Study. *Journal of the American Medical Association, 262,* 914–919.

Winokur, G., & Tsuang, M. (1975). The Iowa 500: Suicide in mania, depression, and schizophrenia. *American Journal of Psychiatry, 132,* 650–651.

Zuckerman, D. M., Kasl, S. V., & Ostfeld, A. M. (1984). Psychological predictors of mortality among the elderly poor: The role of religion, well-being and social contacts. *American Journal of Epidemiology, 11,* 410–423.

Chapter 2

Wardens, Abbots, and Modest Hedonists: The Problem of Permission for Pleasure in a Democratic Society

John Luik

Let us begin with what I call the paradox of pleasure. The paradox is that along with its delight, satisfaction, fulfillment, and joy, pleasure also has been the source of some of humanity's deepest disagreements and persistent dissatisfactions. Something that would at first glance be thought to produce nothing but good carries within it the power to bring great pain.

Part of the reason for this paradox is that pleasure is entwined conceptually, at least in Western culture, with a host of other highly contentious ideas such as good and evil, the nature of humanity, the authority of the state, the nature of truth, the truth of religion, the status of science, and the limits of personal freedom. Thus the history of pleasure is at one level the history of how we have defined right and wrong and good and bad, how we have thought about ourselves as persons, how we have claimed to be certain of anything, and how we have conceived of the state and its power over us. To take one example, it has always been an open question whether, having described something as pleasurable, it also was correct to describe it as good. Pleasure has not been thought of as something intrinsically, analytically, and universally good: It has always required justification and legitimization.

In a word, pleasure has always required permission.

But from where does this permission come? Who or what tells us that pleasure A is acceptable but pleasure D is inappropriate?

THE TRADITION OF THE WARDEN AND THE ABBOT

A full answer to this question is quite obviously beyond the scope of this chapter, in part because of the way in which pleasure is so intimately connected with so many of the strands of our intellectual, cultural, and political history. What I want to do instead is to provide a sketch of two of the more central answers to the question of who legitimizes pleasure. The first of these traditions about the legitimization of pleasure is what I call the tradition of the warden and the abbot. For it is the metaphors of the secular prison and the sacred monastery with their images of enclosure and confinement, of prescription and control, that describe this conception of how pleasure is justified. According to this dominant tradition in our culture, pleasure is something that is first of all insidious and corrupting, something that is far more likely to destroy than to ennoble, something far more likely to be connected with the deeply disturbing aspects of personal and social life than with the truly satisfying and fulfilling. Pleasure in this approach is treated with suspicion and mistrust; it is primarily a problem in that it must be confined lest it spell ruin for individuals and society.

For the Christian, pleasure as such is not intrinsically wrong. But the particular pleasures to which fallen humans turn are inevitably wrong. A corrupted human will and a deformed reason combine, in the Christian tradition, inevitably and universally to produce a corruption of pleasure from what St. Paul describes as the joys of the spirit to the lusts of the flesh. Such a view often is described as Puritan, but this is to reduce a complicated set of widely held views to a particular historical label.

Moreover, this position is not simply a Christian one, as the easy appropriation of the classical tradition by the Christian fathers should remind us. The same sense of pleasure's dangers mixed with the feebleness of reason is to be found in Plato's image of the charioteer who attempts to check, often unsuccessfully, the appetitive passions of the soul.

But if pleasure is likely to be something dangerous, something likely to corrupt, how, and under what circumstances, can so powerful a menace be legitimized? The answer is to be found, once again, in the metaphor. Wardens and abbots are sources of authority: Their function is to authorize, order, proscribe. In this tradition pleasure finds its permission and legitimacy through the authority of a powerful institution, whether the Church and its sacred texts or civil society with its laws or, indeed, often some uneasy combination of the two. As John Stuart Mill (1859/1978, p. 12) notes,

> Society has expended fully as much effort in the attempt . . . to compel people to conform to its notions of personal as of social excellence. The ancient commonwealths

thought themselves entitled to practice, and the ancient philosophers countenanced, the regulation of every part of private conduct by public authority, on the ground that the State had a deep interest in the whole bodily and mental discipline of every one of its citizens.

Indeed, the entire notion of the private is omitted in such a tradition. The central problem with pleasure here is not its expression but its appropriate expression, with "appropriate" having a necessarily social rather than personal, private definition. The question of pluralism of pleasure is inconceivable in this view, because humans are social beings whose pleasures inevitably have a social dimension that must conform rather than conflict (see Chapter 4). Legitimate pleasure, permissible pleasure, is pleasure that, if not assembled by the state, at least bears the state's imprimatur. There is no room for individualistic pleasure. Even if pleasure is a personal experience it is one sanctioned by the state. Pleasure comes completely within the state's paternalistic embrace.

Such a view shares a conceptual space with other monisms, whether of knowing, religion, or politics. All share a similar set of assumptions about persons and society. As for persons, their powers of understanding and their capacity for judgment are too ill developed for them to be left alone to make their way in a world of complicated matters. About society, it is maintained that individuals are too inherently fragile to either tolerate or embrace a plurality of thoughts and ways of living. In all such monisms the state exercises a hegemony of correctness that does not tolerate deviation.

It is perhaps not surprising that such a view about pleasure should dominate Western tradition; there is a certain historical naturalness in society's interest in containing something so powerfully threatening to its stability as pleasure. What may be more surprising is that within the space of a relatively short time this view should come under such sustained attack as to lose its intellectual and legal legitimacy.

INDIVIDUAL HEDONISM AND MODERN DEMOCRACY

The source of this attack on the state as the source of permission for pleasure is the second conception of legitimate pleasure, which I call modest individual hedonism. I refer to it in this fashion to emphasize both that it does not see the end of a fulfilled human life as a constant pursuit of pleasure—rather, it sees pleasure in a more modest and temperate sense—and that it views pleasure from the perspective of the individual. The conceptual home of this view of the legitimacy of pleasure is the Enlightenment. This is not to suggest that there were not previous attempts to root permission for pleasure within an individual context, but rather that these attempts were largely isolated dissents from the prevailing intellectual consensus, not widespread critiques of that consensus.

With the Enlightenment came the first generalized and sustained questioning of the apparatus of monism, that is of the belief that individuals within a particular society must share a wide range of sentiments, beliefs, and behaviors, that there is but one correct way to live one's life. What the Enlightenment did was to use a more optimistic view of human nature—the hope, if not the reasoned evidence, for the perfectibility of persons, along with a more wide-ranging sense of individual liberty. This raises two quite radical questions. First, is it true that there is only one answer to what makes a good life, or are there indeed multiple ways in which individuals and societies might choose to live? Second, should the choice of belief and behavior be left, within certain limits, to individual choice?

In effect, what Enlightenment thinkers wished to argue was that if individuals were genuinely free (that is, if they were, to use an important word, autonomous), then that autonomy quite naturally would reflect itself in a plurality of interests, pursuits, beliefs, values, and pleasures. One consequence of autonomy is thus to change the presumption of the argumentative framework. Previously it was movements away from sameness and control that had to be justified; now it is efforts to enforce conformity that bear the burden of proof.

If individuals have both the right and the ability to shape themselves, the idea of permission for legitimate pleasure takes on a different color. On the one hand pleasure becomes considerably less menacing—it is much less likely to derail the human prospect than to enrich and fulfill it. On the other hand pleasure, primarily because it is more domesticated, falls more comfortably within the purview of individual choice. Pleasure in effect becomes a more legitimately private matter, part of the larger project of the personal governance of the soul. Naturally the choice of one's pleasures is not without limits, as it rests on granting the power for reciprocal choices to others and on the commitment to avoid pleasures that harm others.

Both the most famous and most eloquent expression of this modest individual hedonism is to be found again in the work of Mill (1859/1978). Mill, of course, sees hedonistic freedom, the freedom to choose one's pleasures, as intimately connected to political freedom—the freedom of the citizen. But he realizes, perhaps more clearly than anyone before him, that the freedom of the citizen can have an unfortunate shallowness in that the majority itself can become a tyrant by attaching a range of criminal sanctions to various pleasures, just as surely as an arbitrary ruler can. Again, the conventions of society, particularly the conventions about legitimate, acceptable pleasure, can constrain the autonomy of individuals as tightly as any legal restriction. Liberty, for Mill, must encompass

> tastes and pursuits: of framing the plan of our life to suit our own character, of doing as we like, subject to such consequences as may follow: without impediment from our fellow-creatures, so long as what we do does not harm them, even though they should think our conduct foolish, perverse or wrong. . . . The only freedom which deserves the name, is that of pursuing our own good in our own way, so long as we do not attempt to deprive others of theirs, or impede their efforts to obtain it. Each

is the proper guardian of his own health, whether bodily, or mental and spiritual. (p. 12)

Mill's *On Liberty*, the source of these presumptuous thoughts on permission for pleasure, was published in 1859, and in the century that followed what had started life as a radical doctrine became the liberal consensus of most democratic societies. Pleasure, unless it threatened harm to others, increasingly was accepted as a private matter, a matter of individual choice, and indeed a central part of what was meant by individual autonomy. This does not mean that there were not significant exceptions to pleasure's progress, the United States' experiment with Prohibition and the persistent criminalization of consenting adult sexual behavior being two of the most obvious. But despite such inconsistencies and the occasional emergence of a revived Puritanism, there was still an increasing willingness to accept the definition and pursuit of pleasure as an intrinsic part of individual autonomy.

HEALTH PROMOTERS AS PERMITTERS OF PLEASURE

In the past 20 years, however, modest individualistic hedonism with its belief that permission for pleasure derives from the choices of free persons has come under persistent attack from a seemingly unlikely quarter: the proponents of health or, as they prefer to call themselves, health promoters. What I wish to argue is that health promotion as it is currently conceived and practiced in most of the world represents a return to the tradition of the warden and the abbot, to the belief that because of the threat it poses to health and longevity, permission for pleasure must again be the gift of the state, in this case supported by science.

Such a redefinition of permission for pleasure is far from a trivial encroachment on individual autonomy. It is a radical assault on the key component of what it means to be a free person in a democratic society, and as such it should be vigorously resisted.

Let us begin with a definition of health promotion. Although there are a variety of conceptions of health promotion, I think that it is not unfair to define it minimally as involving the following claims:

1   There is increasing scientific agreement about one healthy and rational way to live that has as its end, to quote the constitution of the World Health Organization (1996), "a state of complete physical, mental and social well-being" (p. 1).

2   Much disease is caused by unhealthy life choices about pleasure and risk.

3   Much disease can be prevented by appropriate lifestyle and behavioral changes, particularly with respect to pleasure.

   4   Individuals have a moral obligation to live their lives in accordance with
their society's accepted norm of healthy behavior and thus avoid inappropriate
pleasures.
   5   The task of health promotion is twofold: to disseminate the truth about
health, disease, lifestyle, and pleasure; and to provide, aided by the state, the necessary persuasive mechanisms for changing both individual and societal beliefs
and behaviors about health, disease, lifestyle, and pleasure.

   It is immediately and indisputably obvious that health promotion falls
squarely within the warden-and-abbot tradition. Pleasure is arrayed against health;
it is the insidious enemy of longevity. Individuals, because their judgments about
pleasure are likely to be inappropriate, require the health promoter's assistance
in determining how to live their lives. Again, there is a revealed truth, vouch-
safed to us by science, about the one correct manner of living that trumps any
notion of pleasure pluralism.
   Now health promoters might well take exception to this characterization of
what their role is. Rather than impeding pleasure and individual autonomy, they
might wish to argue that their job is actually to promote genuine, responsible
pleasure. Is not health, after all, a necessary condition for any really pleasurable
life, let alone any life at all? And is not health the basis upon which both
individual and social autonomy is founded? Pleasure, rightly conceived within
the confines of health promotion, need not be the enemy of health at all. These
claims, however, rest on the false assumption that the conception of health that
is integral to health promotion is a necessary condition of a satisfying, of a
pleasurable, of a good human life such that any rational person would attach a
primacy to health over all other values. For the health promoter the logic appears
straightforward: Health is a necessary condition for any sort of life and thus it
must outweigh, in the scheme of any rational person, any other values that might
conflict with it, particularly the values of any inappropriate forms of pleasure.
   This is certainly true if one accepts the World Health Organization's (1996)
notion of health as a "state of complete physical, mental and social well-being
and not merely the absence of disease or infirmity" (p. 1). But the logic here is
flawed; although it may indeed be true that being alive is a necessary condition
for having a life, it is not at all clear that being healthy in anything like the
health promoter's definition of healthy is a necessary condition for having a
good life. This is not to suggest that health in some sense is not an important
aspect of a pleasant life, a good life, or an autonomous life. It is rather that
individuals whose lives do not measure up to the health promoter's definition
of healthy and good still might lead rich and satisfying lives, and individuals
frequently place a higher value on goods such as pleasure than on health itself.
   Although we might concede that being healthy in the sense of freedom from
debilitating disease can enhance certain kinds of autonomy, it does not follow
that healthy in the all-encompassing sense espoused by the health promoter
is a necessary condition of autonomy. Indeed, the balance between health and

autonomy and health and pleasure is something to be determined not by external fiat, but by the individual. It is the product in the end of autonomous choice, not a socially or medically ordained balance.

The problem is not, however, merely that health promotion fails in its promise of enhancing pleasure and autonomy: It is more seriously that it impedes individual autonomy with respect to pleasure. How does this occur?

First, health promotion's sweeping definition of health, a definition that is simultaneously broad and narrow, allows it a truly totalitarian compass of control over individuals by prescribing what precisely is acceptable behavior. Health becomes the authority against which pleasure becomes permissible. By the narrow sense of health I mean the fact that the health promoter thinks of health largely in terms of longevity. In this sense most of the traditional pleasures are cast as enemies—or at least not friends—of longevity. But at the same time health promotion also embraces a wide sense of health that attempts to bring every aspect of life within the purview of health. Once health is defined in this fashion it brings quite literally everything—character, beliefs, habits, and most importantly pleasures—within the sights of health promotion.

Reasoned and careful argument then become unnecessary. It is enough to simply utter the dreaded word "unhealthy" and pleasures of whatever pedigree are doomed. This is totalitarian in the sense that the project is all-embracing: To save the body we quite literally must engineer the soul. The paradigm of "healthy," whether is construed in the wide or the narrow sense, has little room within its confines for many of the traditional pleasures.

But the assault on pleasure, the attempt to constrict pleasure to the circle of health, the attempt to demand that pleasure once again obtain its sanction from society and not from the individual, often is couched in less aggressive ways through the language of lifestyle. Health promoters appear to fear the consequences of a straightforward discussion about pleasure and the impact of sacrificing pleasure in the interests of longevity. But lifestyle, despite the dissembling, still gives the game away—for what is lifestyle but a discussion about one's life choices, how to balance one's pleasure preferences with the rest of one's life? Put so directly, it is difficult to understand how such an attempt to restrict and curtail the right of individuals to choose their own pleasures would survive a moment's reflection. How is it that health promotion seems so easily to challenge the liberal consensus about permission for pleasure?

I think the answer is to be found in the second sense in which health promotion is a threat to the individual's own definition and pursuit of pleasure—that health promotion passes itself off as scientific. Health, and by extension health promotion, is something that appears to be scientifically determinable, and, however attached we might be to our pleasures and to our individual determination of those pleasures, at the end of the day pleasure must give way to the facts of science.

But is this really the case? Consider the paradigm argument of the health promoter, in which there is some pleasure—let us say eating large amounts of red meat—that Bob wishes to pursue. The health promoter will say to Bob: "It is a scientific fact that if you stop eating so much red meat you will live longer. Therefore you should stop eating so much red meat." The syllogism is however incomplete, and the advice flawed. The health promoter needs an additional premise of the order that, "Bob values living longer more than he enjoys eating red meat." So the argument is now, "It is a scientific fact that if you stop eating so much red meat, you will live longer. Since you value living longer more than you value eating red meat you should stop eating so much red meat."

But as soon as this premise is added, the scientific character of health promotion is exposed for what it is: a thin cheat. Although it might well be science that tells Bob that he will live longer if he eats less red meat, it is not science that tells Bob that he ought to value living longer more than eating his red meat. The "oughts" that health promotion directs to Bob are not scientific oughts but moral oughts, or more particularly the health promoter's moral oughts. Science does not provide us with oughts about pleasure even if it can provide us with facts about pleasure. This does not mean that the health promoter's moral admonitions are unworthy of Bob's attention; it is merely to suggest that they are not the pronouncements of science. They must be justified like every other bit of moral philosophy through careful argument and not by dogmatic pronouncement.

In effect, the scientific character of health promotion extends at best to its claims to knowledge about the causes of disease. Its claims about what to do with this knowledge form no part of science. Indeed, these are as much a part of the arena of personal beliefs and values as are politics and religion. The importance of this to the argument about the permission for pleasure is enormous. What it means is that health promotion's admonitions about pleasure—its pleasure agenda if you will—are built on a very shaky conceptual foundation that has never done the difficult work of providing itself with a compelling moral foundation for why a life of 70 years full of self-chosen pleasures is in some sense inferior to a life of 75 years deprived of many of those pleasures. But this is precisely the kind of argument about the value of pleasure that the health promoter must make. I am not, and let us be clear about this, suggesting that 70 years crammed with pleasure are necessarily better than 75 abstemious years—indeed, I believe it is precisely these choices that are best made by individuals. But this does not relieve the health promoter of the obligation of providing us with compelling reasons why longevity is to be preferred to pleasure.

Health promotion, however, does not wish to allow such a discussion. For at its bottom health promotion is essentially paternalist; it wishes to intervene either indirectly through manipulating the social and intellectual environment (i.e., through social marketing) or directly through regulation, to insure the triumph of its view of pleasure. And it is this aggressive paternalism that represents health promotion's third threat to the hedonist notion of permission for pleasure. If health promotion were merely what the words appear to suggest—arguing for health, and asking that individuals consider health when determining their pleasures—then health promotion would be much less of a problem for pleasure. Stripped of its scientific pretensions and its official standing, funding, and legal sanctions, the moral pronouncements of health promotion would be on a similar footing to those of the Vatican: duly reported, heeded by true believers, and ignored by many others.

But health promotion does not aspire to the diminished clout of 20th-century Roman Catholicism. If anything, it aims for something closer to the prescriptive power with respect to pleasure of the medieval Church. Health promotion fully intends that its moral pronouncements about the correct place of pleasure in the ordered life be both morally and legally binding. Recall the conceptual foundation of the health promoter: Individuals tend to choose pleasure over health even if they understand the consequences, and the state has an obligation to ensure that its citizens come to the correct balance between pleasure and health. The core assumption here is that there is a vast dichotomy of knowledge in society between those few who know the truth about health and pleasure and those many who are ignorant or who are knowing but willful. Failure to head the admonitions of the health promoters is prima facie evidence of irrationality, failure of understanding, or addiction to pleasure.

It is instructive that at its conceptual core, health promotion, like all forms of paternalism, is unfalsifiable. Nothing counts to falsify the thesis that those who choose to order their lives against the prevailing dictates of health fashion, those who choose to ignore the consensus on acceptable as against unacceptable pleasure, are either irrational or in the compulsive grip of desire.

THE CONCEPT OF RISK

The health promoter suggests a regime of permission for pleasure that is at pains to prevent individuals, for their own good of course, from choosing to live their lives outside his or her of a healthy life. The primary means by which such a regime is established is through the concept of risk. Indeed, although the ostensible message of the health promoter is about health and the risks of pleasure, the deeper message almost always is couched in the language of risks. What the health promoter as health paternalist argues for is an involuntary process of collectivized risk. Health promotion as health paternalism seeks to collectively distinguish legitimate from illegitimate risk and thus remove from individuals the right and the responsibility to make their own risk assessments.

Such a collectivization of risk is not simply an attack on pleasure but also a significant assault on individual autonomy in general. For our assessment of risk and the manner in which we calculate risk relative to certain things, pleasures included, are major components of what we mean when we speak about having a life of one's own. Because virtually everything that we do entails risk, the idea of risk provides at least one dimension against which we can plot what we mean by a good life. In the simplest sense this can be done through developing a profile of what things we choose to do in the face of what risks. The risk-and-reward calculus with pleasure—chocolate yes, smoking no, scuba diving no, travel by car yes—is personal, largely ad hoc, and deeply inconsistent. But it constitutes the core of what we mean when we talk about permission for pleasure being an individual choice, as opposed to pleasure being a paternalistic determination.

Such individual decisions about pleasure and risk are arational in the sense that they lie outside the bounds of conventional rationality. By this I mean that rationality cannot pronounce on the legitimacy of an individual's risk calculus with respect to pleasure without introducing some prior, external conception of what a proper ordering of risk and pleasure might be. In effect this means that the modest hedonist holds that pleasure is truly incomparable; the ordering of pleasures of one individual is at one level as genuine as that of any other individual. And indeed, how could things be otherwise? How would reason, simply as reason, be able to say to anyone that "chocolate yes, drinking no" is a rational balancing of pleasure and risk? Surely an answer could be made only from an individual's subjective appraisal of the values of chocolate and drinking against values such as longevity. Risk and the way we use it in thinking about our pleasures serves as a conceptual shorthand for a complex set of values and choices that are at the center of what we mean when we speak about having a distinctive human life. Indeed, charting the topography of those trade-offs that an individual has made between risk and pleasure tells us an enormous amount about what that person considers to be finally a good life.

Health promoters' desire to manage risk then is nothing more than a vast project to usurp not some peripheral, but the central, aspect of being an autonomous chooser of pleasure, of rooting permission for pleasure in the individual. What their pleasure paternalism seeks to do is to replace my values, my weighting of risk and reward, and my pleasures with their risk calculus, their idea of healthy, and their idea of acceptable pleasure. What they wish to do is to expand reason's province from the instrumental—telling me how I might get those pleasures that I desire—to the morally foundational—telling me in the name of society what pleasures I am permitted to desire. By capturing the notion of risk, and with it pleasure, health promoters gain a sweeping power to define and enforce their definition of how personal lives should be lived.

Where within such a vast, ordered, regulated, and carefully engineered edifice is there room for the individual, the idiosyncratic, the autonomous life of pleasure? Health promoters might reply that whatever we might think about the virtues of personal permission for pleasure, their risk calculus, their definition of acceptable trade-offs, their notion of legitimate pleasure is not merely different than mine but somehow better than mine. But in what way better? Better in the sense of more rational than mine.

But this will not work. We have seen that health promoters' notion of legitimate pleasure works only if "rational" is defined in the narrow context of death and injury or illness. Only the one who lives a life has the privileged access to the information about the relative weights of this risk and that pleasure that would allow such a judgment of rationality. Health promoters as pleasure paternalists must in the final count defend the impossible claim that they know more about Bob's values, tastes, and beliefs, and about what mixture of risk and pleasure gives Bob's life the most meaning, than Bob does. They must proclaim without shame that most people do not know what pleasures are good for them, that they cannot do well the most intimate and exhilarating project of human existence—fashioning their own life.

CONCLUSIONS

Does this mean that health promotion must of necessity be a threat to pleasure? Must it inevitably seek to push a view of permission for pleasure that centers permission in an elite class of pleasure police well out of reach of ordinary men and women? I think not, provided—and this is a substantial caveat—that it can move away from three things: first, its often unconscious and therefore uncritical belief that health, by which it often means simply longevity, is the greatest of human goods; second, its tendency to think of health as purely physical health, and thus to see pleasure and healthy as contradictory rather than complementary; and third, its penchant for control, for seeking to change the pleasure preferences of adult citizens. On the positive side this requires a recognition that the state's role in the pleasure business (once again, of course, speaking about pleasures that do not harm others) is to provide its citizens with rigorously objective scientific information about the risks associated with various types of pleasure. This would involve minimally:

1 Stating risk assessments in a way that does not exaggerate harms and allows for individuals to make their own decisions about balancing the risks and rewards of various kinds of pleasures
2 Placing a particular risk assessment about pleasure within a general risk context in a way that allows one to gauge how significant the risk is compared with other risks associated with everyday living (the question thus becomes not simply, "Is this activity risky?" but, "Does it carry a risk that in other circumstances we would consider worrisome?")
3 Conveying the full sense of both the inexactness and the complexity of risk assessment, even in the face of the popular preference for simplicity
4 Acknowledging incorrect risk assessment and changing risk advice when warrented by new scientific evidence.

Such health promotion might take its proper place as one consideration among many which a rational and autonomous person uses in choosing their pleasures and shaping their life.

REFERENCES

Mill, J. S. (1978). *On liberty*. Indianapolis, IN: Hackett. (Original work published 1859).
WHO. (1996). Constitution of the World Health Organization. In *Basic documents* (41st ed., pp. 1–18). Geneva, Switzerland: Author.

Chapter 3

Pleasure in Health Promotion

Michael Daube

Health promotion is the encouragement of health—and pleasure—through the application of sound scientific and medical evidence to people's daily lives and behavior. There is no room in health promotion for biases or scientifically unsupported information and policy. Traditionally, health education has been geared to warning people of the dangers of at-risk behavior of one sort or another. But this fails to capture the larger impact on people's lives of proper health-promotion policy. It is also a far less effective approach than health-promotion, which recognizes, accepts, and encourages pleasure as a central outcome in peoples' lives. Public health policy on alcohol is one area in which the value of recognizing pleasure as a health promotion issue—and the tendency to resist doing so—is most evident.

HEALTH PROMOTION AND PLEASURE

This chapter is based on what I perceive to be the public health perspective. This clearly places me at odds with some of the views expressed by John Luik (see Chapter 2). Far from being a positive or pleasurable viewpoint, his is a depressing view of life. He sees health professionals as ogres akin to Shaw's (1996) "pleasure police" rather than as people seeking to improve the health of the community.

In tagging all health promotion with what he acknowledges is an extreme description, Luik's argument is simply irrelevant to the vast mass of health promotion. It is entertaining and elegant—but nonetheless irrelevant. The actions and advice emanating from governments and health authorities must be evidence-based. There can be no support for those who use a health platform to impose their prejudices without adequate evidence. But there also should be no doubt that governments and health agencies have a right as well as a duty to protect the health of the community on the basis of the best available evidence.

Health promotion traditionally is defined as "any combination of health education and related organizational, economic and political intervention ... designed to predispose, enable and reinforce voluntary adaptations of behavior conducive to health. Such behavior includes individual and collective participation in planning, implementing and evaluating primary health care."

But health promotion also has been defined as the business of making people live miserably so that they can die healthy. The history of health promotion is one in which pleasure has played a fleeting role, and in which suffering appears to be paramount. Rarely are we shown the enjoyment that derives from a healthy life. We are much more frequently shown the miseries and suffering that result from inappropriate behavior. Pleasure does not have a lengthy entry in the health-promotion lexicon.

The history of health promotion as we now know it is in fact fairly short. The term itself did not come into vogue until the 1980s, essentially following the pioneering Canadian Lalonde report, *A New Perspective on the Health of Canadians*. Before then we talked of health education, which had a much more didactic ring to it. And indeed, the development of sophisticated media health-education or health-promotion campaigns only started in the late 1970s and early 1980s. Previously there was health-education advertising, but this was pretty crude stuff: occasional advertisements—rarely shown and even more rarely evaluated.

The past decade has seen an explosion in health promotion around the world. From being a poorly funded Cinderella area, health promotion has emerged in many countries as the belle of the ball: glamorous, exciting, and supported by a growing corps of academic and practical expertise. It is still underfunded in comparison with many other parts of the health system, but there is at least a recognition of the need for more realistic levels of support.

Health promotion also is generally seen as very much more than simply providing advice. It starts with the advocacy required to generate the required activity, follows through to evaluation—and then continues to the advocacy required to start the cycle over again. The basic premises of health promotion were initially fairly clear:

1 Here is something that causes ill health.
2 We must prevent it.
3 We must warn people against it.

Health authorities identified behaviors that seemed inappropriate. The simplest approach thereafter seemed to be to tell people not to do such things, and if they did not listen, to tell them more loudly. This is fine with a product such as tobacco. The evidence on tobacco has been so overwhelming for so many years that nobody concerned for the public health, capable of reading and understanding the evidence, could argue against the benefits of reducing smoking.

But there are two fundamental problems. First, tobacco is unusual in that it is harmful if used as intended, and there is effectively no safe level of use. Secondly, even with tobacco we have learned over many years, often painfully, that shouting loudly in isolation is not necessarily the best approach.

Also, ironically, even with those health behaviors that might lend themselves to positive health promotion, our approach has been so conditioned by the need to warn people off doing what is wrong that we take a negative line. The commercial world of advertising is of course far ahead of us. How many commercial advertisers present a negative message? Commercial advertising is all about the positives. "Use our product and you will feel better, live better, enjoy life more." Commercial advertising is all about the increased pleasure to be derived from one's existence through use of products. Ironically, the promise is often much less likely to be achieved than the promise of greater pleasure through a healthier lifestyle.

For those concerned with promoting health, there are some basic, almost simplistic, arguments in favor of a positive approach—in some cases, indeed, for the use of pleasure. First, a healthy lifestyle by definition promotes greater capacity to enjoy life, and to enjoy the pleasures life has to offer. Second, the longer one lives, the more opportunities one has to derive enjoyment. Ill health manifestly makes enjoyment of life much more difficult, and at times well nigh impossible, for those affected and those around them.

But as we look at the history of what might be termed negative health promotion, the picture is not too encouraging. There have been of course some valuable developments. Cigarette smoking has declined in most developed countries; people in general eat more healthily than they did; there is an awareness of at least some of the risks associated with behaviors such as drinking and driving and illicit drug use; sexual behavior is much more safety-conscious, at least in developed countries; people do take note of screening and other preventive programs; and so on.

But this is simply not good enough. The prize we have to offer is not—as it might be for the commercial advertiser—a more comfortable pair of jeans or a roomier refrigerator. These can be portrayed as providing additional pleasure, but that is to a large extent the artifice of the advertising industry. The prize we have to offer is better health, greater capacity for enjoyment, longer life, and greater enjoyment during that extended life span.

Despite this, any review of the health-education or health-promotion literature shows little interest in pleasure. From the earliest Biblical injunctions there has almost always been an emphasis on negative exhortation. There is not much that is positively phrased in the Ten Commandments. The words "thou shalt not" provide a somewhat forbidding starting point, and since then, we have been exhorted against a range of activities.

We were exhorted against smoking, which is fair enough; against drinking to excess; often against drinking at all; against using illicit drugs; against using pharmaceutical drugs inappropriately; against eating inappropriately; against unsafe sex—again, often in a style that seemed close to be exhorting against any sexual activity. Almost always we were exhorted *against*.

Even straightforward health information was presented in a minatory manner that focused on the dire outcomes of inappropriate behavior. There was little emphasis on the pleasure to be derived along the way. Similarly, regulation of industry is generally about what cannot be said or done, although this can be more readily understood and justified in terms of sheer practicality.

The Biblical precedent to which I previously referred again sets the tone, although an interesting aside is that despite the concerns about alcohol that became high priorities for later Bible-based religions, there is only one incident of drunkenness in the Old Testament, when Noah imbibed overenthusiastically, and the nearest thing to earthly Paradise is described as the period during which "Nation will not take up sword against nation . . ." and "Every man will sit under his own vine and under his own fig tree" (Micah 4.3–4/New International Version).

We have moved on a little—but not far—from our negative past. Those involved in health promotion still are seen as presenting a negative approach and as opponents of behaviors to be avoided. Sartorius (see Chapter 4) has rightly cited here the present definition of health in the constitution of the World Health Organization (WHO, 1996) and the proposed new definition (i.e., "Health is a dynamic state of complete physical, mental, spiritual and social well-being and not merely the absence of disease or infirmity"; WHO, 1998), but it must be said that although it often is quoted in documentation, this positive approach and context have not yet made their way through to most practitioners. Even if apparently positive messages are presented, they still are associated with disease prevention, and not the much more positive context of health and lifestyle promotion.

A COMPREHENSIVE APPROACH TO PROMOTING HEALTH AND PLEASURE

The more positive approach to health promotion has strong historical roots. The basic rationale is that, as the 19th-century British prime minister Benjamin Disraeli wrote, "the first duty of any government is to promote the health of the people." It was clear that Disraeli meant much more than the need for the great public health legislation of the late 19th century—although even these moves to protect the health of the community were attacked on ideological grounds: The London *Times* thundered in 1851 that "every man is entitled to his own dungheap."

In order to be effective, however, health promotion must take a comprehensive approach. This step brings us closer to pleasure. The world we inhabit is not amenable to miracle solutions and either/or resolutions, but to comprehensive approaches. Drug abuse will not be wiped out by either law enforcement or education or treatment, but by a combination of them. Tobacco use will not decline because of education or promotional bans, cessation programs, or tax increases alone: It needs a long-term, comprehensive approach drawing on all these components.

The history of health promotion has been bedeviled by people—often the most ardent advocates for health promotion—who have ruined their case by arguing (a) for a single measure in isolation, and (b) that this single measure in isolation will solve the problem overnight.

But as this volume and the conference upon which it is based recognize, if we need a comprehensive approach, there is one fascinating area on which health promotion has by-and-large missed out. We have talked of primary, secondary, and tertiary prevention. We talk of a comprehensive strategy comprising, if appropriate, legislation and restrictive measures, education, treatment, and so on. We perhaps have moved some way towards the positive in changing our focus from the term *health education* to *health promotion*. We have seen "wellness" programs and a focus on health promotion through "lifestyles," but these programs still tend to lead us back to the same negative injunctions. And rarely if ever do we recognize approaches based primarily on negative injunctions to be truly comprehensive. Indeed, to succeed, we also should talk unashamedly about enjoyment or, in the context of this conference, about pleasure.

Given its Latin root, *placere*, meaning to please or give satisfaction, we can safely see the term "pleasure" as describing much more than, as the 17th-century philosopher John Selden suggested, "nothing else but the intermission of pain." When we talk of pleasure we talk of behaviors, lifestyles, or conditions that enhance life; that are seen as positive; that bring enjoyment, happiness, or contentment; and that entail no evident downsides. Pleasure can be short-term or long-term; it can be physical or emotional.

Where does this fit into health promotion? Health promotion long has been portrayed in the negative. It is about stopping people from doing the things they may enjoy doing—such as smoking, drinking to excess, driving as fast as they like, being lazy, eating fatty foods, or engaging in unprotected sex. And it is about making them do things they do not enjoy—such as having immunizations, avoiding unsafe sex, being screened, or, for those who do not enjoy it, taking regular physical exercise.

But perhaps our disease-prevention origins have steered us away from using one of the most powerful weapons potentially available to us. The vast majority of commercial advertisements focus on three "Ps:" positives, profit, and pleasure. They all show how one will in some way benefit from use of a particular product. Commercial advertising is not only about making profit for the advertiser but about demonstrating how we, the consumers, will benefit from use of the product. Health-promotion advertising normally tells us what we will lose if we act inappropriately. Commercial advertising is above all about pleasure and enjoyment.

There is an important lesson here for health promotion, which has a better basis in science and reality than almost all the commercial advertising we see. Health promotion per se has no ulterior motive: With a few exceptions, it is not based on making money for particular individuals and organizations.

Health promotion is precisely what its name implies: It is about enabling people to live longer, healthier lives. And the two run together. It is not about simply extending our life span so that we can sit inert in wheelchairs for a year or two longer: It is about prolonging our healthy, active life spans. To take a simple example, if infectious disease were eradicated from Aboriginal people in Australia their lifespans would increase by an average of 0.2 years. If smoking and inappropriate drinking were eradicated, their lifespans would increase by 3.5 years for women and 5.9 years for men. And these are not years added on at the tail end of a geriatric existence. They are years of potentially enjoyable middle age for people who die in their 40s and 50s. The same applies to any number of other behaviors health promotion seeks to promote: Screening for cancer of the cervix prevents premature death just as does the safe sex required to avoid HIV infection and AIDS.

But we talk only of the death and disease we can prevent. Rarely if ever do we talk of the pleasure we can bring through enjoyment of longer, healthier lifestyles (see Chapter 23). We do not pursue the theme originated two or three decades ago by Ernst Wynder (see Wynder & Orlandi, 1984) when he spoke of the desirability of "dying young, as late as possible."

We can and we should focus much more on pleasure, not to the exclusion of the negatives, because a comprehensive approach requires that we consider all workable approaches, and often several simultaneously, but as a clear theme or motif in its own right. There is a major role for health promotion in addressing the sheer pleasure and enjoyment to be gained from positive lifestyles. Indeed, it can be argued that a positive lifestyle is a precondition for deriving the maximum possible pleasure and enjoyment from life.

We should, like the commercial advertisers, speak not only about doom and disaster but also about the increased pleasures our populations can enjoy. One need not be a superman or superwoman, but if one is reasonably healthy one will be able to enjoy virtually all aspects of life more. To take some of the examples given previously, the benefits of screening for cervical cancer come not simply from detection of disease, but from the enjoyment of a life free of disease. The benefits of stopping smoking come not simply from prevention of lung cancer or cardiovascular disease, but from the enjoyment to be derived from several years of longer, more active life. The benefits of following HIV-prevention advice come not simply from avoiding an unpleasant, lingering, and often fatal condition, but from much greater enjoyment of both life in general and, indeed, continuing opportunity for the sexual activity that might otherwise have led to the condition in the first place.

PLEASURE AS A GOAL IN ITSELF

In order to promote the pleasure to be gained from better health, there is a worthwhile argument that we should promote the benefits of enjoying life, particularly a healthy, active life. This is not to argue that health promotion should be all about hedonism. It is to argue that unless we talk openly about this enjoyment, unless we move into a mode that sees pleasure and enjoyment as worthwhile ends in themselves, we will not succeed in promoting healthy behavior on the basis that it results in greater pleasure.

So there are two primary reasons for using pleasure or enjoyment of life in health promotion. The first is the pragmatic reason. Commercial advertisers do it successfully. Commercial advertisers have vastly greater budgets not only for their promotional activity but also for their market research. They use the positives, profit and pleasure, to the exclusion of almost all other themes. Perhaps therefore health promotion should take not just the occasional leaf from their book, but a few chapters.

The second reason is that it will work better for us—and hence for the health of the community. If we move away from the negative images we send out we simply will achieve better results.

But there is a third reason for promoting enjoyment or more pleasurable lifestyles that is not solely about improving our health-promotion techniques. An argument worth pursuing is that the encouragement of enjoyment should be a public health objective in its own right. There is now a considerable and growing body of evidence that contented and satisfactory lifestyles lead to longer, healthier lives. Moreover, there is clear evidence from developed countries that there is a socioeconomic gradient in relation to a wide range of conditions. Put bluntly, the better off and better educated you are, the healthier you are likely to be.

There is growing evidence on the impact of depression not only on other mental health problems, but also on various physical conditions. A recent paper in the *British Medical Journal*, for example, focuses on the association between depression and cardiovascular disease (Hippisley-Cox, Fielding, & Pringle, 1998). It is an interesting irony that over the coming decades the two major causes of death and disability worldwide are predicted to be clinical depression and heart disease. There is also strong evidence from a wide range of studies that people who are physically healthy throughout life report more enjoyment of their lifestyles than those who are not. To summarize a substantial body of research (see Chapter 1), promoting greater contentment, enjoyment, or pleasure is a worthwhile objective in that a satisfactory lifestyle leads to better health.

This leads to some further important questions for health agencies and health professionals: Should we promote pleasure in isolation, or only in conjunction with the health behaviors we seek to influence? And what happens in the absence of pleasure? Do we have a responsibility to prevent any negative consequences that might then occur?

THE CRITICAL ROLE OF PLEASURE

The public health perspective that should underpin any community health activity by health and other authorities already has been mentioned. From this perspective, just as we should not impose our own prejudices or moralities as to what members of the community should *not* do unless they are supported by clear medical and scientific evidence, so we should not impose a requirement to engage in pleasurable activity without similar evidence.

But, perhaps paradoxically, there is a middle way. On the one hand, health education and health promotion from the days of the earliest Biblical injunctions to their more recent incarnations have been couched largely in the negative. We tell people what they cannot do, and hope that they will respond positively to this cheerless approach.

Unfortunately, the realities of human nature and experience show that adults accept the validity of the instruction but do not respond well to it. Even in their earliest days, the Ten Commandments must have sounded impressive but would have been observed only sporadically. We are safe in assuming that even those to whom they were addressed not only worshipped other Gods but even coveted their neighbors' oxen, asses, and occasionally their spouses.

On the other hand, we all respond better to the promise of pleasure than to the threat of eternal damnation—or to the promise of ill health, which is much the same thing. So perhaps instead of telling people—on the basis of the best scientific evidence available—what they *cannot* do in order to avoid ill health, we should move to telling them what they *can* do in order to achieve maximum levels of enjoyment. It is true that some health promotion seeks to be constructive. There is indeed a well-recognized approach described as "positive health promotion," but this is generally an afterthought or a very minor component of otherwise largely negative campaigns.

Thus we may find it more fruitful to consider positive health promotion as a starting point for the achievement of better community health. What this means is that, behavior by behavior, instead of telling people what to avoid and what not to do, we tell them what they can and should do that will enable them to lead more pleasurable lives—and, all being well, will yield pleasurable experiences along the way. This advice of course should be based on the best available scientific research. It should be offered in the same way as other health promotion, whether face-to-face by health professionals or through the media.

This does not mean that we offer members of the community complete license to do whatever they wish simply because it pleases them. There are some behaviors that are beyond the pale because they put others at risk, or because the evidence is so strong that they will cause the individual concerned irreparable damage. There are also some important caveats: Alcohol, for example, brings benefit and pleasure when sensibly used—but it must be sensibly used to avoid a range of harmful consequences from road-accident trauma onwards.

That said, we can complement the traditional Ten Commandments with a new set of much more positive edicts that will help to promote health. Instead of telling people the foods to avoid, we should talk of the foods, the diets, and the dietary regimens that they can enjoy. Although the literature on food and diet is probably the most extensive in any health promotion–related area—and certainly the most purchased and eagerly pounced on by the general reader—the complex messages about foods to avoid generally come from health agencies. The simple messages about enjoyment usually come from the commercial sector.

Exercise is traditionally one of the hardest areas to address for health promotion. The evidence on the benefits of regular exercise is clear and fairly frequently presented, particularly to children in school who are already active. But much of our advice on exercise over the years has focused on the desirability of acting like a superstar (or looking like Jane Fonda)—we turn people off almost as soon as they start. And we make it all the more difficult by inventing instruments of torture such as exercise bicycles to give the impression that the only worthwhile exercise is that which causes pain. The truth is that modest daily exercise, especially walking, is the easiest to introduce in the daily regimen and brings consequent benefits to cardiovascular and other aspects of personal health—which in turn lead to a greater capacity to enjoy life.

Even the advice we give on sexual health has been cast largely in the negative. We tell our young people what not to do. We caution against unsafe sex. We warn against any sexual activity that puts people at risk of HIV and other sexually transmitted diseases. But we do not counsel the community about the extensive literature demonstrating the many benefits to be derived from safer sexual activity, let alone the pleasure that it inherently brings.

ALCOHOL, PLEASURE, AND HEALTH

When it comes to alcohol, which provides the focus for this volume, we have traditionally painted pictures so bleak that we have forgotten to consider the positives.

As Sir Richard Doll (1997, p. 1664) wrote recently in the *British Medical Journal*, even in the 1970s "the belief that alcohol was bad for health was so ingrained that the idea that small amounts might be good for you was hard to envisage." In Australia the National Health and Medical Research Council (1987), the country's leading health authority, published a report on alcohol little more than a decade ago that asked whether there was a safe level of drinking. Although there was by then some worthwhile literature in the area, this report essentially plucked some of its recommendations out of thin air. It recommended—for reasons that are as unclear now as they were then—that all drinkers observe two alcohol-free days a week. And although it recognized the existence of evidence on some benefits from alcohol consumption, it expressed caution about letting the public in on this dark secret.

This approach has been overtaken by events and more objective analyses. We know now from Doll (1997, p. 1664) and others that in relation to alcohol "the evidence for a beneficial effect is now massive. It includes not only a reduction of about a third in the risk of vascular disease but also, because vascular disease is such an important cause of death in middle and old age, a reduction in total mortality." We also know that "the beneficial effect is due to the content of ethanol, not to the characteristics of any particular type of drink" (p. 1664).

What are the conclusions for public health, for health promotion, and for the promotion of pleasure? First, as Doll (1997, p. 1666) points out, there is a case for moving away from the earlier approach. "Previous policy could, and generally did, aim to discourage drinking altogether," which, as he notes, was not only based on outdated evidence but also largely unsuccessful.

Second, any moves must be made with caution. The complications range from interpretations of the evidence and the type of community under discussion to the type of product. Third, we must be mindful of the injunction, "First, do no harm." Whatever we do should not undermine measures designed to reduce the recognized harmful consequences of alcohol abuse.

Enthusiasm for a new approach should be seen in the context of a comprehensive program; adopting a new component does not mean giving up all the other, older parts. But that being said, there does now appear to be a case on the community's behalf for telling people what they *can* do, and in this case what they *can* drink—maybe even *should* drink—in the interests of their health.

The evidence thus far enables us to follow Doll's advice (1997, p. 1667) to the public that, "in middle and old age some small amount of alcohol within the range of one to four drinks each day reduces the risk of premature death, irrespective of the medium in which it is taken." It also may be argued that middle-aged and older people are mentioned primarily because these are the age groups in which studies have been carried out (see Chapter 12).

CONCLUSIONS

All this brings us to three questions to illustrate the usefulness—and complexities—of enlisting pleasure in the promotion of health.

First, will our campaigns to reduce the adverse consequences of alcohol abuse be more effective if we focus on the positives, not the negatives—if we tell people what they *can*, maybe *should*, drink rather than what they should *not* drink? With the caveats outlined previously, there is little doubt that this is the case. We will do much better by promoting sensible drinking behavior, by explicitly giving permission—albeit with all the necessary care and caution—for what we know to be beneficial, than by simply exhorting the avoidance of excess. There are significant implications here for the beverage alcohol industry. So long as it does things right—a crucial caveat—it can change the nature of much of its discourse.

Second, do we have a duty in the public interest to make the community aware of the benefits from modest alcohol consumption? This is a debate that has barely begun, but that must inevitably exercise us. The simplistic answer offered here is that we do have such a responsibility—and that it is vital for the public health community and the beverage alcohol industry to work together so that the information is properly presented, presented to the appropriate communities, and presented so that it neither engenders automatic cynicism about the motivation of the messenger nor undermines efforts to reduce abuse of the product.

And third, does this enable us to promote pleasure while promoting health? The answer here is again in the affirmative. We should throw away some of the shackles that for so long have made us embarrassed about the very prospect that in promoting health we also might promote something that is pleasurable. The evidence on the benefits of sensible alcohol consumption gives health promotion a welcome gift. It enables us to demonstrate that we are not kill-joys. It enables us to make common cause with an industry that in my view is almost frightened to recognize the new era in which it could be. It provides as good a rationale as we can find for changing to a more positive approach. Promoting pleasure can and should be commensurate with promoting health.

REFERENCES

Doll, R. (1997). One for the heart. *British Medical Journal, 315,* 1664–1668.

Hippisley-Cox, J., Fielding, K., & Pringle, M. (1998). Depression as a risk factor for ischaemic heart disease in men: Population based case-control study. *British Medical Journal, 316,* 1714–1719.

National Health and Medical Research Council. (1987). *Is there a safe level of daily consumption of alcohol for men and women? Recommendations regarding responsible drinking behaviour.* Canberra, Australia: Australian Government Publishing Service.

Shaw, D. (1996). *The pleasure police.* New York: Doubleday.

WHO. (1996). Constitution of the World Health Organization. In *Basic documents* (41st ed., pp. 1–18). Geneva, Switzerland: Author.

WHO. (1998). *Review of the Constitution and regional arrangements of the World Health Organization: Report of the special group* (Executive Board document EB101/7). Geneva, Switzerland: Author.

Wynder, E.L., & Orlandi, M. (1984). *The American Health Foundation guide to lifespan health.* New York: Dodd, Mead.

Chapter 4

The Cultural Contexts of Pleasure

Norman Sartorius

The exploration of the cultural contexts of a concept faces the difficulty of defining a culture. There are hundreds of definitions of culture (Sartorius, 1979), all learned and excellent, but most of them not easily usable in applied research. The word "culture" conjures up an image of a large assembly of beliefs and rites, habits and attitudes, ways of behaving in various situations, and reactions to stimuli that characterize a defined group of people. In the past, groups belonging to a particular cultural community tended to occupy a defined geographical area; today, in most parts of the world, the same area or country contains people belonging to different cultures. Even within what appears to be a homogenous group, one could speak of cultures of the old, of the young, of females, and of males. Depending on how narrowly cultures are defined the characteristics of a culture can be shared to a larger or lesser degree with others. Cultures also change much faster than ever before, and they do not change at the same rate, in the same place, nor do they change evenly. Despite these differences the concept of culture is nevertheless used and remains useful as shorthand for the variety of characteristics defining groups of people that share them.

Culture affects the expression of our thoughts and feelings. In one culture the shaking of hands is interpreted as an indication of sexual potency (e.g., in Mali); in a neighboring country the shaking of hands is thought to indicate the contrary. The same gestures mean different things in different cultures. Culture affects the ways people think and speak. In some cultures, direct criticism of other people is not tolerable; instead, a criticism is voiced by telling a story that

49

will be understood by the person in question and others who matter. This and other strategies are used in many cultures to avoid confrontation and to prevent the loss of face, thus protecting human relations in a closed group despite errors or misbehavior that some members of the group have committed.

A way of exploring differences among cultures is the investigation of the literal meaning and associative spaces of words. The word "pleasure," for example, is derived, in a number of Western European languages (e.g., English, French, Romanian, Spanish, Portuguese) from the Latin *placere* (related to *placare*, to appease) referring to satisfying an urge, or being comfortable.[1] In Polish, the word used to describe pleasure conveys the notion of receiving something of value. In Greek, pleasure is described by a word composed of two terms, "good" and "joy"—a "good joy"; the same linguistic bases are used for the Greek word for "thank you," bringing the concept of pleasure close to the notion of having received something. In German, the word indicates that urges have been responded to; in Croatian, the word is close to that meaning "life" and thus could be interpreted as an "enhancement of living." In Chinese, the pictogram for pleasure shows a drum similar to those beaten to announce good news. Pleasure here thus might have a broader meaning than in other cultures, expressing the joy felt when learning good news. In Japanese, the word derives from the concepts of joy and relaxation. In Arabic, the word indicates a good feeling, without direct linkage to anything, either the satisfaction of urges or the feeling of being at peace. The word seems to be closest to a generic emotion that could have been caused by any one of a variety of reasons.

Cultures also vary in their use of logical systems. Many cultures—including those in Europe—follow Aristotelian logic: Statements are listed and compared with others, and a conclusion is drawn according to certain fixed rules. If the statements are contradictory, the conclusion is not possible. Other cultures use the Janusian logical system (the name of the system derives from the name of Janus, the Roman god who had two faces so that he could see in two directions at the same time). From the Janusian perspective, even if two statements contradict each other, a conclusion is still possible. Understanding between people using different logical systems is therefore often only partial and has to be assured by a variety of strategies.

Perceptions of the world around us and our relationships with it also differ among cultures. Variations in the comprehension of time, for example, led anthropologists to divide cultures into "now" and the "before-and-after" groups. Cultures of now are those in which the emphasis is on the experience of the present moment and nothing from any other time seems real. Before and after are unimportant. Before-and-after cultures, on the other hand, are conscious of the past and of the future at all points of their existence and often do not consider the experience of a particular moment of time as being of any importance.

The measurement of time also differs among cultural groups. Some cultures use a chronological concept of time, which is seen as a path defined by events that follow one another. Chronological concepts of time have been visualized

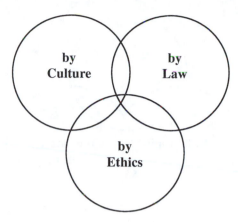

Figure 4.1 Acceptability of behaviors.

somewhat like a necklace, as a series of events that follow one another, as pearls on a necklace do; once events have occurred their position in time is forever defined. Other cultures use a punctual concept of time. Past events do not remain in evidence when new events occur: A new event covers those preceding it. Time conceptualized punctually can be visualized as a book. As soon as a new page is turned, all preceding pages are invisible, covered by it, and no longer can be read.

Predominant logical systems and the conceptualization of time in a culture also affect the comprehension of causality, which is of key importance for any effort to carry out health programs, to educate people, and to make them understand where they could and should intervene if they are to change the way in which things happen. Other features of culture—including, for example, usual coping mechanisms and concepts of honor, gain, loss, and so forth—also matter in this respect and define the acceptability of behavior in a particular culture from the point of view of the culture.

The law of the land—perhaps formulated by a group belonging to a different cultural group or to a period long in the past—may only in part overlap, in its definition of what is permissible, with the cultural definition. And, both of these—the cultural and the legal definitions—only in part overlap with ethical perceptions concerning acceptability.

Figure 4.1 illustrates this: Some behaviors are acceptable by the culture and by ethics, but not by the law; others are acceptable legally and ethically but not by the culture; and so forth. The understanding of these relationships is necessary in order to decide on any public health or social-sector measure aimed at changing the acceptability of a behavior.

Although pleasure is in essence an individual experience, it often is shared in a social context, and its definition is far from purely subjective. An individual may think of a particular experience as pleasurable; this does not mean that the

Figure 4.2   Definition of pleasure.

people with whom the individual interacts or the community as a whole think the same way. The distinct but overlapping perceptions and judgments of the individual, of his or her peers, and of the community jointly define pleasure. A similar Venn diagram therefore can be constructed to illustrate the similarities and differences in the definitions of pleasure by the individual, by his or her community, and by society as a whole (Figure 4.2).

Finally, a third group of overlapping influences on the experience of pleasure are the cultural, biological, and personal factors (Figure 4.3). Those three groups of influences are, to an extent, dependent on each other. Personal preferences and their fulfillment can, for example, be limited by biological age, and culture can make certain of them unacceptable.

We also can use a diagram of overlapping sets (Figure 4.4) to clarify the relationship among pleasure, happiness, and quality of life (see Chapter 23).

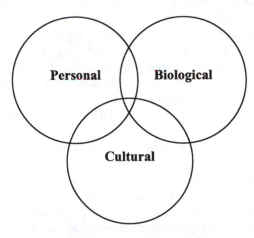

Figure 4.3   Determinants of pleasure.

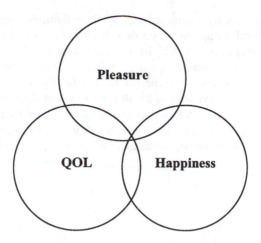

Figure 4.4 Quality of life and pleasure.

The three terms cover similar ground. According to the definition adopted by the World Health Organization, quality of life is defined as the individual's perception of his or her position in life in relation to his or her other goals and expectations and the cultural framework in which he or she lives. This definition is clearly close to the definitions of pleasure and happiness.

Although pleasure has the connotation of a short-lived experience, quality of life usually covers a longer period. Happiness is a pleasurable experience, but pleasure as such cannot be equated with happiness, which usually also involves a feeling of completeness and serenity. The work done on the concept of happiness in different cultures indicates the considerable overlap between the concepts of happiness, pleasure, enjoyment, and good quality of life and other positive statements about one's psychological state (Veenhoven, 1984).

If the assessment of quality of life depends on an assessment of distance from goals, it is clearly necessary to examine who can set these goals and who can measure the (remaining) distance to them (Figure 4.5).

Who measures distance to goals	Who sets goals			
	Self	Close others	Community	Culture
Self				
Close others				
Community				
Culture				

Figure 4.5 Quality of life.

Goals may be set by individuals or by their families, their communities, or the broad cultural groups to which they belong. Equally, the distance to the goals can be measured by oneself, by the community, or by society. Cultures vary in their way of measuring quality of life: In one culture it is perfectly normal for goals for everyone to be set by the family; other cultural groups insist on the need for individuals to be allowed to select their goals themselves. Differences among cultures in this respect can make comparisons of a particular act or experience across cultures very difficult. It is likely that, with the passage of time, such differences among cultures will diminish; it is unlikely, however, that they will disappear.

NOTE

1. This root is the same as that of "placebo," which was first used liturgically to denote the Vespers for the Dead (from the opening words "*Placebo Domino*, . . .") and more recently in psychopharmacology.

REFERENCES

Sartorius, N. (1979). Crosscultural psychiatry. In K. P. Kisker, J. E. Meyer, C. Müller, & E. Strömgren (Eds.), *Psychiatrie der Gegenwart: Forschung und Praxis* [Contemporary psychiatry: Research and practice] (2nd ed., Vol. I/1, pp. 711–737). Berlin, Germany: Springer.
Veenhoven, R. (1984). *Conditions of happiness*. Boston, MA: Reidel.

Pleasure and Health

Nii-K Plange

The discussion that concluded the conference panel on "Pleasure and Health" addressed the substantive issues covered by the speakers, as well as a topic that was barely mentioned: economics. Of particular concern was the conflict between individual choice and social control in relation to health. Among the issues addressed by the discussants were:

1 The role of scientific evidence in providing public health promoters and governments the right to impose behavioral requirements on people. Among the factors that determine the right of institutional third parties to intervene in a health behavior is the scientific evidence of the efficacy or healthfulness of a behavior or policy. One participant maintained that we should not impose our prejudices in lieu of sound scientific evidence. But, as clarified by Michael Daube, scientific evidence in itself is not enough to justify the imposition of public health standards. Among the relevant elements in such a decision are (a) severity of the problem, (b) magnitude or prevalence of the problem, (c) amenability of the problem to treatment, and (d) political and social acceptability of government public health intervention.

2 The role of expectations and outlook in pleasurable experience and health. Alan Marlatt noted that hopefulness—looking forward to things—is a critical factor in health. David Warburton pointed out that important ingredients in any pleasurable experience, apart from the experience itself, are *anticipation* and *expectations* of what its effects will be. The downside to this facet of pleasure is an "optimism bias," according to which people assume that the risks of a behavior will not materialize for them. Health promotion has the task of providing people with realistic information that can successfully counteract this bias.

3   The history and validity of the concept of a "healthy lifestyle."
John Luik emphasized that the idea of a healthy lifestyle is a recent one—
perhaps a hundred years old. Public health advocates have attempted to build
upon medical advances in the elimination of certain diseases in order to prescribe
lifestyles they claim would lead to healthfulness. But the scientific bases for
such prescriptions need to be rigorously defined and scientifically demonstrated,
in order to eliminate the possibility that prescriptions are moral rather than
scientific. For example, Luik questioned how many "good" years on average a
particular health prescription might add to an individual's life—and whether it
is worth it to everyone to cut out an important pleasure in order to extend their
life spans from 85 to 88 years. Others countered that valid health promotion
both extends life and improves its quality.

4   The role of social responsibilities in limiting pleasure. Norman
Sartorius emphasized that pleasure is the result of an interactive process between the individual and his or her social environment. What is considered
permissible or dangerous by a society provides a basis for regulation by the
state. Ole-Jørgen Skog noted that social theorists such as Mill and Durkheim
recognized that uncontrolled individual appetites can escalate, harming society
and leading to anomie. Another commentator emphasized that there is no such
thing as completely individual behavior; in most, if not all, situations proper
behavior implies some responsibility to others. A compromise must be sought
between unbridled individual pursuits and social obligations. This may be best
achieved in a society through the provision of information.

5   The economic costs of health and pleasure. Ann Roche, director
of Queensland Alcohol and Drug Research and Education Center, spoke about
economic factors in support of the state's undertaking an interventionist public
health role. Some behaviors, although gratifying the individual, result in social
costs brought on by diseases and consequent healthcare. Private-sector economic
protection can be provided in some cases through steep insurance levies on
idiosyncratic pleasures posing a potential burden on society as a whole. An
example is higher health-insurance premiums for smokers. Smoking provides
other examples of how a balance may be struck between individual desires and
social needs—for example the restriction of smoking to certain areas.

6   The spiritual dimension in healthcare and promotion. Norman
Sartorius noted that the World Health Organization's executive board has developed a proposal that would expand the current definition of health to include
the attainment of spiritual well-being (WHO, 1998). It has recognized the extent to which spiritual strengths allow people to survive and function in the face
of serious disabilities. Another commentator raised the concern of the extent
to which some spiritual leaders prescribe their followers' lifestyles, sometimes
purely in the leaders' personal interests.

7   The varying functions of alcohol. One participant noted that some
people drink alcohol primarily to mask their suffering and problems. In this
case, there is no obvious pleasure in the experience. Thus, alcohol use may
enhance pleasure in some cases but not in others.

8   Individual freedom versus the need for intervention. A general consensus was that public health interventions could be based on the World Medical

Association's Helsinki Declaration as well as on the Universal Declaration of Human Rights (United Nations, 1948) indicating the need for free, informed choice. There should be no penalty if the individual fails to make the "approved" health choice; this includes the absence of moral coercion of the individual.

REFERENCES

United Nations. (1948). *Universal Declaration of Human Rights.* Available: http://www.unhchr.ch/html/menu3/b/a_udhr.htm.

WHO. (1998). *Review of the constitution of the World Health Organization: Report of the Executive Board special group* (Paper EB.101.R2). Geneva, Switzerland: Author.

Part Two

Pleasure and Alcohol Cross-Culturally

Norman Sartorius introduced the cross-cultural aspects of pleasure in Part 1. The theme of alcohol and pleasure further calls to mind the issue of cultural differences. In Part 2, Dwight Heath provides an overview of the impact of culture not only on drinking patterns and varieties of pleasurable experience associated with alcohol, but also on views of how "permission for pleasure" should fit into public health calculations. On the one hand, public health specialists have resisted acknowledgment of the pleasurableness of drinking. On the other hand, such specialists in developing nations and cultures may see the relationship between these two things very differently from social scientists in the West (see Room, 1984). Thus, the one chapter that deals with a developed nation—France (David)—proposes a cooperation between the alcohol industry and public health sector that is not apparent, and may not yet be possible, in the developing world. This part presents developing world issues in the context of Botswana (Macdonald and Molamu), Latin America (Rosovsky), India (Sharma and Mohan), Japan (Shinfuku), and Ghana (Asare). Among the issues raised in this regard are the following:

1   Psychoactive substance use is universal; in many non-Western societies this involves psychedelics (e.g., peyote, marijuana), opium, coca, and other traditional drugs (Botswana, India, Latin America).
2   Nearly all societies have some traditional exposure to alcohol. In these societies, the supply of alcohol typically has been limited and its use highly regulated socially (Ghana, Japan, Latin America).

3   In some societies, traditional alcohol use, although planned and controlled, involves high levels of consumption and intoxication (Japan, Latin America).

4   Modern societies in which alcohol is a widely available commercial product challenge, but do not eliminate, traditional drinking patterns (Ghana, India, Japan, Latin America).

5   The worst alcohol outcomes involve such disruption of traditional cultural patterns combined with overall cultural degradation and oppression (Botswana).

6   Alcohol regulation in developing nations may be sporadic and nonrationalized (Botswana, Latin America, Ghana).

7   Western styles of drinking among the economically integrated and better off in developing nations often involve more frequent but more moderate imbibing than traditional styles of drinking (Ghana, India, Japan, Latin America).

8   In this sense, the pleasure associated with drinking may need to be redefined from traditional meanings of alcohol if alcohol becomes readily available in a society.

9   Efforts to create regulated drinking in developing societies must call on both traditional and modern patterns and meanings of pleasure.

REFERENCE

Room, R. (1984). Alcohol and ethnography: A case of problem deflation? *Current Anthropology,* 25, 169–191.

Chapter 5

Drinking and Pleasure Across Cultures

Dwight B. Heath

During much of this century, there has been growing awareness of and concern about the many kinds of harm that can result from drinking—physiological and psychic as well as social and economic. During the 1990s, however, there began a countertrend that focuses on the benefits of moderate drinking. Although the physiological benefits—from reduced low-density lipoprotein cholesterol to a lower rate of death from all causes-have had more publicity, the social and psychological benefits have been at least equally important over the long span of the human experience. This chapter characterizes some of those aspects of drinking, after which it suggests how the concept of permission for pleasure (with special reference to drinking) fits into a cross-cultural perspective in the social sciences.

DRINKING FOR PLEASURE

Few people will volunteer, without prompting, that the main reason they drink is "for pleasure," but many of the reasons they do offer appear to be pleasurable and are frankly described as such if fuller discussion probes below the surface of popular slogans and catchwords (see Chapter 15). Some of these benefits, which obviously have brought pleasure to drinkers in various cultures and during many periods of history, are briefly explored here.

Sociability

Drinking together, even more than eating together, serves to bind members of a group in ways that other joint activities do not. In medieval guilds, drinking

61

together was an important symbol of acceptance among those who moved from apprenticeship to membership, and much the same process occurs among groups ranging from college fraternities to dueling clubs, neighborhood ethnic clubs to professional organizations, and among fishermen, lumberjacks, or cowboys in their between-job camaraderie. Public drinking places often are spoken about as "like a second home" to those patrons who are "regulars" (Hunt & Satterlee, 1986).

With alienation and depression seemingly widespread, sociability is an important aim for many people. Drinking appears to meet that aim (or to augment or symbolize it) to the temporary satisfaction of many. In fact, sociability is the primary reason many people give when asked why they drink (Lowe, 1994), and beverage alcohol has been integrated into innumerable social contexts cross-culturally (Akers, 1992). In a double-blind experiment, Smith, Kendrick, and Maben (1992) found that vodka drinkers not only rated themselves "more sociable" than fruit-juice drinkers but also were rated that way by colleagues in the group at various times throughout a long (6.5-hour) "party"; alcohol evidently acts for many people as a "social lubricant," reducing social anxiety.

Relaxation

In nations around the world, people often mention relaxation as a major reason for drinking, and the settings in which drinking takes place are often comfortable, relaxed, and relaxing, as an appropriate complement to one of the principal physiological effects that moderate doses of ethanol are known to have on nearly all human beings.

Whatever the participants consider "comfortable" settings appear to be conducive to drinking that is itself relaxing, sociable, and enjoyable. For some drinkers, quiet also may be important, but for others it is unnecessary, or even antithetical to their needs or expectations. The presence of others in a convivial mood can be supportive but is not essential for many drinkers.

One of the many meanings of the term "time-out" (MacAndrew & Edgerton, 1969) that has come to be used widely with reference to drinking is that of temporary withdrawal from other commitments (whether they be a jangling telephone, the time pressures one might feel whether from an assembly line or a computer screen, or the demands of other people), or simply a subjective feeling of pressure. Drinking for relaxation tends to serve that purpose, except if it interferes with sleep, or if too many drinks in combination with other factors in the setting lead to boisterous or reckless behavior.

Marking Social Boundaries

It is a commonplace that drinking does mark social boundaries, and this often is phrased in terms of "drinking like us," or the clear rejection that is implied when someone will not—or is not invited to—drink with someone else. There are often stereotypes (some accurate, some not) about what members of a particular group drink, and where, when, and how they do it, while doing what else, and so forth.

If an important part of a group's identification is behavior that can be harmful to them or to others (such as assertive masculinity, if that means aggression in any form), drinking to mark boundaries may be problematic. But if the group's behavioral basis is good-natured and has to do with asserting a sense of community, self-esteem, and a positive feeling for the in-group (without necessarily deprecating any out-group), it can be both socially and psychologically beneficial.

Framing of Leisure

In situations in which there is a clear boundary between work and nonwork, drinking can serve as a symbolic marker to set one world off from the other. Gusfield (1987) has written eloquently about this phenomenon in contemporary American culture; the famous afterwork drinking parties among Japanese coworkers also appear to have a similar function (as well as providing a latent escape valve for the informal airing of grievances that are supposedly "forgotten" thereafter) (see Chapter 9). There are various herding groups in sub-Saharan Africa in which men gather around a beer pot (in the yard of a different neighbor each day) and enjoy quiet talk while drinking after they have penned their livestock and before they go home to their families. There are still some kinds of work in which drinking has an integral role—for example, harvesting among the Tarahumara Indians of Mexico, barn-raising among some European and American Protestants, and discussions among editors and journalists. But it is remarkable how many people find a single drink important and effective as a means of "closing the door" on a phase of life over which they have less control and moving to another in which they are "at home" and at ease (figuratively if not literally).

Celebration

One of the most striking findings in any cross-cultural or international study of drinking is the frequency—almost unanimity—with which people speak enthusiastically about drinking as an integral part of or adjunct to celebration. Holidays, rites of passage, arrivals and departures, promotions, winnings, and sundry other reasons for joyous celebration are cited as appropriate occasions for drinking (Heath, 1995).

Toasting is a very special kind of celebration, not just festive in mood but explicitly celebrating someone, something, some event, or some symbol. It focuses attention on whoever or whatever is the subject of the toast, in a way that clearly conveys positive affect from the toaster and from all who join in. The social and psychological benefits of celebration in both the very general and the very specific senses—and of course, in many other senses in between—are woven into the fabrics of most societies, with the drinking of beverage alcohol a frequent accompaniment. So much is that the case that many would feel that they had been cheated, or that the host was stingy, or that the mood of those present was dampened, in the absence of drink. This is not a public health recommendation, but it happens to be true in a great many societies, many more than those in which it is not so.

Transcendence

There are far fewer societies in which transcendence is as popular an activity or goal as celebration, but there are occasions on which the celebration of, for example, a saint's holiday can be the occasion for individuals to "communicate with the gods," or to feel that they are greater than themselves for a time. This should not be difficult to understand, even in Western culture; drunkenness was hailed as one of William James's (1902) varieties of religious experience precisely because it provided a short cut to transcendence of the petty realities of workaday life.

Social Credit

The term "social credit" refers to the fact that exchanges of goods and services (often on a tiny scale) occur with considerable frequency even among people who appear to own little or to control few resources. In relation to beverage alcohol, for example, Waddell (1975) made much of the way in which Papago Indians in bars in towns in the southwestern United States buy a few drinks for friends or neighbors if they have a little extra cash, with the assurance that there will be reciprocity eventually.

The payback is not always in alcohol. It may instead take the form of advice about cheap housing, opportunity for short-term employment, or other informal support. The same is true among Australian aborigines and urban nomads ("homeless people" or bottle gangs) on skid row wherever they occur. Although the terminology of social credit usually is not applied to such settings, there is often an implicit expectation of reciprocity if people attend a cocktail party, a wine-and-cheese reception, or a dinner accompanied by various special drinks. This can be considered an integral part of sociability; it allows hospitality "on a shoestring"; and each such exchange tends to demonstrate (and perhaps to reinforce) the social bonds among the actors.

Signaling of Status

Drinking often is used as a way of signaling the status that one has—or that one aspires to. Certain beverages have prestige or cachet (often commensurate with their cost, but not necessarily so), and their use can be taken to demonstrate, or to imply, the wealth, sophistication, or some other valued attribute of the provider. In the mining communities of South Africa, as in the restaurants of Latin America, bottles are not removed by service persons when they are emptied, but left to accumulate as a demonstration of abundance. Or, at another level, a single beer from a given brewer can represent a major luxury in the life of a person who has little disposable income, but who savors an occasional treat. Serving and talking about wines is construed by many as a marker of cosmopolitan sophistication (Edouard, 1998); the same is true of *grappas* in Italy, single-malt whiskies in Scotland, *pulques* in Mexico (see Chapter 7), *chichas* in Peru, or beers in Belgium, Austria, and many other areas.

Competitive Drinking

Another drinking pattern that deserves special comment in connection with social and psychological pleasure is competitive drinking. To be sure, some of its forms can be dangerous, as when the object is to see who can drink the longest, the fastest, or the greatest quantity. But there are many other forms of competitive drinking that are not inherently risky and that can enhance enjoyment and sociability among members of a group. For example, in Basque country, it may have to do with who can drink from a leather canteen held at the greatest distance. If arm's length is too limiting a factor, this can become a team sport when experts at squeezing the *bota* and aiming its spout are partnered by others who have the rare skill of staying in a stream of wine and swallowing with their mouths open. Somewhat more genteel is the competition that typifies any large meal in the nation of Georgia, where most of those at the table vie with each other, under the direction of a designated toast master, to produce that special combination of eloquence and imaginative hyperbole that typifies their toasting. In ancient China (Xiao, 1995) poems were composed collectively while drinking, the participants taking turns at rhyming on an agreed subject, within strict constraining rules of meter and syllabification, all while quickly carrying forward the overall meaning of an improvised whole. Less formal is the contemporary Costa Rican pattern of improvising vaguely naughty songs, built up of rhyming couplets, with each person, by turns, taking his or her cue from the previous singer. There are hosts of other so-called drinking games or drinking contests (e.g., in Denmark, France, Germany, and Mexico) in which the aim is imaginative creativity, the antithesis of what most people associate with the term "competitive drinking." The spirited and sustained enjoyment of those who play in this manner is ample evidence that we can call it a pleasurable drinking pattern.

Creative Drinking

There is an abundant literature on the relations between alcohol and creativity, although most of it is hampered by vagueness or inconsistency as to what is meant by creativity. Nonetheless, we must recognize that some drinking appears to liberate the imagination of a few individuals in fruitful ways, although excessive drinking often interferes with the discipline or fine control that is needed to move from ideas to products that can be shared with others. The popular witticism about too many Nobel Prize–winning authors being alcoholic (see Goodwin, 1988), or recognition that alcohol provided a significant portion of the calories consumed by the most influential artists early in this century, reflects this little-understood beneficial pattern of drinking that has given pleasure to far more readers than it originally gave to the authors.

PERMISSION FOR PLEASURE

Permission for pleasure has not been among the many aspects of culture that have been subjected to cross-cultural investigation (Naroll, 1983). Writings about norms, values, hedonism, and social control have nibbled at the edges of this subject, but it rarely has been confronted clearly and directly. Although there does exist an elaborately systematic and statistically sophisticated method for comparing qualitative data cross-culturally with respect to correlations between such diverse institutions as value systems, religious beliefs and practices, kinship terminologies, systems of preferential marriage, different kinds of settlement patterns or subsistence activities, the sexual division of labor, warfare, slavery, and so forth, such studies have not been focused on the aspects of culture that are implied in permission for pleasure. Nevertheless, some brief comparative notes about different drinking patterns and their consequences in cultures around the world and throughout history are set out here.

Cultural Perspectives on Pleasure and Alcohol

Peoples in various cultures drink in very different ways (Heath, 1995), and associated with those differing drinking patterns are very different patterns of outcomes (Grant & Litvak, 1998). In other chapters in this part of the book, regional specialists describe some of the specifics of such variation in India, Japan, Latin America, southern and western Africa, and elsewhere, so there is no need for further ethnographic details here. The fundamental anthropological point is that a single relatively simple chemical compound (C_2H_5OH), one that occurs in nature without any human intervention, is treated by the peoples of the world (who are but a single species) in a bewilderingly varied—sometimes diametrically contrasting—number of ways: as food, condiment, drink, or poison; sacrament or abomination; stimulant or relaxant; energizer or soporific; a signal of high status or low; and so forth, almost ad infinitum.

Some might wish for a simple formula that predicts that a given dose of ethanol will stimulate a known response in certain intracerebral receptors, mediated by such-and-such a neurotransmitter. However promising such a microanalytic approach may be for certain kinds of issues, it is far from satisfactory when we deal with questions of social relationships, expectations, drunken comportment, and personal decision making in various contexts, depending on such factors as who one is with and what time it is, what day it is, and so forth.

Although the drinking of beverage alcohol generally is recognized as pleasurable, it must also be recognized clearly and unequivocally as risky. The pleasures of drinking often are described as physiological, psychological, or both (especially relaxation, relief of stress, and altered consciousness). It is evident that many social and cultural associations with drinking are also pleasurable, although they tend usually to be less consciously articulated by the drinkers themselves and less fully described by observers.

This ambivalence can be underscored from two contrasting perspectives. There are, to be sure, some cultures in which the very act of drinking is an abomination in itself, no matter what other pleasures are permitted or even favored. Many Islamic and Hindu societies excel in sheer gusto for sensuousness in many realms of activity, and yet they forbid drinking. By contrast, within many northern European nations, in which people tend generally to be suspicious of pleasure as an aim, men—and, increasingly in recent years, women also— find enjoyment in periodic heavy drinking that often results in general inebriation.

Feelings are so mixed that some devout Muslims find reasons to drink that can be rationalized to fit with both the Koranic prohibition of alcohol and the abundant subsequent scholarly and religious interpretations that support the ban (Badri, 1976). Similarly, people in Denmark, England, Iceland, Sweden, and the United States generally accept drinking, even after having opted for prohibition at various times. This is also the case on Native American reservations and First Nations reserves, or in Alaska Native, Yupik, Inuit, Aleut, or Eskimo communities (some of which alternate with some frequency between being officially wet and dry now that they have the right of local option). After the so-called age of exploration, European colonial powers in all of the Americas, Australia, Oceania, and much of Asia tried repeatedly to impose prohibition on indigenous populations, but they were universally unsuccessful except for brief periods.

However, alcohol was not scorned by the colonial powers (Bradburd & Jankowiak, 1996). On the contrary, it often was used as a tool of exploitation— a cheaply produced commodity providing high value in small volume, easy to transport and store, infinitely divisible, and readily consumed by people unfamiliar with even simple modes of producing it. But the introduction of beverage alcohol did not invariably lead to social and cultural disruption. Sometimes, in fact, drink fitted well into native ways of life, as when the Iroquois incorporated it into their religious ritual of the vision quest (Carpenter, 1959), or when tribes equate a case of beer with a pig in the elaborate ceremonial feasts and exchanges that do so much to keep the peace in highland Papua New Guinea (Marshall, 1982).

Calculating the Risks and Benefits of Alcohol:
Settings and Cultural Typologies

The positive evaluation of drinking often is tempered by a calculus of risks and benefits. The public health or prevention literature of the past few decades (like the temperance literature before it that was associated with regional, statewide, and even national prohibitions earlier in U.S. history) emphasizes only risks, neglecting (or even denying) that there are any benefits. At the same time, proponents of drinking are also selective but in different ways; drunk driving and violation of laws against purchase and possession by young people appear to predominate among the few risks that are mentioned (or even acknowledged) by spokespersons for the several industries that are dependent on beverage alcohol.

Drinking is not unequivocally pleasurable—or even permissible—in a given setting because the setting itself comprises so many relevant variables. Consider time, but not just time of day (some condone a shot of spirits as a morning "eye-opener," some recognize a liter of wine as an appropriate part of breakfast, others who claim to condemn *any* drinking before noon may make exceptions for champagne in scrambled eggs, vodka in orange or tomato juice, and other adjuncts to a gracious brunch). Time matters also in larger units; for example, payday, whether weekly or monthly, may be a significant marker in terms of drinking patterns. Place also matters, so that drinking in church may be frowned on in principle, even by those who take wine in the Eucharist. Jews who would never think of drinking in the temple often have a communal meal with schnapps and socializing in an adjacent room immediately after Sabbath services. To ask for some beverages in a bar is to invite ridicule, just as would not ordering wine with a meal at certain restaurants. As Single (1993) has demonstrated, people drink differently even in the same place, if they are with different numbers of associates, or part of a different gender mix. Even the tempo of background music affects the rate of drinking in public places (Schaefer, 1985). To speak of "the setting" is not simply to speak of place. This single aspect of sociocultural context simply underscores just how many and how varied are the factors that can be relevant in comparing one population's drinking with that of another.

Often called a "social lubricant," alcohol plays a key role in sociability: drinking among guests at a wedding, among friends of the deceased at a wake or funeral, among students at a party, or among viewers at the opening of a gallery, just as much as if friends are visiting, a job is completed, negotiations are finalized, and similar occasions. In a recent volume on cross-cultural aspects of drinking (Heath, 1995), nearly all of the contributing authors, citing public opinion in their countries, emphasized positive evaluations of drinking and its outcomes, which far outweighed the negative. These writers were not solely anthropologists, who have been characterized as "problem deflators" (Room, 1984); they included epidemiologists, medical clinicians, psychiatrists, and specialists knowledgeable in other fields and active in the front line against abuse, who were mostly natives of the 27 countries they described.

When anthropology was first established as an academic discipline and the concept of culture was gaining acceptance among a population reared in ethnocentric unawareness (sometimes coupled with prejudice), the eloquently written book *Patterns of Culture* by ethnographer and poet Ruth Benedict (1934) gained enormous popularity. She characterized "Plains Indians" (actually a regional term she applied indiscriminately to several linguistic and cultural groups) as "Dionysian" or sensation-seeking. She contrasted them with "Pueblo Indians" (similarly, an amalgam of several ethnic groups), whom she called 'Apollonian" or reserved. According to Benedict, Dionysians esteemed pleasure, eagerly sought it by a variety of means, and embraced it if they found it. By contrast, Apollonians held pleasure to be not only suspect but dangerous and deplored any quest for it as risky. They esteemed moderation in all things and assumed that pleasure was in itself unsettling—one might almost say, in today's loose terminology, addicting, inasmuch as people were presumed to be tempted to seek ways to increase, intensify, or prolong it.

That contrast made permission for pleasure a major theme in early contrasts between cultures, although it was never articulated in just those terms. Self-indulgent, demonstrative, exuberant, competitive, and given to extremes, the Dionysian way of life was characterized as the antithesis of Apollonian self-abnegation, conservative, tranquil, and dedicated to moderation in all things.

It should be no surprise that Benedict's book more recently has been relegated to the intellectual dustbin of quaint and curious pioneering efforts, now seen as well intentioned but grossly oversimplified, methodologically wanting, and simplistically selective in what was reported and what was ignored. Nevertheless, it was a milestone in establishing widespread recognition that social and cultural variables must be taken into consideration, in combination with psychological, biochemical, physiological, and other variables, in terms of both perceptions and evaluations of pleasures and permissions among different peoples.

It is evident now that the Apollonian/Dionysian contrast alone is not sufficient for a good understanding of permission for pleasure in cultural context. In plain terms, it tends to focus selectively on those aspects of a way of life that fit with the typological characterization and to ignore those that contrast. But even that critique is too simplistic.

In some senses similar is the "wet/dry" contrast with specific reference to culture that has recently gained some currency in alcohol studies (Levine, 1992). The term "wet" refers to "Southern," "Mediterranean," or "wine" cultures, in which drinking plays a number of important roles throughout each day and during the life of an individual or a community. The contrasting "dry" cultures are "Northern" or "spirits" cultures, generally with a history of temperance ideology. Wetness in that sense refers to the pervasiveness of alcohol, consumed at meals, taken during rest breaks, allowable to women and children, and openly appreciated, as contrasted with dryness, which refers to the compartmentalization of alcohol as separate from the workaday routine of life, restricted from women and children, and even a little shameful.

But if we shift the focus of our attention from the act of drinking to the state of drunkenness, a very different pattern emerges. We find that wet cultures tend to be *less* permissive in that respect, regarding drunkenness as silly, stupid, inappropriate behavior, signaling ineptitude on the part of an injudicious person ignorant of how to drink. By contrast, the supposedly dry cultures tend to accept drunkenness—in an occasional context, usually exclusively male and remote from children—as an important psychic safety valve, with what they call "heroic drinking" (Partanen, 1991) considered appropriate as a periodic demonstration of male bonding and masculinity. Is frequent drinking to be viewed as indulgent, demonstrative, and Dionysian, whereas a predominant pattern of abstention and self-abnegation is more Apollonian? Or, looking at attitudes toward drunkenness, would those labels be reversed? For that matter, just how useful are such concepts as wetness and dryness, or Dionysian and Apollonian?

If the famous but mythical "ethnographer from Mars" were to visit Times Square on New Year's Eve, he or she might come away with a view of permission for pleasure in the United States that is far from usual. The same would be true in Las Vegas or in Salt Lake City at any time, or, for that matter, anywhere in the world where Jews celebrate Purim in the traditional way. We all recognize that, although drinking may take place on almost any occasion, there are some special occasions that virtually "call for" a drink—and people often say exactly that! But permission should not be thought of as a simple dyadic contrast either. It is not just a matter of yes or no; several degrees of permissiveness often are recognized, or even specified. "Yes" and "no" are only two of the possibilities; others on the positive side might be "generally allowed to a few in limited circumstances," "encouraged for many in most circumstances," "people are exhorted to drink," "it's offensive not to drink," and a host of others. Similarly, on the negative side, degrees of nonpermissiveness might include "slightly discouraged," which differs from "illegal," which in turn differs from "immoral," "lightly sanctioned," "severely punished," and so forth. The exact wording is irrelevant, but recognition of degrees of permission or permissiveness is crucial.

CONCLUSION

It is apt that the theme of permission for pleasure be dealt with largely in terms of beverage alcohol as a case study, if only because research and writings on the subject of drinking have for so long been predominantly focused on pathological, negative, or risky aspects, even though the popular consensus on the part of most people is that drinking is positive and pleasurable. It is still, as Bacon (1943) observed over 50 years ago, as if we were trying to understand the role of the automobile by paying attention only to traffic accidents (see Chapter 26). Among the pleasurable social and psychological benefits that have been reported widely by many observers (quite apart from enjoying the taste, enhancing a meal, relieving thirst, and other such common but important reasons that people often give for enjoying drinking) are sociability, relaxation, marking of social boundaries, framing of leisure as distinct from work, stimulation or confirmation of a sense of celebration, transcendence of workaday reality, marking of an event as special, extension of social credit, and low-cost signaling of status (see also Chapter 15).

However, it is premature at best, and indeed unrealistic, to expect to find a simple template that might be applied cross-culturally or internationally as a way of characterizing permission for pleasure as a moral or behavioral phenomenon. As is so often the case with respect to drinking and its outcomes, context is crucial, and that context involves a complex interplay of historical, attitudinal, evaluative, and other factors that tend to be unique to every community. Nonetheless, permission for pleasure is, from a social science perspective, a novel and promising frame of reference, an implied set of questions, and a value orientation that deserves to be explored in greater depth.

REFERENCES

Akers, R. L. (1992). *Drugs, alcohol, and society: Social structure, process and policy*. Belmont, CA: Wadsworth.

Bacon, S. D. (1943). Sociology and the problems of alcohol: Foundations for a sociological study of drinking behavior. *Quarterly Journal of Studies on Alcohol, 4*, 399–445.

Badri, M. B. (1976). *Islam and alcoholism*. Indianapolis, IN: American Trust Publications.

Benedict, R. F. (1934). *Patterns of culture*. Boston: Houghton Mifflin.

Bradburd, D., & Jankowiak, W. (1996). Using drug foods to capture and enhance labor performance: A cross-cultural perspective. *Current Anthropology, 37*, 717–720.

Carpenter, E. S. (1959). Alcohol in the Iroquois dream quest. *American Journal of Psychiatry, 116*, 148–151.

Edouard, D. (1998). *Le vin dans la civilisation américaine, 2: Contemporaine* [Wine in American civilisation, 2: Contemporary]. Unpublished doctoral dissertation, Université de Dijon, France.

Goodwin, D. W. (1988). *Alcohol and the writer*. Kansas City, MO: Andrews & McMeel.

Grant, M., & Litvak, J. (Eds.). (1998). *Drinking patterns and their consequences*. Washington, DC: Taylor & Francis.

Gusfield, J. R. (1987). Passage to play: Rituals of drinking time in American society. In M. Douglas (Ed.), *Constructive drinking: Perspectives on drinking from anthropology* (pp. 73–90). Cambridge, UK: Cambridge University Press.

Heath, D. B. (Ed.). (1995). *International handbook on alcohol and culture*. Westport, CT: Greenwood.

Hunt, G., & Satterlee, S. (1986). Cohesion and division: Drinking in an English village. *Man, 21*, 521–537.

James, W. (1902). *Varieties of religious experience: A study in human nature*. New York: Longmans, Green.

Levine, H. G. (1992). Temperance cultures: Alcohol as a problem in Nordic and English-speaking cultures. In M. Lader, G. Edwards, & C. Drummond (Eds.), *The nature of alcohol and drug-related problems* (pp. 16–36). New York: Oxford University Press.

Lowe, G. (1994). Pleasures of social relaxants and stimulants: The ordinary person's attitudes and involvement. In D. M. Warburton (Ed.), *Pleasure: The politics and the reality* (pp. 95–108). Chichester, UK: Wiley.

MacAndrew, C., & Edgerton, R. B. (1969). *Drunken comportment: A social explanation*. Chicago, IL: Aldine.

Marshall, M. (Ed.). (1982). *Through a glass darkly: Beer and modernization in Papua New Guinea* (Monograph 18). Boroko, Papua New Guinea: Institute of Applied Social and Economic Research.

Naroll, R. (1983). *The moral order: An introduction to the human situation*. Beverly Hills, CA: Sage.

Partanen, J. (1991). *Sociability and intoxication: Alcohol and drinking in Kenya, Africa, and the modern world* (Vol. 39). Helsinki, Finland: Finnish Foundation for Alcohol Studies.

Room, R. (1984). Alcohol and ethnography: A case of problem deflation? *Current Anthropology, 25*, 169–191.

Schaefer, J. M. (1985). The physical setting: Behavior and policy. In E. Single & T. Storm (Eds.), *Public drinking and public policy* (pp. 85–89). Toronto, Canada: Addiction Research Foundation.

Single, E. (1993). Public drinking. In M. Galanter (Ed.), *Research developments in alcoholism* (vol. 11, pp. 143–152). New York: Plenum.

Smith, A., Kendrick, A., & Maben, A. (1992). Use and effects of food and drinks in relation to daily rhythms of mood and cognitive performance: Effects of caffeine, lunch, and alcohol on human performance, mood, and cardiovascular function. *Proceedings of the Nutrition Society, 51*, 325–333.

Waddell, J. O. (1975). For individual power and social credit: The use of alcohol among Tucson Papagos. *Human Organization, 34*, 9–15.

Xiao, J. (1995). China. In D. Heath (Ed.), *International handbook on alcohol and culture* (pp. 42–50). Westport, CT: Greenwood.

Chapter 6

From Pleasure to Pain: A Social History of Basarwa/San Alcohol Use in Botswana

Dave Macdonald and Louis Molamu

Alcohol use among the Basarwa, or San or Bushmen,[1] of southern Africa is an epidemic problem. Moderate drinking is the exception, and alcohol-related dysfunction is widespread in many Basarwa settlements. This situation is the result of both underlying economic and social despair created by oppression and by the problems of adjustment of Basarwa to modern socioeconomic conditions, and the Basarwa's exposure to a modernizing African society in which alcohol is freely available. In this context, alcohol does not convey pleasure as it is typically understood but is predominantly used as a means to relieve pain and despair. Although the prohibition of alcohol might be suggested by this scenario, such a program would seem to be difficult to implement in the free society in which the Basarwa marginally participate.

THE BACKGROUND OF DRINKING BY THE BASARWA

The history of the use of psychoactive or mood-altering substances by Basarwa, the majority of whom reside in remote areas of Botswana, has been the subject of some speculation. Many early accounts by explorers, traders, missionaries, and anthropologists mainly documented the use of tobacco and marihuana (*dagga*) by these indigenous peoples of southern Africa. Stow (1905, p. 52), for example, reported that "the Bushmen were almost passionately fond of smoking" and used a range of mouth pipes, ground pipes, and water pipes. Schoeman, reported in Gordon (1986, p. 182), even suggested that the !Kung Bushmen were so fond of tobacco that they would "trek up to the Kavango river where they would prostitute their wives to migrant workers returning from the mines for a bit of tobacco." Theal (1910, p. 38) also maintained that "the Bushmen were inveterate smokers of dacha or wild hemp" and added other substances to their pipes to complement tobacco and cannabis, such as the kanna-bosch plant, which was dried and powdered and used for chewing as well as smoking. "When mixed with dacha it was very intoxicating" (Stow, 1905, p. 53). In his comprehensive study of cannabis use in Africa, du Toit (1980, p. 15) recognized that such polydrug use by Basarwa "long preceded the arrival of whites in Southern Africa."

Conventional wisdom, however, asserts that the Basarwa had no traditional alcoholic beverages, although there is fragmentary evidence that in parts of the Kalahari Desert some Basarwa groups had sufficient skills and knowledge of their flora to produce mildly alcoholic beverages. The relatively sparse empirical literature on Basarwa alcohol use does not provide any credible account of the purpose of their use of different types of alcoholic beverages. Ambler and Crush's (1992) study, located within the broader framework of southern African historiography, hardly touches on alcohol use among Basarwa. Similarly, other studies on Basarwa contain inadequate data pertaining to drinking as an aspect of culture (Bain, 1936; Duggan-Cronin, 1942; Dunn, 1931; Makin, 1929). What is clear, however, is that the production and consumption of alcohol throughout the whole southern African region was influenced immensely by modern socioeconomic and political changes.

This chapter sketches a sociohistorical portrait of alcohol use among the now relatively sedentary Basarwa communities in the Ghanzi district of Botswana. It stresses at the outset the traditional and relatively inconspicuous role of alcohol in the culture of Naro-speaking Basarwa, which was mainly to produce feelings of *gãe-tcao*, or pleasure or happiness. However, what constitutes pleasure needs to be contextualized within specific cultures and social histories. Pleasure for the Basarwa undoubtedly means something other than the normative middle-class Euro-American version of pleasure that is becoming increasingly globalized. The Naro language, for example, does not have a specific word for pleasure, but has *gãe-tcao*, literally meaning "good-hearted," which is a general word used for happiness or pleasure (Visser, February 27, 1998, personal communication). There is another word, *taia*, which represents that particular form of happiness when someone has returned and brought you something, including him or herself.

In fact, it can be argued that in the contemporary context, pleasure for the impoverished, landless, and marginalized Basarwa is better represented as the absence of pain, or *thŏò*, which is the verb "to hurt" and also can describe wounds and other forms of physical pain, as well as emotional pain. *Thŏò* is also the Naro word for "pity," better translated as the ability to feel the pain of the other. It is the absence of pain rather than the presence of pleasure that best represents the Basarwas' motivational accounts of their reasons for drinking. As with other groups experiencing severe existential pain, "pleasure" derived from drinking is primarily associated with excessive levels of consumption that lead to the physical and psychological obliteration of such pain, at least until the onset of *babalas* (hangover) or more severe symptoms of alcohol abuse. Such a cycle can be only self-perpetuating and is extremely difficult to break.

The Naro farm workers, remote settlement dwellers, and residents of the squatter area in Ghanzi town, provide an important case study on how the traditional pleasures associated with drinking came to be stifled by the impact of broader socioeconomic and political factors. In the analysis that follows, we evaluate the relevance of the conception of pleasure related to drinking and highlight the impact of political and social factors on the changing nature of such pleasure.

THE BASARWA AND ALCOHOL IN THE PRECOLONIAL PERIOD

The legendary Kalahari Desert is a vast and intriguing storehouse of a wide variety of mammal, plant, bird, and reptile life. Interestingly, ethnobotanists have identified five plants of the Kalahari with marked psychoactive properties and a further nine with toxic properties that produce so-called hallucinogenic effects (Winkelman & Dobkin de Rios, 1989). In this environment, obtaining food through hunting and gathering was always a priority for the various hunter-gatherer groups that inhabited the desert (Becker, 1974).

A common feature of precolonial Basarwa communities was the communal participation in seasonal productive activities. Clusters of families, relatives, friends, and visitors, constituting the central units of the various bands, acted collectively on a variety of projects. Cooperative hunting, mainly by male members of the band, was an important element in the lives of the Basarwa. Members of the band also pooled their resources and foraged for veld foods. These included a variety of edible berries, roots, and other fruit from wild plants. In dry areas of the Kalahari plant foods provided the main source of fluids. Anecdotal evidence suggests that from the wide variety of fruits, berries, and honey from wild bees, Basarwa produced some alcoholic beverages. Theal (1910, p. 38) reported that after wild honey was collected, the comb was used for food "but most of the honey was fermented and consumed as an intoxicant." Stow (1910, p. 39) revealingly states that "the great happiness of the Bushmen was in his 'honey harvest'" and it was only then that he could brew his "primitive mead" and "eat, drink, and be merry." Drinking has been perceived traditionally as positive and enjoyable and both Bleek (1928) and Schapera (1963, p. 102) noted that drunkenness was exceptional among the Basarwa, although "they all appreciate alcohol and native beer when it is given to them."

The ethics of sharing and reciprocity among the Basarwa are a well-documented phenomenon (Cashdan, 1985). For a long time one of the documented forms of transaction involved the sharing of meat and veld products. Among the Naro, especially, sharing is a basic principle by which social solidarity is maintained. The group nature of drinking is merely an extension of a fairly well-established principle of sharing and reciprocity.

On closer examination it is clear that, traditionally, there was rarely an abundance of alcohol in Basarwa communities. For many years, prior to the drilling of wells and boreholes, there was a lack of adequate supplies of clear and safe water where most Basarwa resided. This was indeed one of the primary reasons limiting the quantities of alcoholic beverages that could be produced. Because brewing tended to require sweet ground water, grain, sugar and, of course, the money to buy such ingredients, drinking was for most Basarwa an occasional activity. It is against this background that the moderate use of alcohol—often associated with pleasure and leisure—featured modestly in the lives of Basarwa.

The locally brewed alcohol that was produced and consumed reportedly was used to promote community cohesion and for ritual purposes. It seems that alcohol use and a state of mild inebriation were valued, although Dornan (1925, p. 121) reported that "the Masarwas, whether tame or wild, are excessively fond of Kaffir beer, and indeed contrive to get drunk whenever they can." Contradictory historical accounts of alcohol use by Basarwa, such as this account by Dornan and the earlier ones by Bleek and Schapera, reflect the degree of social isolation between Basarwa bands and other ethnic and tribal groups that produced and sold alcohol to them. They further reflect the fact that the term "Bushman" is largely a sociopolitical construct that represents an amalgam of peoples with varying lifestyles and cultures. In contemporary Botswana, for example, there are significant cultural and linguistic differences between distinct groups of the Basarwa such as the !Kung, the !Xo, and the G/wi (Macdonald & Molamu, 1998). Indeed, the main unifying factor of a common Basarwa identity may be that of *sheta*, a shared life of powerlessness, deprivation, and suffering (Guenther, 1996).

The group nature of drinking, primarily for pleasure, was an outstanding feature of the way in which alcohol was used. Alcohol use also was associated, arguably, with religious and therapeutic rituals and folklore sessions. One of the central aspects of Basarwa social life is a campfire where folktales, the unwritten literature of the Basarwa, are told and music is played (Barnard, 1992, p. 144). Other important cultural events such as marriage were marked by the production of alcoholic beverages, and Hutchinson (1979, p. 329) noted that "group and ritual consumption of beer took place frequently." There is no evidence to suggest that drinking alcohol was problematic or dysfunctional in its effects. In the main it was meant to contribute to social cohesiveness. Indeed, consumption of alcohol fitted into the "gregarious, sociable and harmonious nature of their society, where sharing and collaboration form the essential social command" (Mostert, 1992, p. 27) and productive work left much time for outside leisure and social activities (Sahlins, 1974).

Generally in Botswana brewing and beer consumption have been an integral part of village life (Molamu, 1989) and sorghum, a staple food throughout southern Africa, has been a primary ingredient in the production of traditional alcoholic beverages. Crisp (1896, p. 47) noted that beer was a "considerable item of the diet of Bechuana [Batswana]" and in most villages the largely unfiltered opaque beverages were produced for a variety of occasions ranging from agricultural and religious ceremonies to personal and family hospitality. Haggblade (1992, p. 396) stated that "women have been brewing sorghum beer in Botswana since at least the eighteenth century immigration of Tswana peoples to the perimeter of the Kalahari." As Basarwa became incorporated into the village life of the politically dominant Tswana many of them assimilated, inter alia, alcohol-related practices. It is in this context that *bojalwa*, especially, came to play an important role in the lives of many of the Basarwa.

COLONIAL RULE AND ALCOHOL

British colonial rule in the Bechuanaland Protectorate stretched from the close of the 19th century to the mid-1960s. This period was characterized by the consolidation of the position of the Basarwa on the lowest rungs of the social hierarchy (Schapera, 1963), a process that had started long before the colonialists arrived in this part of southern Africa.

In its bid to impose an ordered vision on its colonial possession, one of the objectives of the colonial state was to address the problem of alcohol in the protectorate. Throughout the region, colonial administrations, often in collusion with local elites, implemented strict liquor laws. The chief of the Bangwato tribe, Kgama III, for example, was an early convert to Christianity. He remained a strict prohibitionist throughout his reign from circa 1835 to 1923 (Chirenje, 1978). From the outset in the Bechuanaland Protectorate the colonial administration felt that "European intoxicants," especially spirits, and indigenous alcoholic beverages such as *khadi* were harmful to "the natives." It was felt that the consumption of alcohol tended to disrupt work rhythms and thus affected productivity, particularly on the farms. A series of laws was promulgated in a bid to control the production, sale, and consumption of these types of beverages by the colonized peoples. For many years, the policy on alcohol in the Protectorate was very closely tied to the racist prohibitionist policies that had been introduced in South Africa. Despite the restrictions imposed, the illicit sale of "European liquor" to Africans continued, especially in the 1940s and 1950s (Haggblade, 1992). Similarly, the production and consumption of *khadi* continued, in part as a mode of resistance to colonial rule and domination. Despite prosecutions for contravention of the liquor laws, attempts to control and prohibit the production and distribution of these drinks had limited success.

Legal restrictions on the Basarwa brewing and access to alcoholic beverages persisted until the 1960s. However, the years of prohibition never effectively prevented Basarwa from having access to alcohol. The repeal of the laws, all of which carried criminal penalties, meant that Basarwa, like other Batswana, in this sense at least, could drink freely and openly.

The majority of the Basarwa population now reside in settlements generally remote from the main villages and urban centers. These settlements, established by the Botswana government under the Remote Area Development Program, occupy a unique and somewhat precarious position in the larger economy. They invariably lack the infrastructure needed to promote development. Consequently they are characterized by limited economic opportunities and limited or no social services (Childers, 1976; Mogalakwe, 1986)

The migration to Ghanzi by many Basarwa from neighboring settlements and outlying farms often has been related to these adverse conditions. An increasing number of Naro men and women have entered the Ghanzi labor market, invariably without financial capital and with only limited skills and education. Many of them arrive and seek employment as low-wage and informal-sector workers or just hang around hoping to scrounge some money for alcohol.

The relatively strong social networks among the Naro have tended to channel the migrants into specific neighborhoods, particularly the poor housing section known as the squatter area. Their flight from the devastating poverty of the settlements often culminates in the squalor and poverty of a semiurban squatting environment. Researchers of ethnic inequality view such spatial segregation as part of a broader structural device through which minority groups are denied access to economic opportunities (Telles, 1995).

ALCOHOL SUPPLY AND PRODUCTION

The traditional patterns of beer production have changed significantly over time as the economic and social fabric of Ghanzi and its environs has been transformed. The expansion of the cash economy was accompanied by the increasing production of *bojalwa* and *khadi* for sale. This rapid commercialization of grain-beer production became a pervasive feature of rural and urban communities throughout southern Africa. The output of industrially produced alcoholic beverages increased markedly in the postindependence period from 1966 on, and a variety of products has flooded the market. The fairly sophisticated distribution networks established by Kgalagadi Breweries, Botswana Breweries, and many independent entrepreneurs have ensured that these products are readily available even in remote areas of Botswana. Basarwa communities were simply unprepared for the sheer volume and types of alcoholic beverages that became available, especially after independence in September of 1966.

The main types of alcoholic beverages that are currently available include traditional home brews and industrially manufactured alcoholic beverages. *Bojalwa* and *khadi* are both home-brewed beer-like drinks that differ markedly with respect to alcohol content, consistency, and taste depending on availability of ingredients (such as sugar, sorghum, oranges, and wild berries) and methods of fermentation. *Nyola* is a home-brewed beverage prepared from commercially produced sorghum "beer" powder. These home-brewed alcoholic beverages are invariably significantly cheaper than the Western-type beverages. The latter include Chibuku, a brand name for industrially produced thick sorghum beer that is sold in waxed cardboard cartons. Popularly known as "shake-shake," it often is sold alongside home brews, as its sale does not require a license. Commercial beers such as Castle, Lion, and Black Label and various brands of brandy, whisky, and vodka, referred to as "hot stuff," account for a smaller part of the consumption of beverages, especially because they are more expensive. Proprietary-brand alcoholic beverages such as these are frequently trucked into remote settlements at month's end and sold for inflated prices by illegal entrepreneurs. There are oral reports of Basarwa groups in other parts of the country using both clear and dyed methylated spirits, but there is no evidence of this in Ghanzi district (Molebatsi, September 1, 1997, personal communication).

The marketing outlets of the formal sector include bars, bottle stores, liquor restaurants, and Chibuku depots. In the squatter area and in the settlements, however, the significance of the *shebeen*—also popularly known, as in many parts of South Africa, as a drinking "spot"—is well established. Malahleha (1984, p. 13) defines a *shebeen* as "an unlicensed, unconventional drinking establishment where alcoholic beverages are sometimes brewed, and always sold and dispensed at any time that is convenient to the patrons and the proprietors." These outlets have become an important phenomenon in the social and economic lives of Basarwa, as they have for other impoverished groups throughout the southern African region.

The brewing of traditional sorghum beer, *bojalwa*, and *khadi* on a small scale, for commercial purposes, has turned into one of the primary sources of income for women in Ghanzi and neighboring settlements. This has especially been the case since 1986, when the Presidential Commission on Economic Opportunities legitimized home brewing and recommended that the government remove any existing restrictive regulations "in order to allow all Batswana to engage in various forms of commercial activities in the informal sector. *Shebeens* were accepted as a commercial and social reality" (Molamu & Manyeneng, 1988, p. 86), and by 1986 it was estimated that over 58,000 shebeens operated in Botswana (Haggblade, 1992, p. 405). There are no accurate statistics to show what proportion of Basarwa women are engaged in the production and sale of these beverages. It is clear, however, that because the Basarwa constitute the poorest stratum of rural communities, they often do not possess the necessary excess grain, or indeed money, to establish an economically viable home-based operation. Despite this major obstacle, it is reported that an increasing number of Basarwa women have started to brew beer with the primary objective of selling it on the premises for cash. This socioeconomic phenomenon plays a critical role in the local economies, although Basarwa are still more likely to consume than produce alcohol; production is dominated by other ethnic groups such as the Bakgalagadi, Baherero, and Batswana.

Shebeens, then, are the primary centers of the informal-sector production of alcohol in Basarwa communities and also serve as the main settings for relaxation and socializing for adult men and women who drink, as well as for the increasing numbers of young Basarwa who are turning to alcohol (Macdonald, Malila, & Molamu, 1997). Some individuals and small groups, however, take their beer and spirits into the bush to drink in order to avoid sharing with other Basarwa who have no money to buy alcohol.

THE BASARWA AS AN EXTREME SOCIOECONOMIC UNDERCLASS

An exploration of the various processes of alienation, marginalization, and impoverishment is crucial to an understanding of how problems associated with alcohol abuse have been reproduced among Basarwa. The plight of the Naro, specifically, was a product of the twin land-grab forces of Batswana and later Afrikaner pastoralists. What was once the centerpiece of the hunting ranges of the indigenous people was transformed into pasture for cattle and goats. The marginalization of Basarwa by the Afrikaners from the close of the 19th century was associated with the establishment of pastoral farming as the leading sector of the local economy. The results of this historical process, vividly portrayed by Mogalakwe (1986), find expression, in part, in alcohol abuse. Discrimination, poverty, and violence typically have been daily features of the lives of Basarwa. Within the region generally, Gordon (1992, p. 136) claims that the Bushmen "are in reality the most victimized and brutalized people in the bloody history that is Southern Africa." More specifically, in contemporary Botswana the Basarwa represent an underclass *within* an underclass, or what Kann, Hitchcock, and Mbere (1990, p. 19) describe as "the poorest of the desperately poor." In 1993 and 1994, 48% of all rural households in Botswana fell beneath the official poverty line, and it was estimated that the poorest 10% of rural households (these are Basarwa) had a mean income in cash and kind of approximately US$30 per month. To put this in perspective, in 1991 Botswana, with a population of 1.3 million people, had a per capita gross national product of US$2580 and foreign reserves of over US$4 billion (Government of Botswana, 1993). From being one of the world's poorest countries at independence in 1966, Botswana has in the 1990s become an upper-middle–income country mainly because of wealth generated from the country's vast diamond reserves.

As far as can be ascertained, in the precontact period Basarwa largely lived in independence and dignity as self-sufficient people, although trading networks and other links did exist with the outside world (Denbow, 1984). There are few written records of Basarwa contact with Tswana people prior to the arrival of Europeans. In the case of the Naro, they were reduced to penury and servitude as the dominant Batswana and Afrikaner pastoralists encroached on their traditional water holes and hunting grounds. The radical changes in land use and tenure in the rural areas were accompanied by grave limitations in access to land, water, and natural resources (N'gongola, 1997). Many Basarwa were employed on the farms owned by the descendants of the Afrikaner pastoralists who settled in the area. Guenther (1996, p. 227) describes in detail the harsh conditions under which Basarwa lived and worked and points out that "the farms were on land which, until the Boers' arrival in 1898, had been *n!usa* or *n!ore* [band territory] of the indigenous Naro." Mogwe (1994, p. 4) further contends that a people such as the Basarwa, who have been forcibly removed from their ancestral land, have become "a lost people."

WIDESPREAD ALCOHOL DYSFUNCTION

Shostak (1990, p. 216) has argued that the psychological effects of drastic negative changes in their social and economic circumstances have led the Basarwa to consume increasing quantities of home-brewed alcoholic beverages. In 1992 a report conducted on behalf of the Botswana Council of Churches drew similar conclusions (Mogwe, 1992). In his excellent portrayal, Guenther (1996, p. 228) also refers to "their coping strategies and their [Basarwa] culture's adaptive mechanisms in the face of oppression and deprivation." It is likely that excessive and largely uncontrolled alcohol consumption has featured quite prominently in the whole repertoire of coping mechanisms and that this has been a progressive phenomenon since Botswana's independence in 1966. Lee (1979, p. 418), for example, suggests that a new culture developed among the Dobe !Kung "based on selling and drinking beer, and listening (and dancing) to the hit tunes from Radio Botswana on transistor radios" such that by 1973 "the level of drunkenness had increased to alarming levels."

There undoubtedly has been a marked shift from the earlier and more controlled ceremonial use of alcohol to a more commercial and abusive pattern. In the early days the consumption of alcohol among Basarwa was structured by a combination of the social and ritual imperatives of each group. Alcohol was not always available. However, drinking was for pleasure, conviviality, and the resultant consolidation of group ties. Social breakdown and interpersonal violence attributed to drunkenness, unlike today, were unknown.

The factors that precipitated alcohol abuse among Basarwa were multifaceted. These relate directly and indirectly to the major political, social, and demographic changes experienced over the years. It has been argued that the dislocation of the Basarwa from their ancestral lands and their subsequent incorporation into the cash economy have had a major impact on their cultural lives. Low socioeconomic status, unemployment, inadequate housing, poor community facilities, and inappropriate educational facilities all have played major parts. The institutionalization of hereditary servitude resulted in their social position as *malata*, little more than servants and hereditary vassals, and led to their increasing alienation and social marginalization. For those who ended up as farm workers or squatters on ranches or cattle posts, their lives were equally bleak. As Good (1994, p. 2) poignantly states, their situation in wealthy Botswana "is one of such acute deprivation and exploitation that almost negates the citizenship they possess."

This process of dislocation from ancestral lands is one that still continues in contemporary Botswana. Within the past 2 years the government has "persuaded" Basarwa living in remote settlements in the Central Kalahari Game Reserve (CKGR) to relocate to settlements outside the reserve and nearer to Ghanzi. One group, for example, living in Xade in the CKGR was relocated to New Xade, a settlement outside the reserve where there was no fixed water supply or permanent buildings. Many other Basarwa have been moved out of the CKGR, although there has been some resistance to this. "As one old man said, 'I will not agree to migrate from my ancestral land where my soul and spirits are. I do not understand this rule where people are trucked like cattle that are taken to the Botswana Meat Commission' " ("Botswana: Last," 1998, p. 2).

Regardless of the reasons for the move—some argue that the Basarwa were coerced and threatened into moving and evicted from their homes by a government intent on mining the large diamond deposits recently discovered at Gope in the CKGR and turning the reserve into a "people-free" tourist wildlife area—its effect has been a dramatic increase in alcohol consumption among the relocated Basarwa. This is confirmed by media reports that suggest that the limited compensation paid to heads of families has been spent mostly on alcohol (Bridgland, 1998; Herbert, 1998; "Resettlement," 1997). In New Xade, one report claimed that

> many a Khwe never had that much money in their pocket before. So the first few weeks or months were a time of feasting and indulging in excessive alcohol consumption, as outside traders selling all kinds of brews soon appeared on the scene. It is foreseeable that alcoholism, like in all Bushmen resettlement sites of the country, will soon become a major problem. (Erni, 1997, p. 9)

A more recent report given to the Botswana Christian Council by a clergyman stated that the situation in which Basarwa live in New Xade is now characterized by "abject poverty and absolute suffering" ("Baswara continue," 1998, p. 4).

CONCLUSIONS: PLEASURE AND PAIN IN BASARWA DRINKING

For many years Basarwa have lived in a social context that is characterized by pain. The structural conditions of this "Fourth World" life include intense economic deprivation and a marked degree of social dislocation and marginalization. The chronic insecurity associated with these conditions has contributed to excessive alcohol consumption and abuse by Basarwa. Drinking is no longer primarily for pleasure. Many Basarwa use alcohol, usually excessively, as an analgesic for both existential and physical pain.

Recent research (Macdonald, 1997) suggests that, as with any group of drinkers, the Basarwa's stated reasons for drinking are both complex and shifting. Twenty-three male and female drinkers aged 18 years or more who were interviewed in one settlement near Ghanzi provide a clear illustration of the uneasy alliance and precarious balance between pleasure and pain inherent in motivational accounts of alcohol use by Basarwa. Younger drinkers felt that they had been socialized, and even coerced, into drinking through friends and work colleagues and provided a range of social reasons for drinking such as friendship, relaxation, and "getting girls." Eight of the twenty-three drinkers, however, started to drink to stave off the pangs of hunger and just "to keep going." Logic dictates that if one has money to buy either food or alcohol then one chooses alcohol because it fills one's belly *and* makes one feel good at the same time. Ironically, almost half of the drinkers said that if they had more available money they would drink more often. Most drinking takes place at month end when people have money and usually takes the form of binge drinking. Others drank to forget about unemployment and emotional pain, or *thŏò*, which literally translates as "I can feel pain in my heart."

Expressed preferences for certain types of alcohol given by the drinkers suggest "that they were largely based on notions of self-medication, either to promote health or to avoid sickness" (Macdonald, 1997, p. 9). Alcohol, albeit mistakenly, frequently was referred to as medicine or food. This, of course, did not prevent the contradictory responses given by all of the drinkers that they suffered health problems as a result of their drinking, for example loss of weight, dehydration, malnourishment, palpitations, stomach ulcers, and liver cirrhosis.

Indeed, one of the most interesting findings from the research was that 18 of the 23 drinkers had completely stopped drinking at some stage in their drinking career for periods between 3 months and 2 years, although all had resumed drinking since. Sometimes they had stopped for health reasons, sometimes because of lack of money, and sometimes because they felt ashamed. The longing and craving they all expressed to return to drinking, however, was born more out of suppressing pain than engendering the short-term pleasurable effects of controlled alcohol use. Without substantial changes in their socioeconomic situation, dominated as it is by impoverishment, marginalization, and alienation, it is doubtful whether alcohol can ever bring true *gãe-tcao*, or happiness, to the Basarwa. Although there are signs that some young employed Basarwa practice a form of controlled drinking, for most Basarwa who use alcohol their excessive and largely uncontrolled drinking results in a series of health, social, economic, and spiritual problems. As one old man who had never been able to stop drinking said, "It is not easy for me, I am used to drinking. Even if I am asleep I dream alcohol."

ACKNOWLEDGMENTS

We acknowledge financial support in the preparation of this chapter from NUFU Programme 20/96, The University of Botswana and University of Tromsø Collaborative Programme for San/Basarwa Research.

NOTE

1. The generic term *Basarwa* is used here to refer to that group of people indigenous to southern Africa who are often more pejoratively referred to as "Bushmen." "San" is another ethnic term that has been used extensively to refer to this group. In Botswana, Basarwa are often referred to as *BaTengnyanateng*, meaning "the farthest people," or, as it is sometimes translated, those from "the deep within the deep" (Mogwe, 1992). Some groups of Basarwa now want to be called *N/oakwe*, meaning "the first people" (Hitchcock, 1995).

   At independence in 1966, the constitution of Botswana distinguished between eight major, or principal, tribes and other minor tribes, which had a divisive effect on the country's democratic development and party political practices. The principal tribes are all members of the dominant Tswana ethnic group, for example, Bangwato, Bangwaketse, and Bakgatla, while the minor tribes include members of other ethnic groups such as Bakalanga, Baherero, Bakgalagadi, and Basarwa. Collectively, all citizens of Botswana, whatever their tribal or ethnic origin, are known as Batswana, while individually they are Motswana.

REFERENCES

Ambler, C., & Crush, J. (1992). Alcohol in southern African labour history. In C. Ambler & J. Crush (Eds.), *Liquor and labor in southern Africa* (pp. 1–55). Athens, OH: University of Ohio Press.

Bain, D. (1936). *The Kalahari Bushmen*. Johannesburg: Tillet and Sons.

Barnard, A. (1992). *Hunters and herders of southern Africa: A comparative ethnography of the Khoisan peoples*. Cambridge, UK: Cambridge University Press.

Basarwa continue to suffer. (1998, May 20). *Mokaedi: Monthly Newspaper of the Botswana Christian Council*, p. 4.

Becker, P. (1974). *Tribe to township*. St. Albans, UK: Panther.

Bleek, D. F. (1928). *The Naron, a Bushman tribe of the central Kalahari*. Cambridge, UK: Cambridge University Press.

Botswana: Last "Bushmen" in Kalahari Reserve resist eviction. (1998). *Action Bulletin of Survival International*, p. 2.

Bridgland, F. (1998, January). Forced to march into oblivion. *Weekly Telegraph* (no. 330), p. 24.

Cashdan, E. A. (1985). Coping with risk: Reciprocity among the Basarwa of northern Botswana. *Man, 20,* 454–474.

Childers, G. W. (1976). *Report on the survey investigation of the Ghanzi farm Basarwa situation.* Gaborone, Botswana: Government Printer.

Chirenje, J. M. (1978). *Chief Kgama and his times c. 1835–1923: The story of a southern African ruler*. London: Rex Collings.

Crisp, W. (1896). *The Bechuana of South Africa*. London: Society for Promoting Christian Knowledge.

Denbow, J. R. (1984). Prehistoric herders and foragers of the Kalahari: The evidence of 1500 years of interaction. In C. Schrire (Ed.), *Past and present in hunter-gatherer studies* (pp. 175–193). Orlando, FL: Academic Press.

Dornan, S. S. (1925). *Pygmies and bushmen of the Kalahari*. Cape Town, South Africa: Struik.

Duggan-Cronin, A. M. (1942). *The Bushmen tribes of southern Africa*. Kimberley, South Africa: The Alexander-McGregor Memorial Museum.

Dunn, E. J. (1931). *The Bushmen*. London: Charles Griffin.

du Toit, B. M. (1980). *Cannabis in Africa*. Rotterdam, Netherlands: Balkema.

Erni, C. (1997). Botswana: Resettlement of Khwe communities continues. *Indigenous Affairs*, No. 3/4, 8–11.

Good, K. (1994, August). *Inequalities and the San in Botswana today*. Paper presented at a conference on Text and Images of People, Politics and Power Representing the Bushmen People of Southern Africa, University of the Witwatersrand, Johannesburg, South Africa.

Gordon, R. (1986). Bushmen banditry in twentieth century Namibia. In D. Crummey (Ed.), *Banditry, rebellion and social protest in Africa* (pp. 173–189). London: James Currey.

Gordon, R. (1992). *The Bushman myth: The making of a Namibian underclass*. Boulder, CO: Westview Press.

Government of Botswana. (1993). *Botswana facts*. Gaborone, Botswana: Department of Trade and Investment Promotion.

Guenther, M. (1996). From "lords of the desert" to "rubbish people:" The colonial and contemporary state of the Nharo of Botswana. In P. Skotnes (Ed.), *Miscast: Negotiating the presence of the Bushmen* (pp. 225–238). Cape Town, South Africa: UCT Press.

Haggblade, S. (1992). The Shebeen queen and the evolution of Botswana's sorghum Beer industry. In J. Crush & C. Ambler (Eds.), *Liquor and labor in southern Africa* (pp. 395–412). Athens, OH: University of Ohio Press.

Herbert, R. (1998, March 29). Dumped in a bleak new home, the San try to cling to their culture. *Sunday Independent* (Johannesburg), p. 5.

Hitchcock, R. K. (1995, August). *Settlements and survival: What future for the remote area dwellers of Botswana?* Paper presented at the Basarwa Research Workshop, University of Botswana, Gaborone, Botswana.

Hutchinson, B. (1979). Alcohol as a contributing factor in social disorganization: The South African Bantu in the nineteenth century. In M. Marshall (Ed.), *Beliefs, behaviors, and alcoholic beverages: A cross-cultural survey* (pp. 328–341). Ann Arbor, MI: University of Michigan Press.

Kann, U., Hitchcock, R., & Mbere, N. (1990). *Let them talk: A review of the Accelerated Remote Area Development Programme*. Report to the Ministry of Local Government and Lands and to the Norwegian Agency for Development and Cooperation, Gaborone, Botswana, August, 1990.

Lee, R. (1979). *The !Kung San: Men, women, and work in a foraging society*. Cambridge, England: Cambridge University Press.

Macdonald, D. (1997). Development or destitution? Towards an understanding of alcohol use in Basarwa settlements in Ghanzi District, Botswana. In S. Saugestad (Ed.), *Indigenous peoples in modern nation-states: Proceedings from an international workshop, University of Tromsø, October 13–16 1997* (Occasional Papers Series A, No. 90, pp. 132–139). Tromsø, Norway: University of Tromsø.

Macdonald, D., Malila, I., & Molamu, L. (1997). *Basarwa alcohol abuse action research project: Annual report 1996*. Gaborone, Botswana: University of Botswana.

Macdonald, D., & Molamu, L. (1998). Between a rock and a hard place: Alcohol and Basarwa identity in contemporary Botswana. In A. Bank et al. (Eds.), *The Proceedings of the Khoisan Identities and Cultural Heritage Conference, Cape Town, 1998* (pp. 325–335). Cape Town, South Africa: Institute for Historical Research, University of Western Cape.

Makin, W. J. (1929). *Across the Kalahari Desert*. London: Arrowsmith.

Malahleha, G. M. (1984). *An ethnographic study of Shebeens in Lesotho*. Unpublished doctoral dissertation, University of Surrey, Guildford, UK.

Mogalakwe, M. (1986). *Inside Ghanzi freehold farms: A look at the conditions of farm workers*. Gaborone, Botswana: Applied Research Unit, Ministry of Local Government and Lands.

Mogwe, A. (1992). *Who was (t)here first: An assessment of the human rights situation of Basarwa in selected communities in the Gantsi District, Botswana* (Occasional Paper No. 10). Gaborone, Botswana: Botswana Christian Council.

Mogwe, A. (1994, September). The rights of Basarwa as human rights. In S. Saugestad & J. Tsonope (Eds.), *Developing Basarwa research and research for Basarwa development*. Workshop Report, University of Botswana, Gaborone, Botswana.

Molamu, L. (1989). Alcohol in Botswana: A historical overview. *Contemporary Drug Problems, 16*, 3–42.

Molamu, L., & Manyeneng, W. (1988). *Alcohol use and abuse in Botswana*. Gaborone, Botswana: Government Printer.

Mostert, N. (1992). *Frontiers*. London: Jonathan Cape.

N'gongola, C. (1997). Land rights for marginalized ethnic groups in Botswana with special reference to Basarwa. *Journal of African Law, 41*, 1–26.

Resettlement without consent. (1997, September 5). *Botswana Guardian* (Gaborone), p. 4.

Sahlins, M. (1974). *Stone Age economics*. London: Tavistock.

Schapera, I. (1963). *The Khoisan peoples of South Africa*. London: Routledge, Kegan Paul.

Shostak, M. (1990). *Nisa: The life and words of a !Kung woman*. London: Earthscan.

Stow, G. W. (1905). *The native races of South Africa*. London: Swan Sonnenschein.

Telles, E. E. (1995). Structural sources of socioeconomic segregation in Brazilian metropolitan areas. *American Journal of Sociology, 100*, 1199–1223.

Theal, G. M. (1910). *The yellow and dark-skinned people of Africa south of the Zambezi*. New York: Negro Universities Press.

Winkelman, M. & Dobkin de Rios, M. (1989). Psychoactive properties of !Kung Bushmen medicine plants. *Journal of Psychoactive Drugs, 21*, 51–59.

Chapter 7

Drinking and Pleasure in Latin America

Haydée Rosovsky

The use of alcohol in Latin cultures has a history dating from ancient Indian civilization and reflects the impact of the Spanish conquest, modern industrialization, and international business policies and social trends (such as the liberalization of gender roles). The variety of cultural influences and economic disparities in Latin countries dictates the need for an integrated set of policies that address a range of drinking styles, problems, and social groups. Simple prohibitions do not capture the reality of the drinking practices of these groups, nor do they stand much chance of success. Rather, policies that recognize the realities of drinking—often called *harm minimization*—enhance the effectiveness of public health approaches towards alcohol.

ALCOHOL PROBLEMS, PLEASURE, AND CULTURE

Human consumption of naturally occurring substances to create desired physical and mental sensations is probably universal (Siegel, 1989). Alcohol is undoubtedly the most common substance used for this purpose, and its use is found in practically all cultures. Wherever alcohol is known and used, norms develop to govern when and how to use it and when to abstain; alcohol never has been ignored by societies.

The bulk of research in the medical and public health alcohol literature has stressed the negative outcomes of excessive drinking. On the other hand, research carried out in the social sciences, especially anthropology, mainly has explored the cultural role of alcohol and its different uses. This research has focused on native, nonmodernized groups; in general, anthropologists have not paid attention to urban practices and the negative health and social consequences of drinking (Menendez, 1990). Yet the integration of health and cultural perspectives seems necessary to gain a better understanding of drinking and its consequences.

Over the past decade or two, a number of studies have shown that there are health benefits from low to moderate levels of drinking (see Chapter 12). For most people, drinking alcohol does not represent a menace to their health or well-being; alcohol may be one of the enjoyable experiences in their lives. For a smaller group of people, drinking is related to health and social problems. When, why, and how does drinking become negative or problematic for some people? Do culture and society have a role in shaping these experiences?

Understanding and coping with problematic drinking in a society requires that we also understand nonharmful drinking and abstention in that society. Even if we accept that there is a biological foundation for some people to become alcoholics or alcohol-dependent, there are many people who may develop alcohol-related problems at some point in their lives without being or becoming alcoholics and overcome such problems as their lives progress. Such cases, which represent the most common paths for alcohol problems (Dawson, 1996; Fillmore, 1988), have important implications for the development of effective public health policies in a given society.

Beginning in the 1980s, and increasingly in recent years, alcohol policies in Western societies have been aimed mainly at reducing per capita consumption through measures such as increasing prices and restricting availability (see Chapter 25), on the assumption that such restrictions will produce a corresponding reduction in heavy drinking and alcohol-related problems.

At the same time, alcohol education increasingly has been discredited as a means of preventing alcohol-related problems. The failure of such programs is well illustrated in some developing countries in Latin America (Medina, 1995). The role of alcohol in these societies, the economic and sociocultural context, the different commercial and noncommercial forms of beverage alcohol available, and the diverse patterns of consumption and problems associated with each require a broader approach to designing alcohol policies.

This chapter presents an overview of the historical development of alcohol production and use in Latin America; current drinking practices and cultural variations; the cultural roles of alcohol; alcohol's relationship to economic development; alcohol-related health and social problems; prevalent alcohol policies and their impact on social custom and public opinion; the role and meaning of the pleasure of drinking within Latin societies; and some proposals for policies that could encourage safe drinking while allowing the enjoyable side of alcohol use to flourish.

DRINKING IN LATIN AMERICA: AN HISTORICAL OVERVIEW

Cultural and Racial Background

Latin America is a multiethnic mosaic and also displays extreme variations in levels of economic development. Past and present are mingled: Signs of modernity and the emergence of new identities and lifestyles can be observed alongside ancient traditions and the persistence of poverty. Latin societies struggle for democracy, development, and progress but must contend with internal conflicts and social fragmentation, together with a strong dependency on the developed world in both economic and cultural terms.

A growing urban population has not resulted in better quality of life for the majority. Latin America has huge urban centers surrounded by poverty belts inhabited by people who leave their villages seeking opportunities, or just survival. There are major migration movements to the North American countries fostered by economic and political crises.

Although there are substantial differences within the region in terms of levels of per capita consumption, abstinence rates, and patterns of use, abuse, and dependency, there are many common features among Latin countries concerning the role of alcohol and changes in this role over time.

Before the Spanish and Portuguese conquests during the 16th century, indigenous societies—such as the Inca, Maya, and Aztec—held sway. The conquest of the region was carried out by military power and the forced conversion of the indigenous peoples to the Roman Catholic faith. Soldiers and priests were the new rulers, taking control over land and souls.

Western conquest produced traumatic social changes, destroying indigenous value systems. A racial blending (known as the *mestizaje*) occurred, and most of the current population is a mixture of Spaniards and Indians. In some countries of the region, the population is grouped into two major ethnic classifications: Indians and *ladinos*. The term *ladino* refers to anyone who is not an Indian. The distinction often is made in terms of lifestyle and cultural features rather than physical characteristics. In some countries such as Honduras and Brazil, the descendants of black slaves are an important part of the population and heritage. The population of Latin America also includes many pure descendants of Spaniards and other European immigrants, who usually play powerful roles in the countries' economic and political development.

Traditional Forms and Use of Alcohol

Alcohol production and use is a strong tradition in the Latin American region, dating back to its earliest inhabitants. Many features of drinking in the precolonial era endure into the present. All of the pre-Hispanic cultures produced and consumed fermented beverages, which were used mainly for ceremonial and ritual purposes. These drinking occasions provided very clear measures of social control, including punishments for drinking outside the appropriate social contexts or by those not allowed to drink. Different rituals governed the preparation of the beverages and their use by priests and by commoners to please the gods or to bless crops.

In the huge Inca empire—including territory now occupied by Peru, Ecuador, Colombia, Bolivia, and parts of Chile and Argentina—the main alcoholic beverage was *chicha*, a fermented product made from different fruits or vegetables, particularly maize, a sacred plant for the majority of Indian groups (Mariategui, 1985). In Mexico, *pulque* (or *uctly* in the Nahuatl tongue), a fermented beverage made from a cactus growing in the country's central region, was the main beverage of the Aztecs, and there were special deities that protected alcoholic beverages and drinkers (Celis, 1985). The Maya empire—which covered the lands of the Yucatan peninsula, Guatemala, and several other countries in Central America—produced a beverage called *balché* before the Spanish conquest, using honey, water, and the bark of a tree (Adams, 1995). Many of these beverages still are consumed by peasants, Indian groups, and the working class in poor urban areas.

Anthropological studies carried out in Indian groups still living in Central America, Colombia, and Peru show some characteristic traits involving the Indians' ritual intake, their episodes of excessive drinking, and the properties they attribute to alcohol (Bunzel, 1940; De la Fuente, 1954; Kennedy, 1963; Pozas, 1959). The occasions for alcohol consumption were collective celebrations related to economic transactions, marriages, or the meting out of justice. Some societies, such as the Mapuche, included deliberate and socially accepted drunkenness. During such festivities, the participants changed from glad and cheerful behavior to licentiousness and verbal or physical violence (Medina, 1995). It also is recognized that, for some of these societies, the fermented drinks provided badly needed nutrients (Heath, 1982; Heath, 1995).

Post-Colonial Drinking

The Indian world suffered a crisis in its political and social system under Hispanic colonization. The old social, legal, and religious sanctions against alcohol intoxication vanished. The new system brought stronger alcoholic beverages, which were used as a tool for Western domination, and all sorts of misbehavior and excessive drinking took place among both Spaniards and natives (Mancera, 1996). The mingling of traditional beliefs and native cultural traits with those introduced by the Catholic Church (especially the use of sacramental wine) resulted in distinctive forms of mixed religion, in which drunkenness was intertwined with religious festivities, a pattern that persists in small villages and rural areas today (Sánchez, 1984).

The Spaniards introduced distilled beverages and grapevines into America. The conqueror Hernán Cortés developed the first alcohol sugar-cane distillery in Cuernavaca, Morelos, during the 16th century. This led to the production of spirits in Mexico such as *aguardiente, mezcal,* and tequila, which were incorporated into the population's drinking habits (Rosovsky, 1985). *Chinguirito,* a cheap and strong beverage distilled from sugar cane, was popular among both *mestizos* and black slaves.

Wine was produced in Chile and Peru as early as 1555, and by the end of the 1700s export of wine to other colonies of Spanish America had begun (Medina, 1995). In the second half of the 19th century, the wine industry developed with the importation from France of new varieties of grapevines and modern techniques of cultivation and production. The old fermented drinks continued to be produced and consumed but were in general rejected by the ruling classes. The Spanish crown was sometimes tolerant, sometimes restrictive concerning the production of alcoholic beverages, depending on Spain's economic interests. With time, some controls were introduced over places of sales and consumption, selling hours, and taxation.

The production of both old and new beverages continued to boom in the hands of a few Spaniard and Creole families. Many fiscal measures were implemented by the Spanish crown to protect their wine exports and the sugar-cane industry in the Antilles, making it impossible for local producers to export and trade in their products. In some countries, small-scale industries started to produce alcoholic beverages illegally with the complicity of corrupt officials, a situation that still prevails in some countries of the region, including Mexico. Later, during the 18th century, there were legal changes that allowed the delegate governments of the Spanish crown in the region to regulate the production and sale of sugar-cane alcohol. Although this provided important tax revenue for the governments, it had damaging social effects for the population.

Indians were stigmatized as drunkards and as immoral by the conquerors; along with their intake of alcohol they used other psychedelic substances in their rituals, such as *peyote, ololiuhqui,* and *coca* leaves. But both conquerors and conquered drank heavily, the primary difference being the type of beverage consumed and the context of drinking.

The independence movements of the 1800s in the region meant that other intellectual, economic, and lifestyle influences were felt besides those of Portugal and Spain, such as those coming from France and England. These influences had their greatest impact on the urban class (Mancera, 1996). Alcoholic beverages were consumed by the Indian groups in rural areas and small settlements, and Indians living in cities were ghettoized, attracting the concern of the authorities because of their drunkenness.

CURRENT ALCOHOL PRODUCTION AND CONSUMPTION

Industrial Development

During the 19th century and the beginning of the 20th century, many alcohol industries were family enterprises, producing rum, tequila, beer, and wine in different countries, and some of them started to export their products. The traditional production of fermented beverages and regional spirits continued. The industrialization of many Latin American countries began at the turn of the 20th century and was accelerated after the Second World War, which had important implications for alcohol use. Among the factors shaping Latin societies during the second half of the 20th century have been growing urbanization, foreign cultural influence, and strong dependence on the economies of other countries. New lifestyles, social roles, and gender relationships have appeared in many social groups. In addition, the alcohol industry has shifted its attention to new markets worldwide (Rosovsky & Romero, 1996).

Several multinational alcohol producers and advertising agencies have been established in Latin America, and some governments have encouraged the development of the alcohol industry through financial assistance and by providing lands for growing the necessary crops. Many traditional, family-owned alcohol businesses have been displaced by large corporations, oligopolies controlling the lion's share of markets in spirits, beer, and wine (Rosovsky, 1985). Some alcohol industries control agroindustries, thus concentrating production, distribution, and foreign trade through vertical integration (Quintar, 1983). Although alcohol industries do not generate much employment because of their use of labor-saving technology, they nonetheless represent an important source of income for governments through taxation (Rosovsky, 1985).

Alcohol Consumption and Production

In terms of per capita alcohol consumption, no Latin American country is among the world's leading 20 nations worldwide (World Drink Trends, 1996). Argentina is the country with the highest consumption in the region (an average of 7.2 L per capita between 1993 and 1995); Uruguay, Venezuela, and Chile consumed between 5 and 6 L per capita in the same period; Colombia, Cuba, Brazil, and Mexico between 3 and 5 L. Five of the ten countries worldwide with the highest percentage increase in consumption between 1970 and 1995 were Latin American: Brazil, Paraguay, Cuba, Colombia, and Venezuela. Most of the countries of the region consume mainly beer, although in some wine-producing countries, such as Argentina, Uruguay, and Chile, wine is drunk more than beer. Beer consumption has increased the most in the region during the past two decades.

In terms of production, Mexico is among the 10 biggest beer producers in the world; Argentina is among the main wine manufacturers. Argentina has become a major supplier of wine to European countries, increasing exports by 552% between 1994 and 1995; Chile is one of the main providers of wine for the United States market.

The levels of per capita consumption in Latin America are based on data from the alcohol industry. But in some countries, such as Mexico, an additional 50% of consumption involves unlicensed alcoholic beverages. Beverages like *pulque* in central Mexico and *boj* in Guatemala are produced by small households in rural areas; many small enterprises produce liquor, such as *aguardientes*, outside any sanitary and tax controls (Rosovsky, 1985; Vittetoe, 1995).

Drinking Patterns, Norms, and Attitudes

Patterns of drinking within each society are difficult to assess because of the lack of comparable data among countries. In addition, the type and quantity of use vary according to social groups and between rural and urban populations. In general, men drink more than women, although in urban areas more females are drinking than before as their social roles change. Drunkenness among Indian or peasant women can be observed in some rural areas on specific occasions, such as religious celebrations or market days, and is socially accepted in those contexts.

Drinking may start during childhood or adolescence, either within the family or under the influence of peers. Peer-group drinking, out of the family context, is the more immoderate. Surveys in some countries permit estimates of the prevalence of drinking and patterns of consumption. In Chile, for instance, approximately 20% of the adult population abstains, 65% drinks moderately, and about 10%–15% drinks excessively (Medina, 1995). Alcoholism rates in the region's countries as a whole have been estimated at between 5% and 10% (Pan American Health Organization, 1994), while combining excessive and alcoholic drinkers yields a prevalence figure of perhaps 12%.

Drinking by *ladinos* or European descendants approximates patterns in most Western nations. The upper social classes consume imported beverages as well as prestigious local drinks (tequila in Mexico, wine in Chile and Argentina). Young urban people nowadays prefer beer and distilled liquors (which often are combined with soft drinks), consumed in bars and discos. The dominant pattern among such urban drinkers is moderation without observed problems. But perhaps 10% of this population drinks heavily, mostly in a pattern of infrequent but excessive consumption leading to acute-type alcohol problems (see Chapter 25). A smaller proportion are regular heavy drinkers at risk for developing chronic problems. In some of the region's societies, alcohol is consumed on a daily basis with meals, particularly wine in Chile and Argentina. Regular consumption of beer with food or at social gatherings is observed in some places, such as northern Mexico.

One pattern of drinking beginning in childhood found among Indians (such as the Mapuche in rural central Chile) involves drinking *chupilca* (wine with toasted flour and sugar). Adults drink in groups—such drinking is always viewed as a friendly activity; the solitary drinker is viewed with suspicion and is rejected. Adults drink to become intoxicated for several days at a time, but they do not become alcoholics who drink uncontrollably on their own. Young people drink at parties and social gatherings. When they become adults they are expected to drink more frequently and in higher quantities, because heavy drinking is associated with manhood (Lomnitz, 1969). This pattern is similar to that observed by Heath (1958) in his seminal study among the Camba of Bolivia.

Patterns of alcohol use among indigenous groups show substantial variations. For example, although alcohol use is integrated into all aspects of life among the Chamulas in Chiapas, Mexico (Bunzel, 1940), among the Tarahumaras in Chihuahua alcohol use is restricted to specific occasions (Kennedy, 1963). Modern Mapuches, living in reservations, or *reducciones*, maintain the social role of drinking, mainly by men. However, typical consumption patterns involve fewer days of drunkenness than in the past but more frequent drinking, such as at parties, Catholic celebrations, journeys to the city, and so forth, following the dominant Chilean pattern. Drinking alone is criticized and so is abstention (Medina, 1995).

The Mazahua and *Otomí* peoples living in central Mexico drink *pulque* from childhood, because of both its nutritional properties and the scarcity of water; this is similar to the way the Indians of Alta Verapaz in Guatemala drink *boj* (Adams, 1995). But younger generations prefer beer and commercially distilled alcohol, because traditional drinks increasingly are associated with poverty and are not considered sufficiently urban and modern (Natera, 1995). Such changes in tastes also are reflected in dress and popular music. Alcohol use is considered normal, with some tolerance of excessive drinking by men, especially in rural areas.

Reasons for initiating drinking include curiosity and imitation of adult behavior. Ambivalence towards drinking is common, along with an absence of clear-cut norms as to alcohol use and inebriation. For instance, half the people interviewed in a household survey conducted in central Mexico agreed with the statement, "Drinking is one of the pleasures of life"; 30% considered that "Taking one drink is a way of being friendly." In the same survey, 32% said that "getting drunk is only an innocent way of having fun," and 24% stated that "it's good for people to get drunk once in a while." The majority agreed that "no attention should be paid if a drunk man says something inappropriate when drinking." Nevertheless, 83% of the sample stated that "nothing good can be said about drinking," and 93% said that "drinking is one of the main reasons why people do things they shouldn't have done" (Medina-Mora, 1993).

In terms of social control of drinking, health concerns, prices, misbehavior, and loss of control were mentioned by 90% of the sample as reasons for not drinking; 47% of males and 56% of females said that they would not drink because of their religion, Catholicism. In most of the countries, Protestantism has a growing influence on some Indian rural groups and urban workers, promoting abstinence (Medina-Mora, 1998). Among wealthy young Chileans, no correlation was found between knowledge about the negative effects of immoderate alcohol use and how they drank; among the 98% that had received alcohol education, 12.6% were excessive drinkers (Medina, 1995).

Good and Bad Drinking

Although alcohol research has been aimed at identifying the negative consequences of alcohol use, a growing number of studies have reported benefits from moderate alcohol consumption. Light and moderate drinkers not only have lower mortality rates but also gain other health benefits over abstainers or heavy drinkers. According to a review by Baum-Baicker (1985), moderate alcohol consumption is effective in reducing stress according to both physiological and self-report measures. Low and moderate doses of alcohol have been reported to increase overall affective expression, happiness, euphoria, conviviality, and pleasant and carefree feelings. Tension, depression, and self-consciousness have been reported to decrease with moderate consumption. Low alcohol doses have been found to improve certain types of cognitive performance, including problem solving and short-term memory. Alcohol in low and moderate doses has been effective in the treatment of geropsychiatric problems. Heavy drinkers and abstainers have higher rates of clinical depression than do regular moderate drinkers. (A recent review of the literature on psychosocial benefits of moderate alcohol consumption is provided in Chapter 15).

Alcohol is also associated with adverse health and social consequences. In Latin America, public health problems related to alcohol use derive from both episodic excessive drinking and chronic heavy use. They include traffic accidents, injuries, suicide and homicide, liver cirrhosis, and psychiatric problems (Pan American Health Organization, 1994). The rates of deaths caused by cirrhosis of the liver vary between 6.4 and 34 per 100,000 population; Chile, Mexico, and Puerto Rico, as well as some English-speaking Caribbean countries, are the countries with the highest mortality rates from this cause. Another important alcohol-related problem is traffic accidents: Unlike North American and European countries, most Latin American countries do not have strong measures to prevent drinking and driving. One example is Chile, where 71% of those aged 15 to 24 years who died from traffic accidents had blood alcohol levels higher than 100 mg/100 mL (Pan American Health Organization, 1994).

Alcohol is part of Latin culture, an important means of social integration for most people. Drinking is present in all public and private social gatherings in Latin America. Not accepting a drink often is considered an offense. The prestige of the host is measured by the quality and quantity of the food and alcoholic drinks offered to guests.

Not all groups consider excessive drinking something to be avoided. Drunkenness is the goal of drinking for many groups in Latin America, regardless of their levels of social integration. As Lemert (1991) noted, drunkenness should not always be regarded as a personal failing or as a symptom of a weak social organization; it can be an accepted norm in certain circumstances. Therefore alcoholism and drunkenness should be separated: Alcoholism, in the sense of pathological, addictive, uncontrolled, and compulsive intake of alcohol, is not the same as drunkenness, which can be completely normal in some cultural contexts. This consideration has important implications from the public health perspective.

Many cultural expressions in Latin American countries reflect attitudes and norms about drinking and drunkenness; many films and songs have described the *macho* attitude—a brave, aggressive womanizer as the hero whom everybody admires. Respect also often is given to the man who can drink a lot without making a fool of himself. Some of these values slowly are changing, especially among urban and educated people.

PUBLIC POLICY IMPLICATIONS OF ALCOHOL AND PLEASURE IN A CULTURAL CONTEXT

Drinking can have extremely divergent symbolic meanings in different cultures and even within the same culture, from the sacred to the sacrilegious. Likewise, both in different cultures and within the same culture, drinking may be a pleasant experience if it takes place at the right time and place, but in another context produce feelings of guilt. Taking cultural definitions of drinking into account makes it possible to anticipate whether drinking will be pleasant or not, whether it will be considered relaxing and a social bond or a cause of aggression (Mandelbaum, 1965).

The challenge from a public health perspective is to develop alcohol policies that can meet the needs of different types of drinkers, reducing harmful consequences but accepting the benign or beneficial drinking of the majority. Current alcohol policies aimed at reducing availability through legal measures that regulate alcohol sales and taxation need to be expanded, because alcohol is readily available in Latin American countries, including from illegally produced sources. There are important gaps in current Latin policies and also in their enforcement. A harm-reduction perspective—one that accepts the likelihood of continued drinking and even of problematic drinking but seeks to minimize such problems—has additional benefits over a policy of reducing overall levels of drinking, but this approach still often is overlooked in public policy circles (Gusfield, 1980; Room, 1984; Single, 1994).

Some policies should be directed at the general population (e.g., measures to prevent alcohol-related accidents), and others should be directed at the excessive or problematic drinker. Alcohol policies in Latin America need to include specific measures to reduce alcohol problems but also to allow the use of alcohol in a safe and pleasurable way. Alcohol policies will not work equally well for all social groups; varied policies need to be consistent with one another, to promote public awareness on the issues, and to rally public support in order to be successful. A menu of such suggested policies follows.

Family Education

Alcohol use is a behavior that can be learned and that is shaped by environmental influences. What we learn about alcohol starts in our families. Moderate use of alcohol by the family and the initiation of drinking at an early age in small amounts in a family context, without ambivalence, seem to have positive impacts on attitudes towards alcohol and drinking behavior. Parents therefore should be educated on the advantages of moderate drinking and the value of inculcating this style of drinking in their children, thereby helping their offspring to be able to make healthy drinking decisions throughout their lives.

Public Education

Any measure concerning alcohol availability also should provide information encouraging the consumption of alcohol in moderate and nonharmful ways, in safe contexts, and by individuals at low risk. Alcohol education should not stigmatize all alcohol use but should discourage drinking large quantities at one sitting and offer tips on how to avoid high blood alcohol levels (e.g., drinking with food, spacing of drinks).

School Education

Alcohol education in schools should be integrated with other activities that promote the development of healthy lifestyles and self-care. Programs on alcohol education that are isolated from issues such as the development of assertiveness, creativity, self-esteem, the prevention of accidents, and avoidance of risky sexual behavior have poor results. Schools also should have clear internal rules for managing cases of alcohol use and abuse.

External Control Measures (Including Harm Minimization)

Because laws prohibiting the sale of alcohol to minors are not enforced completely in most societies, auxiliary policies also should be developed. Strict prohibition of alcohol, even for youths, has potential negative effects. It promotes the idea of forbidden fruit and causes some youths to think all laws should be disregarded and avoided. Examples of useful auxiliary measures of control are those that provide safe, clean environments for alcohol use with trained servers, beverages with low alcohol content, and the availability of food. Programs promoting designated drivers or providing transport from bars and discos are other useful examples. Laws regulating the number and location of alcohol outlets should avoid creating situations in which basic goods are less readily available than alcohol. Likewise, pricing of alcoholic beverages should not make them relatively cheap compared with necessary food staples.

Informal Controls

Societies have unwritten rules for controlling different behaviors. Such informal controls—through parents, friends, school, the entertainment industry, and so on—are particularly relevant in the case of alcohol. Useful informal controls take the form of attitudes and behaviors that express disapproval of excessive drinking, drunkenness, and the general misuse of alcohol.

Quality of Alcoholic Beverages

The production and sale of alcohol without proper sanitary controls is very common in Latin American countries and causes many health problems. It is necessary to develop legal measures and the mechanisms for their enforcement to control the quality of commercial alcohol and to minimize the use of illegally produced beverages.

Promotion of Alcohol

The advertising and marketing of alcohol must be socially responsible: Messages that promote or glamorize excessive use of alcohol should be avoided, and moderate consumption should be encouraged and supported.

Early Detection of Alcohol Problems

Services should be in place in schools and health facilities to detect individuals with signs of alcohol-related problems and help them and their families.

Identifying Safe Levels of Drinking

Public education should identify safe drinking levels and how these are influenced by risk factors such as a family history of alcoholism, age, gender, and health status, as well as types of drinking contexts, including those in which drinking should be avoided (e.g., when operating machinery).

REFERENCES

Adams, W. R. (1995). Guatemala. In D. B. Heath (Ed.), *International handbook on alcohol and culture* (pp. 99–109). Westport, CT: Greenwood Press.

Baum-Baicker, C. (1985). The psychological benefits of moderate alcohol consumption: A review of the literature. *Drug and Alcohol Dependence, 15*, 305–322.

Bunzel, R. (1940). The role of alcoholism in two Central American cultures. *Psychiatry, 3*, 361–387.

Celis, R. (1985). *El alcoholismo en México* [Alcoholism in Mexico] (Vol. 4). Mexico City: Fundación de Investigaciones Sociales.

Dawson, D. A. (1996). Correlates of past-year status among treated and untreated persons with former alcohol dependence: United States, 1992. *Alcoholism: Clinical and Experimental Research, 20*, 771–779.

De la Fuente, J. (1954). *Comisión de estudios del problema del alcoholismo en Chiapas* [Working group on the problem of alcoholism in Chiapas]. Mexico: Government of Chiapas, Instituto Nacional Indigenista.

Fillmore, K. M. (1988). *Alcohol use across the life course: A critical review of 70 years of international longitudinal research.* Toronto, Canada: Addiction Research Foundation.

Gusfield, J. (1980). *Symbolic crusade: Status politics and the American temperance movement.* Urbana, IL: University of Illinois Press.

Heath, D. B. (1982). In other cultures, they also drink. In E. L. Gomberg, H. R. White, & J. A. Carpenter (Eds.), *Alcohol, science and society revisited* (pp. 63–79). Ann Arbor, MI: University of Michigan Press and Rutgers Center of Alcohol Studies.

Heath, D. B. (1995). An anthropological view of alcohol and culture in international perspective. In D. B. Heath (Ed.), *International handbook on alcohol and culture* (pp. 330–347). Westport, CT: Greenwood Press.

Heath, D. W. (1958). Drinking patterns of the Bolivian Camba. *Quarterly Journal of Studies on Alcohol, 19,* 491–508.

Kennedy, G. (1963). Tesgüino complex: The role of beer in Tarahumaran culture. *American Anthropology, 65,* 620–640.

Lemert, E. M. (1991). Alcohol, values, and social control. In D. J. Pittman & H. R. White (Eds.), *Society, culture, and drinking patterns reexamined* (pp. 681–701). New Brunswick, NJ: Rutgers Center of Alcohol Studies.

Lomnitz, L. (1969). Función del alcohol en la sociedad mapuche [The role of alcohol in Mapuche society]. *Acta Psiquiatrica y Psicologica de America Latina, 15,* 157–167.

Mancera, S. C. de. (1996). *Entre gula y templanza, un aspecto de la historia mexicana* [Between gluttony and temperance: An aspect of Mexican history]. Mexico City: Foundation for Economic Culture.

Mandelbaum, D. (1965). Alcohol and culture. *Current Anthropology, 6,* 281–294.

Mariategui, J. (1985). Concepción del hombre y alcoholismo en el antiguo Perú [The concept of man and alcoholism in ancient Peru]. *Acta Psiquiatrica y Psicologica de America Latina, 31,* 253–267.

Medina, E. (1995). Chile. In D. B. Heath (Ed.), *International handbook on alcohol and culture* (pp. 31–41). Westport, CT: Greenwood Press.

Medina-Mora, M. E. (1993). *Diferencias por género en las prácticas de consumo de alcohol* [Gender differences in alcohol consumption practices]. Unpublished doctoral dissertation, Universidad Nacional Autónoma de México, Mexico City, Mexico.

Medina-Mora, M. E. (1998). Mexico. In M. Grant (Ed.), *Alcohol and emerging markets: Patterns, problems and responses* (pp. 263–284). Washington, DC: Taylor & Francis.

Menendez, E. (1990). *Morir de alcohol. Saber y hegemonía médica* [To die of alcohol: Knowledge and medical hegemony]. Conaculta, Mexico: Alianza Editorial Mexicana.

Natera, G. (1995). Mexico. In D. B. Heath (Ed.), *International handbook on alcohol and culture* (pp. 179–189). Westport, CT: Greenwood Press.

Pan American Health Organization. (1994). *Health conditions in the Americas.* Washington, DC: Author.

Pozas, R. (1959). Chamula, un pueblo indio de los Altos de Chiapas [Chamula, an Indian village in the highlands of Chiapas]. *Memorias del Instituto Nacional Indigenista, 3,* 72–76.

Quintar, A. (1983). La agroindustria de bebidas alcohólicas: Evolución y structura en México [The agricultural industry of alcoholic beverages: Evolution and structure in Mexico]. In P. V. Molina & M. L. Sánchez (Eds.), *El alcoholismo en México* [Alcoholism in Mexico] (Vol. 2). Mexico City: Fundación de Investigaciones Sociales.

Room, R. (1984). Alcohol control and public health. *American Review of Public Health, 5,* 293–317.

Rosovsky, H. (1985). Public health aspects of the production, marketing, and control of alcoholic beverages in Mexico. *Contemporary Drug Problems, 12,* 659–678.

Rosovsky, H., & Romero, M. (1996). Prevention issues in a multicultural developing country: The Mexican case. *Substance Use and Misuse, 31,* 1657–1688.

Sánchez, O. (1984). Aspectos históricos y psicosociales del alcoholismo en Honduras [Historical and psychosocial aspects of alcoholism in Honduras]. *Revista Médica Hondureña, 52,* 210–216.

Siegel, R. K. (1989). *Intoxication*. New York: Dutton.

Single, E. (1994). Implications of potential health benefits of moderate drinking for specific elements of alcohol policy: Towards a harm-reduction approach for alcohol. *Contemporary Drug Problems, 21*, 273–285.

Vittetoe, K. (1995). Honduras. In D. B. Heath (Ed.), *International handbook on alcohol and culture* (pp. 110–116). Westport, CT: Greenwood Press.

World Drink Trends. (1996). *International beverage alcohol consumption and production trends*. Henley-on-Thames, UK: Produktschap voor Gedistilleerde Dranken in association with NTC Publications.

Chapter 8

Changing Sociocultural Perspectives on Alcohol Consumption in India: A Case Study

Hari Kesh Sharma and Davinder Mohan

In recent years, many developing countries and specific subgroups within them have undergone rapid economic and sociocultural changes. During this process, concomitant changes have occurred in the field of alcohol and drug abuse. Populations have been exposed to an increased availability of alcohol and other psychoactive drugs in forms with which they were unfamiliar. Excessive alcohol consumption in developing countries leads to substantial negative effects on the health and also on the quality of life of drinking individuals and their families. It also causes massive direct and indirect costs to these countries that they can ill afford (Saxena, 1997). The present chapter attempts to review the changing drinking scene in India and traces the historical tradition of alcohol use in the country. It also highlights regional differences, the role of sociocultural variables in the acceptance of alcohol consumption, and the challenges to a developing nation posed by free trade and the growth of transnational corporations.

ALCOHOL USE IN HISTORICAL INDIAN CONTEXT

The Ancient History of Beverage Alcohol

A detailed account of alcoholic beverages in the historical context in India has been provided elsewhere (Mohan & Sharma, 1995). Our main emphasis here is on the availability of alcoholic beverages and normative drinking behavior. Alcoholic beverages in the Indus valley appeared in the Chalcolithic Age (3000–2000 BC) when the invading Aryans settled and Vedic civilization took shape. The cultural assimilation of immigrants resulted in shifting popular preferences for different alcoholic beverages and different patterns of drinking behavior. *Soma* and *sura* were the earliest beverages, traceable to 2000 BC (Chopra & Chopra, 1965). *Soma* was derived from the sarcostemma viminale plant and became identified with the mythical tree of life, the juice of which imparted immortality (Tek Chand, 1972). Its use was confined to nobles and saints. However, there is no mention of its use in the post-Vedic period. *Sura*, a beverage distilled from rice meal, was popular among warriors (Kshatriyas) and the peasant population. It was essentially a drink for day-to-day consumption by the common man. The use of these beverages was well defined within specific social contexts. For example, *soma* was seen as a secular elixir of life and its use restricted to the elites; *sura* and similar beverages fulfilled various functions, depending on the situation. They were, for instance, commonly drunk by warriors (Kshatriyas) as a reward for the sacrifices they made for the country and as a symbol of power to other courtiers. For the lower strata, however, *sura* and other beverages were a means to overcome hunger, day-to-day suffering, and hedonistic urges.

Normative Drinking Behavior

A distinctive feature of ancient drinking was that people comprehended the virtues and drawbacks of alcoholic beverages, but drinking was controlled by religious edicts, proscriptive norms, and social controls on the availability of alcohol. Religious texts such as *Puranas*, *Sutras*, and *Samritis* censured alcohol drinking. The consumption of *sura* was forbidden to the upper castes, especially Brahmins. The other religions of the land also played a crucial role in controlling drinking. Buddhism, which arose in the fifth century AD, denounced drinking, and the commandments of Buddha counseled abstinence from alcohol. This message of abstinence spread across southern and eastern Asia. The other offshoot of the Hindu religion, Jainism, was equally vocal in encouraging abstention towards alcohol. The other contemporary religion of that period (circa the seventh century AD), Islam, likewise condemned the use of wine, and followers were prohibited from consumption of all alcoholic beverages. The Muslim rulers, by and large, discouraged the use of liquor. Sikhism, which appeared in the 15th century, was no less vehement in its advocacy of total abstinence.

These measures, although abstinence-oriented, did not so much eliminate widespread alcohol consumption in many sections of ancient India as serve to check excessive and antisocial drinking (Prakash, 1961). Even during the Mughal period, the puritanical approach to alcohol by rulers could not prevent wine from being used by courtiers and nobles.

The arrival of the British on the Indian scene was a turning point in attitudes towards alcohol consumption. The enactment of excise laws, which provided an important source of revenue for the state exchequer; the establishment of the first distillery in India; and the centralization of distillation under the central distillery system led to a rapid increase in the prevalence of distilled liquor. Distilled spirits indeed were a chief instrument of trade and exploitation at the frontiers of the expansion of the European colony (MacAndrew & Edgerton, 1969; Pan, 1975). Commercial distillation gradually replaced familiar home-brewed alcoholic beverages, and over the years the new emerging Indian elite, bureaucracy, armed forces, and royal princes adopted its products as a status symbol.

The introduction of distilled spirits was marked with protests, and prohibition became a major plank in the freedom movement of the country. On achieving freedom, prohibition was incorporated into the constitution under article 47 of the Directive Principles of State Policy. Following independence, economic development and technological innovation brought sociocultural changes in which the meaning and context of alcohol and drugs were altered, leading the use of alcohol to assume different social and health dimensions.

THE DEVELOPMENT OF MODERN DRINKING TRENDS

The Impact of Modernization on Alcohol Consumption

India is a good example of a developing country in which changes affecting drinking began in the 1970s and accelerated dramatically in the wake of globalization, world trade, and economic-development programs, and their conflict with the cultural status quo. Indian society is a mosaic that is stratified (by caste, gender, age, etc.), culturally heterogeneous, and pluralistic. In the constituent federal state of Punjab, the so-called green revolution of the 1960s introduced advanced agricultural technology to the region. This led to changes in agricultural practices and to a rise in disposable income. Correspondingly, the use of alcoholic beverages during this period increased by 200% to 300% (Deb & Jindal, 1974). The consumption of commercially distilled spirits with their higher ethanol content emerged as a major consumer preference along with home-distilled beverages (Mohan, Sundaram, Neki, Darshan, & Sharma, 1978). This period also saw new drinkers emerge from previously abstinent social groups. This process of "alcoholization" is now being replicated in almost all the federal states of India. In Himachal Pradesh, a hill state in the north, income from programs sponsored by both national and international funding agencies in some instances has been diverted to alcohol consumption. Compensation received by families for natural calamities or disasters similarly has been diverted in the western state of Maharashtra. In the southern state of Kerala, the prosperity acquired by the working class has supported a boom in the liquor trade and an alarming rise in per capita consumption of alcoholic beverages.

The rise in alcohol consumption as a consequence of the development process is often an undesirable outcome in terms of the impact on social institutions and healthcare agencies. This same process also may be occurring in other parts of the developing world, including Asia, Africa, and Latin America.

On the other hand, attributing the increase in the popularity of high-content alcoholic beverages—often replacing traditional Indian drugs such as opium and cannabis—only to the process of globalization or modernization may be too simplistic in the case of a pluralistic society such as India. It is equally important to understand the dynamics and conflicts in contemporary India where, unlike in the West, the tendency is to graft at least parts of old institutions on to new ones. The old and the new tend to coexist and compete for space and resources.

Although alcohol has never been a part of the Indian ethos and was taboo for the middle classes until a few decades ago, alcohol consumption today has become popular among these same classes. The immediate result of economic development in the Orient is a burgeoning middle class that tends to adopt Western-style dietary tastes and consumption habits. Accordingly, the liquor trade and other business enterprises are spawning a new pub culture, particularly in metropolitan areas, to cater to the nouvelle bourgeoisie and the young. In the countryside, nine consecutive good monsoons together with the introduction of improved agricultural technology and modern communications have increased disposable incomes. The inviting urban world suddenly has become accessible to rural villagers. This population has become a part of the alcoholization process.

The Remaining Indian Economic Underclass

A Third World population still exists in India, where 40% of the total population still live below the poverty line in a state of economic and social deprivation. This group finds solace in illicit home-brewed liquor. The rampant use of liquor is taking a heavy toll on society from a public health perspective. A news item from one of the economically backward districts of the country, Kalahandi in Orissa, observed that excessive drinking has increased disease and premature death among men to such an extent that a district of widows had emerged (*Times of India*, 1997).

CURRENT ALCOHOL CONSUMPTION

In the absence of an Indian national research body, we review information from a range of cross-sectional studies (descriptive and analytical) conducted both in the general population and in specific groups from the 1970s onwards.

General Population Surveys

The results of the studies listed in Table 8.1 show broad alcohol consumption trends across India. The prevalence rate of alcohol use during the past 12 months

Table 8.1 General population studies of alcohol consumption.

Investigator	Year	Sample size (n)	Area/population group	Prevalence rate (%)	Remarks
Single-center studies					
Dube	1972	16,725	Agra (R/U)	1.4	Occasional and heavy
Deb & Jindal	1974	1251	Punjab (R)	74.2	Ever used
Lal & Singh	1978	6999	Punjab (R)	25.6	Ever used
Mohan et al.	1978	3600	Punjab (R)	34.1	Used in past year
Varma, Singh, Singh, & Malhotra	1981	915	Chandigarh (U)	19.0	Used in past year
Mohan, Sharma, Sundaram, & Advani	1981	4670	Rajasthan (R)	24.7	Used in past year
Channabasavanna, Ray, & Kaliaperumal	1990	4007	Karnataka	33.5	Ever used
Mohan	1992	11,995	Delhi (U)	13.4	Used in past 30 days
	1992	10,354	Delhi (U)	11.6	Used in past 30 days
Multicenter studies					
Mohan & Sundaram	1983	13,689	Bangalore	36.6	Used in past year
			Delhi		
			Dibrugarh		
			Ranchi		
Sitholey, Mohan, & Purohit	1992	30,000	Delhi	20.3	Used in past 30 days
			Lucknow	16.3	
			Jodhpur	14.9	

Note. Letters in parentheses denote broad categories of populations: R = rural; U = urban.

Table 8.2 Group and gender differences in alcohol consumption.

Name of center	Population group	Prevalence (use in past year), %	
		Males	Females
Bangalore	Rural	24.0	5.2
	Industrial	47.2	—
Delhi	Slum	38.4	2.4
	Industrial	51.0	—
Dibrugarh	Rural	52.8	29.2
	Tea plantation	65.5	47.6
Ranchi	Tribal	63.6	57.1
	Urban	15.8	5.5

Source. Mohan & Sundaram, 1983.

varied between 19% and 37%. Current use, that is, within the preceding 30 days, narrowed the range to 12% to 20%. Assuming that half of those who reported alcohol use within the past 30 days were regular users, this group varied from 6% to 10%. This suggests, through further extrapolation, that perhaps 3% to 5% are hardcore alcohol users, including alcoholics. Alcohol use was largely a male phenomenon (prevalence rate varied between 25% and 74%); women were largely abstainers (over 90%). However, between 28% and 47% of women among tribal subgroups and tea plantation workers were alcohol users (Table 8.2). These subgroups consumed low-content alcoholic beverages made from rice, mahua flowers, and other plant products. Compared with Western nations, the number of current alcohol users, even among men, is quite low, perhaps between 10% and 25% of the population.

Surveys of Specific Groups

Organized workers in manufacturing, mines, transport, and allied jobs rapidly are emerging as groups in which alcohol intake is becoming popular. An Indian Council of Medical Research study indicated that half the industrial workers surveyed had drunk alcoholic beverages during the proceeding 12 months (Mohan & Sundaram, 1983). In a study among industrial workers in Haryana, 40% reported use of alcohol (Federation of Indian Chambers of Commerce and Industry, 1997).

Drinking by students has been fairly well explored. Alcohol use by students varies between 10% and 15% (Table 8.3). A multicenter study conducted in 1976 and 1986 showed that alcohol use among students remained mainly constant over that 10-year period, with some indications of an increase (Mohan & Sundaram, 1987).

Table 8.3 Variations in alcohol use (%) among university students, 1976–1986.

City	Alcohol use (%)	
	1976	1986
Bangalore	—	14.36
Bombay	14.95	15.1
Calcutta	—	7.51
Delhi	8.77	12.2
Hybderabad	8.41	11.8
Jabalpur	6.60	9.3
Jaipur	5.60	9.8
Madras	9.85	9.5
Varanasi	5.18	9.4

Note. Alcohol use in this study was defined as reported alcohol use in the past 12 months.
Source. Mohan & Sundaram, 1987.

DRINKING PATTERNS

Traditional Drinking Patterns

Traditional drinking patterns can be divided into three broad categories:

- Classical drinking traditions
- Regional drinking traditions
- Local drinking traditions

Classical drinking traditions prevail mostly in the tribal groups, which make up 8.8% of the total population spread throughout India. Among men and women in the tribal population, alcohol is held in esteem as a product of nature, as a gift of God, and as both food and medicine. Most traditional alcoholic beverages have a low alcohol content, and tribal peoples have beliefs, attitudes, and rituals that govern alcohol consumption in day-to-day life. However, distilled beverages have been introduced into this traditional mix with planned economic development and increased contacts between tribal peoples and those from the plains. Tribal populations also have acquired the habit of consuming adulterated arrack, another potent alcohol beverage (Reddy, 1971).

Regional drinking patterns refer to the consumption patterns of groups that share special elements that are distinctive to the regional culture; the regional boundaries only in some instances correspond with those of states. The green-revolution belt comprises, for instance, the northern states of Punjab, Haryana, and western Uttar Pradesh. These states currently represent relatively "wet" cultures (Room, 1989), in which comparatively large amounts are spent on licit and illicit liquor as disposable income grows. The emerging alcohol scene occasionally involves celebrations with a bottle of liquor, irrespective of caste hierarchy or economic standing. The broad changes in these regions are matched some-what in less economically advanced states like Rajasthan, in which alcohol is traditionally home-brewed and, similarly, indigenous drugs such as opium and cannabis are home-produced. The northeast regions, because of geographic dif-ferences and varying mixtures of traditional and modern values, display differing regional drinking patterns ranging from complete prohibition in Nagaland to ha-bitual drinking among the working classes of Assam's tea estates.

The regional drinking pattern of the southern states involves intake of arrack (hard liquor) and toddy (fermented palm sap) as well as illicit liquor made from easily available plant bases. The drinking of arrack is favored by both the working classes and the affluent. Toddy is seen as a restorative that has energy-giving and fatigue-relieving effects (Tek Chand, 1964).

Local drinking patterns encompass the narrower traditions of local groups. These are of two types: a) ceremonial and ritualistic and b) convivial. Ritualistic and ceremonial use occurs with ceremonial and festive occasions celebrated in various regions of India. Offerings of alcohol to deities together with animal sacrifices is particularly common among the lower castes. These deities are lo-cal godlings to whom worshippers pray for the well-being of the village and to ward off disease and evil spirits. A logical extension of this idea noted by Mandelbaum (1965) is that alcohol is taboo for gods and for men immersed in cosmic concerns, its use restricted to local blessings and village celebrations. The convivial use of drinking is prominent in another ethnographic account of Rajputs (a Kshatriya group) (Dorchner, 1983), among whom alcohol consump-tion was a group ritual with the sole aim of becoming inebriated as quickly as possible. However, alcohol intake was not confined to a single caste or group but gradually emerged as a general accompaniment to celebrations and other social occasions.

Nontraditional Drinking Patterns

The simultaneous processes of Sanskritizsation (a cultural process of social mo-bility in which "lower" groups adopt the values, rituals, and so forth, of "higher" castes), modernization, and Westernization are paving the way in India for non-traditional drinking in both rural and urban populations. With global communi-cation and the amalgamation of local and national traditions (Redfield, 1956), Western influences have become conspicuously visible among the middle class that began to emerge in the 1960s. The phenomenon of alcohol consumption is more visible in urban society, in which affluence—irrespective of caste and creed—is creating conspicuous consumption and alcohol serves as a mark of hos-pitality and a sign of high social status. Led by elites, the nouveaux riches, and the media, a psychological climate favorable to drinking—and Western drinking patterns in particular—is being created for the conservative middle class. Bars, once the haunt of alcoholics and deviants, are becoming local settings in which to pursue business and social connections.

Table 8.4   Incidence and rate of crimes under prohibition act.

Year	Incidence (no. of cases)	Proportion of total cognizable crimes (%)
1990	594,789	18.1
1991	548,237	16.3
1992	627,426	17.6
1993	600,356	15.8
1994	638,611	16.5

Source. National Crime Records Bureau, 1994.

PROBLEM INDICATORS

In the absence of problem indicators from epidemiological studies, most indicators are based on newspaper articles and other reports of drinking problems. Based on per capita consumption of alcohol, India is categorizable as a "dry culture" (Room, 1989). However, there is a tendency among those who drink to indulge in very heavy drinking (Singh, 1989). This has resulted in a relatively high prevalence of alcohol-related health damage, violence, and social disruption. Approximately 15% to 20% of admissions to psychiatric facilities are for alcohol-related problems or symptoms of alcohol dependence (Ramachandaran, 1991). In 1997, two leading newspapers in the capital city covered around 49 incidents involving illicit liquor, hooch deaths, drunken driving, and so on.

The social and economic consequences of such drinking patterns are equally significant. Every year, more than 600,000 cases are registered under the Prohibition Act, one fifth of which concern women (Table 8.4). In 1994, 961 persons died from consumption of adulterated liquor, including 90 women (National Crime Records Bureau, 1994). Drunk driving also is emerging as a challenge to public health. In a recent study on 1000 drivers of heavy commercial vehicles, 75% reported regular alcohol consumption, and only 10% had accident-free records (Singh & Roy, 1997). Around 50,000 people died in motor-vehicle accidents, alcohol emerging as one of the leading contributory factors.

Gender differences in perceptions of alcohol and drinking problems are critical in India. The link between violence against women and alcohol stands out clearly (Sharma, 1996). Indeed, female sufferers often take up the cudgels against the liquor lobby and inebriated menfolk, and two state governments recently implemented prohibition. However, in both states it was revoked within 2 years because of implementation problems, the emergence of illegal trade, and dwindling funds for development.

CONCLUSION: ALCOHOL—PLEASURE OR PAIN?

"Throughout the thousands of years of human experience with alcoholic beverages, it has been recognized that drinking is a source of both pleasure and harm" (Room, 1997). The historical accounts in the Indian context suggest both traditional pleasures and pitfalls in alcohol intake. Knowledge of the art of fermentation, references to more than 48 alcoholic beverages in the post-Vedic period, themes and images of alcohol connected with rulers and elites, and its selective use among lower classes are some of the indicators of the gradual integration of alcohol consumption into Indian society. Religious censure and condemnation of alcohol by the abstaining upper castes, especially the Brahmins, as well as the portrayal of abstinence as a virtuous and saintly trait, are other traditions reflecting the collective wisdom of a people well aware of the perils of alcohol.

Epidemiological studies conducted during the past two decades showed that between 25% and 40% of men have consumed alcohol at some time in their lives. Abstinence is still a cherished value among women, and more than 90% do not drink at all. The significance of the contemporary alcohol scene lies not in the numbers but in the pattern and availability of Western alcoholic beverages (Indian-made brands of foreign liquor) and indigenous liquor. The upper classes, intelligentsia, high government officials, and the educated young are creating a new climate favorable towards drinking. The urban working class sets its own rituals and rites of passage for drinking (Gusfield, 1987). In urban slums, a perennial feature of city life, alcohol represents the "power of the powerless."

The traditional use of alcohol, although waning, can be traced in varying forms among rural and tribal populations. However, the socio-cultural and economic changes in these populations have altered their lifestyles. High-content alcoholic beverages are becoming commonplace, increasing the incidence of alcohol-related harm to individuals, family, and society. One of the paradoxes of developing nations is the need for revenue collection through such means as the auctioning of liquor licenses and the opening of liquor sales points along national highways, at tourist and sporting locales, and in the interior rural areas. Although providing income and revenue for infrastructure development in urban and rural locations, alcohol also has emerged as a source of corruption that afflicts every area of life.

The answer to the problems created by alcohol is not a whitewash solution such as prohibition or the closing of liquor sales points, but rather the evolution of a rational alcohol policy that is sensitive to public health and supportable over the long term. The European Alcohol Action Plan aims at the prevention of health risks and the harmful social consequences arising from alcohol use and proposes measures that seek to combat high-risk behavior (World Health Organization, 1993). Such a model can be emulated in developing nations as well, although any action in that direction will have to be modified to reflect local realities and customs. At the present juncture, there is a need to identify the appropriate roles of the major actors such as government, the alcohol industry, and the public health community in combating abuse and minimizing risks associated with irresponsible use. The pleasurable aspects of alcoholic beverages can be experienced only if its adverse impacts are minimized. And this, in turn, requires that other stakeholders work together with the public health community to set guidelines for alcohol-abuse prevention.

REFERENCES

Channabasavanna, S. M., Ray, R., & Kaliaperumal, V. G. (1990). *Patterns and problems of non-alcoholic drug dependence in Karnataka*. Bangalore, India: Department of Health and Family Welfare, Government of Karnataka.

Chopra, R. N., & Chopra, I. C. (1965). *Drug addiction with special reference to India*. New Delhi, India: Council of Scientific and Industrial Research.

Deb, P. C., & Jindal, R. B. (1974). *Drinking in rural areas: A study of selected villages of Punjab*. Ludhiana, India: Punjab Agriculture University.

Dorchner, J. (1983). Rajput alcohol use in India. *Journal of Studies on Alcohol, 44*, 538–544.

Dube, K. C. (1972). Drug abuse in northern India: Observations concerning Delhi-Agra region. *Bulletin on Narcotics, 24*, 2.

Federation of Indian Chambers of Commerce and Industry. (1997). *Drug and alcohol prevention programmes at the workplace*. New Delhi, India: Federation of Indian Chambers of Commerce and Industry.

Gusfield, J. R. (1987). Passage to play: Rituals of drinking time in American society. In M. Douglas (Ed.), *Constructive drinking*. Cambridge, UK: Cambridge University Press.

Lal, B., & Singh, G. (1978). Alcohol consumption in Punjab. *Indian Journal of Psychiatry, 20*, 217.

MacAndrew, C., & Edgerton, R. B. (1969). *Drunken comportment: A social explanation*. Chicago, IL: Aldine.

Mandelbaum, G. (1965). Alcohol and culture. *Current Anthropology, 6*, 281–288.

Mohan, D. (1992). *Rapid assessment of drug abuse in an urban community*. New Delhi, India: Indian Council of Medical Research.

Mohan, D., & Sharma, H. K. (1995). Alcohol and culture in India. In D. B. Heath (Ed.), *International handbook on alcohol and culture* (pp. 128–141). Westport, CT: Greenwood.

Mohan, D., Sharma, H. K., Sundaram, K. R., & Advani, G. B. (1981). Prevalence and pattern of alcohol abuse among rural community. New Delhi, India: Ministry of Social Welfare.

Mohan, D., & Sundaram, K. R. (1983). *A collaborative study on non-medical use of drugs in the community* (Base Line Survey Report). New Delhi, India: Indian Council of Medical Research.

Mohan, D., & Sundaram, K. R. (1987). *A collaborative study on drug abuse among university students*. New Delhi, India: Ministry of Welfare.

Mohan, D., Sundaram, K. R., Neki, J. S., Darshan, S., & Sharma, H. K. (1978). *Drug abuse in rural Punjab. Report to the Ministry of Social Welfare*. New Delhi, India: Government of India.

National Crime Records Bureau. (1994). *Accidental deaths and suicides in India*. New Delhi, India: Ministry of Home Affairs.

Pan, L. (1975). *Alcohol in colonial Africa* (Monograph 22). Helsinki, Finland: Finnish Foundation for Alcohol Studies.

Prakash, O. (1961). *Food and drinks in ancient India*. New Delhi, India: Munshi Ram Manohar Lal Publishers.

Ramachandaran, V. (1991). *Prevention of alcohol-related problems*. Presidential Address, 43rd conference of the Indian Psychiatric Society, Calicutta.

Reddy, G. P. (1971). *Where liquor decides everything: Drinking sub-cultures among tribes of India*. New Delhi, India: Social Welfare, Ministry of Welfare.

Redfield, R. (1956). *Peasant society and culture*. Chicago, IL: Chicago University Press.

Room, R. (1989, September). *Response to alcohol-related problems in an international perspective: Characterizing and explaining cultural wetness and dryness*. Paper presented at la ricerca italiana sulle bevande alcoholic nel confiromoto intermazational [Italian research on alcoholic beverages within an international context], Santo Stefano Belbo, Italy.

Room, R. (1997). Alcohol, the individual and society: What history teaches us. *Addiction, 92* (Suppl. 1), S7–S11.

Saxena, S. (1997). Alcohol, Europe and the developing countries. *Addiction, 92*, 43–58.

Sharma, H. K. (1996, September). *Alcohol, aggression and violent acts: A case study of an urban slum in Delhi (India).* Paper presented at the International Conference on Intoxication and Aggressive Behaviour, Addiction Research Foundation, Toronto, Canada.

Singh, G. (1989). Epidemiology of alcohol abuse in India. In R. Ray & R. W. Pickens (Eds.), *Proceedings of the Indo–U.S. Symposium on Alcohol and Drug Abuse* (pp. 3–11). Bangalore, India: National Institute of Mental Health and Neuro Sciences.

Singh, S. P., & Roy, S. (1997). *Unskilled, drunk drivers.* New Delhi, India: Indian Foundation of Transport Research and Training.

Sitholey, P., Mohan, D., & Purohit, D. R. (1992). *A collaborative study on Narcotic Drugs and psychotropic substances.* New Delhi, India: Indian Council of Medical Research.

Tek Chand. (1964). *A study team on alcohol* (Vol. 1). New Delhi, India: Ministry of Planning, Government of India.

Tek Chand. (1972). *Liquor menace in India.* New Delhi, India: Gandhi Peace Foundation.

Times of India. (1997, November 10). Kalahandi: A district of widows.

Varma, V. K., Singh, A., Singh, S., & Malhotra, A. (1981). Extent and pattern of alcohol use and alcohol-related problems in north India. *Indian Journal of Psychiatry, 22*, 331–337.

World Health Organization. (1993). *European alcohol action plan.* Copenhagen, Denmark: WHO, Regional Office for Europe.

Chapter 9

Japanese Culture and Drinking

Naotaka Shinfuku

HISTORICAL PERSPECTIVE

The Ancient Tradition of Sake

According to legend, around the year 2200 BC sake was invented by a man in China and presented to King Wu. King Wu enjoyed sake so much that he became drunk for several days. He then immediately issued a law prohibiting sake, saying: "Sake is so good that people will surely be unable to limit their drinking and will ruin themselves and the country." But this prohibition did not last long. King Wu's son, King Ketu, filled a pond with sake and decked the forest with barbecued meats. This luxuriant lifestyle was thought to have led to the ruin of the kingdom.

In Japan, around the sixth century, sake was produced by chewing rice. Two kinds of sake were produced, one for religious ceremonies and the other for social consumption. Only young virgins could chew the rice to produce sake for religious ceremonies. With the introduction of yeast in Japan during the 7th or 8th century, there was a dramatic increase in output. The production of sake was prohibited to farmers in 646 AD. Since then, prohibitionary laws have been introduced many times in Japan, particularly during famines and epidemics. However, prohibitionary laws have been short-lived in most cases.

The Traditional Benefits of Sake

Attitudes towards sake in Japan were represented in a type of traditional comic play called *kyogen*. In one *kyogen* play called *Mochi-Sake* (Cake and Sake) produced during the Muromachi era, 10 virtues of sake were identified:

113

1   Provides a friend when alone
2   Produces harmony for all people
3   Allows ordinary people to greet nobles with ease
4   Justifies meeting with friends
5   Provides companionship while traveling
6   Promotes long life
7   Is the king of 100 medicines
8   Helps sorrow to disappear
9   Aids recovery from fatigue
10 Warms the body in the cold

During the Ashikaga Shogun era (around the 15th century), *syudo*, a cere-mony of sake drinking, began. The goal was for drinkers at the ceremony not to become drunk but to enjoy the sake and the company based on the spirit of *ichigo-ichie* (savoring a precious time in one's life). *Syudo* was intended to develop the art of sake drinking just as traditional tea ceremonies did for tea. However, *syudo* faded away and is now only an historical memory.

Shinto is the traditional religion in Japan and the emperor is its head. Sake plays a central role in Shinto. Sacred sake is served to the Shinto gods every day with a bowl of rice. Sake is an indispensable element during Shinto weddings. During the Shinto wedding ceremony, the groom and bride exchange small china cups filled with sake three times and drink each cup. These exchanges of cups of sake are a sacred symbol of the unity of the couple and are the highlight of the wedding ceremony.

A book called *Hyakka Seturin* (One Hundred Teachers Preach) of the Edo era cited 10 virtues of sake drinking that are similar to the virtues mentioned in *Mochi-Sake*, although the benefits sound more modern, that is, medical. The volume stressed, among other benefits, that sake (a) helps dispel depression and sad feelings, (b) changes the mood, (c) prevents ill health, (d) cleans poison from the body, and (e) extends the life span. The saying, "Sake is the king of 100 medicines," has been used very popularly throughout Japanese history continuing into modern times.

The Modern Era: The Meiji Era and After

In 1868, a law regulating the production of sake was issued, and in 1918 minors were prohibited from drinking sake. In 1938, a licensing system was introduced for the sale of sake and other alcoholic beverages. The production of alcohol was limited during the Second World War. However, after the war the drinking of whisky, beer, and wine increased as a result of Western influences.

Japanese Culture and Alcohol in Summary

When reviewing the history of sake in Japan, we can summarize by saying that sake, which was highly respected from its origin, has been offered to the gods and regarded as the king of medicine throughout Japan's long history. Its medical effects on psychological sorrows have been greatly valued. In Japan, man and sake have created a beautiful drinking culture with moderation at its center. Sake has been and still is a lifelong friend for many Japanese people.

BIOLOGICAL ASPECTS OF JAPANESE DRINKING

Aldehyde Dehydrogenase Deficiency Among Asians

Physical reactions to alcohol can vary considerably. Almost half the Japanese people lack aldehyde dehydrogenase (ALDH). This group of people, who are called "flushers," cannot efficiently metabolize harmful acetaldehyde that results from alcohol ingestion. Flushers manifest unpleasant symptoms after drinking including flushing of the face and body, palpitations and sweating, headaches, rashes, nausea, and drowsiness. These people are genetically protected from becoming alcoholics because they find alcohol ingestion unpleasant and cannot consume much alcohol.

ALDH-1 and ALDH-2 Differences

There are two types of ALDH deficiency that are linked to specific genotypes. The genotype NN (Normal/Normal) is associated with normal ALDH functioning. The ND (Normal/Deficient) or ALDH-2 deficient, genotype has one 16th of the potency of the NN group in processing ALDH. People with the ND genotype react strongly to alcohol and are unable to drink much. Those with genotype DD (Deficient/Deficient) (ALDH-1 deficient) have no ALDH processing capacity at all and are completely unable to drink alcohol. According to Harada (1984), 30% to 50% of Chinese, 44% of Japanese, 14% to 57% of all Asians, 0% to 7% of North American Indians, and 41% to 69% of South American Indians are ALDH-2 deficient. ALDH deficiencies are not observed among Europeans and Africans. This suggests that ALDH-2 deficiency started among the Mongol population and spread with this population to eastern Asia and then to North and South America through migration over the centuries.

ALCOHOL PROBLEMS IN MODERN JAPAN

Alcohol Beverages in Modern Japan

The traditional Japanese alcohol beverages are sake (rice wine) and syochu (distilled alcohol from sweet potato and grains). Syochu was popular in the southern parts of Japan and the Ryukyu Islands. Syochu contains 25% alcohol; sake used to contain 15% alcohol. In modern Japan, people consume both traditional alcohol beverages and those originally imported from Europe. Although beer is very popular, people also drink whisky, sake, syochu, and wine in their daily lives. The consumption of wine is increasing rapidly in Japan, particularly among young women.

Acute Alcohol Intoxication Among Young Adults

Binge drinking of liquor is common among young Japanese males. *Ikkinomi* (gulping liquor in one shot) commonly is seen as a welcoming ritual in colleges and businesses. The practice is dangerous and leads to acute alcohol intoxication. In 1996 in the metropolitan Tokyo area, 9971 people were taken to the hospital by ambulance because of acute alcohol intoxication; 4725 were in their 20s and 1271 were in their teens (Tokyo Metropolitan Emergency Agency, 1997). In the past 10 years, at least 67 young people (mostly new entrants to colleges) have died from acute alcohol intoxication. This might be related to forced drinking among young males with no ability to process ALDH. Several universities have prohibited *ikkinomi* and an Association for the Prevention of Ikkinomi has been established by family members whose sons have died from the practice. Preventing *ikkinomi* is an important target for alcohol education among the young in Japan.

Increase of Alcohol Dependence Among Japanese Women

Stress and anxiety are factors triggering alcoholism in women. As the opportunities for women to drink have increased in Japan, more women have become alcohol-dependent. According to a survey conducted at 14 alcohol-treatment centers (Alcohol Health Medical Association, 1993), the number of new female clients increased 2.2 times from 1982 to 1986, and the proportion of women among alcohol-dependent patients increased from 6% to 12%. Women become alcohol-dependent more readily than men, requiring only half the consumption level over half the period of time to become alcoholic. This is attributable to biological (see Chapter 13) as well as psychological and social (see Chapter 22) differences. One explanation for the increase in alcohol dependence among women in Japan is the frequent absence of workaholic husbands. While preparing meals in the kitchen and waiting for husbands who never come home on time, some housewives (called "kitchen drinkers") start drinking. Thus male workaholic practices in Japan need to be addressed in conjunction with alcoholism among women.

Alcohol and Driving

Drunk driving is a prevalent problem in Japan, although it is prohibited by the Japanese Transportation Code. In 1996, 330,000 people were prosecuted for drinking and driving offenses. Some 2000 accidents were attributed to drinking and driving and 347 people died in accidents caused by drunk driving. However, mortality rates due to drunk driving have decreased gradually in recent years, perhaps because of the imposition of server liability penalties. Deaths related to drunk driving have decreased as follows: 570 in 1992, 548 in1993, 514 in 1994, 432 in 1995, and 347 in 1996. This successful reduction is a positive example of the results of public education in harmonizing pleasurable drinking with avoiding alcohol harm in modern life.

Drinking Problems of the Aged

The Japanese have the highest average lifespan in the world, and people over 65 years of age outnumber those younger than 15 years old. The number of older alcohol-dependent people has increased as this segment of the population has grown. Retirement, loss of spouse, and a solitary lifestyle sometimes trigger excessive drinking among the elderly and result in alcohol-related physical and mental problems. The Japanese Alcohol Health Association offers the following advice for elderly drinkers:

1 Moderate your drinking.
2 Do not drink during the day.
3 Do not drink alone; drink with family members and friends.
4 Listen to the advice of family members.
5 Do not drink while taking medications.
6 Have regular medical checks, particularly of liver functioning.

Elderly people need to be especially cautious about harmonizing health and pleasure in drinking in order to continue to lead a long and healthy life.

DRINKING AND QUALITY OF LIFE

Drinking and the J Curve

The American Council on Science and Health (ACSH) issued a report in 1993 on the J-curve relationship between drinking and health. It concluded that moderate drinking reduces the overall mortality rate and improves health (see Chapter 12). On the other hand, excessive drinking increases the mortality rate dramatically. Regular intake of moderate amounts of alcohol is particularly effective in preventing coronary heart disease. In Japan, coronary heart disease is the second leading cause of death after cancer. In this context, moderate drinking can contribute to a reduction in one of the most important causes of death in Japan, along with other stress-related diseases.

Sake as a Communication Tool in Modern Japan

Alcohol serves to reduce tension and enhance relaxation. In a 1987 survey by the ministry of coordination, Japanese respondents gave the following reasons for drinking:

1 Recovering from fatigue
2 Conviviality with friends
3 Enhancement of mood

4 Enjoyment at family gatherings
5 Simple enjoyment of drinking
6 Sleep
7 Entertainment of business associates
8 Fondness for the drinking milieu

These responses clearly show that alcohol facilitates everyday social interactions in modern Japanese society, as well as enhancing quality of life (see
Chapter 23).

Sake in Modern Japanese Life

As exemplified in the Shinto wedding ceremony, sake plays an indispensable
role in modern Japanese social ceremonies. The new year starts with the sharing
of *omiki* (sacred sake with a special flavor) among family members. Similarly,
the days at year's end are occasions on which Japanese people organize parties and enjoy sake with friends, family, business associates, and fellow school
alumni. Japanese people have a long tradition of gathering together to enjoy
flowers in the spring, called *hanami* (cherry blossom viewing), and full moons
in autumn, called *tsukimi* (full-moon viewing). Sake is an essential ingredient
for both *hanami* and *tsukimi*. When a new house is built, the Japanese organize
a small ceremony called *jichin-sai* (calming the spirit of the earth-god), which
involves pouring a libation of Sake on the ground.

Japanese Law and Drinking

In Japan, the so-called Drunkeness Prevention Law was promulgated in 1961
for the purpose of "preventing harmful behavior by the public due to excessive
drinking" (Law 103, Chapter 1, 1961). The aim of the law is to minimize
excessive drinking both among individuals and throughout society, to promote
moderate drinking among the Japanese. It directs that people should avoid such
practices as forcing other people to drink, and it prohibits drinking by those
younger than 20 years old.

Ten Principles of Moderate Drinking in
Modern Japan

The Japanese Alcohol Health Association, with the technical assistance of Kurihama Hospital's National Alcohol Center, has provided a modern version of the
10 principles of moderate drinking:

1 Drink with joy and laughter.
2 Do not drink in haste—drink with style and a leisurely pace.
3 Drink together with food.
4 Know and drink the appropriate amount.
5 Take two alcohol-free days per week for the sake of your liver.

6 Do not force other people to drink.

7 Do not drink while taking medicines such as sleeping pills, sedatives, and antidiabetics.

8 Dilute strong alcoholic beverages.

9 Finish drinking at 12:00 midnight at the latest.

10 Have regular medical check-ups of the liver.

CONCLUSION

Misunderstanding of the role of alcohol and its proper use disrupts the harmonious role of alcohol in modern life. It is clear that, in most cultures, moderate drinking can enhance enjoyment and quality of life and is a key to good health. This is likewise the case in Japan, where drinking is a traditional activity with a long social history and many social functions, but where at the same time alcohol misuse is a present danger for many.

ACKNOWLEDGMENTS

The author would like to extend his thanks for the valuable advice provided by Dr. Susumu Higuchi of the National Institute on Alcoholism, Kurihama National Hospital, Japan, and Dr. Kenji Shigemori, Director, Senzoku Mental Health Clinic, Tokyo, Japan.

REFERENCES

Alcohol Health Medical Association. (1993). *Alcohol-related problems in our country*. Tokyo, Japan: Author.

Ellison, R. C. (1993, June). *Does moderate alcohol consumption prolong life?* New York: American Council on Science and Health.

Harada, S., Agawai, D. P., Goedde, H. W. (1981). Al dehydrogenase deficiency as cause of facial flushing reaction to alcohol in Japanese. *Lancet, 2*, 982.

Information Office, Ministry of Coordination. (1987). *Sake and tobacco use among Japanese*. Tokyo, Japan: Author.

Koizumi, T. (1982). *Sake no Hanashi* [Talks on Sake] (Kodansha-Gendai-Shinsyo Series No. 676). Tokyo, Japan: Kodansha.

Law 103, Chapter 1. (1st June Era of Showa 36 [1961]). Tokyo, Japan.

Shigemori, K., Komiyama, T., & Japan Alcohol Health Medicine Association (Eds.). (1997). *Booklet on Alcohol and Health*. Tokyo, Japan: Kirin Beer Company, Socio-Environmental Division.

Tokyo Metropolitan Emergency Agency. (1997, March). *Rescue activities for acute alcohol intoxication*. Tokyo, Japan: Author.

WHO. (1991). *Report of the inter-regional meeting on alcohol-related problems, Tokyo, Japan, April 2–8*. Geneva, Switzerland: WHO Program on Substance Abuse.

Chapter 10

Alcohol Use, Sale, and Production in Ghana

Joseph Asare

Ghana is a largely agricultural country of about 18 million people in West Africa. Since achieving independence in 1957, it has experienced steady urbanization. Documented data on alcohol consumption in Ghana are very limited, and the extent of alcohol consumption and its social consequences are not well known. Traditionally, alcohol has been used in village contexts in socially controlled ways. Modern social trends, and particularly aggressive alcohol advertising, may disturb this historic balance of healthy and pleasurable alcohol use in Ghana.

ALCOHOL USE IN GHANA

The use of alcoholic beverages in the form of locally produced variants has been known in Ghana for a long time. Alcohol traditionally has been used for communal socializing, recreation, religious celebrations, and nutrition. It often is said that "what alcohol can do, water cannot be substituted for." The traditional view of alcohol—which still holds for much of Ghanaian culture—is that it is a way to unite the living soul with the dead. Hence, alcohol is offered at functions such as funerals, meetings, child-naming ceremonies, and weddings in seeking blessing, protection, and goodwill for participants. In other instances, alcohol may be used to curse others or to invoke omens against them.

In most villages and smaller communities, alcohol accompanies communal activities and merry making. The alcohol is drunk from a common receptacle, which is passed from person to person, symbolizing friendship, trust, and to-getherness. People from different households often join together in agricultural work, followed by free drinks and food provided by the organizing household. This is one of the most important traditions in the villages and is reciprocated in turn. The practice has a socially stabilizing effect, leading to social cohesion and improved economic cooperation among villagers.

In these settings, it is unusual for people to get drunk. Those who appear intoxicated are excluded from further rounds of drinking. Some may come to be known for habitually excessive drinking. Frequent drunkenness is stigmatized, and the social stigma extends to the entire family. It is therefore the responsibility of the family to check excessive drinking among its members.

The colonization of Africa brought about many changes in the use of alcohol. In particular, it increased access to European alcoholic beverages. As Ghana was opened to Europeans, gold and other commodities were bartered for alcohol, gunpowder, and tobacco (Pan, 1985). The cocoa boom changed the lifestyles of many farmers, who acquired some wealth and with it greater access to the use of hard liquor. Indeed, in 1927 some Ghanaian chiefs protested against the negative effects of alcohol on their subjects.

PRODUCTION AND SALE OF ALCOHOL IN GHANA

Before the colonial era, Ghana had several forms of alcoholic beverages prepared from local materials. These drinks included *pito* and palm wine. The Europeans brought with them distilled forms of alcohol and beer. In the 1930s, *akpeteshie*, a local form of distilled drink obtained from palm wine, raffia wine, or distilled sugarcane, also was produced for the black market.

Pito

Pito is an alcoholic beverage prepared from Guinea corn, millet, and other grains through a process similar to the brewing of beer. There are some mystic rituals attached to its preparation in order to make it acceptable to the gods and spirits, who are believed to influence its production. *Pito* is highly regarded by the inhabitants of the northern part of Ghana, who treat it as a food because of its Guinea corn content.

The northern part of Ghana is very hot and there is a shortage of water for most of the year. In addition, this region frequently is afflicted by epidemic outbreaks of cerebrospinal meningitis, a potentially fatal condition. In order to protect themselves against disease and dehydration, locals favor the drinking of fluids combined with adequate ventilation and good personal hygiene. Considered a safe fluid because the ingredients are boiled in its preparation, *pito* is often central to this practice.

Pito is cheaper and more easily obtained than commercially manufactured alcohol and is therefore widely and liberally used. Ofori-Atta, Sefa-Dedeh, Ohene, and de-Graft Aikins (in press) identified 168 *pito* brewers in a community study in Ghana's Upper East Region. Of these, 62% were classified as professional brewers. All of the brewers and their workers were female, perhaps because the process of brewing *pito* requires patience, precision, and time—qualities thought to characterize Ghanaian women. More men, however, drink *pito* than women.

Palm Wine

Palm wine is commonly produced in the middle and southern belts of Ghana, where the palm tree thrives. A similar wine is produced from the Raffia palm, which, unlike the palm tree, is not uprooted in the production process. Production of palm wine requires considerable physical strength and may involve such hazards as climbing to the top of the palm trees in order to remove sap; therefore, it is considered mainly a male activity.

Palm wine is an esteemed drink among most tribes in the southern part of Ghana. Its white color and foam signifying purity, it usually is provided at the beginning and at the end of culturally significant gatherings. Traditionally, palm wine collected in pots was offered to the bereaved at funerals. Today, money and other bottled alcoholic beverages frequently are substituted for palm wine.

Palm wine typically is drunk from a special receptacle—a calabash—which is passed from one person to another. Specially molded clay pots are used to store the drink. Nothing is wasted, because any unconsumed surplus is stored in special barrels and allowed to ferment in order to produce distilled *akpeteshie*.

Akpeteshie

Akpeteshie is a name given to the locally distilled gin. It is produced from palm wine, Raffia palm wine, or sugar cane. The name comes from the Ga language spoken in the greater Accra region. It literally means "they are hiding." Popular legend holds that Europeans who lived in Ghana during the colonial era enjoyed palm wine and its intoxicating effects. They decided to distill alcohol from palm wine and hid from the local people when drinking the resulting product. The natives eventually found them out and told others that they were "hiding and drinking," from which the name *akpeteshie* was derived.

Natives soon imitated the process of distillation. Noticing that the local gin was competing with imported drinks, the authorities placed a prohibition on the production, sale, and use of *akpeteshie*. This in turn led to a black market in the product as natives continued consuming *akpeteshie* through the practice of "hiding and drinking." More recently, *akpeteshie* distilleries have developed a simple method of distillation for commercial production.

Beer

Brewing of beer in Ghana began in 1933. Up to that time, beer had been imported from Europe. There are now four major breweries in Ghana. Two of them are

Table 10.1 Beer and stout production in Ghana (no. of cartons).

Year	Beer[1]	Stout[2]
1996	7,736,339	2,703,669
1997	6,362,381	2,282,008

Source. Customs, Excise and Preventive Service of Ghana, unpublished raw data.
[1] One carton contains 12 bottles of 625 ml.
[2] One carton contains 24 bottles of 330 ml.

situated in Accra and two in Kumasi, the country's second-largest city. The two breweries in Accra, the Accra Brewery and Achimota Brewery, are highly competitive.

The Accra Brewery originally was registered in 1931 as the Overseas Brewery Limited. It was the first brewery in the entire West African region. In 1997, the Accra Brewery's net profits were 2,359,228,000 cedis ($980,968.00). This reflected a 7.1% drop in sales of beer, attributed in part to the recent growth in churches that forbid the use of alcohol. As a result, the company has increased both the production and the often aggressive marketing of soft drinks in order to compensate for reduced beer sales. The company also has introduced Club Shandy, a popular beverage containing 2% alcohol.

The Achimota Brewery was established in 1973 as the first and only Ghanaian-owned brewery. It was taken over by the state in 1981, and since then Heineken has gained majority ownership. Kumasi Brewery was established by Heineken International and the United African Company in Kumasi in the mid-1960s. The Achimota and Kumasi breweries are noted for their association with sponsorship of festivals and funerals in many communities. Kumasi Brewery also sponsors a popular Sunday afternoon television musical program entitled *Workers' Rendevous—Killing the Boredom in Life*.

In the view of many, the most successful brewing operation in Ghana is the Guinness brewery. In 1971 a Guinness factory was established in Kumasi. Since then, Guinness has captured a strong market share, primarily through its involvement in many community activities. It also sponsors television programs, including the popular weekend show *Music for Your Dancing Feet*. In an attempt to outmaneuver other companies producing stout, Guinness has started producing larger bottles of stout. Featuring billboards lettered "THINK BIG," the national advertising campaign for the new, larger-sized stout has proven very effective.

Table 10.1 shows quantities of beer and stout produced in Ghana in 1996 and 1997. The figures reflect a recent sudden fall in beer consumption.

Distilled Beverages

There are currently many small-scale, privately owned distilleries in and around Accra. The *akpeteshie* distillers have grouped themselves into cooperatives that control the production, distribution, and sale of the product. They issue licenses to their members and have trained inspectors who collaborate with the police to arrest illegal traders. However, the cooperatives have no on-site inspections of production. Therefore, quality control is inadequate. Since independence, the government has gone a long way towards regulating the legal production and sale of the previously prohibited *akpeteshie*.

Sale of Alcoholic Beverages

The Liquor Licensing Act No. 331of 1970 requires manufacturers of spirits to be licensed and empowers uniformed police to inspect any premises where the illegal distillation of spirits is suspected. The same law forbids sales of spirits without a license. Selling of *akpeteshie* requires a special license; other sections of the law deal with wine and beer. People younger than 18 years old are excluded from the premises of any licensed bar at certain hours. Licensees may not sell alcohol to any drunken person or allow disorderly behavior on their premises. Unfortunately the act is not rigorously enforced and is silent on the sale of alcohol to minors. Lack of identity cards showing the ages of drinkers also presents a problem. Alcoholic beverages are sold in bars, restaurants, kiosks, and shops.

Accredited distributors supply alcohol to retailers. Alcoholic beverages are advertised on the radio and on television and in print media. In the past 5 years, Ghana has witnessed an unprecedented increase in advertisements (particularly for beer) on television. As listening to music and dancing are popular Ghanaian pastimes, the advertisements often center around young boys and girls engaged in such activities. More competitive advertising also includes games that present attractive prizes, including expensive cars. The caps of beer bottles are used for such games. Some companies sponsor festivals, often annual tribal events, at which they promote their products. The increase in competitive advertising seems a dangerous trend, despite the recent decrease in beer consumption. For one thing, the advertisements do not encourage moderate drinking. Their main motive is to get more people to drink, partly in response to efforts by religious bodies to discourage drinking. Apart from Guinness, which has supported the health sector through a community-focused project, most manufacturers concentrate on sports and musical-program sponsorship. Most advertisements target youths and young adults by associating happiness and prosperity with the consumption of specific beers.

MODELS OF ALCOHOL USE IN GHANA

Solitary Use

Solitary use occurs among people suffering from psychological problems such as anxiety and depression or lacking social skills. Other people may choose to drink in isolation because of religious or social sanctions. Some elderly women also tend to drink alone.

Communal

Many consumers drink at social functions, at which beverages are provided by a group of people or a community. Donations usually are offered by participants to the providers of the drink. This model is a commercial variant based on traditional village life.

Funeral ceremonies have become important occasions at which alcohol is consumed. In Ghana, large funerals are prestigious events. Naming ceremonies, which occur on the eighth day following a child's birth, often involve alcohol used for ritual purposes, although smaller quantities tend to be consumed at these events. The child who is named is given alcohol and water three times in succession to teach the child symbolically to differentiate truth from falsehood. Alcohol is poured on the ground with incantations to the ancestral spirits to help the child grow and imitate his or her namesake. Alcohol also is used at parties, marriage ceremonies, and arbitration proceedings. Key elders have customary functions at arbitrations. These may be dependent on alcohol. In urban areas, weekend funerals are common, and some people regularly rely on these occasions to socialize and drink.

Acquired Models

Rapid urbanization and migration of people from rural areas have created problems. Changes in patterns of social behavior that have come about through formal education and exposure to foreign cultures have led to new models or settings for alcohol use. Examples are drinking in hotels, restaurants, bars, and nightclubs; these settings have become part of urban life, usually for those who are more Westernized and with more discretionary income. There are also structures in urban areas resembling village meeting places where drinking occurs; however, one has to pay for the drinks. In most of these places music is provided in the background or there is traditional dancing, making drinking part of a larger context of enjoyment and relaxation.

Alcohol Users in Ghana

Reliable data on alcohol use are not generally available for Ghana. However, a survey conducted by Nortey (1987) revealed that about 30% of youths drank alcohol at least three times a week.

Many Ghanaians do not consider brewed alcohol as alcoholic, despite limitations on alcohol use influenced by religious beliefs. For example, Muslims generally abstain from alcohol use. Nonetheless, Guinness stout is referred to by many inhabitants in the north, where Islamic influence is strong, as *zintim* (blood tonic). This may stem from a hospital practice in which Guinness is provided to blood donors.

The spread of fundamentalist churches has increased since 1980 and has become a threat to the alcohol industry by causing many people to abstain. Regular increases in the price of alcohol also have contributed to a reduction in consumption. This trend has prompted strong competitive activity among beverage-alcohol manufacturers. Competition, in turn, has resulted in the improvement of beverage quality, labeling, and the aesthetic appearance of bottles.

Some types of alcohol, particularly imported beverages, are consumed by the well-off and social elite. In Ghana, apart from *pito* produced in the northern areas, home brewing of wine is limited to a few expatriate homes. The use of *akpeteshie* has spread throughout the country among people at the lower end of the socioeconomic ladder, on account of its affordability and potency. Traditional healers and herbalists also use this spirit to extract essences from plants to make medicines for healing purposes. It is common for people to drink at wayside kiosks, where they buy *akpeteshie* bitters with exotic names for ailments such as constipation, impotence, lack of appetite, and anemia. Others, particularly in the working class, use alcohol to induce an appetite before their main meal; the youth, and boarding students in particular, often eat "kenkey," a fermented boiled corn dough, for its intoxicating effect.

PROBLEMS ASSOCIATED WITH ALCOHOL ABUSE IN GHANA

Although alcohol addiction resulting in psychosis has been found to be extremely common in East Africa (German, 1972), few individuals among general psychiatric admissions in Ghana require psychiatric intervention because of alcohol problems. In 1972, only 18 out of a psychiatric population of 1548 at the Accra Psychiatric Hospital were alcoholics with psychiatric complications (Adomakoh, 1972). This prevalence rate has remained relatively constant to the present. In 1977, 91 (3.4%) out of 2641 total admissions to the hospital were alcohol related. In 1995, 91 (4%) of 2327 psychiatric admissions and in 1996, 99 (3.9%) out of 2540 psychiatric admissions to the same hospital were alcohol-related (Asare, 1997). The figures are equally low in the general hospitals. It would appear that the diagnosis of alcoholism is not readily made, but rather that the physical complications from excessive drinking take precedence over the underlying alcoholism.

The numbers of alcohol-related psychiatric admissions continue to be on the low side. This may be because only extreme cases are referred to the psychiatric hospital. Admission to a psychiatric hospital carries a certain stigma, and therefore alcohol-dependent people who may need help are not seen unless they suffer from psychiatric conditions such as psychosis, delirium tremens, or severe depressive symptoms. A person who is dependent on alcohol is likely to be seen as being cursed or punished for sins committed in the past. The family and fellow workers tend to be protective of such drinkers. The alcohol-dependent person thus may lose his or her job through absenteeism or a chronic physical disability.

The typical alcohol-dependent person loses respect in the community in which he or she lives and is not considered responsible. The treatment options offered are geared towards helping the alcoholic to cope with the physical and psychological problems associated with the use of alcohol. They involve the immediate relatives in helping the person to abstain and to be rehabilitated into the community. Some alcohol-dependent persons may present with seizures, which may compound their problems because epilepsy is highly stigmatized. They also may present with fatal physical disabilities such as liver damage. Unfortunately, most of them return to drinking immediately after discharge, giving the impression of a suicidal orientation.

In the northern part of the country, a high rate of seizure disorders has been observed in annual statistical returns, which many suspect is caused by the increased use of *pito*. However, similar high rates of seizures also have been reported in areas in which onchocerciasis is endemic and *pito* use is not common. Cerebrospinal meningitis is also endemic in the north. Locally distilled alcoholic drinks are highly variable in their alcohol concentrations. It also has been found that some of them contain aldehydes, ketones, and other impurities from the equipment and additives used for distillation.

Even though drinking and the use of cannabis are common among the young, few youths appear among alcohol-related psychiatric admissions. During occasions such as Easter, Christmas, and New Year the number of accidents attributed to careless driving associated with alcohol abuse increases.

PREVENTION OF ALCOHOL ABUSE

Over the years, prevention efforts have been aimed at total abstinence from alcohol use. This approach has not succeeded because alcohol is well established in the cultural life of Ghanaians. Although some Christian churches preach against the evils of excessive alcohol use, others see alcohol use as demonic and condemn its use in all forms. Such churches even have substituted mineral water for wine during Holy Communion.

Until recently, those in the medical field—particularly mental-health personnel—also have preached abstinence for everybody, in keeping with the disease concept of alcoholism. However, this concept fails to explain the realities of alcoholism to the ordinary Ghanaian (Akyeampong, 1995). With a high illiteracy level and beliefs that attribute the origins of disease to supernatural beings, there is a need for education that will be accepted by the common man.

Observations of Ghanaian drinking patterns indicate that most of those who drink do so to seek pleasure, either through social interactions or through the disinhibiting effects of beverage alcohol. A majority of those who drink do not go on to become dependent on alcohol and are able to perform the functions demanded of them by their families and society. Therefore, to preach total abstinence may not be an acceptable method for preventing alcohol abuse. It may be prudent, however, to suggest total abstinence for people who have a family tree replete with alcoholics.

Recent evidence (see Chapters 12 and 13) suggests that moderate alcohol consumption can prove beneficial to drinkers' health. This is beginning to create a more balanced view of alcohol and its impact on the body among public health workers and policymakers.

It also is becoming increasingly clear that people will continue to drink alcohol no matter what laws are enacted. In the 1970s a military officer who was regional commissioner of one of the regions of Ghana banned the sale of *akpeteshie* in his area. The ban was enforced through prevention of imports of the drink from the south. Inhabitants immediately started distilling the beverage from local materials using rusty nails and powdered soap to enhance fermentation. The results were disastrous, and the ban disappeared quietly and completely.

The Ghanaian Ministry of Education recently produced a handbook for coordinators of the school health program that is intended to expose secondary-school students to problems associated with drug and alcohol dependency. This may help school-aged youth to make appropriate decisions on alcohol use. In addition, it could be highly beneficial to identify nonharmful patterns of drinking for this and other groups.

WHO DETERMINES THE QUALITY OF ALCOHOL PRODUCTS?

Each of the beverage-alcohol companies has a quality-control section concerned with maintaining the beverage quality set out in its brewing formulae. Most breweries started with lower concentrations of alcohol than today, for example 3.5%, but some increased this concentration up to around 9% until pressure was put on them to reverse the trend. Currently, apart from Guinness stout which has a concentration of about 7% by volume, all beers contain about 5% alcohol. Unfortunately, there is no association of breweries in Ghana, and therefore the companies act independently. Nonetheless, they are sensitive to public opinion and strive to produce quality products.

The breweries have blamed producers of *akpeteshie* for illnesses caused by alcohol impurities. They claim that because of the increasing cost of beer people are turning to the use of *akpeteshie*, which is produced under poor quality-control conditions, leading in turn to more adverse health effects. Their contention is that beer is the safest drink, that it should be treated differently from the distilled drinks, and that it not be regarded as a harm-inducing substance when adverse health effects of alcohol are discussed.

The proliferation of distilleries that escape the control of established government regulatory systems is likely to put consumers at risk. It therefore may be necessary to create more awareness of the problem, so that communities themselves initiate protective action. The laws on alcohol production and sale are silent on legal hours of sale or the sale of alcohol to minors. These gaps in the law likewise need to be remedied.

CONCLUSION

Alcohol will continue to be consumed in Ghana, as it traditionally has played a very important role in the sociocultural life of Ghanaians. Although alcohol is consumed in large quantities, one cannot say with certainty that alcohol use in Ghana significantly disturbs the well-being of many Ghanaians. However, the increased promotion of alcohol through aggressive and uncontrolled advertisements is likely to increase its use beyond traditionally regulated patterns, creating possible problems in the future. The current effective promotion of beverage alcohol, particularly beer, through association with pleasurable, relaxing aspects of life such as music and dancing, and the targeting of youthful drinkers are both potentially problematic trends. A majority of those who use alcohol does so to derive pleasure. However, the problems of alcohol dependency and the potential for harm that may result from excessive use should be better publicized among consumers. The benefit derived from moderate drinking needs to be highlighted, as well as the dangers inherent in alcohol abuse. In other words, education should focus on appropriate and optimal drinking patterns.

REFERENCES

Adomakoh, C. C. (1972). Mental hospital patients: A Castle Road profile. *Ghana Medical Journal, 11*, 65–70.

Akyeampong, E. (1995). Alcoholism in Ghana: A sociocultural exploration. *Culture, Medicine and Psychiatry, 19*, 261–280.

Asare, J. (1997). [Alcohol-related admissions to the Accra Psychiatric Hospital, Ghana]. Unpublished raw data.

DeHeer, N. A. (1997). *Handbook on health education for basic schools in Ghana*. Accra, Ghana: Ministry of Education.

German, A. (1972). Aspects of clinical psychiatry in Sub-Saharan Africa. *British Journal of Psychiatry, 12*, 461–479.

Nortey, D. N. A. (1987). Epidemiological study of drug abuse among the youth in Ghana. In Division of Educational Sciences, United Nations Educational, Scientific and Cultural Organization (Ed.), *Contents and methods of education*. Geneva, Switzerland: United Nations Educational, Scientific and Cultural Organization.

Ofori-Atta, A. L., Sefa-Dedeh, A., Ohene, S., & de-Graft Aikins, A. (1997). *Implementing a community alcohol programme in Ghana: An investigative and intervention study of the prevalence and consequences of pito drinking in the Upper West Region*. Accra, Ghana: Danida.

Pan, L. (1985). *Alcohol in colonial Africa*. Uppsala, Sweden: Scandinavian Institute of African Studies.

Chapter 11

Promoting Pleasure and Public Health: An Innovative Initiative

Jean-Paul David

This chapter offers a case study as an example of how partnerships can be forged to use pleasure in the promotion of wine from a public health perspective.

VIN-SANTÉ-PLAISIR DE VIVRE

Vin-Santé-Plaisir de Vivre is an initiative of French wine producers and their trade associations. The idea of promoting wine from a public health perspective first was introduced in 1990 at the National Wine Fair of Macon. The idea was well received, and initial meetings were organized during 1990 and 1991 by the economic Junior Chamber International in the Macon region of France to see how pleasure and public health messages might be included in wine promotion.

The timing of the first meeting of Vin-Santé-Plaisir de Vivre presented a political challenge, because it occurred just a month before the French government presented the Loi Evin, new legislation designed to regulate the promotion of alcohol, to the national assembly. The wine producers' trade association responded to this challenge, and the success of the first meeting led to a second one in 1991, Boire, Déboire et Art de Boire (Drinking, Problems, and the Art of Drinking), and then to a third meeting in March 1992. This third meeting, on the topic of love and law, took place during Les Grands Jours de Bourgogne a bi-annual wine trade fair and conference.

Among the topics covered at the third symposium were the mechanisms of excessive behaviors, addiction, and alcoholism, educating the consumer about taste and language associated with taste, and promotion of Èduc'alcool, a social-aspects organization[1] from the Canadian province of Quebec (see David, 1993; Garrier, 1995).

The last meeting of this initiative took place in March 1993 and addressed the ethical implications of the relationship between wine and health under the theme From Prohibition to Balance. Also in 1993, Vin-Santé-Plaisir de Vivre organized the 10th ethics meeting held in Lyon in conjunction with the Association on Health, Ethics, and Freedom (Lery, 1993).

THE SAN FRANCISCO RESOLUTION

Between 1989 and 1993, Vin-Santé-Plaisir de Vivre developed new approaches based on international definitions of health. This 4-year partnership with the wine producers' trade association resulted in the presentation and eventually the adoption of an international resolution by the Office International de la Vigne et du Vin (OIV) in 1993. Named the San Francisco Resolution, this proposal is in keeping with the World Health Organization's European Alcohol Action Plan as defined in Copenhagen in September 1992 (World Health Organization, 1993).

The San Francisco Resolution proposes that:

- further studies be undertaken on the effects of moderate consumption
- OIV member countries encourage individual consumers to avoid dangerous practices involving alcohol
- campaigns to fight the abuse of alcohol concentrate on education rather than exclusively on the reduction of alcohol consumption, and that these campaigns be directed particularly at youth in order to raise awareness of individuals' responsibilities towards themselves and towards society as a whole

Despite some initial skepticism, many public health professionals soon recognized the value of these activities, and in September 1993 the French Department of Health referred to our activities in the journal *Actualités et Dossiers en Santé Publique*. More recently, Vin-Santé-Plaisir de Vivre was made responsible for an intergovernmental report on the topic wine, health and society prepared by the OIV for the Food and Agriculture Organization of the United Nations (David, 1995). The purpose of this report was to review the epidemiological evidence on moderate alcohol consumption and the mechanisms of addiction.

Despite the new and innovative approach this partnership offers, it has proven difficult to extend its activities. Some French health organizations have criticized the approach for not providing concrete prevention programs. The resistance encountered by the partnership has its roots in a number of causes:

- Complexity of the relationships with and among trade associations
- Reluctance among professional health organizations to enter into partnership with the beverage alcohol industry, and at the same time reluctance within the industry to enter into partnership with the public sector or community groups

- Ambiguity of the concept of alcoholism and ambivalence to it by professional associations
- Conflicting economic interests of different sectors of the beverage alcohol industry
- Conflicts between the interests of the beverage alcohol industry and those of public health

Attitudes may be shifting, however. In 1994, the Société Française d'Alcoologie included a discussion of taste education on the program of its annual meeting. More recently, in 1997, the Société Française d'Alcoologie devoted an entire conference to the Alcohol and Pleasure. There appears to be growing recognition within various sectors that a discussion of alcohol and health also can include a discussion of pleasure.

EDUCATIONAL EFFORTS

The proposal to incorporate pleasure and health in the promotion of wine relies heavily on education. These educational services should be provided in conjunction with producers and implemented downstream from the actual sale of alcohol, as so-called after-sales services (David, 1992). These services would include professional training on the industry side to ensure the responsible sale and consumption of alcohol in order to minimize the risk of harm.

Training efforts and after-sales services would be paralleled by education that involves the family and is based on the concept of the individual as a complex being. The synergy achieved between school (i.e., formal education) and the family in this effort must take into account the physiological, psychological, and emotional needs of the individual. Education efforts would be set within the social context of the individual, taking into account culture, social norms and rules, religion, and the individual's need for freedom and happiness. This global approach to human health and contentment may be quite consistent with emergent international definitions of health (see Chapters 4 and 23). A similar framework has been adopted by Éduc'alcool, whose educational policy seeks to explore the historical and cultural contexts of drinking and both disseminate information on the psychological and physiological effects of alcohol and dispell myths related to its consumption (Éduc'alcool, 1998; see also David, 1993).

This approach should not be confused with current advertising efforts by the beverage alcohol industry. Advertising is not education. Any genuine effort at an education campaign must include the following elements:

- Information on the effects of ethanol on the human body, including safe daily consumption levels within the context of a well-balanced diet, taking into consideration both pleasure and moderation
- Education about the savoring and enjoyment of beverages and food (taste education) beginning in early childhood and continuing throughout adulthood

• Education about the mechanisms of abuse and addiction within the context of basic human needs and involving family, friends, and community

Last year, Vin-Santé-Plaisir de Vivre conducted a survey among the French population in the Macon region to determine people's basic knowledge about drinking. The results of the survey suggested that only about 24% of the population know the basics about alcohol. Clearly, much additional education is needed. The challenge is for wine producers and other sectors of the industry to play a role in educating the public.

CIVILIZATION AND ITS DISCONTENTS

When we speak about "permission for pleasure," we also must recognize that there are necessary restraints on humanity's drive to pursue pleasure, or what Freud labeled "the pleasure principle" (Table 11.1). According to Freud, civilization requires that people resolve three dimensions of humanity: the need for love, the need for creativity, and the drive for basic survival requirements such as sustenance, shelter, warmth, and procreation. Three sources of dysfunction that people experience from the failure to successfully resolve these competing needs are failed relationships and isolation, despair or psychological distress, and physical pain or suffering due to the forces of nature.

Among the ways humanity seeks to resolve these competing dimensions of being human are religion and substance use. Although religion represents an apex of civilization, so too have religious excesses created a good deal of human misery. Similarly, seeking personal resolution through substance use has led to addictive excess.

As Freud saw it, both civilization and individual emotional health require the sublimation of individual urges in the service of constructive functioning (Figure 11.1). Recognition of the interdependence of individual desires (singularity) and social connectedness (alterity) allows humans to achieve balance and to avoid addiction. In addition it is this balance that underlies the ethical and moral dimensions of society.

If people fail to communicate appropriately, they often are driven to addiction—or alcoholism—in place of human relationships. They similarly may suffer

Table 11.1 Restraints on the pleasure principle.

Dimensions of humanity	Paths for resolution	Types of dysfunction
Love	Religions	Isolation
Creativity	Substances	Despair/distress
Basic needs (food, shelter, etc.)	Psychological balance	Physical pain/suffering from natural forces

Source. Based in part on Freud (1930/1957).

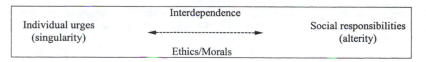

Figure 11.1 Individual urges, society, and ethics. (*Source.* Based in part on Freud, 1930/1957.)

other disorders of excess such as indebtedness, bulimia, promiscuity, violence, and, ultimately, isolation. This is not because of the absence of an effort to communicate as much as because of miscommunication (*incommunicabilité*) (Lejosne & Caussanel, 1993). The opposite of this inability to communicate with others and the resulting excesses and isolation is the ability to love.

The other side of addiction and human relationships is the impact of drug and alcohol excess on those in relationships with addicts or witnessing their behavior. Such victims of the consequences of addiction often react by going to the opposite extreme, towards complete abstinence, just as alcoholics often resolve their own drinking problems by striving to quit drinking altogether. For those in the addict's inner circle, frequently the only choice appears to be either total avoidance of alcohol or unrestrained drinking (Lejosne, 1992). Frequently, it is such people who maintain prohibitionist stances towards alcohol, because they cannot accept emotionally that alcohol can be used constructively.

A more promising approach to prevention is to avoid this artificial dichotomy (see Chapter 26), and instead to inform people of safe and healthy drinking practices. This would begin with the provision of sound medical information on optimal drinking levels (see David, 1995; see also Chapters 12 and 13) and on other alcohol-related topics. A successful prevention program thus will enable young people and others to understand their freedom to make choices and give them guidelines for making such choices.

CONCLUSION

The partnership initiated by the producers of beverage alcohol in Vin-Santé-Plaisir de Vivre represents a novel approach to public health. This approach relies on educating consumers and producers alike so that pleasure and health can be achieved and at the same time the risk for harm from alcohol consumption minimized. The challenge for producers and the public health community is to collaborate as partners and not antagonists in this effort.

NOTE

1. A social aspects organization (SAO) is a national organization funded by the beverage alcohol industry which deals with issues solely concerned with the responsible consumption of alcohol beverages. Although the specific mission of individual SAOs varies depending on the culture of the country in which it operates, SAOs can be distinguished from other organizations such as

trade associations in two respects. First, SAOs are not involved with trade promotion issues; and, second, SAOs are generally intersectoral, i.e., the beverage alcohol companies which fund them have interests across the wine, beer and spirits sectors.

REFERENCES

David, J. P. (1992). Utopie ou défi: Revue des oenologues [Utopia or challenge: Review of oeno-logical studies]. *Vin-Sante-Plaisir de Vivre, 39*, 47–50.

David, J. P. (1993, March). *L'amour et la Loi: De l'usage du vin de la notion d'abus. Débat à propos de l'interdit* [Love and law: Wine drinking in the context of abuse. Debate on the limits of control]. Symposium, Vin-Sante-Plaisir de Vivre.

David, J. P. (1995). Synthesis and conclusions of the intergovernmental group of the FAO on wine consumption and health. *Wine, Health and Society: Bulletin of the Office International de la Vigne et du Vin, 68*, 8–41.

Éduc'alcool. (1998, September 15). *Concrete objectives* [On-line]. Available: http://www.educalcool. qc.ca/concrete.html

French Department of Health. (1993, September). *Repondre aux personnes vivantes avec un problem d'alcohol* [Responding to people living with an alcohol problem]. Actualités et dossiers en Santé publique (Vol. 4, pp. 18–19). Paris: Author.

Freud, S. (1957). *Civilization and its discontents* (J. Riviere, Trans.). London: Hogarth Press and The Institute of Psycho-analysis. (Original work published 1930).

Garrier, G. (1995). *Histoire sociale et culturelle du vin* [The social and cultural history of wine]. Paris: Bordas.

Lery, N. (1993). *Dixième journees d'ethique: Dependence et creativité* [The 10th seminar on ethics: Dependence and creativity]. Lyon, France: Santé, Ethique et Liberté, Hopital du Vinatier.

World Health Organization. (1993). *European Alcohol Action Plan* (EUR/ICP/ADA 035). Copen-hagen, Denmark: WHO, Regional Office for Europe.

Pleasure and Alcohol Cross-Culturally

Jennifer Moyo

A primary issue in the development of alcohol policy is the degree to which ideas developed in Western nations are applicable in developing world contexts. Related to this debate is a further issue: namely, the contrast between a focus on the *amount* of alcohol consumed in different societies and a focus on the *patterns* of consumption in these cultural settings. Despite these issues' central importance, they remain relatively unexamined in the public health and alcohology fields.

1 "Dry" versus "wet" as a cultural distinction. Dwight Heath spoke about the concept of dry cultures, in which little alcohol is consumed overall but in which, when people do drink, they tend to get drunk (e.g., Scandinavian countries). This is not necessarily the case in all dry societies. However, the "dry" model of alcohol use highlights the point that it is not only how much one drinks, but also how one drinks that is important—that is, the importance of patterns of drinking and not just consumption. Once again, the issue of social context in defining how alcohol is used moves to the forefront. Likewise, in defining problems, one needs to examine who is doing the defining. Someone in a given social context may accept its drinking patterns and find them rewarding, even if they are viewed as excessive from outside.

2 Poverty versus pleasure. David Macdonald spoke about use of alcohol in marginalized, impoverished groups. He proposed that alcohol is used to reduce pain rather than to induce pleasure in such settings. Macdonald hypothesized a direct relationship between poverty and excessive use of alcohol. Thus, he surmised, pleasure in relation to alcohol consumption is very specific to cultural context. Following on Macdonald's comments, Louise Nadeau spoke about Canada's Royal Commission on Aboriginal Peoples. The commission had few recommendations on alcohol per se. This was correct, in her view, because alcohol abuse was dwarfed by other problems. Natives themselves saw the issue of autonomy, not alcohol, as primary.

3   The French context: industry and public health collaboration. Jean-Paul David reported on an initiative in France, supported by wine manufacturers, to market wine from a public health perspective. This partnership between public health and manufacturers led in August 1993 to the adoption by the International Wine Organization of its San Francisco Resolution, which was in keeping with the European Regional Office of the World Health Organization's Alcohol Action Plan. The objectives of the European plan against alcoholism include (a) reinforcing practices in the production and distribution sectors that favor the prevention of harm linked to alcohol, (b) creating environments favorable to health that reinforce the motivation and the capacity of the individual to avoid dangerous drinking practices, and (c) encouraging public support of moderate drinking practices through education programs. Some of the elements in the French initiative include, on the industry side, after-sales service and professional training to ensure that alcohol is consumed sensibly leading to as few harms as possible. This is paralleled by education focusing on both the psychological (the needs of the individual) and the physiological (the metabolism of alcohol). The program also engages the entire social context of the individual (for example, looking at the synergy between school and family), part of a larger conception of the individual drinker as a complete human being. In this larger human context, discontents within a society may hinder the satisfactory pursuit of the pleasure principle (perhaps by leading to excessive consumption).

Part Three

Alcohol and Medical, Psychological, and Social Health

This part reviews the range of health benefits that are drawn from moderate consumption of alcohol, and their possible limits in making public health recommendations. Arthur Klatsky provides a general overview of the epidemiological, physiological, and clinical aspects of alcohol's medical benefits. These are primarily caused by reductions in the incidence of coronary heart disease at low to moderate levels of consumption compared with abstinence and create an overall favorable mortality profile for moderate drinkers. However, Klatsky cautions, these results need to be interpreted according to individual medical history and health-risk category.

The primary individual risk group variations that Klatsky identifies are those concerning age and gender interactions, such that women younger than 50 years of age are those least likely to benefit—and most likely to be damaged—by moderate drinking. Carlos Camargo examines the entire range of women's health issues—from heart disease and breast cancer to pregnancy and breast-feeding—for which evidence suggests the possibility of effects of alcohol. Although Camargo indicates that knowledge of alcohol's beneficial effects is likely to enhance pleasurable experiences from drinking, he also notes that most people are not motivated to drink primarily by such benefits.

Ole-Jørgen Skog belongs to a public health tradition that has cautioned against alcohol use and that generally has attempted to control and limit alcohol consumption. In the face of increasing evidence that alcohol conveys health benefits, Skog explores new ground for reservations about alcohol use and for imposing social controls on alcohol and drinking. Among these justifications are the dangers alcohol consumption imposes on others, and the irrational decision making of some individuals and of many or most people under certain circumstances. Finally, Skog addresses a paradox whereby healthy alcohol consumption by individuals may not result in overall health advantages—indeed, quite the opposite—for the society at large.

Finally in this section, Archie Brodsky and Stanton Peele expand the range of benefits associated with moderate alcohol use beyond the standard medical ones into the psychosocial realm. They find substantial evidence that alcohol enhances not just mood and good feelings, but also long-term cognitive functioning. The evidence for the former comes from experimental studies, sociological and anthropological observations, and a host of self-reports of people's motivations for and experiences of drinking. This result therefore seems to have solid footing. Studies of improved cognitive functioning among long-term moderate drinkers (generally the elderly) now have been documented in a series of prospective studies involving a range of populations, and thus this result likewise seems to be robust.

In other areas for which such benefits have been found—including important community studies that have found better mental health and higher salaries among moderate drinkers, along with observations of improved group cohesion and leisure experiences from drinking—results have been less firmly established by modern epidemiological standards. Rather than seeing alcohol to be the cause of the range of benefits claimed, and quite often found, it seems that moderate drinking may be a part of a larger nexus of connecting social, medical, psychological, and lifestyle factors that lead to improved quality of life.

Chapter 12

Is Drinking Healthy?

Arthur L. Klatsky

Beneficial effects from alcohol have been claimed since ancient times. Only in the past 100 years have physicians attempted to define beneficial consumption, and only in the past 20 years has epidemiological research explored the basis, impact, and limits of beneficial alcohol use. This research has established that such benefits occur primarily for coronary disease and are most evident for middle-aged men consuming fewer than three standard drinks daily—for whom they represent a 30% to 40% reduction in relative risk of coronary disease culminating in up to a 10% reduction in overall mortality rate. This benefit varies with individual and group medical risk profiles, occurs mostly through increases in high-density lipids in the blood, and, when graphed, usually take the form of a U- or a J-shaped curve in which mortality and morbidity rates rise sharply at higher consumption levels. Physicians must tailor their recommendations on alcohol to these individual profiles, but such guidelines are difficult to project in a public health context.

DIFFERENTIATING HARMFUL, SAFE, AND BENEFICIAL ALCOHOL DRINKING

Historical Roots of Discovery

In the eloquent terms of Abraham Lincoln in a speech to a temperance society more than 150 years ago, "It is true that many were injured by intoxicating drink, but none seemed to think the injury arose from the use of a bad thing, but from the abuse of a good thing." "Abuse of a good thing" is the key phrase. It seems virtually certain that Mr. Lincoln knew nothing about medical benefits of lighter drinking, but he was perceptive, wise, and brimming with common sense. He enjoyed whiskey as one of life's pleasures. It is best to keep in mind that most people are light or moderate drinkers who choose to drink for nonmedical reasons. Any harm or benefit is incidental.

The medical and social risks of heavier, especially uncontrolled, drinking have been evident for centuries. Also clear has been the relative safety of lighter drinking, leading to serious attempts to define a safe limit. Perhaps the best known such limit has been known for more than 100 years as "Anstie's rule" (Anstie, 1870). Sir Francis Anstie, a distinguished neurologist and public health activist, advised an upper limit of approximately three standard drinks daily. Although this limit was intended to apply primarily to mature men, Anstie emphasized another long-evident aspect of alcohol drinking, namely the individual variation in the ability to handle alcohol. Individual risk-benefit considerations should be a major focus of any discussion.

Philosophic Balance Between "Excess" and "Starvation:" Are These Appropriate Parameters?

In 1926 a Baltimore scientist, Raymond Pearl, became the first investigator (by half a century) to report that light or moderate drinkers were at lower risk of death than abstainers or heavier drinkers. Pearl (1926) described this relationship in a study of 5248 tuberculosis patients and controls. "Heavy/steady" drinkers had the highest mortality rate, "abstainers" were next, and "moderate" drinkers had the lowest mortality rate. Writing during prohibition, Pearl had no biological explanation for his results. His interpretation was appropriately cautious; he concluded that moderate drinking was "not harmful." Perhaps his major contribution was to recognize the fallacy in comparing all drinkers with abstainers, because doing so causes the harmful effects of heavier drinking to mask the apparent benefit of lighter drinking. As an analogy he aptly wrote, "One cannot judge the role of diet by starvation or excess." There has been a strong tendency in the medical literature to attribute the effects of heavier alcohol drinking to *all* drinking. Yet, scientific accuracy requires categorization of drinking when studying health relationships.

The alcohol–mortality rate relationship, graphed as risk of death from abstinence to heavier drinking, is a J-shaped curve (Klatsky, 1995). It nonetheless remains to define the amount of drinking in relation to risk—that is, how much drinking is likely to result in overall benefit and how much is likely to result in overall harm.

THE HEALTH RISKS OF DRINKING ALCOHOL

Health Conditions Associated with Heavier Drinking

Epidemiologic studies have produced compelling evidence of the increased medical risks of heavier drinkers, who are at the highest overall risk of mortality and morbidity when compared to abstainers and moderate drinkers. A multitude of health problems contribute to the increased risks of heavier drinkers. Many, but not all, are noncardiovascular, including liver cirrhosis, accidents, suicide, pancreatitis, gastritis, and certain cancers (Boffetta & Garfinkle, 1990; Klatsky, 1995). There are also cardiovascular conditions related to heavier drinking (Davidson, 1989; Klatsky, 1995), including heart muscle–cell disease or cardiomyopathy (Urbano-Marquez et al., 1989), hypertension or high blood pressure (Klatsky, Friedman, Siegelaub, & Gerard, 1977; Klatsky, Friedman, & Armstrong, 1986; Lian, 1915), heart-rhythm disturbances (Cohen, Klatsky, & Armstrong, 1988), and hemorrhagic stroke (Klatsky, Armstrong, & Friedman, 1989; Van Gign, Stampfer, Wolfe, & Algra, 1993).

Are There Health Risks Associated with Light or Moderate Drinking?

Most of the conditions related to heavier drinking are unrelated in most, but not all studies, to lighter intake of alcohol (Boffetta & Garfinkle, 1990; Klatsky, Armstrong, & Friedman, 1992; Marmot & Brunner, 1991). There are important unresolved questions about the relationships of moderate drinking to risk of female breast cancer, fetal damage in pregnant women, and bowel cancer in both sexes (Friedman & Klatsky, 1993; Hiatt, Klatsky, & Armstrong, 1988; Klatsky, Armstrong, Friedman, & Hiatt, 1988; Klatsky et al., 1992).

In any case, lighter drinking is not risk-free. The most obvious risk is that of addiction. This risk is increased if there is a family history of alcoholism. There is much interest in identifying traits related to risk of alcoholism, including both genetic and environmental factors. It is hoped that the day will come when individuals can be stratified reasonably accurately with respect to risk of uncontrolled drinking.

Benefits of Moderate Drinking

At the same time moderate drinking, compared to abstinence, is associated with lower risk of several medical problems

Coronary Heart Disease   Coronary heart disease (CHD) is, without doubt, the most important of these (Boffetta & Garfinkle, 1990; Jackson, Scragg, & Beaglehole, 1991; Klatsky, 1994; Klatsky, Armstrong, & Friedman, 1990; Klatsky, Friedman, & Armstrong, 1986; Klatsky, Friedman, & Siegelaub, 1974; Klatsky et al., 1992; Marmot & Brunner, 1991; Renaud, Criqui, Farchi, & Veenstra, 1993; Rimm et al., 1991; Stampfer, Colditz, Willett, Speizer, & Hennekens, 1988). CHD is the most common cardiovascular disease and is the single most common cause of death in developed countries. Thus, it has a major impact upon data that lump together all cardiovascular diseases and even has impact upon total mortality data.

Ischemic Stroke   Although less well established than for CHD, moderate drinking probably is associated with lower risk of ischemic stroke (Klatsky et al., 1989; Van Gign et al., 1993), an important cause of injury but with less effect upon total mortality data. To illustrate the complexities of alcohol-health relationships, alcohol apparently *increases* the risk of strokes caused by bleeding (called hemorrhagic strokes) but *decreases* the risk of strokes caused by clots or blockages in blood vessels (Klatsky et al., 1989; Van Gign et al., 1993). The latter (ischemic strokes) are more common but the former are, in general, more serious.

Other Health Benefits   Alcohol drinking decreases the risk of gallstones, a common problem with only minor effect on mortality statistics (Friedman & Klatsky, 1993). Moderate drinking may have other benefits more difficult to measure and with sparser supporting data. Examples are diabetes mellitus and psychiatric problems in older persons (see Chapter 15).

OPERATIONAL DEFINITIONS OF MODERATE AND HEAVY DRINKING

Increased Mortality Rate at More than Three Drinks Per Day

Any discussion of "light," "moderate," or "heavy" drinking must define the terms. All such definitions are intrinsically arbitrary. The definitions used here are based upon the level of drinking in epidemiologic studies above which net harm usually is seen. In many studies, such harm is seen at reported levels of three or more drinks daily. Thus, "lighter" or "moderate" alcohol drinking is used to mean fewer than three drinks per day, and "heavy" or "heavier" alcohol drinking is used to mean three or more drinks per day. This data-based limit is very close to Anstie's commonsense definition.

The composite of these harmful and beneficial effects is often shown as the J-shaped alcohol mortality curve. The heaviest drinkers are at the highest risk because of increased risk for the various conditions already mentioned. The lighter drinkers are at the lowest risk, essentially because of lower CHD mortality. The abstainers are at intermediate risk. Figure 12.1 shows a diagrammatic representation of such a J-curve, derived from Kaiser Permanente studies (Klatsby, Armstrong, & Friedman, 1992; Klatsby, 1994, 1995).

Can Lower and Upper Limits for Benefit Be Well Defined?

Precise limits cannot be defined for several reasons inherent in epidemiologic studies of alcohol drinking and health. Among a number of potential problems, several stand out

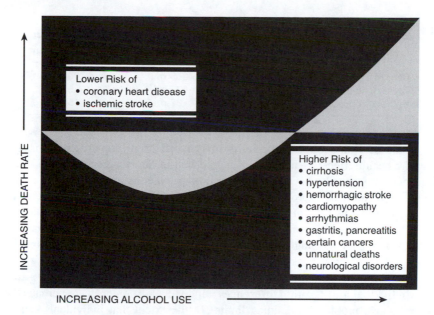

INCREASING DEATH RATE

Lower Risk of
• coronary heart disease
• ischemic stroke

Higher Risk of
• cirrhosis
• hypertension
• hemorrhagic stroke
• cardiomyopathy
• arrhythmias
• gastritis, pancreatitis
• certain cancers
• unnatural deaths
• neurological disorders

INCREASING ALCOHOL USE

Figure 12.1 The J-shaped curve that relates deaths from all causes to alcohol consumption. The J-shaped curve exists primarily because of a reduction in coronary heart disease risk with moderate alcohol use. A major problem with interpreting and applying the curve is that to the extent alcohol consumption is underreported, the threshold of adverse effects appears to be lowered.

Drinking Pattern   In epidemiologic studies a steady habit, rather than a spree pattern, usually is assumed. This is an issue because a binge pattern of drinking is likely to be harmful.

Underreporting of Drinking   In data based upon surveys, systematic "underestimation" (lying) probably tends to lower the apparent threshold for harmful alcohol effects because heavier drinkers appear to be lighter imbibers than they are. There seems no plausible hypothesis for how such underreporting of drinks would lead to assuming a spurious relationship between apparent benefit and light drinking.

Size of Drinks   Because people think in terms of "drinks," not milliliters or grams of alcohol, it is necessary to inquire about habits in such terms and probably also best to describe alcohol relations in terms of drinks per day or week. Fortunately, the amount of alcohol in a standard-sized drink of wine (about 120 mL), liquor (about 37 mL), or beer (about 355 mL) is approximately the same (Table 12.1). A corollary is that clinicians and others always must remember the importance of defining the size of drinks.

Table 12.1 Amount of alcohol per "drink."

Beverage (strength)	Measure	Volume	Alcohol content
Beer (4%)	Can	355 mL	14 mL
Table wine (12.5%)	Glass	120 mL	14.5 mL
Spirits (80 proof)	Jigger	37 mL	15 mL

Role of Nonalcohol Ingredients in Benefits from Beverages Possible specific health effects of nonalcohol ingredients in beverage types (wine, beer, liquor) or in particular beverages represent other potential explanations (or confounding factors) in interpreting these data. Any such apparent differences (as we shall see in the case of wine) also could be caused by personal (or cultural) traits associated with specific beverages, or by drinking pattern differences, as well as by nonalcohol ingredients (Klatsky, Armstrong, & Kipp, 1990; Renaud et al., 1993; Rimm, Klatsky, Grobbee, & Stampfer, 1996).

Individual and Group Differences Individual differences are perhaps the largest single problem in defining limits. To the extent that individuals can be subgrouped usefully, some of these differences in relation to benefits and harms from drinking have been identified.

Gender, Age, and Other Factors Affecting Limit Definitions

It is clear in defining limits that no possible definition is applicable to all persons. Any definition must be qualified so that it allows expressly for individual and group variability in susceptibility to harmful and beneficial effects of alcohol.

Gender Women, because of their smaller size, greater proportion of body fat, and less efficient metabolism of alcohol in the stomach, are generally more susceptible to adverse effects of alcohol (Klatsky et al., 1992; see also Chapters 13 and 22). Women also have specific risks not applicable to men such as breast cancer (Hiatt et al., 1988) and damage to unborn fetuses. Thus, if generalizations must be made, women probably merit a lower "safe" limit for drinking. It is, however, possible that women also enjoy benefits at lighter drinking levels than men (Fuchs et al., 1995; Klatsky et al., 1992).

Age Young persons of both sexes seem to be at higher risk of accidents after lighter drinking than their elders (Klatsky et al., 1992). It is also evident that young persons, at least in the short-term future, obtain less CHD benefit.

Ethnic and Cultural Differences Ethnic and cultural differences in drinking behavior (see Part 2) also may have parallels in differential health risks.

Perhaps drinking patterns express or lead to some of these risks. Other ethnic differences in risks may be biological. This area requires more research.

HAS A BENEFICIAL HEALTH EFFECT FROM LIGHTER DRINKING BEEN ESTABLISHED?

How Well Established is Alcohol's Effect in Reducing CHD Risk?

How well alcohol has been established to yield health benefits depends primarily on the case for a protective effect of alcohol drinking against CHD, because this is the condition for which the evidence of benefit is strongest and because CHD is the most prevalent form of heart disease in developed countries.

The basis of CHD is atherosclerotic narrowing of the coronary arteries, the blood vessels that nourish the heart. The atherosclerotic plaques develop over many years through deposition of fatty and other substances in the linings of the arteries. Problems are caused both by the narrowing of the blood vessels and a tendency for clots to form in narrowed vessels. The established risk factors, identified primarily by prospective population studies, include cigarette smoking, high blood pressure, diabetes mellitus, high levels of low-density lipoprotein (LDL) cholesterol, and low levels of high-density lipoprotein (HDL) cholesterol. There are other less-established risk factors such as other blood lipid components, blood clotting components, homocysteine, blood-vessel lining (endothelial) factors, and, possibly, stress or psychological traits. Other predictors, such as gender and physical activity, most likely operate largely through the established risk factors.

CHD usually progresses without symptoms for years. If clinical problems occur, common manifestations include (a) distress known as angina pectoris; (b) sudden damage to the heart muscle, usually caused by a clot in a narrow vessel (acute myocardial infarction or "heart attack"); and (c) sudden death, usually caused by acute myocardial infarction or certain abrupt arrthythmias.

Satisfaction of Criteria for a Causal CHD Protective Effect

Forms and Symptoms of CHD   Angina pectoris is a common symptom but is subjective and does not readily lend itself to epidemiologic study. Relief of angina by drinking has long been known (Heberden, 1786). Available evidence suggests that this relief is purely subjective. The ischemia persists but is not perceived (Orlando, Aronow, Cassidy, & Prakash, 1976). The data suggest that it is probably dangerous to drink before or during physical exercise. It is not wise to run a marathon while drinking beer.

Acute myocardial infarction and sudden cardiac death are clearly definable events, and both have been extensively studied. Data showing that major coronary events are more likely to develop in abstainers than in alcohol drinkers include international comparisons, time-trend analyses, arteriographic studies, case-control studies, and a number of prospective population studies (Klatsky, 1995; Renaud et al., 1993). Most hospitalization studies show heavier drinkers at similar or lower risk than lighter drinkers. Several population studies using death as an end-point also show a progressive inverse relation with amount of alcohol consumption, but others show a U-shaped curve. Studies of sudden cardiac death, caused mostly by CHD, also show an inverse relation to alcohol use.

Establishing the Benefits of Light Drinking for CHD   The overall problems associated with alcohol inevitably give rise to skepticism, no matter how many studies show a possible beneficial effect of alcohol drinking. The most plausible controversy is based on the thesis that correlates of abstinence and lighter drinking could explain the higher risk of abstainers. For example, one much-publicized hypothesis (the "sick quitter" hypothesis) suggested that movement of persons at high CHD risk into the "abstainer referent group" could explain apparent protection (Shaper, Wannamethee, & Walker, 1988). This hypothesis has been substantially resolved by studies that separate lifelong abstainers from past drinkers and that control for baseline disease or risk (Klatsky, 1995; Renaud et al., 1993).

CHD and Overall Mortality-Rate Benefits

Nurses Health Study   The Nurses Health Study, a large prospective study among women free of baseline CHD, showed a progressive inverse relation of alcohol use to major coronary events, independent of prior reduction in alcohol intake and with detailed control for nutrient intake (Stampfer et al., 1988). The relative risk of CHD among women reporting ingestion of more than 25 g of alcohol daily was 0.4. An analysis of total mortality rate showed that net beneficial effects of moderate alcohol use in women were limited by adverse effects except for women who were at above-average coronary risk (largely those older than 50 years of age).

American Cancer Society Study   The American Cancer Society Study, a large prospective study in men, confirmed the lower relative risk for CHD of drinkers, independent of confounders or baseline disease (Boffetta & Garfinkle, 1990). Coronary mortality rate took the form of a U-curve in relationship to drinking, with a relative risk of 0.8 (versus abstainers) at one or two drinks per day.

Kaiser Permanente Research   The most recent Kaiser Permanente study of hospitalizations in California showed that former drinkers and infrequent drinkers were at levels of risk similar to that of lifelong abstainers; subsets of

Table 12.2   Relative risk[a] for coronary heart disease according to alcohol use.

Alcohol-use category	Hospitalization[b] (N = 756)		Death[c] (N = 600)	
	RR	95% CI	RR	95% CI
Nondrinkers				
Lifelong (reference)	1.0	—	1.0	(—)
Ex-drinkers	1.0	0.7, 1.4	1.0	(0.8, 1.4)
Drinkers				
<1 drink/mo	0.9	0.7, 1.2	0.9	(0.8, 1.2)
<1 drink/d, >1 drink/mo	0.7[d]	0.5, 0.8	0.8	(0.6, 1.0)
1–2 drinks/d	0.6[d]	0.4, 0.8	0.7[d]	(0.6, 0.9)
3–5 drinks/d	0.6[d]	0.4, 0.8	0.6[e]	(0.6, 0.9)
>6 drinks/d	0.6	0.2, 1.1	0.8	(0.5, 1.4)

[a]Computed from coefficients estimated by Cox proportional hazards models with 8 covariates, including age, sex, race, body mass index, cigarette smoking, education, marital status, and baseline coronary heart disease symptoms/risk.
[b]Data from "Relations of alcoholic beverage use to subsequent coronary artery disease hospitalizations," by A. L. Klatsky, M. A. Armstrong, and G. D. Armstrong, 1986, *American Journal of Cardiology, 58*, 710–714.
[c]Data from "Risk of cardiovascular mortality in alcohol drinkers, exdrinkers, and non-drinkers," by A. L. Klatsky, M. A. Armstrong, and G. D. Friedman, 1990, *American Journal of Cardiology, 66*, 1237–1242.
[d]$p < .001$.
[e]$p < .01$.
Note. RR = relative risk; CI = confidence interval.

these groups free of coronary risk or symptoms showed similar relationships (Klatsky, Armstrong, & Friedman, 1986). Lower risk of CHD hospitalization exist for all drinkers, without the U-shaped curve, controlled for a number of potential confounders. For mortality, there was a slight U-shaped curve, with a nadir relative risk at one to five drinks per day (Klatsky, Armstrong, & Friedman, 1990). Table 12.2 summarizes these data.

Other studies reinforce these findings. There has been remarkable consistency in prospective population studies in terms of the lower coronary risk of moderate drinkers.

The Improbability of Mounting Potential Randomized Clinical Trials

The ideal method of studying the risk of primary development of CHD in relationship to lighter alcohol drinking would be a clinical trial, with randomized assignment of eligible, willing persons to abstinence and various levels (and beverage types) of lighter alcohol drinking. The long-term nature of the consequences of CHD mean that such a trial would require complete cooperation over many years, possibly decades. Large numbers of subjects would be needed and the cost would be great. It seems extremely unlikely that such an experiment actually could be done, even for study of secondary prevention of CHD events, that is, myocardial infarction and death after CHD first is evident. Prospective population studies, in which individuals disclose their habits before CHD is evident, probably provide the best data we will ever have.

Plausible Biologic Mechanisms for Alcohol's Protective Effect with CHD

HDL Cholesterol   There are plausible mechanisms by which alcohol drinking might protect against CHD. Best established is a link via HDL cholesterol (Gaziano et al.,1993; Klatsky, 1995; Renaud et al., 1993). The inverse relationship of HDL cholesterol level with coronary risk is well established. In a number of studies alcohol has been shown to raise HDL concentration. Several studies also show a favorable effect upon apoprotein AI and apoprotein AII, which are involved in HDL-particle formation in the liver, but a precise biochemical mechanism for alcohol's effect on HDL cholesterol has not yet been worked out. The hypothesis that the coronary protective effect of alcohol is mediated by higher HDL cholesterol levels in drinkers has been examined quantitatively in three separate studies (Criqui et al., 1987; Gaziano et al., 1993; Suh, Shaten, Cutler, & Kuller, 1992). All three yielded similar findings, suggesting that higher HDL levels in drinkers explained about half of the lower risk. One of these studies (Gaziano et al., 1993) suggests that both major HDL subspecies (HDL2 and HDL3) are involved. HDL3 may be more strongly related to lighter alcohol intake but is probably related as strongly as HDL2 to lower CHD risk.

Anticlotting Effects   Data about antithrombotic (anticlotting) effects of alcohol, another possible protective mechanism, are, so far, less solid (Gaziano et al., 1993; Klatsky, 1995; Renaud et al., 1993). Blood clotting is a complex process; one key component is the tendency for blood platelets to stick together and act as a nidus for clot formation in arteries. Some data support acute antiplatelet aggregatory effects of alcohol, but with a rebound several hours later. Reports of a chronic antiplatelet aggregatory effect, if confirmed, could partially explain lower risk for CHD. Other features of the blood-clotting process also may be affected by alcohol. There are conflicting data that suggest that alcohol lowers blood fibrinogen levels and enhances spontaneous fibrinolysis of blood clots. Thus, multiple mechanisms may play a role in any anticlotting effects of alcohol and may supplement alcohol's beneficial effect caused by the rise in elevation of HDL levels.

The Beverage Type Controversy (the "French Paradox")

Do red wine drinkers fare best in terms of CHD? There are plausible bases for such a hypothesis:

    1 Wine drinkers have the most favorable risk traits for CHD.

    2 The usual pattern of wine consumption, slowly and with meals, may be more protective than the usual patterns of drinking for liquor or beer.

    3 Nonalcohol antioxidant compounds and antithrombotic substances occur in wine, especially in red wine (Gaziano et al., 1993; Klatsky, 1995; Renaud & de Lorgeril, 1992; Renaud et al., 1993). Oxidation of LDL cholesterol plays a role in formation of atherosclerotic lesions. Diets high in antioxidant substances seem to be associated with lower CHD risk, although clinical data on antioxidant supplements remain inconclusive (Hoffman & Garewal, 1995).

The best evidence that wine may be more protective against CHD than beer or liquor comes from international comparison studies of CHD mortality rates (Criqui & Ringel, 1994; Peele, 1997; St. Leger, Cochrane, & Moore, 1979). In these studies, countries in which wine is the preponderant alcoholic beverage have lower CHD mortality rates than beer- or spirits-drinking countries. The "French paradox" has arisen from these data; it derives from the fact that France tends to be an outlier on graphs plotting dietary fat intake against coronary mortality, unless their data are adjusted for wine-alcohol intake. These studies are valuable and provocative, but there are interpretive problems in international comparisons (Rimm et al., 1996):

    1 Drinking patterns are not measured and controlled in these studies, and these patterns could be related to use of different beverages, particularly binge drinking.

    2 International comparisons deal with averages, making it hard to adjust for associated traits, such as smoking, because of lack of data about individuals.

    3 The studies are limited to mortality data; there are no standardized morbidity statistics, and some have questioned the possible effect of international differences in mortality standardization.

Prospective population studies do not provide the basis for a consensus that wine or any other form of beverage alcohol confers additional benefits (Rimm et al., 1996). Various studies show benefit for wine, beer, liquor, or all three major beverage types. In Kaiser Permanente studies, subjects consuming all three major beverage types show evidence of CHD protection relative to abstainers (Klatsky & Armstrong, 1993; Klatsky, Armstrong, & Friedman, 1986, 1990, 1997). In these studies, among those drinkers whose habits indicated a clear preference for one beverage type, both the beer and wine drinkers had lower risk than liquor drinkers for both fatal and nonfatal CHD, drinkers of red and nonred wine faring equally well. However, the wine drinkers had the most favorable coronary-risk profile and the liquor drinkers had the least favorable CHD risk traits, so that for these groups beverage choice cannot be established as the explanation for their differential CHD risk.

Strength of Possible Protective Effect

Reduction of CHD Risk by Light or Moderate Drinking   In most epidemiologic studies the reduced CHD risk for fatal or nonfatal events is about 30% to 40% if lighter drinkers are compared with abstainers. This lower risk is seen at levels of drinking well below one or two drinks per day in some studies, but the optimal drinking level for CHD risk varies from study to study. An apparent risk reduction of this magnitude is not considered large by epidemiologists, because it could be caused by indirect factors related to drinking or CHD. However, no such indirect explanation has been found, despite diligent searches conducted for more than two decades. If causal, a reduction of risk of this magnitude caused by alcohol is quite meaningful clinically and is greater than the impact of many interventions used in managing CHD patients.

Reduction of Total Mortality Risk by Light or Moderate Drinking   Because CHD is the only major factor in lowering total risk of death for lighter drinkers and CHD causes about 30% of deaths in most developed countries, the overall reduction in mortality rate associated with light or moderate drinking is probably 10% or less. Although that percentage is quite meaningful in total numbers of deaths, large population studies are needed to produce statistically significant data in this area. Several studies do show just such numbers.

ADVICE TO THE PUBLIC

Clinical Individual Risk-Benefit Considerations

In considering public health aspects of alcohol use, the major problems of heavier drinking remain of paramount concern (Friedman et al., 1993; Pearson & Terry, 1994). Because increased medical risks predominate among heavier drinkers, any potential coronary benefit is more than outweighed by these problems. All heavier drinkers should reduce their intake or abstain. The drinking habit of established lighter drinkers—the majority of U. S. adults—carries the lowest CHD and overall risk, and most such persons should be encouraged to make no change (Friedman et al., 1993; Pearson & Terry, 1994). Promotion of abstinence by lighter drinkers at substantial CHD risk seems inadvisable in view of the epidemiologic data. Concern about risks of drinking makes it inappropriate to *indiscriminately* advise nondrinkers to drink for health benefit, but *individual* exceptions can be made, based upon age, sex, personal and family history of problem drinking, and risk of CHD, certain cancers (most notably female breast cancer), and other medical problems. Such exceptions require the advising health professional to have personal knowledge of his or her client.

To illustrate the preferred approach, four examples of individuals who might seek advice about alcohol drinking and health are considered, with the author's opinion about advice:

A 30-year-old woman with a healthy lifestyle, no major CHD risk traits, a mother who has breast cancer, and with no current plans to become pregnant but the intention to abstain if she does. This person is at very low risk of CHD for at least 20 years. The long-term risk of breast cancer related to lighter drinking is unknown. She should be advised of the unproven possibility that even lighter drinking might increase this risk. She should be advised that—from the health risk viewpoint—she is probably best off to abstain from alcohol or, at most, to take an average of less than one drink daily.

A 49-year-old man who has had a myocardial infarction and says he has "gone clean:" Specifically, he has given up smoking, eliminated fat from his diet, lost weight, taken up regular exercise, and—although he was never a heavy drinker nor had alcohol-related problems—given up his daily one to two beers per day custom in the belief that this was harmful. With respect to his beer drinking this man made a mistake or was not well advised. He should be told to resume his beer drinking (no more than two 12-oz cans or bottles per day), but to allow for the calories (i.e., reduce the amount of some dietary item). For CHD protection lighter drinking is, of course, only a small part of the picture; control of high blood pressure, blood lipid abnormalities, and diabetes, not smoking, proper diet and exercise, and all the other established preventive measures always need to be emphasized.

A 57-year-old post-menopausal woman with a strong family history of CHD, no family or personal history of alcohol problems, a healthy lifestyle, a border-line positive exercise electrocardiographic test, and low HDL cholesterol, who drinks alcohol infrequently (on special occasions only) but likes wine. This woman is at high risk of a CHD event over the next 5 to 10 years. In conjunction with all other preventive measures, she should be advised that drinking a glass of wine (red or white) daily with dinner would be likely to reduce her risk of CHD or result in later appearance of the condition. In such an instance, drinking carries far more likelihood of benefit than harm.

A 65-year-old man who has CHD (history of angina; has had a coronary bypass operation), and a moderate elevation of LDL cholesterol, is lax about his low-fat diet, is 25 lb overweight, has never had a diagnosed alcohol problem, and has "about three or four" double martinis most days ("it's too much, but it relaxes me and is good for my heart"). This heavy-drinking man has a high risk of future alcohol problems (both cardiovascular and noncardiovascular) and of further CHD events, including sudden death. In addition to losing weight and improving his lifestyle, he needs to sharply reduce his drinking to no more than one or two standard-sized drinks daily (even assuming no underestimation, his report of three or four "doubles" is the equivalent of six to eight standard-sized drinks). Reducing his alcohol intake also would help him to lose weight. If he can control his drinking only with total abstinence, he should abstain.

Public Health Pronouncements Are More Problematic

It is easier for a practitioner to advise an individual about his or her personal risk-benefit balance concerning alcohol drinking than to formulate public health pronouncements. The latter, however, are requested by the public in developed countries and thus are necessary.

The data on CHD protection afforded by moderate drinking have been taken into account by recent governmental guidelines advising the public. The U.S. Department of Agriculture/Department of Health and Human Services 1995 Dietary Guidelines, released in January 1996, included the statement, "Current evidence suggests that moderate drinking is associated with a lower risk for CHD in some individuals." The guidelines concluded with this advice: "If you drink alcoholic beverages, do so in moderation, with meals, and when consumption does not put you or others at risk." Moderation is defined as up to two drinks daily for men and one for women. The most recent U.K. Department of Health Report, *Sensible Drinking* (1995), goes even further, suggesting that a "maximum health advantage" is offered by one to two daily units (small drinks) and that persons in age groups with substantial CHD risk may want "to consider the possible benefits of lighter drinking." The U.K. statements, not surprisingly, caused considerable controversy.

CONCLUSION

Alcohol's cardioprotective effect, caused by a reduction in risk of CHD, is virtually established because it satisfies several important epidemiologic criteria for causality, including consistency in studies and biological plausibility. CHD benefit seems clearest for light to moderate drinking and overall benefit, such as longer life expectancy, is seen only for these drinkers. The benefits from such drinking vary depending on the individual's medical risk profile but represent a 30% to 40% reduction in risk of heart disease for middle-aged men and for women older than 50 years of age at one to two drinks daily, creating perhaps a 10% reduction in total mortality risk. Differences in risk-benefit ratios because of age, gender, and risk-factor profiles require that recommendations be individualized for drinkers. The wine/liquor/beer issue is unresolved at this time. It seems likely that ethyl alcohol is the major factor with respect to lower CHD risk and that the primary operative mechanism is increased HDL cholesterol.

Now that the case for benefit of lighter drinking for many persons has become compelling, it seems as inadvisable to promote general abstinence as to advise the entire population to drink. Much of the public closely follows media reports of scientific study findings and no longer believes oversimplified messages. Hopefully, we have entered an era in which historically established precepts, current governmental guidelines, and scientific evidence have converged into a balanced view of moderate drinking with a reasonable, rational concept of sensible limits for individuals. Health practitioners and public health officials have an obligation to objectively present the entire picture. In the words of Lincoln, who was paraphrasing New Testament scripture for another purpose: "Tell the people the truth and the country will be free.

REFERENCES

Anstie, F. E. (1870). *On the uses of wines in health and disease*. New York: JS Redfield.

Boffetta, P., & Garfinkle, A. (1990). Alcohol drinking and mortality among men enrolled in an American Cancer Society prospective study. *Epidemiology, 1*, 342–348.

Cohen, E. J., Klatsky, A. L., & Armstrong, M. A. (1988). Alcohol use and supraventricular arrhythmia. *American Journal of Cardiology, 62*, 971–973.

Criqui, M. H., Cowan, L. D., Tyroler, H. A., Bangdiwala, S., Heiss G., Wallace R. B., & Cohn, R. (1987). Lipoproteins as mediators for the effects of alcohol consumption and cigarette smoking on cardiovascular mortality: Results from the Lipid Research Clinics Follow up Study. *American Journal of Epidemiology, 126*, 629–637.

Criqui, M. H., & Ringel, B. L. (1994). Does diet or alcohol explain the French paradox? *Lancet, 344*, 1719–1723.

Davidson, D. M. (1989). Cardiovascular effects of alcohol. *Western Journal of Medicine, 151*, 430–439.

Department of Health and Social Security. (1995). *Sensible drinking: The report of an inter-departmental working group*. London: Her Majesty's Stationery Office.

Friedman, G. D., & Klatsky, A. L. (1993). Is alcohol good for your health? *New England Journal of Medicine, 329*, 1882–1883.

Fuchs, C. S., Stampfer M. J., Colditz, G. A., Giovannucci, E. L., Manson, J. E., Kawachi, I., Hunter, D. J., Hankinson S. E., Hennekens, C. H., & Rosner, B. (1995). Alcohol consumption and mortality among women. *New England Journal of Medicine, 332*, 1245–1250.

Gaziano, J. M., Buring, J. E., Breslow, J. L., Goldhaber, S. Z., Rosner, B., VanDenburgh, M., Willett, W., & Hennekens, C. H. (1993). Moderate alcohol intake, increased levels of high density lipoprotein and its subfractions, and decreased risk of myocardial infarction. *New England Journal of Medicine, 329*, 1829–1834.

Heberden, W. (1786). Some account of a disorder of the breast. *Medical Transactions Royal College of Physicians (London), 2*, 59–67.

Hiatt, R. A., Klatsky, A. L., & Armstrong, M. A. (1988). Alcohol consumption and the risk of breast cancer in a prepaid health plan. *Cancer Research, 48*, 2284–2287.

Hoffman, R. M., & Garewal, H. S. (1995). Antioxidants and the prevention of coronary heart disease. *Archives of Internal Medicine, 155*, 241–246.

Jackson, R., Scragg, R., & Beaglehole, R. (1991). Alcohol consumption and risk of coronary heart disease. *British Medical Journal, 303*, 211–216.

Klatsky, A. L. (1994). Epidemiology of coronary heart disease: Influence of alcohol. *Alcohol Clinical Experimental Research, 18*, 88–96.

Klatsky, A. L. (1995). Cardiovascular effects of alcohol. *Scientific American Science and Medicine, 2*, 28–37.

Klatsky, A. L., & Armstrong, M. A. (1993). Alcoholic beverage choice and risk of coronary artery disease mortality: Do red wine drinkers fare best? *American Journal of Cardiology, 71*, 467–469.

Klatsky, A. L., Armstrong, M. A., & Friedman, G. D. (1986). Relations of alcoholic beverage use to subsequent coronary artery disease hospitalizations. *American Journal of Cardiology, 58*, 710–714.

Klatsky, A. L., Armstrong, M. A., & Friedman, G. D. (1989). Alcohol use and subsequent cerebrovascular disease hospitalizations. *Stroke, 70*, 741–746.

Klatsky, A. L., Armstrong, M. A., & Friedman, G. D. (1990). Risk of cardiovascular mortality in alcohol drinkers, exdrinkers, and non-drinkers. *American Journal of Cardiology, 66*, 1237–1242.

Klatsky, A. L., Armstrong, M. A., & Friedman, G. D. (1992). Alcohol and mortality. *Annals of Internal Medicine, 117*, 646–654.

Klatsky, A. L., Armstrong, M. A., & Friedman, G. D. (1997). Red wine, white wine, liquor, beer, and risk for coronary artery disease hospitalization. *American Journal of Cardiology, 80*, 416–420.

Klatsky, A. L., Armstrong, M. A., Friedman, G. D., & Hiatt, R. A. (1988). The relations of alcoholic beverage use to colon and rectal cancer. *American Journal of Epidemiology, 128,* 1007–1015.

Klatsky, A. L., Armstrong, M. A., & Kipp, H. (1990). Correlates of alcoholic beverage preference: Traits of persons who choose wine, liquor or beer. *British Journal of Addiction, 85,* 1279–1289.

Klatsky, A. L., Friedman, G. D., & Armstrong, M. A. (1986). The relationship between alcoholic beverage use and other traits to blood pressure: A new Kaiser Permanente study. *Circulation, 73,* 628–636.

Klatsky, A. L., Friedman, G. D., & Siegelaub, A. B. (1974). Alcohol consumption before myocardial infarction: Results from the Kaiser-Permanente epidemiologic study of myocardial infarction. *Annals Internal Medicine, 81,* 294–301.

Klatsky, A. L., Friedman, G. D., Siegelaub, A. B., & Gerard, M. J. (1977). Alcohol consumption and blood pressure. *New England Journal of Medicine, 296,* 1194–2000.

Lian, C. (1915). L'alcoholisme: Cause d'hypertension artérielle [Alcoholism: Cause of arterial hypertension]. *Bulletin de l'Académie Nationale de Medicine (Paris), 74,* 525–528.

Marmot, M., & Brunner, E. (1991). Alcohol and cardiovascular disease: The status of the U-shaped curve. *British Medical Journal, 303,* 365–368.

Orlando, J., Aronow, W. S., Cassidy, J., & Prakash, R. (1976). Effect of ethanol on angina pectoris. *Annals of Internal Medicine, 84,* 652–655.

Pearl, R. (1926). *Alcohol and longevity.* New York: Knopf.

Pearson, T. A., & Terry, P. (1994). What to advise patients about drinking alcohol. *Journal of the American Medical Association, 272,* 957–958.

Peele, S. (1997). Utilizing culture and behavior in epidemiological models of alcohol consumption and consequences for Western nations. *Alcohol and Alcoholism, 32,* 51–64.

Renaud, S. C., Criqui, M. H., Farchi, G., & Veenstra, J. (1993). Alcohol drinking and coronary heart disease. In P. M. Verschuren (Ed.), *Health Issues Related to Alcohol Consumption* (pp. 81–124). Washington, DC: ILSI Press.

Renaud, S. C., & de Lorgeril, M. (1992). Wine, alcohol, platelets, and the French paradox for coronary heart disease. *Lancet, 339,* 1523–1526.

Rimm, E. B., Giovannucci, E. L., Willett, W. C., Colditz, G. A., Ascherio, A., Rosner, B., & Stampfer, M. J. (1991). Prospective study of alcohol consumption and risk of coronary heart disease in men. *Lancet, 338,* 464–468.

Rimm, E., Klatsky, A. L., Grobbee, D., & Stampfer, M. J. (1996). Review of moderate alcohol consumption and reduced risk of coronary heart disease: Is the effect due to beer, wine, or spirits? *British Medical Journal, 312,* 731–736.

Shaper, A. G., Wannamethee, G., & Walker, M. (1988). Alcohol and mortality in British men: Explaining the U-shaped curve. *Lancet, ii,* 1267–1273.

Stampfer, M. J., Colditz, G. A., Willett, W. C., Speizer, F. E., & Hennekens, C. H. (1988). Prospective study of moderate alcohol consumption and the risk of coronary disease and stroke in women. *New England Journal of Medicine, 319,* 267–273.

St. Leger, A. S., Cochrane, A. L., & Moore, F. (1979). Factors associated with cardiac mortality in developed countries with particular reference to consumption of wine. *Lancet, i,* 1017–1020.

Suh, I., Shaten, J., Cutler, J. A., & Kuller, K. H. (1992). Alcohol use and mortality from coronary heart disease: The role of high-density-lipoprotein cholesterol. *Annals of Internal Medicine, 116,* 881–887.

U.S. Department of Agriculture/Department of Health and Human Services. (1995). *Nutrition and your health: Dietary guidelines for Americans* (4th Ed.). Washington, DC: Goverment Printing Office.

Urbano-Marquez, A., Estruch, R., Navarro-Lopez, F., Grau, J. M., Mont, L., & Rubin, E. (1989). The effects of alcoholism on skeletal and cardiac muscle. *New England Journal of Medicine, 320,* 409–415.

Van Gign, J., Stampfer, M. J., Wolfe, C., & Algra, A. (1993). The association between alcohol consumption and stroke. In P. M. Verschuren (Ed.), *Health Issues Related to Alcohol Consumption* (pp. 43–80). Washington, DC: ILSI Press.

Chapter 13

Gender Differences in the Health Effects of Moderate Alcohol Consumption

Carlos A. Camargo, Jr.

Klatsky (Chapter 12) has provided an overview of the cardioprotective and potential mortality benefits from moderate alcohol consumption in which he emphasizes the need for differential recommendations according to individual characteristics. One drinker characteristic that has received increasing attention in the alcohol literature is gender (Plant, 1997; Wilsnack & Wilsnack, 1997). There is abundant evidence that, compared with men, women drink alcohol less frequently, in smaller quantities, and with lower risk of alcohol-related problems (Fillmore et al., 1997). The historical and sociological aspects of this gender difference are discussed by Nadeau (Chapter 22). The purpose of the present chapter is to summarize some biomedical aspects of this gender difference. The chapter first addresses gender-specific guidelines for moderate alcohol consumption and then points to gender differences in alcohol metabolism and distribution that help explain this gender-specific approach. Potential health risks and benefits of moderate drinking are assessed, with particular attention to several gender-related topics. These include reproductive issues, such as infertility, pregnancy, and breast feeding, and the risk of breast cancer.

MODERATE DRINKING AND PUBLIC HEALTH

In a health-conscious society, awareness of the health effects of alcohol use undoubtedly influences the pleasure of drinking. For much of this century, al-

157

cohol consumption has been viewed in the United States as an unhealthy, even immoral, behavior (Peele, 1993). Indeed, government reports regularly point to alcohol use as a major cause of premature morbidity and mortality, a view that has led to the adoption of reduced national alcohol consumption as a public health goal (National Institute on Alcohol Abuse and Alcoholism, 1997; World Health Organization, 1993). Given this viewpoint, it is not surprising that recent media attention to moderate drinkers' decreased risk of myocardial infarction (MI) has been well received by those who choose to drink.

The cardiac benefits of moderate drinking have caused confusion in the general population, however, because this development appears to contradict evidence that alcohol is a public health problem. This "inconsistency" stems from the numerous and complex health effects of alcohol (especially at different doses), and the complex interaction between these effects and specific character-istics of each drinker (e.g., age, gender, and medical history). Put another way, alcohol-related health benefits (e.g., decreased risk of MI) are of considerable importance for some drinkers, such as middle-aged men at high risk of MI, but of little consequence for others, including adolescents at low risk of MI. Like-wise, alcohol-related hazards are of varying importance according to the specific characteristics of the individual drinker. A better understanding of the net health effect for individual drinkers would facilitate health promotion efforts and could have an important influence on the pleasure of drinking.

GENDER-SPECIFIC GUIDELINES

"Moderate" drinking refers to alcohol consumption that generally does not cause problems for either the drinker or society (National Institute on Alcohol Abuse and Alcoholism, 1992). This construct differs considerably from drinking pat-terns that are accepted by the society in which they occur but that are not necessarily of low risk. A more quantitative definition of moderate drinking (e.g., in drinks per day) is complicated by the familiar observation that a given dose of alcohol affects different people differently. Furthermore, overreliance on *average* daily intake neglects *pattern* of drinking, which also has important health effects (Grant & Litvak, 1998).

With these caveats in mind, moderate drinking has been defined in the U.S. dietary guidelines (U.S. Department of Agriculture/Department of Health and Human Services, 1995) as two drinks or fewer daily for most men, one drink or less daily for most women. Most American drinkers already consume within these limits (Clark & Hilton, 1991). The definition is based on a standard drink, which is assumed to contain roughly 12 g, 15 mL, or 0.5 ounce of alcohol, that is, ethanol, which is the approximate content of 12 oz beer, 4 oz wine, or 1.5 oz liquor. Alcoholic-beverage equivalence extends to the major health effects of moderate drinking, such as coronary artery disease (Rimm, Klatsky, Grobbee, & Stampfer, 1996) and breast cancer (Smith-Warner et al., 1998). Despite claims to the contrary, there is little evidence that these effects are specific to any one type of alcoholic beverage.

ALCOHOL METABOLISM AND DISTRIBUTION

Women have a lower moderate drinking limit (one drink per day) than men (two drinks per day) because women tend to experience higher blood alcohol concentrations at an equivalent dose of alcohol (Jones & Jones, 1976). The principal reasons for this difference are gender differences in the metabolism and distribution of alcohol in the body.

The liver is the main site of alcohol metabolism, but extrahepatic metabolism also occurs. At low doses of alcohol, "first-pass metabolism" of alcohol by gastric oxidation can account for approximately 20% of alcohol oxidation (Di-Padova et al., 1992; Julkunen, Tannenbaum, Baraona, & Lieber, 1985). Frezza and colleagues (1990) reported that gastric alcohol dehydrogenase activity was significantly lower among women than men, thereby leading to decreased first-pass metabolism and higher blood alcohol levels. Furthermore, they found that

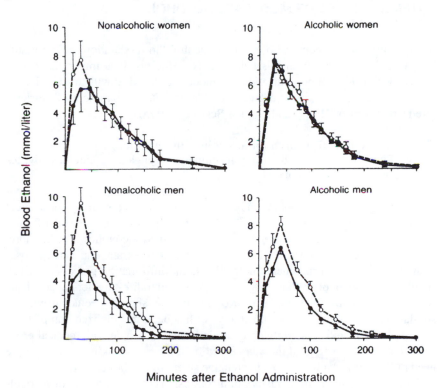

Figure 13.1 Effect of gender and chronic alcohol abuse on blood alcohol concentrations. A moderate dose of alcohol (0.3 g/kg body weight) was administered orally (*solid lines*) or intravenously (*dashed lines*). The area between the solid and dashed lines shows the difference in blood alcohol levels achieved; larger differences indicate larger "first-pass metabolism" of alcohol. (*Source.* "High blood alcohol levels in women: The role of decreased gastric alcohol dehydrogenase activity and first-pass metabolism," by M. Frezza, C. DiPadova, G. Pozzato, M. Terpin, E. Baraona, and C. S. Lieber, 1990, *New England Journal of Medicine, 322*, p. 97. Copyright 1990 by the Massachusetts Medical Society. All rights reserved. Reprinted with permission.)

alcoholism decreased enzyme activity, especially among women, in whom blood alcohol levels were virtually the same whether alcohol was given orally or intravenously (Figure 13.1).

A second explanation of why women have higher blood alcohol concentrations (for an equivalent dose of alcohol) involves the distribution of alcohol in the body. Women tend to have smaller bodies than men. Also, women have proportionally more fat and less body water than men. Because alcohol is more soluble in water than in fat, a given dose becomes more highly concentrated in a women's body water than in a man's larger volume (Goist & Sutker, 1985). Age-related increases in body fat—especially for American men—suggest that a moderate drinking guideline of one drink or less daily might be more appropriate for elderly men (Dufour, Archer, & Gordis, 1992).

POTENTIAL RISKS OF MODERATE ALCOHOL CONSUMPTION

By definition, most people who consume alcohol "in moderation" will not suffer any adverse effect from this behavior. Nonetheless, it is important to recognize two specific contraindications to moderate drinking with which alcohol use may cause major, life-threatening problems (U.S. Department of Agriculture/Department of Health and Human Services, 1995):

- Recovering alcoholism (or alcoholism in remission)
- Plans to drive, handle heavy machinery, or engage in similar activities that require concentration and skill

Although moderate drinking may appear attractive as a strategy for a select number of problem drinkers (Peele, 1992), our prognostic abilities seem far too crude for us to advise alcohol use among established alcoholics. Furthermore, alcohol is an established central nervous system depressant that causes dose-related impairment of judgment, motor skills, and information processing. Even small doses of alcohol produce deficits that may lead to life-threatening accidents (Council of Scientific Affairs, 1986). Recent drinking should preclude driving or similar activities until the consumed alcohol has been metabolized completely.

Moderate drinking is *relatively* contraindicated in people with medical problems that may be worsened or even caused by moderate drinking. These people need individualized advice about the relative safety of alcohol use. At-risk groups include people with a family history of alcoholism (U.S. Department of Agriculture/Department of Health and Human Services, 1995), people taking prescribed and over-the-counter medications (Shinn & Shrewsbury, 1988), and those at an increased risk of gastroesophageal reflux or gastritis (Chari, Teyssen, & Singer, 1993) or hemorrhagic stroke (Camargo, 1989). In some individuals, moderate drinking also can precipitate migraine headache (Peatfield, 1995), and thus they should probably avoid alcohol use. Moderate drinking also can worsen insomnia because bedtime drinking leads to fragmented sleep through several mechanisms, including decreased upper-airway muscle tone with consequent breathing problems (Gillin & Byerly, 1990). Although there is some evidence that moderate drinking may increase risk of colorectal cancer (Klatsky, Armstrong, Friedman, & Hiatt, 1988; Pollack, Nomura, Heilbrun, Stemmermann, & Green, 1984), recent studies have not confirmed this finding (Gerhardsson de Verdier, Romelsjö, & Lundberg, 1993; La Vecchia, Negri, Franceschi, & D'Avanzo, 1993). Individuals with, or at significantly increased risk for, any of these conditions should discuss the relative safety of moderate drinking with their primary care provider.

By contrast, many physicians have commented on the adverse effects of moderate drinking on diabetes mellitus, nutritional status, and obesity, yet the scientific literature does *not* support a proscription of moderate drinking among these groups. For example, recent studies have found that moderate drinking has no adverse effect on glycemic control in healthy, fed diabetics (Meeking & Cavan, 1997). In nondiabetic populations, moderate drinking is associated with increased insulin sensitivity (Kiechl et al., 1996) and decreases risk of developing diabetes (Rimm, Chan, Stampfer, Colditz, & Willett, 1995; Stampfer et al., 1988). Likewise, for most American adults, moderate drinking has little (if any) adverse effect on nutritional intake (Jacques, Sulsky, Hartz, & Russell, 1989). Although the exact relation of alcohol use to obesity is undoubtedly complex, moderate drinking does not appear to contribute significantly to risk of obesity (Hellerstedt, Jeffery, & Murray, 1990).

GENDER-SPECIFIC ISSUES IN MODERATE DRINKING BY WOMEN

Taking into account gender differences in alcohol metabolism and distribution—as is done by the moderate drinking guidelines—all of the preceding observations apply to both men and women. There are several gender-related topics, however, that deserve a more detailed discussion, including the relation of moderate drinking to reproductive outcomes such as infertility, pregnancy, and breast-feeding, and the relation of moderate drinking to risk of breast cancer. Although these topics are of obvious concern to members of both sexes, they are of particular personal interest to women and further complicate moderate drinking recommendations for this group.

Infertility

Although as many as 20% of married women in the United States have experienced infertility during their lifetime (Office of Technology Assessment, 1988), and heavy drinking has been linked with reproductive dysfunction (Wilsnack, Klassen, & Wilsnack, 1984), the data on the effect of moderate drinking on infertility are sparse. Early studies did not find a significant association (Olsen, Rachootin, Schiodt, & Dambo, 1983), but a recent case-control study found that moderate drinking significantly increased risk of infertility caused by an ovulatory factor or endometriosis (Grodstein, Goldman, & Cramer, 1994).[1] A subsequent prospective cohort study (Zaadstra, Habbema, Looman, Karbaat, & te Velde, 1994) did not confirm this finding. Thus, the association remains uncertain, but most studies suggest little cause for concern.

Fetal Alcohol Syndrome

Heavy alcohol consumption during pregnancy also has been linked with fetal alcohol syndrome (National Institute on Alcohol Abuse and Alcoholism, 1997), a condition characterized by growth deficiency, altered morphogenesis, and central nervous system dysfunction. Fetal risk is highest with heavy maternal drinking (at least six drinks per day), especially during the first trimester. As public awareness of fetal alcohol syndrome has increased, so have concerns that less extreme drinking may have hazardous fetal effects. Several ongoing studies are exploring this issue. Although the literature is inconsistent, there already is some evidence for a small reduction in birthweight at average maternal drinking levels of approximately one drink per day (Little, Asker, Sampson, & Renwick, 1986). More importantly, some studies have found that consumption of two drinks per day during pregnancy has adverse physical (Day et al., 1991) and intellectual (Streissguth, Barr, & Sampson, 1990) effects, as measured during early childhood.

The level of drinking in these latter studies, however, does not qualify as truly moderate (no more than one drink per day). Furthermore, mothers' self-reported levels of alcohol intake are probably underestimates (Ernhart, Morrow-Tlucak, Sokol, & Martier, 1988)—that is, these adverse outcomes probably occurred at even higher levels of alcohol intake. Although the sparse evidence of harm has reassured some scientists (Knupfer, 1991), there remain animal studies showing subtle adverse effects on fetal development at considerably lower doses of alcohol. For example, nervous-system abnormalities occurred in primates whose mothers were exposed weekly to low doses of alcohol (Clarren et al., 1990). These abnormalities were observed at a level equivalent to consuming only one alcoholic drink per week. Might subtle neurologic deficits have gone undetected in epidemiologic studies to date? At this point, it seems prudent to counsel pregnant women to avoid alcohol consumption during pregnancy (U.S. Department of Agriculture/Department of Health and Human Services, 1995) but not to become unnecessarily alarmed about an occasional drink.

Breast-feeding

In the postpartum period, nursing mothers face yet another decision regarding the safety of moderate alcohol consumption. Traditionally, mothers have been counseled that alcohol intake enhances their ability to produce and to let down milk (Walter, 1975). However, a minute fraction of consumed alcohol is passed into breast milk, and recent data suggest that this alcohol has an immediate effect on the feeding behavior of infants (Mennella & Beauchamp, 1991): Infants sucked more frequently during the first minute of feedings after their mothers had consumed alcohol, but they consumed significantly less milk. Although the infant received only 0.5% to 3.3% of the one experimentally administered drink, infants have only a limited ability to metabolize alcohol (Pikkarainen & Raiha, 1967) and the infant brain continues to develop during the postpartum period. Until more is known about the consequences of such exposure, for example, on neurologic development and on eventual preference for alcohol, it seems prudent to advise alcohol abstention for nursing women. The benefits of breast-feeding, however, far outweigh any theoretical concerns about an occasional drink during the nursing period. An attractive compromise might be for nursing women to limit moderate drinking to immediately after the last breast-feeding of the day, in which case the amount of alcohol transmitted to the infant is minimized.

Breast Cancer

Unlike the reproductive issues, which pertain to specific times in a woman's life, reports of an association between moderate drinking and risk of breast cancer could influence drinking behavior (and associated pleasure) throughout adult life. Breast cancer is a leading cause of morbidity and mortality in U.S. women (Kelsey & Horn-Ross, 1993). In a recent metaanalysis, Longnecker (1994) found a monotonic increase in breast cancer risk with increasing alcohol consumption. However, he also found statistically significant heterogeneity across studies, raising doubts about whether the finding was applicable to different populations. In early 1998, Smith-Warner and colleagues found very similar results in a pooled analysis of six prospective cohort studies from Canada, the Netherlands, Sweden, and the United States (combined $N = 322,647$ women, with 4335 incident cases). This collaborative study built on the earlier metaanalysis by including additional cohort studies, using uniform exposure categories and covariate definitions across studies, controlling for other dietary factors, evaluating for effect modification, and correcting for measurement error in alcohol intake.

Smith-Warner et al. (1998) found that for alcohol intake of fewer than five drinks per day, risk increased linearly with increasing intake. The pooled multivariate increase in risk was approximately 10% for each one-drink increment, and there was no significant heterogeneity among studies. The authors note that the alcohol–breast cancer link is of particular interest because there are relatively few other lifestyle modifications available to women who want to reduce their risk of this common cancer. On the basis of these data, women at significantly increased risk for breast cancer should be advised to abstain from alcohol.

POTENTIAL BENEFITS OF MODERATE ALCOHOL CONSUMPTION

Coronary Effects

On the positive side of the moderate drinking equation, there now is overwhelming evidence that alcohol has a J-shaped relation to MI and other manifestations of coronary artery disease (CAD). That is, moderate drinkers have lower rates of CAD than either nondrinkers or heavier drinkers, experiencing a 30% to 50% lower risk than nondrinkers (Doll, 1997). This association has been found in both men and women from diverse populations, with women deriving benefit at lower levels of intake than men. Because CAD is a leading cause of morbidity and mortality throughout the world, the risk reductions associated with alcohol consumption are of potentially large public health importance. Although some researchers have cautioned that the higher mortality rate of nondrinkers may result from inclusion of "sick quitters" in the nondrinker group (Shaper, Wannamethee, & Walker, 1988), numerous studies have addressed this concern—and that of potential confounding by diet—and still found a J-shaped relation (e.g., Klatsky, Armstrong, & Friedman, 1990; Rimm et al., 1991).

The most plausible mechanism for the reduced risk involves serum high-density lipoprotein (HDL). Experimental studies show that moderate drinking rapidly increases both HDL cholesterol (by roughly 5 mg/dL) and apolipoprotein AI, and that these effects disappear within a few weeks of abstention (Camargo, Williams, Vranizan, Albers, & Wood, 1985; Haskell et al., 1984); the effect of alcohol on patients with low levels of HDL (less than 35 mg/dL) remains uncertain. Early concerns (Haskell et al., 1984) that moderate drinking preferentially increases HDL3 (over HDL2) have been overstated, as it appears that both subfractions are inversely related to CAD (Stampfer, Sacks, Salvini, Willett, & Hennekens, 1991). Statistical modeling suggests that roughly 50% of the observed protection against CAD is mediated through HDL (Langer, Criqui, & Reed, 1992). The explanation for the residual 50% is unclear, but it is probably caused by alcohol-related changes in thrombotic factors, and measurement error.

Although heavier drinking (i.e., more than two drinks daily) is an established cause of hypertension, there is little evidence that moderate drinking raises blood pressure (Klatsky, 1996). Likewise, other cardiac disorders commonly associated with alcohol use (e.g., arrhythmias, cardiomyopathy) occur at heavier levels of alcohol consumption, such as binge drinking or habitual intake of six drinks or more daily (National Institute on Alcohol Abuse and Alcoholism, 1997). In sum, moderate drinking appears to confer no substantial harm to the heart and ultimately may prove to be of some benefit.

Ischemic Stroke

Moderate drinking also has a J-shaped association with ischemic stroke in predominantly White populations—male and female—but has little (if any) association among populations of Japanese origin (Camargo, 1989). Moderate drinkers' increased risk of hemorrhagic stroke partially offsets the observed protection against ischemic stroke. These complex relations are consistent with ethnic differences in cerebrovascular disease and with the biological mechanisms discussed previously. A recent update of the epidemiologic literature confirms these observations and concludes that moderate drinking does not increase combined risk of stroke (Camargo, 1996).

Other Health Benefits

Other potential health benefits of moderate alcohol consumption include decreased risk of peripheral arterial disease (Camargo et al., 1997). Moderate drinking also may enhance appetite and improve bowel regularity (Lieber, 1982) and decrease risk for symptomatic gallstones (Maclure et al., 1989) and kidney stones (Curhan, Willett, Speizer, & Stampfer, 1998). Preliminary evidence suggests that alcohol may decrease risk of osteoporosis at two or more drinks per day (Felson, Zhang, Hannan, Kannel, & Kiel, 1995), but the effect of lesser amounts of alcohol is uncertain. Although most of these potential benefits have been described in both sexes, some benefits (e.g., in peripheral arterial disease) have not yet been established among women. However, there is little reason to suspect gender differences for these alcohol benefits.

Total Mortality Rate

Moderate drinkers' reduced risk for CAD (and of ischemic stroke in some populations) helps to explain the well publicized J-shaped association between alcohol use and total mortality rate (Poikolainen, 1995). This association has been found in both men and women from diverse populations, women deriving benefit at lower levels of intake than men. As expected, the mortality-rate benefit is most evident in populations at increased risk of cardiovascular death (Fuchs et al., 1995; Thun et al., 1997). Although moderate drinking increases risk of other potentially fatal disorders (such as breast cancer), for most women these adverse effects are outweighed by concomitant reductions in cardiovascular mortality rate (Fuchs et al., 1995; Thun et al., 1997).

Psychological and Lifestyle Benefits

There is considerable evidence that moderate drinking provides psychological benefits (Baum-Baicker, 1985; see Chapter 15) and significantly improves quality of life. Indeed, moderate drinking has been promoted by many gerontologists for its psychological effects, because small doses of alcohol appear to reduce stress, improve mood, and facilitate social interaction among the elderly; the relative contribution, however, of personal expectancy versus pharmacological effect remains controversial.

HEALTH EFFECTS AND THE PLEASURE
OF DRINKING

Among health-conscious individuals, the *perceived* health effects of moderate alcohol consumption undoubtedly influence the pleasure of drinking. People who believe that alcohol use is good for one's health (e.g., through decreased risk for CAD) are likely to find that this understanding enhances pleasure. By contrast, people who believe that alcohol use is hazardous (e.g., through increased risk of adverse reproductive outcomes or breast cancer) are likely to find that this understanding diminishes pleasure. Given the complexity of alcohol's biomedical effects, however, it is not surprising that many people find the overall risk-benefit analysis confusing. Summing alcohol-related health effects is especially complicated for women of reproductive age, who are less likely to benefit from cardiac risk reduction (or to be concerned about such issues) and more likely to worry about harming their children or developing breast cancer.

An important challenge for health professionals is to match perceived health effects with actual health effects as we are best able to describe them. In other words, what actually are the health risks and benefits of moderate drinking for a given individual, and how do these risks and benefits fit into his or her overall health? Just as it makes little sense for people to become frightened (or angry in relation to others' drinking) by an occasional drink during pregnancy, it is unrealistic for smokers to believe that moderate drinking counteracts their risk from smoking. With proper training, primary care providers would be uniquely qualified to correct health-related misconceptions and to provide individual advice on alcohol consumption.

CONCLUSION

The alcohol drinking patterns of men and women differ for a variety of reasons. The present chapter summarizes biomedical explanations of the reasons why women drink less alcohol than men—differences in alcohol metabolism and distribution—and reviews current concepts of the health effects of moderate alcohol consumption. Moderate drinking is contraindicated for specific groups of people but is not an important health hazard for most men and women and may actually confer health benefits. The operative word, of course, is *moderate* (i.e., up to two drinks daily for most men, and up to one drink daily for most women); the medical and social hazards of heavier alcohol use are well known.

After taking into account differences in level of alcohol intake, the scientific literature indicates that the relation between moderate drinking and most health outcomes is similar in men and women. Areas of particular concern for female drinkers include reproductive issues, such as infertility, pregnancy, and breast-feeding, and the risk of breast cancer. The reproductive literature remains equivocal, with the possibility that moderate drinking may have subtle adverse effects. By contrast, the breast-cancer literature now provides persuasive evidence that even moderate drinking modestly increases risk of breast cancer.

Therefore, in addition to promoting gender-specific guidelines for moderate drinking, it seems prudent to advise alcohol abstention at particular times (e.g., before driving and during the first trimester of pregnancy) and for particular people (e.g., alcoholics and women at increased risk of breast cancer). The potential for adverse consequences of alcohol use in these specific situations is too great to advise otherwise. Furthermore, the prospect of heavier drinking and its associated problems—and the evident complexity of alcohol's health effects—preclude any blanket recommendation that lifelong abstainers begin drinking, or that occasional drinkers increase their alcohol consumption. Instead, interested individuals should discuss their drinking habits with their primary care provider, who can help assess the health risks and benefits of any potential behavioral change, and, in that setting, provide individual health advice. Such information would exert a more rational, evidence-based, influence on the pleasure of drinking. It also would assist efforts to enable individual drinkers to increase control over their health and to improve it.

NOTE

1. The authors defined moderate drinking as 100 g of alcohol or less per week. Participants' consumption was estimated on the basis of the following assumptions: 13 g of alcohol/can of beer, 11 g/glass of wine, and 15 g/ounce of liquor.

ACKNOWLEDGMENTS

Dr. Camargo is supported by grant HL-03533 from the National Institutes of Health (NIH), Bethesda, Maryland, U.S.A. The views expressed by the author are not necessarily those of the NIH.

REFERENCES

Baum-Baicker, C. (1985). The psychological benefits of moderate alcohol consumption: A review of the literature. *Drug and Alcohol Dependence, 15*, 305–322.

Camargo, C. A., Jr. (1989). Moderate alcohol consumption and stroke: The epidemiologic evidence. *Stroke, 20*, 1611–1626.

Camargo, C. A., Jr. (1996). Case-control and cohort studies of moderate alcohol consumption and stroke. *Clinica Chimica Acta, 246*, 107–119.

Camargo, C. A., Jr., Stampfer, M. J., Glynn, R. J., Gaziano, J. M., Manson, J. E., Goldhaber, S. Z., & Hennekens, C. H. (1997). Prospective study of moderate alcohol consumption and risk of peripheral arterial disease in U.S. male physicians. *Circulation, 95*, 577–580.

Camargo, C. A., Jr., Williams, P. T., Vranizan, K. M., Albers, J. J., & Wood, P. D. (1985). The effect of moderate alcohol intake on serum apolipoproteins A-I and A-II: A controlled study. *Journal of the American Medical Association, 253*, 2854–2857.

Chari, S., Teyssen, S., & Singer, M. V. (1993). Alcohol and gastric acid secretion in humans. *Gut, 34*, 843–847.

Clark, W. B., & Hilton, M. E. (Ed.). (1991). *Alcohol in America: Drinking practices and problems.* Albany, NY: SUNY Press.

Clarren, S. K., Astley, S. J., Bowden, D. M., Lai, H., Milam, A. H., Rudeen, P. K., & Shoemaker, W. J. (1990). Neuroanatomic and neurochemical abnormalities in nonhuman primate infants exposed to weekly doses of ethanol during gestation. *Alcoholism: Clinical and Experimental Research, 14,* 674–683.

Council of Scientific Affairs. (1986). Alcohol and the driver. *Journal of the American Medical Association, 255,* 522–527.

Curhan, G. C., Willett, W. C., Speizer, F. E., & Stampfer, M. J. (1998). Beverage use and risk for kidney stones in women. *Annals of Internal Medicine, 128,* 534–540.

Day, N. L., Robles, N., Richardson, G., Geva, D., Taylor, P., Scher, M., Stoffer, D., Cornelius, M., & Goldschmidt, L. (1991). The effects of prenatal alcohol use on the growth of children at three years of age. *Alcoholism: Clinical and Experimental Research, 15,* 67–71.

DiPadova, C., Roine, R., Frezza, M., Gentry, R. T., Baraona, E., & Lieber, C. S. (1992). Effects of ranitidine on blood alcohol levels after ethanol ingestion: Comparison with other H2-receptor antagonists. *Journal of the American Medical Association, 267,* 83–86.

Doll, R. (1997). One for the heart. *British Medical Journal, 315,* 1664–1668.

Dufour, M. C., Archer, L., & Gordis, E. (1992). Alcohol and the elderly. *Clinics in Geriatric Medicine, 8,* 127–141.

Ernhart, C. B., Morrow-Tlucak, M., Sokol, R. J., & Martier, S. (1988). Underreporting of alcohol use in pregnancy. *Alcoholism: Clinical and Experimental Research, 12,* 506–511.

Felson, D. T., Zhang, Y., Hannan, M. T., Kannel, W. B., & Kiel, D. P. (1995). Alcohol intake and bone mineral density in elderly men and women: The Framingham Study. *American Journal of Epidemiology, 142,* 485–492.

Fillmore, K. M., Golding, J. M., Leino, E. V., Motoyoshi, M., Shoemaker, C., Terry, H., Ager, C. R., & Ferrer, H. P. (1997). Patterns and trends in women's and men's drinking. In R. W. Wilsnack & S. C. Wilsnack (Eds.), *Gender and alcohol: Individual and social perspectives.* (pp. 21–48). New Brunswick, NJ: Rutgers Center of Alcohol Studies.

Frezza, M., DiPadova, C., Pozzato, G., Terpin, M., Baraona, E., & Lieber, C. S. (1990). High blood alcohol levels in women: The role of decreased gastric alcohol dehydrogenase activity and first-pass metabolism. *New England Journal of Medicine, 322,* 95–99.

Fuchs, C. S., Stampfer, M. J., Colditz, G. A., Giovannucci, E. L., Manson, J. E., Kawachi, I., Hunter, D. J., Hankinson, S. E., Hennekens, C. H., & Rosner, B. (1995). Alcohol consumption and mortality among women. *New England Journal of Medicine, 332,* 1245–1250.

Gerhardsson de Verdier, M., Romelsjö, A., & Lundberg, M. (1993). Alcohol and cancer of the colon and rectum. *European Journal of Cancer Prevention, 2,* 401–408.

Gillin, J. C., & Byerly, W. F. (1990). The diagnosis and management of insomnia. *New England Journal of Medicine, 322,* 239–242.

Goist, K. C. & Sutker, P. B. (1985). Acute alcohol intoxication and body composition in women and men. *Biochemistry & Behavior, 22,* 811–814.

Grant, M., & Litvak, J. (Eds.). (1998). *Drinking patterns and their consequences.* Washington, DC: Taylor & Francis.

Grodstein, F., Goldman, M. B., & Cramer, D. W. (1994). Infertility in women and moderate alcohol use. *American Journal of Public Health, 84,* 1429–1432.

Haskell, W. L., Camargo, C. A., Jr., Williams, P. T., Vranizan, K. M., Krauss, R. M., Lindgren, F. T., & Wood, P. D. (1984). The effect of cessation and resumption of moderate alcohol intake on serum high-density-lipoprotein subfractions: A controlled study. *New England Journal of Medicine, 310,* 805–810.

Hellerstedt, W. L., Jeffery, R. W., & Murray, D. M. (1990). The association between alcohol intake and adiposity in the general population. *American Journal of Epidemiology, 132,* 594–611.

Jacques, P. F., Sulsky, S., Hartz, S. C., & Russell, R. M. (1989). Moderate alcohol intake and nutritional status in nonalcoholic elderly subjects. *American Journal of Clinical Nutrition, 50,* 875–879.

Jones, B. M., & Jones, M. K. (1976). Male and female intoxication levels for three alcohol doses or do women really get higher than men? *Alcohol Technical Report, 5*, 11–14.

Julkunen, R. J. K., Tannenbaum, L., Baraona, E., & Lieber, C. S. (1985). First pass metabolism of ethanol: An important determinant of blood levels after alcohol consumption. *Alcohol, 2*, 437–441.

Kelsey, J., & Horn-Ross, P. L. (1993). Breast cancer: Magnitude of the problem and descriptive epidemiology. *Epidemiology Reviews, 15*, 7–16.

Kiechl, S., Willeit, J., Poewe, W., Egger, G., Oberhollenzer, F., Muggeo, M., & Bonora, E. (1996). Insulin sensitivity and regular alcohol consumption: Large, prospective, cross sectional population study. *British Medical Journal, 313*, 1040–1044.

Klatsky, A. L. (1996). Alcohol and hypertension. *Clinica Chimica Acta, 246*, 91–105.

Klatsky, A. L., Armstrong, M. A., & Friedman, G. D. (1990). Risk of cardiovascular mortality in alcohol drinkers, ex-drinkers and nondrinkers. *American Journal of Cardiology, 66*, 1237–1242.

Klatsky, A. L., Armstrong, M. A., Friedman, G. D., & Hiatt, R. A. (1988). The relations of alcoholic beverage use to colon and rectal cancer. *American Journal of Epidemiology, 128*, 1007–1015.

Knupfer, G. (1991). Abstaining for fetal health: The fiction that even light drinking is dangerous. *British Journal of Addiction, 86*, 1063–1073.

La Vecchia, C., Negri, E., Franceschi, S., & D'Avanzo, B. (1993). Moderate beer consumption and the risk of colorectal cancer. *Nutrition and Cancer, 19*, 303–306.

Langer, R. D., Criqui, M. H., & Reed, D. M. (1992). Lipoproteins and blood pressure as biological pathways for effect of moderate alcohol consumption on coronary heart disease. *Circulation, 85*, 910–915.

Lieber, C. S. (1982). Alcohol and the digestive tract. In C. S. Lieber (Ed.), *Medical disorders of alcoholism.* (pp. 363–411). Philadelphia, PA: W. B. Saunders.

Little, R. E., Asker, R. L., Sampson, P. D., & Renwick, J. H. (1986). Fetal growth and moderate drinking in early pregnancy. *American Journal of Epidemiology, 123*, 270–278.

Longnecker, M. P. (1994). Alcoholic beverage consumption in relation to risk of breast cancer: meta-analysis and review. *Cancer Causes and Control, 5*, 73–82.

Maclure, K. M., Hayes, K. C., Colditz, G. A., Stampfer, M. J., Speizer, F. E., & Willett, W. C. (1989). Weight, diet, and the risk of symptomatic gallstones in middle-aged women. *New England Journal of Medicine, 321*, 563–569.

Meeking, D. R., & Cavan, D. A. (1997). Alcohol ingestion and glycaemic control in patients with insulin-dependent diabetes mellitus. *Diabetes Medicine, 14*, 279–283.

Mennella, J. A., & Beauchamp, G. K. (1991). The transfer of alcohol to human milk. Effects on flavor and the infant's behavior. *New England Journal of Medicine, 325*, 981–985.

National Institute on Alcohol Abuse and Alcoholism. (1992). *Moderate drinking* (Alcohol Alert No. 16). Rockville, MD: Author.

National Institute on Alcohol Abuse and Alcoholism. (1997). *Ninth special report to the U.S. Congress on alcohol and health.* Rockville, MD: Author.

Office of Technology Assessment. (1988). *Infertility: Medical and social choices.* Washington, DC: Congress of the United States, Office of Technology Assessment.

Olsen, J., Rachootin, P., Schiodt, A. V., & Dambo, N. (1983). Tobacco use, alcohol consumption and infertility. *International Journal of Epidemiology, 12*, 179–194.

Peatfield, R. C. (1995). Relationships between food, wine, and beer-precipitated migrainous headaches. *Headache, 35*, 355–357.

Peele, S. (1992). Alcoholism, politics, and bureaucracy: The consensus against controlled-drinking therapy in America. *Addictive Behavior, 17*, 49–62.

Peele, S. (1993). The conflict between public health goals and the temperance mentality. *American Journal of Public Health, 83*, 805–810.

Pikkarainen, P. H., & Raiha, N.C. (1967). Development of alcohol dehydrogenase activity in the liver. *Pediatric Research, 1*, 165–168.

Plant, M. (1997). *Women and alcohol: Contemporary and historical perspectives.* London: Free Association Books.

Poikolainen, K. (1995). Alcohol and mortality: A review. *Journal of Clinical Epidemiology, 48,* 455–465.

Pollack, E. S., Nomura, A. M., Heilbrun, L. K., Stemmermann, G. N., & Green, S. B. (1984). Prospective study of alcohol consumption and cancer. *New England Journal of Medicine, 310,* 617–621.

Rimm, E. B., Chan, J., Stampfer, M. J., Colditz, G. A., & Willett, W. C. (1995). Prospective study of cigarette smoking, alcohol use, and the risk of diabetes in men. *British Medical Journal, 310,* 555–559.

Rimm, E.B., Giovannucci, E. L., Willett, W. C., Colditz, G. A., Ascherio, A., Rosner, B., & Stampfer, M. J. (1991). Prospective study of alcohol consumption and risk of coronary heart disease in men. *Lancet, 338,* 464–468.

Rimm, E. B., Klatsky, A. L., Grobbee, D., & Stampfer, M. J. (1996). Review of moderate alcohol consumption and reduced risk of coronary heart disease: Is the effect due to beer, wine, or spirits? *British Medical Journal, 312,* 731–736.

Shaper, A. G., Wannamethee, G., & Walker, M. (1988). Alcohol and mortality in British men: Explaining the U-shaped curve. *Lancet, ii,* 1267–1273.

Shinn, A. F., & Shrewsbury, R. P. (Eds.). (1988). *Evaluations of drug interactions.* New York: Macmillan.

Smith-Warner, S. A., Spiegelman, D., Yaun, S. S., van den Brandt, P. A., Folsom, A. R., Goldbohm, A., Graham, S., Holmberg, L., Howe, G. R., Marshall, J. R., Miller, A. B., Potter, J. D., Speizer, F. E., Willett, W. C., Wolk, A., & Hunter, D. J. (1998). Alcohol and breast cancer in women: A pooled analysis of cohort studies. *Journal of the American Medical Association, 279,* 535–540.

Stampfer, M. J., Colditz, G. A., Willett, W. C., Manson, J. E., Arky, R. A., Hennekens, C. H., & Speizer, F. E. (1988). A prospective study of moderate alcohol drinking and risk of diabetes in women. *American Journal of Epidemiology, 128,* 549–558.

Stampfer, M. J., Sacks, F. M., Salvini, S., Willett, W. C., & Hennekens, C. H. (1991). A prospective study of cholesterol, apolipoproteins, and the risk of myocardial infarction. *New England Journal of Medicine, 325,* 373–381.

Streissguth, A. P., Barr, H. M., & Sampson, P. D. (1990). Moderate prenatal alcohol exposure: Effects on child IQ and learning problems at age 7 1/2 years. *Alcoholism: Clinical and Experimental Research, 14,* 662–669.

Thun, M. J., Peto, R., Lopez, A. D., Monaco, J. H., Henley, S. J., Heath, C. W., Jr., & Doll, R. (1997). Alcohol consumption and mortality among middle-aged and elderly U.S. adults. *New England Journal of Medicine, 337,* 1705–1714.

U.S. Department of Agriculture/Department of Health and Human Services. (1995). *Nutrition and your health: Dietary guidelines for Americans* (4th ed.). Washington, DC: U.S. Government Printing Office.

Walter, M. (1975). The folklore of breastfeeding. *Bulletin of the New York Academy of Medicine, 51,* 870–876.

Wilsnack, S. C., Klassen, A. D., & Wilsnack, R.W. (1984). Drinking and reproductive dysfunction among women in a 1981 national survey. *Alcoholism: Clinical and Experimental Research, 8,* 451–458.

Wilsnack, R. W., & Wilsnack, S. C. (Eds.). (1997). *Gender and alcohol: Individual and social perspectives.* New Brunswick, NJ: Rutgers Center for Alcohol Studies.

World Health Organization. (1993). *European Alcohol Action Plan.* Copenhagen, Denmark: Author.

Zaadstra, B. M., Habbema, J. D. F., Looman, C. W. N., Karbaat, J., & te Velde, E. R. (1994). Moderate drinking: No impact on female fecundity. *Fertility and Sterility, 62,* 948–954.

Chapter 14

Maximizing Pleasure: Alcohol, Health, and Public Policy

Ole-Jørgen Skog

A large number of studies in recent years has demonstrated that moderate drinkers of alcoholic beverages have lower morbidity and mortality rates than abstainers and very infrequent drinkers (see Chapters 12 and 13). The standard causal interpretation of this observation is that alcohol in moderation may offer protection against certain diseases—coronary heart disease in particular. Biological mechanisms for this effect also have been reported. However, at higher levels of consumption, negative health effects seem to outweigh the alleged protective effects, and the risk of disease increases. Hence, overall mortality rate appears to be a J-shaped function of consumption. Most of the evidence for these calculations derives from nonexperimental, epidemiological studies. The data therefore should be interpreted cautiously, as all confounding variables may not have been controlled for adequately. Abstainers and very light drinkers are different from normal drinkers in many respects and these differences have health consequences (Skog, 1996). Nonetheless, this chapter ignores this difficulty and takes for granted that the observed J-curve is the true relationship between consumption and health outcomes.

In light of the J-curve, some have come to question society's right to regulate and put restrictions on people's consumption of alcoholic beverages. Granted that alcohol can be good for individual health, should people not be allowed to use it freely and without interference from society? This chapter confronts this issue, beginning at the general level and then proceeding to address the more specific issue of the J-shaped curve.

Three facts need to be taken into consideration in attempting to give an answer to the question, "Does society have any right to interfere with people's alcohol consumption choices?"

1   Individual drinking may have detrimental effects on others' well-being.
2   There are both inter- and intrapersonal variations in people's rationality. More or less impaired rationality occurs in some people most of the time, and among all people part of the time.
3   Autonomous agents' social action sometimes produces unintended social consequences, such as in the "prisoner's dilemma" type of situation.

These three facts may suggest the following grounds for some degree of societal control of alcohol consumption:

• Protection of third parties based on the fact that an individual's drinking may have negative consequences for others
• Protection of individuals from themselves based on impaired rationality
• Protection against the unintended consequences of autonomous social action—that is, in the case of the J-shaped curve, the conclusion that the individual optimum is not necessarily the social optimum.

PROTECTING INDIVIDUALS AS A LEGITIMATE BASIS FOR ALCOHOL-CONTROL POLICY

The claim that moderate doses of alcohol may prevent heart disease brings up the old dilemma of weighting pleasure versus pain. Before the age of the J-shaped curve, "pains" included diseases, accidents, and social tragedies; pleasures were just pleasures. Now, health and longevity may join forces in boosting old-fashioned pleasures to tip the balance towards a higher consumption level (see Chapter 23).

Some have argued against alcohol's medical benefits in that those who wish to protect themselves against heart disease could obtain the same benefit by physical exercise or half an aspirin a day. This argument presumes that the effects of exercise, aspirin, and alcohol are not additive. If they are in fact additive, people obtain more by doing all three, and the individual could hardly be criticized for choosing to drink alcohol. Moreover, this argument is somewhat paternalistic. What about people who find exercise unpleasant and boring or who do not like to take aspirin?

That alcohol causes both pleasure and pain suggests that some degree of societal control is necessary. Nonetheless, some would argue, this control should be kept at a minimum—restricted to, for example, age regulations and quality control to prevent poisoning. Others are prepared to accept stricter controls, including a licensing system, price regulation through taxation, state-operated monopolies, and so on.

Those who support substantial restrictions and public regulation of availability of alcohol (and other drugs) base their case on (a) the need to protect citizens against harm, displeasure, and inconveniences brought on by alcohol abuse by others (so-called externalities), and (b) the need to protect certain citizens against themselves. These two arguments are very different in nature. The first derives from the idea that citizens possess certain rights, including the right to protection against offense from third parties. The latter argument adduces an additional limitation on these rights by limiting the right to act in certain self-destructive ways.

Most people probably would subscribe to the first principle. The support for the second principle is likely to be less unanimous. Some would accept that people have the right to destroy their own lives, provided this does not have unreasonable consequences for others; others would reject such a right altogether. A third, intermediate position may allow for self-destructive behavior, but only if the person in question is clearly of sound mind and able to make rational decisions.

The Effects on Others of an Individual's Drinking

People's drinking affects others in several ways. Others may become the victim of an intoxicated driver or, more generally, may be psychologically or physically injured because of the behavior of those under the influence of alcohol. Children may suffer from neglect because of parents' drinking. People's drunkenness may produce feelings of fear and insecurity among others, or this drunkenness simply may be a nuisance. At the societal level, treatment of persons with dependency problems or alcohol-related diseases costs money, and in the final account everyone has to pay for this. Most would agree that such externalities legitimatize some sort of societal control, although there may be differences of opinion with respect to how serious a drinking offense must be before it is considered to deserve a social response.

Protecting People from Themselves

The legitimacy of measures aimed at protecting people against themselves represents a more difficult case from a moral or philosophical point of view. It is most obvious that this is a legitimate policy in the case of children and the mentally ill, because they may be unable to judge what is in their own best interest. Such individuals have preferences and act according to their preferences, but their preferences may be inconsistent, contradictory, or in other ways irrational. Furthermore, their ability to evaluate and take into account the short- and long-term consequences of their actions is limited. They also may more easily fall victims of such irrational traps as self-deception and wishful thinking (see Elster, 1984, for a broad discussion of such issues).

In addition, some adults who are not mentally ill nevertheless are characterized by some of the same traits as children and people with mental disorders. For instance, some people live in the present and do not take the future into account. They may involve themselves in highly self-destructive activities, including excessive consumption of addictive and harmful substances. What about the self-deceptive adult who is otherwise healthy but who jeopardizes his or her life through harmful actions, believing that he or she is invulnerable to harm? Also in this category are those who are *temporarily* in a state of depression or emotional agitation and who are at risk of committing suicide. In these cases, may not society be warranted in intervening even if people's self-destructive behavior may not harm others, in order to protect the individual actor?

Externalities also may offer a reason for societal action in many of these cases. If the person hurts himself or herself, society is obligated to help the person, and this help is costly. Does society have some right to prevent these costs? Even without taking the cost of externalities into account, it still may be argued that society has an obligation to take care of some people, for a society must establish a minimum level of altruism.

This is dangerous territory as it is not always obvious what is a person's own best interest. If the reason for intervention is simply the fact that the person's preferences are bizarre and abnormal, the intervention rightfully may be labeled paternalism. To make deviant choices is not in itself irrational. The standard definition of rationality simply requires that the person's preferences are consistent and that he or she acts according to those preferences. The actual content of the person's preferences is simply a matter of subjective taste. Some people are very risk-aversive; others are risk-loving. Some like to live in the present and do not care much about the future while others are very much concerned about their futures. *De gustibus non est disputandum* ("tastes cannot be discussed").

Thus, society needs very good reasons to intervene to protect people against themselves. One such reason is if a person is temporarily in an atypical mental state and at risk of doing something he or she later will regret. Another is that the person is not entirely rational (or he or she is less rational than people in general) and therefore is occasionally unable to make sound judgments. This person, too, might do things that he or she later would regret.

One criterion to use in deciding if such interventions are legitimate is "anticipated regret," that is, if it seems that people ultimately may regret their current actions. However, it generally is difficult to determine whether or not a certain individual in fact later will regret a current action. And even if there is reason to believe that the person will regret this action, who should society join forces with—the current self who is preferring to do what he or she does, or the future self who may regret the current self's choice?

In *Confessions of an English Opium Eater*, Thomas De Quincey (1822/1994) tells the following story, which clearly illustrates the controller's dilemma when faced with this sort of temporal inconsistency:

> He went so far as to hire men—porters, hackney-coachmen, and others—to oppose by force his entrance into any druggist's shop. But, as the authority for stopping him was derived simply from himself, naturally these poor men found themselves in a metaphysical fix, not provided for even by Thomas Aquinas or by the prince of Jesuitical casuists. And in this excruciating dilemma would occur such scenes as the following:
> "Oh, sir," would plead the suppliant porter—suppliant, yet semi-imperative (for equally if he *did*, and if he did *not*, show fight, the poor man's daily 5s. seemed endangered)—"really you must not; consider, sir, your wife and—"
> *Transcendental Philosopher*—"Wife! What wife? I have no wife."
> *Porter*—"But, really now, you must not, sir. Didn't you say no longer ago than yesterday—"
> *Transcendental Philosopher*—"Pooh, pooh! Yesterday is a long time ago. Are you aware, my man, that people are known to have dropped down dead for timely want of opium?"
> *Porter*—"Ay, but you tell't me not to hearken—"
> *Transcendental Philosopher*—"Oh, nonsense. An emergency, a shocking emergency, has arisen—quite unlooked for. No matter what I told you in times long past. That which I *now* tell you, is that, if you don't remove that arm of yours from the doorway of this most respectable druggist, I shall have a good ground of action against you for assault and battery." (pp. 22–23)

People can be protected against themselves in at least two different ways. First, interventions may be targeted directly at the individuals in question. Compulsory treatment is one example. The legitimacy of such measures then can be questioned, however, if it is not obvious that this is in the person's own best interest. Here, we easily end up in De Quincey's "metaphysical fix."

Second, society may strive to protect people against themselves through the legal and economic framing of individual choices, that is, by primary prevention measures. These measures typically impose some inconveniences on the general public in order to prevent certain individuals from acting foolishly. To take an example, what if the suicide rate in a society can be reduced by 20% by replacing a very poisonous household gas with a less poisonous one, but the safer gas is more expensive by, for example, $100 per year?[1] Should society implement this measure, adding an expense for the general public? Social altruism answers in the affirmative, even if it imposes certain social costs. However, in real life, the size of the cost makes a difference. The decisive question becomes: How much cost or inconvenience can the innocent bystander be expected to tolerate in order to protect a few deviant individuals from themselves?

ADDICTION, RATIONALITY, AND IRRATIONALITY

Freedom of choice is a fundamental democratic right. Most Westerners subscribe to the view that adult, healthy people should be allowed to make their own choices as long as they do not frustrate other people's fundamental rights and as long as they are prepared to take the consequences of their own choices. One tacit premise in this ideology is that people act intentionally and that they are rational: That is, they are able to make sensible deliberations, they have reasonably consistent preferences, and they are able to act according to their own preferences.

Rationality must play a privileged role in any serious social theory. The assumption that people act intentionally and on the basis of rational deliberations is probably necessary to understand other people's conduct and interactions in society. However, most people do not act rationally at all times. Occasionally, each of us acts on the basis of our emotions. Even if we act intentionally and on the basis of deliberation, our rationality may be imperfect. Such imperfections in our rationality surface at times, and much more frequently in some individuals than in others. Hence, the fundamental assumption of rationality need not imply that all people are perfectly rational all the time.

In many areas of social life, small and occasional deviations from rationality are tolerated or ignored for practical purposes. However, irrationality plays a more significant role in relation to goods that are pleasurable in moderate quantities, but strongly addictive and potentially harmful in large quantities. First, addictive substances may represent a particularly hard case for rational choice, as it is difficult to foresee and comprehend their long-term consequences. If so, perfect foresight and full information cannot be realistically assumed, as does Becker and Murphy's (1988) theory of rational addiction. Second, even moderate deficiencies in people's rationality—deficiencies that normally do not matter very much—may greatly elevate the risk in using potentially addictive substances. Hence, although the deviation from rationality is minor, the consequences may be quite substantial and the deviations cannot be ignored.

Thirdly, the addictive life and the addictive substance may cause further deterioration in the person's rationality, making him or her even less able to make free and responsible choices. The hallmark of addiction is that the addicted person may find it very difficult to abstain from performing a certain act, such as drinking. Typically, this craving is sensitive to the context. Under certain circumstances (e.g., if the addict has already performed the act and is "satiated" or if the act would have intolerable consequences), abstaining is not a problem. Other contexts may cause only moderate stress; in still other contexts the addict may experience an irresistible craving.

The addict may or may not wish to get rid of a habit. If the addict wishes to quit but feels that he or she cannot, or that it is extremely difficult for him or her, the addict is a dissonant addict (Orford, 1985). Individuals who do *not* wish to quit under the prevailing circumstances are still considered addicted if, should they try to quit, they would find it very difficult. Such individuals are called consonant addicts.

Because addicted people frequently claim that they would like to stop consuming the substance to which they are addicted but still continue consuming it, they often appear to observers to be irrational. The addict seems to violate the requirement of acting according to one's own preferences. (Obviously, this argument applies to dissonant addicts only. Consonant addicts are not irrational by this criterion.)

However, this argument is not necessarily true, even for dissonant addicts. Becker and Murphy (1988) have demonstrated that even a fully rational person may end up in an addicted state. According to Becker and Murphy, the addict has—through bad luck of one sort or another—been trapped in a suboptimal consumption state. This state is literally a *local* optimum, which is inferior to the nonaddicted *global* optimum. The addict is unable to leave the inferior state because this implies an even bigger setback to the addict's well-being. This setback is temporary and the addict would gain in the long run, but the rational addict is impatient and discounts the prospects of a future improvement so much that it does not counterbalance the immediate setback from quitting. (See Skog, 1999, for a more thorough discussion and critique of the rational addiction theory.)

The rational addict knows that life would be better without the addiction and he or she may form a meta- or second-order preference for abstention (or normal drinking if he or she perceives this as a realistic option). However, the addict is unable to act according to this second-order preference as his or her actual choices are motivated by first-order preferences. According to Becker and Murphy, the addict's basic problem is that his or her first-order preferences have been changed systematically and distorted by the substance abuse. For instance, the salience of alcohol may have increased to the extent that it dominates all other considerations in decision making.

If the addict-to-be knew in advance that this was going to happen, and accepted this consequence from the very start, then it might be that the addict has only himself or herself to blame. In this case, society may have no right—or obligation—to protect the addict against himself or herself. However, it may not be true that addicts actually know this in advance and that they have deliberately taken a calculated risk. Indeed, it may be that nonaddicts really cannot understand what addiction is like—how it feels to have an irresistible urge for something with dramatic negative consequences for oneself and others.

If people cannot be expected to have full knowledge and realistic expectations about the consequences of their own consumption choices, some will make choices that they later regret. Under these circumstances, the issue of protecting people against themselves reappears. If limitations in people's cognitive capacities make them vulnerable to certain problems, this can form a reasonable, nonpaternalistic justification for restricting individual freedom of choice.

The dissonant addict probably regrets his or her former choices—if not, he or she would be a consonant addict.

This argument is based on the premise that many people may be unable to form realistic expectations about the consequences of their choices. The argument also is supported by research finding general deficiencies in people's rationality. First, people display systematic biases in evaluating risks (Kahneman & Tversky, 1979). Second, there is strong evidence to suggest that people in general have a congenital tendency to discount future consequences in such a way that they often fall victim to temptations that they regret later (Ainslie, 1992). The so-called loss-gain asymmetry (Loewenstein & Prelec, 1992), that is, the tendency to discount future gains more strongly that future losses, may have similar effects (Skog, 1998). Younger people tend to discount the future more strongly than older persons (Mischel, Shoda, & Rodriguez, 1992). Hence, young people typically pay less attention to potential future problems caused by their current consumption than they will as they mature.

Such deficiencies in people's cognitive capacities suggest that they cannot always be blamed fully for their misfortunes, even though they have made deliberate choices. If people are allowed to choose freely and without other constraints than the regard for other people's rights, some individuals will make choices that they later will regret, and some of these choices will have quite dramatic consequences. The outcome could be suboptimal for society at large—a state that is less good for some (or all) citizens—while nobody has really gained anything. Or, to use a utilitarian criterion, the overall level of well-being in society may be reduced by free choices compared with a society with slightly more constraints on individual action.

UNINTENDED CONSEQUENCES OF SOCIAL ACTION

If individual actors pursue their own best interest, the aggregate outcome may or may not be the optimum outcome for society. Unfortunately, an optimum outcome is not automatically guaranteed, even if the actors are fully rational. Thus, under certain circumstances, Adam Smith's invisible hand may secure the best outcome for all, but, under other circumstances, the outcome may be suboptimal. The latter could be the case in situations of choice in which the outcome for each depends on the choices of others, as in the prisoner's dilemma. An example is the so-called tragedy of the commons. Several parties have access to the commons, such as a lake or an ocean. If all parties limit their own use of the region and catch only a modest amount of fish, everybody will be reasonably well off. However, each individual actor could increase his or her profit by catching a larger quantity. If everybody decides to maximize his or her profit, overfishing results and in the long run everybody loses. The outcome is suboptimal for all, even if all parties follow their own best interest. Another example is pollution. If all pollute only a little, everybody is reasonably well off.

However, each country may believe it can increase its own standard of living by increasing production and worring less about pollution. Hence, everybody has an incentive to pollute more, but the long-term outcome of such policies is worse for everybody. These examples reflect actual problems, as the continual international negotiations on fishing and pollution demonstrate.

These illustrations serve to show that social action sometimes may have unintended and unwanted consequences. In the view of some, this is almost always the case. In general, we cannot take for granted that the optimal outcome for everybody is obtained if everybody follows his or her own best interest. Suboptimal outcomes are particularly likely to occur whenever people's behavior affects everyone's well-being.

Drinking behavior—like many other types of behavior—is conformist behavior. An individual's drinking habits are shaped and reshaped by other people's drinking, as demonstrated by numerous empirical studies that show the importance of social norms and social modeling in drinking (see Skog, 1980, for a review). Acting very differently from others in the group or community carries a price. Hence, an individual's level of well-being depends not only on his or her own drinking but also on other people's drinking.

As an illustration, imagine a highly simplified scenario in which people have only two consumption choices—drinking little or drinking much. Suppose that all drinkers are equal in terms of their preferences, and that well-being associated with low or high consumption depends only on how other members of society behave. Well-being in this way reflects only people's own subjective valuations, and these may or may not correspond to objective health measures. Consider the choice of a representative individual, given the drinking behavior of the rest of the society. If most other people drink little, it is better for this individual to drink little than to drink much, because of pressure towards conformity. However, if most other people drink much, it is best for this individual to drink much. The situation is depicted in the Schelling diagram in Figure 14.1. The broken line describes how the well-being of an individual choosing to drink much grows from a lower to a higher level as an increasing number of people drink much. The solid line describes how the light drinker's well-being decreases as an increasing number of other people drink a lot. Where the two lines intersect, there is no difference for the individual between the two options. To the right of this point, that is, if a majority drinks much, the individual is better off drinking much; to the left he or she is better off drinking little.

In this highly simplified society, there are two stable equilibria. Either everybody will choose to drink little, or everybody will choose to drink much. In an initial stage in which a majority (say, 70%) drinks much, those who drink little will be better off switching to high consumption, and the number of consumers of large quantities will increase. Those who already drink much have no incentive to change. Ultimately, from this starting point, everybody will end up drinking much. On the other hand, if at some initial stage a majority of this culture should happen to drink small amounts, an individual who drinks

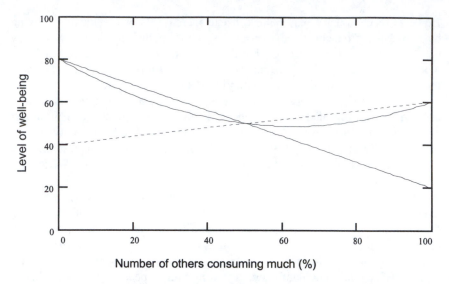

Figure 14.1 Social well-being: the well-being levels associated with consuming much (*broken line*) and consuming little (*solid line*), as they vary according to the prevalence of persons consuming much. The solid curve represents the total well-being of society. The units measuring well-being are arbitary.

much would be better off drinking small amounts. Hence, the number of heavy drinkers would decrease and, in the end, everybody would end up drinking small amounts. Therefore, both equilibrium states can be reached, and which of the two occurs depends on the starting point.

The solid, U-shaped curve in Figure 14.1 depicts the overall level of well-being of this society (its shape is completely determined by the two straight lines). In this particular case, a mix of light and heavy drinkers is the worst outcome, resulting in the lowest total well-being. The state of equilibrium in which everybody drinks much is somewhat better. The state in which everybody drinks little is the best in terms of overall well-being. Hence, if everybody chooses according to his or her best interest, it is possible, but not guaranteed, that the outcome will be the best in terms of overall well-being.[2] As we already have noted, this society very well could end up in a state in which everybody drinks much, although it would be best for all if everybody drank only a little.

Of course, this example is far too simplified to shed much light on the issue in question—the aggregate health effects in the case of a J-shaped curve. The example only serves as an illustration of the fact that social life sometimes gives rise to what Boudon (1982) called "perverse effects." Perverse effects occur if the best outcome in terms of overall well-being is not guaranteed if individuals follow their own best interest. Under those circumstances, some kind of coordination of individual choices is needed in order to secure the best outcome for all—that is, certain limitations on individual freedom must be applied.

SOCIETAL CONSEQUENCES OF THE J-SHAPED CURVE

Because alcohol has both positive and negative effects, these must be weighed against each other. What criterion in the form of an overall summary measure of pleasure and pain can guide the evaluation of different policy options? Such a measure could be simply overall mortality (or morbidity) rate, or it could be a more complex construct that takes psychological well-being and social and economic consequences into consideration. For the sake of simplicity, we can use overall mortality rate as a criterion. The task is then to start out with the individual-level, J-shaped risk curve for death from all causes and try to find out what happens to aggregate overall mortality level under different policies.

If, or when, it becomes widely recognized by the general public that moderate drinking may reduce morbidity and mortality rates, what responses can be expected? On the one hand, abstainers and very light drinkers might start to drink at the optimal level, in which case morbidity and mortality rates in this group would be expected to decrease. And if those who used to drink more than the optimal level should decrease their intake, their risk also would decrease. Alternatively, if people in the latter group were not affected by the health message, but continued to drink at their old pace, there would be no discernable changes in their health. In either case, the overall change for society at large under this scenario would be lowered morbidity and mortality rates.

However, the scenario may be unrealistic for both cognitive and social reasons. On the cognitive side, not all consumers may be fully rational. If science demonstrates that one or two drinks per day is optimal but three or more is suboptimal, this message may not be received without distortion. If consumer X likes to consume three or four drinks per day, he or she very well may reinterpret the message in support of his own preferences. The underlying mechanism could be cognitive dissonance and wishful thinking. And drinkers of larger quantities, say five or more drinks per day, may turn out to be less worried over their own drinking than they used to be, as they now conceive of the first two or three drinks of their daily quota as "medicine," rather than booze. If such drinkers weigh their own personal drinking behavior, they may settle for more rather than less, as some of their drinking has been transformed in their minds from vice to virtue. An empirical study is needed of how people perceive and interpret the message of protective effects from alcohol as it is mediated by the mass media (see the Appendix) and, in particular, the differences among different consumption groups in this respect. My conjecture is that the message of beneficial effects is most eagerly welcomed by those who already drink too much.

The social or interpersonal dynamics also might operate in the direction of increasing, rather than decreasing, the consumption of those who already drink above the optimal level. Drinking is a social act—something people mainly do together (see Chapter 5). Yet numerous empirical studies support the hypothesis that people tend to drink like their peers and that changes in one person's drinking induce changes in other people's drinking (Skog, 1980). This social contagion has the effect of producing strong collective patterns in the drinking culture so as to make the whole population move more or less in concert up and down the consumption scale if changes in drinking habits occur (Skog, 1985).

In the case at hand, an increase in alcohol consumption of those segments of the population that initially drink not at all or drink below the optimal level could induce more drinking among those who already drink above the optimal level. In practice, this could occur because the increase among the former abstainers and light drinkers would create more drinking occasions overall and, as a result, more opportunities to drink even for those who already drink a lot. If this is correct, the net result would be a collective increase in consumption across all segments of the drinking culture.

Such an increase among those who already drink above the optimum would produce an increasing number of drinking problems in that group. Hence, there would be a trade-off between the decreased morbidity rate among former abstainers and light drinkers on the one hand and an increased morbidity rate among the heavier drinkers on the other. The net result could go either way. In some cases, the former effect could be the strongest and the net effect could be a decreased morbidity rate. In other cases the inverse could occur, the net effect being an increased morbidity rate.

In cultures with a low per capita consumption level, the number of very light drinkers is large and the number of persons drinking in excess of the optimal level is small (Skog, 1985). Under these circumstances one would expect that the net effect of an increase in drinking could be reduced overall morbidity and mortality rates. In cultures with a high per capita consumption level, the number of very light drinkers is much lower, and the number of drinkers above the optimum is larger (Skog, 1985). The net result then easily could be the opposite. This would suggest that there is a J-shaped relationship between consumption and mortality rate even at the aggregate level. As per capita consumption increases up to a certain point, morbidity and mortality rates may decrease. Beyond this point, problem rates might increase as the consumption level increases. If this is so, it would be of considerable public health interest to identify the optimum aggregate consumption level, that is, the per capita consumption level at which morbidity and mortality rates are at a minimum.

As yet, the empirical evidence is somewhat ambiguous about the location of the individual-level optimum, that is, the consumption level with the lowest risk for the individual drinker. Some sources suggest one or two drinks per day (U.S. Department of Agriculture/Department of Health and Human Services, 1995); other sources have indicated two or three drinks per day (Department of Health and Social Security, 1995). Furthermore, what is meant by a drink remains open to dispute. The empirical evidence in relation to the location of an aggregate

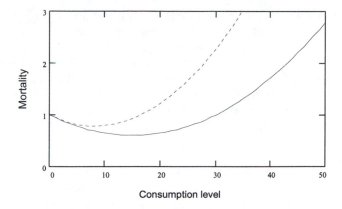

Figure 14.2 Mortality: hypothetical J-shaped risk function describing individual risk of dying as a function of consumption level (*solid curve*) and aggregate relationship between mortality rates and per capita alcohol consumption (*broken curve*). The individual optimum consumption level (*vertical solid line*) is twice as high as the aggregate optimum consumption level (*vertical broken line*). The units are arbitrary.

level optimal point is even smaller. The issue is obviously significant, however, and should be addressed in future research.

It is important to note that the aggregate-level optimum consumption level need not coincide with the individual-level optimum. One cannot simply transform the individual-level optimum consumption level to a per capita consumption figure and presume that this is also the optimum for society. In fact, it may very well be the case that the optimum for society is considerably lower than the individual-level optimum (for the full technical argument for this proposition, see Skog, 1996). My 1996 calculations suggest that the optimum for society very well could be less than half of the optimum for the individual drinker. A realistic scenario is shown in Figure 14.2, in which a hypothetical individual-level risk curve is outlined along with a corresponding aggregate-level relationship. The latter is deduced from the former based on an assumption of collective changes in people's consumption levels (cf. Skog, 1996).

If the individual optimum is two to three drinks per day and the aggregate optimum one half of this, then the optimum consumption level for society in terms of mortality would be 5 to 8 L of pure alcohol per capita per year. In low-consumption cultures such as Norway, a certain increase in alcohol consumption therefore might cause a decrease in mortality rate, provided everything else remained unchanged. However, in many other countries in which the per capita consumption already exceeds 8 L, the positive effects among light drinkers might be more than outweighed by an increased mortality rate among heavy drinkers, and the overall mortality rate may increase rather than decrease. Under these circumstances, conformist actors, pursuing their own best interest, may create a suboptimal consumption state for society at large.

We do not yet have strong empirical data with which to identify an aggregate, optimum consumption level. Hence, no well-founded conclusion can as yet be formulated about aggregate levels of consumption in relation to mortality rate. If the criterion used to evaluate "the common good" is not restricted to mortality rates but is designed to include positive and negative psychological, social, and economic effects as well, our ignorance is even deeper. In order to answer this question, we would have to decide, for example, how many pleasant dinners with wine are needed to balance a fatal accident.

CONCLUSION

Granted that moderate amounts of alcohol are in fact healthy, pertinent questions remain. Should society advise abstainers to drink? And has society the right to implement measures that may restrain some people's drinking at a level below the "optimal" level?

This chapter demonstrates that the resolution of these questions may be complicated and requires accountings of at least the following three factors:

1 *Externalities:* People's alcohol abuse may have negative consequences for third parties' well-being (accidents, violence, etc.) and can be costly to society.

2 *Irrationality:* Cognitive deficiencies through which people do not always act in their own best interest may have particularly dramatic consequences in the case of potentially addictive and harmful consumer goods.

3 *Perverse effects:* Individuals' free choices sometimes may produce suboptimal outcomes for society as a whole.

Acknowledging these factors means that the answer to the first question may not be entirely obvious. Although some abstainers may improve their life expectancy—and perhaps even their quality of life more generally—through drinking more, there may be side effects to advising individuals about optimal drinking levels that also need to be taken into consideration. A public health advisory to drink one or two drinks per day may trigger, under certain circumstances, a process that leads to increased problem rates in society at large.

As to the second question, society's right to impose some limitations on individual freedom is not necessarily a right to impose strict controls over individual choices. Rather, legitimate social control may be first and foremost a right to regulate the legal and economic framing of individual choices. In practice, any society must choose between alternative taxation levels (including zero), alternative regulations for opening hours (including none at all), age limits (including none), licensing rules (including none), and so on. The arguments in this chapter indicate that these choices should take into consideration consequences external to the individual drinker, irrationality in decision making, and perverse global effects that occur as a result of individuals' exercise of personal preferences. A laissez faire policy may not be the best for society. The exact nature and degree of control that a society should choose does not follow from these premises. Some would opt for very light control and others for much stricter control, depending on how the common good is defined, societal values, and the initial levels of alcohol consumption present in society. However, even relying on the simple utilitarian criterion of mortality rates the alcohol industry should be prepared for the possibility that most societies may lose rather than gain from increased consumption of alcoholic beverages, given their current level of consumption. And the temperance movement should get used to the idea that the best of all worlds is not necessarily devoid of alcoholic beverages.

NOTES

1. The British coal gas story (Kreitman, 1976) suggests that this may be a realistic example, as suicide rates decreased substantially when coal gas was replaced with natural gas. The reason is probably that some suicides are performed in a temporary state of agitation in which the availability of means to take one's own life makes a difference. In that particular case, this effect was not planned or expected and the substitution of one gas for another may not have been costly for the consumers. In the hypothetical example, this stipulation has been added to bring out the point more clearly.
2. Note that if the lines corresponding to high and low consumption had been drawn differently, the state at which everybody drinks much could have been the one with the highest overall well-being. However, the basic point would be unaffected by this change, as it would still be the case that society could end up in a suboptimal state.

REFERENCES

Ainslie, G. (1992). *Picoeconomics*. Cambridge, UK: Cambridge University Press.
Becker, G., & Murphy, K. M. (1988). A theory of rational addiction. *Journal of Political Economy, 96*, 675–700.
Boudon, R. (1982). *The unintended consequences of social action*. London: Macmillan.
Department of Health and Social Security. (1995). *Sensible drinking: The report of an Inter-Departmental Working Group*. London: Her Majesty's Stationery Office.
De Quincey, T. (1994). *Confessions of an English opium eater*. Ware, UK: Wordsworth. (Original work published in 1822)
Elster, J. (1984). *Ulysses and the sirens*. Cambridge, UK: Cambridge University Press.
Kahnemann, D., & Tversky, A. (1979). Prospect theory: An analysis of decision under risk. *Econometrica, 47*, 363–391.
Kreitman, N. (1976). The coal gas story: United Kingdom suicide rates, 1960–71. *British Journal of Preventive Social Medicine, 30*, 86–93.
Loewenstein, G., & Prelec, D. (1992). Anomalies in intertemporal choice: Evidence and interpretation. In G. Loewenstein & J. Elster (Eds.), *Choice over time* (pp. 119–145). New York: Russell Sage Foundation.
Mischel, W., Shoda, Y., & Rodriguez, M. L. (1992). Delay of gratification in children. In G. Loewenstein & J. Elster (Eds.), *Choice over time* (pp. 147–164). New York: Russell Sage Foundation.
Orford, J. (1985). *Excessive appetites: A psychological view of addiction*. Chichester, UK: Wiley.
Skog, O.-J. (1980). Social interaction and the distribution of alcohol consumption. *Journal of Drug Issues, 10*, 71–92.
Skog, O.-J. (1985). The collectivity of drinking cultures: A theory of the distribution of alcohol consumption. *British Journal of Addiction, 80*, 83–99.

Skog, O.-J. (1996). Public health consequences of the J-curve hypothesis of alcohol problems. *Addiction, 91*, 325–337

Skog, O.-J. (1999). Rationality, irrationality, and addiction: Notes on Becker and Murphy's theory of addiction. In J. Elster & O.-J. Skog (Eds.), *Getting hooked: Rationality and addiction* (pp. 173–207). Cambridge, UK: Cambridge University Press.

U.S. Department of Agriculture/Department of Health and Human Services. (1995). *Nutrition and your health: Dietary guidelines for Americans* (4th ed.). Washington, DC: U.S. Government Printing Office.

Chapter 15

Psychosocial Benefits of Moderate Alcohol Consumption: Alcohol's Role in a Broader Conception of Health and Well-Being

Archie Brodsky and Stanton Peele

The initial hypothesis and evidence that moderate alcohol consumption reduces the overall mortality rate through its protective effect against cardiovascular disease are now broadly known and accepted (see Chapters 12 and 13). This evidence continues to accumulate, most recently in a study of nearly a half a million middle-aged and elderly people in the United States (Thun et al., 1997). Yet notwithstanding these findings—along with many long-held cultural beliefs that drinking improves health—most people consume alcohol for experiential rather than health reasons (Hall, 1996; Lowe, 1994b; see Chapters 18 and 20 and the Introduction). The critical role of pleasure not only as a motivation for drinking but also as a potential cause or indicator of positive health outcomes is attracting medical attention. As an editorial in the *British Medical Journal* noted, "Public health campaigns have often ignored people's requirement for pleasure" (Cleare & Wessely, 1997, p. 1637). However, clinical medicine has begun to identify global quality of life and level of general functioning as essential dimensions of health outcomes (Wilson & Cleary, 1995; see Chapter 23). Taking into account the psychosocial as well as medical benefits of moderate drinking balances the heretofore exclusively negative public health emphasis on problematic psychosocial consequences of drinking (accidents, violence, addiction), which considers health consequences of drinking exclusively in terms of risk reduction (Edwards et al., 1994).

Baum-Baicker's (1985) earlier review identified five areas of psychosocial benefits from alcohol consumption: (a) stress reduction; (b) mood enhancement; (c) cognitive performance; (d) reduced clinical symptoms, primarily of depression; and (e) improved functioning in the elderly. Taking off from this and the more limited reviews that have appeared in recent years (Midanik, 1995; Pittman, 1996; Poikolainen, 1994), the present authors have updated and expanded Baum-Baicker's framework to include additional areas of benefit, drawing from ethnographic, psychological, and epidemiological research (Peele & Brodsky, 1998). This chapter summarizes these data as an invitation to take stock of their significance. Among the issues to be assessed are:

- The nature of the psychosocial benefits identified with alcohol consumption
- The types of evidence that support each benefit and how firmly established each is
- Whether and which of these benefits assume the J-shaped and U-shaped curves regularly found in mortality rate studies, in which moderate drinkers have better outcomes than either abstainers or heavy drinkers
- The explanatory power for health outcomes of such psychosocial benefits associated with moderate alcohol consumption

In Chapter 26 Peele explores the public health value of acknowledging such benefits in drinking.

METHODOLOGICAL ISSUES

What Constitutes Moderate Drinking?

The definition of optimal drinking for health purposes has been fairly well accepted in the United States and United Kingdom as one or two drinks daily and at the lower end of the range for women (Department of Health and Social Security, 1995; U.S. Department of Agriculture/Department of Health and Human Services, 1995). Going farther afield, however, this range may expand. Grønbæk et al. (1995) found mortality-rate gains for men and women up to three to five drinks of wine daily in Denmark, as did Fuchs et al. (1995) with a sample of women in the United States. Doll (1997) summarized various factors contributing to the relativity of both reported and optimal unit consumption across national boundaries, including extremely different definitions of what constitutes a standard drinking unit and the common underreporting of alcohol consumption. Thus, in Poikolainen's (1995) cross-cultural review, minimum mortality rate was associated with consumption levels ranging from one to five drinks daily. In the current review, which includes ethnographic as well as epidemiologic data and covers a range of cultural settings beyond those involved in typical epidemiologic studies, moderation is an even more variable ideal.

Single (1998; see also Chapter 25) extended this relativity to both quantitative and qualitative dimensions of beneficial drinking, primarily the frequency and distribution of consumption: the person consuming 7 to 14 drinks per week all at one sitting is less likely to experience either the cardiovascular or psychosocial benefits experienced by the person who averages the same number of drinks spread evenly through the week. Single proposed the following dimensions of a beneficial pattern of drinking: frequency of drinking occasions, volume of consumption per occasion, drinking settings (safe and pleasurable, involving diverse activities, ceremonial), characteristics of drinking companions, alcohol expectancies, and the absence of special considerations (medical, cultural, or situational) contraindicating any drinking.

Types of Effects Studied

The studies cited here, reviewed in greater detail by Peele and Brodsky (1998), encompass four general areas of benefit: psychological benefits (subjective health, mood enhancement, stress reduction, mental health), social benefits (sociability, leisure, social cohesion), cognitive and performance benefits, and benefits specific to the young and the elderly. These potential benefits, set out in Table 15.1, are found with varying degrees of confirming evidence using various methods of investigation, including experimental studies, prospective studies in natural environments, general-population or community surveys or correlational studies, self-report questionnaires or interviews, and ethnographic observations. Finally, two levels of exposure to alcohol are considered: immediate and habitual. Experimental studies typically contrast the effects of a single occasion of consumption with those of no consumption. Community studies (prospective or correlational) contrast the cumulative effects for individuals of a pattern of moderate consumption with those of abstinence or persistent heavy consumption. Ethnographic observations may focus on either immediate or longer-term exposure. Our review places greater emphasis on sustained, habitual moderate drinking, pointing to questions of lifestyle and outlook.

PSYCHOLOGICAL BENEFITS

Subjective Health

In a general population survey, Poikolainen, Vartiainen, and Korhonen (1996) found that moderate drinkers have a more favorable self-perception of their health status than either abstainers or heavy drinkers, thus replicating the J-shaped pattern found in actual health outcome studies. This finding is predictable in so far as subjective perceptions of good health have been found to correlate

Table 15.1   Areas of psychosocial benefit from alcohol and associated research on which each is based.

Benefit	Type of research
Psychological	
Subjective health	Correlational
Pleasure, positive experiences	Survey, experimental, observational, correlational, ethnographic
Stress reduction	Experimental, observational, survey
Mental health	Correlational
Social	
Sociability	Survey, experimental, observational, ethnographic
Leisure experience	Survey, observational, ethnographic
Social cohesion	Observational, ethnographic
Performance	
Cognitive	Survey, prospective
Creativity (idea generation, confidence)	Experimental, survey, observational
Income	Correlational
Special age groups	
Youth adjustment	Correlational, ethnographic
Elderly functioning	Experimental, prospective

with objective indicators of good health, which in turn are associated with moderate drinking. Because the researchers did not control for actual health status, various causal explanations may be offered, such as that healthy people (for both medical and social reasons) have more opportunities for social drinking.

Positive Sensations and Experiences

Respondents in surveys in the United States, Canada, and Sweden (Pernanen, 1991), Australia (Hall, 1996; Hall, Flaherty, & Homel, 1992), Finland (Mäkelä & Mustonen, 1988; Mäkelä & Simpura, 1985; Nyström, 1992), and the United Kingdom (Mass-Observation Archive, 1943, 1948) associate drinking predominantly—and routinely—with positive sensations and experiences. These include taste, mood, ritual, relaxation, and socializing. In one U.S. survey, the most common outcome of drinking reported by nonproblem drinkers was "felt happy and cheerful" (Cahalan, 1970). In another, 43% of adult male drinkers always or usually felt "friendly" when they drank, compared with 8% who felt "aggressive" and 2% who felt "sad" (Roizen, 1983).

These self-reports give a picture of normative drinking experiences in various countries without necessarily contrasting the self-reported experiences of drinkers (and nondrinkers) at different consumption levels. Such contrasts do emerge from alcohol expectancy research. For example, by performing a factor analysis of questionnaire responses, Brown, Goldman, Inn, and Anderson (1980) identified six independent expectations drinkers had about alcohol: (a) positive transformation of experience, (b) enhanced social and physical pleasure, (c) enhanced sexual performance and experience, (d) increased power and aggression, (e) increased social assertiveness, and (f) reduced tension. In this pioneering study of how expectancies vary with drinking patterns, less experienced drinkers had more global expectations, while the expectations of more experienced drinkers were more specifically focused on enhanced sexual and aggressive arousal. The implications of these findings for moderate versus heavy drinkers were made clearer in a study by Brown (1985), in which frequent but nonproblem drinkers emphasized expectations of social and physical pleasure, and problem drinkers strongly anticipated tension reduction.

Problem as well as nonproblem drinkers report positive expectations of and reactions to drinking; indeed, problem drinkers' positive as well as negative experiences of drinking are more intense than those of nonproblem drinkers (Cahalan, 1970). Brown's line of research suggests that problem drinkers seek positive effects for ego enhancement and to compensate for personal deficiencies (see Chapter 17), making them susceptible to seeking those sensations to unhealthy excess.

Enhanced Moods in Natural and Experimental Settings

For political, social, and ethical reasons, experimental research rarely has manipulated positive emotions (Stritzke, Lang, & Patrick, 1996; West & Sutker, 1990), although such studies did appear in an earlier, less constrained period. Freed (1978) reviewed a number of such studies, concluding that while nonalcoholics most often anticipate and attain enhanced feelings from drinking, alcoholics experience increasing dysphoria from alcohol. Combined with Brown and her colleagues' (Brown et al., 1980; Brown, Goldman, & Christiansen, 1985) demonstration that alcoholics seek intensely positive experiences from drinking, this finding indicates that moderate drinkers' expectations are more in line with the mood effects that they actually experience than are those of alcoholics.

In the current review, mood enhancement in individuals is considered separately from collective mood enhancement in social groups (termed *sociability* below), which is most commonly documented in naturalistic, ethnographic research. Yet, in the experimental setting as in real life, it is difficult to disentangle the individual's mood from the social context, which both conditions expectations of and interprets reactions to alcohol. Pliner and Cappell (1974), in an experimental variation that is almost unique in the human alcohol literature (Lang & Michalec, 1990), found that subjects experienced greater euphoria drinking in a group than drinking the same quantity alone. In an early experimental test of the effects of low doses of alcohol, the subjects were couples who were already involved with each other. This special kind of social context clearly influenced the finding that "all measures of elation were significantly increased from sober levels" (Smith, Parker, & Noble, 1975, p. 36).

The complexity of the relationship between mood enhancement and social facilitation was explored by Cooper, Russell, Skinner, and Windle (1992). These researchers identified the existence of three distinct motives for drinking: to enhance positive motives, to cope with negative emotions, and to affiliate socially with others. They established that mood enhancement and social motives are interrelated components of a normative pattern of drinking. They also found that people who drink primarily to enhance positive affect tend to drink more heavily than those who drink to regulate negative affect, yet are less likely to report serious drinking problems. Those who drink for enhancement and social motives are more likely to drink in convivial social settings; those who drink to cope are more likely to drink alone or else with one partner. The researchers inferred that social and mood-enhancing drinkers, more so than coping drinkers, benefit from both external (from the social environment) and internal (from greater emotional and behavioral control) constraints on their drinking.

In view of the difficulty researchers have had in documenting (other than naturalistically) the near-universal perception and reported experience that drinking within moderate limits makes people feel better, Lowe's (1996b) work in the United Kingdom is notable for its use of three different methodologies to establish a relationship between alcohol consumption and humor: (a) comparing the reactions of students who were given alcohol and nondrinking students to a film comedy (Lowe & Taylor, 1997), (b) correlating weekly alcohol consumption with frequency of laughter and humor in daily life (Lowe & Taylor, 1993), and (c) observing young drinkers in pubs smiling and laughing more the more alcohol they consumed (Lowe, 1996b). In addition, Warburton (Chapter 1) and his colleagues have demonstrated experimentally that social levels of alcohol consumption (8 g) enhance selective memory of positive words without detracting from ordinary memory.

Reduced Stress

Stress reduction is perhaps the most studied psychological effect of alcohol consumption (Baum-Baicker, 1985; Hull & Bond, 1986; Sher, 1987), bringing together as it does two major strands of alcohol research. On one side of its lineage, stress reduction descends from the tension-reduction model of problem drinking and alcoholism (Cappell & Greeley, 1987). On the other, alcohol's calming effect is also a major motivation for drinking identified in general-population surveys (Hall, 1996; Pernanen, 1991). Thus, stress reduction has been a major concern of both theoretical and empirical research over the whole continuum of moderate to heavy drinkers.

On the theoretical side, stress reduction has been a primary focus of explanatory models of the rewarding properties of alcohol. These include social learning (Abrams & Niaura, 1987), expectancy (Goldman, Brown, & Christiansen, 1987; Lang & Michalec, 1990; Leigh, 1990; see also Chapter 16), and psychophysiological (Stritzke et al., 1996) theories. These theoretical models highlight different ways in which pharmacological, cognitive, and other psychological and social processes may interact to shape people's drinking experiences. At the most general level, they propose that alcohol creates general mood susceptibilities on which social and individual expectancies imprint themselves. Experimental research (designed in many cases to confirm or disconfirm these theories) has explored exhaustively how, when, and with whom alcohol reduces stress. This research has produced complex interactions with respect to individual, gender, ethnic, expectancy, and setting or situational differences (Pohorecky, 1991; Wilson, 1988).

Several naturalistic studies have described how moderate drinkers experience stress reduction in ordinary settings, suggesting essential differences from the way problem drinkers drink in reaction to stress. In daily activity logs, subjects reported that moderate alcohol use had a calming effect even though they did not use it deliberately to reduce anxiety (de Castro, 1990). Culbert (1989) found that moderate drinkers *reduced* their drinking in response to major life stresses, presumably to mobilize higher-order coping mechanisms. Krause (1995) found that alcohol reduces stress arising in a person's less critical social roles but exacerbates stress occurring in more salient roles. These results support the ideas that alcohol is effective for general calming purposes but not as a primary coping tool (Cooper, Frone, Russell, & Mudar, 1995; Cooper, Russell, & George, 1988; Cox & Klinger, 1988) and that, compared with heavy or problem drinkers, moderate drinkers are less intensely and specifically motivated to drink to reduce stress (Brown, 1985; Brown et al., 1985; Brown et al., 1980).

Mental Health

That moderate alcohol consumption may be beneficial to mental health initially was suggested by Bell, Keeley, and Buhl's (1977) seminal correlational study based on interviews with 2000 randomly selected adults in the southern United States. Abstainers (including former heavy drinkers, a confounding factor) scored highest on anxiety and heavy drinkers highest on depression; light or moderate drinkers scored lowest on both. Bell et al. (p. 121) concluded "that the heavy alcohol user cannot be differentiated from the abstainer on the basis of psychopathological symptom configurations." The finding that abstainers often display rigid, avoidant coping styles has been supported by more recent research (Mertens, Moos, & Brennan, 1996; Watten, 1996). These findings suggest that abstainers share certain coping characteristics with problem drinkers or alcoholics, as indeed certain alcoholics alternate between these two extremes.

In another important correlational study, Lipton (1994) found with a southern California population a strong U-shaped relationship between alcohol consumption and depression in the presence of chronic strain combined with negative experiences, replicating a similar finding by Neff and Husaini (1982) in rural Tennessee. Although these studies did not control for the possibility that some abstainers had stopped drinking because of a preexisting health or drinking problem, Lipton found that overall results were unaffected when controlling for self-reported physical health. Moreover, relatively few members of the large proportion of abstainers (66%) in Neff and Husaini's study were likely former problem drinkers, showing that moderate drinkers can have a psychosocial advantage over abstainers even if abstinence is a norm. Studies using other populations and methods also have found superior mental health among moderate drinkers (Liu, Waterbor, & Soong, 1996; Winefield, Goldney, Winefield, & Tiggeman, 1992).

Notwithstanding the dearth of prospective or better-controlled community studies, there is substantial evidence that moderate drinking is an indicator and perhaps a cause of good mental health. The U-shaped curves found in studies in which some controls were applied or age considerations ruled out any substantial proportion of former problem drinkers increase the credibility of these findings, suggesting a parallel with physical health outcomes.

SOCIAL BENEFITS

Sociability

The role of alcohol in facilitating group interactions and enhancing the capacity of individuals to relate to others is a major theme of anthropological research and self-report studies.

Ethnographic Research   The centrality of sociability as a factor in alcohol use is a primary result of ethnographic research, as summed up by Heath (1995, p. 352):

> Drinking is fundamentally a social activity, and sociability is unquestionably the reason for drinking that is most cited in all of the countries that are described here. The same is true in almost all of the populations that have been studied by anthropologists around the world.... We are told that alcohol is "indispensable" for sociability (China, Denmark, Egypt). It is an integral part of "mateship" (male bonding) in Australia, Canada, and New Zealand; and the "regulars" are known and appreciated in pubs in Germany, Italy, and New Zealand. Drinking is "important to community solidarity" in Guatemala and among many of the tribal populations in India; it is said to be integral in relating to friends and general social participation in Spain and Mexico.

Self-report Studies   In population surveys (Lowe, 1994b; Roizen, 1983) as well as smaller-scale diary studies (de Castro, 1990; Wilks & Callan, 1990), sociability and friendliness typically are cited as primary motives for and consequences of drinking. In a survey in four Scandinavian countries, the positive consequences of drinking were "manifested first and foremost by a loss of inhibitions in company with other people and being better able to establish contact with other people" (Hauge & Irgens-Jensen, 1990, p. 652).

Experimental Studies of Sociability   In Pliner and Cappell's (1974) experiment showing that mood-enhancing effects of alcohol are amplified in a group setting, the independent variable was the social environment, not alcohol consumption. Smith, Kendrick, and Maben (1992) demonstrated that people both *feel* and *are perceived* as more sociable when they drink, alcohol consumption here being the independent variable. In this experiment, subjects who were given vodka and juice showed greater sociability; those given juice alone did not. Nonetheless, in other settings alcohol reveals a learned association with sociability, so that nonalcoholic drinks that drinkers believe to contain alcohol produce greater sociability (Darkes & Goldman, 1993; see Chapter 16).

Experimental studies assessing alcohol's effectiveness in reducing "social anxiety" (e.g., Bruch et al., 1992) have yielded the kinds of complex, highly inconsistent findings that characterize the stress-reduction literature generally. This has been especially true with respect to the differential effects of actual alcohol consumption as well as alcohol-related expectancies on men and women (Abrams & Wilson, 1979; de Boer, Schippers, & van der Staak, 1993, 1994; Wilson & Abrams, 1977). The inconsistencies in this line of research may be traceable in part to cultural differences—for example, drinking leads to social anxiety in American women not experienced by Dutch women. Related complex patterns concern self-disclosure by gender as influenced by alcohol expectancies and consumption (Caudill, Wilson, & Abrams, 1987; Hull, Levenson, Young, & Sher, 1983; Schippers, de Boer, & van der Staak, 1997), although in general garrulousness does increase with moderate alcohol consumption (Babor, Berglas, Mendelson, Ellingboe, & Miller, 1983; Higgins & Stitzer, 1988; Stitzer, Griffiths, Bigelow, & Liebson, 1981).

Leisure Enhancement

Despite the pervasive use of alcohol in conjunction with leisure activity worldwide (Argyle, 1987), Kunz's (1997) review of research on alcohol and leisure (including the impact of drinking on leisure and the role of active recreation in preventing alcohol abuse) identified methodological problems that make this line of research inconclusive. Earlier, Simpura (1985) had deplored the exclusion of drinking from systematic research on the use of leisure time.

Thus, the connections between drinking and leisure rely largely on ethnographic and self-report data. MacAndrew and Edgerton's (1969) cross-cultural exploration of the "time out" phenomenon established that people are socialized to know what degree of deviation from nondrinking behavior is acceptable, even during culturally sanctioned periods of alcoholic disinhibition. This classic analysis revealed the persistence of social controls even amid apparent license and mayhem. In a more positive light, American sociology has documented the favorable changes in affect and behavior that occur during transitions from work to play (Gusfield, 1987). College students, for example, experience stress reduction from drinking during such transitional periods (weeknights and early

Friday evenings), but not in the "play" zones of late Friday or Saturday evenings (Orcutt & Harvey, 1991).

Orcutt (1993, p. 390) has summarized the effects of drinking: "disinhibition, relaxation, and sociability signal to self and others the shift from the serious mood of workdays to the more spontaneous and playful mood of evenings and weekends." Drinking that violates these temporal norms (e.g., at work or early in the day) is defined as deviant (Reese & Katovich, 1989). In a telephone survey in the southwestern United States, respondents said they expected alcohol to affect their leisure experiences by (a) facilitating disengagement from responsibilities and tensions, (b) increasing self-assurance and acceptance, and (c) heightening engagement in immediate experience (Carruthers, 1993). Such expectancies apparently mirror actual drinking experiences and rewards.

Social Cohesion

Hunt (1990, pp. 243–244) summarized the way alcohol brings people together into social units, large or small, as a major sociological and anthropological theme: "The use of alcohol is seen as a social cement which along with other group activities binds together the members of the community thereby enhancing group solidarity." Studies of alcohol and social cohesion typically focus on public drinking places such as taverns (Single, 1993), whose social norms determine the level of alcohol consumption, whether moderate or heavy (Clark, 1981; Cosper, Okraku, & Neumann, 1987; Single & Wortley, 1993; Storm & Cutler, 1981; see also Chapter 19). In Canada, for example, adolescents who drink illegally in bars drink more moderately than those who drink away from adults (Smart, Adlaf, & Walsh, 1996). Observational studies consistently describe ritualized sociability in taverns (Fisher, 1981; Single & Storm, 1985); anthropological research has analyzed the shifting functions and benefits of such public drinking establishments throughout history and across cultures (Heath, 1991).

At the culture-wide level of cohesion, nations such as Greece, Italy, and Spain "have acquired a 'cultural immunity' to alcohol 'problems' based on the ways in which alcohol is interwoven into the matrix of the personal, social, and religious lives of the people of these societies" (Gefou-Madianou, 1992, p. 22). There is vast documentation of the moderating influences on drinking and its socialization in general (Blum & Blum, 1969; Maloff, Becker, Fonaroff, & Rodin, 1982; Peele & Brodsky, 1996) and for American subcultures (Greeley, McCready, & Theisen, 1980) such as the Chinese and other Asian groups (Barnett, 1955; O'Hare, 1995), Jews (Glassner & Berg, 1980), and Italians (versus Irish Americans; Vaillant, 1983). Contrasting with these are cultures with proscriptive norms (Akers, 1992), in which abstinence may not convey the psychosocial disadvantages that it does in cultures in which social drinking is the norm (Orcutt, 1991; see Chapter 26). In addition to moderation or abstinence, however, groups can cohere around excessive drinking, as in weekend binge drinking in college fraternities (Kuh & Arnold, 1993; Wechsler, Dowdall, Davenport, & Castillo, 1995).

PERFORMANCE BENEFITS

Long-term Cognitive Functioning

Notwithstanding the impairments of cognitive and psychomotor performance from acute exposure to alcohol (Finnigan & Hammersley, 1992), substantial evidence demonstrates that moderate drinkers show a higher level of cognitive functioning than abstainers. This suggests both that those with a higher level of cognitive functioning are more drawn to moderate drinking and also that there is a possibility of a beneficial long-term effect from alcohol. In a correlational study with a nonclinical sample of 21-year-old women, Bates and Tracy (1990, p. 247) cited the "large number of significant positive correlations between use intensity and cognitive abilities." The failure of a negative tail to appear in this analysis could be explained either by the relatively low levels of drinking in the population or the likelihood that negative long-term effects would not reveal themselves in such a youthful group.

A number of prospective and general-population studies reveal either no relationship in the elderly between cognitive ability and alcohol consumption (Dent et al., 1997; Hebert et al., 1993) or more often a curvilinear (Christian et al., 1995; Iliffe et al., 1991; Launer, Feskens, Kalmijn, & Kromhout, 1996) or a positive (Dufouil, Ducimetière, & Alperovitch, 1997) relationship. Several recent studies with older populations are worth noting. Orgogozo et al.'s (1997) prospective study of a French population yielded a curvilinear relationship between wine consumption and risk for dementia or Alzheimer's disease for both men and women. Hendrie, Gao, Hall, Hui, and Unverzagt (1996) found light drinking to be associated with better cognitive functioning and daily activity in one of the largest community studies among inner-city Black Americans. The study combined both genders and controlled for a range of variables found also to influence the dependent measures. The tested measures included a total cognitive function score, a measure of memory, and an activities-of-daily-living score. Findings obtained in varied populations and for different measures of cognitive functioning lean towards the interpretation that people benefit from drinking moderately in the long term, rather than only that healthier, better-functioning people have more opportunities and desire to drink moderately. Nonetheless, additional prospective studies are needed to strengthen the case that, as with cardiovascular and mortality outcomes, alcohol has such a directly beneficial effect.

Creativity

Studies of the effects of alcohol use on creativity have had mixed results (Lapp, Collins, & Izzo, 1994; Lowe, 1996a; Ludwig, 1990), which may be a function of cultural differences as well as the difficulty of developing adequate research paradigms for this complex phenomenon. Alcohol may facilitate the incubation phase of creativity but obstruct complex intellectual processing (Gustafson & Norlander, 1994; Norlander & Gustafson, 1996), may help inhibited subjects

(Lowe, 1994a), can reduce writer's block (Brunke & Gilbert, 1992), and can be used for self-stimulation (Koski-Jannes, 1985). In two well-designed experimental studies, Lang, Verret, and Watt (1984) found that alcohol consumption did not actually affect creative performance (although subjects who had drunk judged their work more favorably), and Lapp et al. found that drinking had a substantial placebo effect on creativity, but no pharmacological effect.

Income

Work performance, as measured by income, shows a clear advantage for moderate drinkers in several correlational studies done to date. In a study using U.S. survey data (with former drinkers separated for analysis), moderate drinkers (2.0–3.5 drinks per day) had the highest earnings (Heien, 1996). French and Zarkin (1995, p. 319), in a questionnaire survey of randomly selected employees at four U.S. work sites, found that "controlling for other variables and conditional on working, moderate alcohol users have higher wages [peaking at 1.7 to 2.4 drinks per day] than abstainers and heavy drinkers." The parallel to the U-shaped relationship found with drinking and heart disease is striking, although this research is correlational rather than prospective. Possible explanations for the successful work performance of moderate drinkers include both better physical health and psychosocial adjustment.

BENEFITS AT BOTH ENDS OF THE LIFE SPAN

Youth

Heavy, problematic drinking is a hazard of youth (Helzer, Burnam, & McEvoy, 1991). In the United States, concern over concentrated heavy drinking among teenagers and young adults lately has focused on collegiate "binge drinking" (Wechsler, Davenport, Dowdall, Moeykens, & Castillo, 1994; Wechsler et al., 1995). Yet some consider this application of a term that heretofore signified explosive, loss-of-control drinking by alcoholics to be inaccurate and alarmist (Gose, 1997). In Canada, underaged drinkers on the whole are no more likely to be heavy or problem drinkers than are legal drinkers (Smart et al., 1996). Other research indicates that young people who experiment with alcohol may be better adjusted than those who abstain or drink excessively. In Norway, young males who first got drunk in middle adolescence had fewer psychological problems than those who did so earlier or later (Pape & Hammer, 1996). Likewise, in the United States, Nezlek, Pilkington, and Bilbro (1994) found that college students who reported a "moderate" frequency of binge-drinking episodes had more—and more intimate—social interaction than those who reported a greater frequency or none at all. In other words, those who drink normatively (allowing for the risks of such behavior for inexperienced drinkers) are integrated more fully socially and psychologically. As a context for interpreting these data, cultures that successfully inculcate moderate drinking practices (such as the Jewish and Chinese) matter-of-factly accept youthful drinking as an opportunity for learning accepted social behavior—a model of socialization recommended by Lowe and Foxcroft (1993).

Elderly

As a rule, the elderly are moderate, social drinkers (Adams, 1996; Alexander & Duff, 1988; Busby, Campbell, Borrie, & Spears, 1988; Hanson, 1994; Meyers, Hingson, Mucatel, Heeren, & Goldman, 1985/1986) with fewer drinking problems than other age groups (Hilton & Clark, 1991), the exceptions being mainly among isolated individuals (Hanson, 1994). Stall (1986) found that formerly heavy drinkers typically reduce consumption with age in response to reduced tolerance for alcohol and finances. Moreover, for older Americans, like other adult populations, moderate drinking has life-prolonging effects (Mertens et al., 1996; Scherr et al., 1992; Simons, Friedlander, McCallum, & Simons, 1996; Thun et al., 1997).

In addition, research has indicated that elderly drinkers enjoy psychosocial and therapeutic benefits of drinking (see, e.g., Black, 1969; Chien, 1971; Mishara & Kastenbaum, 1974; Volpe & Kastenbaum, 1967). Mishara and Kastenbaum (1980) summarized research showing that patients in geriatric units and nursing homes given beer or wine daily increased social interaction and participation in the milieu relative to control groups and demonstrated improved orientation, morale, general functioning, and cognitive capacity and reduced need for sleeping medications. Analogous findings were obtained among the noninstitutionalized elderly. Dufour, Archer, and Gordis (1992) called these results promising, relying on a study by Mishara, Kastenbaum, Baker, and Patterson (1975) that continued to find the identified benefits and utilized stricter methodological controls than in other research. A recent study reiterated many of these results with elderly drinkers. Examining reports "that retirement communities have a particularly high prevalence of heavy drinking," Adams (1996, p. 1082) found instead in three retirement communities that, although "regular alcohol use was prevalent . . . heavy and abusive drinking were uncommon. . . . Drinking appears to be associated with more social contacts and, possibly, better health status."

CONCLUSION

The disparate research reviewed here broadens the universe of relationships with alcohol consumption beyond health outcomes to psychological adjustment, social integration, productivity, and effective functioning. To a greater degree than either abstainers or heavy drinkers, moderate drinkers experience these indicators of psychological and social well-being. The relationships appear with sufficient frequency across different populations, study variables, and methods of investigation to suggest an underlying pattern analogous to and interlinked with the well established U- or J-shaped relationship between alcohol consumption and increased health benefits and longevity.

The challenge in interpreting such robust yet diverse and complex findings is to say anything meaningful about directions of causality, because ethnographic, self-report, correlational, prospective, and experimental studies justify the assignment of different degrees of predictive power to alcohol consumption as a causal variable. We envision a complex model by which the observed benefits of moderate drinking do not flow directly from the pharmacology of alcohol but are created through positive drinking habits as experienced and interpreted in a context conditioned by culture, social environment, and expectation (Harburg, Gleiberman, DiFranceisco, & Peele, 1994). In this complex causal nexus, alcohol is not the sole cause of cardiovascular and other health benefits associated with it (Peele, 1997; Skog, 1995), but it is likely that moderate alcohol consumption does have independent causal significance in the creation of its psychosocial concomitants.

For now, we can say with some confidence that moderate alcohol consumption is part of a cluster of interrelated factors that we identify provisionally as follows: life orientation (motives, values, resources, decision making); drinking patterns and levels; other health-related behaviors; physical health; psychosocial well-being; and productivity and economic success. More basically, individuals with a positive, health-seeking orientation to life use alcohol within a larger framework of self-regulation and pleasure (Grossarth-Maticek & Eysenck, 1995; Grossarth-Maticek, Eysenck, & Boyle, 1995). Healthful drinking is thus a part of an orientation that includes a range of productive and healthful behaviors that in combination generate positive sensations, health outcomes, and additional reinforcement including social support and cohesion.

REFERENCES

Abrams, D. B., & Niaura, R. S. (1987). Social learning theory. In H. T. Blane & K. E. Leonard (Eds.), *Psychological theories of drinking and alcoholism* (pp. 131–178). New York: Guilford.

Abrams, D. B., & Wilson, G. T. (1979). Effect of alcohol on social anxiety in women: Cognitive versus pharmacological processes. *Journal of Abnormal Psychology, 68*, 168–173.

Adams, W. L. (1996). Alcohol use in retirement communities. *Journal of the American Geriatric Society, 44*, 1082–1085.

Akers, R. L. (1992). *Drugs, alcohol and society: Social structure, process and policy.* Belmont, MA: Wadsworth.

Alexander, F., & Duff, R. W. (1988). Social interaction and alcohol use in retirement communities. *Gerontologist, 28*, 632–636.

Argyle, M. (1987). *The psychology of happiness.* London: Methuen.

Babor, T. F., Berglas, S., Mendelson, J. H., Ellingboe, J., & Miller, K. (1983). Alcohol, affect, and the disinhibition of verbal behavior. *Psychopharmacology, 80*, 53–60.

Barnett, M. L. (1955). Alcoholism in the Cantonese of New York City: An anthropological study. In O. Diethelm (Ed.), *Etiology of chronic alcoholism* (pp. 179–227). Springfield, IL: Thomas.

Bates, M. E., & Tracy, J. I. (1990). Cognitive functioning in young "social drinkers:" Is there impairment to detect? *Journal of Abnormal Psychology, 99,* 242–249.

Baum-Baicker, C. (1985). The psychological benefits of moderate alcohol consumption: A review of the literature. *Drug and Alcohol Dependence, 15,* 305–322.

Bell, R. A., Keeley, K. A., & Buhl, J. M. (1977). Psychopathology and life events among alcohol users and nonusers. In F. A. Seixas (Ed.), *Currents in alcoholism* (Vol. 2, pp. 103–123). New York: Grune & Stratton.

Black, A. L. (1969). Altering behavior of geriatric patients with beer. *Northwest Medicine, 68,* 453–456.

Blum, R. H., & Blum, E. M. (1969). A cultural case study. In R. H. Blum & Associates (Eds.), *Drugs: Vol. 1. Society and drugs* (pp. 188–227). San Francisco, CA: Jossey-Bass.

Brown, S. A. (1985). Expectancies versus background in the prediction of college drinking patterns. *Journal of Consulting and Clinical Psychology, 53,* 123–130.

Brown, S. A., Goldman, M. S., & Christiansen, B. A. (1985). Do alcohol expectancies mediate drinking patterns of adults? *Journal of Consulting and Clinical Psychology, 53,* 512–519.

Brown, S. A., Goldman, M. S., Inn, A., & Anderson, L. R. (1980). Expectations of reinforcement from alcohol: Their domain and relation to drinking patterns. *Journal of Consulting and Clinical Psychology, 48,* 419–426.

Bruch, M. A., Heimberg, R. G., Harvey, C., McCann, M., Mahone, M., & Slavkin, S. L. (1992). Shyness, alcohol expectancies, and alcohol use: Discovery of a suppressor effect. *Journal of Research on Personality, 26,* 137–149.

Brunke, M., & Gilbert, M. (1992). Alcohol and creative writing. *Psychological Reports, 71,* 651–658.

Busby, W. J., Campbell, A. J., Borrie, M. J., & Spears, G. F. S. (1988). Alcohol use in a community-based sample of subjects aged 70 years and older. *Journal of the American Geriatric Society, 36,* 301–305.

Cahalan, D. (1970). *Problem drinkers: A national survey.* San Francisco, CA: Jossey-Bass.

Cappell, H., & Greeley, J. (1987). Alcohol and tension reduction: An update on research and theory. In H. T. Blane & K. E. Leonard (Eds.), *Psychological theories of drinking and alcoholism* (pp. 15–54). New York: Guilford.

Carruthers, C. P. (1993). Leisure and alcohol expectancies. *Journal of Leisure Research, 25,* 229–244.

Caudill, B. D., Wilson, G. T., & Abrams, D. B. (1987). Alcohol and self-disclosure: Analyses of interpersonal behavior in male and female social drinkers. *Journal of Studies on Alcohol, 48,* 401–409.

Chien, C.-P. (1971). Psychiatric treatment for geriatric patients: "Pub" or drug? *American Journal of Psychiatry, 127,* 1070–1075.

Christian, J. C., Reed, T., Carmelli, D., Page, W. F., Norton, J. A., & Breitner, J. C. S. (1995). Self-reported alcohol intake and cognition in aging twins. *Journal of Studies on Alcohol, 56,* 414–416.

Clark, W. B. (1981). Public drinking contexts: Bars and taverns. In T. C. Harford & L. S. Gaines (Eds.), *Social drinking contexts: Proceedings of a workshop, September 17–19, 1979, Washington, D. C.* (NIAAA Research Monograph No. 7, pp. 8–33). Rockville, MD: National Institute on Alcohol Abuse and Alcoholism.

Cleare, A. J., & Wessely, S. C. (1997). Just what the doctor ordered: More alcohol and sex. *British Medical Journal, 315,* 1637–1638.

Cooper, M. L., Frone, M. R., Russell, M., & Mudar, P. (1995). Drinking to regulate positive and negative emotions: A motivational model of alcohol use. *Journal of Personality and Social Psychology, 69,* 990–1005.

Cooper, M. L., Russell, M., & George, W. H. (1988). Coping, expectancies, and alcohol abuse: A test of social learning formulations. *Journal of Abnormal Psychology, 97,* 218–230.

Cooper, M. L., Russell, M., Skinner, J. B., & Windle, M. (1992). Development and validation of a three-dimensional measure of drinking motives. *Psychological Assessment, 4,* 123–132.

Cosper, R. L., Okraku, I. O., & Neumann, B. (1987). Tavern going in Canada: A national survey of regulars at public drinking establishments. *Journal of Studies on Alcohol, 48*, 252–259.

Cox, M., & Klinger, E. (1988). A motivational model of alcohol use. *Journal of Abnormal Psychology, 97*, 168–180.

Culbert, D. S. (1989). Drinking, expectancies, life stress, and social support as predictors of alcohol use. *Dissertation Abstracts International, 51*, 424B.

Darkes, J., & Goldman, M. S. (1993). Expectancy challenge and drinking reduction: Experimental evidence for a mediational process. *Journal of Consulting and Clinical Psychology, 61*, 344–353.

de Boer, M. C., Schippers, G. M., & van der Staak, C. P. F. (1993). Alcohol and social anxiety in women and men: Pharmacological and expectancy effects. *Addictive Behaviors, 18*, 117–126.

de Boer, M. C., Schippers, G. M., & van der Staak, C. P. F. (1994). The effects of alcohol, expectancy, and alcohol beliefs on anxiety and self-disclosure in women: Do beliefs moderate alcohol effects? *Addictive Behaviors, 19*, 509–520.

de Castro, J. M. (1990). Social, circadian, nutritional, and subjective correlates of the spontaneous pattern of moderate alcohol intake of normal humans. *Pharmacology, Biochemistry & Behavior, 35*, 923–931.

Dent, O. F., Sulway, M. R., Broe, G. A., Creasy, H., Kos, S. C., Jorm, A. F., Tennant, C., & Fairley, M. J. (1997). Alcohol consumption and cognitive performance in a random sample of Australian soldiers who served in the Second World War. *British Medical Journal, 314*, 1655–1657.

Department of Health and Social Security. (1995). *Sensible drinking: The report of an interdepartmental working group*. London: Her Majesty's Stationery Office.

Doll, R. (1997). One for the heart. *British Medical Journal, 315*, 1664–1668.

Dufouil, C., Ducimetière, P., & Alperovitch, A. (1997). Sex differences in the association between alcohol consumption and cognitive performance. *American Journal of Epidemiology, 146*, 405–412.

Dufour, M. C., Archer, L., & Gordis, E. (1992). Alcohol and the elderly. *Clinics in Geriatric Medicine, 8*, 127–141.

Edwards, G., Anderson, P., Babor, T. F., Casswell, S., Ferrence, R., Giesbrecht, N., Godfrey, C., Holder, H. D., Lemmens, P., Mäkelä, K., Midanik, L. T., Nostrom, T., Österberg, E., Romelsjö, A., Room, R., Simpura, J., Skog, O.-J. (1994). *Alcohol policy and the public good*. Oxford, UK: Oxford University Press.

Finnigan, F., & Hammersley, R. (1992). The effects of alcohol on performance. In A. P. Smith & D. M. Jones (Eds.), *Handbook of human performance* (Vol. 2, pp. 73–126). London: Academic Press.

Fisher, J. C. (1981). Psychosocial correlates of tavern use: A national probability sample study. In T. C. Harford & L. S. Gaines (Eds.), *Social drinking contexts: Proceedings of a workshop, September 17–19, 1979, Washington, D.C.* (NIAAA Research Monograph No. 7, pp. 34–53). Rockville, MD: National Institute on Alcohol Abuse and Alcoholism.

Freed, E. X. (1978). Alcohol and mood: An updated review. *International Journal of the Addictions, 13*, 173–200.

French, M. T., & Zarkin, G. A. (1995). Is moderate alcohol use related to wages: Evidence from four worksites. *Journal of Health Economics, 14*, 319–344.

Fuchs, C. S., Stampfer, M. J., Colditz, G. A., Giovannucci, E. L., Manson, J. E., Kawachi, I., Hunter, D. J., Hankinson, S. E., Hennekens, C. H., Rosner, B., Speizer, F. E., & Willett, W. C. (1995). Alcohol consumption and mortality among women. *New England Journal of Medicine, 332*, 1245–1250.

Gefou-Madianou, D. (Ed.). (1992). *Alcohol, gender and culture*. London: Routledge.

Glassner, B., & Berg, B. (1980). How Jews avoid alcohol problems. *American Sociological Review, 45*, 647–664.

Goldman, M. S., Brown, S. A., & Christiansen, B. A. (1987). Expectancy theory: Thinking about drinking. In H. T. Blane & K. E. Leonard (Eds.), *Psychological theories of drinking and alcoholism* (pp. 181–226). New York: Guilford.

Gose, B. (1997, October 24). Colleges try to curb excessive drinking by saying moderation is okay. *Chronicle of Higher Education*, p. A61.

Greeley, A. M., McCready, W. C., & Theisen, G. (1980). *Ethnic drinking subcultures.* New York: Praeger.

Grønbæk, M., Deis A., Sørensen, T. I. A., Becker, U., Schnohr, P., & Jensen, G. (1995). Mortality associated with moderate intakes of wine, beer, or spirits. *British Medical Journal, 310,* 1165–1169.

Grossarth-Maticek, R., & Eysenck, H. J. (1995). Self-regulation and mortality from cancer, coronary heart disease, and other causes: A prospective study. *Personality and Individual Differences, 19,* 781–795.

Grossarth-Maticek, R., Eysenck, H. J., & Boyle, G. J. (1995). Alcohol consumption and health: Synergistic interaction with personality. *Psychological Reports, 77,* 675–687.

Gusfield, J. (1987). Passage to play: Rituals of drinking time in American society. In M. Douglas (Ed.), *Constructive drinking: Perspectives on drink from anthropology* (pp. 73–90). Cambridge, UK: Cambridge University Press.

Gustafson, R., & Norlander, T. (1994). Effects of alcohol on persistent effort and deductive thinking during the preparation phase of the creative process. *Journal of Creative Behavior, 28,* 124–132.

Hall, W. (1996). Changes in the public perceptions of the health benefits of alcohol use, 1989 to 1994. *Australian and New Zealand Journal of Public Health, 20,* 93–95.

Hall, W., Flaherty, B., & Homel, P. (1992). The public perception of the risks and benefits of alcohol consumption. *Australian and New Zealand Journal of Public Health, 16,* 38–42.

Hanson, B. S. (1994). Social network, social support and heavy drinking in elderly men: A population study of men born in 1914, Malmö, Sweden. *Addiction, 89,* 725–732.

Harburg, E., Gleiberman, L., DiFranceisco, W., & Peele, S. (1994). Towards a concept of sensible drinking and an illustration of measure. *Alcohol and Alcoholism, 29,* 439–450.

Hauge, R., & Irgens-Jensen, O. (1990). The experiencing of positive consequences of drinking in four Scandinavian countries. *British Journal of Addiction, 85,* 645–653.

Heath, D. B. (1991). Alcohol studies and anthropology. In D. J. Pittman & H. R. White (Eds.), *Society, culture, and drinking patterns reexamined* (pp. 87–108). New Brunswick, NJ: Rutgers Center of Alcohol Studies.

Heath, D. B. (1995). Some generalizations about alcohol and culture. In D. B. Heath (Ed.), *International handbook on alcohol and culture* (pp. 348–361). Westport, CT: Greenwood Press.

Hebert, L. E., Scherr, P. A., Beckett, L. A., Albert, M. S., Rosner, B., Taylor, J. O., & Evans, D. A. (1993). Relation of smoking and low-to-moderate alcohol consumption to change in cognitive function: A longitudinal study in a defined community of older persons. *American Journal of Epidemiology, 137,* 881–891.

Heien, D. (1996). The relationship between alcohol consumption and earnings. *Journal of Studies on Alcohol, 57,* 536–542.

Helzer, J. E., Burnam, A., & McEvoy, L. T. (1991). Alcohol abuse and dependence. In L. N. Robins & D. A. Regier (Eds.), *Psychiatric disorders in America* (pp. 81–115). New York: Free Press.

Hendrie, H. C., Gao, S., Hall, K. S., Hui, S. L., & Unverzagt, F. W. (1996). The relationship between alcohol consumption, cognitive performance, and daily functioning in an urban sample of older Black Americans. *Journal of the American Geriatric Society, 44,* 1158–1165.

Higgins, S. T., & Stitzer, M. L. (1988). Effects of alcohol on speaking in isolated humans. *Psychopharmacology, 95,* 189–194.

Hilton, M. E., & Clark, W. B. (1991). Changes in American drinking patterns and problems, 1967–1984. In D. J. Pittman & H. R. White (Eds.), *Society, culture, and drinking patterns reexamined* (pp. 157–172). New Brunswick, NJ: Rutgers Center of Alcohol Studies.

Hull, J. G., & Bond, C. F. (1986). Social and behavioral consequences of alcohol consumption and expectancy: A meta-analysis. *Psychological Bulletin, 99*, 347–360.

Hull, J. G., Levenson, R. W., Young, R. D., & Sher, K. J. (1983). Self-awareness-reducing effects of alcohol consumption. *Journal of Personality and Social Psychology, 44*, 461–473.

Hunt, G. P. (1990). The anthropology of drinking: A case of cohesion without division. *Alcologia, 2*, 243–247.

Iliffe, S., Haines, A., Booroff, A., Goldenberg, E., Morgan, P., & Gallivan, S. (1991). Alcohol consumption by elderly people: A general practice survey. *Age and Aging, 20*, 120–123.

Koski-Jannes, A. (1985). Alcohol and literary creativity: The Finnish experience. *Journal of Creative Behavior, 19*, 120–136.

Krause, N. (1995). Stress, alcohol use, and depressive symptoms in later life. *Gerontologist, 35*, 296–307.

Kuh, G. D., & Arnold, J. C. (1993). Liquid bonding: A cultural analysis of the role of alcohol in fraternity pledgeship. *Journal of College Student Development, 34*, 327–334.

Kunz, J. L. (1997). Associating leisure with drinking: Current research and future directions. *Drug and Alcohol Review, 16*, 69–76.

Lang, A. R., & Michalec, E. M. (1990). Expectancy effects in reinforcement from alcohol. In W. M. Cox (Ed.), *Why people drink: Parameters of alcohol as a reinforcer* (pp. 193–232). New York: Gardner.

Lang, A. R., Verret, L. D., & Watt, C. (1984). Drinking and creativity: Objective and subjective effects. *Addictive Behaviors, 9*, 395–399.

Lapp, W. M., Collins, R. L., & Izzo, C. V. (1994). On the enhancement of creativity by alcohol: Pharmacology or expectation? *American Journal of Psychology, 107*, 173–206.

Launer, L. J., Feskens, E. J. M., Kalmijn, S., & Kromhout, D. (1996). Smoking, drinking, and thinking: The Zutphen elderly study. *American Journal of Epidemiology, 143*, 219–227.

Leigh, B. C. (1990). The relationship of sex-related alcohol expectancies to alcohol consumption and sexual behavior. *British Journal of Addiction, 85*, 919–928.

Lipton, R. I. (1994). The effect of moderate alcohol use on the relationship between stress and depression. *American Journal of Public Health, 84*, 1913–1917.

Liu, T., Waterbor, J. W., & Soong, S.-J. (1996). Relationships between beer, wine, and spirits consumption and suicide rates in U.S. states from 1977 to 1988. *Omega, 32*, 227–240.

Lowe, G. (1994a). Group differences in alcohol-creativity interactions. *Psychological Reports, 75*, 1635–1638.

Lowe, G. (1994b). Pleasures of social relaxants and stimulants: The ordinary person's attitudes and involvement. In D. M. Warburton (Ed.), *Pleasure: The politics and the reality* (pp. 95–108). Chichester, UK: Wiley.

Lowe, G. (1996a). Creativity: Links with alcohol and other substance use. In D. M. Warburton & N. Sherwood (Eds.), *Pleasure and quality of life* (pp. 131–145). Chichester, UK: Wiley.

Lowe, G. (1996, December). *Drinking behaviour and links with humour and laughter.* Paper presented at the British Psychological Society's London Conference, London.

Lowe, G., & Foxcroft, D. R. (1993). Young people, drinking and family life. *Alcologia, 5*, 205–209.

Lowe, G., & Taylor, S. B. (1993). Relationship between laughter and weekly alcohol consumption. *Psychological Reports, 72*, 1210.

Lowe, G., & Taylor, S. B. (1997). Effects of alcohol on responsive laughter and amusement. *Psychological Reports, 80*, 1149–1150.

Ludwig, A. M. (1990). Alcohol input and creative output. *British Journal of Addiction, 85*, 953–963.

MacAndrew, C., & Edgerton, R. B. (1969). *Drunken comportment: A social explanation.* Chicago, IL: Aldine.

Mäkelä, K., & Mustonen, H. (1988). Positive and negative consequences related to drinking as a function of annual alcohol intake. *British Journal of Addiction, 83*, 403–408.

Mäkelä, K., & Simpura, J. (1985). Experiences related to drinking as a function of annual alcohol intake and by sex and age. *Drug and Alcohol Dependence, 15*, 389–404.

Maloff, D., Becker, H. S., Fonaroff, A., & Rodin, J. (1982). Informal social controls and their influence on substance use. In N. E. Zinberg & W. M. Harding (Eds.), *Control over intoxicant use* (pp. 53–76). New York: Human Sciences Press.

Mass-Observation Archive. (1943). *The pub and the people*. Falmer, UK: University of Sussex Mass-Observation Archive.

Mass-Observation Archive. (1948). *Drinking habits*. Falmer, UK: University of Sussex Mass-Observation Archive.

Mertens, J. R., Moos, R. H., & Brennan, P. L. (1996). Alcohol consumption, life context, and coping predict mortality among late-middle-aged drinkers and former drinkers. *Alcoholism: Clinical and Experimental Research, 20*, 313–319.

Meyers, A. R., Hingson, R., Mucatel, M., Heeren, T., & Goldman, E. (1985/1986). The social epidemiology of alcohol use by urban older adults. *International Journal of Aging and Human Development, 21*, 49–59.

Midanik, L. T. (1995). Alcohol consumption and social consequences, dependence, and positive benefits in general population surveys. In H. D. Holder & G. Edwards (Eds.), *Alcohol and public policy: Evidence and issues* (pp. 62–81). Oxford, UK: Oxford University Press.

Mishara, B. L., & Kastenbaum, R. (1974). Wine in the treatment of long-term geriatric patients in mental institutions. *Journal of the American Geriatric Society, 22*, 88–94.

Mishara, B. L., & Kastenbaum, R. (1980). *Alcohol and old age*. New York: Grune & Stratton.

Mishara, B. L., Kastenbaum, R., Baker, F., & Patterson, R. D. (1975). Alcohol effects in old age: An experimental investigation. *Social Science and Medicine, 9*, 535–547.

Neff, J. A., & Husaini, B. A. (1982). Life events, drinking patterns and depressive symptomatology. *Journal of Studies on Alcohol, 43*, 301–318.

Nezlek, J. B., Pilkington, C. J., & Bilbro, K. G. (1994). Moderation in excess: Binge drinking and social interaction among college students. *Journal of Studies on Alcohol, 55*, 342–351.

Norlander, T., & Gustafson, R. (1996). Effects of alcohol on scientific thought during the incubation phase of the creative process. *Journal of Creative Behavior, 30*, 231–248.

Nyström, M. (1992). Positive and negative consequences of alcohol drinking among young university students in Finland. *British Journal of Addiction, 87*, 715–722.

O'Hare, T. (1995). Differences in Asian and White drinking: Consumption level, drinking contexts, and expectancies. *Addictive Behaviors, 20*, 261–266.

Orcutt, J. D. (1991). Beyond the "exotic and the pathologic:" Alcohol problems, norm qualities, and sociological theories of deviance. In P. M. Roman (Ed.), *Alcohol: The development of sociological perspectives on use and abuse* (pp. 145–173). New Brunswick, NJ: Rutgers Center of Alcohol Studies.

Orcutt, J. D. (1993). Happy hour and social lubrication: Evidence on mood-setting rituals of drinking time. *Journal of Drug Issues, 23*, 389–407.

Orcutt, J. D., & Harvey, L. K. (1991). The temporal patterning of tension reduction: Stress and alcohol use on weekdays and weekends. *Journal of Studies on Alcohol, 52*, 415–424.

Orgogozo, J.-M., Dartigues, J-F., Lafont, S., Letenneur, L., Commenges, D., Salamon, E., Renaud, S., & Breteler, M. B. (1997). Wine consumption and dementia in the elderly: A prospective community study in the Bordeaux area. *Revue Neurologique, 153*, 185–192.

Pape, H., & Hammer, T. (1996). Sober adolescence: Predictor of psychological maladjustment in young adulthood? *Scandinavian Journal of Psychology, 37*, 362–377.

Peele, S. (1997). Utilizing culture and behavior in epidemiological models of alcohol consumption and consequences for Western nations. *Alcohol and Alcoholism, 32*, 51–64.

Peele, S., & Brodsky, A. (1996). *Alcohol and society: How culture influences the way people drink*. San Francisco: The Wine Institute. (Available on-line at http://www.peele.sas.nl/lib/sociocul.html)

Peele, S., & Brodsky, A. (1998). *Psychosocial benefits of moderate alcohol use: Associations and causes*. Unpublished manuscript.

Pernanen, K. (1991). *Alcohol in human violence*. New York: Guilford.

Pittman, D. J. (1996). What do we know about beneficial consequences of moderate alcohol consumption on social and physical well-being? A critical review of the recent literature. *Contemporary Drug Problems, 23*, 389–406.

Pliner, P., & Cappell, H. (1974). Modification of affective consequences of alcohol: A comparison of social and solitary drinking. *Journal of Abnormal Psychology, 83*, 418–425.

Pohorecky, L. A. (1991). Stress and alcohol interaction: An update of human research. *Alcoholism: Clinical and Experimental Research, 15*, 438–459.

Poikolainen, K. (1994). The other health benefits of moderate alcohol intake. *Contemporary Drug Problems, 21*, 91–99.

Poikolainen, K. (1995). Alcohol and mortality: A review. *Journal of Clinical Epidemiology, 48*, 455–465.

Poikolainen, K., Vartiainen, E., & Korhonen, H. J. (1996). Alcohol intake and subjective health. *American Journal of Epidemiology, 144*, 346–350.

Reese, W. A., & Katovich, M. A. (1989). Untimely acts: Extending the interactionist conception of deviance. *Sociological Quarterly, 30*, 159–184.

Roizen, R. (1983). Loosening up: General population views of the effects of alcohol. In R. Room & G. Collins (Eds.), *Alcohol and disinhibition: Nature and meaning of the link. Proceedings of a conference, February 11–13, 1981, Berkeley/Oakland, California* (NIAAA Research Monograph No. 12, pp. 236–257). Rockville, MD: National Institute on Alcohol Abuse and Alcoholism.

Scherr, P. A., LaCroix, A. Z., Wallace, R. B., Berkman, L., Curb, J. D., Cornoni-Huntley, J., Evans, D. A., & Hennekens, C. H. (1992). Light to moderate alcohol consumption and mortality in the elderly. *Journal of the American Geriatric Society, 40*, 651–657.

Schippers, G. M., de Boer, M. C., & van der Staak, C. P. F. (1997). Effects of alcohol and expectancy on self-disclosure and anxiety in male and female social drinkers. *Addictive Behaviors, 22*, 305–314.

Sher, K. J. (1987). Stress response dampening. In H. T. Blane & K. E. Leonard (Eds.), *Psychological theories of drinking and alcoholism* (pp. 227–271). New York: Guilford.

Simons, L. A., Friedlander, Y., McCallum, J., & Simons, J. (1996). Predictors of mortality in the prospective Dubbo study of Australian elderly. *Australian and New Zealand Journal of Medicine, 26*, 40–48.

Simpura, J. (1985). Drinking: An ignored leisure activity. *Journal of Leisure Research, 17*, 200–211.

Single, E. (1993). Public drinking. In M. Galanter (Ed.), *Recent developments in alcoholism: Vol. 11. Ten years of progress* (pp. 143–152). New York: Plenum.

Single, E. (1998, February). *What constitutes a beneficial pattern of drinking: An epidemiological perspective.* Paper presented at the International Conference on Drinking Patterns and Their Consequences, Perth, Australia.

Single, E., & Storm, T. (1985). *Public drinking and public policy.* Toronto, Canada: Addiction Research Foundation.

Single, E., & Wortley, S. (1993). Drinking in various settings as it relates to demographic variables and level of consumption: Findings from a national survey in Canada. *Journal of Studies on Alcohol, 54*, 590–599.

Skog, O.-J. (1995). The J-curve, causality and public health. *Addiction, 90*, 490–492.

Smart, R. G., Adlaf, E. M., & Walsh, G. W. (1996). Procurement of alcohol and underage drinking among adolescents in Ontario. *Journal of Studies on Alcohol, 57*, 419–424.

Smith, A., Kendrick, A., & Maben, A. (1992). Use and effects of food and drinks in relation to daily rhythms of mood and cognitive performance: Effects of caffeine, lunch and alcohol on human performance, mood and cardiovascular function. *Proceedings of the Nutrition Society, 51*, 325–333.

Smith, R. C., Parker, E. S., & Noble, E. P. (1975). Alcohol and affect in dyadic social interaction. *Psychosomatic Medicine, 37*, 25–40.

Stall, R. (1986). Respondent-independent reasons for change and stability in alcohol consumption as a concomitant of the aging process. In C. R. Janes, R. Stall, & S. M. Gifford (Eds.), *Anthropology and epidemiology: Interdisciplinary approaches to the study of health and disease* (pp. 275–301). Boston, MA: Reidel.

Stitzer, M. L., Griffiths, R. R., Bigelow, G. E., & Liebson, I. (1981). Human social conversation: Effects of ethanol, secobarbital, and chlorpromazine. *Pharmacology, Biochemistry & Behavior, 14*, 353–360.

Storm, T., & Cutler, R. E. (1981). Observations of drinking in natural settings: Vancouver beer parlors and cocktail lounges. *Journal of Studies on Alcohol, 42*, 972–997.

Stritzke, W. G. K., Lang, A. R., & Patrick, C. J. (1996). Beyond stress and arousal: A reconceptualization of alcohol-emotion relations with reference to psychophysiological methods. *Psychological Bulletin, 120*, 376–395.

Thun, M. J., Peto, R., Lopez, A. D., Monaco, J. H., Henley, S. J., Heath, C. W., Jr., & Doll, R. (1997). Alcohol consumption and mortality among middle-aged and elderly U.S. adults. *New England Journal of Medicine, 337*, 1705–1714.

U.S. Department of Agriculture/Department of Health and Human Services. (1995). *Nutrition and your health: Dietary guidelines for Americans* (4th ed.). Washington, DC: Authors.

Vaillant, G. E. (1983). *The natural history of alcoholism*. Cambridge, MA: Harvard University Press.

Volpe, A., & Kastenbaum, R. (1967). Beer and TLC in a geriatric hospital. *American Journal of Nursing 67*, 100–103.

Watten, R. G. (1996). Coping styles in abstainers from alcohol. *Psychopathology (Switzerland) 29*, 340–346.

Wechsler, H., Davenport, A., Dowdall, G., Moeykens, B., & Castillo, S. (1994). Health and behavioral consequences of binge drinking in college: National survey of students at 140 campuses. *Journal of the American Medical Association, 272*, 1672–1677.

Wechsler, H., Dowdall, G. W., Davenport, A., & Castillo, S. (1995). Correlates of student binge drinking. *American Journal of Public Health, 85*, 921–926.

West, J. A., & Sutker, P. B. (1990). Alcohol consumption, tension reduction and mood enhancement. In W. M. Cox (Ed.), *Why people drink: Parameters of alcohol as a reinforcer* (pp. 93–129). New York: Gardner.

Wilks, J., & Callan, V. J. (1990). A diary approach to analysing young adults drinking events and motivations. *Drug and Alcohol Review, 9*, 7–13.

Wilson, G. T. (1988). Alcohol and anxiety. *Behavior Research and Therapy, 26*, 369–381.

Wilson, G. T., & Abrams, D. B. (1977). Effects of alcohol on social anxiety and physiological arousal: Cognitive versus pharmacological processes. *Cognitive Therapy and Research, 1*, 195–210.

Wilson, I. B., & Cleary, P. D. (1995). Linking clinical variables with health-related quality of life: A conceptual model of patient outcomes. *Journal of the American Medical Association, 273*, 59–65.

Winefield, H. R., Goldney, R. D., Winefield, A. H., & Tiggemann, M. (1992). Psychological correlates of the level of alcohol consumption in young adults. *Medical Journal of Australia, 156*, 755–759.

Alcohol and Health

Irina Anokhina and Jennifer Moyo

The discussions following presentations on alcohol and health sought to establish specific clinical guidelines for healthy drinking. Numerous complicating factors were noted, both individual and societal in nature. Nonetheless, speakers and commentators felt it was important for physicians to be educated about relationships between drinking and health.

1   **Counseling people to start drinking.** Arthur Klatsky was asked under what circumstances it might be appropriate to advise patients to drink. Klatsky emphasized that such recommendations must be made on a one-to-one basis, because so much depends on the individual's risk profile. The easiest case is the male patient who has had a coronary incident and who has "gone clean" by changing his health habits, including stopping light, daily drinking. This patient might be informed that he was mistaken in making this change. Another case in which a recommendation to increase drinking might be made is an Asian woman (a member of a group that traditionally drinks little) who asks whether it is all right to drink more than once a month. In this case, she might be given a guideline of up to three or four drinks weekly. Older patients who have no tendency to drink heavily would be a group that in general could be advised that drinking might not pose much or any risk.

2   **Applying normative drinking research to cultures with norms of abstention.** A participant pointed out that some developing nations have high levels of abstention, such as India (see Chapter 8), Sri Lanka, and Thailand, in which most of the female and about half of the male population were said to abstain. In these parts of the world, claims of the cardioprotective effects of alcohol are likely to be resisted. Although consumption levels have been rising in

many such areas, their high abstinence rates cloud the epidemiological evidence supporting beneficial claims for drinking.

3   **Ethnic differences in drinking and risk for coronary heart disease.** In response to queries about ethnic differences, Klatsky reported that his studies at Kaiser Permanente involved a wide range of ethnic groups (including many people from Asian groups) and his research found that alcohol reduced coronary heart disease risk equally among these groups. This was particularly interesting because coronary heart disease rates are very low in Chinese Americans but high in South Asians.

4   **Social status, economic differences, and coronary heart disease.** Louise Nadeau reviewed the longitudinal Whitehall (United Kingdom) study, which found a gradient of cardiovascular (and other) diseases occurred in an inverse relationship to status in the bureaucracy, so that those in higher status positions lived longer (Smith, Shipley, & Rose, 1990). The relationship could be explained by differences in lifestyles of those at different status levels, or might simply be due to wealth itself. Control, self-efficacy, even pleasure (see Chapter 1) seem to be directly related to immunity. Thus, other psychosocial factors in addition to alcohol consumption, and even overall lifestyle, influence longevity and health.

5   **Combining the harm reduction and the reduction of consumption models.** Asked whether the introduction of harm-reduction techniques would change the optimal level of consumption in a society, Ole-Jørgen Skog answered that indeed changes in the risk parameters would change the optimum level of consumption.

6   **Conflict between clinical advice and optimum social consumption.** In response to a question about the impact of cautious individual recommendations such as those that Klatsky advocated, Skog indicated that "contagious change in consumption" has been observed in some societies. This refers to the diffusion of the impact of beneficial rises in drinking among lower drinking groups to higher, more risky, drinking in higher drinking groups.

7   **Alcohol and breast cancer risk.** Asked about the solidity of the evidence on breast-cancer risk and drinking, Carlos Camargo indicated that the Nurses' Health Study showed an overall reduction in mortality rate, along with a greater risk of breast cancer, at one drink daily (Fuchs et al., 1995). "If you accept one result from the study, you should accept the other." Likewise, when a member of the audience questioned the significance of a relative risk of 1.5, because it could be a statistical artifact, Camargo said that if that argument were accepted, alcohol mortality benefits of 1.1 and 1.2 also would have to be dismissed. "You can't have it both ways." Camargo then related his wife's personal experience, in which she drank intermittently during her recent pregnancy and moderately following the birth (*after* breast-feeding in the evening, so as not to pass on alcohol to the baby).

8   **Primary care physicians giving advice on drinking.** Asked whether it was realistic to expect primary care physicians to advise patients on drinking in an era of managed care, Camargo noted that physicians spend on average only 8 minutes per patient. Nonetheless he felt that physicians had a valuable role to play, and that they needed to be educated to provide sound information about

alcohol. Currently, there is an unproductive exchange of sound bites—blithely optimisitic views on heart and mortality-rate benefits versus attempts to scare all women away from drinking.

9   The issue of underreporting of drinking levels. Klatsky inquired whether the underreporting of drinking might make the risk of breast cancer appear to occur at a lower level of drinking than it actually did. Nadeau indicated that other data, such as mortality rates, suggest little effect from underreporting. On the other hand, studies showed that heavy drinkers of both genders *do* underreport. Camargo agreed with Klatsky that underreporting of drinking tended to provide lower estimates of optimal levels of drinking, but he pointed out that questioning the applicability of "one drink per day" applied equally to *both* positive and negative results, so that both might actually occur at somewhat higher drinking levels. The point was made that sales data were needed to supplement self-reported drinking levels.

10   Sexism and guidelines for women's drinking. Christa Appel from the Forshungsgruppe Gesundheit und Sucht claimed that separate guidelines for women were paternalistic and sexist. In Germany, these tended to be ignored and people drank a lot because "they enjoy it and it tastes good." Nadeau responded that women are not necessarily the equivalent of men in relation to food and alcohol consumption.

11   Age limits on women's drinking guidelines. A questioner asked whether research had been conducted with women older than 65 years of age and what advice could be given to those in this group. Camargo indicated that larger cohort studies included women of these ages, and that most recommendations applied across this age range.

12   How best to offer advice on healthy drinking levels. Speakers raised a number of issues about offering advice on drinking levels. For example, primary care physicians are themselves confused by conflicting information about alcohol's dangers. Moreover, even if information is given by physicians it is up to the individual consumer to make consumption decisions. In order to gain maximum adherence, advice should not be given as a dictum.

REFERENCES

Fuchs, C. S., Stampfer, M. J., Colditz, G. A., Giovannucci, E. L., Manson, J. E., Kawachi, I., Hunter, D. J., Hankinson, S. E., Hennekens, C. H., & Rosner, B. (1995). Alcohol consumption and mortality among women. *New England Journal of Medicine, 332*, 1245–1250.

Smith, G. D., Shipley, M. J., & Rose, G. (1990). Magnitude and causes of socioeconomic differentials in mortality: Further evidence from the Whitehall Study. *Journal of Epidemiology and Community Health, 44*, 265.

Part Four

Drinking Expectations
and Contexts

The effects of alcohol, both beneficial and harmful, are caused by more than the pharmacological action of ethanol. The "social learning" model of alcohol holds that people learn how to react to alcohol from their social environments. This part of the volume explores the array of factors that add to, modify, or direct human reactions to alcohol. Barbara Leigh describes the body of research on alcohol-related expectancies, expectancies found to be crucial in responses to drinking. People expect a range of experiences—usually positive—from alcohol, including social facilitation, relaxation, and fun, along with such negative effects as loss of control and foolish behavior.

G. Alan Marlatt extends Leigh's treatment of expectancies in relation to drinking problems by exploring the idea that problem drinkers, and alcoholics in particular, seek from alcohol not only pleasure but self-worth, peace of mind, and other essential feelings. These exaggerated expectations are not fulfilled by drinking; rather, such drinkers suffer from their alcohol use. Remedies are to refute such exaggerated expectations while enhancing the problem drinker's capacity to gain satisfaction through other means than alcohol.

People's expectations about alcohol change as they proceed through life. Geoff Lowe notes that young people seek very different experiences from either mature adults or the elderly and that, as a result, they consume alcohol in a different manner. Maturity usually brings more modest but focused expectations about alcohol. Normal drinkers incorporate alcohol along with a range of other daily activities into their lives and social routines in ways that they find gratifying and that often bring them pleasure.

Age is one among a number of factors that direct people towards different settings when they consume alcohol, and these settings in turn affect how people drink. Eric Single and Henry Pomeroy review the range of setting-related factors in drinking. For example, youthful drinking at a club is quite different from drinking at family gatherings. Even within a particular type of setting—a club, say, or a wedding—cultural variables, physical environment, temporal factors, and a host of other considerations affect drinking.

Jan Snel explores drinking as a state-dependent behavior, meaning that people's background and current traits interact with drinking experiences and life outcomes. People are primarily motivated to achieve overall satisfaction, and alcohol generally produces the desired effects that most people experience as positive. Snel's approach, like others in this section, places alcohol in a larger framework involving the individual's outlook, setting, and lifestyle.

Ross Kalucy adds guilt to the drinking equation—the intrapsychic downside of the urge to consume and other life urges. Every human balances restraint and desire. For some, this balance is painful, erratic, and dysfunctional, leading to cycles of excess and intense pain. Self-acceptance, which often comes with maturity, is critical. Sometimes, however, as in the case of an anorexic youth, therapeutic assistance is required. Mature enjoyment reflects social-acceptance and self-acceptance that often leads to pleasure.

A trait that is critical in this section—indeed in this book—is gender. Louise Nadeau describes the divergent realities of men's and women's drinking. Although modern feminist trends may reduce some of these differences slightly, women continue to drink less and have fewer alcohol problems. They also internalize social images that drinking by women, and especially drunkenness, is unfeminine and deplorable. Women thus feel less free to drink, and they are more seriously damaged if they do experience alcohol problems. An ideal drinking style might combine female restraint with male freedom.

Chapter 16

Thinking, Feeling, and Drinking: Alcohol Expectancies and Alcohol Use

Barbara C. Leigh

Research on people's beliefs about the effects of alcohol on their behavior, moods, and emotions is included under the topic of alcohol expectancies. This topic is linked to "social learning" models of alcohol consumption, which hold that people learn styles of drinking, and even how to react to alcohol, from their social and cultural surroundings. Expectancy research is especially relevant to the question of pleasure in relation to drinking because pleasurable experience is strongly influenced by subjective and cultural interpretation (see Chapter 4). Alcohol expectancies also may play a role in the development of drinking problems and in their amelioration.

SCIENTIFIC BACKGROUND

Until recently, expectancies had not been a major focus of research in alcohol studies. Perhaps this area was seen as lacking potential because the effects of alcohol are common knowledge. After all, "everyone knows" that alcohol makes people behave in uncharacteristic ways.

Recent years, however, have seen an explosion of interest in alcohol expectancies. Much of this research follows on the heels of MacAndrew and Edgerton's (1969) influential treatise on alcohol and disinhibition, which argued that the effects of alcohol on behavior are learned culturally rather than directly resulting from pharmacological action. The authors mustered anthropological and historical evidence to show that alcohol-induced transformations in behavior vary widely across cultures and time periods. Thus, the pure pharmacological effect of ethanol cannot account for the changes in social behavior that occur when people drink. MacAndrew and Edgerton (p. 88) proposed that people *learn* the appropriate behaviors to display while intoxicated:

> People learn about drunkenness what their society "knows" about drunkenness; and, accepting and acting upon the understanding thus imparted to them, they become the living confirmation of their society's teachings.

MacAndrew and Edgerton's book inspired subsequent laboratory studies using the "balanced placebo" design (Marlatt & Rohsenow, 1980), which separates actual alcohol ingestion from the belief that alcohol has been consumed. Using this technique, subjects are given either alcohol or a placebo and are instructed that they are receiving either alcohol or plain tonic water. The design, by manipulating both alcohol administration and the belief that one has received alcohol, separates the effects of alcohol consumption from the effects of cognitive set or expectation. In these studies, many behavioral changes are displayed by subjects who only *think* they have imbibed, suggesting that changes in social behavior are caused not by the pharmacological action of alcohol but by the beliefs of the drinker. A large number of studies demonstrate that this cognitive "alcohol set" influences many kinds of social behavior, including aggression, sexual arousal, and self-disclosure (Bushman & Cooper, 1990; Crowe & George, 1989; Hull & Bond, 1986).

Clinical studies on reasons for drinking (Farber, Khavari, & Douglass, 1980) suggest that certain emotional changes resulting from drinking are reinforcing and help to maintain drinking behavior. The focus on expectations rather than pharmacology as the mediator of these effects led to a number of studies showing that people hold a number of common *expectancies* about the behavioral and emotional effects of alcohol (see Critchlow, 1986, for review). An expectancy— essentially an "if . . . then" statement about alcohol effects—can be interpreted as a cognitive representation of one's past direct and indirect experiences with alcohol. Based partly on research showing that these beliefs are correlated with drinking behavior, it has been suggested that expectancies play a role in the initiation and maintenance of drinking (Brown, 1993; Cox & Klinger, 1988; Goldman, 1994; Goldman, Brown, & Christiansen, 1987; Maisto, Connors, & Sachs, 1981). Briefly, the decision to drink is assumed to be driven at least partly by the individual's belief that alcohol will serve certain functions or result in certain desirable consequences, such as relief from tension or enhancement of mood. Drinking then is maintained by ongoing expectations of alcohol's ability to result in these desired outcomes.

Expectancy is thus a key concept in psychosocial models of drinking behavior. Alcohol use, at least in its earlier stages, is taken to be a learned behavior, maintained by anticipation of consequences. This approach stands in contrast to other models that characterize addiction as a biological or medical phenomenon, disease, or moral failing. This social learning model of drinking implies that because drinking is learned, it can be unlearned following the same principles.

WHAT ARE THE EXPECTANCIES ABOUT ALCOHOL EFFECTS?

Folk conceptions of a link between alcohol use and behavioral and personality changes are thousands of years old. Descriptions of alcohol-induced disinhibition appear in Greek and Roman writings, and these representations continue in literature, film, song, and a host of other cultural manifestations. People have believed for centuries that alcohol affects them in desirable ways and at the same time believed that alcohol is a source of immorality, crime, and all manner of deviant behavior.

In the behavioral sciences, the recent focus on cognitive and social aspects of drinking has led to a number of studies that have identified and examined the content of expectancies, as illustrated in Table 16.1.

Surveys and interviews show that people expect largely positive effects from drinking. If they are asked to list the effects that alcohol has on them, they tend to list more positive than negative effects and to list the positive effects first (Gustafson, 1988, 1989; Leigh & Stacy, 1994). Moreover, people view the positive effects as more likely to occur. For example, in Roizen's (1983) analysis of a U.S. national survey, the most commonly reported effects (reported by 70% to 80% of respondents) were generally positive (friendly, talkative, romantic). Unpleasant effects such as feeling sick, aggressive, argumentative, sad, or mean were reported less frequently. Interestingly, it was not the case that some people reported positive effects and others reported negative effects. Instead, people who reported *any* effects mentioned positive ones, and as the number of effects experienced became larger, negative effects were included. Thus, people reported either no effects, positive effects, or both positive and negative effects, but no one reported negative effects without positive effects.

WHAT FACTORS AFFECT THESE EXPECTANCIES?

Age

Beliefs about the effects of alcohol are present in children before their first personal experience with alcohol (Christiansen, Goldman, & Inn, 1982; Christiansen, Smith, Roehling, & Goldman, 1989; Miller, Smith, & Goldman, 1990). Children may acquire these beliefs through observation, vicarious learning, and assimilation of cultural stereotypes (Critchlow, 1986). Young children have predominantly negative beliefs about alcohol (Aitken, 1978; Isaacs, 1977; Jahoda & Cramond, 1972; Johnson & Johnson, 1995; Spiegler, 1983), although some positive beliefs also exist (Christiansen et al., 1982; Christiansen et al., 1989; Miller

Table 16.1   The content of alcohol expectancies: positive and negative effects.

Expectancy category	Effect	
	Positive	Negative
Social	More social Less shy More talkative Enhanced sex	Aggressive Loss of control Loud, obnoxious Stupid, foolish
Physical	Get drunk Increase energy	Hangover Pass out Sick, headache
Emotional	Relax Feel good	Angry Depressed Ashamed, guilty
Negative reinforcement	Forget problems Relieve tension Reduce stress	
Cognitive		Impaired judgment Less alert Poor concentration Decreased motor skills
Fun	Good time Interesting Consciousness alteration Fun, pleasure Happy Buzz Tastes good	
Consequences		Work problems Accidents Trouble with the law Trouble with family or friends

et al., 1990). Once children start experimenting with alcohol in early puberty, expectancies start to shift from negative to positive (Aitken, 1978; Johnson & Johnson, 1995).

Lang and Michalac (1990) suggest that younger children's negative expectancies reflect the discouraging messages of parents and other authority figures, whereas older children may tend to rebel against these figures. Younger children also expect alcohol to make adults' behavior aversive and erratic; these

frightening effects undermine children's security. As children become more sophisticated and capable of tolerating unpredictability, they may find the effects
more appealing (Lang, Murray, & Pelham, 1984).

In a longitudinal study of adolescents, Aas, Leigh, Anderssen, and Jakobsen
(1998) found that the largest increases in positive expectancies of sociability occurred in the year the children had their first drink. These positive expectancies
continued to become stronger during subsequent years of drinking. This pattern
is consistent with a process of assimilation and accommodation in the early
stages of drinking. When drinking begins, positive expectancies about drinking
outcomes change rapidly as these expectancies become assimilated into the individual's new status as a drinker. As drinking continues, gradual changes in
expectancies follow as these expectancies become accommodated.

Cultural and Historical Influences

If expectancies are part of shared cultural understandings, then they should be
different for different cultures during different periods of history. Most cross-
cultural studies of alcohol expectancies suggest that although there are differences in the strength with which the beliefs are held, the content of expectancies
is similar. In studies of expectancies in different ethnic groups, White male college students had stronger expectancies than Black male college students (Reese
& Friend, 1994); Hispanics expected more effects of all kinds (both positive
and negative) than non-Hispanic Americans (Marín, 1996; Marín, Posner, &
Kinyon, 1993; Velez-Blasini, 1997); and Asian American college students expected more tension reduction than non-Asian students, despite their lighter
drinking habits (O'Hare, 1995). In a study of beliefs about alcohol-induced aggression in 10 countries, Lindman and Lang (1994) found that U.S. and Spanish
survey respondents had particularly strong beliefs that alcohol causes aggressive
behavior; French respondents tended to fall at the other end of the scale.

Beverage Type

Positive and negative expectancies are associated differently with different types
of alcoholic beverages. Among young drinkers in Florida and Finland, wine
elicited the most positive expectancies, followed by mixed drinks, beer, and
straight drinks (Lang, Kaas, & Barnes, 1983; Lindman & Lang, 1986). Beer was
associated with lethargy and sleepiness, wine with contentment and romance,
mixed drinks with sociability, and straight drinks with unpleasant consequences
of heavy use, such as passing out and loss of memory. The "unique constellations
of expectations" related to different beverages may arise from the "distinctive
conditions, purposes, and levels of their typical consumption" (Lang et al., 1983).
In addition, such beliefs probably are influenced by advertising and by cultural
stereotypes.

Situation

The effects that people expect from drinking vary across situations. For example, in Roizen's (1983) study, respondents rarely reported that they *always* experienced any effect from drinking; even for the most commonly reported effects, 10% or fewer reported experiencing the effect on every drinking occasion. Similarly, in studies that required respondents to rate the likelihood of an effect occurring, respondents showed an unwillingness to use the endpoints of the scale; instead, they tended to report that alcohol affected their behavior "some of the time" (Leigh, 1987). In one such study (Leigh, 1987), many respondents made unsolicited comments that the effects they experienced when drinking depended on the situation. Roizen (1983, p. 241) noted:

> In this observation would seem a nice demonstration that alcohol is not linked to its various effects in lockstep fashion in popular opinion but is instead regarded very much as a matter of the particularities of the drinking event. That most of us might agree that alcohol may help us to feel friendly does not, then, imply about common opinion that alcohol always or even usually will have this effect.

This lack of certainty and unwillingness to impute any specific effect consistently to drinking suggest that people have a sense of the situational specificity of pharmacological effects. Lay people have a very good idea of what drug researchers already know: that the effects of any drug are dependent on the setting in which it is taken (Lettieri, Sayers, & Pearson, 1980).

HOW DO EXPECTANCIES AFFECT DRINKING?

A large body of research shows that expectancies are correlated with drinking in various groups, including adolescents, social drinking adults, college students, and alcoholics (Goldman, 1994; Goldman et al., 1987; Lang & Michalac, 1990; Leigh, 1989b). The consistency of such a relationship across subject samples has suggested that these expectancies play a role in the initiation and maintenance of drinking (Cox & Klinger, 1988; Goldman, 1994; Goldman et al., 1987; Maisto et al., 1981). According to a social-learning perspective of drinking behavior, people drink in order to achieve certain desirable consequences or to avoid undesirable ones. In this model, people with stronger positive expectancies should drink more, and people with stronger negative expectancies should drink less. However, the picture is not nearly so simple.

Positive and Negative Expectancies

Some research findings show that positive expectancies are more strongly associated with alcohol use than are negative expectancies (Brown, Creamer, & Stetson, 1987; Christiansen & Goldman, 1983; Christiansen et al., 1989; Collins, Lapp, Emmons, & Isaac, 1990; Fromme, Stroot, & Kaplan, 1993; George &

McAfee, 1987; Jackson & Matthews, 1988; Leigh & Stacy, 1993; Rohsenow, 1983; Southwick, Steele, Marlatt, & Lindell, 1981; Stacy, Widaman, & Marlatt, 1990); others show that negative expectancies are as strongly related (Bauman, 1985; Leigh, 1987, 1989a; Mann, Chassin, & Sher, 1987; McCarty, Morrison, & Mills, 1983). In some studies, heavier drinkers saw negative effects as *less* likely to occur than did lighter drinkers (Mann et al., 1987; Roizen, 1983; Young & Knight, 1989); in others, heavier drinkers saw negative effects as *more* likely to occur than did lighter drinkers (Connors, O'Farrell, Cutter, & Thompson, 1987; Leigh, 1987, 1989a; Stacy et al., 1990).

The inconsistency of the relationship of negative expectancies to drinking casts doubt upon a simple reinforcement model whereby people drink because they expect positive effects (Adams & McNeil, 1991). Clearly, heavy drinkers do expect—and experience—negative outcomes from drinking; why do these expectancies not lead to lighter drinking (McMahon & Jones, 1994)?

Negative Effects Are "Swamped" by Positive Effects   As described previously, people who expect negative consequences from drinking also expect positive consequences. Because negative effects reportedly occur less frequently than positive effects, the possibility of their occurrence may be "swamped" by the much more probable likelihood of pleasurable consequences. Thus, although people know that negative effects may occur, they may be more motivated by the more likely positive effects.

Negative Effects Are Evaluated as Not So Bad   Labeling alcohol effects as positive or negative is problematic, given that effects that are desirable for some people may be undesirable for others. A striking example of this subjectivity comes from a study by Leigh and Stacy (1994) in which people were asked to list the positive and negative effects of alcohol. Although 14% of men and 5% of women listed increased sexuality as a positive consequence of drinking, 6% of men and 13% of women mentioned it as a negative consequence. Clearly, some effects of alcohol are positive to some and negative to others.

Heavier drinkers tend to perceive alcohol effects less negatively than do lighter drinkers and nondrinkers (Cahalan & Room, 1974; Critchlow, 1987; Gustafson, 1991, 1993; Leigh, 1987, 1989a, 1989b; McCarty et al., 1983; Roizen, 1983). These perceptions may result from the norms of drinking situations. If heavy drinkers drink mostly with other heavy drinkers who are also experiencing negative consequences, they may accept these consequences as normal (McMahon & Jones, 1994). If bad outcomes are seen as not so bad, these bad outcomes may not effectively limit drinking.

Whether drinking has utility depends on both the probability of the consequences and their desirability. Each of these characteristics varies across individuals. In the case of drinking, some may perceive certain consequences of alcohol consumption as highly likely to occur, and others may see their likelihood as relatively low; some may consider certain consequences as extremely desirable, and others may not. Thus, the relative "payoff" for drinking varies across individuals.

Positive Effects Are More Immediate and More Likely to Be Learned
Many positive effects of alcohol are immediate, "feeling good" consequences, whereas many negative effects are delayed, by minutes (loss of coordination), days (loss of job), or years (loss of liver function). In humans, alcohol effects often demonstrate a biphasic pattern in which an initial increase in excitation, arousal, and euphoria is followed by depression and dysphoria (Mello, 1968). These differing effects may result from rising and falling levels of blood alcohol (Jones & Vega, 1972). The biphasic nature of responses to alcohol may represent a general "opponent process," a model that has been proposed to explain addiction to various drugs and experiences (Shipley, 1987; Solomon, 1980).

From a behaviorist view, a delay between stimulus (drinking) and response (alcohol effects) means that the stimulus-response bonds are weakened, and an association of stimulus to response is not learned. A cognitive model implies that effects that occur closer to the time of drinking are more likely to be encoded in memory with drinking. From either a behaviorist or a cognitive perspective, if negative effects of drinking are delayed in relation to positive effects, they are less likely to be associated with alcohol. The relative importance of desirable and undesirable consequences in drinking motivation might then be a function of the immediacy of the consequence. For drinkers, the pleasurable, reinforcing "ups," being more immediate, may have a greater impact on learning about drinking and its effects than the more delayed "downs." A drinking episode might end badly, but its pleasurable beginnings are more powerful motivators (Marlatt, 1987; Stacy & Widaman, 1987)

In addition, some severe negative consequences of drinking, including accidents and long-term physical damage, are never experienced by most drinkers and thus are not learned by direct experience. Drinkers who have not experienced these consequences perceive them as unlikely to occur in the future, and these consequences may not figure strongly in drinking decisions. Stacy and Widaman (1987) suggest that "beliefs about positive outcomes are more likely to be based on direct experience than are beliefs about negative outcomes, possibly leading to a bias in 'retrievability' favoring positive outcomes" (see also Stacy, 1986). Expectancies that are more easily retrievable are viewed as more probable (Tversky & Kahneman, 1974) and thus may affect intentions to drink more strongly.

Positive and Negative Expectancies: Social Drinkers Versus Problem Drinkers   Relationships between positive expectancies, negative expectancies, and drinking may differ during drinking careers. McMahon, Jones, and O'Donnell (1994) argue that among social drinkers, expectancies of negative consequences should increase with increasing consumption: As these drinkers drink more heavily, they experience more negative consequences and thus expect more negative consequences in the future. At some point, however, if drinking reaches problematic levels, negative expectancy reaches a point at which it begins to influence drinking decisions. Clearly, it is expectations of negative consequences that lead heavy drinkers to moderate their drinking or seek treatment.

In a series of studies of alcohol-dependent patients in treatment, Jones and McMahon (1994a,b, 1996a,b; McMahon & Jones, 1996) found that positive expectancy had little or no relationship to treatment outcome, but that clients with stronger expectations of negative consequences were less likely to relapse within 3 months of treatment and remained abstinent longer. Moreover, the expectancies that were the most strongly related to treatment outcome were expectancies of longer-term consequences of continued drinking (for example, health effects), rather than consequences that happen directly after drinking (for example, unpleasant social behavior) or on the next day (for example, hangover). McMahon, Jones, and O'Donnell (1994) argue that these expectancies of delayed effects are more important in motivating changes in drinking because problem drinkers tend to misperceive the more immediate negative consequences of drinking and underestimate their negative nature.

Stages of Drinking

Because expectancies are learned as drinking experience accumulates (Christiansen et al., 1982; Miller et al., 1990), it is likely that the relationship of expectancies to drinking differs with age and stage of drinking. Expectancies may motivate drinking more strongly in younger drinkers with less experience:

> Expected consequences may play a greater part in influencing a teenager's first drink than an alcoholic's millionth drink. While the new drinker, with no direct drinking experience, might be swayed by the "symbolic power" of alcohol, the experienced drinker may drink more from habit or addiction (Leigh, 1989b, pp. 370–371).

Expectancies and Drinking Initiation   Given that alcohol has little inherent taste appeal for nondrinkers, it is surprising that anyone starts to drink at all. As discussed previously, alcohol expectancies are learned early, before direct experience with alcohol, and it may be these beliefs that influence initiation into drinking.

Although it often is assumed that expectancy drives drinking behavior, the reverse, or some reciprocal combination, is equally plausible. For example, expectancies not only may operate as incentives to drink but may lead the young drinker to perceive drinking situations selectively and seek confirmation of the expected. Thereby, partly through a self-fulfilling prophecy, expectancies are confirmed, which further reinforces the incentives to drink (Aas et al., 1998; Bauman, Fisher, Bryan, & Chenoweth, 1985; Goldman et al., 1987).

Several recent studies have addressed this issue with longitudinal studies, in which adolescents are followed and interviewed over time (Killen et al., 1996).

Expectancies for social enhancement predict drinking onset (Killen et al., 1996; Smith, Goldman, Greenbaum, & Christiansen, 1995), but drinking experience also influences subsequent expectancies (Aas et al., 1998; Kline, 1996; Smith et al., 1995). For example, Aas et al. reported on a 3-year study of Norwegian seventh graders, some of whom already had begun drinking. Aas and colleagues reasoned that as younger teens first begin to gain experience with alcohol, they adjust their expectations in accordance with their behavior; thus, drinking experience influences the subsequent development of expectancies. At the same time, these developing expectancies also act as stronger incentives to drink, influencing concurrent and subsequent drinking behavior. As adolescents become more regular drinkers, previous drinking, rather than expectancies, becomes the most powerful predictor of subsequent drinking (Kandel, Kessler, & Margulies, 1978; Newcomb & Bentler, 1986; Stacy, Newcomb, & Bentler, 1993; Stein, Newcomb, & Bentler, 1986, 1987; Teichman, Barnea, & Ravav, 1989). Thus, at these later stages, expectancy's influence on behavior may weaken.

In Aas et al.'s (1998) study, expectancies for social enhancement from drinking predicted drinking onset among adolescents who began drinking during the study. However, among adolescents who were already drinking in seventh grade, seventh-grade expectancies predicted eighth-grade drinking, but drinking did not influence subsequent expectancy. Because these subjects had begun to drink before the study began, the influence of initial drinking experiences on expectancy already may have taken place. Also, eighth-grade expectancies did not predict ninth-grade drinking, perhaps because drinking patterns had begun to stabilize.

These results are consistent with a model in which expectancies predict initiation into drinking, but early drinking experiences are also important for expectancy development. In initial drinking experiences, the novice drinker with little direct experience of alcohol effects is guided by existing expectations. These expectations may lead to selective perception of alcohol effects such that the effects experienced by the drinker are consistent with expectations. Thus, to the extent that positive outcomes of drinking are expected, they are experienced and reinforced and, along with other sources of reinforcement such as social approval, contribute to continued motivation to drink. This learning process would be more powerful in the very early stages of drinking. As direct experience accumulates and expectancies change, each drinking experience becomes less influential in subsequent expectancy development.

Expectancies and Drinking Cessation   Expectancies figure prominently—either explicitly or implicitly—in cognitive-behavioral treatment models of problem drinking (Brown, 1993; Connors, Maisto, & Dermen, 1992; Miller & Rollnick, 1991; Young & Oei, 1993). For example, Miller's motivational interviewing technique (Miller & Rollnick, 1991) targets the problem drinker's decisional balance, or the balance of positives and negatives of continuing drinking versus stopping. Such a balance is highly idiosyncratic. Because costs and benefits have subjective values, simply listing costs and benefits is insufficient: The importance of the effects to the drinker is more important than the sheer number of positives and negatives. Miller and Rollnick (1991) cite the example of a patient who was experiencing a number of negative consequences of his drinking: He was separating from his partner, had lost his job, and had sustained liver damage. However, it turned out that neither he nor his partner valued the relationship much and both were relieved at separating. He did not like his job anyway and got a substantial severance payment, with which he planned to go into business for himself. Moreover, he did not really understand the information about his health. In fact,

> his prime concern was his dog. Indeed, he eventually decided to quit drinking because when he did drink he neglected his pet, and this was the source of a great deal of personal sorrow. (pp. 239–240)

This drinker's story highlights the subjectivity of evaluations of drinking consequences, and also the necessity for highly personalized assessment (Fromme et al., 1993; Jones & McMahon, 1996b). For many drinkers and drug users, some effects are simply more important than others, so that many negatives can be balanced by one strong positive. As a former heroin addict describes it:

> Hunting for a reason to stop that outweighs the drive to stay hooked is the major problem. During one soul-searching session I neatly listed advantages and disadvantages of taking smack. Potential consequences of using heroin included being charged with an offence, starring in a scandal, losing home, job, health, wealth, friends, and credibility of every kind. Advantages were impossible to find. The following statements appeared on the list of reasons not to stop: "It (heroin) makes life easy"; "I'm scared to stop"; and "I don't feel like it." A moment's thought contradicted the first two and left me confronted by the third. I did not "feel like it." I did not stop, but logic had not assisted the choice. (Stewart, 1987)

Brown (1993) has outlined ways in which expectancies may be altered to help the problem drinker tip the balance, involving either changes in expectancy content or changes in expectancy strength or value.

Changing Expectancy Content   For many drinkers, the effects they *expect* do not always correspond to the effects they *experience*. For example, a study of in-patient alcoholics found that although the alcoholics expected alcohol to make them happier and feel better, they actually felt more depressed when they drank (Tamerin, Weiner, & Mendelson, 1970). In a more recent laboratory study (Laberg, 1986), nondependent and dependent drinkers rated the amount of pleasure they expected to experience after drinking and then drank alcohol. During the drinking session, they rated the amount of pleasure they experienced. Although nonproblem drinkers' expectations of pleasant feelings were highly correlated with the feelings they actually experienced, these feelings were virtually uncorrelated among severely dependent drinkers (Laberg &

Leigh, 1992). This finding supports clinical observations that alcoholics often report drinking to achieve a pleasant state that they do not then successfully attain.

Self-monitoring of drinking, predrinking expectancies, and post-drinking effects can help to highlight this inconsistency between the effects expected and the effects experienced in problem drinkers. By actively attending to situations and expectancies, problem drinkers can be encouraged to actively think about the potential consequences of drinking in high-risk situations, rather than going on "autopilot."

Expectancies also can be challenged by exposing the problem drinker to a situation in which drinking normally would occur and then creating opportunities for the drinker to experience effects *without* drinking. This procedure challenges the drinker's belief that alcohol is necessary to produce these pleasant consequences. Repeating these expectancy challenges creates opportunities to attribute success in the situation to internal factors (for example, coping ability) rather than to alcohol (for example, tension reduction). Studies using this procedure have shown promising results (Darkes & Goldman, 1993, 1998).

Changing Expectancy Strength or Value   Expectancy content can be extremely difficult to change, especially for problem drinkers for whom alcohol is truly functional. Miller and Rollnick (1991) note that rational reflection about these beliefs will not induce change, and that changing the value of alcohol effects is more likely to change behavior. The desirability of an effect might be changed by counterconditioning or by increasing the awareness of adverse consequences of problem drinking. Placing the expectancy in a broader context, examining its importance, and finding alternative means of attaining the effect may alter its importance (Brown, 1993; Brown, Millar, & Passman, 1988). For example, instead of trying to convince a problem drinker that alcohol does not in fact reduce tension, a therapist might encourage the drinker to focus on the negative consequences of problem drinking or to achieve tension reduction by alternative means.

The subjective value of certain expectancies also can be used for matching clients to treatments based on the expectancy. For example, for problem drinkers who are socially anxious, the expectancy that alcohol increases social facilitation is particularly motivating. Such clients may improve more in treatment programs that include a focus on social-skills training.

CONCLUSIONS

- Alcohol expectancies are people's beliefs about how alcohol will affect their emotions and behavior.
- Drinkers have expectations about the effects of drinking, and these expectations influence how and how much they drink.

- Alcohol expectancies are different for different situations, and people do not expect alcohol effects to occur consistently.
- Alcohol expectancies change with age: Children's views of alcohol effects are negative and become more positive as they begin drinking.
- Expectations for social enhancement from drinking predict drinking onset in adolescents, and drinking experience also influences the development of expectancies.
- Heavy or problem drinkers place a lower value on the negative outcomes of heavy consumption than do other drinkers.
- Heavy or problem drinking can be improved if problem drinkers see that negative consequences directly affect their lives in ways that concern them.

Although expectancy research so far has posed more questions than it has answered, it also has contributed a great deal to understanding of psychosocial models of drinking behavior. The promise of expectancy research is the notion that problem drinking is a learned behavior and hence can be unlearned. Alcohol expectancies thus have an important role in both prevention and treatment of problem drinking.

REFERENCES

Aas, H., Leigh, B. C., Anderssen, N., & Jakobsen, R. (1998). Two-year longitudinal study of alcohol expectancies and drinking among Norwegian adolescents. *Addiction, 93*, 373–384.

Adams, S. L., & McNeil, D. W. (1991). Negative alcohol expectancies reconsidered. *Psychology of Addictive Behaviors, 5*, 9–14.

Aitken, P. (1978). *Ten- to fourteen-year-olds and alcohol: A developmental study in the Central Region of Scotland*. Edinburgh, Scotland: Her Majesty's Stationery Office.

Bauman, K. E. (1985). The consequences expected from alcohol and drinking behavior: A factor analysis of data from a panel study of adolescents. *International Journal of the Addictions, 20*, 1635–1647.

Bauman, K. E., Fisher, L. A., Bryan, E. S., & Chenoweth, R. L. (1985). Relationship between subjective expected utility and behavior: A longitudinal study of adolescent drinking behavior. *Journal of Studies on Alcohol, 46*, 32–38.

Brown, S. A. (1993). Drug effect expectancies and addictive behavior change. *Experimental & Clinical Psychopharmacology, 1*, 55–67.

Brown, S. A., Creamer, V. A., & Stetson, B. A. (1987). Adolescent alcohol expectancies in relation to personal and parental drinking patterns. *Journal of Abnormal Psychology, 96*, 117–121.

Brown, S. A., Millar, A., & Passman, L. (1988). Utilizing expectancies in alcoholism treatment. *Psychology of Addictive Behaviors, 2*, 59–65.

Bushman, B. J., & Cooper, H. M. (1990). Effects of alcohol on human aggression: An integrative research review. *Psychological Bulletin, 107*, 341–354.

Cahalan, D., & Room, R. (1974). *Problem drinking among American men* (Monograph No. 7). New Brunswick, NJ: Rutgers Center of Alcohol Studies.

Christiansen, B. A., & Goldman, M. S. (1983). Alcohol-related expectancies versus demographic/ background variables in the prediction of adolescent drinking. *Journal of Consulting & Clinical Psychology, 51*, 249–257.

Christiansen, B. A., Goldman, M. S., & Inn, A. (1982). Development of alcohol-related expectancies in adolescents: Separating pharmacological from social-learning influences. *Journal of Consulting & Clinical Psychology, 50*, 336–344.

Christiansen, B. A., Smith, G. T., Roehling, P. V., & Goldman, M. S. (1989). Using alcohol expectancies to predict adolescent drinking behavior after one year. *Journal of Consulting & Clinical Psychology, 57*, 93–99.

Collins, R. L., Lapp, W. M., Emmons, K. M., & Isaac, L. M. (1990). Endorsement and strength of alcohol expectancies. *Journal of Studies on Alcohol, 51*, 336–342.

Connors, G. J., Maisto, S. A., & Dermen, K. H. (1992). Alcohol-related expectancies and their applications to treatment. *Drug and Alcohol Abuse Reviews, 3*, 203–231.

Connors, G. J., O'Farrell, T. J., Cutter, H. S., & Thompson, D. L. (1987). Dose-related effects of alcohol among male alcoholics, problem drinkers and nonproblem drinkers. *Journal of Studies on Alcohol, 48*, 461–466.

Cox, W. M., & Klinger, E. (1988). A motivational model of alcohol use. *Journal of Abnormal Psychology, 97*, 168–180.

Critchlow, B. (1986). The powers of John Barleycorn: Beliefs about the effects of alcohol on social behavior. *American Psychologist, 41*, 751–764.

Critchlow, B. (1987). A utility analysis of drinking. *Addictive Behaviors, 12*, 269–273.

Crowe, L. C., & George, W. H. (1989). Alcohol and human sexuality: Review and integration. *Psychological Bulletin, 105*, 374–386.

Darkes, J., & Goldman, M. S. (1993). Expectancy challenge and drinking reduction: Experimental evidence for a mediational process. *Journal of Consulting & Clinical Psychology, 61*, 344–353.

Darkes, J., & Goldman, M. S. (1998). Expectancy challenge and drinking reduction: Process and structure in the alcohol expectancy network. *Experimental and Clinical Psychopharmacology, 6*, 64–76.

Farber, P. D., Khavari, K. A., & Douglass, F. M. (1980). A factor analytic study of reasons for drinking: Empirical validation of positive and negative reinforcement dimensions. *Journal of Consulting & Clinical Psychology, 48*, 780–781.

Fromme, K., Stroot, E. A., & Kaplan, D. (1993). Comprehensive effects of alcohol: Development and psychometric assessment of a new expectancy questionnaire. *Psychological Assessment, 5*, 19–26.

George, W. H., & McAfee, M. P. (1987). The effects of gender and drinking experience on alcohol expectancies about self and male versus female other. *Social Behavior & Personality, 15*, 133–144.

Goldman, M. S. (1994). The alcohol expectancy concept: Applications to assessment, prevention, and treatment of alcohol abuse. *Applied & Preventive Psychology, 3*, 131–144.

Goldman, M. S., Brown, S. A., & Christiansen, B. A. (1987). Expectancy theory: Thinking about drinking. In H. T. Blane & K. E. Leonard (Eds.), *Psychological theories of drinking and alcoholism* (pp. 181–226). New York: Guilford Press.

Gustafson, R. (1988). Self-reported expected effects of a moderate dose of alcohol by college women. *Alcohol & Alcoholism, 23*, 409–414.

Gustafson, R. (1989). Self-reported expected emotional changes as a function of alcohol intoxication by alcoholic men and women. *Psychological Reports, 65*, 67–74.

Gustafson, R. (1991). Is the strength and the desirability of alcohol-related expectancies positively related? A test with an adult Swedish sample. *Drug & Alcohol Dependence, 28*, 145–150.

Gustafson, R. (1993). Alcohol-related expected effects and the desirability of these effects for Swedish college students measured with the Alcohol Expectancy Questionnaire (AEQ). *Alcohol & Alcoholism, 28*, 469–475.

Hull, J. G., & Bond, C. F. (1986). Social and behavioral consequences of alcohol consumption and expectancy: A meta-analysis. *Psychological Bulletin, 99*, 347–360.

Isaacs, M. (1977). Stereotyping by children of the effects of drinking on adults. *Journal of Studies on Alcohol, 38*, 913–921.

Jackson, C. P., & Matthews, G. (1988). The prediction of habitual alcohol use from alcohol related expectancies and personality. *Alcohol & Alcoholism, 23*, 305–314.

Jahoda, G., & Cramond, J. (1972). *Children and alcohol: A developmental study in Glasgow.* London: Her Majesty's Stationery Office.

Johnson, H. L., & Johnson, P. B. (1995). Children's alcohol-related cognitions: Positive versus negative alcohol effects. *Journal of Alcohol & Drug Education, 40,* 1–12.

Jones, B. M., & Vega, A. (1972). Cognitive performance measured on the ascending and descending limb of the blood alcohol curve. *Psychopharmacologia, 23,* 99–114.

Jones, B. T., & McMahon, J. (1994a). Negative alcohol expectancy predicts post-treatment abstinence survivorship: The whether, when and why of relapse to a first drink. *Addiction, 89,* 1653–1665.

Jones, B. T., & McMahon, J. (1994b). Negative and positive alcohol expectancies as predictors of abstinence after discharge from a residential treatment program: A one-month and three-month follow-up study in men. *Journal of Studies on Alcohol, 55,* 543–548.

Jones, B. T., & McMahon, J. (1996a). A comparison of positive and negative alcohol expectancy and value and their multiplicative composite as predictors of post-treatment abstinence survivorship. *Addiction, 91,* 89–99.

Jones, B. T., & McMahon, J. (1996b). Changes in alcohol expectancies during treatment relate to subsequent abstinence survivorship. *British Journal of Clinical Psychology, 35,* 221–234.

Kandel, D. B., Kessler, R. C., & Margulies, R. Z. (1978). Antecedents of adolescent initiation into stages of drug use: A developmental analysis. In D. B. Kandel (Ed.), *Longitudinal research on drug use: Empirical findings and methodological issues* (pp. 73–99). Washington, DC: Hemisphere.

Killen, J. D., Hayward, C., Wilson, D. M., Haydel, K. F., Robinson, T. N., Taylor, C. B., Hammer, L. D., & Varady, A. (1996). Predicting onset of drinking in a community sample of adolescents: The role of expectancy and temperament. *Addictive Behaviors, 21,* 473–480.

Kline, R. B. (1996). Eight-month predictive validity and covariance structure of the Alcohol Expectancy Questionnaire for Adolescents (AEQ-A) for junior high school students. *Journal of Studies on Alcohol, 57,* 396–405.

Laberg, J. C. (1986). Alcohol and expectancy: Subjective, psychophysiological and behavioral responses to alcohol stimuli in severely, moderately, and non-dependent drinkers. *British Journal of Addiction, 81,* 797–808.

Laberg, J. C., & Leigh, B. C. (1992, August). *Expected and experienced alcohol effects and desire to drink.* Paper presented at the 36th International Congress on Alcohol and Drug Dependence, Glasgow, Scotland.

Lang, A. R., Kaas, L., & Barnes, P. (1983). The beverage type stereotype: An unexplored determinant of the effects of alcohol consumption. *Bulletin of the Society of Psychologists in Addictive Behaviors, 2,* 46–49.

Lang, A. R., & Michalac, E. M. (1990) Expectancy effects in reinforcement from alcohol. In W. M. Cox (Ed.), *Why people drink: Parameters of alcohol as a reinforcer.* New York: Gardner Press.

Lang, A., Murray, A., & Pelham, W. (1984). *Children's perceptions of the effects of alcohol on adult-child interactions.* Paper presented at the meeting of the Southeastern Psychological Association, New Orleans, LA.

Leigh, B. C. (1987). Beliefs about the effects of alcohol on self and others. *Journal of Studies on Alcohol, 48,* 467–475.

Leigh, B. C. (1989a). Attitudes and expectancies as predictors of drinking habits: A comparison of three scales. *Journal of Studies on Alcohol, 50,* 432–440.

Leigh, B. C. (1989b). In search of the seven dwarves: Issues of measurement and meaning in alcohol expectancy research. *Psychological Bulletin, 105,* 361–373.

Leigh, B. C., & Stacy, A. W. (1993). Alcohol outcome expectancies: Scale construction and predictive utility in higher order confirmatory models. *Psychological Assessment, 5,* 216–229.

Leigh, B. C., & Stacy, A. W. (1994). Self-generated alcohol expectancies in four samples of drinkers. *Addiction Research, 1,* 335–348.

Lettieri, D. J., Sayers, M., & Pearson, H. W. (1980). *Theories on drug abuse: Selected contemporary perspectives* (NIDA Research Monograph No. 12). Washington, DC: U.S. Government Printing Office.

Lindman, R., & Lang, A. R. (1986). Anticipated effects of alcohol consumption as a function of beverage type: A cross-cultural replication. *International Journal of Psychology, 21*, 671–678.

Lindman, R. E., & Lang, A. R. (1994). The alcohol-aggression stereotype: A cross-cultural comparison of beliefs. *International Journal of the Addictions, 29*, 1–13.

MacAndrew, C., & Edgerton, R. (1969). *Drunken comportment: A social explanation*. Chicago: Aldine.

Maisto, S. A., Connors, G. J., & Sachs, P. R. (1981). Expectation as a mediator in alcohol intoxication: A reference level model. *Cognitive Therapy & Research, 5*, 1–18.

Mann, L. M., Chassin, L., & Sher, K. J. (1987). Alcohol expectancies and the risk for alcoholism. *Journal of Consulting & Clinical Psychology, 55*, 411–417.

Marín, G. (1996). Expectancies for drinking and excessive drinking among Mexican Americans and non-Hispanic Whites. *Addictive Behaviors, 21*, 491–507.

Marín, G., Posner, S. F., & Kinyon, J. B. (1993). Alcohol expectancies among Hispanics and non-Hispanic Whites: Role of drinking status and acculturation. *Hispanic Journal of Behavioral Sciences, 15*, 373–381.

Marlatt, G. A. (1987). Alcohol, the magic elixir: Stress, expectancy, and the transformation of emotional states. In E. Gottheil, K. A. Druley, S. Pashko, & S. P. Weinstein (Eds.), *Stress and addiction* (pp. 302–322). New York: Brunner/Mazel.

Marlatt, G. A., & Rohsenow, D. (1980). Cognitive processes in alcohol use: Expectancy and the balanced placebo design. In N. K. Mello (Ed.), *Advances in substance abuse: Behavioral and biological research* (pp. 159–199). Greenwich, CT: JAI Press.

McCarty, D., Morrison, S., & Mills, K. C. (1983). Attitudes, beliefs and alcohol use: An analysis of relationships. *Journal of Studies on Alcohol, 44*, 328–341.

McMahon, J., & Jones, B. T. (1994). Negative expectancy in motivation. *Addiction Research, 1*, 145–155.

McMahon, J., & Jones, B. T. (1996). Post-treatment abstinence survivorship and motivation for recovery: The predictive validity of the Readiness to Change (RCQ) and Negative Alcohol Expectancy (NAEQ) questionnaires. *Addiction Research, 4*, 161–176.

McMahon, J., Jones, B. T., & O'Donnell, P. (1994). Comparing positive and negative alcohol expectancies in male and female social drinkers. *Addiction Research, 1*, 349–365.

Mello, N. K. (1968). Some aspects of the behavioral pharmacology of alcohol. In D. H. Efron (Ed.), *Psychopharmacology: A review of progress* (pp. 787–809). Washington, DC: U.S. Government Printing Office.

Miller, P. M., Smith, G. T., & Goldman, M. S. (1990). Emergence of alcohol expectancies in childhood: A possible critical period. *Journal of Studies on Alcohol, 51*, 343–349.

Miller, W. R., & Rollnick, S. (1991). *Motivational interviewing: Preparing people to change addictive behavior*. New York: Guilford Press.

Newcomb, M. D., & Bentler, P. M. (1986). Frequency and sequence of drug use: A longitudinal study from early adolescence to young adulthood. *Journal of Drug Education, 16*, 101–120.

O'Hare, T. (1995). Differences in Asian and White drinking: Consumption level, drinking contexts, and expectancies. *Addictive Behaviors, 20*, 261–266.

Reese, F. L., & Friend, R. (1994). Alcohol expectancies and drinking practices among Black and White undergraduate males. *Journal of College Student Development, 35*, 319–323.

Rohsenow, D. J. (1983). Drinking habits and expectancies about alcohol's effects for self versus others. *Journal of Consulting & Clinical Psychology, 51*, 752–756.

Roizen, R. (1983). Loosening up: General population views of the effects of alcohol. In R. Room & G. Collins (Eds.), *Alcohol and disinhibition: Nature and meaning of the link* (pp. 236–257). Washington, DC: U.S. Government Printing Office.

Shipley, T. E. (1987). Opponent process theory. In H. T. Blane & K. E. Leonard (Eds.), *Psychological theories of drinking and alcoholism* (pp. 346-387). New York: Guilford Press.

Smith, G. T., Goldman, M. S., Greenbaum, P. E., & Christiansen, B. A. (1995). Expectancy for social facilitation from drinking: The divergent paths of high-expectancy and low-expectancy adolescents. *Journal of Abnormal Psychology, 104*, 32–40.

Solomon, R. L. (1980). The opponent-process theory of acquired motivation: The costs of pleasure and the benefits of pain. *American Psychologist, 35*, 691–712.

Southwick, L. L., Steele, C. M., Marlatt, G. A., & Lindell, M. K. (1981). Alcohol-related expectancies: Defined by phase of intoxication and drinking experience. *Journal of Consulting & Clinical Psychology, 49*, 713–721.

Spiegler, D. L. (1983). Children's attitudes toward alcohol. *Journal of Studies on Alcohol, 44*, 545–552.

Stacy, A. W. (1986). *Attitude and expectancy models of alcohol use: An integration of theoretical perspectives*. Unpublished doctoral dissertation, University of California, Riverside, CA.

Stacy, A. W., Newcomb, M. D., & Bentler, P. M. (1993). Cognitive motivations and sensation seeking as long-term predictors of drinking problems. *Journal of Social & Clinical Psychology, 12*, 1–24.

Stacy, A. W., & Widaman, K. F. (1987, August). *A "positivity" bias in attitude models of alcohol use*. Paper presented at the Annual Meeting of the American Psychological Association, New York.

Stacy, A. W., Widaman, K. F., & Marlatt, G. A. (1990). Expectancy models of alcohol use. *Journal of Personality & Social Psychology, 58*, 918–928.

Stein, J. A., Newcomb, M. D., & Bentler, P. M. (1986). The relationship of gender, social conformity, and substance use: A longitudinal study. *Bulletin of the Society of Psychologists in Addictive Behaviors, 5*, 125–138.

Stein, J. A., Newcomb, M. D., & Bentler, P. M. (1987). An 8-year study of multiple influences on drug use and drug use consequences. *Journal of Personality & Social Psychology, 53*, 1094–1105.

Stewart, T. (1987). *The heroin users*. London: Pandora Press.

Tamerin, J. S., Weiner, S., & Mendelson, J. H. (1970). Alcoholics' expectancies and recall of experiences during intoxication. *American Journal of Psychiatry, 126*, 1697–1704.

Teichman, M., Barnea, Z., & Ravav, G. (1989). Personality and substance use among adolescents: A longitudinal study. *British Journal of Addiction, 84*, 181–190.

Tversky, A., & Kahneman, D. (1974). Judgment under uncertainty: Heuristics and biases. *Science, 185*, 1124–1131.

Velez-Blasini, C. J. (1997). A cross-cultural comparison of alcohol expectancies in Puerto Rico and the United States. *Psychology of Addictive Behaviors, 11*, 124–141.

Young, R. M., & Knight, R. G. (1989). The Drinking Expectancy Questionnaire: A revised measure of alcohol-related beliefs. *Journal of Psychopathology & Behavioral Assessment, 11*, 99–112.

Young, R. M., & Oei, T. P. (1993). Grape expectations: The role of alcohol expectancies in the understanding and treatment of problem drinking. *International Journal of Psychology, 28*, 337-364.

Chapter 17

Alcohol, the Magic Elixir?

G. Alan Marlatt

This chapter explores the possibility that at least some drinkers perceive alcohol as a "magic elixir" capable of transforming emotional states. A prior paper on this topic (Marlatt, 1987) argued that the immediate effects of alcohol consumption often enhance mood or improve affect, a reaction described as "arousal enhancement." For those who are dependent on drinking to enhance pleasurable arousal, alcohol takes on transformative properties:

> Alcohol, viewed from this perspective, takes on the properties of a magic elixir, a substance that can enhance arousal, mood, or affect. Just as the alchemists of centuries past sought out an elixir that would transform lead into gold, so do many of today's problem drinkers turn to alcohol as an elixir to transform negative motional states into positive ones. (Marlatt, 1987, p. 303)

The 1987 paper reviewed two alternative hypotheses about the reinforcing effects of alcohol: (a) the tension-reduction hypothesis, in which drinking is rewarded by the anxiolytic effects of alcohol on tension, anxiety, or pain; and (b) the arousal-enhancement hypothesis, whereby drinking is rewarded through an increase in pleasure or euphoric mood states. The paper concluded that alcohol may have both arousal-enhancing (excitatory) effects and tension-reduction (inhibitory) effects, but that the excitatory effects precede the inhibitory effects in the form of a biphasic response.

The present chapter extends and updates this theoretical model with an emphasis on delineating differential alcohol-outcome expectancy profiles for problem and nonproblem drinkers. After a summary of the main points presented in the 1987 paper, new extensions of the expectancy model are applied to the

234 DRINKING EXPECTATIONS AND CONTEXTS

analysis of cases of both alcohol abuse and dependence. It is hypothesized that expectancy profiles for problem drinkers are often linear and unidimensional, for example, more drinking leads to greater pleasure or relief from pain. Research is reviewed showing that this unidimensional expectancy is incongruent with the actual biobehavioral effects of alcohol. Recent studies on the biphasic response to alcohol consumption strongly suggest that outcome expectancies are shaped primarily by the immediate (first-phase) arousal-enhancing properties of the biphasic reaction. The delayed (second-phase) effects of alcohol, which tend to be relatively unpleasant or dysphoric in quality, often are discounted in terms of motivational incentive. Case studies are provided to illustrate differences in the biphasic response for alcohol abuse and alcohol dependence. Both forms of problem drinking then are compared with moderate or nonproblem drinking. The chapter concludes with a brief discussion of the implications of this expectancy model for the prevention and treatment of alcohol problems.

ALCOHOL OUTCOME EXPECTANCIES AND THE BIPHASIC RESPONSE

Set and Setting in Alcohol Outcomes

Research on alcohol outcome expectancies dates back to early studies utilizing the balanced-placebo design (Marlatt, Demming, & Reid, 1973; Marlatt & Rohsenow, 1980). Four groups are compared in this design: expect alcohol/receive alcohol; expect alcohol/receive placebo; expect placebo/receive alcohol; and expect placebo/receive placebo. This design is required in order to independently vary the belief or expectancy that a drink contains alcohol with the actual alcohol content of the drink. A review of research employing this design (Hull & Bond, 1986) found that expectancy effects predominate for behaviors that otherwise are inhibited socially (e.g., increased sexual or aggressive response). Research using the balanced-placebo design shows that drinkers who are expecting to consume alcohol show disinhibited responsiveness, regardless of the actual alcohol content of the beverage. Alcohol administration, however, tends to have a deleterious effect on nonsocial behaviors such as motor performance or reaction time (e.g., impaired driving), regardless of the expectancy set.

In studies employing the balanced-placebo design, expectancy of beverage content (whether or not it contains alcohol) is manipulated by instructional set (Marlatt & Rohsenow, 1981). Drinkers are told that their drink either does or does not contain alcohol as a means of manipulating and eliciting expectancies about the effects of consuming alcohol. These outcome expectancies are thought to be influenced by both the drinker's cognitive "set," that is, whether the individual expects to drink an alcoholic or a nonalcoholic beverage, and the environmental setting or context in which drinking occurs. In short, both set and setting influence outcome expectancies.

Expectancies and Evaluations of Alcohol Outcomes

Following research with the balanced-placebo design, researchers turned their attention to assessing the content of alcohol outcome expectancies. Early research on this topic using the Alcohol Expectancy Questionnaire revealed several expectancy factors (Brown, Goldman, Inn, & Anderson, 1980). The first factor identified in the questionnaire administered to a wide range of drinkers portrays alcohol as a "global, positive transforming agent" (sample items: "Alcohol seems like magic," "Drinking makes the future seem brighter"). In a factor analysis of the AEQ, two thirds of the items had a significant loading on this factor of general transformation, that is, alcohol as a magic elixir.

In another study conducted by Brown and her colleagues (Brown, Goldman, & Christiansen, 1985), the AEQ scores of adult alcoholics were compared with those of college students and medical patients. The findings showed that alcoholics were found to maintain stronger alcohol expectancies, even if demographic differences between groups were controlled for in the analysis. The typical expectancy profile for alcoholics indicated more global, positive expectancies; increased interpersonal assertiveness; and more physical as well as social pleasure than the other populations tested.

Much research has been conducted on alcohol expectancies in subsequent years, as reviewed by Barbara Leigh (see Chapter 16). Expectancy questionnaires have been modified and improved to include assessment of potential moderating or mediating variables such as drinking setting or context (Fromme, Stroot, & Kaplan, 1993), different types of alcoholic beverages (Lang, Kaas, & Barnes, 1983), and low versus high dose of alcohol consumed (Southwick, Steele, Marlatt, & Lindell, 1981). As noted by Leigh (1998), it is also important to assess the value attached by the individual to the expected outcome of drinking.

> To more fully understand the nature of expectancies, we need to know about the valuations that people attach to them. Whether drinking has utility depends both on the probability of the consequences and the desirability of the consequences. . . . Thus, the relative "payoff" for drinking will vary among individuals, and in order to examine this payoff we need to know about both the subjective probability of experiencing an effect and the perceived desirability of the effect.

In support of this point, Leigh and Stacy (1994) found that although 14% of men and 5% of women listed increased sexuality as a positive consequence of consuming alcohol, 6% of men and 13% of women in the same sample described it as a negative consequence. This finding is consistent with a conclusion stated in the Marlatt (1987) review.

> Outcome expectancies for the effects of alcohol lie in the "eye of the beholder." For some beholders, alcohol is believed to possess highly attractive powers; for others, it is seen in a much more negative light, regardless of objective evidence as to its

"real" effects. The way in which we evaluate alcohol and label it as good or bad (positive or negative outcome expectancies) determines much of our behavior toward it. (Marlatt, 1987, p. 305)

Expectations and Actuality in Alcohol Outcomes

Several studies have shown that what a drinker expects to experience is often incongruent with the actual effects of alcohol. In early studies of drinking by alcoholics by Mendelson and his colleagues, alcoholics were asked to describe their initial expectancies about the effect of alcohol on their feelings and moods before a scheduled drinking period in a research-ward setting. Almost all of the alcoholics anticipated that alcohol would make them feel more relaxed, more comfortable, and less depressed. These expected effects were found to be the direct opposite of the actual dysphoric effects of prolonged drinking during the intoxication phase of the study (McGuire, Mendelson, & Stein, 1966; Tamerin, Weiner, & Mendelson, 1970).

In a more recent laboratory drinking study, Laberg and Leigh (1992) compared dependent and nondependent drinkers on the degree of congruence between the expected effects of alcohol and the actual experience of drinking. Prior to drinking, all participants were asked to rate the amount of pleasure they expected to feel after drinking. They then rated the amount of pleasure they experienced during the drinking session itself. Results showed a high correlation between expected and experienced pleasure for nonproblem drinkers only. Problem drinkers did not show this pattern, showing little or no correlation between their expected enhancement of pleasurable feelings and the actual effects. Even among nonproblem or social drinkers, expectancy effects may be moderated by drinking context.

Biphasic Effects of Alcohol   What accounts for the discrepancy between expected and actual effects of alcohol, and why is this incongruency stronger for problem drinkers? One possible explanation for the discrepancy may be that although outcome expectancies tend to be linear and unidimensional ("The more alcohol I drink, the better I will feel"), the actual effects of drinking are biphasic or bidimensional in nature. Research dating back several decades has affirmed that alcohol exerts a biphasic effect as a function of time and dose. In an early review of the psychopharmacological effects of drinking, Mello (1968, p. 789) concluded that "alcohol acts as a stimulant at low doses and its depressive functions are evident only at higher concentrations." Low doses of alcohol appear to increase heart rate and skin conductance, whereas higher doses tend to depress these measures of arousal (Knott & Beard, 1982; Rush, Higgins, Hughes, Bickel, & Wiegner, 1994).

Jones and Vega (1972) were the first to show that the biphasic response to alcohol maps onto the ascending limb of the blood alcohol curve (associated with arousal-enhancement effects) followed by the descending limb (associated with dysphoric or depressant effects). More recently, a biphasic alcohol-effects scale has been developed and validated by Martin, Earleywine, Musty, Perrine, and Swift (1993).

Various research studies have continued to explore individual differences in the behavioral and subjective effects of alcohol in human drinkers (deWit, Uhlenhuth, Pierri, & Johanson, 1987), including those with and without a family history of alcoholism (deWit & McCracken, 1990). The initial rewarding phase of the biphasic response is considered by some to be mediated by endogenous opioid mechanisms (Ulm, Volpicelli, & Volpicelli, 1995).

In addition to physiological mechanisms such as endogenous opioids and dopamine release that may mediate the rewarding first phase of the biphasic response to alcohol, learning and conditioning factors also play an important role. Solomon (1980) hypothesized that an underlying biphasic response may be common to a variety of emotional states, including the affective and hedonic response to alcohol and other psychoactive drugs. According to this theoretical model, eliciting of a particular emotional response automatically triggers a response of the opposite affective tone. This "opponent-process" system is thought to be designed as a basic homeostatic balancing mechanism to protect the organism from extreme affective states (Solomon & Corbit, 1974).

Extending this approach, Siegel (1983) has argued that these homeostatic or compensatory responses can be conditioned to alcohol or other drug cues. The conditioned compensatory response, elicited by alcohol-related conditioned stimuli (e.g., the sight and smell of an alcoholic beverage), is predicted to be opposite in hedonic quality to the pharmacological effects of alcohol itself. The body's compensatory response to a depressive drug such as alcohol (in an experienced drinker) is hypothesized to be an initial increase in arousal, in order to compensate for the anticipated depressive effects of alcohol on the nervous system. This initial increase in compensatory arousal, followed by the delayed depressive effects, parallels the two phases of the biphasic response to alcohol.

Biphasic Responses in Alcohol Abuse or Dependence   For heavy drinkers who are more tolerant to either the pleasure-enhancing or the adverse effects of alcohol, alcohol outcome expectancies may be far from the actual pharmacological or physiological effects. This "disconnect" between expectation and reality is especially strong in dependent drinkers, as documented previously. Unlike the process of metabolic or behavioral tolerance to alcohol, outcome expectancies do not show an increased tolerance effect over time; if anything, they remain robustly euphorogenic.

Research consistently shows that outcome expectancies, regardless of their accuracy in predicting future emotional states, are consistent and strong predictors of drinking behavior for both social drinkers (Stacy, 1997) and alcoholics (Brown, 1985). Through studies of the development and influence of alcohol expectancies, a new understanding of what is meant by "psychological dependence" is beginning to emerge. In the following section, outcome-expectancy profiles used as markers of psychological dependency are compared for problem and nonproblem drinkers.

OUTCOME EXPECTANCY PROFILES FOR PROBLEM AND NONPROBLEM DRINKERS

As an illustration of different expectancy profiles for problem drinkers, consider the following two case studies. The first case presents a young male whose drinking fits the criteria for alcohol abuse (hazardous binge-drinking pattern). In the second case, a middle-aged woman with alcohol dependence (chronic physical and psychological dependence) is presented. Both cases are presented as composite profiles, based on the author's clinical experience with a large number of similar cases.

Case 1: College Male Binge Drinker

Jack is a 19-year-old college freshman who belongs to a fraternity at a large West Coast university in the United States. Like many of his fraternity brothers, Jack likes to "party." As part of a research project designed to assess and modify "binge drinking" patterns in college students (Marlatt et al., 1998), Jack was asked to keep track of his drinking for a 2-week period and to fill out various research questionnaires to assess drinking problems, alcohol outcome expectancies, and other measures. Jack reported drinking between 40 and 50 drinks per week (mostly bottles of beer), spread out between Wednesday night (fraternity-sorority party night) and Saturday. His drinking style fits the minimal criteria for binge drinking as defined by Wechsler and colleagues: drinking five or more drinks in a row (Wechsler, Dowdall, Davenport, & Rimm, 1995).

When asked why he needed to drink 22 beers on one Saturday night party at the fraternity house, Jack replied, "If you want to mash, man, it's better to do it wearing beer goggles!" Asked to translate, Jack responded, "Mashing is making out, man, and if you don't like the way your date looks at the beginning of the party, she always looks great later at night looking at her through beer-goggles." Jack's outcome-expectancy questionnaire illustrates the "alcohol as magic elixir" profile. For Jack, alcohol is perceived as an elixir that can transform his perception of his date: she appears more attractive as seen through his "beer goggles." Jack further reported that he believed that he also was seen as more attractive by his date after an evening of heavy drinking. He believed that alcohol was a basic necessity for "making out" or having sex, quoting the old adage, "Candy is dandy, but liquor is quicker" in defense of his belief. For Jack, there is no upper limit to this effect: More is better.

Jack's magic elixir profile is presented in Figure 17.1. His expectancy profile is linear and unidimensional: Jack expects that he will feel more and more pleasure from a greater number of drinks. Often he anticipates that this pattern of drinking will culminate in a jackpot of sexual pleasure. Jack does not see

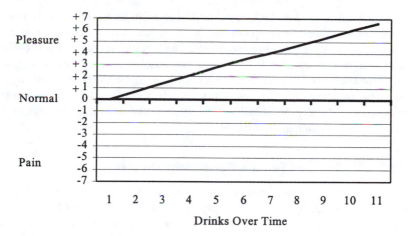

Figure 17.1 Magic elixir expectancy profile for binge drinking.

his drinking as a problem, nor does he see it as abnormal. In fact, his drinking is normative for his fellow fraternity members. However, he did admit to the research interviewer that he drank so much on some occasions that his sexual performance was impaired and that he was unable to recall much the next day about the previous evening's activities.

Jack's actual drinking experience is illustrated by the biphasic curve in Figure 17.2. Jack begins drinking in a normal or emotionally neutral state. Because he drinks in a binge pattern, he feels the "buzz" more quickly than

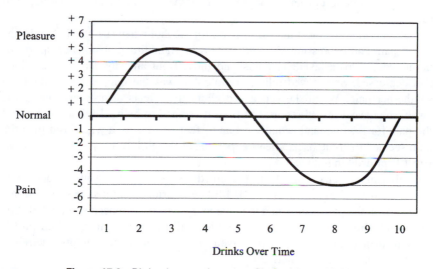

Figure 17.2 Biphasic experience profile for binge drinking.

most social drinkers. For Jack, the subjective high he experiences is one of positive reinforcement, in sharp contrast to the negative reinforcement pattern in the next case. Wanting an even greater high—and its sexual fringe benefits—Jack continues to drink long after the "point of diminishing returns" has been passed in the biphasic curve. As his blood alcohol level rises above the 200 mg/mL level, approximately after 10 beers, his speech begins to slur and his partner appears more sexually provocative than ever. Later that night he passes out before he can consummate his desires.

Case 2: Middle-Aged Female Dependent Drinker

Jill is a 42-year-old woman, married and with two children aged 8 and 11 years. Jill has been struggling with marital problems since her husband began having a serious affair. She sought counseling for depression and began drinking heavily during this period. Her therapist recommended in-patient treatment for her combined depression and drinking problems, and she was diagnosed as alcohol-dependent. She committed herself to abstinence after completion of the treatment program and was referred to the author for out-patient relapse prevention therapy (Marlatt & Gordon, 1985). Although Jill was able to maintain abstinence during the year following her completion of the residential treatment program, she experienced two serious lapses. On the first occasion, her husband initiated a marital separation and moved to another house, taking the children with him because, as he put it, "Jill is an alcoholic and cannot take care of our children." Jill responded by sinking into a deep depression. After the first night alone, she reported, "I just couldn't take it any more," and she drank continuously for the next 2 days before she was able to pull out of the lapse. Her husband used this drinking episode to bolster his argument that she was a helpless alcoholic, unfit to be a mother.

Jill reported the most intense craving for alcohol when she was in the depths of her pain and depression. All her success in maintaining abstinence up to this point seemed to no avail: Her husband moved out anyway, leaving her alone and depressed. She craved relief, and alcohol was the only elixir available to soothe her pain. When she was asked about the effects of drinking during the lapse, she gave a mixed report: "At first, it seemed to help—I felt a numbing of the pain for a while, and actually began to feel normal for a while. But then the pain seemed to come back when I experienced the guilt of having relapsed—but I just kept drinking anyway."

Jill's magic elixir profile is presented in Figure 17.3. Unlike Jack, who began "partying" in a normal mood, Jill began drinking in a state of emotional pain (−6 on the pain scale), and to some extent she experienced some relief. She reported feeling "normal" for a short period. Jill illustrates a magic elixir profile for self-medication. Alcohol is perceived to transform the pain, to provide relief, and to restore a sense of normality.

Although expectancy profiles for both Jack and Jill are unidimensional and linear (the more alcohol, the more reinforcing the effect), each starts at a different

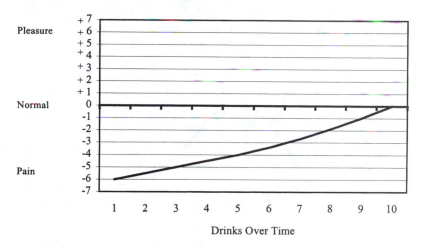

Figure 17.3 Magic elixir expectancy profile for self-medication drinking.

point on the pleasure-pain axis. Jack starts off drinking in a normal state and seeks greater pleasure from increased drinking ("More is better"). Jill, on the other hand, begins drinking when she is unable to withstand the pain without drinking ("I can't stand it any more").

For Jill, the expected payoff or "jackpot" from drinking is to feel normal again, to escape or avoid an ongoing painful experience. But normality is often short-lived, and the guilt Jill felt ended up making matters worse for her in the long run. She later reported that the first experience undermined her self-confidence to the extent that it may have contributed to a second lapse that occurred several months later (also triggered by her husband's behavior). Thus, Jill's experience is consistent with the research reviewed previously showing a disconnection between the problem drinker's expectancies about drinking and the experienced effects. In Jill's case, the experienced effects are illustrated in Figure 17.4. As can be seen, Jill begins drinking in a painful emotional state (−6) and experiences self-medicating effects that make her feel normal for a short period. But the second phase of the biphasic response plunges her back into a state of dysphoria (overlaid with guilt), a downside that she continues to try to escape by drinking even more. This pattern of negative reinforcement can lead to a vicious cycle that keeps Jill locked into drinking and at greater risk of relapse.

Expectancy Differences Between Problematic and Moderate Drinking

Both Jack's and Jill's expectancy profiles are linear and unidimensional. More drinking leads to greater pleasure (Jack) or greater relief from pain (Jill). Neither expectancy profile maps well onto the actual alcohol effects experienced by Jack

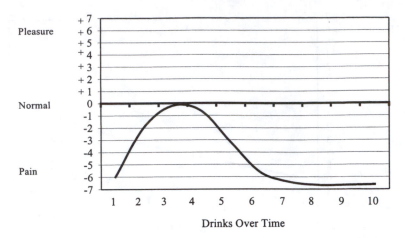

Figure 17.4   Biphasic experience profile for self-medication drinking.

or Jill. Jill's actual experience, shown in Figure 17.4, reveals a biphasic (two-dimensional) effect, characterized by negative reinforcement in the initial phase followed by increased dysphoria in the second phase.

How does moderate or nonproblem drinking compare with the profiles for Jack's binge drinking (alcohol abuse) and Jill's self-medication drinking (alcohol dependence)? Most moderate or social drinkers drink to enjoy the pleasurable effects associated with the initial phase of the biphasic response (positive reinforcement). They space their drinking over time, in contrast with Jack's "chug-a-lug" binging style. Moderate drinkers tend to "know their limit" and do not drink beyond the peak of the initial phase of the biphasic response (the "point of diminishing returns"). As such, moderation is characterized by drinking that serves to enhance or maintain a positive emotional state. Alcohol dependence, in contrast, is characterized by the drinker's attempt to self-medicate or transform a prior negative emotional state (negative reinforcement).

Table 17.1 illustrates the differences between moderate drinking and drinking as a form of self-medication (Marlatt, 1987). In this figure, three stages of affect or mood are portrayed: (a) the prior mood, or the individual's emotional state prior to drinking; (b) the biphasic drug response showing the immediate and delayed changes in mood after drinking; and (c) residual mood following drinking.

Looking first at moderate drinking, we consider the case in which an individual chooses to drink in a context associated with a positive mood state, such as a wedding reception for a good friend (+ prior mood). The initial effects of two or three glasses of champagne consumed in this celebratory context are experienced as an enhanced positive mood (+/+), or "feeling high." By drinking in a moderate fashion and keeping the blood alcohol level below intoxicating levels (below 80 mg/mL for most social drinkers), the individual experiences minimal

Table 17.1 Moderation versus self-medication drinking: Mood transformation effects.

	Prior Mood	Biphasic Drug Response		Residual Mood
		Immediate Effect (+)	Delayed Effect (-)	
Moderation	+	+/+ Enhanced Positive (Feeling High)	+/- Neutral Affect	Equilibrium
Self-Medication	-	-/+ Restored Neutral (Normalization)	-/- Delayed Negative	Disequilibrium

delayed negative effects, perhaps limited to a mild feeling of fatigue associated with the second phase of the biphasic response. Any negative aftereffects are offset or neutralized by the combined positive effects of the prior mood state and the initial arousal phase of the biphasic response. As a result, the individual's mood state following the drinking episode is essentially neutral (+/−), and the final outcome is one of emotional balance or equilibrium. Moderation leaves no negative emotional aftereffects.

In the case of self-medication drinking, the transformation of emotional states follows quite a different course, as depicted in the lower half of Figure 17.4. As in the case of Jill, before drinking the individual is likely to be experiencing a negative emotional state (−), often arising from a stressful life situation and/or the delayed negative physical effects of prior heavy drinking (e.g., hangover, withdrawal symptoms). After downing a few drinks, Jill experiences some temporary relief from the initial effects of alcohol. She reports feeling normal for a short period as the alcohol brings about a "restored neutral" emotional state (−/+). This neutral or normal mood is short-lived, however, because of the delayed negative effects of the biphasic response. As a result, the cumulative effect is emotionally negative, leaving Jill with a continued desire for more alcohol in a vain attempt to gain relief.

In comparison with the equilibrium of moderation (+/−), Jill's end state is one of disequilibrium (−/−). This state of imbalance often sets up a vicious cycle of self-medication drinking. The disequilibrium experienced after one drinking occasion sets the stage for repeated use as an attempt to restore balance. Any short-term effect soon is dispelled by the delayed negative effects, which in turn give rise to another attempt to gain relief.

IMPLICATIONS FOR PREVENTION AND TREATMENT

As noted by Leigh (see Chapter 16), alcohol outcome expectancies represent cognitive processes that may be subject to modification through preventive education and cognitive-behavioral therapy. Research on interventions that challenge drinking expectancies shows that this approach may have important implications for the prevention of problem drinking (Darkes & Goldman, 1993). In a recent study by these investigators (Darkes & Goldman, 1998), high-risk young male drinkers were assigned to expectancy challenges designed to mediate unrealistic expectations about alcohol's effects on arousal and sociability. The expectancy-challenge procedure involves administering either alcohol or a placebo beverage to drinkers in a group setting who then engage in tasks designed to focus on the expected effects of drinking. Participants are asked to identify which participants received alcohol and which did not, based on their observations of one another's behavior. Almost all participants made errors in their attempts to identify who had received alcohol and who had not. This provided the impetus for the expectancy challenge: "These identification errors were exploited to initiate and enhance the presentation of information on the development, maintenance, and operation of alcohol expectancies" (Darkes & Goldman, 1998, p. 68). Results showed that the expectancy-challenge procedure resulted in reduced alcohol consumption and altered expectancies post-treatment and following a short "booster" session six weeks later.

Another intervention that can be used to educate high-risk drinkers about alcohol outcome expectancies involves the use of a decision-matrix exercise (Marlatt & Gordon, 1985). In this procedure, the individual is asked to identify expected consequences of a choice involving drinking. As an example, Table 17.2 depicts a decision matrix involving a choice between moderate consumption and binge drinking. The top half of the figure shows the expected outcomes for moderate drinking and is contrasted with outcomes expected for heavy or binge drinking in the bottom half. In using the decision matrix, the interviewer or therapist begins by asking the respondent to identify his or her expected outcomes for both styles of drinking. First to be assessed are the immediate consequences, both positive and negative, of drinking in moderation. Then the delayed consequences (parallel to the second phase of the biphasic response) of moderate drinking are evaluated. As can be seen by the examples given in Table 17.2, both the immediate and delayed positive consequences far outweigh the expected negative outcomes.

The expected outcomes for binge drinking are in sharp contrast to the outcome expectancies for moderate drinking. Although several positive immediate effects are identified, negative effects predominate for both the immediate and

Table 17.2 Decision matrix for moderate vs. binge drinking.

Choice	Immediate consequences		Delayed consequences	
	Positive	Negative	Positive	Negative
Moderate drinking	Enhanced pleasure Socialization Mild disinhibition Enhanced appetite	Weight gain Drowsiness Less efficient Slowed reaction	Low dependence Increased longevity Social pressures Wine-connoisseur skills	Weight gain Stigma of being a drinker in a zero-tolerance society Financial costs (wine cellar)
Binge drinking	Enhanced pleasure Socialization and drinking games Extreme disinhibition ("getting wasted") Sexual disinhibition Risk-taking thrills Self-medication of pain	Injuries Blackouts Assaults Date rape Drink driving	Chronic relief	High tolerance High dependence Low self-esteem High health costs Decreased longevity Increased risk of family problems Legal costs Employment loss Treatment

delayed time periods. Exploration of these subjective expectations can be used to help high-risk drinkers become more informed consumers. Therapists can focus on the risk of delayed negative consequences in order to counter the appeal of the immediately gratifying effects. Use of the decision matrix as a prevention or treatment strategy is congruent with behavior-economic theory, an approach that treats drinkers as informed consumers who are capable of analyzing the pros and cons, or the benefits and costs, of their drinking behavior (Marlatt, Tucker, Donovan, & Vuchinich, 1997).

In a comprehensive relapse-prevention approach, problem drinkers often complete the decision matrix as part of a "functional analysis" to identify motives for drinking. Once the functions of drinking have been identified for a given individual, alternatives to drinking can be introduced that have the same functional outcome. If a client believes that drinking is the only way to reduce his or her anxiety, alternative relaxation procedures can be introduced—such as meditation or exercise—that fulfill this outcome. More recently, pharmacotherapeutic agents have been introduced that may influence outcome expectancies. Some studies show that problem drinkers who are administered naltrexone (an opioid antagonist) report less craving for alcohol over time (Weinrieb & O'Brien, 1997). Future combinations of cognitive-behavioral interventions coupled with adjunctive pharmacotherapy may show particular promise in this regard.

CONCLUSION

Alcohol expectancies are important elements in drinking behavior, but expectancies about alcohol's effect, evaluations of their outcomes, and corresponding drinking behavior differ among different types of problem drinkers and normal or moderate drinkers. Normal drinkers and nondependent problem drinkers generally anticipate pleasurable effects from alcohol; dependent drinkers more often are motivated by the desire to eliminate pain. Although expectations and outcomes are generally synchronized for normal drinkers, problem drinkers and alcoholics typically show discordance between expectations and outcomes, such that anticipated benefits do not materialize and they instead experience increasingly negative or painful effects as they continue to consume more alcohol. Clinically, these factors can be utilized to address problematic drinking through such methods as disabusing problematic drinkers of unrealistic expectations about the results of their drinking, or other cognitive, behavioral, and pharmacological methods for remediating such expectancies, and alternative ways for achieving desired feelings and outcomes can be developed.

REFERENCES

Brown, S. A. (1985). Reinforcement expectancies and alcoholism treatment outcome. *Journal of Studies on Alcohol, 46*, 304–308.

Brown, S. A., Goldman, M. S., & Christiansen, B. A. (1985). Do alcohol expectancies mediate drinking patterns of adults? *Journal of Consulting and Clinical Psychology, 53*, 512–519.

Brown, S. A., Goldman, M. S., Inn, A., & Anderson, L. R. (1980). Expectations of reinforcement from alcohol: Their domain and relation to drinking patterns. *Journal of Consulting and Clinical Psychology, 48*, 419–426.

Darkes, J., & Goldman, M. S. (1993). Expectancy challenge and drinking reduction: Experimental evidence for a mediational process. *Journal of Consulting and Clinical Psychology, 61*, 344–353.

Darkes, J., & Goldman, M. S. (1998). Expectancy challenge and drinking reduction: Process and structure in the alcohol expectancy network. *Experimental and Clinical Psychopharmacology, 6*, 64–76.

deWit, H., & McCracken, S. G. (1990). Ethanol self-administration in males with and without alcholic first-degree relatives. *Alcoholism: Clinical and Experimental Research, 14*, 63–70.

deWit, H., Uhlenhuth, E. H., Pierri, J., & Johanson, C. E. (1987). Individual differences in behavioral and subjective responses to alcohol. *Alcoholism: Clinical and Experimental Research, 11*, 52–59.

Fromme, K., Stroot, E. A., & Kaplan, D. (1993). Comprehensive effects of alcohol: Development and psychometric assessment of a new expectancy questionnaire. *Psychological Assessment, 5*, 19–26.

Hull, J. G., & Bond, C. F. (1986). Social and behavioral consequences of alcohol consumption and expectancy: A meta-analysis. *Psychological Bulletin, 99*, 347–360.

Jones, B. M., & Vega, A. (1972). Cognitive performance measured on the ascending and descending limb of the blood alcohol curve. *Psychopharmacology, 23*, 99–114.

Knott, D. H., & Beard, J. D. (1982). Effects of alcohol ingestion on the cardiovascular system. In E. M. Pattison & E. K. Kaufman (Eds.), *Encyclopedic Handbook of Alcoholism* (pp. 332–342). New York: Gardner.

Laberg, J. C., & Leigh, B. C. (1992). *Expected and experienced alcohol effects and desire to drink*. Paper presented at the 36th International Congress on Alcohol and Drug Dependence, Glasgow, Scotland.

Lang, A. R., Kaas, L., & Barnes, P. (1983). The beverage type stereotype: An unexplored determinant of the effects of alcohol consumption. *Bulletin of the Society of Psychologists in Addictive Behaviors, 2*, 46–49.

Leigh, B. C., & Stacy, A. W. (1994). Self-generated alcohol outcome expectancies in four samples of drinkers. *Addiction Research, 1*, 335–348.

Marlatt, G. A. (1987). Alcohol, the magic elixir: Stress, expectancy, and the transformation of emotional states. In E. Gottheil, K. A. Druly, S. Pashko, & S. P. Weinstein (Eds.), *Stress and Addiction*. New York: Brunner/Mazel.

Marlatt, G. A, Baer, J. S., Kivlahan, D. R., Dimeff, L. A., Larimer, M. E., Quigley, L. A., Somers, J. M., & Williams, E. (1998). Screening and brief intervention for high-risk college student drinkers: Results from a two-year follow-up assessment. *Journal of Consulting and Clinical Psychology, 66*, 1–12.

Marlatt, G. A., Demming, B., & Reid, J. B. (1973). Loss of control drinking in alcoholics: An experimental analogue. *Journal of Abnormal Psychology, 81*, 233–241.

Marlatt, G. A., & Gordon, J. R. (Eds.). (1985). *Relapse prevention: Maintenance strategies in the treatment of addictive behaviors*. New York: Guilford Press.

Marlatt, G. A., & Rohsenow, D. J. (1980). Cognitive processes in alcohol use: Expectancy and the balanced placebo design. In N. K. Mello (Ed.), *Advances in substance abuse: Vol. 1* (pp. 159–199). Greenwich, CT: JAI Press.

Marlatt, G. A., & Rohsenow, D. J. (1981). Think-drink effect. *Psychology Today, 15*, 60–69.

Marlatt, G. A., Tucker, J. ., Donovan, D. M., & Vuchinich, R. E. (1997). Help-seeking by substance abusers: The role of harm reduction and behavioral-economic approaches to facilitate treatment entry and retention. In L. S. Onken, J. D. Blaine, & J. J. Boren (Eds.), *Beyond the therapeutic alliance: Keeping the drug-dependent individual in treatment* (National Institute on Drug Abuse Research Monograph 165, pp. 44–84). Rockville, MD: U.S. Department of Health and Human Services.

Martin, C. S., Earleywine, M., Musty, R. E., Perrine, M. W., & Swift, R. M. (1993). Development and validation of the biphasic alcohol effects scale. *Alcoholism: Clinical and Experimental Research, 17,* 140–146.

McGuire, M. T., Mendelson, J. H., & Stein, S. (1966). Comparative psychosocial studies of alcoholic and non-alcoholic subjects undergoing experimentally-induced ethanol intoxication. *Psychosomatic Medicine, 28,* 13–25.

Mello, N. K. (1968). Some aspects of the behavioral pharmacology of alcohol. In D. H. Efron (Ed.), *Psychopharmacology: A review of progress* (U.S. Public Health Service Publication No 1836, pp. 787–809). Washington, DC: U.S. Government Printing Office.

Rush, C. R., Higgins, S. T., Hughes, J. R., Bickel, W. K., & Wiegner, M. S. (1994). Acute behavioral and cardiac effects of alcohol and caffeine, alone and in combination. *Behavioural Pharmacology, 4,* 562–572.

Siegel, S. (1983). Classical conditioning, drug tolerance, and drug dependence. In R. G. Smart, F. B. Glaser, Y. Israel, H. Kalant, R. E. Popham, & W. Schmidt (Eds.), *Research advances in alcohol and drug problems: Vol. 7* (pp. 207–246). New York: Plenum Press.

Solomon, R. L. (1980). The opponent-process theory of acquired motivation: The costs of pleasure and the benefits of pain. *American Psychologist, 35,* 691–712.

Solomon, R. L., & Corbit, J. D. (1974). An opponent-process theory of motivation: Temporal dynamics of affect. *Psychological Review, 81,* 119–145.

Southwick, L., Steele, C., Marlatt, G. A., & Lindell, M. (1981). Alcohol-related expectancies: Defined by phase of intoxication and drinking experience. *Journal of Consulting and Clinical Psychology, 49,* 713–721.

Stacy, A. W. (1997). Memory activation and expectancy as prospective predictors of alcohol and marijuana use. *Journal of Abnormal Psychology, 106,* 61–73.

Tamerin, J. S., Weiner, S., & Mendelson, J. H. (1970). Alcoholics' expectancies and recall of experiences during intoxication. *American Journal of Psychiatry, 126,* 1697–1704.

Ulm, R. R., Volpicelli, J. R., & Volpicelli, L. A. (1995). Opiates and alcohol self-administration in animals. *Journal of Clinical Psychiatry, 56*(Suppl. 7), 5–14.

Wechsler, H., Dowdall, G. W., Davenport, A., & Rimm, E. B. (1995). A gender specific measure of binge drinking among college students. *American Journal of Public Health, 85,* 982–985.

Weinreib, R. M., & O'Brien, C. P. (1997). Naltrexone in the treatment of alcoholism. *Annual Review of Medicine, 48,* 477–487.

Chapter 18

Drinking Behavior and Pleasure Across the Life Span

Geoff Lowe

Children, adolescents, young adults, mature adults, and older persons view and drink alcohol differently. What are these differences, and can they be related to varying conceptions of pleasure at different ages? This chapter emphasizes *what* people say about their drinking and pleasures and *how* they say it.[1] To illustrate my approach, I turn to Laurie Lee's autobiographical trilogy, which describes her progress and education in the art of drinking in the first part, *Cider with Rosie* (1965). In this literary work, one reads of childish lemonade and ginger beer, beer-drinking uncles, and of course, memorably, cider: "Never to be forgotten, that first long secret drink of golden fire, juice of those valleys and of that time, wine of wild orchards, of russet summer, of plump red apples." Reviewing data from recent surveys, other empirical studies, and from the Mass-Observation Archive (in the United Kingdom), this chapter first outlines the main common, and differentiating, characteristics of drinking patterns across the age groups. These patterns are related to different kinds of drinking expectancies, from initial development through subsequent strengthening or modification, and to the varieties of reasons for drinking (see Christiansen, Goldman, & Inn, 1982; Corcoran & Segrist, 1993; Leigh, Chapter 16; Rohsenow, 1983; Wilks & Callan, 1990).

THE DEVELOPMENT OF DRINKING OVER
THE LIFE SPAN

Age-Group Differences in Drinking:
The Young and the Elderly

Within a period of about 10 years, young people change from individuals who have never had an alcoholic drink to individuals who, as an age group, are the heaviest drinking section of the population (Edwards, 1984; Goddard, 1991). Media messages (both positive and negative) may be significant modifiers of adolescents' attitudes towards alcohol (Guild & Lowe, 1998). Continually surrounded by attractive and sophisticated images of the pleasures of alcohol, adolescents are strongly motivated to at least experiment with alcohol— a phase that some behavioral researchers refer to as *sensation seeking* (Beck, Thombs, Mahoney, & Fingar, 1995; Cato, 1992; Earleywine & Finn, 1991). Many youngsters report having their first drink between the ages of 9 and 11 years (Hawker, 1978; Lowe, Foxcroft, & Sibley, 1993), and a substantial proportion of older teenagers drink excessively (Dorn, 1983; Ghodsian & Power, 1987; Plant, Bagnall, & Foster, 1990). Although young problem drinkers are a major source of concern, surveys consistently have portrayed teenage drinking as a normal development in the context of the psychosocial environment (e.g., Grant, Harford, & Grigson, 1988; Sharp & Lowe, 1989a). Drinking is predominantly a social behavior and is widely regarded as a key indicator of adult status (Budd, Eiser, Morgan, & Gammage, 1985; Thombs & Beck, 1994).

In other studies in which we looked at underage drinking and alcohol expectancies (Sharp & Lowe, 1989b), we found certain reasons for drinking to be universally confirmed, that is, across all age groups for both boys and girls: because "they like the taste," it "makes a party fun," or "to get drunk." Most denied that they drink because it is expected of them. In a study of 16- to 18-year-old youth trainees (Foxcroft & Lowe, 1991), we noted that the majority of respondents—typically older females and younger males—usually drank to "get merry." More males, especially older ones, than females drank "to get drunk."

The elderly typically decrease their drinking and moderation is the rule, although elderly women and people older than 75 years of age frequently abstain from alcohol (Adams, 1996; Cahalan & Cisin, 1986; Harford & Mills, 1978; Helzer, Burnham, & McEvoy, 1991; Hilton, 1987). This is understandable because, apart from other reasons (Glass, Prigerson, Kasl, & Mendes de Leon, 1995), older people have proportionately less body water, i.e., a smaller volume for distribution of alcohol, and so quickly reach higher blood alcohol levels (Vogel-Sprott & Barrett, 1984). Even the drinking of heavy drinkers and alcoholics generally tails off with old age (Stall, 1986, 1987).

Cross-sectional Surveys

A major problem in interpreting cross-sectional surveys is whether the age effect reflects the aging process or represents instead a generational or cohort effect. Thus, an over-60 group in 1990 not only is older than a young adult group but also reflects the different attitudes and social values of the 1950s, when the older group was in its 20s. Such generational differences, rather than age differences per se, could be responsible for some of the drinking differences noted (including pleasures).

In addition, cross-sectional age comparisons do not portray the drinking pattern for any one individual growing older. The older group typically may report lower drinking levels than those of young people today, but this does not necessarily mean that they are drinking less today than they did when they themselves were younger. However, most individuals do drink less as they get older. Changes in drinking patterns (usually declines) are related to frail health, decreases in metabolic efficiency and alcohol tolerance, poverty, bereavement, and social isolation (Dufour, Archer, & Gordis, 1992; Midanick, Klatsky, & Armstrong, 1990).

Fillmore (1987) used both cross-sectional and longitudinal designs to assess age-related drinking differences in men over two decades. The longitudinal studies showed a modest continuity between drinking levels in middle age and those in adolescence and young adulthood. But incidence of *heavy* drinking declined as men aged from their 20s through their 50s.

The literature in general shows that teens and young adults drink less frequently but in greater amounts—including binge drinking—compared with more frequent, lighter drinking among older adults. Frequency and overall consumption generally decrease as people become elderly, although the extent of elderly alcohol use is strongly influenced by such demographic factors as gender, marital status, and size of the community in which people live (Adams, 1996; Ekerdt, Labry, Glynn, & Davis, 1989; Mooney, Fromme, Kivlahan, & Marlatt, 1987).

PLEASURES OF DRINKING AND OTHER SUBSTANCE USE

Although a few studies suggest a possible neurochemical basis for alcohol's pleasurable effects (cf. Johnson, Campling, Griffiths, & Cowen, 1993), that alcohol is an inherently positive (or pleasurable) reinforcer is not clear. Many data suggest that the emotional experiences associated with moderate drinking depend on the environment, and especially social context (see Gustafson, 1991). Most research in this area uses social-learning/expectancy constructs and ethnographic perspectives. Such an approach, according to Peele and Brodsky (1998; see also Chapter 15), suggests that the benefits and pleasures of drinking are not directly attributable to alcohol's pharmacological properties but arise through particular contexts conditioned by culture, social environment, and expectations (Peele & Brodsky, 1996; Pittman & White, 1995; Room, 1997; Simpura, 1985).

Individual Reports and Ethnographic Research on Pleasurable Drinking

> I was very well brought up. As a first proof of so categorical a statement, I shall simply say that I was no more than three years old when my father poured out my first liqueur glass of an amber-coloured wine which was sent up to him from the Midi, where he was born: the muscat of Frontignan.
>
> The sun breaking from behind the clouds, a shock of sensuous pleasure, an illumination of my newborn taste buds! This initiation ceremony rendered me worthy of wine for all time. A little later I learned to empty my goblet of mulled wine, scented with cinnamon and lemon, as I ate a dinner of boiled chestnuts. At an age when I could still scarcely read, I was spelling out, drop by drop, old light clarets and dazzling Yquems. Champagne appeared in its turn, a murmur of foam, leaping pearls of air providing an accompaniment to birthday and First Communion banquets, complementing the grey truffles from La Puisaye.... Good lessons, from which I graduated to a familiar and discreet use of wine, not gulped down greedily but measured out into narrow glasses, assimilated mouthful by spaced-out, meditative mouthful.
>
> It was between my eleventh and fifteenth years that this admirable education programme was perfected. My mother was afraid that I was outgrowing my strength and was in danger of a "decline." One by one, she unearthed, from their bed of dry sand, certain bottles that had been aging beneath our house in a cellar, hewn out of fine, solid granite.... As an accompaniment to my modest, fill-in meals we often drank Chateau-Laffittes, Chambertins, and Cortons which had escaped capture by the "Prussians" in 1870. Certain of these wines were already fading, but most of them retained their aristocratic ardour and their invigorating powers. The good old days! (Colette, 1966, p. 11).

Colette was a deeply sensuous human being with a deep love, a passion, for food and, above all, wine. She was born in Burgundy into a family in which the values of wine were well understood. As she said herself, "Since childhood I have known French wine, and been well acquainted with it."

Johnson (1993) advocates ethnographic alcohol studies that

> are concerned, almost by definition, with describing a particular group's drinking behavior and placing it within the context of values and norms that direct the group and give its actions meaning. Psychological studies of drinking could greatly benefit from a cultural orientation that seeks to anchor group drinking to the larger context in which it develops, is maintained, and changes over the life trajectory. (p. 28)

Among ethnographic approaches to the study of drinking behavior (Demers, Kishchuk, Bourgault, & Bisson, 1996; Douglas, 1987), longitudinal or panel research investigates the process of drinking as it unfolds over individual life trajectories (Newcomb, Bentler, & Collins, 1986). Such exploration frequently uncovers great variability and change over the life span. Thus, we must bear in mind that studies that simply offer snapshots of drinking in one time frame are limited, and their results may be misleading.

The Mass-Observation Archive

The Mass-Observation (M-O) Archive at the University of Sussex is a remarkably rich store of predominantly qualitative material about many facets of British life during the past half century. The early M-O data came from active observers who infiltrated particular environments, supplemented by questionnaire surveys. During the 1940s Mass-Observation carried out several studies of people's drinking habits (Mass-Observation Archive, 1943, 1948). The latest stage of the M-O has recruited a panel of several thousand M-O volunteers in the 1980s and 1990s. Two or three times a year a special directive is sent out that invites these observers to write about various aspects of British life and their own everyday lifestyles. Several recent M-O directives concerned substance use and pleasure.

Although M-O respondents cover the range of age, gender, occupation, and regional groups, they are predominantly middle-aged, middle-class, and female and thus do not make up a representative sample of the general population. M-O respondents are best regarded as being mature, well-seasoned, responsive, and responsible—but "ordinary"—people who represent the traditional backbone of British society and whose attitudes and opinions therefore are valued by social scientists and the media. The data they provide are qualitative, and respondents highlight whichever aspects of questions are important or relevant to their own lives. Overall, the data this study provides are incomparably rich in descriptive and emotional detail, offering unique and fascinating insights that supplement those from such standardized research techniques as questionnaires.

Mass-Observation Data on Pleasure   One Mass-Observation directive (in 1993) asked respondents to write about pleasure and good times or moments. The database from this *Pleasure* directive consisted of hundreds of written reports, each comprising 1 to 20 pages. The respondents were adult women (74%) and men (26%). Their average age was 56 years, with an age range from 16 to 92 years. M-O respondents are mostly middle-aged or older, and in our sample 87% were in the over-40 age group.

One of the interesting aspects from an initial sampling of those reports was the amazing variety of pleasures that people reported (see Table 18.1). Pleasures featuring places, scenery, art, music, love and sex, books, food and drink, films and concerts, memories, children, and so on were common. But there were also many idiosyncratic or unusual pleasures:

> Several incidents of really gross misbehavior that I still smile at in retrospect. (Male, 40 years old)

Table 18.1 **Pleasure categories by age and sex of respondents.**

	<40 years old		≥40 years old	
	Males	**Females**	**Males**	**Females**
Most frequent categories	Reading Food and drink Love/sex Home and garden Friends Music Nature/scenery Sport and exercise	Food and drink Family/children Entertainment Love/sex Reading	Food and drink Music Family/children Reading Sport and exercise	Family/children Food and drink Nature/scenery Entertainment Reading
Least frequent categories	Driving Humor Memories Mental Indoor pastimes Art Security/money Special occasions Spiritual/religious Places	Smoking Smells Art Sounds Humor Health	Sounds Special occasions Smells Smoking Indoor pastimes	Sounds Health Driving Humor Mental Cosiness

Cessation of pain/discomfort. The more I write about my "pleasures" I realise that many of them are related to the contrast. I might be "content" living in an even temperature, not too cold, not too hot; but this is not really "pleasure." If I hadn't been horribly sea-sick I wouldn't have felt the joy of stepping on to dry land. (Female, 71 years old)

When I have a splinter and my wife can look and find it. (Male, 47 years old)

Nothing can compare to the pleasure gained from pulling a lovely long strip of wallpaper off. (Female, 55 years old)

Seeing elderly couples walking hand-in-hand. It gives me faith in humanity to see these people. I get a warm feeling from looking at them. (Female, 26 years old)

There was much emphasis on social pleasures, and many respondents rated friendship highly:

The laughs, the support, the bottles of wine, the trips to the theatre, opera, the holidays, barbecues and feeling of camaraderie. The pleasure of close friends is probably the most important thing to me. (Male, 33 years old)

My second pleasure is enjoying the company of friends and having a laugh, a drink, a discussion, a gossip, an exchange of views to relax at the weekend and unwind. The pub is the place we go for every occasion as well. (Female, 51 years old)

Relaxing in a nice bath was a firm favorite of some:

To wallow unashamedly in a deep, hot bath complete with a sherry and/or radio or book. (Female, 63 years old)

Pleasures and Substance Use Across the Ages

Hardly any research has tracked the normative development of drinking pleasures—which, of course, are a more complex phenomenon than level of alcohol consumption. Although younger children frequently are intrigued by alcohol (because they often observe pleasurable drinking among adults) and request a sip, they typically find that the taste of alcohol is unpleasant. It is only older adolescents who specifically mention taste as a pleasurable aspect of drinking (Sharp & Lowe, 1989b). The acquired nature of pleasurable drinking resembles many other pleasures. Although few teenagers enjoy classical music and opera, for instance, many more find this music pleasurable as mature adults.

Romanova and Petrakova (1992) noted that, although children acquire basic information about the effects of alcohol by age 6 or 7 years, "between 9 and 11 years of age, children demonstrate more insight into this issue through observing effects of alcohol intoxication in adults drinking and through their own experience with isolated trials of drinking" (p. 22). The authors stressed that familiarity with the ritualistic aspects of drinking precedes learning to enjoy the consumption of alcohol. This process was demonstrated in the earlier quote from Laurie Lee, and we shall see that ritualistic aspects frequently are mentioned in respondents' reports of pleasurable drinking experiences.

Western society employs many substances for pleasure, such as tea, coffee, alcohol, cigarettes, and chocolate. We recently undertook another project that focuses on people's pleasures and enjoyments (Crook & Lowe, 1998). This project aimed to investigate how people's reported use of these social substances may affect their daily experience and perceived quality of life. A specific hypothesis was that substance users may have different orientations towards pleasure compared with those who abstain. We also were able to examine possible age- and sex-related differences among pleasure categories.

In this research, respondents aged 18 to 74 years were asked to anonymously provide details on up to 20 pleasurable activities, in addition to demographic information. Questions about alcohol, smoking, and other substance use, diet, and life events also were included, along with a subjective quality-of-life measure (see Chapter 23). Independent raters sorted respondents' pleasures into 15 main categories. Among these, nature (e.g., animals, pets, trees, gardens, country walks), family, work, and social pleasures varied with age, gender, and substance use, as well as with employment and marital status. Many pleasures also were related to quality of life.

Overall, demographic characteristics were more important than substance use in predicting pleasure types. For instance, 51- to 70-year-olds reported more nature pleasures than did 18- to 30-year-olds, who had more social pleasures than 41- to 50-year-olds. Women reported more creative, nature, and social pleasures than did men, who reported more work pleasures. Amount of alcohol drunk (as a variable) was not associated markedly with any differences in reported pleasures, nor was other substance use. This may be simply because use of alcohol and the other substances considered is so widespread and accepted. However, heavy drinkers had more active (including sports, dancing, driving) pleasures and eating/drinking/smoking pleasures than other types of drinkers. Nondrinkers enjoyed more family pleasures. And there were slight differences in pleasures among individuals drinking different types of alcohol (probably more related to different age groups). Wine drinkers reported more family pleasures and spirit drinkers reported more self-indulgent pleasures than did other types of drinkers. This may reflect the more common consumption of beer, lager, and wine than spirits, so that a glass of whisky perhaps is seen as more of a treat than a beer or glass of wine.

Respondents aged 50 to 69 years reported significantly more nature-based pleasures than those younger than 39 years. Those aged 20 to 29 years reported more sex pleasures and those younger than 20 years more social pleasures than those aged 50 to 59; those younger than 30 as a whole reported more active and more self-indulgent pleasures than other age groups. And those aged 30 to 39 years reported slightly more eating/drinking/smoking pleasures than did other groups. Elderly respondents reported more family pleasures than did the young (almost three times as many). Compared with men, women reported significantly more nature, social, family, and holiday-based pleasures, but their alcohol consumption was lower.

Substance use does seem to have consequences for people's pleasure preferences, especially ones such as active pleasures, nature pleasures, work, social, and family pleasures, which also vary in importance at different times in the life span.

Substance Pleasures and Quality of Life

Many commentators have highlighted the apparent conflict between society's health-related messages that decry pleasurable substance use and individuals' use of such substances in sensible ways that bring enjoyment. Although it is likely that some pleasurable substances are, in some circumstances, be really bad for us, it is even more likely that enjoyable pleasures really are good for us (Lowe, 1994). Our M-O research has confronted this issue in considering the extent to which people appreciate the pleasures of socially enjoyed substances and their contribution to quality of life.

Most recent research that assesses the quality-of-life dimension is primarily health-related or medically related. Attempts are being made to measure, in objective terms, a person's quality of life as a sufferer from a particular illness or after recovery from a medical intervention or treatment. The M-O data consider quality of life from the point of view of the ordinary (generally healthy) person, who engages in certain pursuits that add a bit of pleasure, enjoyment, satisfaction and contentment to life—and thereby enhance the quality of experience. M-O respondents considered the pleasures of socially enjoyed substances—tea, coffee, chocolate, cigarettes, and alcohol—along with a wide range of other pleasures of daily existence in terms of their contribution to quality of life (Lowe, 1996).

Although many surveys show that substance users, both young and old, ingest primarily for positive sensations (e.g., for the taste, for the "buzz," to feel relaxed, to get "high," and to "feel good"), M-O reports highlight important ritualistic aspects of substance use. Most of these substances, if used for pleasure, have a regular temporal pattern. Moreover, sensible drinking and other substance use can be regarded as a skilled behavior; and the greater the familiarity and skill in use, the more and better the pleasure and enjoyment. For instance, *bons viveurs* and wine connoisseurs greatly refine some aspects of the quality-of-life dimension.

Furthermore, these substances frequently are consumed in particular places. Society needs to ensure that appropriate substance-oriented places, such as pubs, cafes, and other comfortable places outside the home, are readily available to appropriate groups of people. Provision of such places acknowledges the need to relax and unwind, accompanied often by socially enjoyed substances (Oldenburg,

1989). Skillful enjoyment of such pleasures in the proper context seemingly enhances quality of life both individually and culturally.

Pleasures of Drinking and Substance Use of M-O Participants

A 16th-century *bon viveur* remarked: "There are five reasons for drinking: the visit of a friend, present thirst, future thirst, the goodness of the wine, or any other reason." This commentator highlighted company, thirst, quality of beverage, and a rather large set of miscellaneous reasons that foster drinking as a pleasurable activity. M-O respondents illuminated various social aspects of drinking, including social pressure and expectancies:

> An old friend of mine, now, alas, deceased, used to say that he only consumed alcohol in order to make himself a more pleasant companion for those he drank with! I echo these sentiments. (Male, retired)

Even observations about drinking excesses included pleasurable social references:

> Yes. I drank much too much when I was young. I remember, as a student, consuming gallons of some beer, and having terrible hangovers. Oh, the wickedness and excitement of it all. (Female, 71 years old)

Some respondents reflected on quality beverages they greatly enjoyed:

> Good wine can make me feel orgasmic. The nose, taste, and glow one gets can be overwhelming. I have occasionally had wine so delicious it has almost brought tears to my eyes. The ability to taste different spices, fruits, flowers, herbs within one glass of wine differentiates good wines to bad wines for me, and a good wine requires time and thought to be enjoyed fully. However it is not for me, a thing to be deeply discussed, analysed as to what the definitive taste or nose is, but something to be slowly explored and quietly enjoyed. If I were to be marooned on a desert island I would have a good case of wine as my luxury (plus a corkscrew and a large glass!). (Female, 35 years old)

> A pint or two of Guinness—with a stimulating companion. This isn't necessarily the best of the items—it just struck me that it is a very important thing to me. Guinness helps me relax and be myself—rather than muddle my mind, it sharpens it and I can be much more decisive in what I am saying. (Male, 53 years old)

> I am sitting outside a cottage/farmhouse in the evening somewhere in France (or maybe anywhere else in southern Europe) on a warm evening. It's a rural area—there is no traffic noise, no dogs barking, nobody asking me to do things for them. I have a good novel and a glass of red wine. In the background the crickets are

chirping. Perhaps I am sitting with my wife who is reading a book as well, or perhaps I am with a group of 6 male friends who I go cycling with every other year and we have been for a meal and some drinks in the local bar. This for me is probably the ultimate pleasure! (Male, 42 years old)

This group of sensible, ordinary people who responded to the M-O directive was almost unanimous in highlighting the importance of ritualistic aspects in their consumption of social substances. Among those older than 50 years, in particular, there was a sense of pride in their ritualistic approaches to drinking alcohol, coffee, and tea, and they saw the rituals as pleasurable in and of themselves. This contrasts with more contemporary trends towards adjunctive smoking and drinking, for example straight from cans, which demote substance use to mere accompaniment of other primary activities.

Such adjunctive behavior occurs mainly among younger smokers and drinkers. Several studies (e.g., Doyle & Samson, 1985, 1988) suggest that schedule induction (whereby subjects receive intermittent reinforcement from video-game slot machines, for instance) may be more important in the formative stages of an individual's drinking history. Many of our observations from teenage and student respondents are consistent with this notion. Eventually, of course, this drinking style becomes less a product of schedule control and more a reinforced pattern under stimulus control, whereby sensory quality and taste are predominant. Comments from our mature students and older respondents seem to bear this out.

DRINKING AS SKILLED BEHAVIOR

"Sensible" drinking and other substance use can be regarded as a skilled behavior, and the greater the skill, the greater the pleasure and enjoyment. For instance, *bons viveurs* and wine connoisseurs add refined gradations to the quality-of-life dimension (Kunz, 1997).

Skill in drinking involves practical knowledge such as how to ingest the substance, the names and qualities of specific beverages and substances, and what quantities or doses are appropriate to each. Knowledge about customs, rituals, rules, and meanings of consumption are picked up en route through socialization. Consumers learn through this process when, where, and what types of consumption are appropriate to which contexts, and *how* to consume. At the same time, they learn to distinguish their consumption so that they develop a repertoire of drinking and ingestion styles to be used on different occasions and for different purposes in different contexts.

Altogether, skill in drinking and consuming other substances requires balancing dose, purpose, and context. To have good experiences of drinking and substance use, all three elements need to be harmonized. As with many other skilled behaviors—sports, cooking, musical skills, and so on—the more skilled the practitioner, the higher the degree of pleasure and enjoyment. In this vein, reading and writing about pleasurable activities generally leads to the greater enjoyment of such pleasures, presumably by increased activation of expectancy processes.

CONCLUSIONS

A consideration of drinking behavior and pleasures across the life span suggests that most people are well capable of adjusting their drinking and pleasure seeking according to their changing circumstances. Although there is evidence of general age-related trends in both these domains, there is also a wide range of individual differences that emerge in the qualitative observations drawn from *what* people say about their drinking and pleasures and *how* they say it. Notwithstanding the uniqueness of individual preferences, the following generalizations emerge from this chapter:

- The context in which drinking occurs contributes substantially to its pleasurable or positive aspects; "time out" and ritualistic elements are important in that respect.
- Most people report positive aspects (taste, enjoyment, pleasure) of drinking, with heavier drinkers expecting more positive and pleasurable consequences.
- Younger respondents tend to focus more on the fun, party, and sociable aspects of drinking, whereas older drinkers are more serious in taking their pleasures and also emphasize ritual.
- There is more adjunctive drinking in younger groups—in which drinking frequently accompanies other primary activities and is more schedule-controlled. Older drinkers, on the other hand, operate more under stimulus control, with the emphasis on the quality and sensory pleasures of special types of alcohol beverage or other substances.
- Types of pleasures vary markedly with age, and drinking pleasures are simply one subset within a wide range of other pleasures; older people typically report wider varieties of pleasure.
- Drinking may be viewed as a skilled behavior. Young people have to learn to drink sensibly, whereas older, experienced, sensible drinkers are generally more proficient in matching dose, function, and context appropriately to maximize positive enhancement and to minimize negative effects.

NOTE

1. The present chapter represents one focus on an area in which multiple and complementary strategies are likely to be more fruitful than any single research model. In no sense were our samples of respondents formally representative, although they offer a rich spectrum of observations and insights. Such observations highlight attitudes, feelings, and behaviors that often remain uncovered by conventional research designs. The excerpts presented here portray some of the vividness of what respondents have to say, but rigorous scientists are shy of anecdotes, however alluring. "We must therefore try to find a way of exploiting such rich material within a design which allows conjectures to be refuted. Otherwise we may simply be fascinated and intrigued—even deeply moved, but may be sadly misled" (Edwards, Oppenheimer, & Taylor, 1992). However, with a triangulation of methods the research world can surely meet this dilemma.

REFERENCES

Adams, W. L. (1996). Alcohol use in retirement communities. *Journal of the American Geriatric Society, 44*, 1082–1085.

Beck, K. H., Thombs, D. L., Mahoney, C. A., & Fingar, K. M. (1995). Social context and sensation seeking: Gender differences in college student drinking motivations. *International Journal of the Addictions, 30*, 1101–1115.

Budd, R. J., Eiser, J. R., Morgan, M., & Gammage, P. (1985). The personal characteristics and life-style of the young drinker: The results of a survey of British adolescents. *Drug and Alcohol Dependence, 16*, 145–157.

Cahalan, D., & Cisin, I. H. (1986). American drinking practices: Summary of findings from a national probability sample. *Quarterly Journal of Studies on Alcohol, 29*, 130–151.

Cato, B. M. (1992). Youth's recreation and drug sensations: Is there a relationship? *Journal of Drug Education, 22*, 293-301.

Christiansen, B. A., Goldman, M. S., & Inn, A. (1982). Development of alcohol-related expectancies in adolescents: Separating pharmacological from social-learning influences. *Journal of Consulting and Clinical Psychology, 50*, 336–344.

Colette. (1966). *Earthly Paradise*. Secker & Warburg.

Corcoran, K. J., & Segrist, D. J. (1993). Personal expectancies and group influences affect alcoholic beverage selection: The interaction of personal and situational variables. *Addictive Behaviors, 18*, 577–582.

Crook, R., & Lowe, G. (1998, March). *Pleasures, guilt and health: A questionnaire study*. Paper presented at the British Psychological Society Annual Conference. Brighton, UK.

Demers, A., Kishchuk, N., Bourgault, C., & Bisson, J. (1996). When anthropology meets epidemiology: Using social representations to predict drinking patterns. *Substance Use & Misuse, 31*, 847–871.

Dorn, N. (1983). *Alcohol, youth and the state: Drinking practices, control and health education*. London: Croom Helm.

Douglas, M. (Ed.). (1987). *Constructive drinking: Perspectives on drink from anthropology*. Cambridge, UK: Cambridge University Press.

Doyle, T. F., & Samson, H. H. (1985). Schedule-induced drinking in humans: A potential factor in excessive alcohol use. *Drug and Alcohol Dependence, 16*, 117–132.

Doyle, T. F., & Samson, H. H. (1988). Adjunctive alcohol drinking in humans. *Physiology and Behavior, 44*, 775–779.

Dufour, M. C., Archer, L., & Gordis, E. (1992). Alcohol and the elderly. *Clinical Geriatric Medicine, 8*, 127–141.

Earleywine, M., & Finn, P. R. (1991). Sensation seeking explains the relation between behavioral disinhibition and alcohol consumption. *Addictive Behaviors, 16*, 123–128.

Edwards, G. (1984). Drinking in longitudinal perspective: Career and natural history. *British Journal of Addiction, 79*, 175–183.

Edwards, G., Oppenheimer, E., & Taylor, C. (1992). Hearing noise in the system: Exploration of textual analysis as a method for studying change in drinking behaviour. *British Journal of Addiction, 87*, 73–81.

Ekerdt, D. J., Labry, L. O., Glynn, R. J., & Davis, R. W. (1989). Change in drinking behaviors with retirement: Findings from the normative aging study. *Journal of Studies on Alcohol, 50*, 347–353.

Fillmore, K. M. (1987). Prevalence, incidence and chronicity of drinking patterns and problems among men as a function of age: A longitudinal and cohort analysis. *British Journal of Addiction, 82*, 77–83.

Foxcroft, D. R., & Lowe, G. (1991). Adolescent drinking behaviour and family socialization factors: A meta-analysis. *Journal of Adolescence, 14*, 255–273.

Ghodsian, M., & Power, C. (1987). Alcohol consumption between the ages of sixteen and twenty-three in Britain: A longitudinal study. *British Journal of Addiction, 82*, 175–180.

Glass, T. A., Prigerson, H., Kasl, S. V., & Mendes de Leon, C. F. (1995). The effects of negative life events on alcohol consumption among older men and women. *Journal of Gerontology, 50B*, S205–S216.

Goddard, E. (1991). *Drinking in England and Wales in the late 1980s*. London: Her Majesty's Stationery Office.

Grant, B. F., Harford, T. C., & Grigson, M. B. (1988). Stability of alcohol consumption among youth: A national longitudinal survey. *Journal of Studies on Alcohol, 49*, 253–260.

Guild, T., & Lowe, G. (1998). Media messages and alcohol education: A school-based study. *Psychological Reports, 82*, 124–126.

Gustafson, R. (1991). Does a moderate dose of alcohol reinforce feelings of pleasure, well-being, happiness and joy? A brief communication. *Psychological Reports, 69*, 220–222.

Harford, T. C., & Mills, G. S. (1978). Age-related trends in alcohol consumption. *Journal of Studies on Alcohol, 39*, 207–210.

Hawker, A. (1978). *Adolescents and alcohol*. London: Edsall.

Helzer, J. E., Burnham, A., & McEvoy, L.T. (1991). Alcohol abuse and dependence. In L. N. Robins & D. A. Regier (Eds.), *Psychiatric disorders in America* (pp. 81–115). New York: Free Press.

Hilton, M. E. (1987). Drinking patterns and drinking problems in 1984: Results from a general population survey. *Alcoholism: Clinical and Experimental Research, 11*, 167–175.

Johnson, B. A., Campling, G. M., Griffiths, P., & Cowen, P. J. (1993). Attenuation of some alcohol-induced mood changes and the desire to drink by 5-HT-sub-3 receptor blockade: A preliminary study in healthy male volunteers. *Psychopharmacology, 112*, 142–144.

Johnson, P. B. (1993). The value of ethnographic alcohol studies: A psychologist's perspective. *Social Science and Medicine, 37*, 27–30.

Kunz, J. L. (1997). Associating leisure with drinking: Current research and future directions. *Drug and Alcohol Review, 16*, 69–76.

Lee, L. (1965). *Cider with Rosie*. London: Hogarth Press.

Lowe, G. (1994). Pleasures of social relaxants and stimulants: The ordinary person's attitudes and involvement. In D. M. Warburton (Ed.), *Pleasure: The politics and the reality* (pp. 95–108). Chichester, UK: Wiley.

Lowe, G. (1996). Pleasure, relaxation and unwinding. In D. M. Warburton & N. Sherwood (Eds.), *Pleasure and quality of life* (pp. 67–77). Chichester, UK: Wiley.

Lowe, G., Foxcroft, D. R., & Sibley, D. (1993). *Adolescent drinking and family life*. Chur, Switzerland: Harwood Academic.

Mass-Observation Archive. (1943). *The pub and the people*. Falmer, UK: University of Sussex Mass-Observation Archive.

Mass-Observation Archive. (1948). *Drinking habits*. Falmer, UK: University of Sussex Mass-Observation Archive.

Midanik, L. T., Klatsky, A. L., & Armstrong, M. A. (1990). Changes in drinking behavior: Demographic, psychosocial, and biomedical factors. *International Journal of the Addictions, 25*, 599–619.

Mooney, D. K., Fromme, K., Kivlahan, D. R., & Marlatt, G. A. (1987). Correlates of alcohol consumption: Sex, age, and expectancies relate differentially to quantity and frequency. *Addictive Behaviors, 12*, 234–240.

Newcomb, M. D., Bentler, P. M., & Collins, C. (1986). Alcohol use and dissatisfaction with self and life: A longitudinal analysis of young adults. *Journal of Drug Issues, 16*, 479–494.

Oldenburg, R. (1989). *The great good place*. New York: Paragon House.

Peele, S., & Brodsky, A. (1996). *Alcohol and society: How culture influences the way people drink*. San Francisco: The Wine Institute.

Peele, S., & Brodsky, A. (1998). *Psychosocial benefits of moderate alcohol use: Associations and causes*. Unpublished manuscript.

Pittman, D. J., & White, H. R. (Eds) (1995). *Society, culture, and drinking patterns reexamined*. New Brunswick, NJ: Rutgers Center of Alcohol Studies.

Plant, M. A., Bagnall, G., & Foster, J. (1990). Teenage heavy drinkers: Alcohol-related knowledge, beliefs, experiences, motivation and the social context of drinking. *Alcohol and Alcoholism, 25*, 691–698.

Rohsenow, D. J. (1983). Drinking habits and expectancies about alcohol's effects for self versus others. *Journal of Consulting and Clinical Psychology, 51*, 752–756.

Romanova, O. L., & Patrakova, T. I. (1992). Socio-psychological mechanisms of children's introduction to the tradition of alcohol drinking. *Voprosy Psikhologii, 5/6*, 22–25.

Room, R. (1997). Alcohol, the individual and society: What history teaches us. *Addiction, 92* (Suppl. 1), S7–S11.

Sharp, D. J., & Lowe, G. (1989a). Adolescents and alcohol: A review of recent British research. *Journal of Adolescence, 12*, 295–307.

Sharp, D. J., & Lowe, G. (1989b). *Asking young people why they drink*. Paper presented at the BPS Scottish Branch Annual Conference, University of Strathclyde. Glasgow, Scotland.

Simpura, J. (1985). Drinking: An ignored leisure activity. *Journal of Leisure Research, 17*, 200–211.

Stall, R. (1986). Respondent-independent reasons for change and stability in alcohol consumption as a concomitant of the aging process. In C. R. Janes, R. Stall, & S. M. Gifford (Eds.), *Anthropology and epidemiology: Interdisciplinary approaches to the study of health and disease* (pp. 275–301). Boston: D. Reidel.

Stall, R. (1987). Research issues concerning alcohol consumption among aging populations. *Drug and Alcohol Dependence, 19*, 195–213.

Thombs, D. L., & Beck, K. H. (1994). The social context of four adolescent drinking patterns. *Health Education Research, 9*, 13–22.

Vogel-Sprott, M., & Barrett, B. (1984). Age, drinking habits and the effects of alcohol. *Journal of Studies on Alcohol, 45*, 517–521.

Wilks, J., & Callan, V. J. (1990). A diary approach to analysing young adults' drinking events and motivations. *Drug and Alcohol Review, 9*, 7–13.

Chapter 19

Drinking and Setting: A Season for All Things

Eric Single and Henry Pomeroy

"To every thing, there is a season"

Book of Ecclesiastes, used as lyrics by Pete Seeger in the song, "Turn, Turn, Turn."

According to the Bible, drinking—like everything else—has a season. In the context of this quotation, "season" is more than a temporal concept. It is also means a place in people's lives, both as a part of everyday experience and as a part of special occasions. In this chapter we explore the "seasons" for drinking, focusing on settings and activities associated with alcohol consumption. We then review research regarding typical drinking environments, the characteristics of persons who drink in different settings, and the problems and benefits associated with different drinking settings. We conclude from this analysis that drinking *per se* is rarely the sole cause—and sometimes not even the major cause—of drinking problems. The magnitude and nature of problems often are determined by other factors, including the manner in which people drink and the setting in which drinking takes place. We end the chapter by noting some of the conditions that appear to minimize the risks of drinking and those that enhance the pleasurable aspects of drinking.

ALCOHOL USE IN HUMAN HISTORY

Alcohol clearly had a place in the lives of people in biblical times. But the use of alcohol long precedes that era. The first written reference to alcohol

noted a daily beer allowance for workers on a temple in Mesopotamia in 5000
BC. Throughout Greek and Roman times, acceptance of alcohol was the rule,
although concern over immoderate consumption also was expressed. Plato advocated abstinence for those aged fewer than 18 years, moderate consumption for
those up to 30 years old, and no limits for those over 40. He was 43 years old at
the time. It was not until the 18th century, however, that attitudes toward alcohol
hardened and the temperance movement gained momentum. This was caused in
no small measure by the excesses in the first half of that century when, for example, production of British gin rose 20-fold and Hogarth bitterly satirized Gin
Lane, where one could be drunk for a penny and dead drunk for twopence—
the straw being free. Regardless of prevailing attitudes, the consumption of
alcohol has been a regular feature of life in Western societies for a considerable period; its use may vary in character among societies and alcohol may be
subject to greater or lesser controls, but there always has been a "season" for
drinking.

There is clearly a wide variety of reasons why people drink and occasions
when they do so. Drinking may be a normal accompaniment to eating, serving
both a nutritional and social function. For many it may be routine to drink at
certain social activities or entertainments, such as sporting events or artistic per-
formances, or when celebrating special occasions such as a birthdays, holidays,
personal successes or milestones. Or drinking may be just a way to relax after
work or with friends. Indeed, the consumption of alcohol is often a "time out"
behavior, used to mark those occasions when the problems and worries of everyday life are put aside. Drinking is often part of social, cultural, and religious
rituals (see Chapter 5). For example, in the Christian ritual of communion, wine
is used as a symbol of the blood of Christ, consumed to express an intimate
bond between the deity and ordinary humans.

THE IMPORTANCE OF SETTINGS IN
DRINKING BEHAVIOR

Expert Informant Data

A source of information regarding the nature of drinking locales and characteristics of persons who drink in different settings is the WHO Study of Public
Drinking (Single et al., 1997). This study involved the collation of information
on public drinking from addiction experts in 12 countries: Australia, Canada,
Chile, Congo, Fiji, Finland, France, India, Israel, Japan, Poland, and Trinidad
and Tobago. The expert informants were asked a series of questions regarding
alcohol consumption, common drinking locales, and problems associated with
drinking. In addition to providing information from every continent, the countries represented in the informant survey range from large nations such as India
with a population of more than 844 million in 1991 to relatively small countries
such as Fiji with a population of less than 4 million.[1]

Drinking in these countries occurs in an enormous variety of venues, ranging from large to small and from commercial establishments to open public areas, in conjunction with eating or religious functions or simply for its own sake. A wide variety of public drinking locales was identified by the expert informants, and there is no classification of public drinking venues that could be applied to every country. The most commonly identified types of public drinking locales were bars and restaurants, which were almost universal; clubs, nightclubs, cafés, taverns, and cultural events were also frequently mentioned. Many types of venues are associated with particular activities or types of patrons. For example, in several countries it was noted that the patrons of nightclubs and discotheques generally are young adults. Drinking at social and religious functions generally is associated with lower- and middle-income groups but includes somewhat younger drinkers as well. In India, drinking in bars and restaurants is associated with middle- and higher-income groups, especially young adults aged 20 to 35 years, and it is mostly the older, higher socioeconomic groups who drink in private clubs. In Japan, drinking groups frequently consist of coworkers and colleagues. In Poland, drinking in bars is associated with lower-class males, while cafés have a more middle-class clientele.

Tavern Studies

Another source of information is the research conducted in public places where drinking behavior is observable. In the United Kingdom about half the adult population visits a pub once a week, and half of those have a regular place that they visit. In North America and most Western European countries, tavern-going is generally less common than in the United Kingdom, but it is nonetheless a routine activity for many people. Taverns and pubs are considered by both regular and infrequent patrons to offer increasingly good value for money for an evening out (Brewers and Licensed Retailers Association, United Kingdom, personal communication, 1998).

A search of literature based on tavern studies has identified five major sets of situational determinants of drinking behavior: temporal variations, characteristics of the drinking group, the length of time spent on one drinking occasion, the characteristics of the physical environment, and price differences (Single, 1985). As these studies generally are conducted by public health specialists concerned with the prevention of alcohol-related problems, the data understandably focus on the problematic aspects of drinking rather than its pleasurable aspects.

Temporal variables, such as weekends versus weekdays, are perhaps the most obvious and some of the strongest correlates of drinking rates. Possibly because of their very obviousness, variations in drinking according to day of the week and hour of the day have been relatively neglected in epidemiological research on alcohol.

A situational factor that has received a great deal of research attention has been the influence of the drinking group. A number of studies have shown that the drinking rate of confederates is a strong influence on consumption and that the influence of low-rate drinking companions is less than that of high-rate drinking companions (Caudill & Marlatt, 1975; De Ricco, 1978; De Ricco & Garlinton, 1977; De Ricco & Niemann, 1980). It would appear that the drinking norms described by Bruun in 1959 among subjects in a small-group drinking experiment continue to have wide applicability. Bruun observed that it was permissible for a group member to drink more than other members of the group but not less. Several studies in North America and the United Kingdom have found that intake tends to be higher in exclusively male groups (Single, 1985). This is consistent with the perception that excessive drinking is common in fraternities, among sports supporters—for example, the "lager louts" of British football—and in other male-dominated activities.

A second way in which drinking in groups may influence patrons to drink more is through its effect on length of stay at the drinking spot. In a study of Edmonton beer parlors, Sommer (1965) found that isolated drinkers consume less than persons drinking in groups, but he attributed this to their shorter stays in drinking establishments. The finding that group drinkers tend to consume more than isolated drinkers has been replicated in Canada (Ratcliffe et al., 1980; Storm & Cutler, 1981) and in the United States (Foy & Simon, 1978).

Another influence on length of stay is the physical environment. By providing television, games, and other activities, bars and taverns increase the length of patron visits and thus increase consumption. Even the tempo of music can influence drinking: According to Bach and Schaefer (1979), the slower the tempo of country-and-western music played in bars in western Montana in the United States, the faster the patrons consumed their drinks. Ratcliffe and colleagues (1980) found that in Alberta beverage rooms in which dancing and games were provided, the patrons who participated in these activities stayed longer and consumed more than nonparticipants. Sommer (1965) contrasted the Edmonton beer parlors with English pubs and attributed the short stays by isolated drinkers in the former setting to the lack of anything to do other than sit and drink.

The physical environment can influence drinking behavior in other ways. Cloyd (1976) detailed how the layout of "market-place" bars is designed to maximize patrons' discretionary powers to initiate and control encounters with other patrons. Cavan (1966) described bars as "open regions" in which patrons have the right to initiate conversation with others and an obligation to accept overtures from others. As Ratcliffe and his colleagues pointed out (1980), the degree of such "openness" is controllable; the closed nature of lounges tends to foster a genteel atmosphere and greater privacy as compared with the more open nature of taverns and pubs. Contrary to expectations, however, Ratcliffe et al. found no support for the assumption that the lounge environment fosters moderate drinking. Thus, the physical layout of a drinking establishment affects the nature of the drinking group, the atmosphere within the setting, and the length of drinking occasions, but its net impact on consumption levels is not clear-cut.

The composition of the drinking group also can influence drinking behavior. Drinking in family groups with young children present is much more common in the United Kingdom than in North America, where state and provincial legislation often forbids underage persons from entering licensed premises. Even in the United Kingdom, opinion is split on the issue of whether children should be allowed in pubs. Although 30% of patrons consider the admission of children to be a positive aspect in choosing pubs, about 20% feel that children should not be admitted into pubs at all. The presumed rationale for exclusion of children from licensed establishments is to protect children from alcohol-related problems, such as aggressive behavior by drinkers, and from the influences that might lead them to become heavy drinkers. On the other hand, a case can be made that exposing underage persons to drinking situations helps them to develop responsible drinking practices. In any case, drinking in family groups and mixed gender groups tends to be associated with more moderate consumption and fewer problems (Single, 1985).

Survey Data on Drinking Locales

Tavern studies have been supplemented by data from general-population surveys concerning individual variations in the amount of drinking in different situations in the United States (Clark, 1985), Canada (Single & Wortley, 1993), Finland (Sulkunen, personal communication, 1997), and Israel (Barr & Elder, 1987). Single and Wortley estimated the proportion of total drinking in different social situations for each respondent in a national survey in Canada and validated the results against sales data. The proportion of total drinking in different settings was strongly related to sociodemographic variables. Age was strongly related to both venue and level of consumption within particular venues. Younger persons were more likely to go to public drinking establishments, while older respondents were more likely to stay at home. Furthermore, younger persons generally reported higher rates of drinking in all situations except if they stayed at home. In addition to the age pattern, it has been found that male, high-income, and well-educated respondents consume a relatively high proportion of their total drink intake in bars and taverns but female, low-income, and less well-educated respondents have a relatively greater share of their consumption at home.[2] In line with these patterns, it has been found in the United Kingdom that regular pub goers tend to be more socially active than people who rarely or never go to pubs (Brewers and Licensed Retailers Association, United Kingdom, personal communication, 1998).

In sum, there is an enormous variety of drinking settings around the world. Tavern studies indicate that certain situational variables in the drinking environment affect drinking behavior, and general-population surveys show that the situational distribution of alcohol consumption is strongly related to level of drinking and sociodemographic characteristics. Socially active people such as unattached young adult males tend not only to drink more but also to drink a greater share of their total consumption at on-premise outlets such as bars and taverns.

PROBLEMS AND BENEFITS OF DRINKING AT SOCIAL OCCASIONS

Problems Associated with Drinking at Social Occasions

Excessive drinking undoubtedly carries a certain degree of risk. Although chronic drinking can lead to alcohol dependence, the most common problems associated with drinking at social occasions involve adverse consequences of intoxication, ranging from alcohol-related aggression to impairment in carrying out tasks requiring skill and care, such as operating a motor vehicle, complex work activities, or caring for children.

The expert informants in the World Health Organization study cited previously (Single et al., 1997) were asked a series of questions regarding health and social consequences of drinking in their respective societies. Family discord, poor productivity, and unemployment often were seen as significant issues but rarely attributed to alcohol use. The most commonly mentioned problems ascribed to drinking were alcohol dependence, alcohol-related traffic injuries, alcohol-related violence,[3] and cirrhosis of the liver.[4] Public intoxication generally is not viewed as a major social problem in most of the countries in the survey. Indeed, in most countries either it has been decriminalized or the existing laws against being intoxicated in a public place are not enforced.[5] Other problems associated with drinking were noted, including intoxicated pedestrians (Finland and Poland), child and spouse abuse (Poland), and poor school performance (Congo).

Many of these problems, particularly acute problems such as impaired driving and alcohol-related violence, do not stem solely from the amount of alcohol that a person drinks. There is considerable evidence that an individual's drinking pattern and the setting in which drinking takes place exert significant influence on the probability and nature of problems that might result. A person's pattern of drinking, particularly if it involves drinking to intoxication, may be a more reliable predictor of problems than his or her overall level of drinking. Analyses of national survey data in Australia (Stockwell, Hawks, Lang, & Rydon, 1994), Canada (Single & Wortley, 1993), and the United States (Midanik, Tam, Greenfield, & Caetano, 1994) have found consistently that the number of heavy drinking occasions is a stronger predictor of drinking problems than level of consumption. Furthermore, there is an interaction between the number of heavy drinking occasions and level of consumption, with particularly high rates of alcohol problems among low-level drinkers who occasionally drink immoderately. Indeed, the likelihood of experiencing drinking problems is greater for a low- or moderate-level drinker who occasionally drinks immoderately than for a high-level consumer who rarely or never drinks immoderately. This may be associated with physical tolerance as well as the tendency for high-volume drinkers to develop social supports and other mechanisms to minimize the adverse consequences of their drinking.[6] For many acute alcohol problems, such as impaired driving and alcohol-related violence, relatively low-level consumers who occasionally drink immoderately contribute substantially to problem levels.

The drinking setting also has an impact. We know that drinking in bars and taverns is associated with higher levels of drinking and drinking to intoxication. A Finnish study found that high-risk drinkers were much more likely than others to visit licensed establishments such as bars and restaurants (Sulkunen, personal communication, 1997). Almost two thirds of men reported visiting restaurants or medium beer bars, and more than 40% report doing so when drunk. More than 60% of women had visited licensed establishments, and 20% report doing so when drunk. In Canada, the higher the level of drinking, the higher the relative share of total consumption that occurs in bars and taverns (Single & Wortley, 1993). These findings are potentially significant to prevention programming and research. Although drinking in certain settings such as bars, restaurants, and other licensed establishments is related to higher alcohol consumption and an increased chance of drinking to intoxication, the causal order in this relationship is not clear. It is noteworthy, for example, that many of the respondents in the Finnish study arrived at a bar or restaurant in an intoxicated state. To some extent these environments may stimulate excessive drinking, but it also must be recognized that to some extent they are attractive to heavy drinkers, particularly young male adults.

Benefits of Drinking at Social Occasions

Thus, drinking problems are often the result of a person's drinking pattern and the setting in which drinking takes place, rather than simply the amount of alcohol consumed. Not surprisingly, the same drinking patterns and settings that are the least likely to lead to a problem tend to be those that are most likely to provide a positive and pleasurable experience to drinkers. For example, the consumption of food with drinking slows the absorption of alcohol into the blood. At the same time, drinking can add a pleasurable element to eating occasions. In North America and the United Kingdom an increasing number of pubs and taverns effectively become restaurants during eating hours. An appealing aspect for consumers is that eating in a pub or tavern is seen as an informal social occasion that does not require advanced planning if they do not want to cook at home (Nelson, 1997).

The benefits of drinking have received increased scientific attention with the growing recognition that consumption of small amounts of alcohol has cardiovascular benefits. Long before there was evidence of this physiological health benefit, however, it was obvious that drinking must convey a wide variety of subjective psychological and social benefits—if only because humans have been producing and consuming alcohol since the beginning of written history. There are clearly positive psychological effects of alcohol: Drinking produces an improved sense of well-being and quality of life, and there is evidence of potential cognitive effects in enhancing creativity and reducing stress (see Chapter 15). But apart from physiological effects, drinking sometimes has social benefits. For example, drinking may be used to convey both subtle and obvious messages concerning social status. In parts of the Far East, a businessperson who orders expensive cognac from distinctive designer bottles (recognizable even in dark nightclubs) may be signaling an ability to distinguish the finer qualities of premium products, which in turn connotes a higher social status. In such situations it is not the type of drink or how much that is important, but the quality of what is being drunk (see Chapter 5).

A recent set of papers commissioned by the International Center on Alcohol Policies attempted to address the issue of what constitutes a "beneficial" pattern of drinking (see Chapter 27). Several panels of experts were contacted to specify and delineate the key aspects of this concept from different perspectives. Based on input from the epidemiology panel, a statement was prepared regarding beneficial patterns of drinking (Single, 1998). The statement points out two key considerations: Beneficial patterns are those that (a) maximize the potential benefits of drinking and (b) minimize the risk of harm. Although there was considerable evidence regarding aspects of drinking behavior that are associated with an increased risk of harm, minimal evidence exists regarding specific patterns of drinking that maximize the benefits of drinking. There is some evidence that highly infrequent drinking and binge drinking are unlikely to convey any benefits. This would suggest that regular, low-level consumption would maximize both the psychological benefits and the positive cardiovascular impacts of drinking, but the exact pattern is not yet known. On the other hand, there was considerable evidence regarding factors that lower the risks of drinking. Low risk of harm is associated with low quantity and frequency of drinking, rarely or never drinking to intoxication, drinking in combination with eating or socializing with friends in safe and pleasurable surroundings, drinking in the company of persons who exert a moderating influence, and avoiding excess drinking or not drinking at all in special circumstances—for instance, when engaging in activities that require skill and care such as operating machinery or a motor vehicle.

Alcohol research focuses on the minority of drinkers who experience relatively severe problems as the result of their drinking rather than the majority of drinkers who do not (Harburg, Gleiberman, DiFranceisco, & Peele, 1994). It is not surprising, therefore, that there is so little information on patterns of drinking associated with benefits. The author of the statement of the epidemiology panel on beneficial patterns of drinking concluded with the story about an inebriated man who loses his car keys. The drunk looks for the lost keys under a street lamp, not because he lost them there but because that is where the light is best. Like this proverbial drunkard futilely looking for his keys under the street lamp, the alcohol-research community is in the dark about the benefits of drinking because it has been shining its light solely on problem drinking. Thus, there is considerable understanding of drinking patterns that involve serious risk of harm, but comparatively little is known about settings leading to beneficial drinking. Until more attention is given to normal, unproblematic drinking, we will remain in the dark about how to encourage the positive aspects of alcohol. Without such knowledge, our understanding of alcohol and its effects remains incomplete.

CONCLUSIONS

In this presentation, we have discussed the nature of drinking settings and their influence on drinking behavior. We offer the following general conclusions:

- Drinking conveys benefits as well as risks. In the words of Poikolainen (1995), "Of course there are benefits to drinking—otherwise, people wouldn't so it so much."
- Drinking involves risks of both chronic and acute adverse consequences, but an individual's overall level of drinking is rarely the problem. The magnitude and nature of problems, particularly acute problems, are very much determined by other factors, specifically the individual's drinking pattern and the setting in which drinking takes place.
- Some conditions minimize the risks from drinking: The risk of experiencing a problem as a result of one's drinking can be minimized by avoiding intoxication, drinking in combination with eating or socializing in a safe environment, drinking with persons who exert a moderating influence, and minimizing consumption or abstaining altogether in special circumstances such as when driving a vehicle or in other situations requiring care and attention.
- Some conditions enhance the positive aspects of drinking: Obviously, drinking under the conditions that minimize the risk of problems likely will enhance the positive aspects of drinking. It is also reasonable to assume that the positive aspects of drinking will be enhanced if drinking is in the company of family or friends in a pleasant environment.

Beyond this, however, it is difficult to say more, as research has thus far placed almost all its attention on drinking problems, giving comparatively little attention to normal, unproblematic drinking. To provide a more complete understanding of drinking behavior, greater attention needs to be given in the future to those aspects of drinking that enhance the drinking experience.

NOTES

1. There is also a wide range of variation with regard to industrialization and modernization. Annual levels of alcohol consumption range from 3.5 L of absolute alcohol per capita in Trinidad and Tobago to 16.8 L in France. There is also considerable variation in the predominant type of alcoholic beverage. In the majority of these countries, beer is the alcoholic beverage of choice

(Australia, Canada, Congo, Fiji, Finland, and Trinidad and Tobago). However, there are two wine-drinking countries (France and Chile), a spirits-drinking country (Poland), and three countries in which no one type of beverage accounts for most of the alcohol consumption (India, Israel, and Japan).

2. In Canada high income is associated with a relatively high proportion of consumption in restaurants; low-income drinkers consume a greater proportion of their total consumption in bars and taverns (Single & Wortley, 1993). In Israel, however, income is not clearly related to drinking venue. The Canadian study also found that marital status is related to the proportion of alcohol consumption within particular venues. Overall, the proportion of total consumption in bars or taverns is higher among individuals who are either single (23%), separated, or divorced (15%) than among those who are married (6%) or widowed (3%). These figures corroborate observational studies of tavern behavior that detail how these locales frequently are structured to maximize contact between strangers and otherwise function as sexual marketplaces.

3. Alcohol-related violence was noted as a particular concern in Australia, Fiji, Finland, Israel, and Japan. Alcohol was considered to be related to 73% of assaults in Australia and 80% in Fiji. The correlation of violent crimes and alcohol use does not necessarily imply a causal connection. For example, consider a person who consumed alcohol prior to committing a crime. Even if this person had been intoxicated, it is not clear whether the crime can be attributed to alcohol consumption. Nonetheless, it is clearly widely believed that alcohol is a major factor in many crimes of violence in some societies, even if not all crimes involving intoxication can be attributed causally to the use of alcohol.

4. Alcoholism (alcohol dependence) was mentioned almost universally as a major health concern. Only in Japan was alcohol dependence not seen as an important health issue. However, the WHO/ADAMHA (NIH) Joint Project on Diagnosis and Classification of Mental Health and Alcohol and Drug Related Problems found sometimes quite startling differences in perceptions and diagnoses of alcohol dependence in nine nations worldwide (Room, Janča, Bennett, Schmidt, & Sartorius, 1996). Alcohol-related traffic injuries were reported to be a significant health issue in Fiji, India, Japan, Canada, and Australia. Cirrhosis was sometimes indicated as a health issue that the public sees as significant, particularly in the Congo and in Fiji, but it was not considered a major health issue in India, Poland, Canada, or Trinidad and Tobago. The other alcohol-related health problems generally were not seen as major public health issues, with the exception of poisoning of adulterated alcohol, which is reported to be a significant concern in India. With regard to "other" health problems, it is noteworthy that the impact of alcohol on sexuality was viewed as a health issue in Israel.

5. However, public intoxication is considered a major problem in some countries. For example, in Finland the rate of arrests per capita for public drunkenness is among the highest in the world (Mäkelä, Österberg, & Sulkunen, 1981, Table 1). Although the rate of arrests declined somewhat during the late 1970s and 1980s, it remains very high (Rahkonen & Sulkunen, 1988). Interestingly, another exception is Chile, where social attitudes toward public intoxication are the most tolerant among those countries surveyed. In 1990 there were more than 222,000 arrests for public intoxication in Chile. It would appear that social norms accepting or disapproving of drunken comportment have a greater impact on behavior than on legislation: Either those countries in which public drunkenness is frowned upon have no laws against public intoxication, or such laws are ignored. On the other hand, the country with the most tolerant attitudes toward public drunkenness has the greatest number of arrests for public intoxication.

6. Of course, heavy drinkers cannot control certain adverse consequences: over time, heavy drinking will greatly elevate the risk of chronic health consequences such as liver cirrhosis.

REFERENCES

Bach, J., & Schaefer, J. (1979). The tempo of country music and the rate of drinking in bars. *Journal of Studies on Alcohol, 40*, 635–651.

Barr, H., & Elder, P. (1987). *Drinking patterns of the Israeli public* [text in Hebrew]. Jerusalem: Israeli Institute of Applied Social Research.

Bruun, K. (1959). *Drinking behaviour in small groups* (Vol. 9). Helsinki: Finnish Foundation for Alcohol Studies.

Caudill, B. D., & Marlatt, G. A. (1975). Modelling influences in social drinking: An experimental analogue. *Journal of Consulting and Clinical Psychology, 43*, 405–415.

Cavan, S. (1966). *Liquor license: An ethnography of a bar*. Chicago, IL: Aldine.

Clark, W. (1985). Alcohol use in various settings. In E. Single & T. Storm (Eds.), *Public drinking and public policy* (pp. 49–70). Toronto: Addiction Research Foundation.

Cloyd. J. W. (1976). The market-place bar: The interaction between sex, situation and strategies in the pairing ritual of homo ludens. *Urban Life, 5*, 293–312.

De Ricco, D. (1978). Effects of peer majority on drinking rate. *Addictive Behaviour, 3*, 29–34.

De Ricco, D., & Garlinton, W. (1977). The effect of modeling and disclosure of experimenter's intent on drinking rate of college students. *Addictive Behaviors, 2*, 135–139.

De Ricco, D., & Niemann, J. (1980). In vivo effects of peer modeling on drinking rate. *Journal of Applied Behavioral Analysis, 13*, 149–152.

Foy, D. W., & Simon, S. J. (1978). Alcoholic drinking topography as a function of solitary versus social context. *Addictive Behaviours, 3*, 39–41.

Harburg, E., Gleiberman, L., DiFranceisco, W., & Peele, S. (1994). Towards a concept of sensible drinking and an illustration of measure. *Alcohol and Alcoholism, 29*, 439–450.

Mäkelä, K., Österberg, E., & Sulkunen, P. (1981). Drink in Finland: Increasing alcohol availability in a monopoly state. In E. Single, P. Morgan, & J. de Lint (Eds.), *Alcohol, society and the state: The social history of control policy in seven countries* (pp. 31–60). Toronto: Addiction Research Foundation.

Midanik, L., Tam, T., Greenfield, T., & Caetano, R. (1994). *Risk functions for alcohol-related problems in a 1988 U.S. national sample*. Berkeley, CA: California Pacific Medical Center Research Institute, Alcohol Research Group.

Nelson, T. (1997). *Attitude and usage survey*. Unpublished report commissioned by the Brewers and Licensed Retailers Association, United Kingdom.

Poikolainen, K. (1995). Comments at the International Symposium on Moderate Drinking and Health, Toronto. Helsinki, Finland: A-Clinic Foundation.

Rahkonen, K., & Sulkunen, P. (1988, June). *The cruel welfare state: A case of public drunkenness arrests in Finland*. Paper presented at the annual Alcohol Epidemiology Symposium, Berkeley, California.

Ratcliffe, W. D., Nutter, R. W., Hewitt, D., Flanders, P. L., Caverhill, K. M., & Gruber, G. P. (1980). *Drinking behaviours in lounges and taverns* (Research report). Edmonton, Alberta: Alberta Alcoholism and Drug Abuse Commission.

Room, R., Janča, A., Bennett, L. A., Schmidt, L., & Sartorius, N. (1996). WHO cross-cultural applicability research on diagnosis and assessment of substance use disorders: An overview of methods and selected results. *Addiction, 91*, 199–220.

Single, E. (1985). Studies of public drinking: An overview. In E. Single & T. Storm (Eds.), *Public drinking and public policy* (pp. 5–34). Toronto: Addiction Research Foundation.

Single, E. (1998, February). *What constitutes a beneficial pattern of drinking: An epidemiological perspective*. Paper presented at the International Conference on Drinking Patterns and Their Consequences, Perth, Australia.

Single, E., Beaubrun, M., Mauffret, M., Minoletti, A., Moskalewicz, J., Moukolo, A., Plange, N. K., Saxena, S., Stockwell, T., Sulkunen, P., Suwaki, H., Hoshigoe, K., & Weiss, S. (1997). Public drinking, problems and prevention measures in twelve countries: Results of the WHO project on public drinking. *Contemporary Drug Problems, 24*, 425–448.

Single, E., & Wortley, S. (1993). Drinking in various settings: Findings from a national survey in Canada. *Journal of Studies on Alcohol, 54*, 590–599.

Sommer, R. (1965). *Personal space: The behavioural basis of design*. Englewood Cliffs, NJ: Prentice-Hall.

Stockwell, T., Hawks, D., Lang, E., & Rydon, P. (1994). *Unraveling the prevention paradox*. Perth, Australia: National Centre for Research into the Prevention of Drug Abuse.

Storm, T., & Cutler, R. E. (1981). Observations of drinking in natural settings: Vancouver beer parlors and cocktail lounges. *Journal of Studies on Alcohol, 42*, 972–997.

Chapter 20

State-Dependent Lifestyles and the Pleasure of Alcohol

Jan Snel

The moderate use of alcohol is a pleasure that people have known from the earliest times. Both pleasure and moderate use have been proven to be healthy (see Chapters 1 and 12). But the benefits of alcohol, together with the enjoyment of drinking, are threatened in the current atmosphere in which only the negative effects of alcohol are emphasized.

This chapter develops the view that an individual's lifestyle is the crucial factor in achieving optimal mental and physical states. Alcohol is just one contributor to such an optimizing lifestyle. Alcohol has a number of characteristics that assist in achieving this aim, and research on the effects of alcohol on cognitive functioning and stress reduction indicates that alcohol is a functional, useful component of lifestyle. Moreover, the pleasure derived from responsible drinking is an important means to achieve an optimum state.

BACKGROUND

Since ancient times, humans have sought and found peace and satisfaction in beverage alcohol. Alcohol was consumed as part of religious rituals and services, celebrations, and other communal social events. Some alchemists maintained that alcohol was the long-sought elixir of life; indeed the name *whisky*, like the less common *usquebaugh*, comes from the Gaelic words *uisge beatha* which mean "water of life." The same meaning is found in the word *aquavit*, or *akavit*, the spirit drunk by Scandinavians, and in the French *eau de vie*. Although alcohol is still consumed widely today, its use nonetheless has become highly controversial.

The preponderance of alcohol research creates the impression that alcohol is a substance that has only harmful effects on people's health and cognition, and that drinking must lead eventually to addiction. Thus, if people accepted the opinions of many health scientists, they would decide that alcohol is a poison that should be banned. Yet the large majority of those who drink do so in a sensible way and with no apparent harm to their health. For example, in 1996, a quality-of-life survey conducted by the Dutch Central Bureau of Statistics noted a rise in the number of moderate drinkers and a decline in the number of abstainers. The results indicated that 65% of those older than 18 years consumed one or two glasses per day, compared with 61% in 1990; 7% of Dutch citizens older than 18 consumed more than three glasses per day, and the proportion of abstainers in the general population declined from 32% in 1990 to 28% (Central Bureau of Statistics, 1996). Eighty-four percent of men reported drinking, and 61% of women. In the United States, Harburg, Gleiberman, Difranceisco, and Peele (1994) refer to a national survey in which over 76% of men and 64% of women older than 18 years drink, including 30% and 42% respectively who drink fewer than 15 drinks per month.

Alcohol as a Part of Lifestyle

A great deal of research has been done into who drinks what, where, and how they do so. A critical question is *why* people enjoy alcohol or other substances, drink in a responsible and socially accepted way, and integrate alcohol into a positive lifestyle. First, some methodological issues in the alcohol literature should be considered.

Methodological Issues

Orientation Towards Alcoholism   Most methods used in studying ordinary drinking are simply the methods used for studying drinking problems and alcoholism. For example, Bergman (1985) assumed that the cognitive tests in which alcoholics showed impairment and that best discriminated alcohol-dependent patients from a random control sample also would be potentially most sensitive for the detection of cognitive deficits in social drinkers. Furthermore, a rule of pharmacology is that substances may have beneficial effects on health and functioning at a specific dose, but not at other dosage levels. Examples are digitalis, curare, caffeine, taxol, and many others. It would be unusual if alcohol were the exception. Yet Hill and Ryan (1985) hypothesized a linear dose-response relationship between alcohol ingestion and impairment. However, the index that best correlated with neurobehavioral deficits in alcoholics was the *number* of years of heavy drinking; the measure that typically correlated with performance in social drinkers was the *quantity* per occasion. Although both of these drinking styles do have measurable impacts on cognitive function, apparently their impact is quite dissimilar. Nonetheless, methods that assume this dose-response relationship generally tend to submerge potential beneficial effects found in social drinkers by examining them only as hangover or withdrawal effects.

Biased Interpretations   A consequence of the focus on alcoholism is that research on social drinking generally is interpreted in terms of the linear dose-effect model, that is, in terms of negative effects rather than actual positive effects. For example, Arbuckle, Chaikelson, and Gold (1994) concluded that neuropsychological functioning was hardly affected by the amount of alcohol consumed over a lifetime. Seemingly disbelieving this result, they suggested that the tests they used might not have been sensitive enough, and that such a conclusion would be premature. The arguments they used in favor of this position were that their subjects were a selected sample in excellent health who might have recovered cognitive functioning that actually was damaged by alcohol!

Similar reasoning is evident in other studies. In interpreting a positive correlation of about 25% (explaining a nonsignificant 3% to 7% variance) between quantity per occasion (in ml) and neuropsychological functioning in heavier lifetime consumers, Hill and Ryan (1985) indicated that the results were caused by tolerance effects. Hannon et al. (1987) studied the relationship between increased levels of social drinking and performance on various neuropsychological tests. The investigators found several correlations in the predicted, inverse direction, but also significant correlations in the positive direction. Nevertheless, the conclusion was that the weak and inconsistent nature of the correlations suggested that the many *positive* correlations probably were spurious and caused purely by chance.

Harper, Kril, and Daly (1988) studied whether "moderate" alcohol intake (30–80 g/d) could damage the brain. It is well known that maturation of the brain is accompanied by an active myelination process involving a decrease in water content and an increase in lipid content. Although the authors found these changes in the moderate drinking group, they dismissed their results as too insignificant compared with the control group of nondrinkers and alcoholics. Once again, by extrapolating the effects of alcohol abuse to hypothesized effects of social drinking, these authors were looking in the wrong direction, making it difficult to examine socially accepted, sensible alcohol use and its effects in an unbiased way.

The cognitive-causal hypothesis (Parsons, 1986) asserts that heavier drinking is associated with lower intelligence. Interpreting this in keeping with the linear dose-response relationship model, inhabitants of countries with the highest per capita consumption, such as Luxembourg, France, and Portugal (see Single & Leino, 1998) should be less intelligent than those people living in, for example, Morocco, Malaysia, and Tunisia, a clearly unwarranted conclusion. The same line of reasoning appears—and fails—with the assumed negative relationship between vocabulary and drinking level. Results in this direction have proven weak and of marginal clinical significance at best. Indeed, other findings even have been in the direction opposite to that hypothesized. Hannon et al. (1987), for example, found higher vocabulary scores for women who were social drinkers than for women who abstained from drinking for 2 weeks. Similarly, Orgogozo et al. (1997) found in a prospective study of wine drinking and cognitive functioning that light drinkers (from two units per week to two units per day), moderate drinkers (three to four units per day), and even *heavy* drinkers (five or more units per day) showed a *lower* incidence of dementia compared with nondrinkers (see discussion of the cognitive benefits of moderate drinking in Chapter 15).

SOCIAL DRINKING

Social-drinking limits vary remarkably within Europe and around the world. In Sweden, an upper limit of 6.7 g/d is advocated by the state alcohol monopoly, Systembolaget; in France an upper limit of virtually 10 times this amount (60 g/d) is recommended by the French Academy of Science.

Social-drinking conceptions might be derived from the Sensible/Problem Drinking Classification (Harburg et al., 1994). In general, answers on the scale refer to socially regulated drinking without the negative symptoms after drinking: drinking as a positive family ritual, as a part of joyous encounters, and so on, or drinking as a means to relax, to find enjoyment, and to attain a positive mood. The implicit meaning of such a view of drinking is that the drinker concerned is well integrated socially. As a result, drinking is the outcome of a lifestyle that is focused on fitting in with society, obeying laws, and maintaining a positive attitude.

Sensible drinking (Harburg, Gleiberman, Difranceisco, & Peele, 1994; Harburg, Gunn, Gleiberman, Difranceisco, & Schork, 1993), in contrast to problem drinking, is marked by drinking smaller amounts, a lower frequency of drinking, fewer attempts to quit, less impulsivity and neuroticism, and fewer negative life events. Harburg et al.'s distinction between types of drinking could be utilized in public health campaigns aimed at increasing sensible, and reducing problem, drinking.

STATE

Lifestyle is the cognitive-behavioral expression of an individual's neurobehavioral state. This state is influenced by long-term and short-term cultural, sociodemographic, and other environmental factors that have an impact on the individual.

Long-Term Versus Short-Term Factors

Factors determining an individual's neurobehavioral state can be characterized as either long-term (chronic) or relatively short-term (acute). Long-term, relatively stable factors include, for example, personality, age, gender, and intelligence. As an illustration of the importance of such factors, Harburg and colleagues (1994) found that levels of impulsiveness and neuroticism were the most significant independent predictors of drinking subtypes ranging from sensible to problem drinking. These data also support findings that impulsiveness is a dominant factor for primary (male) alcoholism and that various levels of neuroticism have a prominent place in the so-called secondary alcoholism more common in women. In addition to these relatively stable characteristics of an individual's neurobehavioral state, there are short-term factors such as mood and physical or mental fatigue.

Environmental and Sociodemographic Factors

Environmental or sociodemographic determinants of the individual's condition include such long-term or chronic factors as climate and season, positive and negative life events, and housing and other living conditions. More acute factors are daily hassles and uplifts, time of day, and tasks the individual faces.

Among the chronic factors, sociodemographic variables are the subject of several studies of young people's lifestyles. Friedman and Humphrey (1985) found that important antecedents of college drinking were ethnicity and race, gender, and the size of students' home towns. Other factors concerned familial characteristics such as fathers' occupations, parents' marital status, and the relative closeness of a problem drinker to the subject. The importance of psychosocial factors as determinants of alcohol use is underscored in Friedman and Humphrey's finding that problem drinkers, in comparison with sensible or social drinkers, are more often single (widowed and divorced) and less religious. The latter may indicate a lack of social support—a factor that is known to have a significant impact on drinking behavior. In contrast, sensible drinkers are generally older and are more likely to be married and religious. Social-drinking models may have a particularly striking influence on the drinking behavior of certain sensitive individuals.

Burda and Vaux (1988) assessed the importance for social drinking of social support processes in 205 male college students. Responses were consistent with other research in demonstrating that social drinking within peer groups plays an important role in the social support network of college males. In fact, results showed that the psychosocial environment of young people was the essential factor in determining a positive drinking pattern. Individuals without social supports tended to drink more heavily (Collins, Parks, & Marlatt, 1985).

Evidence that drinking depends on lifestyle as determined by sociodemographic and cultural factors is provided by Brown (1985). She showed that demographic predictors such as ethnicity, gender, religiosity, and social and economic status were strong predictors of drinking and, taken together, were a better predictor of drinking outcomes than expectancies. This was especially true for the moderate-frequent style of drinking. Viewed in light of such evidence, alcohol education should concentrate on manipulable sociodemographic factors instead of on alcohol use per se.

A further indicator of the impact of sociodemographic factors on drinking was provided by a study by Emmerson, Dustman, Heil, and Shearer (1988). The investigators assessed the neuropsychological performance of males aged 23 to 42 years, whom they grouped in four categories based upon their drinking histories. The categories ranged from nondrinkers to long-term sober (more than 30 days) alcoholics. Their data showed that performance of the four groups was very similar across all measures and was independent of alcohol use. These results underscore the importance of studying factors other than alcohol use itself in the neuropsychological functioning of individuals with specific drinking patterns.

LIFESTYLE AND ALCOHOL USE

In a way, one could say that each individual is continuously enmeshed in a changing neurophysiological and behavioral state that is directed towards achieving optimal functioning and well-being. The individual strives to reach such a state by using the many possibilities available to him or her. The structure for this motivated behavior is called lifestyle. It may take such forms as sensation seeking, sheltering oneself from the cold, resting, drinking coffee, using alcohol, or consuming other substances. Lifestyle is a self-regulating, continuous process that leads to satisfaction and pleasure if it achieves its goals. Use of alcohol as a method for reaching an optimal state is based on the pleasure experienced in attaining, or even anticipating, the goal of its consumption.

Noble (1983) posed the question of how some of the negative factors associated with drinking should be balanced with the effects alcohol has in enhancing sociability, euphoria, romance, and, for some, relief from pain and stress. This question may be answered best by directing research towards lifestyle and its determinants rather than focusing predominantly on consumption variables. Once again, viewing drinking primarily in relation to excessive consumption hinders such exploration. Social drinking and its lifestyle determinants are rarely the object of open and rational discourse, even though most people would acknowledge that objective, unbiased knowledge of this type could help people make more successful choices about their life and drinking styles.

Diet

Diet as a component of lifestyle was the subject of a study by LaVecchia, Negri, Francheschi, Parazzini, and Decarli (1992). LaVecchia et al. examined frequency of consumption of 30 selected food items, nutritional and caloric intake, drinking, smoking, and education in 1774 healthy men and women from 45 to 74 years of age. There was an association of heavy alcohol consumption, tobacco smoking, and lower educational levels with a diet poor in fresh fruit and green vegetables and high in such foods as sausages and canned meat. The more alcohol that was drunk, the more coffee was consumed and cigarettes were smoked. Alcohol drinking, cigarette smoking, and other variables were thus important indicators of subjects' socioeconomic status, which, in turn, correlated with dietary patterns. This pattern not only showed the interrelationships among alcohol and other lifestyle variables but also suggested that improving socioeconomic status may lead to a healthier lifestyle and more appropriate alcohol use. If the authors' claim in this regard is true, these results may offer valuable perspectives for public health interventions.

Concurrent Use of Substances

People not only enjoy drinking alcohol but often consume it in combination with other substances such as nicotine and caffeine, each in more or less healthy ways (Hughes & Oliveto, 1993; Istvan & Matarazzo, 1984; Kemper, 1995; Kozlowski et al., 1993; Leibenluft, Fiero, Bartko, Moul, & Rosenthal, 1993; Pihl, Assaad, & Bruce, 1998). Such behavior may reflect a certain lifestyle as well as being geared to attaining a certain joint or interactive effect.

Although most substances often are used concurrently with another, the majority of attention has been given to measuring consumption levels for each product separately and determining how changes in the individual levels of each may affect health and psychosocial functioning. Indeed, research (Istvan & Matarazzo, 1984; Klatsky & Armstrong, 1992; Rehm, Fichter, & Elton, 1993; Shu, Hatch, Mills, Clemens, & Susser, 1995) tends to show that (a) alcohol and nicotine consumption are highly correlated; (b) smokers consume more coffee on average than nonsmokers; (c) smoking seems to increase the clearance of caffeine; and (d) caffeine alone or in combination with alcohol (Pritchard, Robinson, DeBethizy, Davis, & Stiles, 1995) does not appear to play a role in the link between smoking and coffee drinking. Thus, in evaluating the influence of one of these behaviors, the accepted practice is to control for the use of the other. These controls were applied in our social-drinkers study (Zeef, Snel, & Maritz, 1998), in which social drinkers who smoked were excluded, just as Lorist (1995) recruited coffee drinkers who did not smoke.

In the longitudinal Amsterdam Growth and Health study (Kemper, 1995), we examined cooccurring smoking and alcohol use in subjects between the ages of 14 and 27 years. Those subjects who used alcohol were about three times more likely to smoke as well. Furthermore, the dichotomized lifestyle factors of drinking alcohol, smoking, inactivity, and high calorie intake were clustered and used as an outcome variable. For the 16- to 27-year-old age range, the personality factors of rigidity and inadequacy predicted a high score on this "unhealthy lifestyle" cluster; for the 21- to 27-year-old age range, dominance, inadequacy, and low rigidity predicted this cluster. Using the cluster as a predictor, the higher (i.e., the more unhealthy) the lifestyle score was, the higher the body mass index and the worse the aerobic conditioning were as well.

The hypothesis tested by Schwarz, Bischof, and Kunze (1994) was whether coffee drinking is associated with a lifestyle unhealthier than that of a tea drinker. Coffee and tea drinking were studied in relation to four lifestyle factors—drinking, smoking, physical activity, and nutrition—in 2400 randomly selected 25- to 64-year-old men and women. They were questioned on 22 behavioral factors, including intake of fat, cakes, meat, sweets, coffee, and tea. Independent trends were found for coffee and tea consumption in relation to alcohol use. These trends were independent of age and gender and were similar below and above the age of 45 years for both men and women.

Griffiths, Bigelow, and Liebson (1976) tried to isolate the *mechanisms* by which alcohol and smoking interacted. Their speculation was that alcohol might alter the reward value of cigarettes or vice versa. It appeared that the consumption of alcohol increased the length of time people spent smoking, the number of puffs taken on each cigarette, and the amount of tobacco burnt. There were also strong subjective effects, with subjects looking forward to more smoking after alcohol and reporting greater smoking satisfaction after alcohol. It is obvious that advanced methodologies are needed to study the processes by which the consumption of one drug influences the consumption of another. Smoking and drinking are just one example; other cases of combined use involve alcohol with nicotine, cocaine with ethanol or marijuana (see Glautier, Clements, White, Taylor, & Stolerman, 1996), and so on.

A related question is whether there are theories or models that explain the use of any or all of these substances. Unfortunately, such theories are still to be developed, and the question then is whether they will gain wide acceptance, especially if they focus on social or moderate use of substances taken separately or concurrently. This point is relevant because genetic or behavioral factors apparently related to *heavy* use of substances may be absent or quite different if *moderate* use is studied. Interestingly, Istvan and Matarazzo (1984) found that drinking was related to a more global and smoking to a more specific risk-taking orientation or behavior. Drinking, but not smoking, was related to global risk taking ($r = 0.26$), whereas smoking was *inversely* related to using seat belts while driving ($r = -0.23$). The same might apply to individuals who use either licit or illicit psychoactive substances, thereby expressing different behavioral styles and a greater inclination than nonusers to take risks that are more likely to lead to physical illness and injury.

Based on observations suggesting that the effects of substances and their patterns of use may extend to commonalities in the mechanisms that underlie the addictive processes themselves, Kozlowski et al. (1993) assessed whether the frequency of tobacco use was related to the frequency of licit and illicit substance use, including alcohol. The most important finding was that use of alcohol, nicotine, and caffeine were directly related. An absence of similar positive relationships between levels of illicit drug use and the intake of nicotine and caffeine suggests that use of these other drugs may be controlled by a separate set of factors. Unfortunately, alcohol and drug researchers and clinicians have tended to ignore cigarette smoking or other substance use. Yet the majority of alcohol and drug abusers rate their urges for cigarettes as at least as strong as their greatest urges for their main substance of abuse, such as alcohol (Kozlowski et al., 1993). Although the previous relationship may apply only to *abuse* of these substances, the least that can be done in research on *social* or sensible use of these substances is to find out which interrelationships are operative and what mechanisms account for them. One view is that there is a common genetic basis for those substances that affect the pleasure and reward systems in the brain—most likely at the receptor level of the dopaminergic system (Blum, Cull, Braverman, & Comings, 1996).

In conclusion, there are many studies that have shown that the use of certain substances often correlates with that of other substances. These studies also suggest that concurrent use of several substances (a) occurs in certain interrelated ways, (b) seems to be related to personality, and (c) may have a common genetic basis. For these reasons, studies of social drinking should pay particular attention to such interrelationships in order to understand more clearly why individuals use alcohol in particular, and substances in general. Again, such research could guide and inform the public in using alcohol in a responsible and sensible way.

Stress and Alcohol

Another issue pertaining to lifestyle and an individual's neurobehavioral state is the relationship between stress and alcohol use. Clinical stress is the inability to cope with prevalent stressors. Stress is viewed almost exclusively as the negative outcome of a person's experience of a stressor. Stress-related incapacities, however, can be divided into two types. In one, eustress, the individual cannot cope with stimuli of a positive nature, such as winning a big prize in the lottery or the victory of one's favorite soccer team. In the other, negative stress—or distress—arises in the case of inadequate control if unpleasant, negatively experienced occurrences take place. In both cases, stress can be viewed as the physical and mental consequence of stressors with which one cannot deal adequately; in other words, stress leads to a deviation from the optimal state towards which individuals strive.

It is important for understanding the role of social drinking in alleviating stress to examine the situational and cognitive factors that come into play. In order to do so, one should ask under which conditions, at which doses, in what people, and by which measures alcohol reduces stress. Hull (1981) showed the utility of this approach. Combining cognitive factors and personality traits into a self-awareness model of alcohol intoxication, Hull in fact included the whole lifestyle context of variables such as demographic factors, personality, gender, and so forth. His results demonstrated a consistent, reliable, and predictable relationship between alcohol and psychological stress. Hull's view is that alcohol directly affects information processing and this, combined with the demands of the situation, gives alcohol its unique power to alter subsequent emotions and behavior. In this conception, alcohol reduces tension or dampens stress and may become a preferred technique for coping with a specific stressor.

By using what can in certain circumstances be an appropriate way to handle the situation, whether it is stressful or relaxing, one is able to optimize one's state effectively. In fact, by adjusting their coping strategy appropriately to the situation, individuals may find alcohol to be not only tension-reducing but also pleasure-inducing, as they approach or attain their optimal state. Interestingly, Volpicelli's notion (cited in Sayette, 1993) that alcohol consumption replenishes depleted endorphin levels fits this idea on a neurophysiological level.

That the capacity of alcohol to improve mood has consequences for health was demonstrated by Cohen, Tyrel, Russel, Jarvis, and Smith (1993). The researchers inoculated 400 male and female volunteers with a cold virus. Drinkers who did not smoke were in better mood and were more resistant to colds than nondrinkers, dose-dependently up to three drinks per day (see Chapter 1). Among those consuming two or three glasses a day, 85% had a greater resistance than nondrinkers. After extensively reviewing the relevant literature, Turner, Bennett, and Hernandez (1981) and Bates and Tracy (1990) concluded that moderate social drinking (i.e., up to and including five drinks per day) as a response to stress seldom led to adverse effects on the body. In fact, they found beneficial effects in terms of reduced risk of myocardial infarction, improved quality of life in the elderly, and general stress relief. Clearly, stress-response reduction mitigates the negative effects of stress and optimizes the drinker's state.

According to Steele, Southwick, and Pagano (1986), the reduction of psychological stress by alcohol stems largely from its impairment of cognitive processes that, in conjunction with a distracting activity, blocks out stress-inducing thoughts. In particular, alcohol's effects assist the subject's narrowing of perception to more immediate cues, thereby restricting attention to only the most salient stimuli. This "alcohol myopia" can be viewed positively as well as negatively (Josephs & Steele, 1990). Suppressing passive attention enables subjects to strengthen their active attention, which means an improvement of the signal-noise ratio. Without distraction, the individual can focus more directly and intensely on salient, stressor-related aspects with which he or she must cope. The ability of alcohol to positively relieve distress depends on the possibility it creates for the individual to focus attention selectively on the stressor and thereby improve the likelihood of coping with it successfully.

Similar arguments apply to situations in which the processing demands of the task exceed the control-processing abilities of the individual. According to Josephs and Steele (1990), such a situation could lead to frustration and, if the performance is then evaluated, anxiety. Indeed Logue, Linnoila, Wallman, and Erwin (1981) found that performing complex psychomotor tasks increased anxiety as a function of increasing blood alcohol levels. Self-evidently, alcohol in and of itself cannot diminish frustration and anxiety (Schaeffer & Parsons, 1986). Rather, for a specific activity to act as a suitable distractor from psychological stress, it should redirect attention without inducing frustration and anxiety. Such a distractor has the advantage of mobilizing the individual's available attention to cope with the stressor only. By facilitating the ability to deal with the stressor, alcohol may further reduce frustration and anxiety.

To evaluate the effects of responsible alcohol use on stress and its concomitant anxiety and frustration, these effects have to be studied in relation to both eustress and distress and under conditions that permit realistic coping. Individuals should be convinced that it is possible to manipulate their condition in such a way as to achieve their optimal sense of well-being. Therefore, pleasure from drinking might be seen as a consequence of stress reduction because the act of drinking assists in achieving an optimum state. In this view, the sensible consumption of alcohol is, for some, a daily, positive life event and, hence, a pleasurable occasion (see Chapter 18).

CONCLUSION

Balance between pleasure and guilt is disturbed if only the harmful effects of a potentially healthy activity are emphasized and the positive effects are ignored. Just as pleasure has proven to be beneficial for health, a negative mood, such as a sense of guilt, may threaten health. As demonstrated in this chapter drinking sensibly and moderately may heighten pleasure and thereby improve health, and refraining from alcohol can deprive an individual of these benefits. The capacity of the individual to achieve functional states and feelings of well-being is an asset that has to be learned and, once achieved, should be polished and fostered.

Lifestyle is the cognitive-behavioral expression of an individual's unique neurobehavioral characteristics and of his or her sociodemographic, cultural, and environmental background. These characteristics form important, interrelated factors that determine lifestyle. Alcohol research should focus on lifestyle and look at alcohol use as one of the many components of lifestyle.

This view also has consequences for the way alcohol research could be conducted. First, its methodology should encompass factors that determine lifestyle. Second, it should be prospective, using large random samples that take account of subjects' background variables and giving preference to natural research settings. And third, the information gathered in this way could then be used to inform and guide the public in responsible—and pleasurable—use of alcohol.

REFERENCES

Arbuckle, T. Y., Chaikelson, J. S., & Gold, D. P. (1994). Social drinking and cognitive functioning revisited: The role of intellectual endowment and psychological distress. *Journal of Studies on Alcohol, 55,* 352–361.

Bates, M. E., & Tracy, J. I. (1990). Cognitive functioning in young "social drinkers:" Is there impairment to detect? *Journal of Abnormal Psychology, 99,* 242–249.

Bergman, H. (1985). Cognitive deficits and morphological cerebral changes in a random sample of social drinkers. In M. Galanter (Ed.), *Recent developments in alcoholism* (Vol. 3, pp. 265–277). New York: Plenum Press.

Blum, K., Cull, J. G., Braverman, E. R., & Comings, D. E. (1996). Reward deficiency syndrome. *American Scientist, 84*, 132–145.

Brown, S. A. (1985). Expectancies versus background in the prediction of college drinking patterns. *Journal of Consulting and Clinical Psychology, 53*, 123–130.

Burda, P. C., & Vaux, A. C. (1988). Social drinking in supportive contexts among college males. *Journal of Youth and Adolescence, 17*, 165–171.

Central Bureau of Statistics. (1996). *Statistical Yearbook 1996.* The Hague, Netherlands: Sdu/Publishers.

Cohen, S., Tyrel, D. A. J., Russel, M. A. H., Jarvis, M., & Smith, A. P. (1993). Smoking, alcohol consumption and susceptibility to the common cold. *American Journal of Public Health, 83*, 1277–1283

Collins, R., Parks, G., & Marlatt, G. (1985). Social determinants of alcohol consumption: The effects of social interaction and model status on the self-administration of alcohol. *Journal of Consulting and Clinical Psychology, 53*, 189–200.

Emmerson, R. Y., Dustman, R. E. J., Heil, J., & Shearer, D. E. (1988). Neuropsychological performance of young nondrinkers, social drinkers, and long- and short-term sober alcoholics. *Alcoholism: Clinical and Experimental Research, 12*, 625–629.

Friedman, J., & Humphrey, J. A. (1985). Antecedents of collegiate drinking. *Journal of Youth and Adolescence, 14*, 11–21.

Glautier, S., Clements, K., White, J. A. W., Taylor, C., & Stolerman, I. P. (1996). Alcohol and the reward value of cigarette smoking. *Behavioural Pharmacology, 7*, 144–154.

Griffiths, R. R., Bigelow, G.E., & Liebson, I. (1976) Facilitation of human tobacco self-administration by ethanol: A behavioral analysis. *Journal of the Experimental Analysis of Behavior, 25*, 279–292.

Hannon, R., Butler, C. P., Day, C. L., Khan, S. A., Quitoriano, L. A., Butler, A. M., & Meredith, L. A. (1987). Social drinking and cognitive functioning in college students: A replication and reversibility study. *Journal of Studies on Alcohol, 48*, 502–506.

Harburg, E., Gleiberman, L., Difranceisco, W., & Peele, S. (1994). Towards a concept of sensible drinking and an illustration of measure. *Alcohol & Alcoholism, 29*, 439–450.

Harburg, E., Gunn, R., Gleiberman, L., Difranceisco, W., & Schork, A. (1993). Psychosocial factors, alcohol use and hangover signs among social drinkers: A reappraisal. *Journal of Clinical Epidemiology, 46*, 413–422.

Harper, C., Kril, J., & Daly, J. (1988). Does a "moderate" alcohol intake damage the brain? *Journal of Neurology, Neurosurgery and Psychiatry, 51*, 909–913.

Hill, S. Y., & Ryan, C. (1985). Brain damage in social drinkers? Reasons for caution. In M. Galanter (Ed.), *Recent developments in alcoholism* (Vol. 3, pp. 277–288). New York: Plenum Press.

Hughes, J. R., & Oliveto, A. H. (1993). Coffee and alcohol intake as predictors of smoking cessation and tobacco withdrawal. *Journal of Substance Abuse, 5*, 305–310.

Hull, J. G. (1981). A self-awareness model of the causes and effects of alcohol consumption. *Journal of Abnormal Psychology, 90*, 586–600.

Istvan J., & Matarazzo, J. D. (1984). Tobacco, alcohol, and caffeine use: A review of their interrelationships. *Psychological Bulletin, 95*, 301–326.

Josephs, R. A., & Steele, C. M. (1990). The two faces of alcohol myopia: Attentional mediation of psychological stress. *Journal of Abnormal Psychology, 99*, 115–126.

Kemper, H. C. G. (Ed.). (1995). *HK sport science monograph series: Vol. 6. The Amsterdam growth study.* Champaign, IL: Human Kinetics.

Klatsky A. L., & Armstrong, M. A. (1992). Alcohol, smoking, coffee and cirrhosis. *American Journal of Epidemiology, 136*, 1248–1257.

Kozlowski, L. T., Henningfield, J. E., Keenan, R. M., Lei, H., Leigh, G., Jellinek, L. C., Pope, M. A., & Haertzen, C. A. (1993). Patterns of alcohol, cigarette, and caffeine and other drug use in two drug abusing populations. *Journal of Substance Abuse Treatment, 10*, 171–179.

LaVecchia, C., Negri, E., Franceschi, S., Parazzini, F., & Decarli, A. (1992). Differences in dietary intake with smoking, alcohol, and education. *Nutrition and Cancer, 17*, 297–304

Leibenluft, E., Fiero, P. L., Bartko, J. J., Moul, D. E., & Rosenthal, N. E. (1993). Depressive symptoms and the self-reported use of alcohol, caffeine and carbohydrates in normal volunteers and four groups of psychiatric outpatients. *American Journal of Psychiatry, 150*, 294–301.

Logue, P. E., Linnoila, M., Wallman, L., & Erwin, C. W. (1981). Effects of ethanol on psychomotor tests on state anxiety: Interaction with menstrual cycle in women. *Perceptual and Motor Skills, 52*, 643–648

Lorist, M. M. (1995). *Caffeine and human information processing.* Unpublished doctoral dissertation, University of Amsterdam, the Netherlands.

Noble, E. P. (1983). Social drinking and cognitive function: A review. *Substance and Alcohol Actions/Misuse, 4*, 205–216.

Orgogozo, J.-M., Dartigues, J-F., Lafont, S., Letenneur, L., Commenges, D., Salamon, E., Renaud, S., & Breteler, M. (1997). Wine consumption and dementia in the elderly: A prospective community study in the Bordeaux area. *Revue Neurologique, 153*, 185–192.

Parsons, O. A. (1986). Cognitive functioning in sober social drinkers: A review and critique. *Journal of Studies on Alcohol, 47*, 101–114.

Pihl, R. O., Assaad, J.-M., & Bruce, K. R. (1998). Cognition in social drinkers: The interaction with nicotine and caffeine. In J. Snel & M. M. Lorist (Eds.), *Nicotine, caffeine and social drinking: Behaviour and brain function* (pp. 347–362). Reading, UK: Harwood Academic Publishers.

Pritchard, W. S., Robinson, J. H., DeBethizy, D. J., Davis, R. A., & Stiles, M. F. (1995). Caffeine and smoking: Subjective, performance, and psychophysiological effects. *Psychophysiology, 32*, 19–27.

Rehm, J., Fichter, M. M., & Elton, M. (1993). Effects on mortality of alcohol consumption, smoking, physical activity and close personal relationships. *Addiction, 88*, 101–112.

Sayette, M. A. (1993). An appraisal-disruption model of alcohol's effects on stress responses in social drinkers. *Psychological Bulletin, 114*, 459–476.

Schaeffer, K. W., & Parsons, O. A. (1986). Drinking practices and neuropsychological test performance in sober male alcoholics and social drinkers. *Alcohol, 3*, 175–179.

Schwarz, B., Bischof, H. P., & Kunze, M. (1994). Coffee, tea and lifestyle. *Preventive Medicine, 23*, 377–384.

Shu, X. O., Hatch, M. C., Mills, J., Clemens, J., & Susser, M. (1995). Maternal smoking, alcohol drinking, caffeine consumption, and fetal growth: Results from a prospective study, *Epidemiology, 6*, 115–120

Single, E., & Leino, V. E. (1998). The levels, patterns, and consequences of drinking. In M. Grant & J. Litvak (Eds.), *Drinking patterns & their consequences* (pp. 7–24). Washington, DC: Taylor & Francis.

Steele, C. M., Southwick, L., & Pagano, R. (1986). Drinking your troubles away: The role of activity in mediating alcohol's reduction of psychological stress. *Journal of Abnormal Psychology, 95*, 173–180.

Turner, T. B., Bennett, V. L., & Hernandez, H. (1981). The beneficial side of moderate alcohol use. *Johns Hopkins Medical Journal, 48*, 52–63.

Zeef, E., Snel, J., & Maritz, B. M. (1998). Selective attention and event related potentials in young and old social drinkers. In J. Snel & M. M. Lorist (Eds.), *Nicotine, caffeine and social drinking: Behaviour and brain function* (pp. 301–314). Reading, UK: Harwood Academic Publishers.

Chapter 21

Guilt, Restraint, and Drinking

Ross Kalucy

The topic of pleasure introduces the question of restraints on pleasure, particularly internal constraints, which may result in guilt. This chapter explores the
links between restraint, pleasure, and guilt. Pleasure often has been seen in the
literature as an immature motivation, although Engel and Szasz have recognized
mature and immature versions of pleasure seeking. At the same time, restraint
on pleasure can be accompanied by guilt. It also can alternate with excessive
behavior and may result in a disorder per se, such as anorexia or bulimia. Mature, integrated pleasure seeking may, by contrast, offer valuable insights into
public health models.

PLEASURE

The author makes the following declarations about his approach to the topic of
pleasure:

- Psychoanalytic concepts are very useful in his daily life as a clinician.
- He understands that this is an unfashionable and unscientific view.
- He is not a psychoanalyst.
- He finds object-relationship theory particularly apt in examining the
questions posed by this topic.

In exploring pleasure, there is little to turn to in the research literature.
Pleasure often is equated with the most immature forms of instant gratification of
urgently felt needs, e.g., the persistent and demanding cry of a hungry baby who,
once fed, is contented and falls asleep. Sexual behavior likewise can be viewed

in terms of its most basic, orgiastic components, although this is not usually an accurate description. Sexual behavior is determined by multiple factors, is surrounded by many complex social rituals, and involves mutuality as well as a degree of integration between the self and internalized objects and between the self and one's partner.

There are things, events, people, groups, and experiences that consistently and reliably can result in pleasure. In this sense, pleasure has a fundamental quality, overlapping the concept of social capital (Cox, 1995). But pleasure seems to involve more conscious input than other affective experiences. This is particularly true in relation to the more painful affects such as guilt and shame. Pleasure can be refined and is subject to choice. People choose, for instance, different foods and beverages for different occasions, friends, moods, or groups. Pleasure as a reinforcing affective experience can involve a great deal of selectivity and particularity, allowing for the socially legitimated role of the expert, the connoisseur, and even the eccentric.

People choose hobbies, particular coffees or beers, books or music. Within these categories there is an infinite array of possibilities. Pleasure emerges as an integrating emotion. It brings the self and internalized objects into new arrangements and automatically compares and contrasts these with external objects. As long as it is not pursued in an overwhelmingly self-centered or narcissistic manner, the affective experience of pleasure promotes well-being, personal growth, and a sense of harmony. Nevertheless, pleasure does allow room for a degree of self-indulgence.

These reflections are directed towards mature forms of pleasure. According to psychoanalytic principles, the capacity for this experience depends in part on previous experiences extending back to infancy. These experiences build on one another. Traumatic episodes early in life, for instance, may complicate, distort, or even deny the capacity to experience pleasure later. Perhaps the current, most frequently cited example of this phenomenon is sexual abuse in childhood. Linked with this unfolding of experience is the Ericksonian concept of critical developmental phases (Erickson, 1963), made more complex by Piaget's (1954) theory of cognitive development processes. In essence, this means that people show different capacities for—and attach separate meanings to—various pleasurable objects and activities over the life span.

Amid the sparseness of research on pleasure, George Engel and Thomas Szasz each have made valuable contributions to the topic. In his classic text, *Psychological Development in Health and Disease*, Engel (1962) introduces an informative way of understanding the role of affect in the workings of the adult mental apparatus—despite the considerable emphasis on painful vis-à-vis pleasurable affects, to which he accords 28 and 1.5 pages respectively. Engel sees

these [pleasurable] affects as indicative of self-judgments of intactness, success and gratification. For the most part they are less urgent and less intense than affects indicating unpleasure, except when the achievement or success is of unusual degree, or follows great effort. In contrast to the unpleasure affects, the ego processes involved act to facilitate the continuation or repetition of the conditions responsible for the feelings of pleasure.

Engel includes an array of feeling states under the rubric of pleasure including contentment, confidence, joy, pride, and hope. The presence of these affects indicates that:

1　One is at ease with oneself and with one's internal objects. Furthermore, there may a degree of fusion of self and object (without the accompanying fear of damaging the object or the self—a common fear in adolescence).

2　There is commonly an experience of mastery that in its own right negates anxieties, such as performance anxiety, preceding and accompanying the pleasurable affects.

3　The ego's perception, or self-judgment, is of success in finding solutions to conflict and (often simultaneously) the gratification of needs experienced intrapsychically.

Like many psychoanalysts, Engel notes a developmental sequence in the unfolding of pleasure before it reaches a mature form of expression. He argues that the earliest experiences of pleasure occur in relation to gratification of urgently felt needs (such as hunger, being seen and stroked by parental objects, and, once self-mastery of bodily functions has been achieved, the relief of bodily wants). Later development can be affected critically by satisfactory, or unsatisfactory, earlier experiences. Clinical experience has demonstrated that serious trauma at earlier points, such as severe emotional deprivation and physical or sexual abuse, can cause significant developmental arrest so that some aspects of the personality never fully mature. In these cases, the individual may never be able to fully experience pleasure in the mature manner described, in which the pleasurable affects are reasonably in concert with reality and are not symptoms of hypomania or of denial of serious threats to the person's well-being. It is indicative of health if feelings of well-being match reality.

Szasz's treatment of the question of pleasure is much more exhaustive than Engel's, but arrives at the same core conclusions. Szasz (1957) believes that pleasure has been ignored in recent theory and research as an important motivating force and notes that the great thinkers of antiquity such as Plato and Aristotle regarded pleasure as the "highest of all goods achieved by action." He suspects that psychologists avoid the question of satisfaction "through the association of satisfaction [pleasure] with hedonism."

In order to properly study the role of pleasure, Szasz strongly recommends freeing the term from preconceptions that it is simply the result of the absence of pain or, secondarily, the satisfaction of some pressing physical need. He recommends against taking all concepts of pleasure back to "something erotic," which would suggest either that pleasure is purely "sexual" or, more broadly, that it is synonymous with bodily processes, fulfilling oral, anal, or genital needs. It is not simply that the pleasure principle draws up the agenda for life or that the reduction of tension is the sole purpose of the ego's activities.

Szasz notes that mastery and object seeking are at least as common sources of pleasure as instinct gratification. Indeed, pleasure may be associated with not a reduction but rather a rise in tension, such as in a state of heightened arousal. Quoting Fairbairn, he notes that "from the point of view of object-relationships theory explicit pleasure-seeking represents a deterioration in behavior" (p. 192). "The fact is that simple tension-relieving is really a safety valve process. It is thus not a means of achieving libidinal aims, but a means of mitigating the failure of these aims."

This conceptualization is particularly important if we look at the addictive or biological dependency components of alcohol use. The intake of alcohol in such a situation is characterized by the need to stem craving. As a result, it gratifies a basic—albeit derived—need but does not lead to a sense of mastery or comfort in relation to internalized objects. Instead, dependency often results in widening gaps between the self and internalized objects as well as between the self and external representations of those objects. Dependency leads in particular to false presentations of the self, to secrecy, and to an inability to distinguish between the particular activity, drinking alcohol, and the personal and social context in which alcohol is consumed.

Szasz feels that we experience pleasure from doing things that we enjoy and *not* as a dividend or an accessory to what we are doing. This is almost the exact opposite of the pleasure principle as originally enunciated by psychoanalysts— although it nonetheless seems consistent with Freud's dictum that to "love and work" are the point of life.

In expounding upon this view of pleasure, Szasz sets considerable store in its developmental nature, which he refers to as the "hierarchical development of the concept pleasure." He proposes that the first stage, or "primary model of pleasure," involves the satisfaction of physiological needs. This is followed by the second stage, in which pleasure is gained from "object contact." This stage involves the novel but intuitively sensible idea of "pleasure as an added substance." With this concept, Szasz describes the end result of a process by which children come to associate pain (and anxiety) with the notion of loss and, conversely, pleasure with the notion of gain.

Finally, Szasz notes that pleasure takes on a quality of "communicative meaning." Here, pleasure is the result or expression of a satisfactory relationship between ego and body. Subsequently, the concept of pleasure becomes extended to include relationships between the ego and others. Pleasure gains a high level of independence from any reference to physiological needs. Instead, it becomes chiefly an index of the satisfactoriness of personal relationships.

THE DANGERS OF RESTRAINT

In some cases, the desire to exercise restraint, to control and master, paradox-ically predicts loss of control. Guilt both initiates failure of restraint and is a consequence of this failure. Moreover, guilt inhibits the capacity to experi-

Table 21.1   Revised eating restraint scale.

1. How often are you dieting? Never; rarely; sometimes; often; always. (Scored 0–4)
2. What is the maximum amount of weight (in pounds) that you have ever lost within one month? 0–4; 5–9; 10–14; 15–19; 20+. (Scored 0–4)
3. What is your maximum weight gain within a week? 0–1; 1.1–2; 2.1–3; 3.1–5; 5.1+. (Scored 0–4)
4. In a typical week, how much does your weight fluctuate? 0–1; 1.1–2; 2.1–3; 3.1–5; 5.1+. (Scored 0–4)
5. Would a weight fluctuation of 5 lb affect the way you live your life? Not at all; slightly; moderately; very much. (Scored 0–3)
6. Do you eat sensibly in front of others and splurge alone? Never; rarely; often; always. (Scored 0–3)
7. Do you give too much time and thought to food? Never; rarely; often; always. (Scored 0–3)
8. Do you have feelings of guilt after overeating? Never; rarely; often; always. (Scored 0–3)
9. How conscious are you of what you are eating? Not at all; slightly; moderately; extremely. (Scored 0–3)
10. How many pounds over your desired weight were you at your maximum weight? 0–1; 1–5; 6–10; 11–20; 21+. (Scored 0–4)

Source. "Restrained eating," by C. P. Herman and J. Polivy, 1980, in A. J. Stunkard (Ed.), *Obesity*, p. 212. Copyright 1980 by A. J. Stunkard. Reprinted with permission.

ence pleasure. Some of the most notable work on restraint was done by those interested in obesity and eating control (Herman & Mack, 1975). The issue here resembles the paradox of the regulatory control of alcohol intake, that is, those most desirous of limiting their intake are the most vulnerable to loss of control.

Herman and Mack (1997) devised an Eating Restraint Scale, which attempted to quantify dieting behavior, body weight, and consciousness of food, including the desire to control intake and the feelings of guilt associated with overeating. Subjects could score anywhere from 0 to 35 on the scale, with women scoring 16 and above and men scoring 12 and above considered restrained eaters (Polivy & Herman, 1983) (Table 21.1).

The researchers conducted a series of elegant experiments comparing the eating behavior of "restrained eaters" (i.e., those who most consciously restrained their intake in the interest of weight control) with "unrestrained eaters." In one study, restrained and unrestrained eaters (subjects were normal female college students) were tested for the amount of ice cream they consumed (the students were told that the purpose of the experiment was to rate the taste of the ice cream) after having been "preloaded" with zero, one, or two milkshakes. The effects of preloading were dramatic, but in opposite directions, for the two types of eaters (Figure 21.1). Unrestrained eaters reduced their intake of ice cream substantially with one milkshake and, after two milkshakes, consumed less than half the ice cream of the no preload condition. Restrained eaters, on the other hand, actually consumed more after preloading.

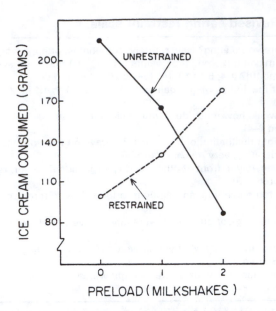

Figure 21.1 Response to preload in restrained and unrestrained eaters. (*Source.* "Restrained eating," by C. P. Herman and J. Polivy, 1980, in A. J. Stunkard [Ed.], *Obesity*, p. 214.) Copyright 1980 by A. J. Stunkard. Reprinted with permission.

This result was very similar to the findings of Schachter (1968) and his colleagues, who showed that food intake in obese persons was greater if they were offered food after a meal than if they had had nothing to eat beforehand. Factors associated with excessive eating by restrained eaters include:

- *Disinhibition:* The restrained eaters felt that they were part of an experiment that required them to eat, so they suspended their attempts to diet "for the sake of the study" and then behaved as if they had temporarily suspended their efforts at self-control.
- *Anticipation:* Restrained eaters salivated much more than the unrestrained when looking at, smelling, and anticipating attractive foods.
- *Taste:* Restrained eaters ate more if they perceived that the food tasted good and also if it actually tasted good—perception and actual taste were synergistic.
- *Perception of caloric content of the preload food:* Irrespective of the actual caloric content of the food, if the restrained eaters believed that the content was high they subsequently ate more; this might be described as the "in for a penny, in for a pound" phenomenon.
- *Emotionality:* Restrained eaters ate if they were anxious, depressed, or in a state of stress (this a problematic issue for restrained eaters because dieting is a stressor and a cause of depression in its own right); dysphoric states have the opposite effect on unrestrained eaters, who consume less when stressed.

- *Social influences:* Restrained eaters did not overeat if a member of the study team remained in the room during the course of the study (but if the study team member pretended to be a fellow subject and ate a large amount, both restrained and unrestrained eaters ate more).

In recent years, similar results have emerged with restrained drinkers (Collins, Gollinsch, & Izzo, 1996). Restrained drinking (often associated with a strong sense of temptation to drink) correlates with more extreme patterns of alcohol consumption, a higher proportion of drinking occasions that result in intoxication, more external styles of alcohol consumption, and more alcohol-related negative consequences (Weinberger & Bartholomew, 1996). Drinking restraint is a risk factor for developing problems with alcohol (Curry, Southwick, & Steele, 1987). Studies using alcohol along the lines noted in the restrained-eating experiments are not nearly as common as those with food. In one such study, however, restrained drinkers did not increase intake if the alcohol was disguised—it was only if the subjects fully understood that they were consuming alcohol that the restrained drinkers exhibited disinhibition (see Marlatt, Demming, & Reid, 1973).

ANTAGONISTIC SPLITS IN THE MIND

The paradoxical nature of restraint and the complex multidimensional and developmental nature of pleasure provide the groundwork for considering some of the root causes of guilt in relation to the experience of pleasure, as well as loss of control and subsequent abuse, in the conscious presence of a wish to exercise restraint, control, and mastery.

Conceptions of antagonistic splits in the mind in the manner of Freud's concept of the ego and the superego or in Fairbairn's object-relationships theory assist in this understanding. These formulations imagine internalized self and parental representations, especially in this case parental images that prohibit gratifying behaviors or that are intolerant of personality facets that do not fit with the parental style (see for example Winicot's concepts of "best-fit" and "good-enough mothering"). These parental objects then are taken to speak for the outside world. Because the parents are not, and cannot be, perfect representations of the attitudes, beliefs, and tolerances of the world into which the individual grows, splits develop in the internal representations of the social milieu. The healing of these splits and the integration of the divided representations is an essential component of maturity and the eradication of excessive, self-destructive guilt.

Splits of this kind occur as part of normal development. In childhood, an object must be internalized as a first step before integration can occur. In adolescence, individuals sometimes veer between asceticism, self-denial, and austerity on the one hand, and gross self-indulgence on the other. Splits also occur after gross trauma in which dissociative mechanisms come into play (routinely found in post-traumatic stress disorders that may be characterized by intermittent loss of control) and in disorders associated with depression, anxiety, and panic. Addictive and dependency states create splits because the demand for gratification is so great that the addict often identifies his or her drug with derogatory bodily images, as exemplified in the common phrases "shooting up shit" and "getting pissed" for heroin and alcohol use respectively.

SOCIAL RESTRAINT: CASE HISTORIES

Case 1

The depressed mother of a 3-year-old boy expressed great exasperation with her son, who had an interesting temperamental trait. He was very attracted to machinery and loved to take machinery apart. She was working in the garden when she heard her son talking very loudly inside the house. She crept inside where she could hear her son shouting, "Roger, that's very naughty—you're very bad. How many times do I have to tell you don't touch that." When she looked into the room where Roger was shouting, she saw that this monologue was occurring as her son was taking the lounge-room clock apart!

This case illustrates the early stages of resolving conflict—the internalized admonishing mother and the curious mechanically minded self are brought together in, as it were, the same mental space; both have equal space and both are kept happy. Integration is under way but obviously has a long way to go.

Case 2

An 18-year-old girl presented at our hospital's Weight Disorder Unit with classical abstaining anorexia nervosa (weight 35 kg, amenorrhoea for 6 months). She achieved all weight loss by abstaining from food, denied herself any previously enjoyed pleasure, was ascetic in her world view, became something of a recluse, and avoided friends because she felt she worried them and they wanted her to gain weight.

Her background was that of an adopted, only child of a farming family from a very small town some 700 km from Adelaide. She was described as a compliant, somewhat shy, and sensitive child who set herself high standards. She was outstanding at school and had an "artistic temperament." She spent hours in her room quietly drawing. Her teachers reported that she was a delight to teach and her mother felt that she was an "easy" child but she sometimes seemed young for her age and a bit too serious.

At age 13 years her father was asked to come and see the headmaster of the local high school, who told the father, "She is the best student the school has had for a very long time and she should go to university." He felt that the parents would have to encourage her studies because few of her peers had any real interest in academics and "many were likely to go off the rails in their mid-teens."

The patient's father and mother talked this over with her (sparing none of the details about how adolescent girls can go astray). They added that she would need to stop her drawing (which was seen as time-wasting). She knuckled down under the new regime without complaint. She ultimately got an outstanding result in her final examinations.

The following year she went off to Adelaide to study humanities at the university. There she found herself overwhelmed by the size of the place and the mass of students, who she felt "all seemed to know much more about life than me." Many seemed much older than her; she felt intimidated and socially incompetent. To make matters worse, many of the students were at least as bright as she. She said that because there was no question of quitting, which she felt would let her parents down, the only device she saw available was to study even harder than she had before. She felt desperately lonely and isolated but noticed that if she missed meals and resisted chocolates and other "comfort" foods she felt more in control and less depressed. She also noticed that thin girls were more popular. Within 2 months she developed full-blown anorexia nervosa. After 6 months her peers became very worried on her behalf and convinced her to go to the university doctor, who in turn referred her to our clinic.

Somewhat reluctantly, she accepted treatment, which was begun on an out-patient basis. (We confidently expected that she would require in-patient care; told this, she stated that she would feel this was a personal failure.) Treatment consisted of support from the team and a community nurse, simple nondirective psychotherapy, and nutritional advice. She gained weight steadily to 44 kg. Her hormonal state returned to normal and preoccupations became adolescent in nature, albeit at a level more typical of a 13- to 15-year-old than of an 18-year-old, her actual age at the time. Her psychotherapy (a mixture of insight-oriented and cognitive-behavior therapy) picked up intensity and became more specific. She became significantly depressed and preoccupied with "letting everybody down," and a course of antidepressant medication was added to her treatment with good results. At 52 kg, she stopped all contact with the unit. In our experience, this usually means that patients want to escape to return to their anorexia or that they have drifted into out-of-control patterns of bulimia nervosa. Unfortunately, it rarely means that healthy self-assertion has taken place.

The unit's policy is to write to such patients and, after 3 months, to call them to check on how they are doing. We called the patient, who was amazed that we still thought of her and wanted to come back and see us *that day*. She turned up at the unit dressed completely in black with a punk hairstyle, several diamond studs in her nose and ears, and wearing masses of purple and green make-up. She reported that she was binging and vomiting in secret many times a day, that she was drinking heavily, often to the point of collapsing, and that she was smoking 40 to 50 cigarettes and drinking "gallons of coffee" a day. She had become promiscuous but gained no pleasure from sex. She was up most of the night partying and slept a lot during the day. Her studies had suffered, but not disastrously. Her parents were, naturally, extremely worried and perplexed about the profound change in their daughter.

We felt that the situation was totally out of hand—as did she—and negotiated for her to come into hospital during her university holidays in 2 months' time. In the meantime, we reinstituted the program as it was at the time she left the unit but placed much greater emphasis on issues of control and mastery. Our goal was to help her achieve a normal and moderate range of gratification-oriented behaviors, a more coherent sense of self, a less unrealistic view of her internalized parents, and a more confident sense of self and a greater ability of self-assertion. Again, antidepressants had a beneficial effect.

As the 2 months prior to her admission passed, she stopped her out-of-control behavior, settled on modest levels of alcohol and coffee intake, developed a more normal sleep pattern, still strange but entirely consistent with her peers, settled on a boyfriend, and returned to A-level performance at the university. She was gaining weight at about 1.5 kg per week. The diamond studs and bizarre haircut were gone. Sensing the direction of our thinking she declared, "I still want my time in hospital." She saw this as "her right and her property"—a time when she could reflect on what she had been through and consolidate her position. We agreed that the agenda was an important part of our program and therefore said that we would keep her bed available.

Two days before the time for admission she called to say that she thought it was completely silly that we should want her in the hospital and that she could see no point to admitting herself. In the staff's assesment, a split remained between an internalized parent and the self. She thus was projecting her own assessment of the situation onto the staff and claiming that it was our opinion and not hers which was inappropriate. She continued treatment and some 3 months later called to say "you are going to be very angry with me." When asked what she meant, she replied, "I have left university and started arts school." Again the split was obvious. In saying we would be angry, she presumably saw the therapeutic staff in a similar role to her internalized father who stopped her painting at the age of 13 years. In fact, it seemed quite a healthy thing for her to assert her own needs and, in any event, it was fairly easy to talk these issues through with her. After a few months at arts school, she was back to her normal weight at 52 kg, her menstrual periods had returned, and she appeared quite content with life. We concluded that an important step in her maturation had occurred, so that she was now much more tolerant of her own feelings about what she enjoyed and had a much more secure sense of her own identity.

This case dramatically exemplifies the splits that can exist within an individual. Moreover, it demonstrates the way in which such splits manifest themselves as illnesses characterized by exaggerated restraint followed by inappropriate, grossly unrestrained behavior. Typically, the unrestrained behavior then is associated with guilt and, in this case, with the use of alcohol, coffee, and sex as attempts to ward off feelings of guilt.

Case 3

When I first came to Adelaide in 1977, I was invited by a number of colleagues around the city to a Sunday afternoon lunch. The lunch was held on an open patio on a day resplendent with deep blue sky and warm sunshine. The patio was covered with a vine of seedless sultana grapes, whose bunches hung liberally around us. The meal was in three courses, beautifully prepared, and delicious to the taste. It was accompanied by the best of South Australian wines and beautiful music. The afternoon was suffused with pleasure and somewhat soporific. Later in the afternoon one of our friends said, "I wonder what the poor people are doing."

This seems to be a case of mature, pleasurable experience. A slight proviso relates to the question concerning "the poor people." All involved were very aware of the immense privilege of the afternoon—and the pleasure it had given everyone—yet enough residue remained from our upbringings, generally Protestant, to experience a tiny degree of guilt generated by our internalized religious parents.

A situation like this is not truly an example of social restraint, but rather of social enhancement. The situation did not provoke fear of violence, rudeness, or contentiousness. There was no need to be on guard; one did not have to watch oneself. The atmosphere was enhancing, infectious, calming, inclusive, and confirming of group values. People were open, frank, and self-revealing, and the humor avoided severe cynicism or skepticism; that is, it did not portray an inner prohibitor or the interpersonal envy, jealousy, or greed reflective of inner as well as external conflicts.

Control arose out of the joy of mutuality, a comfort with the group norms, a sense of solidarity, and the feeling of belonging, as well as out of the enjoyment of pleasurable activities. There was no sense of imposed values. Situations of this degree of existential bliss are not common, but approximations are common and can be promoted. For example, the work of Walsh and others has looked at the way in which English pubs could be designed so as to promote pleasure and control and diminish the tendency towards violence.

There is not an equal playing field for the capacity to feel pleasure, mastery, or control, nor to experience the validation of one's self and one's group. Differences abound in developmental experiences, temperament, addictive proclivities, and proneness to violence—the last of these being facilitated by pervasive feelings of helplessness, despair, and hopelessness and by situations that marginalize the individual or group. Perhaps the best intrapsychic mechanisms in adverse circumstances are sublimation and suppression rather than repression and denial, the former representing mature and the latter primitive defense mechanisms.

Can more mature defense mechanisms be promoted in the social sphere? It is a not uncommon result of good psychotherapy that a patient moves from denial to repression, and then to suppression plus or minus a degree of sublimation. Social mechanisms that enhance this shift are those that facilitate communication, acknowledge common personal traumas (e.g., sexual abuse), and diminish stereotyping and marginalization. In our society, for example, we have made considerable (if incomplete) progress in assuring that inherited status does not determine one's social position. As a result, being a woman, Black, a foreigner, or a homosexual today is much less apt to involve exclusion, stigmatization, or deindividualization than it was 20 or 30 years ago. Have these movements resulted in a decrease in violence and an increase in the capacity for experiencing pleasure? In Australia, one could assert an answer in the affirmative.

The ability and willingness to discuss forbidden topics—key components of sound psychotherapy—have made considerable headway in Australia during the past decade or so. Indeed, topics such as sexual abuse, rape, and abortion now can be freely discussed, and their effects on internal objects and the self readily and easily explored. This reduces internal splits and promotes a sense of acceptance by self and others.

In this way, social movements and one-to-one situations in a psychiatric office or in communications between friends converge to enhance the ability to experience pleasure and to decrease the unpleasurable. Or, in other words, the capacity to master or control is promoted and the secret, perhaps hidden, fears and experiences that lead to shame and guilt are diminished.

CONCLUSION

Pleasure is linked to a reasonably harmonious integration of the inner life—or internal objects—which, in turn, are linked with external objects and activities. The capacity for pleasure is diminished if there are induced splits between internal objects or between the self and the desired external world, the latter producing marginalization and isolation.

In such circumstances, disturbances in appetitive behaviors are common if, in order to suppress anxiety, fear, or depression, people engage in eating or drinking to excess or abuse drugs. Addictive behaviors are reminiscent of the most primitive levels of pleasure, at which, as with infants, self-gratification is extremely time-limited. Such overindulgence deepens negative feelings and creates dysphoria in its own right.

The patient who overindulges often then seeks to exercise restraint, which, in turn, can lead to even greater loss of self-control. The feeling of many of these patients is that the restraint is externally imposed. This imposition becomes identified with punitive or constraining internalized objects as well as with those in the outside world who suggest restraint.

The problems that alcohol generates in our society, such as road accidents and violence, may or may not be outweighed by the benefits of moderate alcohol consumption. This balancing of benefits and risks is consistent with working to reduce the risk components of alcohol abuse. Most people who drink do so moderately. Health is not their major reason for drinking. They drink instead for pleasure, the enhancement of fellowship, and other similar motives (see Chapter 15).

However, clinicians and public health workers have to face the fact that many of the messages and policies they use are tied to a restraint-promotion model (see Chapter 3). This approach at times may cause harm, particularly in adolescence. Thus, it may be appropriate for the public health community not only to consider the promotion of pleasure as a desirable public health outcome, but also to promote settings and contacts that maximize the chances of pleasure in moderation.

REFERENCES

Collins, R., Gollnisch, G., & Izzo, C. (1996). Drinking restraint and alcohol-related outcomes: Exploring the contributions of beverage instructions, beverage content and self-monitoring. *Journal of Studies on Alcohol, 57*, 563–571.

Cox, E. (1995). *A truly civil society: 1995 Boyer lectures*. Sydney, Australia: Australian Broadcasting Commission.

Curry, S., Southwick, L., & Steele, C. (1987). Restrained drinking: Risk factor for problems with alcohol? *Addictive Behaviors, 12*, 73–77.

Engel, G. (1962). *Psychological development in health and disease*. Philadelphia, PA: Saunders.

Erickson, E. H. (1963). *Childhood and society* (2nd ed.). New York: W. W. Morton.

Herman, C. P., & Mack, D. (1975). Restrained and unrestrained eating. *Journal of Personality, 43*, 647–660.

Herman, C. P., & Polivy, J. (1980). Restrained eating. In A. J. Stunkard (Ed.), *Obesity* (pp. 208–225). Philadelphia, PA: Saunders.

Marlatt, G. A., Demming, B., & Reid, J. B. (1973). Loss of control drinking in alcoholics: An experimental analogue. *Journal of Abnormal Psychology, 81*, 223–241.

Piaget, J. (1954). *The construction of reality in the child*. New York: Basic Books.

Polivy, J. & Herman, C. P. (1983). *Breaking the diet habit: The natural weight alternative*. New York: Basic Books.

Schachter, S. (1968). Obesity and eating. *Science, 161*, 751–756.

Szasz, T. (1957). *Pain and pleasure*. London: Tavistock.

Weinberger, D., & Bartholomew, K. (1996). Socio-emotional adjustment and patterns of alcohol use among young adults. *Journal of Personality, 64*, 495–527.

Chapter 22

Gender and Alcohol: The Separate Realities of Women's and Men's Drinking

Louise Nadeau

Today, both men and women drink. They drink alone, in mixed groups, in same-sex groups. If the alcohol molecule is identical for both genders, the drinking experience undergone by the genders is dissimilar. The manner in which alcohol is consumed, the participation in drinking situations, and the ideas, feelings, and ideals associated with drinking and drunkenness in a given environment differ for men and women. This chapter examines drinking patterns, attitudes, expectancies, and social representations in an attempt to grasp the differential experiences of drinking between the genders. These data are used to highlight a significant and crucial part of the drinking experience, that is, the pleasure of drinking and its unique flavor for each gender.

CONSUMPTION PATTERNS AND PROBLEMS BY GENDER

Alcohol is the masculine psychoactive substance of choice. In all countries and historical periods for which there are general-population survey data, compared with men, women drink alcohol in smaller quantities and consume it less frequently. Metaanalysis of data from 39 longitudinal general-population surveys of 15 countries shows that in every country and age group represented, women were less likely than men to drink frequently or heavily and to report drinking-related problems (Fillmore et al., 1991; Wilsnack & Wilsnack, 1995). For instance, in a survey among 22,102 American adults (Dawson & Archer, 1992), men were more likely to report having consumed alcohol, and their overall level of alcohol consumption was about twice as high as that of women. In Quebec (Kurminski & Demers, 1998), men, in comparison to women, drank on average one drink more per drinking occasion; consumed twice as much alcohol per year; reported twice as often having drunk at least five drinks per occasion in the past 12 months (in 1994, 63% versus 32%); consumed a higher average maximum amount per occasion; and had more alcohol-related problems (in 1994, 14% versus 7%). In a population survey in the United States in which more than 7% of the respondents met the DSM-IV one-year-window criteria (American Psychiatric Association, 1994) for an alcohol disorder, males were almost three times as likely as females to meet the criteria (Grant et al., 1994). Studies in psychiatric epidemiology (Bland, Newman, & Orn, 1992; Helzer, Bucholz, & Robins, 1992; Kessler et al., 1994; Légaré, 1995) have found comparable results. Consequently, women enter treatment less frequently than men. The ratio ranges from 3:1 to 5:1, depending on the treatment modality and the geographical area (Dawson, 1996). The mortality rate for alcohol dependency is considerably lower for women than for men (by a 6:1 ratio) (Adrian, Jill, & Williams, 1989).

The social and economic emancipation of women that has taken place in recent decades has caused many researchers to speculate about the convergence between men and women's drinking patterns that could be taking place (Ferrence, 1980; Fillmore, 1984). Neve, Drop, Lemmens, and Swinkels (1996) set out four hypotheses to explain why such narrowing of ratios in drinking patterns could be expected since the 1960s. First, female participation in the labor force has increased, and employment is positively related to drinking. Second, the number of children is decreasing, and parenthood is a deterrent to drinking. Third, the difference in educational levels between men and women is decreasing, and education is associated with drinking. Finally, secularization has lead to a greater reduction in churchgoing for women than for men, and religious nonattendance is associated with drinking. In short, convergence appears as the logical result of the changes that have occurred between genders in recent decades.

In spite of this logic, studies that have examined this hypothesis have not confirmed the expected trend. American surveys conducted over the past two decades have found little evidence of major changes in drinking levels or drinking problems among women in general (Wilsnack & Wilsnack, 1991). However, these authors believe that change may be occurring within certain subgroups defined by age, ethnicity, employment, and marital status. Neve, Drop, Lemmens, and Swinkels (1996) did observe some convergence since 1960, but this change was attributable to a decrease in consumption among men. Although the investigators observed an increase in consumption among women older than 40 years of age, they rejected the hypothesis of a convergence between the genders in abstinence and heavy drinking. In Quebec, from 1978 to 1994, the proportion of current drinkers diminished by 10 percentage points for men and 8 percentage points for women, as did rates of daily drinking, from 16% to 6%

Table 22.1 Percentages of men and women who reported having used alcohol in the preceding 12 months in Quebec.

	Men	Women	Ratio (Men/Women)
1979	90.6	80.7	1.12:1
1987	84.9	74.8	1.13:1
1992	83.7	74.8	1.12:1

Note. Data taken from *Et la santé, ca va? Rapport de l'Enquête Santé Québec 1987: Tome 1. Rapport de l'Enquête Santé Québec, Ministère de la Santé et des Services sociaux.* [And how is your health? Report of the Quebec Health Survey 1987: Vol. 1. Report of the Québec Health Survey, Ministry of Health and Social Services], Santé Québec, 1988, Québec, Canada: Les publications du Québec; *Et la santé, ça va? Rapport de l'Enquête sociale et de santé 1992–93 (Vol. 1).* [And how is your health? Report of the 1992–93 social and health survey (Vol. 1). Report of the Québec Health Survey, Ministry of Health and Social Services], Santé Québec, 1995, Montréal, Canada: Ministry of Health and Social Services; Aspects sociaux reliés à la santé *Rapport de l'Enquête sociale et de santé 1992–93 (Vol. 2).* [Social aspects relating to health. Report of the 1992–93 social and health survey. Vol. 2], Santé Québec, 1995, Montréal, Canada: Ministry of Health and Social Services.

for men and from 3% to 2% for women (Neve et al. found similar results in the Netherlands). Finally, in North America, the 6:1 ratio in alcohol-related mortality rates between the genders has not changed in the past 50 years (Adrian, Jill, & Williams, 1989; Ferrence, 1980; Fillmore, 1984).

Health and psychiatric surveys and clinical and mortality data show that discrepancies between the genders increase as the severity of the indicators of both drinking patterns and alcohol-related problems increases (Nadeau, Guyon, & Bourgault, 1997; Santé Québec, 1988, 1995a,b). The ratios obtained from Quebec data illustrate this point in Tables 22.1 and 22.2.

Table 22.2 Drinking profile by gender.

	Men, %	Women, %	Ratio (Men/Women)
1 to 6 drinks per week	36%	41.1%	0.88:1
7 to 13 drinks per week	18.0	10.0	1.8:1
14 or more drinks per week	13.0	2.8	4.8:1
29 or more drinks per week	2.5	0.2	12.5:1
Alcohol dependence	10.0	2.8	3.6:1
CAGE questionnaire	19.1	7.4	2.6:1

Note. Data taken from *Et la santé, ca va? Rapport de l'Enquête Santé Québec 1987: Tome 1. Rapport de l'Enquête Santé Québec, Ministère de la Santé et des Services sociaux.* [And how is your health? Report of the Quebec Health Survey 1987: Vol. 1. Report of the Québec Health Survey, Ministry of Health and Social Services], Santé Québec, 1988, Québec, Canada: Les publications du Québec; *Et la santé, ça va? Rapport de l'Enquête sociale et de santé 1992–93 (Vol. 1).* [And how is your health? Report of the 1992–93 social and health survey (Vol. 1). Report of the Québec Health Survey, Ministry of Health and Social Services], Santé Québec, 1995, Montréal, Canada: Ministry of Health and Social Services; Aspects sociaux reliés à la santé *Rapport de l'Enquête sociale et de santé 1992–93 (Vol. 2).* [Social aspects relating to health. Report of the 1992–93 social and health survey. Vol. 2], Santé Québec, 1995, Montréal, Canada: Ministry of Health and Social Services.

In a secondary analysis of the 1987 Quebec Health Survey (Nadeau, Guyon, & Bourgault, 1997), not only were heavy drinkers predominantly men, but heavy-drinking women clearly came from populations more generally at risk. These female respondents more often were characterized by low education, poverty, stress, and psychological distress than their male counterparts and than women from the general population. On the other hand, studies using clinical samples show that women manifest more comorbidity than men (Hesselbrock, Meyer, & Keener, 1985; Schuckit & Morrissey, 1979; Turnbull & Gomberg, 1988). In Quebec public treatment centers (Guyon & Landry, 1996), women presented higher rates of psychiatric diagnosis and a higher incidence of life-time suicide attempts compared with men, evaluated by the Addiction Severity Index (McLellan, Lubrosky, & O'Brien, 1981). One can hypothesize that women who abuse alcohol experience greater personal distress, or that alcohol abuse causes greater damage to women's self-esteem, or both (for a review, see Nadeau, 1994).

Since the first papers published on the subject (Lindbeck, 1972; Lisanski, 1957; Schuckit, 1972; Wall, 1937), women's drinking has been conceptualized as being more environmentally related than men's. More recent data also show significant linkages between women's drinking and aspects of their social environments, including gender of coworkers and drinking behavior of significant others (Wilsnack & Wilsnack, 1991). Moreover, a body of data associates the onset of drinking problems with life events (Gorman, 1986, 1987; Gorman & Brown, 1992; Gorman & Peters, 1990; Nadeau, 1990). Among women in Quebec who drink the same volume as men, those who reported feeling somewhat or very stressed had, respectively, five or more and eight or more times the rate of reporting at least one alcohol-related problem of those who did not report any stress (Kurminski & Demers, 1998). By way of illustration, Wilsnack, Wilsnack, and Hiller-Sturmhöfel (1994) have shown from a 10-year longitudinal study with 911 women that those with a history of problem drinking reported childhood sexual abuse twice as often as women without such a history. In addition, sexual dysfunction was the strongest single predictor of continued problem drinking. Clinical data concur with general-population data in showing the vulnerability of women who have been sexually abused to addiction (Windle, Windle, Scheidt, & Miller, 1995).

In summary, women drink less than men, and the prevalence ratios for women versus men increase as indicators of drinking severity increase. Alcohol-related problems in women appear to be associated with stress as experienced in, for example, life events, chronic personal problems, childhood neglect, and sexual abuse. For these women, alcohol abuse appears to be a coping strategy in response to adversity.

BIOLOGICAL VULNERABILITY

Biological vulnerability to alcohol consumption is greater for women (see Chapter 13). The survey data presented previously were not adjusted for differences in body composition, weight, and water content. Had they been, such adjustments would have reduced substantially the discrepancy in the male to female ratio of consumption (Dawson & Archer, 1992; Lo & Globetti, 1995; Neve, Drop, Lemmens, & Swinkels, 1996; York & Welte, 1994). The total volume of body fluid is less for women because of their higher ratio of fat and lower average body weight. To obtain similar alcohol consumption values for both genders, alcohol intake on drinking days should be expressed in grams of ethanol per kilogram of total body fluid. Furthermore, because smaller quantities of the enzyme alcohol dehydrogenase have been found in their gastrointestinal tract, female alcoholics may have greater risk of tissue damage from exposure to alcohol (Frezza et al., 1990). Wechsler, Dowdall, Davenport, and Rimm (1995) have documented that women who report having drunk four drinks in a row are as likely to experience drinking-related problems as men who typically drink five drinks in a row. As a result, unadjusted consumption measures (such as those used in the Quebec research presented previously) yield more conservative estimates of binge drinking and related measures for women. However, using four drinks or more for women and five or more drinks for men as measures of binge drinking would not dramatically change the relationship on most measures.

The greater physical vulnerability of women who abuse alcohol has been demonstrated repeatedly (Blume, 1991; Hill, 1995; Lex, 1994; Morgan & Sherlock, 1977; Urbano-Marquez et al., 1995). For instance, American data have shown that women with an alcohol disorder demonstrated higher rates than men on all measures of *physical* morbidity. Female-to-male risk rates of experiencing a morbid condition were 1.5 to 2.0 (Chou, 1994). Several studies have confirmed the "telescoping" effect of alcohol abuse in women, that is, the more rapid presentation of alcohol disorders in women than in men who hypothetically started to drink at the same time (Dawson, 1996; Lex, 1994; Schuckit, Anthenelli, Bucholz, Hesselbrock, & Tipp, 1995). Women enter treatment sooner after the onset of heavy drinking or alcohol-related problems than men (Dawson, 1996). For women who abuse alcohol, greater environmental vulnerability acts together with greater biological vulnerability to increase health and other risks.

ATTITUDES

In 1991 and again in 1996, two representative sample surveys of the French-speaking population of Quebec ($N = 512$, Gauthier, 1991; $N = 1004$, Gauthier, 1996) inquired about attitudes towards alcohol. In 1996, 58% of the respondents agreed that alcohol produced pleasure, an increase of five percentage points over the 1991 survey. Notwithstanding this evolution towards more permissive attitudes, two thirds of the men agreed that alcohol was pleasurable but only one half of the women did. When the respondents were asked if most people are able to drink without abusing alcohol, 58% of the men and 48% of the women agreed. When asked if alcohol, even taken in moderation, can be detrimental to health, 41% of the men and 47% of the women agreed. This gender difference in the permissiveness of attitudes towards alcohol is standard in the literature.

Children

Studies have indicated that knowledge concerning alcohol is acquired at a very young age, when children are still in primary school. Awareness of social norms associated with alcohol also develops before actual drinking starts. Research (Casswell, Brasch, Gilmore, & Silva, 1985; Fossey, 1993; Spiegler, 1983) conducted on 5- to 10-year-old children has found that a double standard relative to male and female intoxication develops during this period. Children of all ages tended to judge female drinkers more harshly than they did male drinkers. In addition, female children in the Fossey study were more condemnatory of female drinkers than were males. However, one should keep in mind that as children grow into adolescence, they become somewhat more tolerant towards drinking.

College Students

A study done in 1984 in Australia (Wilks & Callan, 1984) measured attitudes towards alcohol demonstrated by father-mother-son triads and by father-mother-daughter triads. The children were college students and the families were middle-class. For the father-mother-son triads, results on sociability and reduction of inhibitions indicated that both fathers and sons agreed more than mothers that one gets on better with others after a drink. Sons were more likely than their mothers to agree that drinking helps people have fun and to disagree that women should not drink because they need to look after their children. As for sanctions, fathers, mothers, and sons had similar attitudes (see examples of "sanction" items subsequently). When the benefits of moderate drinking were evaluated, there was more disagreement on the part of mothers that having a drink was a sign of friendship and that people should be able to buy alcohol close to their homes. Parents were more likely than their sons to disagree that people could drink as much as they like as long as they kept out of trouble. Mothers were thus more severe than their sons and husbands, even (or especially) concerning drinking by women and by mothers.

The analysis of the father-mother-daughter triads revealed that fathers and daughters agreed more often than mothers. This was the case with items measuring the benefits of moderate drinking (i.e., people can drink as much as they like as long as they keep out of trouble). In comparison with their parents, daughters felt that drinking made them more self-confident. On the items pertaining to sanctions against female drinking and drinking in general, the daughters disagreed most about women not drinking because they need to look after their children, followed by fathers and then by mothers. On items measuring sanctions against heavy drinkers, mothers were more severe than fathers and daughters when asked whether (a) heavy drinkers should be fired from their jobs; (b) alcoholics should be prevented from rearing children; (c) there was nothing worse than heavy drinkers; and (d) they would refuse to have a friend who was a heavy drinker.

Although this study was conducted in the early 1980s, it nonetheless exemplifies the generational gap in attitudes towards alcohol and, more specifically, that between mothers and daughters. Mothers have more censorious attitudes in several areas, including sociability benefits from drinking and attitudes towards heavy drinkers. Nevertheless, as the investigators noted, there generally seemed to be more similarities than differences between parents and their university-educated children. Moreover, this research leaves open whether children's attitudes become similar to their parents as they mature or whether there are real differences between the cohorts.

EXPECTANCIES

A corpus of research deals with expectancies about alcohol (see Chapters 16 and 17). Expectancies mainly have been measured with the Alcohol Effects Questionnaire (AEQ) developed by Brown, Goldman, Inn, and Anderson (1980). The AEQ scale identifies six expectancy factors: (a) global positive changes, (b) sexual enhancement, (c) social and physical pleasure, (d) social assertiveness, (e) tension reduction, and (f) arousal and feelings of power.

A Swedish study (Gustafson, 1991) using the AEQ revealed that men expect more sexual enhancement than women. They rated enhanced sexual functioning, physical and social pleasure, and increased sexual assertiveness as more desirable than women did. Differences were greater between the genders among college students than in the adult sample. These youths anticipate greater behavioral and emotional transformation when they become intoxicated. Men in college expected more global positive changes from alcohol than their female counterparts and than older men. Older men, however, had stronger expectancies for enhanced sexual functioning. Nevertheless, heavy consumers in this study had higher expectations of change, and consumption was a stronger predictor of expectancies than was gender.

In an American study using the AEQ, Rohsenow (1983) also found gender differences in the expected effects of alcohol among college students. Results showed that women have lower expectations of pleasure and relaxation and anticipate more cognitive and motor impairment after a few drinks. In comparison with men, women thought that others generally would be more affected by alcohol than they themselves would be, particularly in terms of social and physical pleasure, aggression and power, and social assertiveness. There were no gender differences in expectations of sexual enhancement, aggression, expressiveness, or irresponsibility. Rohsenow interpreted these results as a manifestation of greater disapproval by women of intoxication.

Another study conducted on the social context of drinking and sensation seeking found that, for both genders, alcohol was used in a context of social facilitation and disinhibition. For women, high-intensity drinking was described as taking place in a context of emotional pain; for men, sex seeking was significantly more frequent. For both genders, the context was more important for drinking motivation than sensation seeking (Beck, Thombs, Mahoney, & Fingar, 1995).

The measurement of expectancies attests that men and women place different values on the pleasure associated with alcohol, men attaching a higher value to the positive outcomes of an altered state of consciousness induced by alcohol. Men drink to enhance gratification within a male cultural context characterized by positive attitudes about drinking. The female drinking culture has more constraints. Such results from expectancy research confirm findings from epidemiological surveys that women who get intoxicated are more likely to use alcohol to cope with negative feelings.

SEXUALITY

A body of studies specifically has examined the expectations of men and women relative to the alleged aphrodisiac properties of alcohol (Nahoum-Grappe, 1991; see Chapter 16). Female subjects reported that alcohol has positive effects on sexual feelings, yet laboratory studies suggest that alcohol suppresses physiological sexual responsiveness in women (Beckman & Ackerman, 1995). Wilsnack (1984) has suggested that drinking serves as a cue for men to initiate sexual activity. Because this initiation traditionally has been defined as a male activity, Klassen and Wilsnack (1986) have proposed that alcohol consumption may mean that women are assuming a nontraditional attitude towards sex and a more disinhibited state. Scenario studies have shown that, if women drink, they are perceived as more sexually interested, available, and promiscuous than nondrinking women (Leigh & Aramburu, 1996).

Leigh and Aramburu (1996) constructed a drinking scenario involving potential sexual activity in which the alcohol consumption of the subject and of the virtual partner varied. Subjects were college students of both sexes. The results indicated strong gender differences in subjects' choices, judgments, and feelings. Men more frequently chose scenarios that led to ultimate sexual activity and were consistent in their gender-role stereotypes. They also manifested more attraction and sexual desire for the virtual women throughout. However, in this study the effects of alcohol were weak. Nevertheless, among the few women who opted to pursue the hypothetical sexual adventure to its end, those who had been drinking chose more frequently to have protected sex. Having drunk alcohol appeared to influence women's decision to engage in fictitious sexual intimacy but did not affect the decision to use protection. Drinking did not affect men's willingness to have sex, but those who imagined they had drunk chose to use condoms less frequently. In a study with undergraduate students, Mooney (1995) found that men who express sexual insecurity believe that alcohol facilitates sexual experience and drink significantly more per episode than men who have less sexual insecurity. This type of expectation was not a predictor of drinking patterns for women. If men and women are confronted with alcohol in relation to sexual situations women drink heavily to compensate for perceived social deficits and men both to remedy sexual deficits and to enhance positive experiences and mood states.

SOCIAL REPRESENTATIONS

Sociologists (Demers, Kishchuk, Bourgault, & Bisson, 1996) and anthropologists (Gefou-Madianou, 1992; Papagaroufali, 1992) have studied expectations from the perspective of social representations. The point of departure of this research is that social representations are mechanisms by which socially accepted attitudes are translated into individual drinking practices (Demers et al., 1996). The main results observed in these studies are that women associate drinking with negative states, such as loneliness or sadness, and men report using alcohol for relaxation and social drinking. This group of studies also has shown that alcohol often is perceived as a sign of virility for men and immorality for women, or as an aphrodisiac for both genders (for a review, see Demers et al., 1996). In a Quebec study examining the social representations in a general population survey, 12 distinct representations emerged. Eight factors emerged from a factor analysis explaining 44% of the variance in responses. Results indicate that women rate representations of convivial, disinhibitory, relaxing, sexually enhancing, compensatory, socially enabling, and conventional drinking lower than do men. The eighth factor, harmful effects, was not significant. The investigators indicate that the prevalence of a representation is a good indicator of its importance in a culture. From this standpoint alcohol is not as present in the beliefs and behaviors of women as it is for their male counterparts. Should a female drinking culture be emerging, it is not yet as pervasive and dynamic as that of men.

ATTITUDES TOWARDS POLICY

Men and women also are divided on their judgments concerning alcohol policy. In a 1994 study of Quebec, for instance (Kurminski & Demers, 1998), 42% of the women wanted to raise the legal drinking age compared with 32% of the men. More men than women (38% versus 23%) wanted to lower alcohol taxes, while more women (26% versus 18%) wanted to raise taxes. More women (74% versus 64%) wished that there were more alcohol treatment programs. Six women out of 10 (compared with 47% of men) wanted more antialcohol advertising. Three quarters of women and 62% of men favored warning labels on alcohol bottles. Women favored more restrictive positions on all proposals that would lead to increased alcohol accessibility and perceived the need for added treatment resources.

WOMEN'S AMBIVALENCE TOWARDS ALCOHOL

Contemporary data reported here show that women are more ambivalent—or negative—towards alcohol than men. The surveys are clear: The egalitarian dream in reference to alcohol is not with us, even if data are adjusted for differences in body weight and composition. The biological vulnerability of women is indeed greater, but genetics and physiology cannot themselves explain the separate experiences of men and women regarding alcohol. A more severe moral onus is placed on intoxicated women by children, and girls are harsher towards these women than boys. Intoxicated women are perceived as less respectable than their male counterparts. Women are more fearful than men that drinking, and *a fortiori* drunkenness, could harm them. If women experience more pleasure, then men could be more seductive and demanding and women more vulnerable to having sex without consent or sex they later regret. If alcohol increases male aggressiveness, including sexual aggression, then drinking constitutes a potential threat to women's well-being and safety. In short, the double standard relative to female drinking and drunkenness is present in alcohol attitudes and expectancies, sexual expectancies, social representations of alcohol, and attitudes towards alcohol policy. Moreover, women appear to more readily endorse this double standard than do men. Finally, women who do abuse alcohol drink as a coping strategy because and when they are in distress. Two centuries after the onset of the temperance movement, women still retain powerful remnants of Victorian attitudes that define differential drinking practices, beliefs, and ideals for men and women.

THE CONTINUING DOUBLE STANDARD AND ITS ORIGIN

The Role of Women in the Temperance Movement

The actual division in the drinking practices and attitudes of men and women originated in the 19th century, shaped by the temperance movement. Women were an important component and often leaders in the temperance crusade (Levine, 1980; Nadeau & Harvey, 1995).

Understanding the role of the temperance movement requires some comprehension of the changes in gender roles that transformed life for a growing segment of the population. In most middle-class families around the mid-1800s, professional pursuits took men outside the home, leaving women behind as household managers and full-time caretakers of children. The intensification of the mother-child bond raised the status of motherhood to almost mythic proportions. Blocked in their access to paid work, married women's prestige and authority rested on their maternal and housekeeping role. American historians (Cott, 1977; Smith-Rosenberg, 1985) have referred to this development in the last third of the century as "the cult of true womanhood." Womanhood became the metaphor for all that was missing in men's "economic" world, and women were deemed superior because of their more developed moral sense, which was attributed to maternal instinct.

In Canada as in the United States (Bernard, 1991), membership in the first temperance societies consisted exclusively of men. Beginning around 1830, the movement passed from a temperance (moderation) position to one that insisted on abstinence, and prohibition became the answer to the uncontrollable evil of alcohol. The prohibitionists formed a powerful lobby, often religiously based, and worked for social and legal reforms. It was in this context of extreme intolerance towards drunkards and of strong commitment to the implementation of moral reforms that women moved to the forefront of the temperance movement (Levine, 1980; Nadeau & Harvey, 1995).

Women organized their crusade through the Woman's Christian Temperance Union. This organization held it as women's moral duty to protect the home against the social ills of drinking. Women, particularly wives and mothers, had the responsibility of preventing alcohol abuse. Women paid a heavy price for this responsibility: It was up to them to reform the drinking habits of their mates. Alcohol became an object of contention between the genders, women having the role of putting the brakes on men's drinking. This scenario turned on the image of men who became brutes when drinking, and whose brutishness could only be quelled by the virtuousness of a kind and loving woman. Abstention from alcohol became essential to the very definition of what was considered female. The femininity of women who drank was called into question (Tyrrell, 1991), and female alcohol abusers were seen as "fallen angels"—failed women (Fillmore, 1984). In fact, drunkenness deprived fathers and husbands of the female labor considered essential to their continued well-being. Society strongly censured the alcoholic woman who put her desires before those of husband and child. In short, the temperance discourse served the dual purpose of criticizing male behavior and requiring women to police male drinking habits. It also threw a cloak of invisibility around women who drank.

The Modern Version of the Double Standard

At the turn of the 21st century, we might think that Western society has transcended "the cult of true womanhood." Women no longer are denied access to paid work. Many would not consider women's maternal instinct and moral sense as core features of female identity. Feminism has challenged the naturalness of family relationships organized around rigid gender roles. One might hypothesize that the social and economic emancipation of women has allowed them to overcome their 19th-century social heritage, including their roles vis-à-vis alcohol. Emotional and attitudinal changes, however, may proceed more slowly than socioeconomic transformations.

Indeed, in some ways, the rise of the modern alcoholism movement has solidified aspects of the particular meanings assigned to female drinking. Likewise, the special role of women in protecting against male alcoholism now has clinical support. In the 1950s, the notion of the wife's responsibility for male drunkenness found its way into the scientific literature under the hypothesis of the disturbed personality. In a first attempt to conceptualize alcoholism as a process within the married couple, Whalen (1953) described four types of women married to alcoholic men—the suffering Susan, the controlling Catherine, the wavering Winifred, and the punitive Pauline—all of whom were held accountable for their husbands' alcoholic excesses. These women were seen as having chosen their husbands because of some form of psychopathology that preceded their marriage. In a paper published the following year, Jackson (1954) was the first of many subsequent authors to question that point of view, placing emphasis on the effects of the husband's inebriety on the wife. Nevertheless, Whalen's view persists in many popular works about female "codependency" and its relationship to male alcoholism.

The powerful image of the virtuous woman, central to the construction of the middle-class ideal of the family, may have survived the passage of Victorian times. In most families, in spite of professional pursuits, women still remain principally responsible for the household and child-rearing. Consequently, as in the previous century, female drinking still can be seen an insidious force that threatens to topple both women's maternal and married roles. In addition, because of ongoing, and legitimate, concerns for sexual and physical victimization, intoxication retains its status as risk behavior, the "fallen angel" having given way to preoccupations with nonconsensual sex.

How can one explain the ongoing additional pain for women who abuse alcohol? Jellinek (1960) was one of the first to suggest that in societies that tolerate only moderate alcohol consumption those who abuse alcohol and present significant psychological vulnerability have a higher risk of becoming addicts. Thus, those women who abuse alcohol may be those who experience particularly high levels of emotional and social distress and have more risk factors such as familial alcoholism or abuse. At the same time, lower rates of heavy alcohol consumption and drinking problems in women may be compensated for partly by greater use of minor tranquilizers by women (Laurier, Dumas, Grégoire, & Duval, 1990).

CONCLUSION

Women, although drinking less, abstaining more, and experiencing fewer alcohol-related problems than men, nevertheless display special vulnerabilities to alcohol. Excessive drinking by women results in worse social and health outcomes and more often occurs because of or concurrent with serious emotional distress. Women expect fewer benefits from drinking, anticipate greater dangers, and suffer more disapproval (including internal disapproval) because habitual or episodic intoxication. Women, retaining a role they were assigned in the 19th century, have sterner attitudes towards even moderate alcohol consumption. In these ways, alcohol consumption appears to be a less pleasurable experience for women in general than it is for men.

This basic difference in drinking behavior, attitudes, and beliefs notwith-standing, some signs of change are emerging. Surveys conducted in 1991 and 1996 in Quebec on the use of and attitudes towards alcohol showed a five-point increase over the intervening period in the percentage of women who agreed that alcohol produces pleasure. This change may be caused by the diffusion of research results announcing potential health benefits from regular, moder-ate drinking (Rehm & Sempos, 1995; see also Chapters 12 and 13), which may preserve women's traditional roles in maintaining family life and health and provide them with permission to take pleasure in moderate drinking for themselves and their spouses. Furthermore, Demers and Bourgault (1996) found that 22% of women (and 40% of men) in a representative sample of Montreal residents ($N = 3155$) drank alone, predominantly in the home, in moderate amounts (not exceeding one or two units). Although "maleness" was a signifi-cant predictor of this practice, substantial nonpathological solitary drinking may be a sign of increased acceptance by women of their right and ability to enjoy drinking.

Finally, that moderation is universally more characteristic of women's than of men's drinking suggests that women may serve as models of positive drink-ing. The ideal world would be one in which women would borrow from men their positive attitudes towards drinking and preserve the moderation that has more typically characterized women's drinking. Because, as they say in Quebec, "moderation tastes so much better."

REFERENCES

Adrian, M., Jill, P., & Williams, R. (1989). *Statistics on alcohol and drug use in Canada and other countries: Vol. 1. Statistics on alcohol use, data available in 1988.* Toronto, Canada: Addiction Research Foundation.

American Psychiatric Association. (1994). *Diagnostic and statistical manual of mental disorders* (4th ed.). Washington, DC: Author.

Beck, K. H., Thombs, D. L., Mahoney, C. A., & Fingar, K. M. (1995). Social context and sensation seeking: Gender differences in college student drinking motivations. *International Journal of the Addictions, 30,* 1101–1115.

Beckman, L. J., & Ackerman, K. T. (1995). Women, alcohol, and sexuality. In M. Galanter (Ed.), *Recent developments in alcoholism: Vol 12. Alcoholism and women* (pp. 181–197). New York: Plenum Press.

Bernard, J. (1991). From fasting to abstinence: The origins of the American Temperance Movement. In S. Barrows & R. Room (Eds.), *Drinking: Behavior and belief in modern history* (pp. 337–354). Berkeley, CA: University of California Press.

Bland, R. C., Newman, S. C., & Orn, H. (1992). Alcohol abuse and dependence in Edmonton, Canada. In J. E. Helzer & G. J. Canino (Eds.), *Alcoholism in North America, Europe, and Asia* (pp. 97–113). New York: Oxford University Press.

Blume, S. B. (1991). Women, alcohol, and drugs. In N. S. Miller (Ed.), *Comprehensive handbook of drug and alcohol addiction* (pp. 147–177). New York: Marcel Dekker.

Brown, S. A., Goldman, M. S., Inn, A., & Anderson, L. R. (1980). Expectations of reinforce-ment from alcohol: Their domain and relation to drinking patterns. *Journal of Consulting and Clinical Psychology, 48,* 419–426.

Casswell, S., Brasch, P., Gilmore, L., & Silva, P. A. (1985). Children's attitudes to alcohol and awareness of alcohol-related problems. *British Journal of Addiction, 80*, 191–194.

Chou, S. P. (1994). Sex differences in morbidity among respondents classified as alcohol abusers and/or dependent: Results of a national survey. *Addiction, 89*, 87–93.

Cott, N. (1977). *The bonds of womanhood, "Woman's sphere" in New England, 1780–1853*. New Haven, CT: Yale University Press.

Dawson, D. A. (1996). Gender differences in the probability of alcohol treatment. *Journal of Substance Abuse, 8*, 211–225.

Dawson, D. A., & Archer, L. (1992). Gender differences in alcohol consumption: Effects of measurement. *British Journal of Addiction, 87*, 119–123.

Demers, A., & Bourgault, C. (1996). Changing society, changing drinking: Solitary drinking as a non-pathological behaviour. *Addiction, 91*, 1505–1516

Demers, A., Kishchuk, N., Bourgault, C., & Bisson, J. (1996). When anthropology meets epidemiology: Using social representations to predict drinking patterns. *Substance Use and Misuse, 31*, 847–871.

Ferrence, R. G. (1980). Sex differences in the prevalence of problem drinking. In O. J. Kalant (Ed.), *Research advances in alcohol and drug problems: Vol 5. Alcohol and drug problems in women* (pp. 69–124). New York: Plenum Press.

Fillmore, K. M. (1984). "When angels fall:" Women's drinking as cultural preoccupation and as reality. In S. C. Wilsnack & L. J. Beckman (Eds.), *Alcohol problems in women* (pp. 7–37). New York: Guilford Press.

Fillmore, K. M., Hartka, E., Johnstone, B. M., Leino, E. V., Motoyoshi, M., & Temple, M. T. (1991). Preliminary results from a meta-analysis of drinking behavior in multiple longitudinal studies. *British Journal of Addiction, 86*, 1203–1210.

Fossey, E. (1993). Young children and alcohol: A theory of attitudes development. *Alcohol and Alcoholism, 28*, 485–498.

Frezza, M., De Padova, C., Pozzato, G., Terpin, M., Baragna, E., & Lieber, C. S. (1990). High blood alcohol levels in women. *New England Journal of Medicine, 322*, 95–99.

Gauthier, C. (1991). *Les Québécois et l'alcool* (Sondage d'opinion réalisé pour Communication bleu blanc rouge inc. Rapport inédit) [Quebecers and alcohol (Survey conducted for Communication bleu blanc rouge inc.)] Montréal, Canada: CROP.

Gauthier, C. (1996). *Les Québécois et l'alcool*. (Sondage d'opinion réalisé pour Éduc'alcool) [Quebecers and alcohol (Survey conducted for Éduc'alcool)]. Montréal, Canada: CROP.

Gefou-Madianou, D. (1992). Alcohol commensality, identity transformations and transcendence. In D. Gefou-Madianou (Ed.), *Alcohol, gender and culture* (pp. 1–33). New York: Routledge.

Gorman, D. M. (1986). Comment on D. J. Cooke and C. A. Allen's "Stressful life events and alcohol abuse in women." *British Journal of Addiction, 81*, 637–638.

Gorman, D. M. (1987). Measuring onset of "caseness" in studies of stressful life events and alcohol abuse. *British Journal of Addiction, 82*, 1017–1020.

Gorman, D. M., & Brown, G. W. (1992). Recent developments in life-events research and their relevance for the study of addictions. *British Journal of Addiction, 87*, 837–849.

Gorman, D. M, & Peters, T. J. (1990). Types of life events and the onset of alcohol dependence. *British Journal of Addiction, 85*, 71–79.

Grant, B. F., Harford, T. C., Dawson, D. A., Chou, P., Dufour, M., & Pickering, R. (1994). Prevalence of DSM-IV alcohol abuse and dependence: United States, 1992 (Epidemiologic Bulletin No. 35). *Alcohol Health and Research World, 18*, 243–248.

Gustafson, R. (1991). Is the strength and the desirability of alcohol-related expectancies positively related? A test with an adult Swedish sample. *Drug and Alcohol Dependence, 28*, 145–150.

Guyon, L., & Landry, M. (1996). L'abus de substances psychoactives, un problème parmi d'autres? Portrait d'une population en traitement [The abuse of psychoactive substances: A problem among many? Profile of a population in treatment]. *Psychotropes, Revue Internationale des Toxicomanies, 1*, 61–81.

Helzer, J. E., Bucholz, K., & Robins, L. N. (1992). Five communities in the United States: Results of the Epidemiological Catchment Area Survey. In J. E. Helzer & G. J. Canino (Eds.), *Alcoholism in North America, Europe, and Asia* (pp. 71–95). New York: Oxford University Press.

Hesselbrock, M. N., Meyer, R. E., & Keener, J. J. (1985). Psychopathology in hospitalized alcoholics. *Archives of General Psychiatry, 42*, 1050–1055.

Hill, S. Y. (1995). Mental and physical health consequences of alcoholism in women. In M. Galanter (Ed.), *Recent developments in alcoholism: Vol 12. Alcoholism and women* (pp. 181–197). New York: Plenum Press.

Jackson, J. K. (1954). The adjustment of the family to the crisis of alcoholism. *Quarterly Journal of Studies on Alcohol, 15*, 562–586.

Jellinek, E. M. (1960). *The disease concept of alcoholism.* Schenectady, NY: New College and University Press.

Kessler, R. C., McGonagle, K. A., Zhao, S., Nelson, C. B., Hughes, M., Eshleman, S., Wittchen, H., & Kendler, K. S. (1994). Lifetime and 12-month prevalence of DSM-III-R psychiatric disorders in the United States. *Archives of General Psychiatry, 51*, 8–19.

Klassen, A. D., & Wilsnack, S. C. (1986). Sexual experience and drinking among women in a U.S. national survey. *Archives of Sexual Behavior, 15*, 363–392.

Kurminski, F., & Demers, A. (1998). *Evolution et déterminants de la consommation d'alcool et de drogues au Québec. Analyses secondaires des données d'enquêtes nationales.* [Evolution and factors underlying alcohol and drug consumption in Québec: Secondary analysis of national survey results]. Montreal, Canada: Groupe de recherche sur les aspects sociaux de la santé et de la prévention (GRASP), Département de sociologie, Université de Montréal.

Laurier, C., Dumas, J., Grégoire, A., & Duval, J. P. (1990). *L'utilisation des tranquillisants, sédatifs et sommifères: Analyse des données de l'Enquête Santé Québec. Enquête Santé Québec 87 (Cahier technique #2)* [Use of tranquilizers, sedatives and sleeping pills: Analysis of the results of the Santé Québec survey. (Santé Québec survey 87)]. Québec, Canada: Ministry of Health and Social Services.

Légaré, G. (1995). *La prévalence des troubles mentaux dans le Bas-Saint-Laurent.* [The prevalence of mental health problems in Bas-Saint-Laurent]. Rimouski, Canada: Central agency for public health, Bas-Saint-Laurent.

Leigh, B. C., & Aramburu, B. (1996). The role of alcohol and gender in choices and judgements about hypothetical sexual encounters. *Journal of Applied Social Psychology, 26*, 20–30.

Levine, H. (1980). Temperance and women in the19th century United States. In O. J. Kalant (Ed.), *Research advances in alcohol and drug problems: Vol. 5. Alcohol and drug problems in women* (pp. 25–67). New York: Plenum Press.

Lex, B. W. (1994). Women and substance abuse: A general review. In R. R. Watson (Ed.), *Drug and alcohol abuse reviews: Vol. 5. Addictive behaviors in women* (pp. 279–327). Totowa, NJ: Humana Press.

Lindbeck, V. L. (1972). A review of the literature. *International Journal of Addictions, 7*, 567–580.

Lo, C. C., & Globetti, G. (1995). Letters to the editor. *Addiction, 90*, 1547–1551.

McLellan, A. T., Lubrosky, L., & O'Brien, C. P. (1981). An improved evaluation instrument for substance abuse patients. *Journal of Nervous and Mental Disorder, 168*, 26–33.

Mooney, D. K. (1995). The relationship between sexual insecurity, the alcohol expectation for enhanced sexual experience, and consumption patterns. *Addictive Behaviors, 20*, 243–250.

Morgan, M. Y., & Sherlock, S. (1977). Sex-related differences among 100 patients with alcoholic liver disease. *British Medical Journal, 1*, 939–941.

Nadeau, L. (1990). L'alcoolisme, la santé mentale et l'homosexualité: Trois cas de femmes lesbiennes [Alcoholism, mental health and homosexuality: Three cases of lesbian women]. *Santé mentale au Québec, 15*, 237–243.

Nadeau, L. (1994). Les femmes et l'alcool: État de la question [Women and alcohol: The state of research]. In P. Brisson (Ed.), *L'usage des drogues et la toxicomanie* [Drug use and addiction] (Vol. 2, pp. 231–254). Montréal, Canada: Gaëtan Morin.

Nadeau, L., Guyon, L., & Bourgault, C. (1997). Heavy drinkers in the general population: comparison of two measures. *Addiction Research, 5*, 1–25.

Nadeau, L., & Harvey, K. (1995). Women's alcoholic intoxication: The origins of the double standard in Canada. *Addiction Research, 2*, 279–290.

Nahoum-Grappe, V. (1991). *La culture de l'ivresse* [The culture of drunkenness]. Paris: Quai Voltaire.

Neve, R. J., Drop, M. J., Lemmens, P. H., & Swinkels, H. (1996). Gender differences in drinking behaviour in the Netherlands: Convergence or stability? *Addiction, 91*, 357–373.

Papagaroufali, E. (1992). Uses of alcohol among women: Games of resistance, power and pleasure. In D. Gefou-Madianou (Ed.), *Alcohol, gender and culture* (pp. 48–71). New York: Routledge.

Rehm, J., & Sempos, C. T. (1995). Alcohol consumption and all-cause mortality. *Addiction, 90*, 471–480.

Rohsenow, D.J. (1983). Drinking habits and expectancies about alcohol's effects for self versus others. *Journal of Consulting and Clinical Psychology, 51*, 752–756.

Santé Québec. (1988). *Et la santé, ca va? Rapport de l'Enquête Santé Québec 1987: Tome 1. Rapport de l'Enquête Santé Québec, Ministère de la Santé et des Services sociaux.* [And how is your health? Report of the Quebec Health Survey 1987: Vol. 1. Report of the Québec Health Survey, Ministry of Health and Social Services]. Québec, Canada: Les publications du Québec.

Santé Québec. (1995). *Et la santé, ça va? Rapport de l'Enquête sociale et de santé 1992–93* (Vol. 1) [And how is your health? Report of the 1992–93 social and health survey (Vol. 1)]. Montréal, Canada: Ministry of Health and Social Services.

Santé Québec. (1995). *Aspects sociaux reliés à la santé: Rapport de l'Enquête sociale et de santé 1992–93* (Vol. 2) [Social aspects relating to health: Report of the 1992–93 social and health survey (Vol. 2)] Montréal, Canada: Ministry of Health and Social Services.

Schuckit, M. A. (1972). The alcoholic woman: A literature review. *Psychiatry in Medicine, 3*, 37–43.

Schuckit, M. A., Anthenelli, R. M., Bucholz, K. K., Hesselbrock, V. M., & Tipp, J. (1995). The time course of development of alcohol-related problems in men and women. *Journal of Studies on Alcohol, 56*, 218–225.

Schuckit, M. A., & Morrissey, E. R. (1979). Drug abuse among alcoholic women. *American Journal of Psychiatry, 136*, 607–611.

Smith-Rosenberg, C. (1985). *Disorderly conduct: Visions of gender in Victorian America.* New York: Oxford University Press.

Spiegler, D.L. (1983). Children's attitudes toward alcohol. *Journal of Studies on Alcohol, 44*, 545–552.

Turnbull, J. E., & Gomberg, S. L. (1988). Impact of depressive symptomatology on alcohol problems in women. *Alcoholism: Clinical and Experimental Research, 12*, 374–381.

Tyrrell, I. (1991). Women and Temperance in international perspective: The world's WCTU, 1880's–1920. In S. Barrows & R. Room (Eds.), *Drinking: Behavior and belief in modern history* (pp. 217–242). Berkeley, CA: University of California Press.

Urbano-Marquez, A., Estruch, R., Fernandez-Sola, J., Nicolas, J. M., Paré, J. C., & Rubin, E. (1995). The greater risk of alcoholic cardiomyopathy and myopathy in women compared with men. *Journal of the American Medical Association, 274*, 149–154.

Wall, J. H. (1937). A study of alcoholism in women. *American Journal of Psychiatry, 93*, 943–952.

Wechsler, H., Dowdall, G. W., Davenport, A., & Rimm, E. B. (1995). A gender-specific measure of binge drinking among college students. *American Journal of Public Health , 85*, 982–985.

Whalen, T. (1953). Wives of alcoholics: Four types observed in a family service agency. *Quarterly Journal of Studies on Alcohol, 14*, 632–641.

Wilks, J., & Callan, V. J. (1984). Similarity of university students' and their parents' attitudes toward alcohol. *Journal of Studies on Alcohol, 45*, 326–333.

Wilsnack, S. C. (1984). Drinking, sexuality, and sexual dysfunctions in women. In S. C. Wilsnack & L. Beckman (Eds.), *Alcohol problems in women* (pp. 189–227). New York: Guilford.

Wilsnack, S. C., & Wilsnack, R. W. (1991). Epidemiology of women's drinking. *Journal of Substance Abuse, 3*, 133–157.

Wilsnack, S. C., & Wilsnack, R. W. (1995). Drinking and problem drinking in U.S. women. In M. Galanter (Ed.), *Recent developments in alcoholism: Vol 12. Alcoholism and women* (pp. 29–59). New York: Plenum Press.

Wilsnack, S. C., Wilsnack, R. W., & Hiller-Sturmhöfel, S. (1994). How women drink: Epidemiology of women's drinking and problem drinking. *Alcohol Health and Research World, 8,* 173–180.

Windle, M., Windle, R. C., Scheidt, D. M., & Miller, G. B. (1995). Physical and sexual abuse and associated mental disorders among alcoholic inpatients. *Journal of Psychiatry, 152,* 1322–1328.

York, J. L., & Welte, J. W. (1994). Gender comparisons of alcohol consumption in alcoholic and nonalcoholic populations. *Journal of Studies on Alcohol, 55,* 743–750.

Rapporteur's Report

Drinking Expectancies and Contexts

Irina Anokhina and Mohan Isaac

Two larger realms were combined in this session—the *internal* one of expectations and the *external* one of contexts. The two are united in that both see alcohol effects as being crucially determined by nonpharmacological factors.

In the discussion of expectancies, participants explored social variations in anticipated effects from drinking and ways to change such expectations if they led to drinking problems.

1 Expected effects of different beverages. A questioner asked if people associated different expectations with different beverages. Barbara Leigh said that only a little research had been conducted in this area, primarily by Alan Lang and his associates (Lang, Kass, & Barnes, 1983). They found that beer was linked to sleepiness, wine to contentment and romance, mixed drinks to sociability, and straight spirits to unpleasant consequences. There were cultural differences and ethnic differences within the United States in these expectations (Lindman & Lang, 1986). The same research group also found differences in perceptions of whether alcohol leads to aggression in different cultures (Lindman & Lang, 1994). In the United States, expectations of violence in connection with drinking are high; in Spain they are low.

2 Sources of problems go beyond expectations. The therapy for transforming alcohol expectancies should go beyond teaching people what alcohol does. Instead, behavior and the ability to gain satisfaction should be the focus of change, as in teaching people how to date and to be sociable without relying on drinking. The case described by Alan Marlatt of the woman whose husband's infidelity led to her alcoholic outbursts was cited; the suggestion was that dumping the husband would be the best therapy. (Indeed, Marlatt said, Jill's urge to drink had been reduced now that she had begun divorce proceedings.)

3 Methods for changing people's expectancies. Marlatt described the process of "expectancy challenge" treatment, which he deemed a way to shift the focus from alcohol. Many young individuals have never had two drinks and then stopped. They go to parties expecting that they will drink. The effort is to reshape their approach to social events. For example, they may be given nonalcoholic drinks that they are told contain alcohol, after which they find they feel sociable and interact readily with others. When they are told they have not had alcohol, they realize that it is not drinking but their expectations about drinking that make them sociable.

4 Removing the "disconnect" between current actions and future reactions. The point had been made that, in problem drinking, the drinker discounts the connection between current behavior and future, negative consequences. The question was raised how to address this disconnect. The work of George Ainslie (1992) was cited on the economics of behavior (including the values people attach to short- and long-term outcomes) (see Chapter 14). Leigh spoke of efforts to extend the time-limited nature of people's expectations, because people more readily recall positive than negative outcomes. Marlatt described a number of techniques for accomplishing this, such as Alcoholics Anonymous's recommendation to "hink through the drink," cue exposure (in which people are exposed to stimuli that arouse the urge to drink but do not drink, thereby learning that they can resist the immediate pressure), vouchers people sign indicating that they will lose something if they take a drink, and showing people videos of their behavior after drinking to remove the view they have when actually drinking that their behavior is more attractive.

5 Group influences on drinking expectations. Immediate peer influences are quite important for expectancies. Marlatt noted that, at the University of Washington, although 40% of the students do not drink at all, and others drink moderately, binge drinkers are simply reacting to their immediate peer group, in which binge drinking is the norm.

6 Biological factors in excessive drinking. Irina Anokhina discussed the impact of biology as an important contributor to problem drinking, in which the drinker gains a dwindling effect from continued drinking. Marlatt noted that expectancies were not simply psychological effects but triggered physiological reactions and thus were part of a "biopsychosocial" model.

7 Early childhood learning. A participant described a situation in Zambia, in which children were studied who were alert to and observed the use of psychoactive substances (alcohol, tobacco, and marijuana) in their environments but had not yet learned to use these substances. Leigh noted that expectancy research has shown that children form expectancies towards alcohol at very early ages, before they themselves drink.

8 Creating appropriate expectancies about alcohol. Given that exaggerated expectations about alcohol lead to excessive and problem drinking, ways were discussed for creating more appropriate and moderate alcohol expectancies. This task involves advertising and depictions of alcohol on television and in the movies that do not create larger-than-life expectations about the benefits alcohol can produce in people's lives, particularly their social lives.

The discussion that followed the presentations on social controls centered around the issues of restraint and excess:

1 Loss of community. The costs of the loss of community in the United States and elsewhere were noted. Today, there are fewer public places for people to gather communally (a "third place" away from home and work; see Oldenburg, 1989), where social control is exerted over individual behavior. Instead, people spend more of their spare time isolated in residential structures, which in some cases may be associated with problem drinking. This can be an unintended, and perhaps dysfunctional, consequence of laws such as those raising the drinking age, lowering the limit for blood alcohol level while driving, and banning smoking in bars.

2 Taverns as opportunities to learn moderate drinking. Eric Single noted that a countermovement exists in efforts such as those to allow minors in drinking establishments in order to normalize the drinking in these environments. Taverns are controlled environments in which young people can learn moderate drinking practices. At the same time, Single refuses to go to pubs in the United Kingdom, because smoking is permitted in them.

3 Restraint and excess: the campus and the pub. In many countries, people are losing opportunities for "controlled excess," in which people are given legitimized chances to "lose control" in an otherwise controlled environment. Rituals such as getting drunk once a week may serve as a valuable safety valve. Ross Kalucy noted that modern equivalents to occasions like fiestas exist, such as sporting events and music festivals for the young. Cultures can find ways to express what may be a part of human nature. One participant described a process of "inversion," defined as "turning the world upside down," also known as "time out." Swedish bureaucrats do this once a week, because they operate under such tight constraints most of the time. A Zambian participant described an angry medical student whose anger was managed and dissipated by allowing him to get drunk, after which he proceeded to graduate normally from medical school.

4 Should excessive drinking be eliminated from college campuses? The vestigial need for excess may account for ritualized drunkenness on college campuses. Indeed, there may be a valuable role for college settings to play in providing environments in which young people can experiment. Imposing rigid controls on campus drinking, on the other hand, actually can increase certain kinds of alcohol-related problems. Marlatt noted that, following a tragic drinking incident at the University of Washington, the University began to strictly regulate fraternity parties, for example prohibiting kegs and inspecting identification cards to check people's age. As a result, however, there was more drinking of distilled spirits like vodka and more private drinking in dorm rooms, where no one would notice if an individual passed out. In this regard, the pub can be the working-class equivalent for the middle class's opportunity to experiment in the safety of the college campus. The Zambian example of "shebeens" (unlicensed drinking establishments) also was cited, in which proprietors were at pains to regulate drinking and thereby maintain order because any unruly behavior would call attention to the place and probably get it shut down.

5　**Research methods for measuring pleasure.** In the 1940s, Geoff Lowe noted, the Mass-Observation Archive method was for researchers to observe working-class people as they drank—a practice that led some to regard the investigators as peeping Toms. In the 1980s, the study shifted to recruiting panels to write about their experiences. These panels predominantly were made up of middle-class, older, and female (60%–70%) respondents, because they tended to have the time and facilities to participate fully in the study's new survey method. In addition, Lowe recommended that research methodologies be expanded and refined in order to incorporate pleasure in standard, quantitative drinking surveys.

6　**Negative examples easier to agree on than positive models.** Although it is easy to cite negative models of drinking behavior, the creation of acceptable models that recognize and support positive or pleasurable drinking poses a considerably greater challenge. Indeed, the root of this challenge lies in developing a public health consensus on what constitutes positive drinking behavior.

REFERENCES

Ainslie, G. (1992). *Picoeconomics*. Cambridge, UK: Cambridge University Press.

Lang, A. R., Kaas, L., & Barnes, P. (1983). The beverage type stereotype: An unexplored determinant of the effects of alcohol consumption. *Bulletin of the Society of Psychologists in Addictive Behaviors, 2,* 46–49.

Lindman, R. E., & Lang, A. R. (1986). Anticipated effects of alcohol consumption as a function of beverage type: A cross-cultural replication. *International Journal of Psychology, 21,* 671–678.

Lindman, R. E., & Lang, A. R. (1994). The alcohol-aggression stereotype: A cross-cultural comparison of beliefs. *International Journal of Addictions, 29,* 1–13.

Oldenburg, R. (1989). *The great good place: Cafes, coffee shops, community centers, beauty parlors, general stores, bars, hangouts, and how they helped you through the day.* New York: Paragon.

Part Five

Pleasure and Alcohol Policy

For most drinkers, alcohol creates pleasure, which is the main reason that they drink—an observation at the same time obvious, simple, and profound. The fact of pleasurable drinking is so fundamental that it *cannot* be ignored in formulating alcohol policy.

John Orley describes the expansion of conceptions of health embodied through the development of "quality of life" as an essential health indicator. Both clinically and in terms of public health, outcomes and benefits cannot be assessed without understanding how the individual experiences his or her existence. The World Health Organization Quality of Life project gave the imprimatur of the world's most prominent health body to this emergent reality. Orley describes the cross-national process through which an internationally useful measure of such a highly subjective concept was formulated.

In response to the notion that alcohol consumption in the developing world is a different creature from drinking in the West, Olabisi Odejide and Biola Odejide address the use of alcohol in the most populous nation in Africa— Nigeria. They describe a complex environment in which strong but variegated traditions regarding the consumption of alcohol coexist with commercial forces, changing values, and behaviors in a modernizing environment (see also Part 2). Alcohol policy in Nigeria must take account of two contrasting elements: on the one hand, strong, traditional indigenous feelings about the pleasures of alcohol associated with moderate consumption, and on the other, the effects of urbanization and cultural dislocation.

It is clear that people are not about to sacrifice their own views of pleasure to notions of outside public health forces of where their best interests lie.
Yet unregulated marketing would create a free-for-all atmosphere that is unlikely to lead to optimal drinking outcomes. Odejide and Odejide take on the
challenge of describing the dimensions of a sensible alcohol policy in a developing nation; namely, a policy that recognizes people's urges for pleasure and
self-determination in the context of modern public health goals.

Tim Stockwell and Eric Single tackle the contemporary public health challenge with the liberating conception of "harm minimization." This radical perspective on drinking opposes the notion that the only worthwhile goal of policy
is the elimination, or at least the sharp reduction, of a substance's use—clearly
a non sequitur in the case of alcohol, which is ubiquitous and legal throughout much of the world. Through a combination of state actions (e.g., graded
taxation, drunk-driving laws and enforcement), industry participation (e.g., advertising codes), and assessment of data with appropriate policy adjustments
based on the evidence, the researchers propose a platform for formulating a
practicable and flexible alcohol policy, that is, one that is not seen to be at war
with those it is intended to benefit.

Taking an entirely different slant on what it means to interact constructively with a population about its alcohol use, Stanton Peele describes historical
and contemporary social conceptions of alcohol and its effects. Peele postu-
lates that temperance traditions in the United States and elsewhere that view
alcohol use only in terms of negative consequences have become sorely out of
focus. Indeed, education programs embodying temperance messages may result
in dysfunctional drinking outcomes such as the bursts of unregulated drinking
that Stockwell and Single outline as the most hazardous of consumption patterns.
In place of this "war on alcohol" model, Peele suggests a healthy integration of
drinking with overall prohealth values and lifestyles.

Taken together, these chapters argue for a radical rethinking of alcohol
policy.

Chapter 23

Pleasure and Quality of Life

John Orley

Quality of life (QOL) is becoming an increasingly important consideration in the health field, reflecting the growing concern with the elements of health that are more than the simple absence of disease. The World Health Organization (WHO) Quality of Life project is the broadest effort yet to develop a universal QOL instrument. Pleasure is surely an important ingredient in such calculations, although as yet only items preliminarily concerned with pleasure in the form of measures of positive feelings have been incorporated. WHO collaborators in some cultures have expressed interest in including more hedonistic items such as food and drink if these are considered essential to the quality of existence; indeed, these extra items make a significant contribution to the overall scale's coverage and to global quality of life in, for instance, Hong Kong. We may see more of this in future efforts to combine QOL and health assessments.

THE ROLE OF PLEASURE AND PAIN IN QOL

What is the contribution of pleasure to QOL? The answer to this requires a definition of pleasure and a definition of QOL. Pleasure is a positive emotional experience related to enjoyment, contentment, and happiness. Pleasure often is used in reference to a particular situation or activity, such as reading a book, listening to music, seeing a certain view, being with certain people, eating a meal, or some combination of these. These references are usually limited temporally to moments; indeed, pleasure probably would stop being a positive experience if it went on for days or weeks at a time.

QOL, on the other hand, describes a situation over a longer term. The concept of QOL in this chapter derives from the development of the World Health

Organization's instrument for the assessment of quality of life (the WHOQOL) (WHOQOL Group, 1998). In this instance, "life" need not be a whole life from birth to death but should comprise a period lasting at least a few weeks to a few months in order to allow assessment of its quality. The quality of a life cannot be judged from the quality of a moment in that life. QOL assessments therefore should not be carried out daily, expecting change from day to day. Certain experiences, such as pain, may be assessed in that way, but assessments of a person's QOL must examine pain over the long term and judge how moments of pain affect the many other different facets of life that also reflect its quality. Indeed, most assessments that attempt to assess the impact of pain examine how pain has been experienced over a reasonably long period (Melzack, 1975).

Pain and discomfort—unpleasant physical sensations—are just one facet among many that affect quality of life. A summary of the moments of pain experienced over days and weeks gives us an idea of how unpleasant physical sensations affect life quality. It may be, however, that one factor has some qualitative content that cannot be expressed as a summation of quantities. Friendship, for example, cannot be described adequately as a numerical sum of interactions with a friend. Adding together relatively short periods of pain can help describe the overall experience of pain, although it is likely that intermittent periods of pain adversely affect the quality of life between such experiences. To the extent that they do, this is in part because of the apprehension that a person feels knowing that the pain will recur.

Conversely, it is certainly true that a life with many moments of pleasure has a quality that goes beyond the simple summation of these intermittent positive experiences. Moments of pleasure are likely to smooth the rough edges in other parts of someone's life, and expectations of pleasure create anticipation that itself adds quality to life. Such expectations function in a similar way to a good friendship: The friendship supports us even at times when we are not in contact with that friend, simply because we know the friendship is there.

THE MEASUREMENT OF QOL

The Relationship Between Health and QOL

The public health sector has become increasingly interested in the issue of QOL in recent years. The traditional view of medical practice is that its purpose is to treat or prevent disease. The WHO's 1948 definition of health started this broadening process by maintaining that health incorporates more than the absence of disease or infirmity; it is also a state of complete physical, mental, and social well-being (WHO, 1996). In this view, health practitioners should work not just to eliminate disease by treatment or prevention, but also to promote well-being (Orley & Birrell Weisen, 1998).

This issue continues to be debated, however. Some have argued that any extension of the field of medicine in this way smacks of medical imperialism beyond its legitimate boundaries. Indeed, few practitioners go beyond treatment and prevention of disease in order to create well-being, and most healthcare consumers and payers may not wish to fund anything so global. Yet the overall trend is certainly to consider health from a broader perspective.

The assessment of QOL in health and disease is particularly important in those with chronic conditions or who require long-term care. Sometimes little can be done to prevent or slow the course of a disease, but it may be possible to do things to improve the quality of a patient's life. A concern for QOL is particularly appropriate for those who are dying in a health facility. Their whole lives are in the hands of health professionals, who may stick so much to their medical trade that they deny their patients access to nonmedical means of adding pleasure to—and thereby improving the quality of—their lives. A QOL assessment can remind the health professional that nonmedical care also may be beneficial for patients. Such nonmedical care would include, for example, support from friends or family, or access to some form of spiritual comfort. Health professionals may not be qualified to provide this help, but by recognizing patients' needs in these areas they can at least assist in gaining such help from other quarters.

Measurement of QOL

If QOL is a goal, then it should be measured, just as disease, disability, and mortality are measured to evaluate the success rate of standard disease-related therapies. So far, the effort to assess QOL has emphasized its multidimensionality (Bowling, 1997; Bullinger, 1993; Patrick & Bergner, 1990). QOL clearly encompasses a very broad range of issues. Measuring changes in the size of a person's bank account is not in itself enough to determine how sudden increases in disposable income affect QOL; nor is a list of new possessions, such as cars or houses, a sufficient indicator if taken alone. The old adage that money cannot buy everything is an important consideration in QOL assessment.

A scale's multidimensionality should reflect a practitioner's concern for the "whole person" and not just a preoccupation with a particular disease. What is more, the scale must reflect the fact that QOL is determined not just by an absence of problems but also by the presence of positive features in the patient's life (Hyland, 1992).

One approach to QOL is first to determine which factors impact life quality and then to assess each factor to the extent possible. The WHOQOL study, which examined the content of QOL in many different cultures worldwide, tapped, for example, additional dimensions to those originally indicated by the WHO definition of health. Although the WHO definition of health focuses on physical, social, and mental dimensions, the WHOQOL study's final list of six QOL domains included physical and psychological dimensions, levels of independence, social relationships, environment, and spiritual, religious, and personal beliefs. The level-of-independence category has some features in common with the physical-health domain; indeed, it turned out to correlate quite well with it. The environmental domain, by contrast, resembles the more sociological approach to QOL, generating social indicators. The spiritual domain was added because of the strong support it received from the various focus groups organized in different parts of the world. In fact, within the past year or so there has been discussion in WHO's governing bodies of a possible expanded definition of health that would include spiritual well-being (WHO, 1998).

To a certain degree, measurement of QOL poses similar problems to that of stress (Cohen, Kessler, & Gordon, 1995). Some measures quantify the extent to which an individual is exposed to (presumably) stress-inducing life events, situations, and difficulties—also known as "stressors." Other measures have been designed to quantify the effects of such stressors on the individual's behavioral (sleep), emotional (worry), or physiological (cortisol levels) condition.

Assessing QOL similarly requires examining the presence or absence of QOL-related features in an individual's environment as well as the individual's reaction to such features and the more "internal" features such as positive and negative affective states, or simply satisfaction. These various aspects of life are important to explore in order to know how to improve QOL.

The Facets of QOL

How then can we conceive of a QOL model in which certain factors affect QOL directly as well as indirectly through their influence on other factors? One might propose to measure QOL directly by asking individuals, "How would you rate your quality of life?" A more reliable indicator, however, is to ask survey subjects about the presence or absence of factors they generally associate with QOL. Within the WHOQOL project, focus-group work around the world led to the adoption of 24 such QOL factors or facets (Table 23.1).

Although some of the facets listed in Table 23.1 may interact (e.g., the experience of pain and discomfort could affect personal relationships or financial resources), attempts were made to choose facets that would not correlate too highly with each other (WHOQOL Group, 1995). Thus, QOL may be conceived in this case as the core of a model that only can be described (crudely) by the set of facets that comprise it and explored through further examination of each facet. In order to examine the facets listed in Table 23.1, the WHOQOL study asked questions such as the following:

- Have you enough money to meet your needs?
- How safe do you feel in your daily life?
- Do you have enough energy for daily life?
- How satisfied are you with your personal relationships?

These questions relate to the QOL facets of financial resources, physical safety and security, energy and fatigue, and personal relationships, respectively.

Table 23.1 Facets by domain in WHOQOL.

Domains	Facets incorporated within domains
Physical health	1. Energy and fatigue
	2. Pain and discomfort
	3. Sleep and rest
Psychological	4. Bodily image and appearance
	5. Negative feelings
	6. Positive feelings
	7. Self-esteem
	8. Thinking, learning, memory and concentration
Level of independence	9. Mobility
	10. Activities of daily living
	11. Dependence on medicinal substances and medical aids
	12. Work capacity
Social relationships	13. Personal relationships
	14. Social support
	15. Sexual activity
Environment	16. Financial resources
	17. Freedom, physical safety and security
	18. Health and social care: accessibility and quality
	19. Home environment
	20. Opportunities for acquiring new information and skills
	21. Participation in and opportunities for recreation/leisure
	22. Physical environment (pollution/noise/traffic/climate)
	23. Transport
Spirituality/religion/ personal beliefs	24. Religion/spirituality/personal beliefs

These 24 identified facets are conceived of as "first order" (Figure 23.1). Many other factors of course do affect QOL, but in the main, these can be understood as acting through one of the previously identified 24 facets. Thus, if we are exploring QOL psychometrically, the 24 facets listed should suffice.

Other facets of a "second order" are those that may affect a first-order facet. One could, for instance, tease out personal relationships into family relationships and other friendships, and family relationships could, in turn, be explored in terms of interactions with parents, siblings, or other significant relations such as uncles and cousins. In essence, however, all of this can be addressed under the question, "Do you feel happy about your relationships with your family members?"

A different sort of factor is "having good eyesight." This was not included in the WHOQOL because the distribution of responses within a normal population is too skewed towards complete satisfaction with eyesight. It therefore does not offer much opportunity for differentiating individuals in terms of QOL. Moreover, if poor eyesight affects QOL it primarily does so through one or more of the 24 facets already tapped such as mobility, capacity to work, or participa-

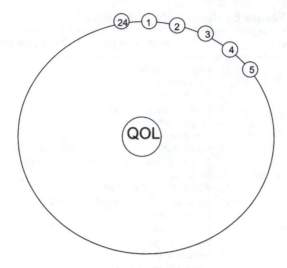

Figure 23.1 Model of quality of life showing first-order facets.

tion in leisure activities. Good vision is, however, necessary to experience and appreciate beautiful people, objects, or surroundings, which can enhance one's QOL, and in that way it may be said to resemble a first-order factor. The QOL model can thus be expanded to include an outer concentric circle of second-order factors (Figure 23.2).

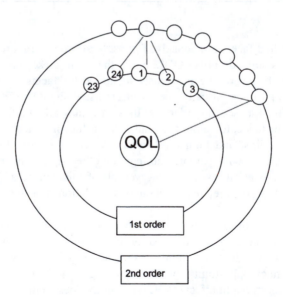

Figure 23.2 Model of quality of life expanded to include second-order facets.

QOL can be conceived of as something akin to a sense of well-being and satisfaction with life. Some facets are included in the QOL assessment because they express that sense of well-being in a very direct way, that is, they *reflect* QOL. Other facets, such as living in an unsatisfactory environment, are included because they very directly influence an individual's perception of well-being— for better or worse. These facets can be said to *affect* QOL rather than reflect it. This is a difficult distinction to make; it is useful to think of facets as either affecting or reflecting quality of life.

Is QOL Subjective or Objective?

In seeing where pleasure fits with QOL, it is appropriate to examine QOL's subjective elements. There is general agreement that QOL should refer to a subjective state (Gill & Feinstein, 1994; WHOQOL Group, 1994). An expert opinion about an individual's QOL only can be formulated by that individual. A person's QOL is what he or she says it is and, if we are exploring its facets, these can be judged only by the individual. If we wanted to judge mobility, for instance, rather than QOL, we could (a) objectively measure the range of movement in an individual's joints, (b) see how far he or she could walk without pain or other hindrance, or (c) review the individual's capacity to perform life's daily activities (Katz & Apkom, 1976).

These kinds of measures are not, however, indicators of an individual's QOL. The kinds of QOL questions that need to be asked are "How well can you move about?" or "How satisfied are you with your ability (or capacity) to move around?" The subjects then are expected to answer according to their own expectations and standards; the measure should not be a professional judgment based on some population norm. Similarly, the way that sleep relates to QOL is explored by questions such as "How well do you sleep?" and not by recordings taken in a sleep laboratory. This is not to denigrate objective measurements. They can be extremely useful as one aspect of assessment, but subjective evaluations are at the heart of QOL.

The field of psychiatry may be able to determine fairly precisely whether a patient experiences hallucinations and to categorize these according to type, frequency, and other descriptors. It is also possible to measure the effects of certain medications against such criteria. What is sometimes forgotten is to inquire how "bothered" the patient is by such phenomena (Orley, Saxena, & Herrman, 1998). One object of treatment should be to reduce the level of "bother" to the point at which it is balanced by any increasing bother caused by the medication. Such levels of disturbance or annoyance caused by symptoms are seldom assessed. The answer to the question "How bothered are you by (hallucinatory) voices?" would better reflect QOL than a question that asks how frequently they are heard.

The addition of an environmental domain to the WHOQOL took it beyond many other health-related QOL models and other social indicators, such as the Human Development Index developed by the United Nations Development Programme (UNDP, 1995). This stresses the importance of human development in enabling people to lead long and healthy lives, to acquire knowledge, and to have access to the resources needed to attain a decent standard of living. Scales of human development, however, must balance improved health, knowledge, and skills against the use made of these elements for productive purposes, for leisure, for creating moments of pleasure, or for being active in cultural, social, and political affairs.

The purpose of development is to enlarge all human choices, not just income. Economic growth models deal with an expanding gross national product but not the quality of human lives. The WHOQOL approach is very different from that of the Human Development Index. The WHOQOL assessment of economic and other resources is set against subjective standards, that is, levels of satisfaction with financial resources, living space, or physical environment. No attempt is made in the WHOQOL assessment to determine an absolute figure in dollars or square meters for these elements. Incidentally, this enables QOL comparisons to be made more easily between very different groups. There really would be no possible way to compare the housing of, for example, a psychiatrist in New York with a pavement dweller in Calcutta using an absolute measure (such as square meters of floor space). The level of satisfaction with their respective accommodation reflects their QOL in a more meaningful—if still imperfect—way.

INCLUDING PLEASURE IN THE WHOQOL

We return now to the role of pleasure in QOL. Most measures of QOL used in medical settings place little emphasis on the positive aspects of life that might fall under the category of "pleasure." The SF36 is a measure of a person's functional status (Ware, Snow, Kosinski, & Gandek, 1993) that also is used widely to measure of QOL in relation to health and disease. The questions on this scale primarily are focused on physical and psychological problems, without inquiring into the facet of pleasure. The nearest the scale gets to such an inquiry is when it asks "Have you been a happy person?" and "Have you felt calm and peaceful?"

Questions in the WHOQOL that Tap Pleasure

Pleasure is a positive feeling that surely contributes to life's quality. In the WHO instrument, pleasure's contribution to QOL is tapped by the question, "How much do you experience positive feelings in your life?" But this is one question out of a hundred. Other questions in the same facet also tap into the contribution of pleasure—such as "How much do you enjoy life?"—but even the whole facet is only one of 24. The other facet of the WHOQOL that is likely to be contributing to or reflecting the experience of pleasure is the one concerned with "Participation in . . . recreation and leisure" with, for instance, the question "How much are you able to relax and enjoy yourself?" (WHOQOL Group, 1998).

In much of the WHOQOL focus-group work, little emphasis was given to sociable eating and drinking—certainly not enough to justify having a facet or even an item on the overall scale devoted to this area. However, centers were encouraged to add questions on certain topics if they felt that they were sufficiently important to have an impact on the QOL in their culture. The contribution of answers to these additional items in the QOL measure could be analyzed to see if they added something to the QOL assessment not captured by other means. There are in fact cultures in which meal times, with communal eating and drinking, are almost sacred. Examples are the French and Chinese cultures. Colleagues in France felt that the addition of such items to the WHOQOL was worthwhile, but unfortunately this was not done. The Chinese center in Hong Kong was so adamant about the importance of this aspect of life that it included extra items on eating and food in its version of the WHOQOL. The inclusion was justified in that the items did group together and make a significant, separate contribution to explaining QOL (Leung, Tay, Cheng, & Lin, 1997). Colleagues in Hong Kong suggested that the contribution was as much because of social interaction at meals as the quality of the food.

One can only guess at this stage why the WHOQOL study played down this kind of contribution to QOL. There were perhaps too many academic participants coming from rather severe cultural backgrounds, who were loathe to admit that the pleasures of food and drink should be seen as contributing to life's quality. Indeed, for some, the notion that pleasure makes any contribution to QOL might seem to be a sinful indulgence.

The Importance of Positive Feelings Measured in the WHOQOL

Given then that the WHOQOL does not contain a facet labeled "pleasure," what can be derived in regard to pleasure from existing data? We can get some idea by looking at the partial correlation coefficients of the various facets against overall QOL—this being assessed by questions that ask people directly about their QOL, such as "How would you rate your quality of life?" In examining which facets are associated with the set of questions on "overall quality of life," we find that it is indeed positive feelings that correlate most highly (with a coefficient of about 0.75; see Table 23.2). Although we further note that many other facets also correlate highly with overall QOL, only one of these—"participation in and opportunities for recreation and leisure"—stems from the eight facets found in the environmental domain (see item 7 in Table 23.2).

It might be concluded then that all other facets that correlate highly with overall QOL do so by affecting positive feelings. To explore this supposition, we can "partial out" positive feelings and look again at these correlations. If we do

Table 23.2 Correlation of different facets of life with overall quality of life.

Facet	Correlation, *r*
1. Positive feelings	0.749
2. Activities of daily living	0.678
3. Energy and fatigue	0.676
4. Negative feelings	0.602
5. Work capacity	0.567
6. Self-esteem	0.564
7. Leisure activities	0.537
8. Personal relationships	0.531
9. Pain and discomfort	0.530
10. Sleep and rest	0.528

so, however, we see that all of the remaining facets still correlate significantly with overall QOL, many with sizable residual coefficients. (We can carry on with this procedure and partial out the next highest facet, yet even then all except "sleep and rest" remain significantly correlated). For those who like numbers, it should be added that the 24 facets in the WHOQOL contribute 60% of the overall variance in the set of questions that directly asks about QOL, which is a very substantial percentage of its meaning (WHOQOL Group, 1998).

The point of all this is to show that QOL indeed seems to be a multidimensional construct and that we need to look at very many different aspects of life to describe its quality. Although positive feelings contribute strongly to our QOL, there are many other aspects of life that independently contribute to and reflect its quality. What we have not shown, but only surmised, is the contribution of pleasurable experiences to overall positive feelings in life. The contribution of pleasure could be examined in a scientific way by, for example, examining subjects' self-reports about their experiences of pleasure in the recent past, their sense of positive feelings, and their sense of the quality of their lives. It seems likely that these would be highly correlated, although it should be kept in mind that there are many factors besides positive feelings and pleasure that heighten QOL.

Nevertheless, it is their rich mental life that singles human beings out from other members of the animal kingdom. We therefore need to value all those aspects of life that contribute to that richness. Pleasure is surely one such aspect, and the times of enjoyment and sharing that frequently accompany food and drink are a potent source of pleasure for most people.

CONCLUSION

The WHO has taken a broad view of health as more than a matter of attacking disease. It has sponsored a substantial project to measure QOL as an aspect of positive health. This exercise has entailed, first, developing a concept of QOL and, second, determining the factors that most directly contribute to it. Six primary domains that foster QOL were identified in worldwide assessments: physical health, psychological factors, levels of independence, social relationships, environmental factors, and spiritual factors. These in turn encompass 24 facets, or factors, that contribute to the measurement of QOL.

QOL is a subjective measurement; thus, people's individual reactions are more critical than their objective levels of material possessions, for instance. Pleasure would seem to be one component of such subjective assessments. However, little attention was given to pleasure per se in the WHOQOL. "Positive feelings," on the other hand, was the facet that best correlated with overall QOL. Leisure activities also were highly associated with QOL.

Future QOL assessments may reveal more about the reality of people's inner lives and the place that pleasure holds there—including such pleasurable activities as eating and drinking. Although taking this step may represent a bold departure from previous efforts at health assessment, it now seems a natural one.

REFERENCES

Bowling, A. (1997). *Measuring health* (2nd ed.). Buckingham, UK: Open University Press.

Bullinger, M. (1993). Indices versus profiles—Advantages and disadvantages in quality of life assessment: Key issues in the 1990s. In S. R. Walker & R. M. Rosser (Eds.), *Quality of life assessment: Key issues in the 1990's* (pp. 209–220). Dordrecht, The Netherlands: Kluwer Academic Publishers.

Cohen, S., Kessler, R. C., & Gordon, L. U. (Eds.). (1995). *Measuring stress. A guide for health and social scientists*. New York: Oxford University Press.

Gill, T. M., & Feinstein, A. R. (1994). A critical appraisal of the quality of quality-of-life measurements. *Journal of the American Medical Association, 272*, 619–626.

Hyland, M. (1992). A reformulation of quality of life for medical science. *Quality of Life Research, 1*, 267–272.

Katz, S., & Apkom, C. A. (1976). Index of ADL. *Medical Care, 14*, 116–118.

Leung, K. F., Tay, M., Cheng, S. W., & Lin, F. (1997). *Hong Kong Chinese version, World Health Organization Quality of Life Measure: Abbreviated version*. Hong Kong: Hong Kong Hospital Authority.

Melzack, R. (1975). The McGill Pain Questionnaire: Major properties and scoring methods. *Pain, 1*, 277–299.

Orley, J., & Birrell Weisen, R. (1998). Mental health promotion: What it is and what it is not. *International Journal of Mental Health Promotion, 1*, 41–44.

Orley, J., Saxena, S., & Herrman, H. (1998). Quality of life and mental illness: Reflections from the perspective of the WHOQOL. *British Journal of Psychiatry, 172*, 291–293.

Patrick, D. L., & Bergner, M. (1990). Measurement of health status in the 1990's. *Annual Review of Public Health, 11*, 165–183.

UNDP. (1995). *Human development report 1995*. New York: Oxford University Press.

Ware, J. W., Snow, K. K., Kosinski, M., & Gandek, B. (1993). *SF36 health survey manual and interpretation guide*. Boston, MA: The Health Institute, New England Medical Center.

WHO. (1996). Constitution of the World Health Organization. In *Basic documents* (41st ed., pp. 1–18). Geneva, Switzerland: Author.

WHO. (1998). *Review of the Constitution and regional arrangements of the World Health Organization: Report of the special group* (Executive Board document EB101/7). Geneva, Switzerland: Author.

WHOQOL Group. (1994). The development of the World Health Organization quality of life as-
    sessment instrument (WHOQOL). In J. Orley & W. Kuyken (Eds.), *Quality of life assessment:
    International perspectives* (pp. 41–57). Berlin, Germany: Springer.
WHOQOL Group. (1995). The World Health Organization quality of life assessment (WHOQOL):
    Position paper from the World Health Organization. *Social Science and Medicine, 41*, 1403–
    1409.
WHOQOL Group. (1998). The World Health Organization quality of life assessment (WHOQOL):
    Development and general psychometric properties. *Social Science and Medicine, 46*, 1569–
    1584.

Chapter 24

Harnessing Pleasure for Population Health Ends

Olabisi A. Odejide and Biola Odejide

Although the imagery of pleasure is prevalent in Nigerian cultures, attitudes towards pleasure are mixed. Pleasure on the one hand is regarded as healthy and desirable but on the other hand also is considered destructive in excess. In fact, this ambivalence is descriptive of attitudes towards alcohol as well; the social consensus that favors integrated, social drinking similarly disapproves of excessive drinking. In this chapter, we examine beverage alcohol consumption according to the context-of-use approach advocated by Roche and Evans (1998); more specifically, we attempt to reveal the beliefs and social practices surrounding consumption and thereby understand the meaning that alcohol has for users in Nigeria. We conclude by making policy recommendations in line with the specific images of drinking and pleasure prevalent in Nigerian society.

METHODOLOGY

For the studies described here, four focus groups were created, each comprising 8 to 10 persons ranging in age from 18 to 65 years and including drinkers and nondrinkers, males and females, and Christians and Moslems. The individual groups were drawn respectively from (a) junior workers (e.g., drivers, office assistants, cleaners) in a health institution, (b) university students from various faculties, (c) inhabitants of a rural village about 40 km from Ibadan, and (d) lecturers in Yoruba studies from various tertiary institutions. The latter group was included in particular for its expertise in Yoruba traditional beliefs and practices.[1]

This investigation of various socioeconomic strata of Nigerian society found that there was a consensus about the concept of pleasure. For the respondents, pleasure had two essential dimensions: (a) its relationship with emotional states, and (b) its commonly gregarious nature as an activity. Pleasure was defined by these respondents as "satisfying oneself" and "making oneself happy" (male lecturer). Its pursuit was seen as a congenial activity involving friends, family and coworkers, occuring most commonly in the form of recreation after work or the celebration of special occasions such as *idawo* (announcing the birth of a child), naming ceremonies, burials, and house warmings.

Pleasure further involved enjoyment, having a nice time, drinking alcohol, smoking cigarettes, dancing, playing games, and, among the men, "relaxing with women." Notably, the female lecturers in the fourth group were less tolerant of this last category, that is, the men's reference to women as objects of pleasure. However, the participants were unanimous in feeling that pleasure occurs if one is not under tension or pressure, or depressed—indeed, if one is totally at ease with oneself. In summary, respondents felt pleasure is healthy and desirable.

DRINKING AND PLEASURE

In all four groups, alcohol was strongly linked with pleasure. Its use was seen as a *sine qua non* of all celebrations, "an obliterator of sadness" (male villager), a promoter of social discourse, and an aid in resolving conflict. Alcohol was seen as important in ensuring societal harmony through its disinhibiting effects; as one of the male junior workers put it, "a drinker holds no malice." The lecturers in Yoruba studies adduced "evidence" from the Ifa Corpus (Yoruba divination system) to show that alcohol helps resolve issues by relaxing participants, unearthing deep-seated feelings, aiding recall of events, and facilitating amicable settlement of conflicts. Drinking is considered so vital to the resolution of any serious conflict that, after the settlement, the two warring parties are made to drink from the same calabash to seal the agreement.

The university students drew attention to the importance of alcohol use in celebrating significant life events of the Yoruba man such as at ceremonies concerning naming, marriage, and death. One male university student noted:

> Alcohol is spiritual. The essence of the Yoruba man is not complete without alcohol. It is essential for libation. There are a lot of wrong impressions concerning alcohol use—that is, that alcohol use is the source of intoxication, especially in our society today. Take a Yoruba community, when someone is getting married, the ceremony is never complete without the use of alcohol.

Social drinking also creates linkages that facilitate group help for people of lower socioeconomic status in, for example, the securing of employment. For this group, alcohol use is not only useful in celebrations, it is also acceptable, worthwhile, and respectable. They believe that "a drinker is one who socializes; he never loses popularity." One male villager said, "Once you see palm wine in front of a person, you don't ask him again if all is well." In contrast, a teetotaler was perceived as a "dangerous person," "an introvert," a person with a "deep, unfathomable mind," "a withdrawn person," and "a person to be feared."

The pattern of drinking preferred is convivial drinking, because it limits excessive use and encourages sharing. In contrast, individual drinkers are perceived as being miserly and prone to become alcoholic. If taken in moderation, alcohol was regarded as an energizing substance which improves the quality of people's physical and emotional health. This view tends to support recent scientific evidence that moderate consumption of alcohol reduces risk of cardiovascular disease and all-cause mortality rates (Holman, 1995, as cited in Roche & Evans, 1998; U.K. Department of Health and Social Security, 1995; WHO, 1994).

These findings support reports from previous studies (Netting, 1964; Odejide, 1978, 1979, 1982, 1989; Odejide & Olatawura, 1977; Ohaeri & Odejide, 1993; Ohaeri et al., 1996; Pan, 1975), which show that alcohol plays a socially harmonizing role in Nigerian communities. The respondents' attitudes also buttress suggestions that the current focus on drinking problems should shift from alcohol as a substance to the consequences of mixing its use with other behaviors that thereby may become hazardous, such as driving and certain workplace tasks (Roche & Evans, 1998; see also Chapter 25).

CULTURAL CONSTRAINTS ON DRINKING

There is evidence in Nigerian culture of alcohol's very negative potential for individuals and their social circles. There was a consensus among those in the focus groups that societal sanctions do prevent excessive drinking. Such sanctions mentioned by respondents included exclusion from clubs, financial penalties, verbal disapproval, and enforcement of consumption limits by members of organizations. Excessive use was condemned and moderation commended. The negative connotations of unacceptable alcohol use may be summed up in the pejorative terms for excessive drinking. Derived from intoxicated behavior manifest in intoxicated drunkards, such terms include *O te nile ana* (the one who disgraces himself in his in-laws' house); *Paa laa gbaju* (the one who slaps others); *Fidi gbogi* (the one who crawls on his backside); and *O tele koo* (one who marches around aggressively). A drunkard was described as a "despicable person" (male university student). The general attitude towards drinking was summed up with the words, "A person with good upbringing can drink but he must not drink to excess." Drunkards were perceived as even less discerning than were insane people.

Religious prohibition of drinking was reported to be enforced more effectively among devotees of traditional religions than among adherents of imported faiths like Islam and Christianity. This was particularly true in the case of followers of such gods as Obatala, the Yoruba god of creation, who prohibits consumption of alcohol. Jokes frequently were made about drinking among Christians and Muslims even if they resided in ostensibly "dry" states. However, worship of some traditional gods such as Ogun, the god of iron, required abundant drinking.

Although alcohol was perceived as aiding productivity among persons in the armed forces and the entertainment industry, certain occupational constraints on drinking were recognized. These constraints were noted in particular among those who require dexterity and mental acuity for their tasks, such as roof builders, palm-wine tappers, traditional surgeons, drivers, electrical workers, and grinding-machine operators.

Gender and age were important constraints to drinking. Women's roles as homemakers and nurturers of children prevented them from drinking alcohol except for so-called "women's drinks," unfermented beverages. This was tied to the cultural belief that women cannot keep secrets. Exceptions to this rule were made for female palm-wine sellers, commercial sex workers, or "overly liberated women." Underage drinking, that is, drinking before puberty, was frowned upon and thought to lead to delinquent behavior and danger of addiction. One of our respondents, a male university student, noted:

> The use of alcohol shows the level of maturity as well, because somebody who takes alcohol and knows how to handle it and does not get intoxicated—he's someone who's actually very mature. Our elders gather round and use alcohol appropriately. They will not allow children to use it because they believe they are not mature enough.

The concept of moderate drinking was operationalized as "knowing one's limit," "drinking to one's capacity," or "being able to control one's intake." Moderate drinkers drink when they go to special occasions and when friends offer them alcohol. In addition, they eat before drinking, restrict their number of drinks, and do not drink in the mornings. One of the villagers concluded that alcohol is good in moderation, but not if it causes unseemly or violent behavior.

Taken together, respondents reflected the view that alcohol consumed in moderation is pleasurable and desirable but that unwise consumption practices can lead to excessive drinking, intoxication, and embarrassing or inappropriate behavior. Indeed, even the social settings in which alcohol consumption was considered appropriate were quite well delimited. These included bars, clubs, and hotels but excluded social contexts in which, for example, a person may be interacting with his or her in-laws.

ALCOHOL POLICIES IN NIGERIA

Alcohol Importation and Local Production, Distribution, and Sales

Obot (1992) noted that drugs as well as alcohol were considered a problem long before Nigeria became independent from Great Britain in 1960. Colonial administrators were influenced by a home policy that encouraged temperance, voiced concerns about alcohol-related problems, and promulgated laws to control the "booming trade in alcoholic beverages, opium and its derivatives" (p. 482). They tried to control trade liquor in Africa for both social and economic reasons. Thus, the earliest attempts to curb alcohol use in Nigeria were tied to the temperance movement in Britain. Missionaries and colonial administrators were joined in their war against alcohol by local chieftains like Malike, the "Mohammedan Emir of Nupe in the Niger who had written to Bishop Ajayi Crowther, the first African bishop in Nigeria, to beg the English queen to prevent the bringing of rum into this land ... to spoil this country" (Pan, 1975, p. 11).

Economic considerations included a trade rivalry between Britain and Germany, the latter of which had increased its importation of liquor and was undermining the British cotton trade. In 1917 and 1918, Native Liquor Ordinances were passed to control the sale and manufacture of alcohol in all the African colonies. Between 1886 and 1919, eight major initiatives were taken by the colonial government to regulate alcohol importation, distillation, sale, and possession (Obot, 1992). However, "[alcohol] abolition was a failure. Nigerian gin produced from palm wine became illicit gin by law. The criminalization of a long entrenched way of life demanded consistent enforcement which was a difficult task to perform in a colonial set-up as it is in more modern settings" (Obot, 1992, p. 487). The manufacture and sale of local gin was prohibited for many years.

Today, however, alcohol is a legal substance and one that is widely consumed. One reason for its legalization in the 1970s was to support breweries whose brewing processes removed noxious additives often found in illicit alcoholic beverages (Odejide, Ohaeri, & Ikuesan, 1988). Beer breweries increased from 7 in 1977 to 34 in 1985 (Federal Office of Statistics, 1985), and by 1989 there were four distilleries and nine wine-producing plants. The volume of wines and spirits imported into the country jumped from 1.0 million hL in 1982 to 5.9 million hL in 1983 (Odejide, 1989).

The only exception to the free sale and use of alcohol is in certain states to the north where Islam is prevalent. Yet even in such places, as our focus groups and Ifabumuyi's (1982) study showed, covert use is commonplace. With alcohol no longer considered a drug by the majority of Nigerians, strife frequently arises from attempts to enforce antidrinking laws in dry states that have substantial non-Muslim populations.

There is an absence of strict government control over the production, consumption, or sale of domestically produced alcoholic beverages. In fact, the government's primary roles are to (a) determine the quantity and types of both raw materials and alcoholic beverages to be imported, (b) grant licenses to the respective importers, and (c) license local alcohol manufacturers. One result of the government's limited activity in the beverage-alcohol market is the lack of comprehensive records of local beverage alcohol produced. Statistics are available, however, on the number of breweries in Nigeria and the annual quantity of alcohol imported—the majority of which comes from Europe and North America.

Alcohol Marketing

There is a ready market for alcohol from the giant multinational corporations in Europe and America that produce under local license. The industry's marketing strategies are drawn largely from those of the Western world and currently are regulated less stringently than in the West. As Wallack and Montgomery (1992) observed, expanded delivery systems, proliferating communication channels, and increased privatization all are creating unprecedented opportunities for transnational advertisers to market heavily advertised products abroad. The products they advertise range from soft drinks, cigarettes, beer, and wine to processed foods, over-the-counter drugs, and toiletries. Alcoholic beverages are advertised freely in the media as products that create strength, success, and status. The value of alcohol as a "blood tonic" is prominently emphasized in television advertisements. So also is alcohol's association with the most desirable events in life, such as naming ceremonies, house warmings, and success at work.

Critics have criticized the advertising's potential for increasing the illegal use of alcohol among minors. A general code for advertising has been put in place by the Advertising Practitioners Council of Nigeria, but the only specific product it covers is cigarettes. There is currently no legislation comparable to that of some Western nations that restricts broadcasting time for advertisements or prohibits sponsorship of sporting events by certain industries. In fact, the government gains substantial revenue from trade in alcoholic beverages through taxes on manufacturers, excise duties on goods or commodities produced or sold within the country, duties on imported raw materials, income tax, and revenue from ancillary institutions.

Enforcement

The federal and most state governments in Nigeria do not at present regulate the availability or consumption of alcohol. In the southern part of the country, alcohol vendors are not restricted as to the hours of sale. Many sales outlets, especially those in residential buildings, are not licensed. Alcohol sales are illegal in motor parks or roadside rest stops, but this law is not enforced. Young people, regardless of age, are allowed to purchase alcohol even though drinking by prepubescent children is illegal. And although drunk-driving laws are enforced by the Federal Road Safety Corps, the absence of breathalyzers and defined blood alcohol levels makes their application a discretionary act on the part of law enforcement. The corps, however, has initiated primary prevention campaigns in all states of the federation to caution drivers against drunk driving.

RESEARCH INTO PATTERNS OF ALCOHOL USE

Epidemiological Studies

Studies of alcohol use in Nigeria have shown that, in rural communities, alcohol is most commonly used during festivals and parties. On such occasions, people may drink to acute intoxication, the effects of which wear off over several days (Odejide, 1979; Odejide & Olatawura, 1977). Moderate or heavy drinking is uncommon before the age of 35 years, and it is mainly a male affair—even after the sudden increase in alcohol production and availability that began with the oil boom in 1977. Studies of alcohol-consumption patterns have been hampered by the fact that people rarely complain of alcohol problems to their doctors. Working in Kaduna in the north, Ifabumuyi (1982) found that a high percentage of newly registered patients in out-patient clinics had definite indications of alcoholism. Other studies based on nonhospital populations revealed that women were drinking more than previously—often openly in social clubs (Odejide, 1982). Youths also seemed to have increased consumption (Anumonye, 1980; Ebie & Pela, 1981; Ebie, 1988; Ihezue, 1988; Nevadomsky, 1981; Oshodin, 1981).

Several authors have bemoaned the availability of and easy access to alcohol in Nigeria. As observed in focus groups, the use of alcohol in Nigeria is accepted as a normal pattern of behavior. This may have encouraged state governments of the federation to allow the rapid establishment of alcohol manufacturing industries during the country's oil boom. Since then, preference has grown for commercially manufactured alcoholic beverages over locally brewed ones. Commercial alcoholic beverages are supposed to be sold under license in Nigeria, but the laws cannot be enforced.

As previously mentioned, there is no age limit on alcohol purchases, no limit on the hours during which alcohol sales are permitted, and no defined limit for blood alcohol level when driving a vehicle. The lack of precise policies in these areas permits young people to use alcohol freely in peer-group settings outside the home. Odejide, Ohaeri, Adelekan, and Ikuesan (1987) referred to this scenario as part of sociocultural change. They noted, "We found that youths now prefer a more regular use of alcohol at social clubs and in the evenings. This may be an indication of the beginning of a socio-cultural shift from the traditional to the more western style" (p. 232).

Although these studies reveal a rapid increase in alcohol use and the social and physical health consequences of this consumption, social responses to these trends in terms of policy formulation and treatment have been inadequate. It is noteworthy, however, that the premise of these studies is that alcohol is a potential health hazard; they do not consider drinking as a source of pleasure or recreation that can be accommodated and kept within bounds in a particular social milieu.

Clinical Studies

Studies on alcohol use in Nigeria have focused primarily on the medical model of health and disease. In support of Ledermann's (1956) single-distribution theory, researchers in Nigeria have concentrated on the quantity of alcohol consumed and its direct social and health impact (Adelekan, Abiodun, Obayan, Oni, & Ogunremi, 1992; Ebie, 1988; Nigeria Drug Law Enforcement Agency, 1992, 1993; Odejide, 1989; Odejide et al., 1987; Odejide, Ohaeri, Adelekan, & Ikue-san, 1989; Ohaeri & Odejide, 1993).

In almost all the studies cited here, alcohol consumption was evaluated in terms of units of alcohol consumed per day, week, or month, without relating it to the contexts or circumstances surrounding drinking episodes. A good example of this is the epidemiological study conducted by the Drug Demand Reduction Unit of the Nigerian National Drug Law Enforcement Agency (1992, 1993) in the cities of Lagos and Kano. These studies used stratified samples, targeted alcohol (among other substances), and measured variables that included units of alcohol consumed per day or per week, frequency of use, and the health or social impact of alcohol use. The underlying assumption was a linear correlation between the amount of alcohol consumed and the eventual damage to the individual or society. No attempt was made to identify the at-risk or hazardous episodes of drinking, nor the environment in which alcohol consumption by the students occurred (see Chapter 25).

A common observation in the studies was the early age at which alcohol use began (Nevadomsky, 1981; Odejide & Sanda, 1976; Ohaeri & Odejide, 1993). This pattern of adolescent drinking is at variance with the traditional Nigerian drinking culture. Odejide et al. (1987) drew attention to this change in the pattern of alcohol use in their study of drinking behavior and social change among youths in two cities of Nigeria: "In the last decade ... there has been a noticeable trend of youths getting more and more involved in alcohol use" (p. 232). This was attributed to increased availability of alcoholic beverages combined with the absence of regulations.

In addition to indicating increased drinking by females, some of the studies noted also have shown various pathologies associated with alcohol use in Nigerian youths; alcohol users were found to be more involved in accidents and the use of the other psychoactive drugs than nonusers. For the purpose of education and prevention, however, it would have been more informative to identify the environmental context in which adolescent alcohol and drug use occurred.

Another area that research has investigated in the past two decades is the pathology associated with alcohol use. Ohaeri and Odejide (1993) studied admissions for drug- and alcohol-related problems in Nigerian care facilities in 1 year. The authors found that more than 800 youths, especially males, were admitted for drug-related problems. Commonly, the young patients were multiple drug-users (especially alcohol and cannabis) and they were reported to have been involved in traffic accidents or, as a result of aberrant behaviors when intoxicated, in delinquent acts at school or at home. Physical damage such as liver cirrhosis, brain damage, or pancreatitis and psychological complications such as delusional jealousy and alcoholic hallucinosis were common symptoms in the middle and older age groups. The differences in symptoms between young and middle-aged patients indicate that different treatment approaches are needed for each population segment. The results also support the need to focus on problems not associated with chronic drinking but rather with acute or episodic drinking (Roche & Evans, 1998; see Chapter 25). From a prevention perspective, it is necessary to identify high-risk drinking situations and circumstances within different cultures in order to establish harm-minimizing principles and practices.

Case Study of Pleasurable Alcohol Use

If the premise of the studies discussed previously is that alcohol is basically a potential health hazard, Ohaeri et al.'s (1996) study of alcohol use among a nationwide university student club called the Kegites presents a fascinating picture of the pleasurable uses of alcohol (palm wine) within a regulated drinking setting. Among other activities, the club seeks to promote moderate consumption in correspondence with traditional African culture and customs. Official engagements of the club are characterized by *gyrations*, exuberant singing, drumming, and dancing in which the only alcoholic beverage allowed is the locally brewed palm wine. In addition, there are strict rules to prevent intoxication. As noted by the authors, "The Kegites are very conscious of what others think about them and like to guard their reputation jealously" (p. 181). Hence, anyone wearing the regalia and found drinking industrial brews, even outside the official setting, faces severe punishment. An important goal of the Kegites is to prevent intoxication; hence the popular greeting *"Wa ka without fall,"* meaning "May you never stagger as drunken people do" (p. 181). The authors argue that there are elements within the Kegite club's ideals that can be used for preventive drug education in institutions of higher learning in Nigeria. These include, in particular, the discouragement of heavy drinking and the enforcement of rules relating to drinking norms.

OBSERVATIONS AND RECOMMENDATIONS

Recommendations about alcohol use have to be placed in a cultural perspective—
especially those concerning acceptable drinking patterns. As Whitehead (1996)
observes, the "effectiveness of control measures depends on the particular drinking culture of the country in question" (p. 163). The focus-group findings reviewed in this chapter, combined with other systematic research, support this
observation. Among the resulting observations and recommendations concerning
alcohol use in Nigeria are the following:

- There is a strong link between alcohol and pleasure.
- Drinking is approved of, but drunkenness is not.
- Drinking per se is not disapproved of or stigmatized.
- There are strong traditional cultural constraints on drinking.
- The preference is for convivial as opposed to solitary drinking.
- Although the oil boom was seen to encourage more drinking, the sub-
sequent decline in the nation's economy has acted as a constraint on excessive
drinking.
- Existing regulatory laws are not being enforced.
- Despite the previous point, self-imposed limits and social sanctions are
very effective in creating moderate, safe drinking practices.
- Nigeria's drinking norms prohibit drinking by children and, by extension,
imply a minimum drinking age.
- Blood alcohol levels must be established and regulated for persons engaged in occupations involving activities such as driving and operating machinery.
- The government should regulate the hours during which alcohol may be
purchased legally.
- Advertising practices that glamorize alcohol use and may induce children
to experiment prematurely with drinking must be evaluated and controlled, either
informally or formally.
- Awareness must be created that occasional bouts of excessive drinking
among moderate drinkers can be hazardous to the self and society.

PLEASURE AND POLICY

The concept of pleasure in relation to alcohol use adds another dimension to
alcohol policy. The views expressed by the focus-group respondents support
recent observations that we need to expand beyond the per capita consumption theory to recognize patterns of use of alcohol and drinking occasions (see
Chapter 19). This is particularly true because "the number of heavy drinking
occasions has better predictive power for drinking patterns than the level of alcohol consumption" (Roche & Evans, 1998, p. 250; see also Stockwell, Hanks,
Lang, & Rydon, 1996). Individuals, groups, and communities therefore need to
be better informed about the risks associated with acute alcohol consumption.

The following policy recommendations respond to this perspective as well as to observations elicited from our field reports.

Information, Education, and Communication

Although alcohol has been used in Nigeria for ages, little attention has been paid to the risk factors associated with occasional intoxication among otherwise moderate drinkers. Factors such as the circumstances under which alcohol is consumed, the individual's susceptibility to the effects of alcohol, and frequency of intense consumption usually are downplayed. Such factors, however, may influence typically low- or moderate-level consumers to become intoxicated and manifest maladaptive behaviors. This would seemingly contribute to the preventive paradox theory (Kreitman, 1986), which argues that although low to moderate consumers are a low-risk group, they collectively produce the majority of alcohol problems because they number much more than the heavy drinkers.

Group and occasional drinking are popular in Nigeria, and thus it is important for drinkers to have appropriate information on hazardous drinking patterns. Such information could be included in the educational programs of primary, secondary, and tertiary schools. As previously argued by Odejide et al. (1989, p. 234), "Education on drug and alcohol use should be considered part of the individual's needed equipment to take responsibility for his own health and lifelong promotion of good health. Such an education should be aimed at giving the pupils requisite qualifications for their independent and responsible decision, both in principle and in concrete choice regarding their own use."

Furthermore, because drinking usually takes place in bars, hotels, and social gatherings, it is necessary to work out training programs on harmful alcohol use for people working in such places. Saltz (1987) found that server training aimed at reducing the risk of customers' intoxication was found to reduce the chances of intoxication by one half. In fact, similar methods of server control are already in practice in traditional settings where fellow drinkers, especially older people, stop excessive drinking by others.

Another strategy for reducing episodes of intoxication is the use of public health messages targeted at youths and adults respectively. There is diversity in the drinking patterns of these different groups and they each need different prevention messages. Government agencies, nongovernmental organizations, and local communities should be involved in the conception and implementation of these educational policies.

Minimum Drinking Age

In traditional Nigerian culture, children are not allowed to drink alcohol. The accepted premise is that they are not mature enough and that drinking is thus hazardous for such individuals. This belief easily can be translated into a socially accepted policy that sets a minimum age for alcohol purchase and use. Furthermore, as Whitehead (1996) argued, young drinkers are at increased risk because they are both inexperienced drinkers and inexperienced drivers.

Drinking and Driving

Nigeria has one of the highest traffic-fatality rates in the world (Federal Road Safety Corps, 1988). Alcohol probably contributes to this high rate of accidents; public-transport drivers are known, for example, to take *ogogoro* (a locally brewed gin) to increase their alertness before starting on long journeys. The Federal Road Safety Corps has embarked on an aggressive anti–drinking-and-driving campaign, which includes preventive and punitive measures. Jingles in the media, prominent billboards along the highways, road patrols, lectures, and fines are all being utilized.

As mentioned previously, however, Nigeria has no policy on an appropriate legal blood alcohol concentration for drivers. In the Western world, the limit varies from country to country, ranging from 80 mg/100 mL in the United Kingdom to 20 mg/100 mL in Sweden. The existence of blood alcohol concentration policies often serves as a deterrent to drivers. In order to reduce fatal crashes on Nigeria's roads, policies must be established that clearly define drunk driving. Such policies will be widely accepted, but enforcement agents will need to be monitored to ensure that they apply the law.

Licensing Hours

Community standards make it unacceptable to drink alcohol in the mornings. A policy that seeks to limit hours for the purchase and use of alcohol to the evening period is thus likely to be accepted. From the focus groups, it is clear that this is already in operation in locations such as university campuses, where sales are limited to the hours between 4 and 10 PM in student union buildings. This type of local policy could be applied nationally and alcohol sales could be restricted to licensed premises.

Local Alcoholic Beverages

Before the introduction of commercial alcoholic beverages in Nigeria, there were varieties of locally fermented alcoholic beverages such as palm wine; *ogogoro*, a distillate of palm wine; and *burukutu*, a fermented by-product of Guinea corn. These local drinks are still the favorites of peasant farmers living in rural areas, who comprise 60% to 70% of Nigeria's population. The current decline in the nation's economy has reintroduced local drinks, and especially palm wine, to better-educated people in urban centers.

Data are needed to determine the patterns of consumption of these local beverages in order to devise suitable strategies for their nonhazardous use. The distillation of palm wine into *ogogoro* is similar to the process for industrial spirits, but the product has many impurities. Regular users often get addicted and eventually die of malnutrition or concurrent infections such as tuberculosis (Odejide, 1978). Educational campaigns to encourage moderate use of these local alcohols in rural as well as urban areas is urgent.

CONCLUSION

As shown in this study and in previous research, Nigerians closely associate alcohol use with pleasure. Moreover, they commonly believe that moderate alcohol use promotes good health but excessive use destroys health and impairs social relationships. The focus in the past decades had been on controlling per capita alcohol consumption as a means to reduce adverse social and health consequences of excessive and prolonged use. Minimal attention has been paid to the context in which alcohol is used and the factors that constitute high risk to low- and moderate-level drinkers.

There are indications, however, that the circumstances under which alcohol is used, and episodes of intoxication, binge drinking, and other hazardous uses of alcohol, predict drinking problems better than does the level of consumption. The current study tends to support this observation, pointing to the need to reorient prevention strategies towards harm reduction—especially in the areas of acute risk such as intoxication, drunk driving, and binge-drinking episodes.

In creating such strategies and policies, governmental and public health officials must build on existing beliefs and patterns concerning alcohol consumption in Nigeria. Such indigenous attitudes support moderate drinking and restrictions on hazardous alcohol use, and they offer a strong basis for developing a usable, modern alcohol policy. The involvement of local communities in the development and promulgation of such policies, along with prevention and treatment programs, is both plausible and desirable. Furthermore, another strategy worth exploring is enlistment of both local and international alcohol manufacturer cooperation in creating sensible drinking practices through both the responsible promotion of alcohol use and restrictions on the local sale and consumption of beverage alcohol.

ACKNOWLEDGMENTS

The authors acknowledge the assistance of Dr. Olajide Morakinyo who gathered part of the data, and of the following groups: the Yoruba Studies Association, University of Ibadan students, staff of the University College Hospital, and residents of Bare village (via Ibadan).

NOTE

1. Yoruba is one of the three major language and ethnic groups in Nigeria; the Yoruba people are located in the southwestern part of the country.

REFERENCES

Adelekan, M. L., Abiodun, O. A., Obayan, A. O., Oni, G., & Ogunremi, O. O. (1992). Prevalence and pattern of substance use among undergraduates in a Nigerian university. *Drug and Alcohol Dependence, 29*, 255–261.

Anumonye, A. (1980). Drug use among young people in Lagos, Nigeria. *Bulletin in Narcotics, 32*, 39–45.

Ebie, J. C. (1988). *Report of a research project on substance abuse in some urban and rural areas of Nigeria*. Lausanne, Switzerland: International Council on Alcohol and Addictions.

Ebie J. C., & Pela, O. A. (1981). Some socio-cultural aspects of drug use among students in Benin City, Nigeria. *Drug and Alcohol Dependence, 8*, 265–301.

Federal Office of Statistics. (1985). *Industrial Profile*. Lagos, Nigeria: Author.

Federal Road Safety Corps. (1988, June). *Report, January 1985 to June 1988*. Lagos, Nigeria: Author.

Ifabumuyi, O. I. (1982). Alcoholism: A missed diagnosis. In O. E. Erinosho & N. W. Bell (Eds.), *Mental health in Africa* (pp. 115–121). Ibadan, Nigeria: University of Ibadan Press.

Ihezue, U. H. (1988). Alcohol and drug taking among medical students at a Nigerian university campus. *Journal of the National Medical Association, 80*, 191–195.

Kreitman, N. (1986). Alcohol consumption and the preventive paradox. *British Journal of Addiction, 81*, 353–364.

Ledermann, S. (1956). *Alcool, alcoolisme, alcoolisation* [Alcohol, alcoholism, alcoholization] (Cahier 29, Institut National d'Etudes Démographiques). Paris: Presses Universitaires de France.

Netting, R. M. (1964). Beer as a locus of value among the West African Kofyar. *American Anthropologist, 66*, 375–384.

Nevadomsky, J. J. (1981). Patterns of self-reported drug use among secondary school students in Bendel State. *Bulletin in Narcotics, 33*, 9–19.

Nigeria Drug Law Enforcement Agency. (1992). *1992 Drug Data Collection*. Lagos, Nigeria: Author.

Nigeria Drug Law Enforcement Agency. (1993). *1993 Drug Data Collection*. Lagos, Nigeria: Author.

Obot, S. I. (1992). Ethical and legal issues in the control of drug abuse and drug trafficking: The Nigerian case. *Social Science and Medicine, 35*, 481–493.

Odejide, A. O. (1978). Alcoholism: A major health hazard in Nigeria? *Nigerian Medical Journal, 8*, 230–232.

Odejide, A. O. (1979). Alcohol use in a sub-group of literate Nigerians. *African Journal of Psychiatry, 1*, 15–20.

Odejide, A. O. (1982). Pattern of psychotropic drug use: A survey of civil servants in Ibadan, Nigeria. In *Proceedings of the 3rd International Congress on Alcoholism and Drug Dependence, Tangiers, Morocco* (pp. 33–34). Lausanne, Switzerland: International Council on Alcohol and Addictions.

Odejide, A. O. (1989, February 9). *A nation at risk: Alcohol and substance abuse among Nigerian youths*. University of Ibadan Inaugural Lecture, Ibadan, Nigeria.

Odejide, A. O., Ohaeri, J. U., Adelekan, M. L., & Ikuesan, B. A. (1987). Drinking behaviour and social change among youths in Nigeria: A study of two cities. *Drug and Alcohol Dependence, 20*, 227–233.

Odejide, A. O., Ohaeri, J. U., Adelekan, M. L., & Ikuesan, B. A. (1989). Alcohol treatment systems in Nigeria. *Alcohol and Alcoholism, 24*, 347–353.

Odejide, A .O., Ohaeri, J. U., & Ikuesan, B. A. (1988). Alcohol use among Nigerian youths: The need for drug education and alcohol policy. *Drug and Alcohol Dependence, 23*, 231–235.

Odejide, A. O., & Olatawura, M. O. (1977). Alcohol use in a Nigerian rural community. *African Journal of Psychiatry, 3*, 69–74.

Odejide, A. O., & Sanda, A. O. (1976). Observation on drug abuse in Western Nigeria. *African Journal of Psychiatry, 2*, 303–309.

Ohaeri, J. U., & Odejide, A. O. (1993). Admissions for drug and alcohol-related problems in Nigerian psychiatric care facilities in one year. *Drug and Alcohol Dependence, 31*, 101–109.

Ohaeri, J. U., Oduyela, S. O., Odejide, A. O., Dipe, T. M., Ikwuagu, P. U., & Zamani, A. (1996). The history and drinking behaviour of the Nigerian students' palmwine drinking club. *Drugs, Education, Prevention and Policy, 3,* 171–183.

Oshodin, G. O. (1981). Alcohol abuse in a case study of school students in rural area of Benin District, Nigeria. *Drug and Alcohol Dependence, 8,* 207–213

Pan, L. (1975). *Alcohol in Colonial Africa* (Vol. 22) Helsinki: Finnish Foundation for Alcohol Studies.

Roche, A. M., & Evans, K. R. (1998) The implications of drinking patterns for primary prevention, education and screening. In M. Grant & J. Litvak (Eds.), *Drinking patterns and their consequences* (pp. 243–265). Washington, DC: Taylor & Francis.

Saltz, R. F. (1987). Roles of bars and restaurants in preventing alcohol-impaired driving: An evaluation of server intervention. *Evaluation and Health Professions, 10,* 5–27.

Stockwell, T., Hawks, D., Lang, E., & Rydon, P. (1996). Unravelling the preventive paradox for acute alcohol problems. *Drug and Alcohol Review, 15,* 7–15.

U.K. Department of Health and Social Security. (1995). *Sensible drinking: The report of an interdepartmental working group.* London: Her Majesty's Stationery Office.

Wallack, L., & Montgomery, K. (1992). Advertising for all by the year 2000: Public health implications for less developed countries. *Journal of Public Health Policy, 13,* 204–223.

Whitehead, S. (1996). The impact of alcohol control measures on drinking patterns. In M. Grant & J. Litvak (Eds.), *Drinking patterns and their consequences* (pp. 153–164). Washington, DC: Taylor & Francis.

WHO. (1994). *Cardiovascular disease risk factors: New areas for research* (WHO Technical Report 841). Geneva: World Health Organization.

Chapter 25

Reducing Harmful Drinking

Tim Stockwell and Eric Single

This chapter outlines some basic concepts and directions for programs and policies designed to reduce the harm sometimes associated with drinking alcohol.

There can be no doubting the great cost of alcohol-related harm in social,
health, and economic terms. Estimates in Australia, Canada, and the United
States indicate that alcohol accounts for 2% to 3% of total mortality, as well as
for large numbers of hospitalizations. The economic costs of alcohol misuse have
been estimated in the billions of dollars, accounting for 1.1% of gross domestic
product in Canada (Single, Robson, Xie, & Rehm, 1998), 1.4% in Australia
(Collins & Lapsley, 1991), and 1.7% in the United States (Rice, Kelman, Miller,
& Dunmeyer, 1990). This chapter outlines a risk- and harm-reduction approach
to reducing alcohol-related harm that is concerned with the overall amounts of
alcohol people drink, their patterns of consumption over time and place, and
other individual and environmental factors that increase risk. Although drinking
is not inevitably harmful, certain patterns and levels of drinking increase the
risk of various harms—risk that in turn, is further increased by a host of other
factors. A comprehensive national strategy to address alcohol problems must
seek to reduce the extent to which people engage in a variety of high-risk
drinking patterns.

WHAT IS HARMFUL DRINKING?

High-Risk Drinking Patterns

Different patterns or styles of drinking alcohol each carry with them their own
set of potential risks and benefits. A useful way to classify the many harms

associated with drinking is first to classify the major varieties of drinking patterns and then to identify the harms potentially associated with each. An early form of such a classification was Jellinek's (1960) description of types of alcoholism with each denoted by a letter of the Greek alphabet. Gamma and delta alcoholism both were considered to be varieties of the full-blown disease of alcoholism. Gamma alcoholism was characterized by a sporadic pattern of loss-of-control drinking whereby just one or two drinks invariably led to drunkenness, whereas delta alcoholism was characterized by a pattern of continuous heavy drinking spread evenly across all days and an "inability to abstain." Gamma and delta alcoholism reflect a fundamental distinction between acute and chronic excessive drinking patterns and problem consequences.

Thorley (1980) classified the broader range of alcohol-related problems according to three major patterns of excessive alcohol consumption: problems of intoxication (car crashes, violence, poisoning), problems of long-term use (liver disease, cancers, brain damage), and problems of dependence (withdrawal symptoms, possible disruption of social functioning). In answer to the question "What is harmful drinking?" this classification system suggests that drinking can be problematic if too much is drunk on one occasion, if alcohol is consumed in sufficient amounts over a period of many years, and, finally, if dependence on alcohol has developed. Each of these three instances, however, requires further definition: How much is "too much" on one occasion; what is a "sufficient amount" over many years; and what is "dependence?"

These are complex questions with which alcohol research has grappled for several decades. A number of conclusions, however, can be reached on the basis of current knowledge. First, it is not possible to define any specific amount of alcohol as inevitably harmful—whether in the short or long term. Nor can one identify with certainty the amount of alcohol that would need to be drunk over a given period for alcohol dependence to be established. Instead, it is possible to describe in general terms increasing levels of *risk* for a variety of harms as alcohol consumption also increases and continues. Second, the level of risk for an individual is further influenced by many factors other than the sheer amount of alcohol consumed. Such factors include differences in the rate at which alcohol is metabolized, the activities that accompany or follow drinking (e.g., driving versus watching television), use of other drugs, and other lifestyle and biological factors that reduce or increase risk of injury and illness.

If drinking an amount of alcohol is not invariably harmful, it follows that some harm reduction strategies might not necessarily require a reduction in consumption. Elsewhere we have defined this as a risk- and harm-reduction approach to alcohol-related problems (Single, 1997; Stockwell, Single, Hawks, & Rehm, 1997). Although most risk- and harm-reduction strategies require a reduction in alcohol consumption, this is not always the case. Thus the risk of alcohol-related crashes can be reduced by a variety of means, such as designated-driver schemes and improved public transportation, which even may allow individuals to drink more alcohol so long as they are not driving. Furthermore, the same level or pattern of consumption may incur extremely low or no risk for one kind of harm but high risk for another. For example, a pattern of drinking for a young adult male of four drinks (of 10 g of alcohol) four times per week probably does not pose long-term health risks. Four drinks in one hour, however, could significantly impair driving ability.

The Importance of Problems of Intoxication

At the total population level (and alcohol policy needs to be made at this most general level), all three of Thorley (1980) major varieties of alcohol problems must be considered. For example, to provide treatment services only for persons severely dependent on alcohol is to miss the nature and cause of most alcohol-related deaths. Only 10% of alcohol-related deaths can be directly linked to alcohol dependence. Furthermore, it is not sufficient to develop strategies that aim solely to reduce the incidence of such chronic conditions as liver cirrhosis, because the most recent estimates show that the majority of alcohol-related deaths are acute rather than chronic in nature. In fact, the more telling statistic, total potential years of life lost (PYLLs), points to the primacy of acute alcohol-related deaths, because such deaths often involve younger people. An Australian study found that 67% of all PYLLs were caused by alcohol are caused by single episodes of intoxication (English et al., 1995). A more recent Canadian study similarly estimated that 66% of all PYLLs caused by alcohol were caused by accidents and other acute causes (Single, Robson, Rehm, & Xie, 1999).

Responses to drinking problems have tended to ignore problems of intoxication. Most examples of research effort, services, and educational campaigns over the past few decades have focused on dependence and chronic health problems (Rehm et al., 1996; Stockwell, 1998). For example, English et al.'s (1995) major metaanalysis of the international literature on alcohol use and health problems found hundreds of studies linking levels of alcohol use to long-term health problems such as cancer, cirrhosis, and heart disease, but relatively few focusing on injury. A limitation of this research literature has been the failure to measure patterns of drinking, without which it is not possible to calculate the contribution of binge-style drinking over and above that of volume of alcohol consumed over longer periods of time.

Treatment services in most countries do not focus on the less-dependent drinkers for whom a goal of controlled drinking is often feasible (Heather & Robertson, 1981). Advice on low-risk drinking to the general population is almost invariably based on epidemiological studies biased towards measures of drinking volume and chronic health problems. As a consequence, few countries provide guidelines for safer drinking that distinguish between low-risk drinking on a single occasion and the average of consumption across all occasions. New Zealand is a rare exception (Alcohol Advisory Council of New Zealand, 1995).

Although problems of dependence and long-term drinking should not be ignored, drinking to intoxication also can be considered a gateway to these other
types of drinking problem. Occupational categories in which there is a high risk
for alcohol dependence such as writers, entertainers, and construction workers
(Parker & Harford, 1992) also have reputations for tolerating drunkenness. A
pattern of frequent heavy drinking, usually defined as more than five drinks per
occasion, has been found to contribute to the risk of a wide variety of health
and social problems over and above what would be predicted by the sheer volume of alcohol consumed over the long term (Rehm et al., 1996). Analyzing
U.S. national survey data, Greenfield (1996) found that persons consuming five
or more drinks at least twice a week accounted for the great bulk of reported
alcohol-related problems, both acute and chronic. A community survey of drinking patterns and signs of dependence in Australia found that as many as one
in five drinkers reported sometimes finding it hard to stop drinking until intoxicated and that this was the most commonly reported sign of alcohol dependence
(Stockwell, Sitharthan, McGrath, & Lang, 1994). Other studies have suggested
that such a loss-of-control style of drinking is the earliest sign of dependence
to emerge in the drinking careers of persons with severe alcohol dependence
(Orford & Hawker, 1974).

In summary, if one looks objectively at the patterns of alcohol use most
associated with death, injury, and illness, drinking to intoxication emerges as a
major contributor to short-term harm and, subsequently, to longer-term problems
including dependence. Drinking to intoxication, especially on a regular basis,
is high-risk drinking and worthy of close attention by those who wish to improve public health and safety. It is also a highly prevalent behavior. Oddy and
Stockwell (1995) calculated that 47% of the volume of all alcohol consumed
in Western Australia was in excess of four Australian standard drinks per day
for men and two for women—the nationally recommended levels for low-risk
consumption. Greenfield (1996) estimated that 80% of all alcohol consumed in
the United States was in excess of national drinking guidelines of up to 24 g
per day for a man and 12 g per day for a woman.

What is a High-Risk Drinking Level?

Different national authorities have arrived at widely different definitions of safe,
or low-risk, levels of alcohol consumption (International Center for Alcohol
Policies, 1996). Different criteria have been applied by different authorities in
weighing the evidence that has guided recommendations. Thus Ashley et al.
(1997) reviewed both the empirical evidence and professional opinion in the
development of a standard set of drinking guidelines for Ontario, Canada. Although acknowledging the existence of a more liberal school of thought, the
researchers concluded with a recommendation of no more than two drinks per
day for men and one for women on average and no more than two per day on
any one occasion (one drink was defined as 13.6 grams of ethyl alcohol.)

By contrast, English et al. (1995) plotted average daily drinking levels against the risk of an alcohol-related death and reported that the Australian drinking guidelines of 40 g per day for men and 20 g for women identified the point at which the risk curve escalated and risk of death from all causes began to significantly exceed that for abstainers. This metaanalysis provides the most precise basis for drinking advice about average daily levels of consumption that are low in risk for premature death from alcohol-related causes.

In relation to problems of intoxication, a number of studies based on large surveys of drinkers in different countries suggest that for men the risk of experiencing some acute problem from drinking on one occasion becomes significant at above 60 g and for women above 40 g. Single and Wortley (1993) reported that a frequency of five or more drinks (at 13.6 g) per day is a strong predictor of a variety of alcohol-related problems for Canadians. Crawford (1993) reported that frequency of drinking in excess of 64 g per occasion (eight British standard drinks) predicts a variety of mainly acute alcohol-related problems. Shepherd (1994) similarly reported that the risk of an alcohol-related injury becomes significant at a level of consumption of above 64 g. And Stockwell, Hawks, Lang, and Rydon (1996) reported that drinking in excess of 60 g for men and 40 g for women in an Australian survey was highly predictive of one of six types of acute alcohol-related problem.

More recently, McLeod, Stockwell, Phillip, and Stevens (1998) have reported the first case-control study of the contribution of alcohol to the risk of having an injury with controls drawn from the wider community. The study found that the risk of an injury only became significant above 60 g for women and above 90 g for men when consumed over six hours. Clearly the risk of having a road crash is elevated at far lower levels of consumption than this. Two controlled studies have estimated that the risk of having a road crash approximately doubles with a blood alcohol level (BAL) of above 50 mg/100 mL (Borkenstein, Crowther, Shumate, Ziel, & Zylman, 1974; McLean, Holubowycz, & Sandow, 1980).

Studies of persons in treatment for alcohol dependence rarely find individuals reporting average daily consumption of less than 60 g. A standard instrument for measuring alcohol dependence assesses quantity and frequency of alcohol intake, the lowest point of which corresponds to 64 g per day (Stockwell, Murphy, & Hodgson, 1983).

In conclusion, we suggest that on the basis of current knowledge, high-risk drinking can be defined in the following ranges:

- For chronic health problems: above 40 g alcohol on average per day for men and above 20 g per day for women.
- For acute health problems: above 60 g for men and 40 g for women on any one day—unless driving, operating machinery, or any other reason for not drinking.[1]

These are guidelines only, and individual circumstances and other factors, e.g., pregnancy or other drug use, may increase or decrease the level of drinking that is low-risk.

Other Risk Factors Concerned with Drinking Settings and Activities

Over and above the level and pattern of drinking itself, other individual and situational factors determine the extent of risk associated with drinking alcohol. The risk of alcohol-related brain damage could be substantially reduced through the provision of thiamine in alcoholic drinks (Connelly & Price, 1996). Alcohol-related cognitive impairment is partly caused by a thiamine deficiency in chronic excessive drinkers that could be rectified, in theory, without altering the actual drinking pattern.

Many of the 40 conditions that have been shown to be in part causally attributable to alcohol consumption themselves have numerous other environmental and genetic or other biological risk factors. For example, hypertension, the various types of cancer related to alcohol use, and indeed most of the causes of chronic disease attributable to alcohol have "etiologic fractions" (the proportion of total cases attributable to alcohol consumption) that are well below 1.0 and often below 0.5, indicating that other risk factors play an even more determinative role.

Observational studies of licensed drinking settings in which violence takes place have found that although intoxication among customers is one risk factor for violent incidents, other situational predictors such as a confrontational security staff, poor entertainment, overcrowding, and a predominantly young male clientele also contribute to violent outcomes (Graham & Homel, 1997). One review of the literature on alcohol and violence concluded that intoxication per se was only a risk factor for violence in situations in which there was already frustration and conflict sufficient for there to be a preexisting risk (Stockwell, 1995).

A similar list of variables other than alcohol consumption can be identified in relation to all types of acute and chronic alcohol-related problems. In many instances, additional controlled research is required to identify these more precisely. Clearly high-risk drinking is more than just drinking to intoxication; it is also a matter of who this drinking is done with, where, and in what context (see Chapter 19).

ADVANTAGES OF FOCUSING ON HIGH-RISK DRINKING VERSUS ALL DRINKING

Although we believe that the evidence linking per capita consumption of alcohol to general levels of alcohol-related harm is incontrovertible, pursuing a reduction in per capita consumption tends to encounter substantial resistance (Stockwell et al., 1997). A focus on risk and harm reduction, however, can overcome that resistance and may be more likely to achieve the same public policy objectives.

Public Support for Risk Reduction versus Consumption Reduction Policies

A major source of resistance to the idea of reducing alcohol problems by lowering overall consumption seems to come from the general community, at least in English-speaking countries in which public opinion on this issue has been tested. The Australian National Household Survey for the National Drug Strategy repeatedly has found that public support is weakest for alcohol policies that operate by influencing everyone's drinking, such as raising the price of alcohol, reducing the hours of sale, reducing the density of outlets, and increasing the legal drinking age from 18 to 21 years (National Drug Strategy, 1996).

Table 25.1 summarizes Australian and international opinion research indicating levels of support for alcohol control policies characterized in two ways:

- "Across-the-board strategies" that clearly effect everyone and are designed to either reduce everyone's consumption or to reduce the availability of alcohol to a significant section of the community
- Specific strategies that focus on harm and risk behavior and are identified as "focused strategies"

Table 25.1 contrasts these approaches in relation to raising the price of alcohol, to reducing drinking problems of young people, and to reducing problems of intoxication on licensed premises. In each case, a harm-and-risk reduction approach attracts greater public support and is likely to be just as effective as one based on a reduction of overall consumption—even if the latter were politically viable.

One of the most unpopular policies of all in most opinion surveys is raising the price of alcohol—at least if this is only justified on the implicit or explicit basis of reducing consumption (Flaherty, Homel, & Hall, 1991; Room, Graves, Giesbrecht, & Greenfield, 1992; Single, 1996). However, several surveys in both Australia and the United States show that a substantial majority of the population would support a small rise in the price of alcohol if the proceeds were used to fund treatment and prevention programs (Beel & Stockwell, 1993; Flaherty et al., 1991; Room et al., 1992). Although the effect of such an initiative almost certainly would be to reduce overall alcohol consumption, promoting such a policy on this basis would be to miss the point and would be unlikely to succeed. In other words, it is possible to gain support for a rise in the price of alcohol if this is portrayed as a harm-reduction initiative.

There is strong evidence from Australian and overseas studies that it is comparatively easy for people within 1 or 2 years of the legal drinking age to gain access to alcohol on licensed premises (Grube, 1997; Lang, Stockwell, Rydon,

Table 25.1 Public support for alcohol-control policies.

Policy objective	Across-the-board strategies	Focused strategies
Raise price of alcohol to reduce harm	*Explanation: Reduce consumption* Australia 35% Canada 25% United States 51%	*Explanation: Pay for treatment and prevention programs* Australia 70%–74% United States 82%
Reduce drinking by young people	*Raise legal age* Australia 38%–55% Canada 38% United States 30%	*Enforce laws* Australia 56%–95% United Kingdom 92% *Pub identification cards* Australia 77%–82%
Reduce intoxication on licensed premises	*Reduce hours* Australia 13%–30% Canada 11% United States 58% *Reduce outlets* Australia (−2%) United Kingdom 45% United States 63%	*Enforce laws* Australia 78%–92% New Zealand 87% *Prevent drunks from being served* Canada 76% United States 83%

Source. Data from "Public attitudes to alcohol control policies," by B. Flaherty, P. Homel, and W. Hall, 1991, *Australian Journal of Public Health, 15*; "Public perceptions of responsibility and liability in the licensed drinking environment," by E. Lang, T. Stockwell, P. Rydon, and A. Lockwood, 1993, *Drug and Alcohol Review, 12*; *Trends in public opinion about alcohol policy initiatives in Ontario and the U.S., 1989–1991*, by R. Room, K. Graves, N. Giesbrecht, and T. Greenfield, 1992, Paper presented at the 36th International Congress on Alcoholism and Drug Dependence (ICAA), August 16–21; "Public opinion on alcohol and other drug issues," by E. Single, 1996, in P. Macneil and I. Webster (Eds.), *Canada's Alcohol and Other Drug Survey 1994: A discussion of the findings*, Ottawa, Canada: Ministry of Supply and Services Canada.

& Lockwood, 1993). There is compelling evidence that denying young people access to licensed premises significantly reduces road-crash injuries and fatalities (Wagenaar, 1993). However, as shown in Table 25.1, there is only modest public support in Australia, Canada, and elsewhere for raising the legal drinking age. By contrast, there is an overwhelming level of support both in Australia and overseas for enforcing existing laws denying access to persons younger than 18 years of age to licensed premises. In addition, Australian opinion research shows strong public backing for the use of laminated photographic identity cards for young people to be presented whenever purchasing alcohol. It would appear likely, therefore, that some benefits similar to those that have been sought in the United States through raising the legal age can be achieved by simply enforcing existing drinking laws more effectively, that is, by raising the de facto drinking age to the actual legal drinking age. This clearly would be an example of creating an effective policy that at the same time has wide public support. In addition, although specific data are lacking, it seems likely that the proposal that the probationary driving period with a lower permissable BAL be extended to 3 years also might be both effective and broadly acceptable (Smith, 1984).

In relation to reducing problems associated with alcohol consumption on licensed premises, Table 25.1 also illustrates the far greater acceptability of "server responsibility" and law-enforcement approaches compared with attempts to restrict access to alcohol on licensed premises. Indeed, programs designed to prevent intoxicated persons from being served alcohol are the single most popular alcohol strategy in Canada (Single, 1996). This represents a significant innovation in strategy, because current laws regarding the service of alcohol to intoxicated customers are enforced rarely, at least in the United Kingdom, the United States and Australia, where this issue has been closely examined (Stockwell, 1997). There is now highly promising scientific evidence that enforcing laws on serving intoxicated customers and also requiring the compulsory training of licensees, managers, and serving staff (Holder & Wagenaar, 1994) can generate tangible benefits such as a reduction in road-traffic crashes. McKnight and Streff (1994) calculated that, for every dollar spent on such an enforcement program to prevent the serving of drunk customers, between $90 and $280 were saved in the cost of traffic accidents.

Random breath testing is a classic harm-reduction strategy that now enjoys almost universal support in Australia. In a recent random household survey of two Australian states, up to 97% of respondents supported random breath testing (Beel & Stockwell, 1995). Support for lowering the legal BAL to 50 mg/100 mL also has enjoyed continued support from up to two thirds of the population (Beel & Stockwell, 1995). These policies do not require a reduction in population consumption of alcohol to be effective, although they may cause a shift in drinking patterns. For example, there may be an increase in home consumption or more frequent designation of "skippers" (designated drivers), that is, individuals who remain abstinent while their friends are free to drink perhaps even more than if there were no designated driver.

These examples also constitute cases in which it is possible to identify prevention strategies that combine effectiveness and high levels of public acceptability. As in the classic case of drunk-driving laws, alcohol control policies may be more acceptable if they focus on high-risk behaviors and situations rather than on all drinking on all occasions.

Harm and Risk-Reduction Strategies Acknowledge Low-Risk and Beneficial Drinking Patterns

The converse of targeting high-risk drinking for prevention programs is the acceptance and even encouragement of low-risk drinking patterns. The beneficial effects of moderate drinking, that is, drinking regularly at a low level, as a preventive measure against heart disease for persons aged more than 45 years of age now are accepted widely (Poikolainen, 1995). Health educators and medical authorities now must address seriously the issue of whether one or two drinks per day should be recommended to persons older than 45 years of age who are at risk for heart disease but are not at risk for drinking problems or other drinking-related maladies (e.g., breast cancer) (see Chapters 12 and 13). Evidence is growing, however, that these protective benefits are lost if what amounts to an overall moderate amount of alcohol per week is consumed in just one or two sittings during the week (Puddey, Rakic, Dimmitt, & Beilin, 1998).

Most drinkers believe that they experience personal and social benefits from their consumption of alcohol and that they are unlikely to experience alcohol-related harm (Lang et al., 1993). The more popular harm-and risk-reduction strategies discussed here would not have an impact on low-risk or beneficial drinking patterns at all or, in the case of a modest harm-reduction tax, usually would do so only minimally in comparison with a high-risk drinking pattern. Other harm-reduction interventions such as promoting the use of shatter-proof glassware in high-risk licensed premises (Shepherd, 1998), or the addition of thiamine to beer to reduce the incidence of Korsakov's psychosis, do not require any reduction in ethanol intake.

The promotion of low-alcohol products is an attempt to maintain social benefits of drinking and reduce actual ethanol intake. One well-conducted social-drinking experiment showed that college students at a party—a high-drinking group if there ever was one—could not tell the difference between 3% and 7% beer if the alcohol content was disguised (Geller, Kalsher, & Clarke, 1991). In Australia there has been a burgeoning market for low- (around 2.5%) and midstrength (around 3.5%) beers stimulated by tax concessions for retailers of beers below 3.8% alcohol by volume in most states. Industry market-share data consistently have revealed a growing and substantial market share for these products, perhaps as a synergistic response to the vigorous enforcement of drunk-driving laws in Australia (cf. Gruenewald, Stockwell, Beel, and Dyskin, 1999).

Alcohol Problems Are Not Restricted to Alcoholics

The alcohol industry and other opponents of alcohol-control policies regularly express the view in policy debates that the problems associated with alcohol consumption are caused by the deviant behavior of a small number of alcoholics. Why punish the entire population if 1% to 2% of the population experience actual alcoholism? Some industry sources have even argued that it is only 1% to 2% of their products' drinkers who exceed low-risk drinking levels (see, for example, Stockwell, Lang, & Lewis, 1995). A clear focus on high-risk drinking patterns should circumvent this objection, because only intoxicating and high-volume drinking would be targeted. The results of such policies may impact consumption more than expected in some quarters, however, as drinking to intoxication is widely practiced and is responsible for a substantial proportion of all alcohol consumed in the United States, Australia, and presumably most other countries (Greenfield, 1996; Oddy & Stockwell, 1995). Although many harm-and risk-reduction approaches target specific types of harm in specific high-risk situations, high-risk drinking is so prevalent and costly that policies that affect the drinking of the entire population have to be entertained. Nonetheless, even these policies are best justified, in our opinion, in terms of their impact on high-risk drinking.

EVIDENCE-BASED STRATEGIES FOR REDUCING ALCOHOL-RELATED HARM

This section contains a set of recommendations for priority strategies that should be applicable in any jurisdiction. These are not intended to be an exhaustive list, and a range of other effective strategies has been described in more detail elsewhere (see Plant, Single, & Stockwell, 1997). The recommendations in this section are based on the following principles:

- Strategies should be supported by either direct or indirect evidence of effectiveness in the reduction of alcohol-related harm. Direct evidence would be from well-designed trials of effectiveness. Indirect evidence would be that in favor of a general principle or approach on which the strategy is based.
- Strategies should be likely to enjoy popular support, as evidenced by public opinion polls, and also the support of key stakeholders with influence on the formation of public policy; that is, they should be broadly acceptable.
- The strategies adopted should be comprehensive, mutually compatible, and, ideally, synergistic in their actions across different sectors and levels of society.

Tax Policies

Alcohol taxation should be structured with public health and safety issues in mind. Taxes should be based on the type of beverage and alcoholic strength. This should in time replace all sales taxes as a way of providing price incentives for drinkers to choose lower-strength alcoholic beverages.

With this in mind, a policy based on a three-tier system of taxation might be optimal. A simpler tax system that only taxes alcohol according to ethanol content (without taking type of beverage into account) fails to reflect the higher production and distribution costs involved in producing beer and most wines and would result in a much lower price per unit of ethanol for spirits. By contrast, a three-tier tax system conceivably could structure taxes so that (a) the prices consumers pay per unit of ethanol are approximately equal for all major types of beverages, and (b) low-alcohol products within the major beverage categories are taxed at a lower rate to promote moderation. The main guidelines of such a taxation system would be as follows:

- Drinks with very low alcohol content (in the Australian context less than 3% alcohol by volume), consumption of which is unlikely to lead to intoxication, should be taxed no more than soft drinks.

- A range of tax rates should be applied corresponding to three major categories of alcoholic beverages in excess of 2.9% alcohol by volume: those under 7% (mainly beer and wine or spirit "coolers"), those between 7% and 20% alcohol by volume (mainly table wines, fortified wines, and some specialty drinks), and those over 20% alcohol by volume (mainly spirits).
- Within these three major beverage classes, the tax rates should be set according to ethanol content, such that, for example, beer with a strength of 3.5% would be taxed at a lower rate than regular or overstrength beers.

Any small, overall increase in revenue from a three-tier taxation system should be used to fund prevention and treatment programs. Moreover, a principle should be established that the revenue collected from alcohol at least match the net economic costs to a particular jurisdiction as a whole.

Server Responsibility

The international trend is towards requiring greater responsibility from alcohol servers, a policy that requires the support of effective regulation. The use of licensing controls as a means of promoting public health, safety, and order should be acknowledged in the objectives of liquor acts and the goals of licensing authorities through the following means:

- Effective and credible enforcement of the laws regarding service of alcohol to underage and intoxicated persons
- Mandatory training of licensees and managers in responsible service and business practices
- Photographic identity cards for young people wishing to buy alcohol
- Extended probationary driving periods, such as 2 to 3 years, with a lower permissible legal BAL.

Enforcement of Drink-Driving Laws

Effectiveness of drink-driving laws is attained through creating perceptions among drivers of a high probability of being breath-tested and apprehended if they are over the limit (Beel & Stockwell, 1995; Homel, 1988). This perception can be established by random breath testing with low BAL limits, and extensive point of sale and media publicity.

An effective level of deterrence does not necessarily require the application of severe penalties and is best created by a high level of enforcement of whatever penalties apply. Within that constraint, and only within that constraint, deterrence of drinking and driving might be achieved by administrative means such as license suspensions and fines that do not, in the first instance, necessarily involve the criminal justice system.

In terms of inexperienced drivers, they are often also inexperienced drinkers, which contributes to the overrepresentation of young people in road-crash statistics. We recommend the concept of graduated licensing with the provision that new drivers (who are generally teenagers or young adults) are not allowed to drive with any alcohol in their systems for a probationary period of 2 to 3 years.

Local Choice on Availability of Alcohol

Legislation and regulatory authorities should provide clear opportunities and the flexibility for communities to regulate the supply of alcohol in their locality, including, at a minimum, the ability to influence sales hours and numbers of outlets. Such an opportunity is especially important in some remote Aboriginal communities in which excessive drinking and related harm are of epidemic proportions (e.g., Midford, Daly, & Holmes, 1994).

Clear Public Health Information on the Risk and Benefits of Different Drinking Patterns

National drinking guidelines involving specific amounts consumed per day or per occasion should be formulated by leading medical, health, and safety experts (as well as international drinking guidelines formulated by an appropriate international agency such as the World Health Organization). These standards should be promulgated widely according to the following conditions:

- Notwithstanding the need for consistent standards, advice must be tailored for different risk groups (see Chapters 12 and 13).
- Advice must be specified for different circumstances (e.g., pregnancy, operating equipment, driving).
- A distinction must be drawn between how much is safe to drink on a single occasion as opposed to an average across all days of the week (as in New Zealand, where males are advised to drink no more than 40 g/d on average and no more than 60 g on any one occasion—provided the individual is not driving or engaged in other tasks requiring judgment and accuracy).

Recommendations then can be reinforced via (a) the media; (b) various medical specialties; (c) health-promotion advice in schools, colleges, and workplaces; (d) drunk-driving campaigns and police; and (e) alcohol manufacturers. In terms of the last, product labeling, for example, could be utilized to communicate to the main target group, regular high-risk drinkers who see the messages most often (Greenfield, Graves, & Kaskutas, 1993). In order to be effective, however, labels should provide (a) clear information about alcoholic volume and strength, presented at a minimum according to alcohol content in grams or, preferably, in terms of standard drinks or units of alcohol that contain a fixed amount of ethanol (cf. Stockwell & Single, 1997); and (b) specific advice about low-risk levels of drinking which support national drinking guidelines.

CONCLUSION

Prevention policies for alcohol-related problems should focus on high-risk drinking patterns—and drinking to intoxication in particular—as well as on overall levels of drinking. Focusing on harmful drinking enjoys strong public support and leads to a number of prevention strategies that have been shown to reduce harmful drinking patterns. What is required now is strong and coordinated action from government and other sectors to attack high-risk alcohol consumption and encourage low-risk consumption. The beverage alcohol industries can contribute in some areas, but in others they may have too strong a conflict of interest to self-regulate effectively. There is a need for:

- Appropriate alcohol regulations, taxation policies, reasonable advertising controls and industry action (including self-regulatory codes) that promote moderation and control practices that promote high-risk drinking
- Information systems to monitor high-risk drinking and associated harms at the community, regional, state, and national levels
- National, regional, and local coordination of programs to avoid duplication of effort or contradictory messages
- Continuing evaluation of programs and feedback of outcomes

The alcohol industry often argues that governments should adopt a less paternalistic view of alcohol prevention and treat drinkers as responsible individuals who are capable of making sensible choices. But the industry can do more to promote moderation and control practices that lead to high-risk drinking. Besides continuing its own prevention efforts, the industry also should support government and public health prevention efforts. Moreover, producers of alcoholic beverages should ensure that their customers have the information they need to make responsible choices, for example by stating on product labels the amount of alcohol contained using an international standard unit. The alcohol industry thus can play an important role in reducing alcohol-related problems.

ACKNOWLEDGMENTS

The first author is funded by the Commonwealth Government of Australia's National Drug Strategy. The views expressed in this chapter, however, should not be understood to represent those of the Australian government or any of its relevant departments.

NOTE

1. Regularly drinking in excess of these particular levels further increases the risk of both chronic health problems and the development of alcohol dependence.

REFERENCES

Alcohol Advisory Council of New Zealand. (1995). *Upper limits for responsible drinking: A guide for health professionals*. Wellington, New Zealand: Author.

Ashley, M. J., Ferrence, R., Room, R., Bondy, S. J., Rehm, J., & Single, E. (1997). Moderate drinking and health: Implications of recent evidence for clinical practice, *Canadian Family Physician, 43*, 687–694.

Beel, A., & Stockwell, T. (1993). *The introduction of 0.05 legislation in Western Australia: A preliminary research report*. Perth, Australia: National Centre for Research into the Prevention of Drug Abuse.

Beel, A., & Stockwell, T. (1995) *The impact of Western Australia's .05 legislation on drivers' attitudes, perceptions and behaviours*. Perth, Australia: National Centre for Research into the Prevention of Drug Abuse.

Borkenstein, R., Crowther, P., Shumate, R., Zeil, W., & Zylman, R. (1974). Role of the drinking driver in traffic accidents (The Grand Rapids Study). *Blutalkohol, 11*(Suppl. 1): 132P.

Collins, D., & Lapsley, H. (1991). *Estimating the economic costs of drug abuse in Australia* (National Campaign Against Drug Abuse Monograph No. 15). Canberra, Australia: Australian Government Publishing Services.

Collins, D., & Lapsley, H. (1996). *The economic costs of drug misuse in Australia in 1988 and 1992*. Canberra, Australia: Commonwealth Department of Human Services and Health.

Connelly, L., & Price, J. (1996). Preventing the Wernicke-Korsakoff syndrome in Australia: Cost-effectiveness of thiamine-supplementation alternatives. *Australian and New Zealand Journal of Public Health, 20*, 181–187.

Crawford, A. (1993). Much ado about nothing. Commentary on the "Preventive paradox: A critical examination" by Sinclair, J. D., Sillanaukee, P. *Addiction, 88*, 595–598.

English, D., Holman, D., Milne, E., Winter, M., Hulse, G., Codde, G., Bower, C., Corti, B., De Klerk, C., Lewin, G., Knuiman, M., Kurinczuk, J., & Ryan, G. (1995). *The quantification of drug caused morbidity and mortality in Australia, 1992*. Canberra, Australia: Australian Government Publishing Services.

Flaherty, B., Homel, P., & Hall, W. (1991). Public attitudes to alcohol control policies. *Australian Journal of Public Health, 15*, 301–306.

Geller, E. S., Kalsher, M. J., & Clarke, S. W. (1991). Beer versus mixed-drink consumption at fraternity parties: A time and place for low-alcohol alternatives. *Journal of Studies on Alcohol, 52*, 197–204.

Graham, K., & Homel, R. (1997). Creating safer bars. In M. Plant, E. Single & T. Stockwell (Eds.), *Alcohol: Minimising the harm. What works?* (pp. 171–192). New York: Free Association Books Ltd.

Greenfield, T. K. (1996). *Consumption and risk patterns: Who buys and who pays?* Berkeley, CA: Alcohol Research Group Western Consortium for Public Health.

Greenfield, T., Graves, K., & Kaskutas, L. (1993). Alcohol warning labels for prevention: *National survey findings. Alcohol Health and Research World, 17*, 67–75.

Grube, J. W. (1997). Preventing sales of alcohol to minors: Results from a community trial. *Addiction, 92*(Suppl. 2), S251–S260.

Gruenewald, P., Stockwell, T., Beel, A., & Dyskin, E. (1999). Beverage sales and drinking and driving: The role of on-premise drinking places. *Journal of Studies on Alcohol, 60*, 47–53.

Heather, N., & Robertson, I. (1981). *Controlled drinking*. Cambridge, UK: Cambridge University Press.

Holder, H., & Wagenaar, A. (1994). Mandated server training and reduced alcohol-involved traffic crashes: A time series analysis of the Oregon experience. *Accident Analysis and Prevention, 26*, 89–97.

Homel, R. (1988). *Policing and punishing the drinking driver: A study of general and specific deterrence*. New York: Springer.

International Center for Alcohol Policies. (1996). *Safe alcohol consumption: A comparison of* Nutrition and your health: Dietary guidelines for Americans *and* Sensible drinking (ICAP Reports 1, Suppl.). Washington, DC: Author.

Jellinek, E. M. (1960). *The disease concept of alcoholism.* Schenectady, NY: New College and University Press.

Lang, E., Stockwell, T., Rydon, P., & Lockwood, A. (1993). Public perceptions of responsibility and liability in the licensed drinking environment. *Drug and Alcohol Review, 12,* 13–22.

McKnight, A. J., & Streff, F. M. (1994). The effect of enforcement upon service of alcohol to intoxicated patrons of bars and restaurants. *Accident Analysis and Prevention, 26,* 79–88.

McLean, A. J., Holubowycz, O. T., & Sandow, B. L. (1980). *Alcohol and crashes: Identification of relevant factors in this association* (Report No. CR11). Adelaide, Australia: Department of Transport, University of Adelaide.

McLeod, R., Stockwell, T., Phillip, M., & Stevens, M. (1998, February 1–5). *The relationship between alcohol consumption patterns and injury.* Paper presented at the Second International Conference on Drinking Patterns and Their Consequences, Perth, Western Australia.

Midford, R., Daly, A., & Holmes, M. (1994). The care of public drunks in Halls Creek: A model for community involvement. *Health Promotion Journal of Australia, 4,* 5–8.

National Drug Strategy, Commonwealth Department of Health and Family Services. (1996). *National household survey, 1995.* Canberra, Australia: Australian Government Publishing Service.

Oddy, W., & Stockwell, T. (1995). How much alcohol in Western Australia is consumed in a hazardous or harmful way? *Australian Journal of Public Health, 19,* 434.

Orford, J., & Hawker, A. (1974). Note on the ordering of onset of symptoms of alcohol dependence. *Psychological Medicine, 4,* 281–288.

Parker, D., & Harford, T. (1992). The epidemiology of alcohol consumption and dependence across occupations in the United States. *Alcohol Health and Research World, 16,* 97–105.

Plant, M., Single, E., & Stockwell, T. (Eds.). (1997). *Alcohol: Minimising the harm. What works?* New York: Free Association Books.

Poikolainen, K. (1995). Alcohol and mortality: A review. *Journal of Clinical Epidemiology, 488,* 445–465.

Puddey, I. B., Rakic, V., Dimmitt, S. B., & Beilin, L. J. (1998, February 1–5). *Influence of pattern of drinking on cardiovascular disease and cardiovascular risk factors.* Paper presented at the Second International Conference on Drinking Patterns and Their Consequences, Perth, Western Australia.

Rehm, J., Ashley, K. J., Room, R., Single, E., Bondy, S., Ferrence, R., & Giesbrecht, N. (1996). On the emerging paradigm of drinking patterns and their social and health consequences. *Addiction, 91,* 1615–1621.

Rice, D., Kelman, S., Miller, L., & Dunmeyer, S. (1990). *The economic cost of alcohol and drug abuse and mental illness 1985* [DHHS Publication No. (ADM) 90-1694]. San Francisco, CA: Institute for Health and Aging, University of California.

Room, R., Graves, K., Giesbrecht, N., & Greenfield, T. (1992, August 16–21). *Trends in public opinion about alcohol policy initiatives in Ontario and the U.S., 1989–1991.* Paper presented at the 36th International Congress on Alcoholism and Drug Dependence (ICAA), Glasgow.

Shepherd, J. (1994). Violent crime: The role of alcohol and new approaches to the prevention of injury, *Alcohol and Alcoholism, 29,* 5–10.

Shepherd, J. (1998). The introduction of shatter-proof glasses to prevent injuries from bar-room brawls. *Addiction, 93,* 5–7.

Single, E. (1996). Public opinion on alcohol and other drug issues. In P. Macneil & I. Webster (Eds.), *Canada's Alcohol and Other Drug Survey 1994: A discussion of the findings.* Ottawa, Canada: Ministry of Supply and Services Canada.

Single, E. (1997). The concept of harm reduction and its application to alcohol: The 6th Annual Dorothy Black Lecture. *Drugs: Education, Prevention and Policy, 4,* 7–22.

Single, E., Robson, L., Rehm, J., & Xie, X. (1999). Morbidity and mortality attributable to substance abuse in Canada. *American Journal of Public Health, 89,* 385–390.

Single, E., Robson, L., Xie, X., & Rehm, J. (1998). The economic costs of alcohol, tobacco and illicit drugs in Canada, 1992. *Addiction, 93,* 983–998.

Single, E., & Wortley, S. (1993). Drinking in various settings as it relates to socio-demographic variables and level of consumption: Findings from a national survey in Canada. *Journal of Studies on Alcohol, 54,* 590–599.

Smith, I. (1984). *Effect of low prescribed blood alcohol levels on the traffic accidents of newly licensed drivers.* Perth, Western Australia: Western Australian Alcohol and Drug Authority.

Stockwell, T. (Ed). (1995). *Alcohol misuse and violence No. 5: An examination of the appropriateness and efficacy of liquor licensing laws across Australia* (2nd ed.). Canberra, Australia: Australian Government Publishing Services.

Stockwell, T. (1997). Regulation of the licensed drinking environment: A major opportunity for crime prevention. *Crime Prevention Studies, 7,* 7–34.

Stockwell, T. (1998). Towards guidelines for low-risk drinking: Quantifying the short- and long-term costs of hazardous alcohol consumption. *Alcoholism: Clinical and Experimental Research, 22*(Suppl. 2), 63S–69S.

Stockwell, T., Hawks, D., Lang, E., & Rydon, P. (1996). Unravelling the preventive paradox for acute alcohol problems. *Drug and Alcohol Review, 15,* 7–15.

Stockwell, T., Lang, E., & Lewis, P. (1995). Is wine the drink of moderation? *Medical Journal of Australia, 162,* 578–581.

Stockwell, T., Murphy, D., & Hodgson, R. (1983). The severity of alcohol dependence questionnaire: Its use, reliability and validity. *British Journal of Addiction, 78,* 145–155.

Stockwell, T., & Single, E. (1997). Standard unit labelling of alcohol containers. In M. Plant et al. (Ed.), *Alcohol: Minimising Harm.* London: Free Association Books.

Stockwell, T., Single, E., Hawks, D., Rehm, J. (1997). Sharpening the focus of alcohol policy from aggregate consumption to harm and risk reduction. *Addiction Research, 5,* 1–9.

Stockwell, T., Sitharthan, T., McGrath, D., & Lang, E. (1994). Measurement of alcohol dependence and impaired control in community samples. *Addiction, 89,* 167–174.

Thorley, A. (1980). Medical responses to problem drinking. *Medicine, 35,* 1816–1822.

Wagenaar, A. (1993). Research affects public policy: The case of the legal drinking age in the United States. *Addiction, 88*(Suppl.), 75S–82S.

Chapter 26

Promoting Positive Drinking: Alcohol, Necessary Evil or Positive Good?

Stanton Peele

Historically and internationally, cultural visions of alcohol and its effects vary in terms of how positive or negative they are and the likely consequences that they attach to alcohol consumption. The dominant contemporary vision of alcohol in the United States is that alcohol (a) is primarily negative and has exclusively hazardous consequences, (b) leads frequently to uncontrollable behavior, and (c) is something that young people should be warned against. The consequences of this vision are that when children do drink (which teenagers regularly do), they know of no alternative but excessive, intense consumption patterns, leading them frequently to drink to intoxication. This chapter explores alternative models of drinking and channels for conveying them which emphasize healthy versus unhealthy consumption patterns as well as the individual's responsibility to manage his or her drinking. The ultimate goal is for people to see alcohol as an accompaniment to an overall healthy and pleasurable lifestyle, an image they enact as moderate, sensible drinking patterns.

MODELS OF ALCOHOL'S EFFECTS

Selden Bacon, a founder and long-time director of the Yale (then Rutgers) Center of Alcohol Studies, remarked on the strange public health approach to alcohol taken in the United States and elsewhere in the Western world:

Table 26.1 Views of alcohol in the United States.

	Alcohol is bad	Alcohol is good	Alcohol is bad/good	An integrated approach
Model of alcohol use	Temperance/proscriptive	Nontemperance/permissive	Ambivalent/prescriptive	Nontemperance/prescriptive
Key ingredient	Abstinence; formal controls	Excessive drinking	Informally regulated drinking	Moderation; self-regulation
Consequence	Nonoptimal drinking/ health	Nonoptimal drinking/ health	Mixed or oscillating drinking	Healthy drinking

Current organized knowledge about alcohol use can be likened to ... knowledge about automobiles and their use if the latter were limited to facts and theories about accidents and crashes. ... [What is missing are] the positive functions and positive attitudes about alcohol uses in our as well as in other societies. ... If educating youth about drinking starts from the assumed basis that such drinking is bad ... full of risk for life and property, at best considered as an escape, clearly useless per se, and/or frequently the precursor of disease, and the subject matter is taught by nondrinkers and antidrinkers, this is a particular indoctrination. Further, if 75–80% of the surrounding peers and elders are or are going to become drinkers, there [is] ... an inconsistency between the message and the reality. (Bacon, 1984, pp. 22–24)

When Bacon wrote these words, the coronary and mortality benefits of alcohol were only beginning to be established, while the psychological and social benefits of drinking had not been systematically assessed. His wry observations seem doubly relevant today, now that the life-prolonging effects of alcohol are on a firm footing (Doll, 1997; see also Chapter 12) and the conference on which this volume is based has begun the discussion of the ways in which alcohol enhances quality of life (see also Baum-Baicker, 1985; Peele & Brodsky, 1998; Chapter 15). In other words, if science indicates that alcohol conveys significant life advantages, why does alcohol policy act as though alcohol were evil?

This chapter examines different views of alcohol as being either evil or good (Table 26.1). Two different typologies of social attitudes towards alcohol are employed. One is the distinction between temperance and nontemperance Western societies. In the former, major efforts have been mounted to ban alcoholic beverages (Levine, 1992). Less alcohol is consumed in temperance societies, with more outward signs of problematic use. In nontemperance societies, by contrast, alcohol is used almost universally, drinking is socially integrated, and few behavioral and other alcohol-related problems are noted (Peele, 1997).

An alternate typology has been used by sociologists to characterize norms and attitudes towards alcohol in subgroups within the larger society. Akers (1992) lists four such types of groups: (a) groups with *proscriptive* norms against the use of alcohol; (b) *prescriptive* groups that accept and welcome drinking but establish clear norms for its consumption; (c) groups with *ambivalent* norms that invite drinking but also fear and resent it; and (d) groups with *permissive* norms that not only tolerate and invite drinking but do not set limits on consumption or on behavior while drinking.

This chapter contrasts these different views of alcohol and the ways of approaching alcohol education and policy suggested by each. It additionally juxtaposes the potential consequences of each view and its educational approach.

VISIONS OF ALCOHOL

Alcohol is Bad

The idea of alcohol as evil took root 150 to 200 years ago (Lender & Martin, 1987; Levine, 1978). Although this idea has varied in its intensity since then, antialcohol feeling has resurfaced and consumption has declined since the late 1970s in much of the Western world, led by the United States (Heath, 1989). The idea that alcohol is bad takes a number of forms. Of course, in the 19th and 20th centuries, the temperance movement held that alcohol is a negative force that must be eliminated from society because (in its view) of the following characteristics of alcohol:

- Alcohol is an addictive substance whose use inevitably leads to increased, compulsive, and uncontrollable use.
- Alcoholism underlies most, indeed practically all, modern social problems (unemployment, wife and child abuse, emotional disorders, prostitution, and so on).
- Alcohol conveys no discernible social benefits.

Alcoholism as a Disease: The Inbred Alcoholic The essential attributes of alcoholism as a disease were part of the temperance movement's view of alcohol. These were consolidated and reintegrated into the modern disease theory of alcoholism both through the development of Alcoholics Anonymous (AA), beginning in 1935, and in a modern medical approach, beginning in the 1970s and espoused currently by the directorship of the National Institute on Alcohol Abuse and Alcoholism (NIAAA). AA popularized the idea that a small subgroup of individuals has a deeply ingrained form of alcoholism that prevents its members from drinking moderately. In the modern medical view, this has taken the form of the idea of a heavy genetic loading for alcoholism.

AA actually wished to coexist with alcohol in the post-prohibition era,[1] because the signs were inescapable that the nation would no longer support national prohibition. If only certain individuals are stricken with alcoholism, then only they have to fear the evils that lurk in the beverage. For this limited group, however, the evils of alcohol are unlimited. They progressively lead the alcoholic (the drunkard or inebriate in temperance terms) to a total collapse of ordinary values and life structure and the ultimate depredations of death, the insane asylum, or prison.

A standard temperance view of alcohol was provided in the set of prints drawn by George Cruikshank, entitled *The Bottle*, included in Timothy Shay Arthur's 1848 *Temperance Tales* (see Lender & Martin, 1987). *The Bottle* comprised eight prints. After first sampling alcohol, the protagonist descends rapidly into a drunkard's hell. In short order he loses his job, the family is evicted and must beg on the streets, and so on. In the seventh print, the man kills his wife while he is drunk, leading to his commitment to an asylum in the last print. This sense of the imminent, horrible danger and death in alcohol is an integral part of the modern medical disease viewpoint as well. G. Douglas Talbott, president of the American Society of Addiction Medicine, wrote, "The ultimate consequences for a drinking alcoholic are these three: he or she will end up in jail, in a hospital, or in a graveyard" (Wholey, 1984, p. 19).

Alcohol Dependence and the Public Health Model The modern medical viewpoint, despite its allegiance to genetic causality of alcoholism, is less committed than AA to the idea that alcoholism is in-born. For example, an NIAAA general population study (Grant & Dawson, 1998) assessed the risk of developing alcoholism to be much higher for youthful drinkers (a risk that was multiplied if alcoholism was present in the family). The model underlying this view of alcoholism's development is alcohol dependence, which holds that individuals drinking at a high rate for a substantial period develop a psychological and physiological reliance on alcohol (Peele, 1987). (It should be noted that the Grant and Dawson study (a) did not distinguish between those who first drank at home and those who drank with peers outside the home and (b) asked about first drinking "not counting small tastes or sips of alcohol" (p. 105), which more likely indicates first drinking other than within the family or at home.)

In addition to the disease and dependence views of alcohol's negative action, the modern public health view of alcohol is a drinking-problems model, which holds that only a minority of alcohol problems (violence, accidents, disease) are associated with alcoholic or dependent drinkers (see Chapter 25). Rather, it holds, drinking problems are spread across the population and can appear either because of acute intoxication even in occasional drinkers, cumulative effects from lower levels of nondependent drinking, or heavy drinking by a relatively small percentage of problem drinkers. In any case, according to the most popular public health viewpoint, alcohol problems are multiplied by higher levels of drinking society-wide (Edwards et al., 1994). The public health model sees not only alcohol dependence but all alcohol consumption as inherently problematic, in that greater consumption leads to greater social problems. The role of public health advocates in this view is to diminish alcohol consumption through whatever means possible.

Alcohol is Good

The view of alcohol as beneficent is ancient, as old at least as the idea that alcohol produces harm. The Old Testament describes alcoholic excess, but it also values alcohol. Both the Hebrew and Christian religions include wine in their sacraments—Hebrew prayer bestows a blessing on wine. Even earlier, the Greeks considered wine a boon and worshipped a god of wine, Dionysius (the same god who stood for pleasure and revelry). From the ancients to the present, many have valued wine and other beverage alcohol for either their ritualistic benefits or their celebratory and even licentious aspects. The value of alcohol certainly was appreciated in colonial America, which drank freely and gladly, and where minister Increase Mather termed alcohol the "good creature of God" (Lender & Martin, 1987, p. 1).

Before Prohibition in the United States and from the 1940s through the 1960s, drinking alcohol was accepted and valued as was perhaps even excessive drinking. Musto (1996) has detailed cycles of attitudes towards alcohol in the

United States, from the libertarian to the prohibitionistic. We can see the view of drinking and even alcohol intoxication as pleasurable in American film (Room, 1989), including also the work of such mainstream and morally upright artists as Walt Disney, who presented an entertaining and drunken Bacchus in his 1940 animated film, *Fantasia*. Television dramas in the 1960s casually depicted drinking by doctors, parents, and most adults. In the United States, one view of alcohol—the permissive—is associated with high consumption and few restraints on drinking (Akers, 1992; Orcutt, 1991).

Most drinkers throughout the Western world view alcohol as a positive experience. Respondents in surveys in the United States, Canada, and Sweden predominantly mention positive sensations and experiences in association with drinking—such as relaxation and sociability—with little mention of harm (Pernanen, 1991). Cahalan (1970) found that the most common result of drinking reported by current drinkers in the United States was that they "felt happy and cheerful" (50% of male and 47% of female nonproblem drinkers). Roizen (1983) reported national survey data in the United States in which 43% of adult male drinkers always or usually felt "friendly" (the most common effect) when they drank, compared with 8% who felt "aggressive" or 2% who felt "sad" (see Chapters 15 and 16).

Alcohol May Be Good or Bad

Of course, many of those sources for the goodness of alcohol also drew important distinctions among styles of alcohol use. Increase Mather's full view of alcohol was outlined in his 1673 tract *Wo to Drunkards*: "The wine is from God, but the Drunkard is from the Devil." Benjamin Rush, the colonial physician who first formulated a disease view of alcoholism, recommended abstinence only from spirits, and not wine or cider, as did the early temperance movement (Lender & Martin, 1987). It was only in the middle of the 19th century that teetotaling became the goal of temperance, a goal that was adopted by AA in the next century.

Some cultures and groups instead accept and encourage drinking, although they disapprove of drunkenness and antisocial behavior while drinking. Jews as an ethnic group typify this "prescriptive" approach to drinking, which allows frequent imbibing but strictly regulates the style of drinking and comportment when drinking, a style that leads overwhelmingly to moderate drinking with a minimal number of problems (Akers, 1992; Glassner, 1991). Modern epidemiologic research on alcohol (see Chapters 12 and 13) embodies this view of alcohol's double-edged nature with the U- or J-shaped curve, in which mild to moderate drinkers display reduced coronary artery disease and mortality rates, but abstainers and heavier drinkers show depreciated health outcomes.

A less successful view of the "dual" nature of alcohol consumption is embodied by ambivalent groups (Akers, 1992), which both welcome alcohol's intoxicating effects and disapprove (or feel guilty about) excessive drinking and its consequences.

Alcohol and the Integrated Lifestyle

A view consistent with that in which alcohol may be used in either a positive or a negative fashion is one that sees healthful drinking not so much as the cause of either good and bad medical or psychosocial outcomes but as a part of an overall healthful approach to life. One version of this idea is embedded in the so-called Mediterranean diet, which emphasizes a balanced diet lower in animal protein than the typical American diet, and in which regular, moderate alcohol drinking is one central element. In line with this integrated approach, cross-cultural epidemiologic research has shown that diet and alcohol contribute independently to coronary artery disease benefits in Mediterranean countries (Criqui & Ringle, 1994). Indeed, one can imagine other characteristics of Mediterranean cultures that lead to reduced levels of coronary artery disease—such as more walking, greater community supports, and less stressful lifestyles than in the United States and other temperance, generally Protestant, cultures.

Grossarth-Maticek (1995) has presented an even more radical version of this integrated approach, in which self-regulation is the fundamental individual value or outlook, and drinking moderately or healthily is secondary to this larger orientation:

> "Troubled drinkers," i.e. people who both suffer from permanent stress and also impair their own self-regulation by drinking, only need a small daily dose to shorten their lives considerably. On the other hand, people who can regulate themselves well, and whose self-regulation is improved by alcohol consumption, even by a high dose, do not manifest a shorter life span or a higher frequency of chronic illnesses.

DRINKING MESSAGES AND THEIR CONSEQUENCES

Never Drink

The proscriptive approach to alcohol, characteristic for example of Moslem and Mormon societies, formally rules out all alcohol use. Within the United States, proscriptive groups include conservative Protestant sects and, often corresponding to such religious groupings, dry political regions. If those in such groups drink, they are at high risk for drinking excessively, because there are no norms to prescribe moderate consumption. This same phenomenon is seen in national drinking surveys, in which groups with high abstinence rates also display higher-than-average problem-drinking rates, at least among those who are exposed to alcohol (Cahalan & Room, 1974; Hilton, 1987, 1988).

Control Drinking

Temperance cultures (i.e., Scandinavian and English-speaking nations) foster the most active alcohol-control policies. Historically, these have taken the form of prohibition campaigns. In contemporary society, these nations enforce strict parameters for drinking, including regulation of the time and place of consumption, age restrictions for drinking, taxation policies, and so on. Nontemperance cultures show less concern in all these areas and yet report fewer behavioral drinking problems (Levine, 1992; Peele, 1997). For example, in Portugal, Spain, Belgium, and other countries, 16-year-olds (and those even younger) can drink alcohol freely in public establishments. These countries have almost no AA presence; Portugal, which had the highest per capita alcohol consumption in 1990, had 0.6 AA groups per million population compared with almost 800 AA groups per million population in Iceland, the country that consumed the least alcohol per capita in Europe. The idea of the need to control drinking externally or formally thus coincides with drinking problems in a paradoxically mutually reinforcing relationship.

At the same time, efforts to control or ameliorate drinking and drinking problems sometimes have untoward effects. In regard to treatment, Room (1988, p. 43) notes,

> [We are in the midst] of a huge expansion in the treatment of alcohol-related problems in the United States [and industrialized nations worldwide] ... In comparing Scotland and United States, on the one hand, with developing countries like Mexico and Zambia, on the other hand, in the World Health Organization Community Response Study, we were struck with how much more responsibility Mexicans and Zambians gave to family and friends in dealing with alcohol problems, and how ready Scots and Americans were to cede responsibility for these human problems to official agencies or to professionals. Studying the period since 1950 in seven industrialized nations, ... [when] alcohol problem rates generally grew, we were struck by the concomitant growth of treatment provision in all of these countries. The provision of treatment, we felt, became a societal alibi for the dismantling of long-standing structures of control of drinking behavior, both formal and informal.

Room noted that, in the period from the 1950s through the 1970s, alcohol controls were relaxed and alcohol problems grew as consumption increased. This is the perceived relationship underlying the public policy approach of limiting consumption of alcohol. However, since the 1970s, alcohol controls in most countries (along with treatment) have increased and consumption has *declined*, but individual drinking problems have *risen* markedly (at least in the United States), particularly among men (Table 26.2). Around the point at which per capita consumption began to decline, between 1967 and 1984, NIAAA-funded national drinking surveys reported a doubling in self-reported alcohol-dependence symptoms without a concomitant increase in consumption among drinkers (Hilton & Clark, 1991).

Table 26.2 Dependence-drinking problems among U.S. drinkers.

| Year | Respondents reporting at least one dependence symptom over prior year (%) | |
	Men	Women
1967	8	5
1984	19	8

Note. Data from "Changes in American drinking patterns and problems, 1967–1984," by M. E. Hilton and W. B. Clark, 1991, in D. J. Pittman and H. R. White (Eds.), *Society, culture, and drinking patterns reexamined* (pp. 157–172), New Brunswick, NJ: Center of Alcohol Studies.

Drink for Enjoyment

Most people drink in line with the standards of their social environments. The definition of enjoyable drinking varies according to the group of which the drinker is a part. Clearly, some societies have a different sense of the enjoyment of alcohol relative to its dangers. One definition of nontemperance cultures is that they conceive of alcohol as a positive pleasure, or as a substance whose use is valued in itself. Bales (1946), Jellinek (1960), and others have distinguished the very different conceptions of alcohol that characterize temperance and nontemperance cultures such as, respectively, the Irish and the Italian: In the former, alcohol connotes imminent doom and danger and at the same time freedom and license; in the latter alcohol is not conceived as creating social or personal problems. In Irish culture, alcohol is separated from the family and is used sporadically in special circumstances. In the Italian, drinking is conceived as a commonplace, but joyous, social opportunity.

Societies characterized by the permissive social style of drinking also might be seen to conceive of drinking in a predominantly enjoyable light. However, in this environment, excessive drinking, intoxication, and acting out are tolerated and are in fact seen as a part of the enjoyment of alcohol. This is different from the prescriptive society, which values and appreciates drinking but which limits the amount and style of consumption. The latter is consistent with nontemperance cultures (see Chapter 5). Just as some individuals shift from high consumption to abstinence and some groups have both high abstinence and high excessive-drinking rates, permissive cultures can become aware of the dangers of alcohol and shift as a society into ones that impose strict alcohol controls (Musto, 1996; Room, 1989).

Drink for Health

The idea that alcohol is healthy is also ancient. Drinking throughout the ages has been thought to enhance appetite and digestion, assist in lactation, reduce pain, create relaxation and bring rest, and actually attack some diseases. Even in temperance societies, people may regard a drink of alcohol as healthful. The health benefits of moderate alcohol consumption (as opposed to both abstinence and heavy drinking) were first presented in a modern medical light in 1926 by Raymond Pearl (see Chapter 12). Since the 1980s, and with greater certainty in the 1990s, prospective epidemiologic studies have found that moderate drinkers have a lower incidence of heart disease and live longer than abstainers (see Chapters 12 and 13).

The United States typifies a modern society with a highly developed and educated consumer class characterized by an intense health consciousness. Bromides, vitamins, and foods are sold and consumed widely on the basis of their supposed healthfulness. There are few cases, if any, in which the healthfulness of such folk prescriptions is as well established as in the case of alcohol. Indeed, the range and solidity of the findings of medical benefits of alcohol rival and exceed the empirical basis for such claims for many pharmaceutical substances. Thus, a basis has been built for drinking as a part of a regulated health program.

Yet, residual attitudes in the United States—a temperance society—conflict with a recognition and utilization of alcohol's health benefits (Peele, 1993). This environment creates conflicting pressures: Health consciousness presses towards consideration of the healthfulness and life-prolonging effects of drinking, but traditional and medical antialcohol views work against presenting positive messages about drinking. Bradley, Donovan, and Larson (1993) describe this failure of medical professionals, out of either fear or ignorance, to incorporate recommendations for optimal drinking levels in interactions with patients. This omission both denies information about life-saving benefits of alcohol to patients who might benefit and fails to take advantage of a large body of research that shows that "brief interventions," in which health professionals recommend reduced drinking, are highly cost-effective tools for combating alcohol abuse (Miller et al., 1995).

WHO GIVES DRINKING MESSAGES AND WHAT DO THEY SAY?

Government or Public Health

The view of alcohol presented by government, at least in the United States, is almost entirely negative. Public announcements about alcohol are always of its dangers, never of its benefits. The public health position on alcohol in North America and Europe (WHO, 1993) is likewise strictly negative. Government and public health bodies have decided that it is too risky to inform people at large of the relative risks, including the benefits, of drinking because this may lead them to greater excesses of drinking or serve as an excuse for those already drinking excessively. Although Luik (see Chapter 2) views the government's discouragement of pleasurable activities (such as drinking), which he accepts as being unhealthy, as paternalistic and unnecessary, in fact, in the case of alcohol, such discouragement is counterproductive even as far as health goes. As Grossarth-Maticek and his colleagues have shown (Grossarth-Maticek & Eysenck, 1995; Grossarth-Maticek, Eysenck, & Boyle, 1995), self-regulating consumers who feel they can control their own outcomes are healthiest.

Industry Advertising

Nongovernmentally supported, non–public health advertising, that is, commercial advertising by alcohol manufacturers, frequently advises drinkers to drink responsibly. The message is reasonable enough but falls far short of encouraging a positive outlook towards alcohol as part of an overall healthful lifestyle. The industry's reticence in this area is caused by a combination of several factors. Much of the industry fears making health claims for its products, both because of the potential for incurring governmental wrath and also because such claims could expose them to legal liability. Thus, industry advertising does not suggest positive drinking images so much as it seeks to avoid responsibility for suggesting or supporting negative drinking styles.

Schools

The absence of a balanced view of alcohol is as noteworthy in educational settings as in public health messages. Elementary and secondary schools simply fear the disapprobation and liability risks of anything that might be taken to encourage drinking, particularly because their charges are not yet of the legal drinking age in the United States (compare this with private schools in France, which serve their students wine with meals). What may be even more puzzling is the absence of positive drinking messages and opportunities on American college campuses, where drinking is nonetheless widespread. Without a positive model of collegiate drinking to offer, nothing appears to counterbalance the concentrated and sometimes compulsive nature (termed "bingeing," see Wechsler, Davenport, Dowdall, Moeykens, & Castillo, 1994) of this youthful imbibing.

Family, Adults, or Peers

Because contemporaneous social groups provide the greatest pressures and supports for drinking behavior, families, other present adults, and peers are the most critical determinants of styles of drinking (Cahalan & Room, 1974). These different social groups tend to affect individuals, particularly young individuals, differently (Zhang, Welte, & Wieczorek, 1997). Peer drinking, among the young in particular, connotes illicit and excessive consumption. Indeed, one reason to allow young people to drink legally is that they then are more likely to drink with adults—related or otherwise—who as a rule tend to drink more moderately. Most bars, restaurants, and other social drinking establishments encourage moderate drinking, and thus such establishments and their patrons can serve as socializing forces for moderation.

Of course, social, ethnic, and other background factors influence whether positive modeling of drinking will occur in these groups. For example, young people with parents who abuse alcohol would do best to learn to drink outside the family. And this is the central problem with instances in which the family provides the primary model for drinking behavior. If the family is unable to set an example for moderate drinking, then individuals whose families either abstain or drink excessively are left without adequate models after which to fashion their own drinking patterns. This is not an automatic disqualification for becoming a moderate drinker, however; *most* offspring of either abstinent or heavy-drinking parents gravitate towards community norms of social drinking (Harburg, DiFranceisco, Webster, Gleiberman, & Schork, 1990).

Not only do parents sometimes lack social-drinking skills, those who possess them are often under attack from other social institutions in the United States. For example, totally negative alcohol education programs in schools liken alcohol to illicit drugs, so that children are confounded to see their parents openly practicing what they are told is a dangerous or negative behavior.

What Should Young People Learn About Alcohol and Positive Drinking Habits?

Thus, there are substantial deficiencies in the available options for teaching, modeling, and socializing positive drinking habits—exactly the ones Bacon identified 15 years ago. Current models leave a substantial gap in what children and others learn about alcohol, as shown by the 1995 Monitoring the Future data (Survey Research Centers, 1998a, 1998b) for high-school seniors (see Table 26.3). These

Table 26.3   1997 Monitoring the Future high-school senior data.

Survey findings	Student response, %
Drinking behaviors	
Drank in past year	75
Been drunk in past year	53
Drinking attitudes (disapproved of)	
Have 5+ drinks 1 or 2 times/weekend	65
Have 1 or 2 drinks nearly every day	70

Note. Data from *The Monitoring the Future Study: Table 4* [On-line], by Survey Research Center, Institute for Social Research, 1998, available: http://www.isr.umich.edu/src/mtf/mtf97t4.html; *The Monitoring the Future Study: Table 10* [On-line], by Survey Research Center, Institute for Social Research, 1998, available: http://www.isr.umich.edu/src/mtf/mtf97t10.html

data indicate that, although three quarters of high school seniors in the U.S. have drunk alcohol over the year, and more than half have been drunk, 7 in 10 disapprove of adults drinking regular, moderate amounts of alcohol (more than disapprove of heavy weekend drinking). In other words, what American students learn about alcohol leads them to disapprove of a healthful style of drinking, but at the same time they themselves drink in an unhealthy fashion.

CONCLUSION

In place of messages that lead to a dysfunctional combination of behavior and attitudes, a model of sensible drinking should be presented—drinking regularly but moderately, drinking integrated with other healthy practices, and drinking motivated, accompanied by, and leading to further positive feelings. Harburg, Gleiberman, DiFranceisco, and Peele (1994) have presented such a model, which they call "sensible drinking." In this view, the following set of prescriptive and pleasurable practices and recommendations should be communicated to young people and others:

1   Alcohol is a legal beverage widely available in most societies throughout the world.

2   Alcohol may be misused with serious negative consequences.

3   Alcohol is more often used in a mild and socially positive fashion.

4   Alcohol used in this fashion conveys significant benefits, including health, quality-of-life, and psychological and social benefits.

5   It is critical for the individual to develop skills to manage alcohol consumption.

6   Some groups use alcohol almost exclusively in a positive fashion, and this style of drinking should be valued and emulated.

7   Positive drinking involves regular moderate consumption, often including other people of both genders and all ages and usually entailing activities in addition to alcohol consumption, where the overall environment is pleasant—either relaxing or socially stimulating.

8   Alcohol, like other healthful activities, both takes its form and produces the most benefit within an overall positive life structure and social environment, including group supports, other healthful habits, and a purposeful and engaged lifestyle.

If we fear communicating such messages, then we both lose an opportunity for a significantly beneficial life involvement and actually *increase* the danger of problematic drinking.

NOTE

1. Prohibition was repealed in the United States in 1933.

REFERENCES

Akers, R. L. (1992). *Drugs, alcohol and society: Social structure, process and policy.* Belmont, CA: Wadsworth.

Bacon, S. (1984). Alcohol issues and social science. *Journal of Drug Issues, 14,* 7–29.

Bales, R. F. (1946). Cultural differences in rates of alcoholism. *Quarterly Journal of Alcohol Studies, 6,* 480–499.

Baum-Baicker, C. (1985). The psychological benefits of moderate alcohol consumption: A review of the literature. *Drug and Alcohol Dependence, 15,* 305–322.

Bradley, K. A., Donovan, D. M., & Larson, E. B. (1993). How much is too much? Advising patients about safe levels of alcohol consumption. *Archives of Internal Medicine, 153,* 2734–2740.

Cahalan, D. (1970). *Problem drinkers: A national survey.* San Francisco: Jossey-Bass.

Cahalan, D., & Room, R. (1974). *Problem drinking among American men.* New Brunswick, NJ: Rutgers Center of Alcohol Studies.

Criqui, M. H., & Ringle, B. L. (1994). Does diet or alcohol explain the French paradox? *Lancet, 344,* 1719–1723.

Doll, R. (1997). One for the heart. *British Medical Journal, 315,* 1664–1667.

Edwards, G., Anderson, P., Babor, T. F., Casswell, S. Ferrence, R., Giesbrech, N., Godfrey, C., Holder, H. D., Lemmens, P., Mäkelä, K., Midanik, L. T., Norstrom, T., Österberg, E., Romelsjö, A., Room, R., Simpura, J., & Skog, O.-J. (1994). *Alcohol policy and the public good.* Oxford, UK: Oxford University Press.

Glassner, B. (1991). Jewish sobriety. In D. J. Pittman & H. R. White (Eds.), *Society, culture, and drinking patterns reexamined* (pp. 311–326). New Brunswick, NJ: Rutgers Center of Alcohol Studies.

Grant, B. F. & Dawson, D. A. (1998). Age at onset of alcohol use and its association with DSM-IV alcohol abuse and dependence: Results from the National Longitudinal Alcohol Epidemiologic Survey. *Journal of Substance Abuse, 9,* 103–110.

Grossarth-Maticek, R. (1995). *When is drinking bad for your health? The interaction of drinking and self-regulation* (Unpublished presentation). Heidelberg, Germany: European Center for Peace and Development.

Grossarth-Maticek, R., & Eysenck, H. J. (1995). Self-regulation and mortality from cancer, coronary heart disease, and other causes: A prospective study. *Personality and Individual Differences, 19,* 781–795.

Grossarth-Maticek, R., Eysenck, H. J., & Boyle, G. J. (1995). Alcohol consumption and health: Synergistic interaction with personality. *Psychological Reports, 77,* 675–687.

Harburg, E., DiFranceisco, M. A., Webster, D. W., Gleiberman, L., & Schork, A. (1990). Familial transmission of alcohol use: I. Parent and adult offspring alcohol use over 17 years—Tecumseh, Michigan. *Journal of Studies on Alcohol, 51,* 245–256.

Harburg, E., Gleiberman, L., DiFranceisco, M. A. & Peele, S. (1994). Towards a concept of sensible drinking and an illustration of measure. *Alcohol & Alcoholism, 29,* 439–450.

Heath, D. B. (1989). The new temperance movement: Through the looking glass. *Drugs and Society, 3,* 143–168.

Hilton, M. E. (1987). Drinking patterns and drinking problems in 1984: Results from a general population survey. *Alcoholism: Clinical and Experimental Research, 11,* 167–175.

Hilton, M. E. (1988). Regional diversity in United States drinking practices. *British Journal of Addiction, 83,* 519–532.

Hilton, M. E., & Clark, W. B. (1991). Changes in American drinking patterns and problems, 1967–1984. In D. J. Pittman & H. R. White (Eds.), *Society, culture, and drinking patterns reexamined* (pp. 157–172). New Brunswick, NJ: Rutgers Center of Alcohol Studies.

Jellinek, E. M. (1960). *The disease concept of alcoholism.* New Brunswick, NJ: Rutgers Center of Alcohol Studies.

Lender, M. E., & Martin, J. K. (1987). *Drinking in America* (2nd ed.). New York: Free Press.

Levine, H. G. (1978). The discovery of addiction: Changing conceptions of habitual drunkenness in America. *Journal of Studies on Alcohol, 39,* 143–174.

Levine, H. G. (1992). Temperance cultures: Alcohol as a problem in Nordic and English-speaking cultures. In M. Lader, G. Edwards, & C. Drummond (Eds.), *The nature of alcohol and drug-related problems* (pp. 16–36). New York: Oxford University Press.

Miller, W. R., Brown, J. M., Simpson, T. L., Handmaker, N. S., Bien, T. H., Luckie, L. F., Montgomery, H. A., Hester, R. K., & Tonigan, J. S. (1995). What works? A methodological analysis of the alcohol treatment outcome literature. In R. K. Hester & W. R. Miller (Eds.), *Handbook of alcoholism treatment approaches: Effective alternatives* (2nd ed.). Boston, MA: Allyn & Bacon.

Musto, D. (1996, April). Alcohol in American history. *Scientific American,* pp. 78–83.

Orcutt, J. D. (1991). Beyond the "exotic and the pathologic:" Alcohol problems, norm qualities, and sociological theories of deviance. In P. M. Roma (Ed.), *Alcohol: The development of sociological perspectives on use and abuse* (pp. 145–173). New Brunswick, NJ: Rutgers Center of Alcohol Studies.

Peele, S. (1987). The limitations of control-of-supply models for explaining and preventing alcoholism and drug addiction. *Journal of Studies on Alcohol, 48,* 61–77.

Peele, S. (1993). The conflict between public health goals and the temperance mentality. *American Journal of Public Health, 83,* 805–810.

Peele, S. (1997). Utilizing culture and behavior in epidemiological models of alcohol consumption and consequences for Western nations. *Alcohol and Alcoholism, 32,* 51–64.

Peele, S., & Brodsky, A. (1998). *Psychosocial benefits of moderate alcohol use: Associations and causes.* Unpublished manuscript.

Pernanen, K. (1991). *Alcohol in human violence.* New York: Guilford.

Roizen, R. (1983). Loosening up: General population views of the effects of alcohol. In R. Room & G. Collins (Eds.), *Alcohol and disinhibition: Nature and meaning of the link* (pp. 43–45). Rockville, MD: National Institute on Alcohol Abuse and Alcoholism.

Room, R. (1988). Commentary. In Program on Alcohol Issues (Ed.), *Evaluating recovery outcomes.* San Diego, CA: University Extension, University of California, San Diego.

Room, R. (1989). Alcoholism and Alcoholics Anonymous in U.S. films, 1945–1962: The party ends for the "wet generations." *Journal of Studies on Alcohol, 83,* 11–18.

Survey Research Center, Institute for Social Research. (1998a). *The Monitoring the Future Study* [On-line]. (Available: http://www.isr.umich.edu/src/mtf/mtf97t4.html)

Survey Research Center, Institute for Social Research. (1998b). *The Montoring the Future Study* [On-line]. (Available: http://www.isr.umich.edu/src/mtf/mtf97t10.html)

Wechsler, H., Davenport, A., Dowdall, G., Moeykens, B., & Castillo, S. (1994). Health and behavioral consequences of binge drinking in college: National survey of students at 140 campuses. *Journal of the American Medical Association, 272,* 1672–1677.

WHO. (1993). *European Alcohol Action Plan.* Copenhagen: WHO Regional Office for Europe.

Wholey, D. (1984). *The courage to change.* New York: Warner.

Zhang, L., Welte, J. W., & Wieczorek, W. F. (1997). Peer and parental influences on male adolescent drinking. *Substance Use and Misuse, 32,* 2121–2136.

Pleasure and Alcohol Policy

Alan Haworth

The discussion on pleasure and alcohol policy was launched by a brief but im-passioned presentation from Morris Chafetz, a distinguished alcohol and public health official who had been the first director of the U.S. National Institute on Alcohol Abuse and Alcoholism. His remarks sparked a heated discussion.

1   The need for an individualist approach to alcohol. Chafetz indicated that he had "neither slides nor studies to present," but that, after his 44th year in the field, he had valuable personal perspectives to share. The first such per-spective resulted from a visit he had recently made to China, where he learned that "the Chinese venerate old people like me." This was because, first, old peo-ple "are no longer competition." Second, "they have a historical perspective." Third, old people "are very comfortable saying, 'I don't know.'" That is, they recognize "that certainty may not be possible."

Each person, Chafetz emphasized, is unique, including even identical twins. "So no one has ever existed like you and never will again." Therefore, in talking about pleasure and drinking, "we cannot homogenize human beings. Pleasure is like beauty in the eyes of the beholder." Any formal definition of pleasure "would have no personal significance" to listeners.

Likewise with scientific models. Chafetz noted that the so-called public health model was a great achievement in the history of medicine. "At the begin-ning of this century, life expectancy, at least in the United States, was 47, and now, because of the removal of infectious disease, life expectancy approaches almost 80 in this country." Even more importantly, we have remedied the situ-ation present at the beginning of this century, when "50% of the children were dead by age five."

2   Public health research and the lack of critical distinctions. But the public health model is not really applicable in the case of alcohol:

PLEASURE AND ALCOHOL POLICY

The triad of the public health model is agent, host, and environment. Now the host and environment still operate. But when it comes to the agent, that was a living organism in the original public health model, and no matter what bad things people say about alcohol, I have yet to hear someone claim it to be a living organism.

Furthermore, for Chafetz, the whole of social sciences is a misnomer:

> Calling the study of human beings a science may be the greatest oxymoron that anyone has ever expressed.... Each person is an individual; we don't know what they're feeling, thinking. They sometimes don't know themselves ... all of the things that may or may not influence their lives.
>
> And so consequently we are limited in our understanding, and we don't like to be limited because we like to believe there's a formulaic way of telling people how to live.

As a result, Chafetz advised, "We'd better go back to respecting the individual as an individual—not as a product of a sample, or a risk management endeavor, but as a human being."

3 Alcohol as an enhancement to individual experience. Chafetz himself would "contend that alcohol enhances the quality of life, but I don't base it on studies." Rather, this is his personal experience. Chafetz cited the uncertainty of knowing whether an accident attributed to a person with a blood alcohol level of 100 mg/100 mL really was caused by the drinking that person did, or a combination of a large number of situational and personal factors. But, in the same vein, "If we who drink moderately come up with statistics that indicate we have fewer heart attacks, aren't we guilty of the same thing?"

Chafetz concluded,

> I'm going to be hypocritical. I have said that giving advice, especially advice you don't have to take, or following social studies and statistical analysis where you can't control all the variables, and coming to conclusions, and giving all kinds of people mechanisms for how they ought to live their lives is based more on theory than reality. But I, now, want to give you a piece of advice. Trust and respect yourself.

In the discussion that followed, it was apparent that Chafetz had struck a chord in many participants.

1 Pleasure cannot be measured by standard epidemiologic means. A participant indicated that pleasure, as a feeling, could not be measured by standard epidemiological means, that taking the concept into account would require a paradigm shift and a shift in methodologies. Another participant pointed out that existing methods in ethnography and other qualitative and observational research already offer many insights into pleasure and related questions (see Chapter 15). Quantitative research, which is often more succinct, is seemingly the most attractive to researchers but is not sufficient by itself. It also was pointed out that rich ethnographic descriptions simply often take more space.

2 Is the health field overreaching by expanding its views of health?
Morris Chafetz made the provocative statement that democratic societies always
face a danger from fascism: "We have to be afraid of the 'good' people who
want to tell us what to do." John Orley's presentation concerning the expansion of health and quality-of-life measurement to include a spiritual dimension
were criticized by one participant who noted that medical experts did not have
qualifications to advise people about spirituality. Orley responded that the health
sector was not limited to physicians, and that it could accomplish more if it did
not compartmentalize people by considering them solely as the sum of their
illnesses. For example, in treating patients with chronic disease, the health professional needed to take account of all facets of the person, including reaching
out to professionals who can respond to the individual's spiritual needs as applicable.

**3 Cultural variations extend even to the biomedical level of func-
tioning.** Stanton Peele noted some remarkable variations in measured impact of
alcohol according to levels of consumption. In Australia, he pointed out, recommended limits to daily levels of drinking were about twice those in the United
States or up to four drinks daily for men and two drinks daily for women. Peele
also noted that two studies considering cognitive functioning in old age among
very different populations—an African American population in the United States
(Hendrie, Gao, Hall, Hui, & Unverzagt, 1996) and a French population from a
wine-producing area (Orgogozo et al., 1997)—found optimal functioning in the
first study at three or four drinks a week, and in the second at three or four
drinks *daily*. Ross Kalucy replied that the specific question of recommended
daily consumption levels was a political as well as a medical one. Although
medical benefits may be established clearly at one level, societies might vary in
how permissive they are of drinking at just up to that level of optimal drinking
or of going somewhere beyond it to the point at which measured risk really rose
(see Chapter 25). Guidelines are determined by the question being addressed
(e.g., purely pharmacological benefits versus enjoyment).

**4 Considering variations within the developing world is crucial when
developing approaches.** Another participant cautioned about creating overarching approaches that supposedly encompass all societies. In India, for example,
a largely dry culture, those who do drink tend to drink excessively, creating a
different profile for alcohol use. Ethnographic research would reveal that moderation meant something very different in India. When the dominant form of
alcohol was home brew, moderation was dictated by the simple fact of limited
availability. With British rule came mass-produced alcohol, which the population
was not equipped to handle. At the same time, existing social structures were
destroyed. According to a specialist from the region, Davinder Mohan, "Cultural
variations are not only important, they are *profoundly* important."

5 Can positive cultural drinking patterns be taught to young people?
Ole-Jørgen Skog was asked whether it was necessary for young people in temperance cultures to go through a period of excess before settling on moderation
(and described his own experience in taking 20 years to learn to drink moderately). In response, Archie Brodsky discussed traditional cultural models (e.g.,
Jewish, Chinese, Italian) of inculcating moderate drinking, such as introducing
alcohol to the young in moderate amounts in controlled social settings, thereby

removing the "forbidden fruit" element of drinking. Such cultures also hold people strictly responsible for controlling their consumption and avoiding antisocial drinking behavior. As a whole, the discussion can perhaps best be summed up by stressing a point previously noted by Haworth and Acuda (1998), namely, the importance of taking relativity of experience and viewpoint into account in understanding the complexity and difficulty of linking pleasure and alcohol policy.

REFERENCES

Haworth, A., & Acuda, S. W. (1998). Sub-Saharan Africa. In M. Grant (Ed.), *Alcohol and emerging markets: Patterns, problems, and responses* (pp. 19–90). Philadelphia, PA: Taylor & Francis.

Hendrie, H. C., Gao, S., Hall, K. S., Hui, S. L., & Unverzagt, F. W. (1996). The relationship between alcohol consumption, cognitive performance, and daily functioning in an urban sample of older Black Americans. *Journal of the American Geriatric Society, 44*, 1158–1165.

Orgogozo, J.-M., Dartigues, J.-F., Lafont, S., Letenneur, L., Commenges, D., Salamon, E., Renaud, S., & Breteler, M. (1997). Wine consumption and dementia in the elderly: A prospective community study in the Bordeaux area. *Revue Neurologique, 153*, 185–192.

Part Six

Conclusions

Rapporteur's Report

Conference

Cynthia Chasokela and Eva Tongue

PLEASURE AND HEALTH

The point of departure of this conference is that health goes beyond the simple presence or absence of disease to include emotional and spiritual elements, political and social context, and the overall interaction between the individual and his or her environment. This definition is critically linked to what is now called "quality of life." There is evidence that pleasure contributes to physical health as traditionally defined. But pleasure is also crucial for health, because it addresses the subjective elements that have recently come to the fore in considering healthfulness.

Lifestyle is crucially related to emerging definitions of health in a number of ways. Of course, lifestyle has been determined to have a major impact on health and longevity. But lifestyle also embraces issues such as personal values and subjective enjoyment (i.e., pleasure) that are part of the new, broader view of health. As a result, public health increasingly has addressed lifestyle issues. But the state's role in governing individual lifestyles opened considerable debate at the conference. On what grounds can the state insist on a "proper" lifestyle? Arguments against government control are those of personal choice—for example, some people may prefer behaviors that have negative effects on long-term health. But longevity is not everyone's goal.

A conference consensus seemed to accept the role of a public health sector that develops and disseminates a neutral and scientifically well grounded body of health information. This information, constantly updated, can offer individuals a sound basis for making informed lifestyle choices that reflect personal values, enjoyments, and acceptance of risk. This program seems to fall within the bailiwick of "health promotion," a somewhat separate category of public health from prevention of specific diseases (most notably infectious ones) that often entails a larger and more active role for government.

Both traditional views of health and the broader definition embraced at this conference leave considerable room for the consumption and enjoyment of beverage alcohol. Available scientific evidence simply does not point to the cessation of consumption of alcohol for individuals who drink moderately and who enjoy drinking.

DRINKING AND PLEASURE CROSS-CULTURALLY

The fundamentals of "alcohol and culture" are that people drink primarily for pleasure and that alcohol use is primarily a social phenomenon. Societies create the settings, patterns, and limits of drinking for people. The amount of alcohol consumed, and especially patterns of consumption, are important in epidemiology, and they vary substantially across cultures. Moreover, drinking problems and pleasure are defined culturally—including conceptual, economic, and personal dimensions and meanings. Culturally approved lifestyles and concepts about self-control also influence the way alcohol is consumed.

Impoverished, disempowered societies are more vulnerable to drinking that serves to alleviate pain, and thus there is a relationship between poverty, disenfranchisement, and alcohol abuse. Developing and developed nations both attach highly specific meanings to drinking that cannot be separated from their specific cultural settings and share certain issues surrounding alcohol. One common area across the board for developing nations is their relationship to external commercial forces that market alcohol in their countries.

ALCOHOL AND MEDICAL, PSYCHOLOGICAL, AND SOCIAL HEALTH

That moderate drinking reduces coronary heart disease is well established and is information to be utilized in dealing with the health of individuals and communities. It also has an impact on the pleasurableness of drinking, because understanding that something may be good for you reinforces the direct pleasurable sensations produced by the experience.

The health and demographic traits of the individual have a critical impact on whether, in what amounts, and how alcohol affects health. Thus, we are on the safest ground in describing healthy drinking for a given individual; public health pronouncements are more problematic. The possibility exists that sound individual recommendations about healthy consumption levels nonetheless will have deleterious effects on health society-wide.

Drinking can benefit people's psychological health, while at the same time it can also affect their socio-economic status and physical health. Healthy drinking is thus a highly synergistic matter, both resulting from and contributing to the healthfulness of the individual's lifestyles and his or her social integration.

DRINKING EXPECTATIONS AND CONTEXTS

Individual and cultural expectations about alcohol govern drinking patterns and alcohol's effects in important ways. What a society believes and conveys about alcohol may lead to better or worse public health outcomes, because wider cultural beliefs—reinforced or modified by family and peer group beliefs—affect how individuals approach and respond to alcohol. Thus media and public health messages about alcohol are critical components of alcohol policy. Larger-than-life conceptions of alcohol can harm both societies and individuals. Typical drinkers, on the other hand, have moderate, realistic expectations about how they will enjoy the effects—physiological, social, and psychological—of alcohol.

Both the traits and condition of drinkers are essential to their drinking experiences. At any time, alcohol consumption represents a complex interaction between the individual and his or her environment, as well as with all the other types of consumption in which an individual engages. Each individual can be viewed as a mechanism attempting—generally with good results—to bring about optimal functioning through self-regulation.

The study of people's daily pleasures reassures us that people are well-regulated mechanisms who can learn and seek out what brings them pleasure. One prominent example of such pleasure seeking, among many others, is beverage alcohol. Sometimes, however, people cannot balance self-restraint and consumption and instead veer between abstinence and excess. This does not mean that they cannot rectify this imbalance and learn to enjoy pleasure comfortably.

Age and gender are two prototypical factors influencing how much, how, when, and with what effects people drink. Young people are more prone than their elders to seek sensation and approval, sometimes leading to excesses in drinking; women generally drink less but experience more pain as both a cause and a result of alcoholism.

Likewise influential in the drinking equation are the people and settings with whom and in which people drink. These factors are some of those most readily influenced by social engineering and should be considered an important part of alcohol policy. In addition, the overall integration of a society is a factor in alcohol consumption. Community standards are strong regulators of drinking. Unfortunately, we see that such informal social controls are disappearing rapidly in both developed and developing nations.

PLEASURE AND ALCOHOL POLICY

The participants in this conference were very much concerned with the need to expand research paradigms and methodologies beyond the standard quantitative epidemiologic and social scientific public health research. This broadened research is needed to address the qualitative aspects of pleasure, as well as to validate cultural approaches underlying patterns of alcohol consumption, which are critical to public health outcomes. A deeper understanding of both individuals and cultures is required in order to design appropriately specific informational campaigns and prevention strategies.

A range of policy options is available to governments in order to regulate the consumption of alcohol. In evaluating any such options—including taxation, licensing of outlets and hours of operation, drunken-driving laws, and policies towards youthful drinking—the acceptability of the policies to those who will be subjected to them is a critical issue. Sometimes identical policies presented in alternate ways generate far different reactions. One conception of public policy toward alcohol is termed "harm reduction," in which combining restrictive policies with those that encourage beneficial drinking (e.g., drinking that involves a lesser degree of episodic excess) can lead towards an optimal policy mix.

Some cultures have such clear patterns of moderate consumption that substantial public health efforts might be redundant. These cultures carefully introduce alcohol to young people and indicate to them when and how to drink and the need to avoid excess. The question of safe limits in any society is a cultural one and depends on the circumstances and political aims as much as it does on epidemiologic data and medical science.

Individual responsibility in drinking is consistent with group support for moderation. It also requires that people be shown respect by providing them with sound information with which to make choices. The development of drinking guidelines in a society must be preceded by ethnographic and demographic research in order to generate sound scientific information and valid public health recommendations.

As for the young, it is futile to ignore the fact that they will be exposed to alcohol. The challenge rather is to educate the young about and initiate them into drinking so as to create lifelong pleasurable drinking practices. Often, public health approaches are impeded by cultural baggage—such as the remnants of temperance traditions in some societies—that undermines the development of sound policies and the communication of sound information about beverage alcohol.

THE ROLE OF THE MEDIA

Much at this conference indicates that images of drinking and of alcohol influence drinking problems and pleasure. At the same time, evidence about healthy and risky behavior generally is filtered through the media. The role of the media is thus a crucial one—for spreading messages about health risks and benefits, in depicting the glamorous life, and in marketing campaigns to make products and activities appealing to consumers.

The media are not the servants of researchers. They have an independent role to play in critically reviewing scientific data and pronouncements. Likewise, censorship of reporting on health issues to reflect politically correct or government-approved messages is undesirable. Independent media are required as much—perhaps more—in the area of health as they are in the political arena.

The media are being required to perform more functions than ever before. On the one hand, the popular media are obligated to make sense of scientific data—even if this information is contradictory, changeable, or in dispute. Both the scientific community and the popular media must take responsibility for better communication of sound scientific information and at the same time educate people to realize that science entails uncertainty, change, and disagreement. Thus independent media must learn more about and liaison better with the scientific community.

If public health is unduly problem-oriented, the media can err in either of two directions. On the one hand, they can pick up and amplify alarmist health messages, some of which may be unfounded. Indeed, there could be said to be a market for "scare" messages. On the other hand, an entirely different segment of the media (e.g., food and features) informs the public about the accouterments of the good life, promoting pleasure and its sources. Thus the *New York Times* may on one page talk about the enjoyment of wine and on another recommend against drinking. There is need in the case of alcohol to shift attention from the minority of those who misuse alcohol to the overall population of drinkers.

The media's role grows more complex along with the globalilization of information technology, creating new responsibilities for advertisers and electronic, print, and visual media. The media have to recognize, respect, and respond to the different cultural contexts in which their messages may be received. Thus, accuracy of reporting must be matched with a sensitivity to cultural settings, because the same message creates different responses depending upon who hears it and where.

The conference also called on the alcohol industry to exercise responsibility in marketing and observe codes of ethical practice. Beyond this, the industry must recognize its public health obligations as it creates images of alcohol and promotes drinking in the developing world.

Chapter 27

Conclusion

Marcus Grant

Although the Permission for Pleasure conference did not issue a consensus statement, the participants at the conference—on which this volume is based—did agree on several critical issues. This final chapter consists of a commentary on the four general conclusions of the conference, as well as a summary of material from several additional International Center for Alcohol Policies (ICAP) projects relevant to the topics and goals of Permission for Pleasure.

1. The function of pleasure in relation to drinking needs to be considered in the context of many other individual, socioeconomic, and cultural variables, including gender and age.

How people drink, for better or worse, is influenced strongly by who they are and in which situations they drink. Their patterns of consumption and behavior while drinking are functions of individual attributes such as their age and gender, the circumstances in which they are drinking, larger cultural patterns of alcohol consumption, and the cultural balance and economic well-being of their society.

Alcohol consumption is generally a part of a much broader landscape of human activity—including eating, talking, sharing time with family and friends, relaxing, and celebrating. This is the major theme of another book in the ICAP series on alcohol in society (Heath, 2000) that has considerable relevance to the topic of pleasure and alcohol. For most people, most of the time, drinking is naturally integrated with other aspects of their lives that they find pleasurable.

Public policy needs to accept and accentuate both (a) that drinking takes place in such a larger cultural context and (b) that drinking is in the main accepted, benign, and enjoyable. Pathological drinking may be defined as drinking that dominates—or is isolated from—other cultural considerations that ordinarily rein in excessive drinking. The challenge, both for making drinking pleasurable and for wider public policy considerations, is to focus on the development of drinking that is positive, responsible, and pleasurable, rather than on pathological drinking. This approach to policy coordinates health with people's pursuit of pleasure—these should not be approached in opposition to one another.

2. *The individual choice whether or not to drink should be based on accurate and balanced information.*

The first book in the ICAP series on alcohol in society is entitled *Drinking Patterns and Their Consequences* (Grant & Litvak, 1998). It demonstrates, both theoretically and empirically, that drinking patterns are a better predictor of positive and negative drinking outcomes than is per capita consumption. This approach opens the door to a more pragmatic style of alcohol policy that accepts alcohol use but seeks to direct individual and community choices towards reducing alcohol-related harm without necessarily curtailing alcohol availability or opportunities to drink. The new formulation suggests the need to search for a replacement to models that mechanistically link levels of problems to levels of consumption, in the belief that such a new approach can be both more sensitive and more broadly acceptable to the public. There is no conflict between reducing reckless drinking and promoting responsible drinking—the two are actually mutually reinforcing.

Increasingly, evidence suggests that moderate consumption of alcohol confers physiological, psychological, and social benefits and improves an individual's quality of life. Although the existence of beneficial effects is generally recognized, little attention has been paid to them within the public health context and the published literature on benefits associated with alcohol consumption is thus far modest (see Hall, 1995; Hauge & Irgens-Jensen, 1988). Even more modest than research on benefits is any existing attempt to describe beneficial patterns of drinking. Single (1998) noted that drinking patterns that minimize the risk of harm are somewhat understood, but research is lacking on the specific patterns likely to maximize the benefits of drinking. Similarly, harm-reduction and prevention strategies have focused primarily on the potential for harm associated with excessive or reckless alcohol consumption. What is missing from the equation is a description of beneficial drinking patterns with which to replace detrimental ones.

An assumption often made is that for alcohol consumption, "risk" and "benefit" lie at the extreme ends of a single continuum. Yet, as pointed out by Roche, Single, and Heath (in press), risk and benefit may coexist separately, and the relationship between them may be one of two parallel or even intersecting axes. For this reason, risk as well as benefit should be assessed separately and in the context of drinking patterns, of individual characteristics of the drinker, and of the role alcohol plays within an individual's overall existence.

Although available literature on beneficial patterns may be scant, informal definitions of what makes up such drinking patterns exist in practice. Such definitions are inherent in each public health message delivered on the risks and benefits of alcohol and in each recommendation on responsible drinking. Over the course of the past 2 years, ICAP has undertaken a project to examine current definitions of beneficial drinking patterns accepted by international experts from various key disciplines involved in alcohol issues. The disciplines chosen for this project are public health, clinical medicine, sociology, epidemiology, and the beverage alcohol industry.

As a point of departure, five panels were formed: one each from the four academic disciplines mentioned, the fifth from the beverage alcohol industry.[1] In each case, a panel chair was appointed and charged with the task of conducting a survey among an international sample of colleagues within the field to assess their views on beneficial drinking patterns. Concurrently, a survey conducted within the beverage alcohol industry focused on what definitions of beneficial drinking patterns were in use by social aspects organizations[2] in the promotion of prevention and education messages. The approaches adopted by the panel chairs ranged from open-ended questions on the nature of beneficial drinking patterns to structured surveys containing specific questions aimed at determining which circumstances and variables render certain drinking patterns beneficial and others not.

As the results of the surveys show, there was generally agreement on three basic issues: (a) Beneficial patterns of drinking do indeed exist; (b) they are multidimensional and may extend into virtually every aspect of human activity; and (c) they are largely shaped by the culture and context of the individual drinker. With this in mind, it may be useful to view benefits as falling into discrete domains that sometimes overlap. Three overarching domains appear: psychological, physiological, and social. These beneficial patterns can be broken down further into the following groups of benefits:

- Psychological: relaxation, happiness, pleasure
- Cognitive: intellectual acuity, creativity
- Social: sociability, social networks and boundaries, celebrations, social exchange, leisure time
- Medical: disease prevention and lowering of specific disease risks, stress reduction
- Health: physical condition, subjective well-being
- Gustatory: taste and texture, complement to food
- Spiritual and existential: religious feeling, transcendent experience

Some benefits are established readily through straightforward epidemiological research; others may be largely subjective and dependent upon an individual's circumstances, state, and cultural perspective, including the culture's delineation of what is acceptable or pleasurable. Many depend on an individual's subjective expectations of the harm or benefit that he or she may experience as a result of drinking (as outlined by Leigh, see Chapter 16). Whatever its genesis, a drinking pattern or outcome that qualifies as beneficial nonetheless can be described as in some way contributing to health and quality of life.

Survey respondents did not agree uniformly on all of the dimensions of beneficial patterns. However, there was a relatively high level of agreement on the potential beneficial effects of alcohol on coronary heart disease and on general health, on sociability, and on the subjective well-being of the individual. The effects of intoxication also were included as sometimes beneficial by respondents in several disciplines, but this rating was highly culture- and situation-specific. Some respondents also included celebratory events and holidays in beneficial drinking patterns, although this response once again was dependent largely upon culture and context. There was also consensus about the relevance of special considerations such as the medical condition of the individual drinker or circumstances under which drinking may not be advisable and the only recommended pattern can be abstinence.

In summary, beneficial patterns of drinking can be defined as those that not only minimize the risk of harm but maximize the potential benefits of drinking (Roche, Single, & Heath, in press). In addition, beneficial drinking patterns emerge as those in which the salience of alcohol is not foremost, but rather drinking is seamlessly integrated into other life activities, contributing to the overall richness of life (Saunders, 1998).

3. Health, quality of life, and responsible drinking can be interconnected, but their relationship to each other needs to be better understood.

Key definitions of health (including the one enshrined as the first principle in the preamble to the World Health Organization Constitution) are not limited to the absence of disease but also include a subjective sense of well-being, as is evident in the assessment of quality of life (see Chapter 23). Alcohol is thus interrelated, through moderate consumption, with health as traditionally measured and with expanded definitions that incorporate subjective well-being, including (potentially) pleasure. In this volume, Klatsky (Chapter 12) and Camargo (Chapter 13) review the medical health benefits of alcohol, most notably in the prevention and reduction of risk for cardiovascular disease and mortality, along with potential health costs from drinking. Brodsky and Peele (Chapter 15) elaborate research findings on a range of psychological and social benefits that have been associated in complex interacting patterns with moderate drinking.

All of these benefits interact in specific cultural contexts. As one conference participant noted (referring to India, a highly heterogeneous society), "Cultural variations are not only important, they are *profoundly* important." In other words, the entire configuration of what moderate drinking comprises, as well as its interrelationships with other social currents and mechanisms, has to be transformed over and over again to meet the specific characteristics of different cultures. Apart from the highly idiographic nature of individual cultures, developing nations as a group share particular concerns. That is, time and again we witness existing, indigenous social support for locally defined patterns of moderate alcohol consumption, upon which is superimposed an internationalization of modern lifestyles, including "Western" styles of drinking alcohol (see Chapters 8, 10, and 24).

It is unlikely that cultures can take on new, ready-made patterns; at the same time, many individuals in these cultures are being challenged to adopt new behaviors and to adapt to new information and customs. Both public health advocates and the beverage alcohol industry should recognize and seek to understand these cultural patterns, and to build on them in a positive way. As well as respecting individual self-determination by providing accurate and complete information about alcohol, public health advocates and beverage alcohol manufacturers need to respect cultural patterns of dealing with alcohol.

4. Public health advocates, scientists, governments, the media, and the beverage alcohol industry all have distinct, and sometimes overlapping, roles and responsibilities when it comes to addressing the place of alcohol in society. The dialogue at this conference is part of a partnership through which to guide the future.

The most notable feature of the group of participants at the conference on which this volume is based was their diversity. Scientists, public health specialists, psychologists, psychiatrists, physicians, scholars, public health advocates, community leaders, government officials, representatives of the media and of the beverage alcohol industry—all came together in New York in the early Summer of 1998 with a rare willingness to find common ground and build upon it. All have sincere concerns and positions to articulate. All need to be heard.

ICAP is committed to the principle of partnership. Every ICAP project involves individuals from public health and from the beverage alcohol industry working together as equals. Of course, other kinds of partnership are equally important: partnerships across geographical and political frontiers or between competing academic disciplines; between scholars and practitioners; between drinkers and abstainers. It is through partnerships that it will be possible to build upon the success of the conference and to take forward the remarkably broad range of ideas covered by this volume.

The four conference conclusions are simply cornerstones for a structure whose dimensions are unknown. What is important is that the ideas which emerged during the conference and which are elaborated in this volume contribute to a public policy that values education and information, that recognizes the autonomy of individuals and communities, and that rises above worn-out ideologies. The challenge is to build a scientifically sound approach that also will be of practical utility in making people's lives healthier, of higher quality, and more pleasurable.

NOTES

1. The panel chairs selected were Dr. Eric Single (epidemiology), Dr. Ann Roche (public health), Dr. John Saunders (clinical practice), Dr. Dwight Heath (sociology), and Mr. Peter Mitchell (beverage alcohol industry).

2. A social aspects organization (SAO) is a national organization funded by the beverage alcohol industry which deals with issues solely concerned with the responsible consumption of alcohol beverages. Although the specific mission of individual SAOs varies depending on the culture of the country in which it operates, SAOs can be distinguished from other organizations such as trade associations in two respects. First, SAOs are not involved with trade promotion issues; and, second, SAOs are generally intersectoral, i.e., the beverage alcohol companies which fund them have interests across the wine, beer and spirits sectors.

REFERENCES

Grant, M., & Litvak, J. (Eds.). (1998). *Drinking patterns and their consequences*. Washington, DC: Taylor & Francis.

Hall, W. (1995). Changes in the public perception of the health benefits of alcohol use, 1989 to 1994. *Australian and New Zealand Journal of Public Health, 20*, 93–95.

Hauge, R., & Irgens-Jensen, O. (1988). The experience of positive and negative consequences in four Scandinavian countries. *British Journal of Addiction, 85*, 645–653.

Heath, D. (2000). *Drinking occasions: Comparative perspectives on alcohol and culture*. Philadelphia, PA: Taylor & Francis.

Peele, S., & Brodsky, A. (1998). *Psychosocial benefits of moderate alcohol use: Associations and causes*. Unpublished manuscript.

Roche, A., Single, E., & Heath, D. (in press). *What constitutes a beneficial pattern of alcohol consumption: A multidisciplinary review.*

Saunders, J. (1998). *Defining beneficial patterns of alcohol consumption: Results of a survey of clinicians*. Washington, DC: International Center for Alcohol Policies.

Single, E. (1998, February). *What constitutes a beneficial pattern of drinking: An epidemiological perspective*. Paper presented at the International Conference on Drinking Patterns and Their Consequences, Perth, Australia.

Media Panel

Mohan Isaac

A media panel was convened at the Permission for Pleasure conference to explore the joint issues of (a) how—and how well—scientific information is interpreted by the media and then communicated to the public, and (b) how better to work through the media to reach the public with scientific data about beneficial uses and experiences with alcohol to counteract a perceived negative bias in available information concerning beverage alcohol.

The media panel was moderated by Andrew Barr, a freelance journalist, and included Leslie Laurence, contributing editor at *Glamour*, Laurie Abraham, features editor at *Mirabella*, and John Illman, medical correspondent for *The Observer*. Barr introduced the panel by describing its mission as to explore the role of the media in communicating alcohol-related issues in terms of both the plusses and minuses of their fulfillment of this role.

1 **"Mixed messages."** Leslie Laurence reviewed the reporting of alcohol-related issues in the U.S. media from December 1997 to June 1998. Most material reported health risks and benefits from alcohol on the basis of studies published in medical journals. There was a dichotomy in reporting—articles in the food and features sections of newspapers focused on the pleasures of drinking; other sections focused on the "sinfulness" of drinking. In the United States, a new temperance movement could be discerned, a seemingly Puritanical view at war with hedonistic tendencies. She cited the case of a Denver, Colorado, school principal who was placed on administrative leave from his job following a trip to France during which children were permitted to taste wine with a meal (Robey, 1998; Cortez & Robey, 1998). Overall, she opined, "The media are

sending mixed messages. This reflects the ambivalence of our culture toward alcohol."

2   Scientific findings potentially slanted. Laurie Abraham discussed the difficulty journalists face in interpreting statistical data on the risks and benefits of alcohol reported in medical journals. She cited specifically a study by Smith-Warner et al. (1998) on alcohol as a risk factor in breast cancer, which featured the finding that two to four drinks per day increased the risk of breast cancer by 40%. Abraham asked why these particular daily levels of drinking were the focus of the study. Fewer than two drinks daily was not associated with much risk of cancer; the greatest leap in cancer risk occurred at five drinks daily. She speculated that the data were reported in this way to grab media attention, reflecting the pressure on the media to report "spectacular" results. She felt that such reporting was deficient because journalists had an obligation to present helpful information, rather than to write simply to draw readers' attention.

3   Avoidance of pleasure as a topic. Most articles, according to Abraham, focus on the risks of alcohol consumption as the safer course. Journalists hesitate to write that "most people drank because they liked a little mind alteration" and the use of alcohol is a "way to relax." The only case in which people's pursuit of pleasure through drinking is frankly discussed is in the context of connoisseurship. She noted the absence, for the most part, of public health researchers at a conference devoted to pleasure.

4   Stereotypes in the media. John Illman maintained that journalists do poorly because they rely on the scientific community as sources, and that the medical evidence does not add up to much. Ilman took the position that "the more we learn, the more the confusion." The media prefer very simple stories. Thus they might overplay the importance of alcohol in the diet and downplay the importance of such dietary components as fruit and vegetables. Because of contradictory stories, the public takes little notice of recommended drinking levels. All in all, he considered that science has done the public a great disservice.

5   Conflict between public health sector and beverage alcohol industry approaches. Andrew Barr noted the conflicting approaches of government and industry in Great Britain. Although the government focuses on the public health model, which seeks to reduce the overall consumption of alcohol, the beverage alcohol industry stresses primarily drunk driving in its educational programs.

6   Communicating with the public: risk percentages. One of the conference participants recommended discontinuing the presentation of health dangers in terms of percentage risk, because this is inherently sensationalistic and misleading. Any such percentage must be placed in a broader context. The question was asked by another participant whether the media's job was to report or educate. Journalists have an obligation, in the view of some, to educate, which is the opposite of propagandizing.

7   Cross-cultural responsibilities. It was suggested by a member of the audience that English-language scientific research—and related reporting—has a disproportionate impact on cultures around the world. Journalists need to recognize a responsibility in this regard by being aware, at the same time as they wrote for readers in their own language, of the influence their writing could have in other countries and language groups in which their work was translated and understood in different ways. Another conference participant discussed the hold that developed countries have over worldwide media, and also the vast influence over the media in developing nations exercised by alcohol manufacturers.

8   The use of media by public health sources for greater exposure. It was pointed out during the discussion that public health researchers are under increasing pressure, not only to publish results, but to be cited in the press in order to increase their own exposure. Science could make good headlines. Although the media has responsibilities, the scientific community has a responsibility not to sensationalize research findings.

9   The role of electronic media. A speaker referred to the role of the electronic media in advertising enticing images of drinking without being bound by ethical guidelines that may apply to the conventional media. This is particularly evident in developing countries, where codes employed in the developed world are not observed.

10   The press as watchdogs: alcopops. The example of alcoholic sodas— perceived by some to be an enticement to young people to drink—was cited as a case in which the media served a useful watchdog function. However, the media soon went too far in playing the story up, claiming that underage drinkers drank *only* alcopop (actually they preferred cheap cider). Meanwhile, the Portman Group (a British industry education organization) was cited positively for getting this phenomenon under control and for its other work with underage drinking and drunk driving.

REFERENCES

Cortez, A., & Robey, R. (1998, May 15). Parents push for principal reprieve: School's governing board also wants say. *The Denver Post*, p. B1.

Robey, R. (1998, May 14). Principal in hot water over wine. *The Denver Post*, p. A1.

Smith-Warner, S. A., Spiegelman, D., Yaun, S. S., van den Brandt, P. A., Folsom, A. R., Goldbohm, R. A., Graham, S., Holmberg, L., Howe, G. R., Marshall, J. R., Miller, A. B., Potter, J. D., Speizer, F. E., Willett, W. C., Wolk, A., & Hunter, D. J. (1998). Alcohol and breast cancer in women: A pooled analysis of cohort studies. *Journal of the American Medical Association, 279*, 535–540.

Index

(